A HISTORY OF
ENGLISH DRAMA
1660-1900

A HISTORY OF
ENGLISH DRAMA
1660-1900

BY

ALLARDYCE NICOLL

*Professor of English Language and Literature
in the University of Birmingham*

VOLUME VI

A SHORT-TITLE
ALPHABETICAL CATALOGUE OF PLAYS
PRODUCED OR PRINTED IN ENGLAND
FROM 1660 TO 1900

CAMBRIDGE
AT THE UNIVERSITY PRESS
1965

PUBLISHED BY
THE SYNDICS OF THE CAMBRIDGE UNIVERSITY PRESS
Bentley House, 200 Euston Road, London, N.W. 1
American Branch: 32 East 57th Street, New York, N.Y. 10022

©

CAMBRIDGE UNIVERSITY PRESS

1959

First printed   1959
Reprinted   1965

Printed in Great Britain at the University Printing House, Cambridge
(Brooke Crutchley, University Printer)

PREFATORY NOTE

IN the earlier volumes of this series grateful acknowledgement has been made to several students of English theatrical history, and in particular to Sir St Vincent Trowbridge, who have kindly drawn my attention to obscure plays, as well as to sources of information concerning authorship and production dates for plays already recorded. In preparing the present catalogue, further help has come from Professor Beecher Hogan (who provided me with a list of hitherto un-noted Dublin performances) and from Mr Anthony M. Parish (who has given me items of information based on his examination of nineteenth-century printed texts). I wish also to take this opportunity of thanking Mr P. F. Hinton for furnishing me with a catalogue of the R. Crompton Rhodes Collection now in the Birmingham Reference Library.

A. N.

THE SHAKESPEARE INSTITUTE
(UNIVERSITY OF BIRMINGHAM)
STRATFORD-UPON-AVON

February 1958

INTRODUCTION

THIS volume is much more than an index.

Normally, and properly, an index is dependent upon the book to which it acts as a guide, and consequently it does not pretend to possess other than a subsidiary value. It is true that the pages of this volume do have as their first aim the object of thus serving as a guide, but they are designed to go considerably beyond such an immediate purpose and thus to have a positive, and to a certain extent independent, value of their own. In one sense, while the catalogue presented here may be regarded as an index to what is more fully given elsewhere, it seeks to be a substantive list, as complete as possible, of dramatic works produced in England from the Restoration to the end of the nineteenth century.

If this had been merely an index, nothing more would have been required, or expected, than short-title entries of plays, followed by volume and page references. The present list provides further information in three specific ways:

First, it indicates, in addition to the play-titles, the names of their authors (where known), together with the years of original production, publication or submission to the licensing authority. For immediate reference, therefore, the catalogue stands independent of the Handlists in the other volumes of this series, even although, of course, these contain more detailed information than could here be presented.

Secondly, it should be observed that this catalogue presents some material not in the Hand-lists themselves. During its compilation a number of fresh titles from the earlier periods came to light, as well as new information on the authorship of some dramas previously classed as anonymous. Such additional material has been incorporated here, with symbols to indicate the items or the supplementary information provided for the first time.

Thirdly, there has been introduced into the catalogue an element of a unique kind. From Archer's primitive play-catalogue of 1656, on through Langbaine's *An Account of the English Dramatick Poets* (1691) and Baker's *Biographia Dramatica* (1812), to the *Stage Cyclopaedia* of 1909, various efforts have been made to provide alphabetically-arranged records of English dramatic activity; but in none of these is any attempt made to list more than the main titles (quite apart from the fact that, as the Hand-lists have demonstrated, hundreds and indeed thousands of plays remained unrecorded). Often, however, short main titles fail to offer the help that a student needs: everyone working in this field must realise that frequently a play originally presented under one title was later acted under another name and that even more frequently dramas with sub-titles became popularly, and even professionally, known not by their main but by their alternative titles. A student unacquainted with Dryden's works, for example, might search in vain for *The Maiden Queen*, the name under which his *Secret Love* was usually performed, and he would fail to find *The City Wives' Confederacy*, the name under which Vanbrugh's *The Confederacy* was commonly acted. These are but two examples out of many. Now, it is obvious that a student engaged in elucidating theatrical references in contemporary diaries, correspond-ence or playhouse documents may be saved a great deal of trouble, or even may be provided with information which otherwise might elude him, if he has available a catalogue not only of main titles but of sub-titles and alternative titles as well. Accordingly, although it has entailed a great deal of additional labour, the present catalogue has been expanded so as to include at least the majority of such alternative names for plays of the period 1660–1900.

Expansion of the catalogue, however, had to be halted somewhere. The original plan called for the listing of all sub-titles and for the attaching to these of author and date references similar to those used for the main titles. The carrying out of a plan of this kind would obviously have swollen this volume, already lengthy, to inordinate proportions, and some modifications had perforce to be adopted. To save space, most of the Italian operas which appear in the Hand-lists have been omitted here—the only exceptions being those early operas of Addison's time which mingle English with their Italian and those of later date which have English translations prepared by known dramatic authors. Since the Italian operas are given alphabetically in the Hand-lists, their omission should not cause any difficulty if reference has to be made to them. Similarly, the repertoire of the French and Italian comedians presented in London early in the eighteenth century has not been included in the catalogue.

While the leaving out of this material resulted in a certain saving, clearly more was demanded; and hence arose the two chief modifications in the plan originally proposed. First, no author or date references are given for the sub-titles. This means that anyone consulting the catalogue may on occasion be referred back from a subtitle to a main title which belongs to two or more separate plays and that consequently a further short search may be necessary before the particular drama concerned is located. Clearly, it would have been best to make all the references specific: equally clearly, this could not have been done within reasonable limits—and between a choice of adopting the present procedure or leaving out the sub-titles altogether no doubt can be felt which is the preferable. In any case, for the majority of references no problem arises.

A second modification concerns those many pantomimes which so actively attracted audiences during the eighteenth and nineteenth centuries. Not only were these very numerous, they often indulged in sprawling titles, such as *King Hal the Bluff, Anne Boleyn the Fair; or, Harlequin Herne the Hunter and the Good Little Fairies of the Silver Ferns* and *Harlequin Blue Beard; or, The Red Rover, the Fairy of the Golden Locks and the Genie of the Magic Key*. Because of the number and length of these titles it was decided that only the main titles should be recorded except for the pantomimes of the early eighteenth century, which, as a scrutiny of Weaver's list shows, are often unlocatable unless we know the alternative names under which they were performed. Perhaps the loss here is not so serious: after all, the student is less likely to require the aid of sub-titles in this pantomimic sphere than when he is dealing with the more formal categories of plays.

The method followed in the catalogue may be briefly outlined. With the exceptions noted above, all the entries in the Hand-lists to the volumes of this series are recorded alphabetically and, save for pantomimes after 1750, all sub-titles and alternative titles are given with indications of the main titles to which they belong.

(1) The normal entry presents the short main title with (in brackets) the author's surname and initials followed by the year, and the appropriate volume and page references, as in:

Way of the World (Congreve, W., 1700),
I. 74, 190, 193, 236, 242–3, 341, 398;
II. 125, 147

The year date usually is the earliest recorded, whether of production, publication or submission to the Lord Chamberlain's Office. For a few plays two dates appear: this indicates that a drama published at a certain time was not acted until several years later. To save space the various dates of similarly named pantomimes are given together, not separately. For plays written by two authors only references to the main entries in the Hand-lists are given.

(2) All initial definite and indefinite articles are omitted, except (*a*) when they form part of a proverb or quotation, as in *The Greatest of These*—; and (*b*) when the deliberately archaic 'Ye' is employed, as in *Ye Battell of Bosworth Field*.

(3) The original spelling forms are retained, as in *Old Batchelour*, but minor variations, such as *Busie-Body* and *Busie Body* are ignored. When confusion might arise, cross-references are supplied from the old-spelling to the modern-spelling forms.

(4) Occasionally plays appear in the Hand-lists twice, once under the name by which they were performed and once under that by which they were licensed. In such instances the form used is as in:

Fisherman's Hut (Tobin, J., 1819)=
Fisherman, IV. 413, 461, 614, 625

Those consulting the catalogue should observe that for some of these double entries part of the relevant information appears in one Hand-list entry, part in another. Thus in the example given above, IV. 413 gives the title under which this melodrama was performed and the date, IV. 461 records the title it had when submitted to the Lord Chamberlain and gives reference to the manuscript, while IV. 614 gives information concerning a printed version of the songs included in the production. Entries under both titles should be consulted.

(5) A + sign before an entry indicates that the play in question does not appear in the Hand-lists but has been added to this catalogue. Similarly a + sign before an author's name or a date draws attention to additional information incorporated here. Other notes are given in square brackets.

(6) Sub-titles and alternative titles are presented with the symbol =, followed by the main title to which they belong, as in:

Manoeuvring = Two make a Pair

It should be observed that the = sign may indicate (*a*) a sub-title (e.g. 'Mayor in a Hamper=Peeping Tom' refers to a play entitled *Peeping Tom; or, The Mayor in a Hamper*); (*b*) an original title abandoned before production (e.g. 'Bertrand and Suzetta=Marriage of Reason' refers to a play acted as *The Marriage of Reason* but submitted to the Lord Chamberlain as *Bertrand and Suzette*); or (*c*) a title substituted at a revival of the play or in a printed text (e.g. 'Brothers = Wolf and the Lamb' refers to a piece acted as *The Wolf and the Lamb* but later published as *The Brothers*). In addition, the same symbol is used to call attention to divergent spellings (e.g. *Boadicia* for *Boadicea*).

(7) In all instances, adaptations and translations are given under the names of the authors concerned in adapting or translating: thus, for example, Kemble's *Hamlet* is listed under Kemble's name, not under Shakespeare's, and *Rosmersholm* under Archer's, not under Ibsen's. Fundamentally, this is a catalogue of dramatic activity in England and any procedure other than that adopted here would have raised serious problems. *Rosmersholm* is, of course, only a translation, but it would have been impossible to draw an exact line between such a drama and *Breaking a Butterfly*, which is an adapted version of *A Doll's House*: Kemble's *Hamlet* is, in the main, merely a cut version of Shakespeare's tragedy, but from this we move on to adaptations of all kinds, going so far even as an independent melodrama called *Hamlet Prince of Denmark*, with songs for Hamlet and Ophelia. Apart from the fact that some of the 'Shakespeare' titles refer to lost plays concerning the text of which we have no other information, clearly it would have been inadvisable to list all of these under 'Shakespeare', and precisely the same conclusion must be reached in dealing with dramas derived from foreign originals, stretching all the way from literal versions to what are virtually separate works.

(8) Where a single title applies to several plays, the order of entry is (*a*) by authors, alphabetically; (*b*) by dates for anonymous pieces; and (*c*) by sub-titles. For example:

> Adrift on the World (Bousfield, F., 1868), v. 270
> — (Twist, J. C., 1894), v. 605
> — (1874), v. 638
> — = Outcast Joe

This indicates (*a*) that there are two plays of known authorship, in 1868 and 1894; (*b*) that there is one, in 1874, which is anonymous; and (*c*) that the same title is attached as a variant to a drama the main title of which is *Outcast Joe*.

(9) The arrangement of entries is strictly alphabetical, so that, for example, *Only a Farmer's Daughter* comes before *On Parade* and *Son's Revenge* before *Son Tricked*. Where a title has *Dr Faustus*, this is not altered to *Doctor Faustus*; where it has *No. 17*, this is not altered to *Number 17*.

(10) Numbers are inserted alphabetically as they are commonly pronounced. Thus £110 *Pounds* appears as though it were 'A Hundred and Ten Pounds', and 1873 as though it were 'Eighteen Seventy Three'. Names of monarchs followed by numbers (as in *Henry VIII*) are placed in numerical order first in their appropriate categories, and variants, such as *Henry the Fifth* for *Henry V*, are regularised. Thus the Henry monarchs come before, say, *Henry Adams* and *Henry VIII* comes after, not before, *Henry V*.

Undoubtedly, there must be a number of duplicates in this catalogue, even although a considerable amount of effort has been made to identify entries of the same piece listed under two varying titles. It has, however, been thought wiser to leave possible duplicates standing without comment rather than risk guesses which might wrongly bring two distinct dramas under one name. No doubt the detailed study of individual dramatists, with the exact examination of manuscripts and printed texts, will result in the identification of many among the 'Lord Chamberlain' plays with plays listed under other names; but until such detailed examination is made the titles must perforce remain separately recorded. It is tempting, for example, to hazard the suggestion that *Under Suspicion*, licensed on 5 June 1894 for a minor London hall, is a revised version of another *Under Suspicion* licensed for Margate on 22 April 1893, and acted there on 29 May of that year as *The New Boy*; but we cannot be sure. It might be thought that *Little Ben Bolt*, licensed for the Bijou, Nashville Gardens, in 1876, is the same as Edwin Keene's *Little Ben Bolt*, acted at the Subscription Ground, Gravesend, in 1879; but again any basis for making a sure judgment is denied us. In the present state of knowledge concerning dramatic activity of these years the student is far more likely to be aided by having as full a list of titles as possible, even if he comes to discover that some of them are variant duplicates, than by having these variant titles attached together on no certain foundation of proof. Similarly, he is less likely to be confused if the attempt is made to keep as strictly as possible to the contemporary ascriptions of authorship for the plays recorded here.

A SHORT-TITLE
ALPHABETICAL CATALOGUE OF PLAYS

PRODUCED OR PRINTED IN ENGLAND
FROM 1660 TO 1900

A Apple Pie (1866), v. 638

Abaellino, the Great Bandit (Dunlap, W., 1802), IV. 582

+ Abandondero, the Bloodless (Byron, H. H.: *Dicks* (in *Sensation Dramas*))

Abandoned Irishman = Pat and his Potatoes

Abarbance the Hebrew (1849), IV. 423

Abbaye de Castro (Boucicault, D., 1851), v. 779

Abbé Buonaparte (1891), v. 638

Abbé de l'Epée = Deaf and Dumb

Abbé Laffarge (1876), v. 638

Abbess of Santa Maria = Modern Vittoria Bracciano

Abbé Vaudreuil and the Court of Louis XV (Addison, H. R., 1860), v. 235

Abbey Lands (1824), IV. 423

Abbey of Glenthorn = Murderer's Dream

Abbey of San Marco = Proof Presumptive

Abbey of St Aubert = Ellinda

Abbot (Beverley, H. R., 1820), IV. 94, 267, 572

Abbot of San Martino (Dibdin, T. J., 1819), IV. 302

A.B.C. (Dibdin, T. J., 1833), IV. 423, 619

— (Newton, H. C., 1898), v, 503

Abdalla (Delap, J., 1803), IV, 165, 289

— (Wallace, J., 1845), IV, 416

Abdallah (Barham, F. F., 1820), IV. 569

— (1891), v. 638

Abdelazer (Behn, A., 1676), I. 101, 120, 390

Abd el Kador, the Napoleon of Algeria (1848), IV. 423

Abdellac the Terrible (1824), IV. 619

Abdicated Prince (1690), I. 11, 439

Abdication of Ferdinand (Mayo, R. W., 1809), IV. 423, 619

Abduction of Bianca (Sapte, W., Jr. and Yorke, C. M., 1888), v. 556

Abduction of the Jew's Daughter = Fortune-teller

Abelard and Heloise (Buckstone, J. B., 1837), IV. 275

Abel Drake (Taylor, T. and Saunders, J., 1874), v. 594

Abel Drake's Wife (1872), v. 638

Abel Flint (Hazlewood, C. H., 1868), v. 797

Abelino (1805), IV. 423

Abigail (1849), IV. 423

Abimelech (Jago, R., 1784), III. 348, 388

Abon (Tabrar, J., 1885), v. 589

Abon Hassan (1793), III. 318

— (O'Neil, A., 1869), v. 507

Abou Hassan (Dimond, W., 1825), IV. 145, 307, 581

— (Gilbeigh, and Grimes, G., 1850), v. 638, 793, 795, 826

— (Talfourd, F., 1854), v. 590

— (Upton, W., 1810), IV. 423, 619

Abou Hassan, the Sleeper of Bagdad and the Fairy Elves of the Enchanted Mosque (Marchant, F., 1862), v. 638, 805, 826

Aboukir Bay (Sicklemore, R., 1799), III. 307

About Town (À Beckett, A. W., 1873), v. 233

Above and Below (Stirling, E. 1846), IV. 37, 408

— (1847), IV. 423

Above Suspicion (Capel, G., 1882), v. 302

Abradates and Panthea (Edwards, J., 1808), IV. 309

3

Adventures of a Night = Alasnum and his Cottage Queen

Adventures of an Umbrella = Memoirs of an Umbrella

Adventures of a Sealed Packet = Nabob's Fortune

Adventures of a Servant Girl = Mary Price

Adventures of a Shilling (1845), IV. 424

Adventures of a Ventriloquist (Moncrieff, W. T., 1822), IV. 359

— (1826), IV. 424

Adventures of a Young Man (Lee, N. Jr., 1860), V. 802

Adventures of Becky Sharp (1899), V. 638

Adventures of Charley-wag (1846), IV. 424

Adventures of Cheek and Plant = Cheek and Plant

Adventures of Don Quixote = Don Quixote

Adventures of Five Hours (Tuke, Sir S., 1663), I. 2, 9, 26, 33, 38, 66, 69, 101, 127, 171, 192, 197, 219, 264, 346, 347, 348, 435; III. 114

Adventures of Florio the Foundling Prince = Dark King of the Black Mountains

Adventures of Four Years = Abdicated Prince

Adventures of Half an Hour (Bullock, C., 1716), II. 211, 301

Adventures of Harlequin in Spain (1741), II. 365

Adventures of Robin Hood, Earl of Huntingdon (1730), II. 365 [Probably = Robin Hood, II. 448]

Adventures of Jerry Abbershaw (1826), IV. 424

Adventures of John Sheppard = Prison Breaker

Adventures of Paddy O'Rafferty = Irishman's Fortune

Adventures of Prince Headstrong and Princess Bloomingbell = Enchanted Tower

Adventures of Roderick Random (Dibdin, T. J., 1818), IV. 96, 301

Adventures of Roderick Random, and his Friend Strap = (1) Pretenders; (2) Volunteers

Adventures of the Count de Monte Cristo (Smith, H. J., 1899), V. 572

Adventures of the Halibut Family = Life in Paris

Adventures of the Prince of Seville (1790), III. 318

Adventures of the Weasel Family = Pop goes the Weasel

Adventures of Tom and Jerry = Ashantees

Adventures of Tom Trip (Siddons, H., 1796), III. 307

Adventures of Twelve Hours = Love in the East.

Adventures of Ulysses (Mendham, 1811), IV. 355

Adventures of Venice = Perjur'd Husband

Adventuress (Amory, T. S., 1882), V. 240

— (Hilton, B. H., 1871), V. 422

Adversity (1861), V. 638

Advertisement (Burges, Sir J. B., 1817), IV. 276

— (Fennell, J., 1791), III, 259

— (Gardner, Mrs Sarah, 1777), III. 262

Advertisement for a Husband (Lawler, D., 1814), IV. 342

Advertisements (1868), V. 638

Advertisement—Wanted, Wives and Husbands (1854), V. 638

Advice Gratis (Dance, C., 1837), IV. 288

Advice to Husbands (Lancaster, C. S., 1846), IV. 341

— = Hints to Wives

Advocate (Lander, C., 1886), V. 447

— (1859), V. 638

— = Last Cause

Advocate and his Daughter (Ebsworth, J., 1852) = Advocate's Daughter, V. 353, 789, 826

Advocate of Durango (Wynne, J., 1853), V. 634

Advocate's Daughter (Ebsworth, J., 1856) = Advocate and his Daughter, V. 638, 789, 826

Advocate's Wife = Fatal Duel of the Glacis

Adzuma (Arnold, Sir E., 1893), V. 243

Æneas (Granville, H. S., 1868), V. 388

Aladdin (Hewson, J. J., 1896), v. 640, 798, 826
— (Lisle, M., 1896), v. 460
— (Locke, F., 1889), v. 462
— (Milton, A. and Milton, P., 1897), v. 640, 807, 826
— (O'Keeffe, J., 1788), III. 294 (the same as the pantomime listed, III. 318)
— (O'Neill, J. R.), v. 808
— (Pike, A. E., 1896), v. 524
— (Pratt, F. W., 1889), v. 639, 811, 826
— (Ramsdale, T., 1889), v. 534
— (Ramsdale, T., 1892), v. 534
— (Ratton, E. R., 1897), v. 535
— (Reece, R., 1881), v. 539
— (Rogers, T. S., 1897), v. 549
— (Rogers, T. S., 1898), v. 549
— (Smith, A. R. and Kenney, C., 1844), IV. 402, 611
— (Soane, G., 1826), IV. 403
— (Soutar, R., 1868), v. 575
— (Spry, H., 1879), v. 577
— (Sturgess, A. and Lennard, H., 1896), v. 586
— (Summers, W., 1898), v. 640, 818, 826
— (Thorne, G., 1889), v. 598
— (Thorne, G., 1890), v. 598
— (Thorne, G., 1898), v. 599
— (Townrow L., Jones, J. W. and Mulholland, J. B., 1896), v. 441
— (White, J. W., 1893), v. 620
— (1810, 1811, 1826, 1833), IV. 424
— (1861), v. 640
— (1873, 1875), v. 639
— (1875), v. 640
— (1876, 1877, 1878, 1879, 1880, 1881, 1882, 1883, 1884, 1885, 1886, 1887, 1888, 1889, 1890), v. 639
— (1890, 1891, 1892, 1893, 1895, 1896, 1897, 1898, 1899), v. 640
Aladdin, a Lad with a Wonderful Lamp (Conquest, G. and Spry, H., 1895), v. 323
Aladdin and his Cloud Palace (1830), IV. 424
Aladdin and his Wonderful Lamp (Green, F. W., 1881), v. 391
Aladdin and the Flying Genius (1881), v. 640

Aladdin and the Forty Thieves (Reece, R., 1885), v. 539
Aladdin and the Lamp (George, G. H., 1873), v. 377
Aladdin and the Wonderful Lamp (Blanchard, E. L., 1865), v. 264
— (Blanchard, E. L. and Greenwood, T. L., 1878), v. 265
— (Jones, J. W., 1894), v. 441
— (Lennard, H., 1889), v. 455
— (McArdle, J. F., 1879), v. 466
— (Morton, J. M., 1856), v. 496
— (Spry, H., 1874), v. 576
— (Taylor, E., 1856), v. 820
— (1856), v. 640
Aladdin at Sea (Zangwill, I., 1893), v. 637
Aladdin, in another Shape (Horncastle, J. H., 1844), IV. 328
Aladdin in Luck (Craven, T., 1893), v. 329
Aladdin's Lamp (Best, W., 1883), v. 260
Aladdin the First (1871), v. 640
Aladdin the Great (1875), v. 640
Aladdin, the Lad with the Wonderful Lamp (Conquest, G. and Spry, H., 1884), v. 322
Aladdin the Second (Thompson, A., 1870) = Aladdin the Third, v. 597, 640, 820, 826
Aladdin the Third (Thompson, A., 1870) = Aladdin the Second, v. 597, 640, 820, 826
Aladdin up-to-date (Thorne, G., 1895), v. 599
A-lad-in and well out of it (Smith, B., 1889), v. 572
À la Française (Bartholeyns, A. O'D., 1893), v. 252
Alanna, the Child of Clare (1894), v. 640
Alan's Wife (Bell, Mrs H., 1893), v. 256
Alarbas (1709), II. 234, 365
Alaric and Eliza (1808), IV. 424
Alarm (1776), III. 398
Alarm Bell = Twelve at Night
Alarming Incidents (1845), IV. 424
Alarming Sacrifice (Buckstone, J. B., 1849), IV. 275, 575
Alarmist (Roberdeau, J. P., 1803), IV. 395
Alasco (Shee, Sir M. A., 1824), IV. 203–5, 400

Alasnum and his Cottage Queen (1816),
IV. 424

Alban and Aphanasia (O'Keeffe, J.),
III, 294

Albanio = Fatal Accusation

Alberic, the Consul of Rome (Dwarris,
Sir F. W. L., 1832), IV. 582

Alberta (Carter, J., 1787), III. 242

Albert and Adelaide (Birch, S., 1798),
III, 45, 101–2, 238, 378

Albert and Elmira (1820), IV. 425

Albert and Emma = Treacherous Baron

Albert and Louise = Soldier Girl

Albert and Rosalie (Wharton, F. F.,
1808), IV. 419

— = Fire King

Albert Arnall = Adolph Arnal

Albert de Rosen (Lane, Mrs S., 1875),
V. 448

Alberto and Lauretta (Lynch, T. J.,
1806), IV. 425, 619

Alberto and Rosabella = Brazen Mask

Albert's Mystery (1899), V. 640

Albina, Countess Raimond (Cowley,
Mrs H., 1779), III. 83, 248

Albion (Cooke, T., 1724), II. 260, 316

Albion and Albanius (Dryden, J., 1685),
I. 40, 43, 44–8, 65, 135, 141, 158–9,
406

Albion Queens (Banks, J., 1704), I. 52–
3, 167, 389

Albion Restored (Stevens, G. A., 1758),
III. 318, 396, 398

Alboin (Gurney, A. T., 1846), IV. 322

Album (James, H., 1895), V. 433

Albumazar (?Garrick, D., 1747), II.
437

— (Garrick, D., 1773), III. 113, 263, 385

Album of Beauties (1884), V. 641

Album of Beauty (1879), V. 641

Alcaid (Kenney, J., 1824), IV. 144, 337,
592

Alcamanes and Menalippa (Phillips,
W.), I. 423

Alcantara (Woolf, B. E., 1879), V. 632,
824

Alcestis (Spicer, H., 1855), V. 576

— (Todhunter, J., 1879), V. 600

Alcestis burlesqued (Styrke, I., 1816),
IV. 409

Alcestis, the Original Strong-minded
Woman (Talfourd, F., 1850), V. 590

Alchemist (Shillingford, O., 1897), V.
563

— (1782), III. 318. See also Alchymist

Alchemist of Modena (Charlton, F.,
1868), V. 308

Alchymist (Fitzball, E. and Bayly, T. H.,
1832), IV. 314, 584

— (Garrick, D., 1774), III. 264

— (Moser, J. additional scene, 1809),
IV. 364

Alchymy (Dibdin, C. I. M., 1817), IV.
294

Alchymyst's Daughter (Oxenford, J.,
1844), IV. 367

Alcibiades (Otway, T., 1675), I. 39, 40,
120, 165, 348, 422

Alcide (1821), IV. 425

Alderman (Mortimer, J., 1887), V. 494

Alderman No Conjurer = Cuckolds-
Haven

Alderman's Bargain = Luckey Chance

Alderman's Gown (Abrahams, H.,
1851), V. 235

Alderman's Last Wish = Bow Bells

Aldgate Pump (Faucit, J. S., 1841), IV.
311, 583

Alerame, the Knight of the Lion
(Denvil, 1833), IV. 290

Alexander and Statira (Wallis, G.),
III. 314

Alexander Balus (Morell, T., 1748), II.
388

Alexander Selkirk (1845), IV. 425

Alexander's Successors = Humorous
Lieutenant

Alexander the Great (Egville, J. d',
1795), III, 258, 398

— (Kemble, J. P., 1795), III. 279

— (Ozell, J., 1714), II. 347, 442

— (1715), II. 388

— (1770), III. 59, 318

— = Chiselling

Alexander the Great and Thalestris the
Amazon (Dibdin, C. I. M., 1822), IV.
295

Alexander the Great! in Little (Dibdin,
T. J., 1837), IV. 305

Alexander the Little (1764), III. 318

—— (1791), III. 318

Alexandra (1893), V. 641

Alexina (Knowles, J. S., 1866), V. 445

Alexis (Vallings, H., 1885), V. 606

Alexis (1831), IV. 425
Alexis and Dorinda (1725), II. 365
Alexis's Paradise (Newton, J., ?1722), II. 346
Alfonso and Claudina, the Faithful Spouse (1862), V. 641
Alfonso, King of Castile (Lewis, M. G., 1801), IV. 163, 195, 345
Alfred (Garrick, D., 1773), III. 263
— (Gower, Lord F. L., 1840), IV. 320
— (Home, J., 1778), III. 94, 272
— (Lindsay, Sir C., 1848), IV. 595
— (Mallet, D. and Thomson, J., 1740), II. 343, 440, 445
— (Mallet, D. and Thomson, J., 1751), III. 286
— (O'Keeffe, J., 1796), III. 295
— (Rhodes, E., 1789), III. 61, 318, 394, 398
— (1861), V. 641
Alfred and Elvida = Patriot King
Alfred and Emma (1806), IV. 87, 425
Alfred and Matilda (1825), IV. 425
Alfred le Grand, roi d'Angleterre (Aumer, 1823), IV. 425, 619
Alfred the Great (Almar, G.), IV. 253
— (Brough, R. B., 1859), V. 278
— (Faucit, Mrs J. S., 1811), IV. 311
— (Hamilton, S., 1829), IV. 425, 619
— (Knowles, J. S., 1831), IV. 79, 112, 172, 339
— (Lawler, D., 1811), IV. 425
— (Lonsdale, M., 1798), III. 318, 391, 398
— (Magnus, T., 1838), IV. 597
— (Milner, H. M., 1824), IV. 357
— (Pocock, I., 1827), IV. 46, 112, 387
— (1823), IV. 425
— = Alfred
Alfred the Great at Athelney (Redcliffe, Lord Stratford de, 1876), V. 536
Alfred the Great, Deliverer of his Country (1753), III. 318
Alfred the Ingrate (Bayley, W. V., 1871), V. 253
Al Fresco (1899), V. 641
Algerian (McDonough, G., 1893), V. 469
Algerine Corsair = Alzira
Algerine Slaves (Cobb, J., 1792), III. 244
Algernon the Blind Guide (Pitt, G. D., 1847), IV. 374

Algonah (Cobb, J., 1802), IV. 280
Alhambra (Smith, A. R., 1851), V. 572
Alhamor the Moor (Fitzball, E., 1849), IV. 317 [The entry under *Almahar* on IV. 425 should be deleted]
Ali Baba (Byron, H. J., 1863), V. 296
— (Colman, G. the Younger, 1806) = Forty Thieves, IV. 425
— (Locke, F., 1898), V. 462
— (Moreton, F. L. and Mountford, H., 1897), V. 493
— (O'Neil, J. R., 1852), V. 808
— (Pratt, F. W., 1892), V. 641, 811, 826
— (Taddei, E., 1871), V. 590
— (1811), IV. 425
— (1850), V. 826
— (1865), V. 641
— (1868), V. 826
— (1873, 1879, 1883, 1895), V. 641
Ali Baba à la mode (Reece, R., 1872), V. 537
Ali Baba and the Forty Thieves (À Beckett, G. A., 1866), V. 233
— (À Beckett, G. A., 1871), V. 233
— (Byron, H. J., Gilbert, W. S., Burnand, F. C. and Reece, R., 1878), V. 299
— (Chatterton, F. B. and Grattan, H. P. 1881), V. 308
— (Douglass, J. T., 1878), V. 348
— (Green, F. W., 1872), V. 794
— (1878, 1879, 1880, 1884, 1896), V. 641
Ali Baba, M.P. (Scarlett, W., 1893), V. 557
Alice Aukland (Parry, T., 1843), IV. 368
Alice Gray (1833), IV. 425
Alice Grey (Haines, J. T., 1839), IV. 323, 587
Alice Home (1843), IV. 425
Alice in Wonderland (Clarke, H. S., 1886), V. 313, 826
— (1886), V. 641, 826
Alice Lowrie, the Forger's Victim (1861), V. 641
Alice May (Fitzball, E., 1852), V. 368
Alice Wingold (Lacy, M. R., 1862), V. 446
Alienated Manor (Baillie, J., 1836), IV. 258
Aliens (Rowe, B., 1889), V. 552
Alina (1844), IV. 425

Alina (1851), v. 641

Aline (Stirling, E., 1843), IV. 407

Aline, reine de Golconde (Aumer, 1823), IV. 425, 619

Ali Pacha (Payne, J. H. and Planché, J. R., 1822), IV. 377

Ali Pasha (1836), IV. 425

Alive and Merry (Brown, 1796), III. 240

— (Dance, C., 1839), IV. 289

Alive or Dead (Hall, R. W., 1876), v. 400

— (Webb, C., 1843), IV. 425, 619

All about a Bonnet (Harraden, H., 1891), v. 404

All about a Lost Will = Capers

All about Love and Jealousy (Bolton, G., 1846), IV. 425, 619

All about the Battle of Dorking (Burnand, F. C. and Sketchley, A., 1871), v. 290

All Abroad (Burnside, W., 1892), v. 293

— (Hall, O. and Tanner, J. T., 1895), v. 400

— (Law, A., 1890), v. 450

Alladine and Palmonides (Archer, W., 1899), v. 242

All a Fetch (Dibdin, T. J., 1826), IV. 304

All Alive and Merry (Johnson, S., 1737), II. 340

— (1740), II. 451

— = (1) Happy Hero; (2) Wanton Trick'd

All Alive at Liverpool (1809), IV. 619

All Alive at the Races = Epsom Downs

All Alive in Auld Reekie = Royal Visit

All Alive, Oh! (1897), v. 641

All a Mistake (Phillips, Mrs N., 1890), v. 523

— (1825), IV. 425

+ Allario and Adelina; or, The Village Inn and the Count Out (Byron, H. J.: *Dicks* (in *Sensation Dramas*))

All Asleep at Noon = Modern Breakfast

All at C (Millet, and Wilcox, 1873), v. 489

All at Coventry (Moncrieff, W. T., 1816), IV. 358

All at Home (1804), IV. 425

All at Cross Purposes = Contrarieties

All at Sea (Grundy, S., 1873), v. 205, 396

All at Sea (Law, A., 1881), v. 449

All at Sixes and Sevens (Dibdin, C. I. M., 1829), IV. 296

All Bedevil'd (Browne, M., 1723), II. 215, 300

All but lost (Warrington, F., 1869), v. 615

All but One (Travers, W., 1868), v. 602

All by Chance (Belverstone, J., 1879), v. 257

All Change Here (Keith, R., 1898), v. 442

All comes to he who waits = Waiter

All Correct = Marriage of Gamacho

Allegro, il Penseroso ed il Moderato (Jennens, S., 1740), II. 388, 439

Allendale (Phillpotts, E. and Burgin, G. B., 1893), v. 524

All Fair in Fair Time = Cousin Campbell's Courtship

All for Error = What a Blunder!

All for Fame! (Cherry, A., 1805), IV. 279, 576

All for Gold (Griffiths, J. C., 1878), v. 394

— (Hopkins, F., 1878), v. 426

— = Found Dead in the Streets

All for her (Simpson, J. P., 1875), v. 568

All for himself (Wills, C., 1874), v. 626

All for Love (Dryden, J., 1677), I. 115, 136, 172-3, 177, 179-80, 350, 406; II. 70

— (Coyne, J. S., 1838), IV. 284

All for Money (Thierre, G. le, 1869), v. 595

All for Nothing (Aidé, H., 1880), v. 236

All for Number One = Gay Musketeers

All for our Country = Inundation

All for St Paul's = Britain's Brave Tars!!

All for the Best (1846), IV. 425

— (1880), v. 641

All for the Better (Manning, F., 1702), II. 50, 140, 160, 170, 343, 440

All for Them (Lyste, H. P., 1876), v. 465

All Hallows' Eve (Forbes, Mrs and Whitbread, J. W., 1891), v. 370

— (Leclercq, M., 1859), v. 641, 802, 826

— (Towers, E., 1865), v. 821

— (1838), IV. 425

— (1882), IV. 641

Altamira = Generall

+Altamont and Lavinia (Smock Alley, Dublin, 8/3/1776)

Altar of Revenge = Nick of the Woods

Altemira (Boyle, R., 1701), I. 100, 106–7, 394; II. 299, 432

Alternative (1796), III. 318 [The date of acting should be 6/1/1796]

Alternative, Tyranny or Liberty = King Henry VII

Altogether (Dowsett, E., 1894), v. 350

Altogether Moral Trilby (Kay, C. B., 1896), v. 442

Alva (1840), IV. 619

+Alvarez (Talfourd, F., 1850), v. 819

— (1835), IV. 426

Always Intended (Wigan, H., 1865), v. 622

Always Ready (Callender, E. R., 1873), v. 300

Always sit up for your Husband (Sorrell, W. J., 1873), v. 574

Always Wrong and Try Again (1829), IV. 426

Alwyn and Bertholdy (Almar, G., 1831), IV. 426, 619

Alzira (Hill, A., 1736), II. 65, 72, 109, 336, 438

— (1809), IV. 426

Alzora and Nerine (+Leclerq, P., 1818), IV. 426

Alzuma (Murphy, A., 1773), III. 43, 53, 76–7, 290

Amadan (Boucicault, D., 1883), v. 269

Amadis (Rich, J., 1718), II. 133, 253, 365

— (1724), II. 446

Amakosa (Fitzball, E., 1853), v. 368

Amalasont, Queen of Goths (Hughes, J., 1696), I. 415

Amalderac the Black Pirate (1840), IV. 426, 593

Amalderac, the Black Rover (Lancaster, E. R.), IV. 426, 593

Amana (Griffith, Mrs E., 1764), III. 266

Amanthis (1820), IV. 426

Amasis King of Egypt (Marsh, C., 1738), II. 39, 58, 71, 111, 343

Amateur Detective (Lloyd, A., 1898), v. 461

Amateur Wife (Lancaster-Wallis, E., 1897), v. 447

Amateurs and Actors (Peake, R. B., 1818), IV. 145, 369

Amazonian Warriors (1861), v. 826

Amazon Queen (Weston, J., 1667), I. 101, 437

Amazon Queen of Denmark and Norway = Landgartha

Amazons (Pinero, Sir A. W., 1893), v. 525

Amazon's Oath (1858), v. 641

Amazon Sisters = (1) Ida and Carelia; (2) Sisters

Ambassador (Hobbes, J. O., 1898), v. 422

+ — (8°, 1832)

Ambassador from Below = Mephistopheles

Ambassador's Lady (Wilkes, T. E., 1843), IV. 421

Ambassadress (À Beckett, G. A., 1838), IV. 84, 250

— (Mellers, H., 1848), IV. 84, 355

— (Reece, R., 1868), v. 537, 812

Amber Box (1800), IV. 426

Amber Girl (Gordon-Clifford, E. and H., 1894), v. 385

Amber Heart (Calmour, A. C., 1887), v. 300

Amber Witch (Chorley, H. F., 1861), v. 784

— (? Faucit, J. S., 1851), v. 363, 791

Ambiguous Lover (Sheridan, Miss, 1781), III. 184, 305

Ambition (Fomm, L., 1899), v. 370

— (Mayhew, T., 1830), IV. 355, 598

— (Phillips, F. L., 1857), v. 641, 810, 826

— (Walford, H. L., 1870), v. 611

— (1836), IV. 426

— (1854), v. 641

Ambition's Slave (Fox, J., 1883), v. 371

Ambitious Father = Injur'd Lovers

Ambitious Mrs Moresby (White, E., 1898), v. 620

Ambitious Queen = Siege of Memphis

Ambitious Slave (Settle, E., 1694), I. 101, 149–50, 429

Ambitious Statesman (Crowne, J., 1679), I. 56, 150, 399

Ambitious Step-Mother (Rowe, N., 1700), II. 50, 98, 351, 443

Ambitious Vengeance (Merry, R., 1790), III. 287

Ambitious Widow (Woty, W., 1770), III. 317

Amboyna (Dryden, J., 1673), I. 78, 405

Ambrose Gwinett (Jerrold, D. W., 1828), IV. 331

+ Ambrosius (Berry, Alice, 8°, 1879)

Ambuscade at Inkerman (1860), v. 641

Amelia (Carey, H., 1732), II. 31, 32, 235–6, 302

— (Cumberland, R., 1768), III. 251, 381

Amergau (McSwiney, P., 1881), v. 472

America (Barber, J. H., 1805), IV. 258

— (Dibdin, T. J., 1812), IV. 299

American (Derrick, J., 1882), v. 343

— (James, H., 1891), v. 433

— (Wood, G. M., 1883), v. 630

American Adventurers = Coup de Main

American Assurance (Sidney, F. W., 1894), v. 565

American Belle (Seton, H., 1897), v. 561

American Bride (Young, Sir W. L. and Noel, M., 1892), v. 637

American Citizen (Ryley, M. L., 1899), v. 554

American Girl = (1) Sunny Florida; (2) Spin for Life

American Heiress (Branscombe, A. and Day, G. D., 1899), v. 274

American Heroine (1790), III. 318

— (1792), III. 319

— (1796), III. 319

— (1797), III. 319

American Indian (Bacon, J., 1795), III. 235

American in England (1855), v. 641

American Lady (Byron, H. J.,1874),v. 298

Americans (Arnold, S. J., 1811), IV. 255

Americans Abroad = Jonathan in England

American Savage = Tombo-Chiqui

American Singer Downstairs (Locke, T. and Downes, J. F., 1899), v. 462

American Sketches = Belle of the Hotel

American Slavery (1862), v. 641

American Slaves (McLaren, A., 1792), III. 284

American War of 1780 = Spy of the Neutral Ground

Amethyst Ring (1838), IV. 426

Amiable Mistake = Ranger in Wedlock

Am I a Princess? = Rosine

Amilie (Haines, J. T., 1837), IV. 322

Am I Myself or Another? = Irishman's Dream

Aminta (Dancer, J., 1660), I. 400

— (Du Bois, P., 1726), II. 224, 320, 435

— (Oxenford, J., 1852), v. 509

Amintas (Ayre, W., 1737), II. 224, 296, 432

— (Oldmixon, J., 1698), I. 422; II. 347, 442

— (Rolt, R. and Tenducci, F., 1769), III. 303

Amintas et Sylvie (1802), IV. 426

Aminte et Sylvie (1814), IV. 426

Among the Amalekites (Bennett, E., 1889), v. 258

Among the Breakers (Brougham, J., 1868), v. 281

Among the Mormons (Ward, A., 1866), v. 613

Among the Relics (Palmer, T. A., 1869), v. 511

Amorel of Lyonnesse (Brown, W. H. and Lawrence, S. B., 1890), v. 282

Amores da Gileso Scroggini e Molli Brownini (Lemon, M., 1843), IV. 344

Amorous Adventure (1730), II. 365

Amorous Adventures = Marriage A-la-Mode

Amorous Alderman (1773), III. 319

Amorous Bigotte (Shadwell, T., 1690), I. 187, 431

Amorous Fantasme (Lower, Sir W., 1660), I. 420

Amorous Fryars = Rome's Follies

Amorous Gallant = Amorous Orontus

Amorous Goddess (1744), II. 365

Amorous Jilt = Younger Brother

Amorous Knight, and the Belle Widow = Valentine's Day

Amorous Miser (1705), II. x, 209–10, 233, 365, 441, 446

Amorous Old-woman (1674), I. 17, 439

Amorous Orontus (Bulteel, J., 1664), I. 101, 394

Amorous Prince (Behn, A., 1671), I. 83, 140, 266–7, 390

Amorous Quaker = Fox and Geese

Amorous Quarrel (Foote, S., 1762), III. 384

Amorous Sportsman (1732), II. 365

Amorous Widow (Betterton, T., 1670), I. 17, 188, 259, 281, 347, 392; III. 114

Amos Clark (Phillips, W., 1872), V. 523
Amos Tyrrell (1892), V. 641
Amour (1819), IV. 426
Amour A-la-Mode (Kelly, H., 1760),
    III. 278
Amour et la folie (1817), IV. 426
Amourettes (Percival, J., 1885), V. 520
Amour fugitif = Anacreon
Amours among the Moors = Cadi
Amours de Glauque et Circe (1809), IV.
    426
Amours de Mars et Vénus (1811), IV.
    426
Amours de Paris (1834), IV. 426
Amours of Billingsgate = Cobler's Opera
Amours of Harlequin (1749), II. 451
Amours of Harlequin and Miss Cadiere
    = Father Girard the Sorcerer
Amours of Lord Flame = Cheshire
    Comics
Amours of Mars and Venus (1746), II.
    365
Amours of Sir John Falstaffe = Comical
    Gallant
Amours of Thalestris to Alexander =
    Amazon Queen
Amours of the Great = Vanelia
Amphitryon (Dryden, J., 1690), I. 188,
    231, 308, 352, 407; III. 113
— (Echard, L., 1693), I. 410
— (Hawkesworth, J., 1756), III. 113, 267
— (1872), V. 641
Ample Apology (Roberts, G., 1865), V.
    544
Ample Security (Stephenson, C. H.,
    1872), V. 582
Amurath, the Great Emperor of the
    Turks (1730), II. 365
Amusements on the Road of Life =
    Euphrosyne
Amy (Somerset, C. A., 1847), IV. 405
Amy Arlington (Stewart, D., 1863), V.
    641, 826
Amoroso, King of Little Britain
    (Planché, J. R., 1818), IV. 152, 376
Amy Lawrence, the Freemason's
    Daughter (Bidalles, A. H., 1851), V.
    261
Amyntas (Stockdale, P., 1770), III. 70,
    309, 396
Amy Robsart (Halliday, A., 1870), V.
    401

Amy Robsart (Kingthorne, M., 1880),
    V. 445
— (Markwell, W. R.), V. 477
— (Weatherley, F. E. and Harris, Sir A.,
    1893), V. 617
Amy the Golden (1860), V. 642
Amy the Skipper's Daughter (Barnett,
    C. Z., 1847), IV. 261
Anaconda (Milliken, R. A., 1822), IV. 426
— (1818), IV. 426
Anacreon (1810), IV. 426
Anacreontics Revived (1800), IV. 426
Anarchist (Gieve, E., 1894), V. 378
Anarchy (Mackaye, J. S., 1887), V. 471
— (1899), V. 642
Anato (1850), V. 642
Anatomist (Ravenscroft, E., 1696), I.
    63, 191, 256, 426; III. 114
— (1771), III. 114, 319
An Bratach (Dibdin, C. I. M., 1805), IV.
    291
Ancestors of Leopold = Landgrave's
    Leap
Ancestral Incubus = Sir Reginald
Ancestress (Lemon, M., 1837), IV. 343
— (Lemon, M., 1840), IV. 344
Anchora Machree (1867), V. 642
Anchorite (1825), IV. 426
Anchor of Hope (Stirling, E., 1847), IV.
    408
Anchor's Weighed (Taylor, T. R.,
    1883), V. 592
— (1849), IV. 426
Ancient and Modern Fashions (1797),
    III. 398
Ancient and Modern Magic (Coletti, A.,
    1860), V. 317
Ancient Animosities = Juvenile Friend-
    ship
Ancient Britons (À Beckett, G. A., and
    Reed, G., 1875), V. 234
Ancient Chivalry = Ferdinand of Spain
Ancient Times (Strutt, J., 1808), IV. 409
And One Suffered (1889), V. 642
Andrea Hofer (1838), IV. 426
Andrea of Hungary (Landor, W. S.,
    1839), IV. 199, 341
Andrea the Painter (Neil, R., 1883), V.
    502
— (1888), V. 642
Andreas Hofer (Fitzball, E., 1832) =
    Hofer, IV. 314, 584

André the Miner, the Son of Toil (Faucquez, A., 1861), v. 642, 791, 826

André the Mountaineer = My Nadine

Andrew (Mohamed and Marlen, 1895), v. 490

Andrew Mills (1876), v. 642

Andrew Paterson (Vynne, N. and Hankin, St J. E. C., 1893), v. 609

Andrian (1772), III. 319

Androboros (?1700), II. 365

Androcles and the Lion (Planché, S., 1893), v. 528

Androcles, the Slave (1829), IV. 426

Andromache (Crowne, J., 1674), I. 98, 124, 399

Andromeda (Seaton, R., 1890), v. 559

— (1662), I. 252, 439

— (1897), v. 642

Andronicus (1661), I. 438, 439

Andronicus Comnenius (Wilson, J., 1664), I. 50, 438

Andy Blake (Boucicault, D., 1854), v. 268

Anecdote from the "Times" = Lord Mansfield's Wig

Angela (Kingston, L., 1878), v. 642, 801, 826

— (Wardhaugh, M., 1871), v. 614

Angela Teresa = Teresa

Angelica (1758), III. 319

Angelina (Cooper, W., 1889), v. 324

— (Goldsmith, M., 1804) = Walcot Castle, IV. 319, 550, 585, 642

Angeline (Cherry, A., 1811), IV. 576

— (1840), IV. 426

— (1854), v. 642

Angeline de Lis (Haines, J. T., 1837), IV. 322

Angel King (Neil, R., 1884), v. 502

Angelo (À Beckett, G. A., 1852), v. 233

— (Coe, E. O., 1880), v. 784

— (Cooper, F. F., 1835), IV. 80, 426, 577, 619

— (Reade, C., 1851), v. 535

Angel of Darkness (Conquest, G., 1859), v. 642, 785, 826

Angel of Death (Conquest, G., 1861). v, 320

— = Angel of Midnight

Angel of Islington (Blanchard, E. L., 1840), IV. 268

— (1855), v. 642

Angel of Midnight (Brougham, J., 1862), v. 280

— (Suter, W. E. and Lacy, T. H., 1861), = Spirit of Death, v. 588, 753, 819, 847

Angel of Peace and Pardon (1863), v. 642

Angel of the Attic (Morton, T., Jr., 1843), IV. 364

Angel or Devil (Coyne, J. S., 1857), v. 328

Angels and Lucifers (Blanchard, E. L., 1838), IV. 268

Angels of Paris (Rogers, F. and Wilkinson, M., 1894), v. 548

Angel's Visit (Abel, W. H., 1870), v. 234

Angel's Whisper (King, H. N., 1869), v. 444

Angiolina del' Albano (Stuart-Wortley, Lady Emmeline, 1841), IV. 613

Angler (Le Clercq, 1817), IV. 426, 619

Anglers = Queen of the Thames

Angling in Troubled Waters (Towers, E., 1872), v. 601

Animal Magnetism (Inchbald, Mrs E., 1788), III. 275, 388

Animal Sympathy (Dibdin, T. J., 1821), IV. 303

Animated Effigy (Scott, J. M., 1811), IV. 426, 619

Animated Fig (1811), IV. 426

Animated Portrait (Bourdon, 1816), IV. 426, 619

Animated Statue (1869), v. 642

Ankle Jack (Pitt, G. D., 1835), IV. 373

Anna (Cuthbertson, Miss, 1793), III. 253

— (1821), IV. 426

Anna Boleyn (Dickinson, A., 1877), v. 344

Anna Bullen (?1681), I. 439

— = Vertue Betray'd

Anna Maria's Piano (Robinson, N., 1872), v. 547

Anna of Norway (Reeve, W., 1869), v. 540

Anna Ruina (Field, M., 1899), v. 366

Anne Blake (Marston, J. W., 1852), v. 479

Anne Boleyn (Edwardes, C. T. M., 1872), v. 354

Anne Boleyn (Dodson, R., 1873), v.
346
— (Grover, H. M., 1827), IV. 321
— (Lee, N., 1856), v. 642, 802, 826
— (Milman, H. H., 1826), IV. 167, 356
— (Taylor, T., 1876), v. 594
— (1825), IV. 426
Anne Bracegirdle (1847), IV. 426
Annette (1837), IV. 619
Annette Carline (Pitt, G. D., 1848), IV.
375
Annette and Lubin (Dibdin, C., 1778),
III. 118, 255, 381
Anne Mie (Scott, C. W., 1880), v. 558
Ann Grandet (1835), IV. 427
Annie Laurie = Bonnie Annie Laurie
Annie Monksworth (Seaman, W., 1859),
v. 642, 815, 826
Annie of Edenside (Vynne, C., 1868), v.
609
Annie of Tharau (Zoblinsky, Mme,
1880), v. 637, 825
Annie Tyrell (Serle, T. J., 1852), v. 561
Annira (Waterhouse, B., 1822), IV. 616
Anniversary (1758), III. 319
— = (1) Guilt; (2) Waterloo Bridge
Anniversary of St Patrick = Shamrock
Ann Jane Thornton (1835), IV. 427
Anno Domini 1838 = Murphy's Weather
Almanac
Anno Domini 670 = Shadow of the
Cross
Anonymous (1838), IV. 427
Anonymous Letter (Ambient, M. and
Latimer, F., 1891), v. 240
— (Talfourd, F., 1854), v. 642, 819, 826
Anonymous Letters (Jacques, F., 1888),
v. 432
Another (Hodson, E., 1885), v. 423
Another Cup (1881), v. 642
Another Daughter of the Danube
(1847), IV. 619
Another Drink (Clarke, H. S. and
Clifton, L., 1879), v. 312
Another Elopement (De Lara, F., 1888),
v. 341
Another Fish out of Water = Recom-
mendations
Another Glass = Drunkard's Glass
Another Maid and Another Magpie
(+ Dibdin, C. I. M., 1815), IV. 148,
427

Another Man's Crime = Forgery
Another Man's Money (Payne, W. B.,
1884), v. 518
Another Man's Wife (Vaughan, W. J.
and Mackay, R. F., 1893), v. 607
Another Matinée = Stage Coach
Another Mistake (1883), v. 642
Another Mummy (1833), IV. 427
Another Pair of Shoes (Hay, F., 1875),
v. 411
Another Piece of Presumption (Peake,
R. B., 1823), IV. 427, 619
Another Retreat from Moscow = Great
Russian Bear
Anster Fair (Pocock, I., 1834), IV. 385
Answer Paid (Burnand, F. C. and
Austin, W. J., 1878), v. 291
Antarctic (Farnie, H. B., 1875), v. 362
Anthony and Cleopatra (1891), v. 642
Anthony, Cleopatra and Harlequin
(Dibdin, C. I. M., 1804), IV. 91, 291
Anthony Jolt (Bedwell, H., 1896), v. 255
Anthony's Legacy (Charleson, A. J.,
1891), v. 308
Anthropos (1898), v. 642
Antichristian Opera (Paul, G., 1755),
III. 296
Antigallican = Heiress
Anti-garotte (Collins, C. J., 1857), v.
642, 785, 826 [and see under My
Knuckleduster, v. 628]
Antigone (Bartholomew, B., 1845), IV.
262
— (Blanchard, E. L., 1845), IV. 268
— (Fitzball, E., 1821), IV. 312, 427, 584
— (Whitelaw, R., 1890), v. 621
Anti-matrimonial Society (Beauchamp,
E., 1876), v. 254
Antiochus (Mottley, J., 1721), II. 110,
346
— (Shuckburgh, C., 1740), II. 355
Antiochus the Great (Wiseman, Mrs J.,
1702), II. 104, 160, 364, 446
Antipodes (Allen-Jefferys, J., 1896), v.
239
— (Taylor, T., 1867), v. 593
Antiquarian (Stead, G., 1889), v. 580
Antiquary (Murray, W. H., 1820), IV.
93, 365
— (Pocock, I., 1818), IV. 93, 384
— (Pocock, I. and Terry, D., 1820), IV.
28, 66, 77, 93, 384

Antiquary and the Bluegown Beggar (1832), IV. 93, 427

Antiquity (1808), IV. 427

Antoine, the Savage (Fitzball, E., 1828), IV. 427, 619

Antoinette (Warren, E., 1886), V. 614

Antonia (Galt, J., 1812), IV. 585

Antonio (Godwin, W., 1800), IV. 194, 319

Antonio and Leonora (1814), IV. 427

Antony and Cleopatra (Brooke, H., 1778), III. 57, 240

— (Burnand, F. C., 1866), V. 289

— (Capell, E. and Garrick, D., 1758), III, 57, 241, 378

— (Draper, J. F., 1870), V. 350

— (Miller, A., 1896), V. 488

— (Sedley, Sir C., 1677), I. 120, 348, 428

— (Selby, C., 1842), IV. 398

— (Kemble, J. P., 1813), IV. 335

— (1810), IV. 90, 427

Antony and Cleopatra Married and Settled (Selby, C., 1843), IV. 399

Antony and Octavius (Landor, W. S., 1856), IV. 341

Anxious Time (Reynolds, E., 1889), V. 541

Any Other Gal = Jeannie Deans

Any Port in a Storm (Stocqueler, J. H., 1853), V. 585

Any, rather than Fail = Maid's Last Prayer

Anything Else (Racer, P., 1892), V. 532

Anything for a Change (Brooks, C. W. S., 1848), IV. 271

Any Thing New (Pocock, I., 1811), IV. 383

Any Wife better than None = Intriguing Harlequin

Apartments (Brough, W., 1851), V., 278

Ape and the Infant = Crom-a-boo'

Apelles and Campaspe (1782), III. 319

Apelles et Campaspe (1818), IV. 427

Ape of Brazil = Jocko

Ape of the Forest = Knight and his Page

Ape of the Island = Walooka and Noomahee

Ape of the Prairies (1861), V. 642

Apocriphal Ladies (Cavendish, M., 1662), I. 396

Apollo (Roberts, Sir R., 1888), V. 545

Apollo and Daphne (Hughes, J., 1716), II. 260, 338

— (Theobald, L., 1726), II. 135, 136, 138, 359

— (Thurmond, J., 1723), II. 253, 360

— (1734), II. 236, 365

Apollo and the Flying Pegasus (1858), V. 642

Apollo and the Muses celebrating the Nuptials of Thetis and Pallas = Parnasso in Festa

Apollo Daggerwood (1819), IV. 427

Apollo's Choice (1815), IV. 427, 636

Apollo's Decree = Appeal to the Muses

Apollo's Festival (1814), IV. 427

Apollo's Holiday (Cawdell, J., 1792), III. 242

Apollo turn'd Stroller (Oldmixon, Sir J., 1787), III. 295

Apostate (Galt, J., 1814), IV. 318, 636

— (Sheil, R. L., 1817), IV. 166, 400

Apostate Moor (1832), IV. 427

Apothecary turned Doctor = Physick lies a Bleeding

Apotheosis of Punch (Macnally, L., 1779), III. 285

Apparition (Cross, J. C., 1794) = Flesh and the Spirit, III. 98, 102, 250, 380

— (1713), II. 50, 53, 173, 365

— (1828), IV. 427

Apparition of the Cliffs = Sicilian Romance

Apparition on the White Horse = Leonora

Appeal (Galt, J., 1818) = Witness, IV. 427, 585

Appeal to the Audience (Brown, A., 1852), V. 282

Appeal to the Feelings (Palmer, T. A., 1875), V. 512

Appeal to the Muses (Cawdell, J., 1778), III. 242

Appeal to the Public (Oxenford, J., 1848), IV. 427

Appearance is against Them (Inchbald, Mrs E., 1785), III. 47, 184, 275

Appearances (Simpson, J. P., 1860), V. 567

Appearances are Deceitful = Cherry and Blue

Appel des Fées (1831), IV. 427

Appius (Moncrieff, J., 1755), III. 287

Appius and Virginia (Betterton, T., 1669), I. 392

— (Dennis, J., 1709), II. 20, 31, 56, 86, 214, 318

Apple Blossoms (Albery, J., 1871), V. 237

Apples (Sturgis, J., 1887), V. 586

Appointed Spot (1845), IV. 427

Apprentice (Murphy, A., 1756), III. 21, 179–80, 188, 289

— = Acting Mad

Apprentice's Opera (Dibdin, C. I. M., 1826), IV. 296

April Day (O'Hara, K., 1777), III. 208, 291

— (1782), III, 319

April Folly (Hurst, J. P., 1885), V. 431

April Fool (Fitzball, E., 1841), IV. 316

— (Halliday, A. and Brough, W., 1864), V. 400

— (Macnally, L., 1786), III. 113, 285

— (1788), III. 319

— (1822), IV. 427

— (1895), V. 642

— = Davenport Done

April Fools (Dibdin, C. I. M., 1817), IV. 294

— (1883), V. 642

April Jest (1893), V. 642

April Rain (Outram, L. S., 1886), V. 509

April Showers (Romer, F. and Bellamy, G. S., 1889), V. 549

Apt Pupil (1896), V. 642

Aquatic Harlequin (1809), IV. 427

— = Fashion's Fools

Aquatic Prize (Dibdin, C. I. M., 1805), IV. 291

Aqua Triumphalis (Tatham, J., 1662), I. 434

A qui le victoire? = Cannon-mouth and Pistol-shot

Arab (Cumberland, R., 1785), III. 79, 252

— (1809), IV. 427

— (1812), IV. 427

Arab and his Steed (Rede, W. L., 1846), IV. 391

Arab Boy (1846), IV. 427

Arabella (Moser, J., 1808), IV. 364

Arabella Stuart (Neil, R., 1879), V. 502

Arabian Courtezan = Harlequin Hermit

Arabian Eve (1894), V. 642

Arabian Martyr = Abdallah

Arabian Nights (Grundy, S., 1887), V. 396

Arabian Night's Entertainments (1847), IV. 427

Arabian Vow = Almyna

Arab of the Desert (1831), IV. 427

— = Caliph Haroun Alraschid

Arab of the Desert and his Faithful Steed (Cooke, W., 1856), V. 324

Arab of the Niger = Mungo Park

Arab of the Red Desert = Battle of Navarino

Arab's Faith (Farrell, J., 1822), IV. 427, 619

— = Elphi Bey

Arab's Leap = Hassan Pacha

Arabs of the Desert (1837), IV. 427

— = Bedouins

Arab Spy = Lily of the Desert

Arab's Sacrifice = Leah and Nathan

Arajoon (Coyne, J. S., 1838), IV. 284

Aramanthus (Smith, H., 1821), IV. 402

Arbitration (Reynolds, F., 1806), IV. 391

Arcades of Flora = Florist

Arcadia (Blanchard, E. L., 1841), IV. 268, 573

— (Lloyd, R., 1761), III. 282

— (1849), IV. 427

— (1860), V. 642

Arcadian Brothers (O'Neil, J. R., 1852), V. 507

Arcadian Nuptials (1764), III. 319

Arcadian Pastoral (Craven, E., 1782), III. 249

Arcadie (Burton, J., 1888), V. 294

Archer rides to win = Demon Jockey

Archers of Islington and the Hog of Highbury = Red Cow

Archers of Ludgate = Citizen's Daughter

Archibald Danvers (Southam, G. and Armitage, E., 1893), V. 575

Archibald of the Wreck = Press-Gang

Archie Lovell (Burnand, F. C., 1874), V. 290

Architect (Gypsum, N., 1807), IV. 322

Architopia, Unlimited (Earle, A. E. and Sim, E. H., 1894), V. 353

Archives of the Poor = Halfpenny Club

Archon's Daughter = Lazaria the Greek

Arrah Niel (1872), v. 642
Arrah-No-Brogue (Shelley, 1865), v. 642, 816, 826
Arrangement (De Trueba, J. T., 1831), IV. 428, 619
Arrant Knave (Mackaye, J. S., 1889), v. 471
Arrested on Suspicion (1877), v. 642
Arrival of Redgauntlet = Practical Jokes
Arrivals (Lennox, W., 1821) = Incog., IV. 428, 619
Ar-rivals (Banero, J. M. and Pincroft, A. D., 1884), v. 248
Arrivals and Marriages = Love and Gout
Arrivals from College = Honour
Arrived at Crow-Street (1796), III. 319
Arrived at Last (1823), IV. 428
Arrived at Portsmouth! (Pearce, W., 1794), III. 204, 297
Arrogance brought down (McLaren, A., 1824), IV. 352
Arrogant Boy (1802), IV. 428
Arrow, the Apple and the Agony = William Tell
Arrow which killed the King = Knight of the Sepulchre
Arsaces (Hodson, W., 1775), III. 70, 83, 270
Arsinoe (Henderson, A., 1752), III. 268
Arsinoe, Queen of Cyprus (Motteux, P. A., 1705), II. 36, 226, 231, 234, 266, 389
Art (Brigdman, C., 1874), v. 275
— (Reade, C., 1855), v. 536, 812
— (1881), v. 642
Art and Love (Dubourg, A. W., 1877), v. 351
Art and Nature (Miller, J., 1738), II. 13, 146, 182, 203-4, 344, 441
Artaxerxes (Arne, T. A., 1762), III. 28, 69, 197, 233
— (Hoole, J., 1767), III. 387
— (1811), IV. 428
Artful Automaton (Law, A. and Hall, K., 1878), v. 449
Artful Cards (Burnand, F. C., 1877), v. 290
Artful Dodge (Blanchard, E. L., 1842), IV. 268
Artful Girl (Ridge, W. P., and Pearce, J. E., 1892), v. 543

Artful Husband (Taverner, W., 1717), II. 157, 171, 358; III. 116, 170
Artful Little Spouser (Robertson, L. and Comerford, M., 1882), v. 545
Artful Patriot = Patriot
Artful Plans (1895), v. 642
Artful Trick and Love in the Dark = Fireman and the Volunteer
Artful Wife (Taverner, W., 1717), II. 197, 358
Arthur and Emmeline (1784), III. 58, 319
Arthur, Monarch of the Britons (Hilton, W., 1776), III. 269
Arthur Orton (Stephens, W., 1874), v. 581
Arthur's Bakery Co. (Silvester, F., 1898), v. 566
Arthur's Round Table Restored = Institution of the Garter
Article 47 = Louisiana Creole
Artifice (Centlivre, Mrs S., 1722), II. 156, 306; III. 115
— (Miles, W. A., 1780), III. 287
Artificial Flower Maker (Hazlewood, C. H., 1871), v. 414
Artipadiades, King of Queeramania (1822), IV. 428
Artisan's Daughter (1842), IV. 428
— (1861), v. 642
Artisan's Triumph (Wood, A., 1861), v. 630, 642, 826
Artist (Wibrow, G. V., 1894), v. 621
Artist and his Family (Phillips, F. L., 1859), v. 642, 810, 826
Artiste de Terracina (1853), v. 643
Artistic Dilemma (Fenton, C., 1893), v. 365
Artist of Cas (1846), IV. 428
Artist of Rome = Graven Image
Artist's Ghost = Love and Art
Artist's Model (Hall, O. and Greenbank, H., 1895), v. 400
— (Lynn, N., 1892), v. 465
— (1894), v. 643
Artist's Muddle = Eugénie
Artist's Wife (À Beckett, G. A., 1838), IV. 250
— (1854), v. 643
Artizan and his Daughters (Archer, T., 1845), IV. 255
Artless Cinderella (Field, H. K. H., 1895), v. 365

Art of Love = Calypso
Art of Management (Charke, Mrs C., 1735), II. 23, 261, 306
Art of Modern Poetry = Harlequin-Horace
Art of Pleasing = Chameleon
Art of Seeing = Eyes and No Eyes
Arts and Crafts (James, A. and James, D., 1897), V. 432
Arts in an Attic = Lofty Projects
Arviragus (Tasker, C., 1795), III. 310
As a Man sows (Ramsay, A. and De Cordova, R., 1898), V. 534
Asancesado (1837), IV. 428
Ascot (Fendall, P., 1879), V. 364
Asgard, the Demon Hunter (Scott, J. M., 1812), IV. 397
As Gold through Fire (1873), V. 643
— (1879), V. 643
As Good as Gold (Coghlan, C. F., 1869), V. 316
Ashamed to Own It = All in the Dark
Ashantee Prince (1842), IV. 428
Ashantees (Almar, G., 1825), IV. 568
Ashantee War (Lowe, W., 1874), V. 464
— (Sandford, J., 1874), V. 555
— = King Coffee
Ashbrooke Blacksmith = Ding Dong Will
Ashby Manor (Allingham, W., 1883), V. 59, 239
Ashes (Collins, E. and Saunders, R., 1894), V. 318
Ashlynn (1870), V. 643
Ashore and Afloat (Hazlewood, C. H., 1864), V. 412
Asiatic (Yeo, 1790), III. 318, 398
As in a Glass (Rodway, J. and Lauri, C., 1887), V. 548
As in a Looking Glass (Grove, F. C., 1887), V. 160, 395
As it Should Be (Oulton, W. C., 1789), III. 185, 296
Ask No Questions (Selby, C., 1838), IV. 398
— = Father Matthias
As Large as Life (Shirley, A., 1890), V. 564
Aslan the Lion (Barrymore, W., 1824), IV. 262
Aslar and Ozines (Haines, J. T., 1842), IV. 323

Asleep or Awake (1823), IV. 428
As Like as Two Peas (Lille, H., 1854), V. 459
Asmodeus (1885), V. 643
Asmodeus, the Devil on Two Sticks (1859), V. 643
Asmodeus, the Little Demon (Archer, T., 1843), IV. 84, 254
Aspacia (Hughes, Mrs A., 1790), III. 274
Asprand (1805), IV. 428
As Pretty as Seven (1887), V. 643
A.S.S. (Maddox, J. M., 1853), V. 472
Assassin (Bell, R., 1816) = Watchword, IV. 428, 619
— (Hill-Mitchelson, E., 1890), V. 422
— = Man in the Cloak
Ass-ass-ination (Hook, T. E., 1810), IV. 328
Assassin Labourer (1827), IV. 428
Assassin of Dijon (1831), IV. 428
Assassin of Nantes = Julie de Moin
Assassin of Silesia = Fatal Precept
Assassin of Stebonheath = Man of Mile End
Assassin of the Rocks = False Friend
Assassins of Aveyron = Wild Girl
Assassins of Istria = Bertha
Assassins of Paris = Courier
Assassins of the Forest = Frederick the Great and the Deserter
Assassins of the Roadside (Douglass, J. T., 1865), V. 643, 788, 826
Assassins of the Roadside Inn = Assassins of the Roadside
Assault and Battery = Welcome Visit
+ Assembly (Worsdale, J., Smock Alley, Dublin, 18/4/1740)
— (1722), II. 365
— (1752), III. 319
Assignation (À Beckett, G. A., 1837), IV. 249, 567
— (Dryden, J., 1672), I. 191, 230, 405
— (Fisher, 1812), IV. 318, 583
— (Lee, S., 1807), III. 281; IV. 343
— (1826), IV. 428
Assignation, Dissipation and Starvation (1830), IV. 428
Association = Downfall
Assommoir (Foote, J., 1879), V. 370
— (Sidney, W., 1879), V. 566
— (1879), V. 643
— (1882), V. 643

Assumptions (1823) = Guardians Outwitted, IV. 428, 619

Assurance Company (Fitzball, E., 1836), IV. 315

Assyrian Spy (1852), V. 643

As the Night Cometh (Grogan, W. E., 1899), V. 395

As the World Goes (Horde, T.), III. 273

Aston Hall (1854), V. 643

Astonishment (1818), IV. 428

Astounding Phenomena (Mathews, C. J., 1847), IV. 354

Astray from the Flock (1881), V. 643

Astrea Appeased (Olivari, F., 1797), III. 295

Astrologer (Dibdin, C. I. M., 1810), IV. 292

— (Ralph, J., 1744), II. 350

Astrologer's Star = Bertha the Broom Girl

Astronomer (Amphlett, 1802), IV. 254

+ — (Dibdin, C. I. M.: R.A., 1798)

Astronomy a Farce = Philosophic Whim

As You Find It (Boyle, C., 1703), II. 154, 232, 299, 432

As You Like It (Kemble, J. P., 1815), IV. 335

— (Macready, W. C., 1842), IV. 353

— (Moser, J., additional scene, 1809), IV. 364

— (1746), II. 365

— (1824), IV. 428

+ As you make your bed so you must lie in it (*French*)

At a Health Resort (Paull, H. M., 1893), V. 516

Atala and Chactas (Dibdin, C. I. M., 1825), IV. 295

Atalanta (Hawtrey, G. P., 1888), V. 410

— (Talfourd, F., 1857), V. 590

Atalanta in Calydon (Swinburne, A. C., 1865), V. 589

At All in the Ring (Dibdin, T. J., 1817), IV. 301

At Anchor in the Bay of Naples (1794) = Naples Bay, III. 319, 398

At any cost = Desperate Man

At Bay (Lander, C. and Cassilis, I. L., 1888), V. 447

At Break of Day (Tracey, F. T., 1894), V. 602

Atchi— (Morton, J. M., 1868), V. 496

At Dead of Night (Whyte, H., 1897), V. 621

At Duty's Call (Gerant, J., 1898), V. 377

Athalia (Humphreys, S., 1733), II. 390, 439

Athaliah (Duncombe, W., 1724), II. 320, 435

Athanase (Roberts, E. F., 1847), IV. 608

Atheist (Otway, T., 1683), I. 188, 423

Athelstan (Brown, J., 1756), III. 82, 240

Athelstane (1854), V. 643

Athelwold (Hill, A., 1731), II. 108-9, 116, 336, 438

— (Smith, W., 1843), IV. 303 [The author's full name is William Henry Smith]

Athenian Captive (Talfourd, T. N., 1838), IV. 48, 142, 177, 410

At Home (1813), IV. 428

At Home and Abroad = Face to Face

Atlantic Jack (Travers, W., 1860), V. 822

Atlantis (Dalton, M. and Genet, E., 1886), V. 333

Atlantis Destroyed = Apostate

At Last (Clarance, L., 1883), V. 311

— (Gough, H. and Edwards, M., 1896), V. 386

At Mammon's Shrine (Landeck, B., 1887), V. 447

Atonement (Fisher, C. A., 1894), V. 367

— (Poole, J., 1836), IV. 387

— (Muskerry, W., 1872), V. 500

Atreus and Thyestes (Sinnett, E., 1821), IV. 401

Atrocious Criminal (Simpson, J. P., 1867), V. 567

At Santa Lucia (Grist, W., 1894), V. 395, 795

At Sea (1882), V. 643

At Stake (Killick, J. M., 1870), V. 444

Attack of the Caravan = Horse Banditti and their Forty Steeds

Attack of the Diligence (Amherst, J. H., 1829), IV. 254

Attack of the Dragoons = Brigands of Ancona

Attack on Monterreau = Grand Army

Attack on the Convoy (1828), IV. 428

Attack upon the Mail = Courier of Lyons

Attar Gull (Almar, G., 1832), IV. 252

Attempt to please = Touch at the Times
At the Cross Roads (Dilley, J. J., 1894), v. 345
At the Ferry (Fawcett, Mrs, 1897), v. 364
At the Foot of the Altar (Jarman, F., 1897), v. 434
At the Foot of the Ladder (Travers, W., 1869), v. 603
At the Harbour Side (Pinkerton, P. and Grist, W., 1900), v. 525, 810
At the Kirk Arms (Malyon, E. J. and James, C., 1897), v. 473
At the Madonna's Shrine (1847), iv. 428
At the Mercy of the World = Wrecked in London
At the Pantomime (Grain, R. C., 1890), v. 388
At the Sword Point (Lashbrooke, H. and Perry, R. D., 1884), v. 449
Attic Drama (James, F., 1898), v. 433
Attic Science and Mimic Art = Scheming and Seeming
Attic Story (Morton, J. M., 1842), v. 352
+ Attila (8°, 1840)
Attila, my Attila (Field, M., 1896), v. 366
At Zero (Teale, L. and Hughes, T., 1898), v. 594
Auberge des Adrets (Selby, C., 1834), iv. 428, 619
— = Two Murderers
Auchindrane (Scott, Sir W., 1830), iv. 397
Auction (Cibber, T., 1757), ii. 314, 437; iii. 116, 243
Auctioneer (Dibdin, T. J. ?1796), iii. 382
— (Morton, J. M. and Reece, R., 1898), 497
Auction of Pictures (Foote, S., 1748), ii. 329
Augusta (Poole, J., 1823), iv. 386
Augusta's Triumph = Brutus of Alba
August First (1831), iv. 428
Augustus (Biddle, E., 1717), ii. 298
Augustus and Gulielmus (Holland, W. A., 1806), iv. 328
Augustus Buggins (Selby, C., 1834), iv. 428, 619
Au Japon (1896), v. 643

Auld Acquaintance (Dilley, J. J., 1878), v. 345
Auld Lang Syne (Gordon, G. L., 1877), v. 385
— (Hood, B., 1892), v. 425
— (Lee, N., 1846), iv. 342
— (Leigh, N., 1891), v. 454
— (Stirling, E., 1843), iv. 407
— = Rob Roy Macgregor
Auld Robin Gray (Arnold, S. J., 1794), iii. 19, 206, 234
— (Byrne, J., 1814), iv. 277
— (Fitzball, E., 1858), v. 368 [probably = the play listed without date, iv. 317]
— (Hazlewood, C. H., 1856), v. 643, 796, 826
— (Macfarren, G., 1828), iv. 350
— (Roy, G., 1883), v. 552
Aunt Agatha's Doctor (Harraden, H., 1891), v. 404
Aunt Charlotte's Maid (Morton, J. M., 1858), v. 486
Aunt Chimpanzee (Williams, R. A. P., 1897), v. 625
Aunt Dorothy (1855), v. 643
Aunt Hannah (1899), v. 643
Auntie (Byron, H. J., 1882), v. 299
Auntie's Motor (John, G. and War, C., 1899), v. 437
Auntie's Young Man = What! More Trouble!
Aunt Jack (Lumley, R. R., 1889), v. 464
Aunt Jemima (1894), v. 643
Aunt Madge (1898), v. 643
Aunt Margaret (Pease, S., 1897), v. 518
Aunt or Uncle (Wilson, A. J., 1885), v. 628
Aunt Rebecca (Atwood, A. and Vaun, R., 1895), v. 245
Aunt's Advice (Sothern, E. A., 1861), v. 575
Aunt Tabitha (Morland, F. H., 1894), v. 493
Aurelia = Roman Empress
Aurelian (1897), v. 643
Aurelio = Aurelio and Miranda
Aurelio and Miranda (Boaden, J., 1798), iii. 72, 238, 378
Aureng-Zebe (Dryden, J., 1675), i. 24, 68, 101, 115, 345, 346, 405; iii. 58
Au Revoir (1896), v. 643

Auromania (Pritchard, J., 1871), v. 531
Aurora (Noble, 1817), IV. 428, 620
— (1865), v. 643
— (1893), v. 643
Aurora Floyd (Ashley, J. B. and Melton,
  C., 1885), v. 244
— (Cheltnam, C. S., 1863), v. 309
— (Hazlewood, C. H., 1863), v. 412
— (Johnstone, J. B., 1863), v. 800
— (Webster, B. the Younger, 1863), v.
  618
— (1863), v. 643
Aurora's Nuptials (1734), II. 365
Austerlitz (Haines, J. T., 1831), IV.
  322
Australia (Stanley, A. G. and Archer,
  W., 1881), v. 579, 778
Australia Felix (1862), v. 643
Austrian Peasant (1791), III. 319
Author (Foote, S., 1757), III. 172, 259
— (Greville, E. E., 1891), v. 394
Author on the Wheel (1785), III. 319
Authors (Jones, L., 1755), III. 277
Author's Box (1896), v. 643
Author's Farce (Fielding, H., 1730), II.
  21, 41, 232, 255, 263, 323, 381
Author's Triumph (1737), II. 366
Automaton (Beckwith, 1832), IV. 428,
  620
Autumnal Dream = Camille
Autumn Manoeuvres (Stow, W. R.,
  1871), v. 585
Autumn Sheaves (1872), v. 643
Avalanche (Harris, A. G., 1854), v. 404
— (Taylor, T. P.), IV. 614
Avare (Ozell, J., 1732), II, 347, 442
Avare corrigé (1790), III. 319
+Avarice (Emson, F. E., 8°, ?1877)
— (?Johnstone, J. B., 1857), v. 643, 800,
  826
Avenger (Lee, H., 1824), IV. 428, 620
— (Lovell, G. W., 1835), IV. 347
— (Moule, F., 1899), v. 498
— (1838), IV. 428
— (1846), IV. 428
Avenger's Vow (Linders, G., 1863), v.
  804
Avenging Gift = Storm Visitor
Avenging Hand (Bartlett, H., 1899), v.
  252
Avenging Hand of Fate and the Shilling
  Legacy = Life of Guilt

Average Man (Courte, S. X., 1895), v.
  325
Avventura di Scaramuccia (1836), IV.
  428
Awakening (Benham, A., 1892), v. 257
Awaking (Clarke, C., 1872), v. 151, 311
Away down East = Yankee Courtship
Away with Melancholy (Morton, J. M.,
  1854), v. 495
Awful Experience (Dening, Mrs C.,
  1893), v. 342
Awful Rise in Spirits (Taylor, T., 1863),
  v. 593
Awkward (1885), v. 643
Awkward Affair (Hay, F., 1878), v. 411
Awkward Dilemma (Scarlett, W., 1893),
  v. 557
Awkward Mistake (1881), v. 643
Awkward Recruit (1805), IV. 428
Axe and the Sword = Headsman
Axel and Valborg (Chapman, J. F.,
  1851), v. 783
Ayesha (1836), IV. 428
Aylma's Dream (1886), v. 643
Aylmere (Conrad, R., 1846), IV. 282
Ayrshire Tragedy = Auchindrane
Azael (Fitzball, E., 1851), v. 367, 792
— (Rodwell, G. H., 1851), v. 548
— = Prodigal Son
Azael the Prodigal of Memphis (Fitz-
  ball, E., 1851), v. 367, 792
Azamoglan (Dixon, W. H., 1845), IV.
  581
Azel the Arab (James, C. S., 1851), v.
  433
Azim (Dibdin, T. J., 1818), IV. 301
Azim and Alzira = Silver Valley
Azor and Zemira (Ball, W., 1831), IV.
  428, 620
Azurine (1860), v. 643

Bab (1882), v. 643
Babbage's Puppets (1884), v. 643
Bab-Ballad Monger (Lindo, F., 1892),
  v. 460
Babbler (1762), III. 319, 398
Babble Shop (Rose, E., 1893), v. 550
Babes (Paulton, H., 1884), v. 516
Babes and Beetles = Babes in the Wood
Babes in the Wood (À Beckett, G. A.,
  1867), v. 233
— (Bailey, W. E., 1898), v. 247

Babes in the Wood (Bowyer, F., 1898), v. 272
— (Byam, M. and Wyke, E. B., 1891), v. 294
— (Byam, M., Graham, F. and Vincent, W. T., 1897), v. 295
— (Capel, G., 1884), v. 302
— (Chute, J. H., 1858), v. 784
— (Daly, B. and East, J. M., 1896), v. 334
— (Gordon, G. L. and Anson, G. W., 1877), v. 384
— (Grahame, J. C. and Artlett, B., 1895), v. 387
— (Hall, F., 1880), v. 399
— (Jones, J. W., 1894), v. 441
— (Jones, J. W., 1898), v. 441, 800
— (Jourdain, J., 1888), v. 442
— (Lander, G., 1873), v. 448
— (Locke, F., 1886), v. 804
— (McArdle, J. F., 1881), v. 644, 804, 827
— (McCabe, C. W. and Belmore, G., 1893), v. 467
— (Mead, T., 1873), v. 483
— (Merion, C., 1875), v. 485
— (Ramsdale, T., 1891), v. 534
— (Rice, C., 1874), v. 542
— (Robson, W., 1843), IV. 395
— (Roe, J. E., 1870), v. 814
— (Rogers, T. S., 1884), v. 644, 814, 827
— (Sturgess, A. and Collins, A., 1897), v. 586
— (Summers, W. J., 1899), v. 645, 818, 827
— (Taylor, T., 1860), v. 593
— (Thorne, G., 1888), v. 598, 820
— (Thorne, G., 1890), v. 598
— (Thorne, G., 1894), v. 821
— (Woolfe, J. H., 1896), v. 644, 824, 827
— (1824), IV. 428
— (1855), v. 643, 827
— (1856), v. 645
— (1857, 1858), v. 826
— (1859, 1860), v. 827
— (1869), v. 643
— (1872), v. 827
— (1875, 1876, 1877, 1878, 1879, 1880, 1881, 1884, 1885, 1886), v. 643-4
— (1887), v. 827

Babes in the Wood (1887, 1889), v. 644
— (1889), v. 827
— (1890, 1892, 1893, 1894, 1896, 1897, 1898, 1899), v. 644-5
— (1899), v. 827
Babes in the Wood and Bold Robin Hood (Lennard, H., 1892), v. 455, 803
— (1894), v. 645
Babes in the Wood and the Good Little Fairy Birds (Byron, H. J., 1859), v. 295
Babes in the Wood, Robin Hood and his Merry Men, and Harlequin who killed Cock Robin (Harris, Sir A. G. H., Blanchard, E. L. and Nichols, H., 1888), v. 405
Babes of the Castle (Dibdin, C. I. M., 1809), IV. 292
Babes out of the Wood = Little Offsprings
Babette (Murray, A. and Mosenthal, J. G., 1888), v. 500
Babil and Bijou (Boucicault, D. and Planché, J. R., 1872), v. 269
Babington (Doubleday, T., 1826), IV. 428, 582, 620
Babiole (Reece, R., 1879), v. 538
Baboon of Paraguay (1830), IV. 428
Baboo or Prince? (Daly, C., 1897), v. 334
Baby (Cowell, A. E., 1892), v. 327
— (Greville, Lady V., 1890), v. 394
— (Hook, W., 1888), v. 425
— (Soutar, R. and Herbert, F. H., 1890), v. 575
— (Waldron, W. R. and Ellis, L., 1896), v. 611
— (1883), v. 645
Baby and the Bachelor = Runaways
Baby and the Regimentals (Graham, J. H., 1850), v. 387
Baby Bunting (1897), v. 645
Baby's Birthday (Bucklaw, A., 1893), v. 286
Baby's Engagement (Rogers, R., 1892), v. 549
Baby's Hat (1891), v. 645
Baccarat (Suter, W. E., 1865), v. 588
Bacchanalian Festival = Charioteers
Bacchus (1855), v. 645

Bacchus and Ariadne (Leclercq, 1841), IV. 594

— (Mereweather, C., 1891), V. 806

— (1734), II. 366

— (1861), V. 645

Bacchus and Cupid (1715), II. 366

Bacchus Festival (Jordan, T., 1660), I. 415

Bachelor of Arts (Hardwicke, P., 1853), V. 403

Bachelor of Duddington (Ebsworth, J.), IV. 309

Bachelor Quarters = Bungalow

Bachelors (Aldred, A. A., 1884), V. 238

— (Buchanan, R. and Vezin, H., 1884), V. 284

— (Wharton, C. H. M., 1885), V. 619

Bachelors and Married Men = Balance of Comfort

Bachelor's Box (1882), V. 645

Bachelor's Buttons (Stirling, E., 1837), IV. 406

Bachelors' Fare = Helpless Animals

Bachelors' Hall (Gordon, G. L., 1877), V. 384

— = Bachelors

Bachelors' Miseries (1818), IV. 429

Bachelor's Romance (Morton, M., 1896), V. 497

Bachelor's Vow (Phillips, E., 1849) = Prejudice, IV. 429, 604, 620

Bachelor's Widow (O'Hare, J. F., 1897), V. 506

Bachelor's Wife (Watson, F., 1858), V. 615

Bachelors' Wives (Beazley, S. Jr., 1817), IV. 263

— (Bousfield, F., 1886), V. 270

— = P.Q.

Bachelor, the Maid, the Wife and the Widow = Domestic Arrangements

Back-Biter (1836), IV. 429

Back from India (Stevens, P. and Dick, C., 1879), V. 583

Back from the Grave = Church and Stage

Back from the Land of Yesterday = Not Guilty

Back in Five Minutes (Johnson, H. T., 1891), V. 437

Backing the Favourite (Gordon, G. L., 1875), V. 384

Back in Town (Grain, R. C., 1894), V. 388

Backsheesh (Grain, R. C., 1884), V. 387

Backslider (Shillingford, O., 1895), V. 563

Backwoodsman's Daughter = David Hunt

Back to Life = Mad

Bad Bargain (Grundy, S., 1879), V. 396

Bad Boys (Scott, C. W., 1885), V. 558

Bad Business (1832), IV. 429

Bad Customers (1810) = Who Pays the Piper, IV. 429, 620

Baden Baden (Bateman, R., 1872), V. 253

Bad D(j)inn and the Good Spirit = Camaralzaman and the Fair Badoura

Badinage de Provence (1735), II. 366

Bad Lot (Paulton, H. and Tedde, M., 1887), V. 517

Bad Luck's Good Luck with Good looking after = Leprechaun

Bad Neighbours (Arnold, S. J., 1810) = Plots, IV. 429, 620

Bad Penny (Lestocq, W., 1882), V. 457

Bad Quarter of an Hour (Costello, Miss, 1896), V. 325

Baffled (1878, 1881, 1884), V. 645

Baffled Crime (McCabe, C. W., 1896), V. 467

Bagging a Barrister (Stockton, E., 1896), V. 585

Baghran-Ho (1812), IV. 429

Bag of Gold (Hillyard, J., 1852), V. 422

Bag of Tricks (Potter, M., 1896), V. 529

Bagpipes (1895), V. 645

Bagshot Heath Camp (1792), III. 319

Bailie Bewitched = Bogle of the Clyde

Bailiff (Broughton, F. W., 1890), V. 282

Bailiff and the M.P. = Contrivances

Bailiff's Bet = Walk for a Wager

Bail Up (Hughes, J., 1893), V. 430

Bairn (Duncan, G., 1878), V. 352

Bakarak, the Miser (1824), IV. 429

Baker's Bride = Kitchen

Baker's Daughter = Fire of London

Baker worried by Buckstone = Keeley worried by Buckstone

Balaam (Davy, C., 1787), III. 351, 381

Balaclava (Johnstone, J. B., 1878), V. 438

Balaclava Day (1856), V. 645

Balaclava Heroes = Duty
Balaclava Joe (Emery, C. P., 1892), v. 358
Balance of Comfort (Bernard, W. B., 1854), v. 259
— (Raymond, R. J., 1836), IV. 389
Balcony Beau = My Wife's Dentist
Bald Head (1840), IV. 429
Baldur (Anderton, H. O., 1893), v. 241
Balet de la Paix (1660), I. 440
Ballad Girl (1866), v. 645
Ballad Monger (Besant, W. and Pollock, W. H., 1887), v. 260
Ballad Singer (Craven, T., 1891), v. 329
— (Moncrieff, W. T., 1839), IV. 361
Ballanasloe Boy (Hazlewood, C. H., 1867), v. 413
Ballet des Sauteurs et Voltigeurs (1788), III. 319
Ballet et Musique pour le divertissement (1674), I. 440
Ballet Girl (Tanner, J. T., 1897), v. 591
Ballet-girl and the Jew = Honour and Shame
Balloon (Darnley, J. H. and Fenn, G. M., 1888), v. 337
— (1812), IV. 429
Balloonacy (Burnand, F. C. and Stephens, H. P., 1879), v. 291
Balloon Agent = Mad or Not Mad
Balloon in Turkey (1837), IV. 429
Ball upon Deck = On Board the Mars
Ballybaggerty Bequest (Cleaver, M., 1852), v. 314
Ballyhooley (Bogue, J. R., 1898), v. 266
Ballynavogue = Row of Ballynavogue
Ballyvogan (Lloyd, A., 1887), v. 461
Bal Masqué (Ward, A. H., 1898), v. 613
— (1848), IV. 429
— = Any Port in a Storm
Baltic Fleet (1854), v. 645
Bamboozell = Lock and Key
Bamboozle (1860), v. 645
Bamboozling (Wilks, T. E., 1840), IV. 421
Bambuzleum (1872), v. 645
Bamfyde Moore Carew (Jerrold, D. W. + Surrey, 21/5/1824), IV. 331
Bampfyde Moore Carew (+ Moncrieff, W. T., 1816), IV. 331, 620
Bandalero the Bandit (Barrie, Sir J. M., 1877), v. 778

Bandit (Burges, Sir J. B., 1817), IV. 276–7
— (1814), IV. 429, 635
Bandit Farmer = When the Clock Strikes
Bandit Host (Rogers, W., 1839), IV. 609
Bandit Innkeepers (1832), IV. 429
Bandit King (1895), v. 645
Bandit Merchant (1847), IV. 620
— = Maid of Genoa
Bandit of Bohemia = Geraldi Duval
Bandit of Corsica (1840), IV. 620
Bandit of Otranto = Justinio
Bandit of Sicily (Courtney, J., 1860), v. 786
Bandit of the Blind Mine (Milner, H. M., 1821), IV. 356
Bandit of the Charmed Wrist = Spoglioni
Bandit of the Rock = Female Courage
Bandit Queen (1861), v. 645
Bandits = Malak the Jew
Bandit's Bride = Hag of the Glen
Bandit's Daughter = Salvatori
Bandit's Revenge = Castle of de Courcy
Banditti (D'Urfey, T., 1686), I. 221, 274, 409
— (O'Keeffe, J., 1781), III. 292
Banditti of the Cavern = When the Bell Tolls
Band of Death (1821), IV. 429
Band of Patriots = Constantine Paleologus
Bang Up! (Dibdin, C. I. M., 1810), IV. 292
Banished Brother (1818), IV. 429
Banished Cavalier = Rover
Banish'd Duke (1690), I. 440
Banished from Home (Griffiths, J. C., 1875), v. 394
Banished General (1731), III. 366
+ Banished Lord (8°, 1842)
Banished Star (Buckstone, J. B., 1840), IV. 275
Banishment of Cicero (Cumberland, R., 1761), III. 77, 125, 251
Banish't Cavaliers = Rover
Banker's Clothes Philosophy = Fact and Fancy
Banker's Daughter (Foster, W. C., 1876), v. 371
Banker's Son (1883), v. 645

Banker's Son and the Felon's Daughter = Leap for Life

Banker, the Thief and the Will = Two London Locksmiths

Bank Holiday (Cooper, H. B., 1886), v. 324

Bank Note (Macready, W., 1795), III. 116, 170–1, 285

Bank Robbery (Dawson, F., 1896), v. 339

Bankrupt (Campbell, A. V., 1835), IV. 278

— (Foote, S., 1773), III. 174, 260

Bankrupt Cobbler (1806), IV. 429

Banks and Breaks (O'Byrne, 1869), v. 506

Banks of Allan Water (Barnett, C. Z., 1831), IV. 259

Banks of the Boyne Water (1884), v. 645

Banks of the Delaware = Recluse

Banks of the Elbe = All in the Dark

Banks of the Hudson (Dibdin, T. J., 1829), IV. 305

Banks of the Lee = Bells of Shandon

+Banner (Pemberton, C. R.; 8°, 1843, (in *The Life and Literary Remains*))

Bannian Day (Brewer, G., 1796), III. 239

Bannister's Budget with the Shipwreck (1814), IV. 429, 620

Bannockburn (Milner, H. M., 1827), IV. 429, 620

Banquet (Freeth, F., 1888), v. 373

Banquet Gallery = (1) Feudal Times; (2) Silver Knight

Banquet of Wiles = Bilker Bilk'd

Banshee (Levey, J. C., 1876), v. 458

Banshee's Spell (Watson, J. S. W., 1882), v. 616

Bantry Bay (Bond, S., 1897), v. 267

— (Reynolds, G. N., 1797), III. 301

Bar and the Stage = T.T.S.

Barark Johnson (Reeve, W., 1844), IV. 391

Barataria (Pilon, F., 1785), III. 114, 298

Barbara (Jerome, J. K., 1886), v. 436

— (Kenney, J., 1838), IV. 338

Barbara Allen (Dibdin, C. I. M., 1803), IV. 291

Barbarossa (Brown, J., 1754), III. 82, 208, 240

Barbarous Idea (1857), v. 827

Barbazon (Matthison, A., 1887), v. 481

Barbe Bleue (Kenney, C. L., 1869), v. 801

Barber (Fitzball, E., 1822), IV. 312, 584

— (1892), v. 645

Barber and his Brothers (1826), IV. 429

Barber and the Bravo (Vernier, I., 1846), IV. 415

Barber and the Hairdresser (1828), IV. 429

Barber and the Olive Merchant = Mill of Bagdad

Barber, Barber, Shave the Cat (Seaman, W., 1859), v. 645, 815, 827

Barber Baron (Thackeray, T. J., 1828), IV. 412

Barber Barrister (1838), IV. 429

Barber Blue (1869), v. 645

Barber Bravo (Reynoldson, T. H., 1846), IV. 393

— (1846) = Barber and the Bravo, IV. 429 (*and see* 415)

Barber Duellist = Modern Honour

Barber of Bagdad (Browne, E. M., 1891), v. 283, 780

— (1826), IV. 429

Barber of Bath (Farnie, H. B., 1879), v. 362

Barber of Bishopsgate = Blood-spiller

Barber of Cadiz (1869), v. 645

Barber of Fleet Street = Sweeney Todd

Barber of Paris (O'Neil, J. R., 1853), v. 507

— (1842), IV. 429

Barber of Pera (Moser, J., 1808), IV. 364

Barber of Seville (Fawcett, J. and Terry, D., 1818), IV. 311, 583

— (Griffith, Mrs E., 1776), III. 119, 266, 386

— (1824), IV. 429

— (1831), IV. 429

Barbers at Court (Mayhew, H. and Smith, G., 1835), IV. 429, 620

Barbers of Bassora (Morton, J. M., 1837), IV. 362

Barber's Petition (1796), III. 319

Barber's Secret (Archer, T., 1846), IV. 255

Barber's Trip to Paris (1876), v. 645

Barbier de Cadiz (1855), v. 827

Barcarolle (1847), IV. 429, 620

Bard and his Birthday = Shakespearian Reverie

Bard Bewitched = Christabelle

Bardes = Ossian

Bard, the Baron, the Beauty = Princess Charming

Bardwell versus Pickwick (Hollingshead, J., 1871), V. 424

— (Gem, T. H., 1881), V. 377

Barefaced Imposters (Taylor, T., 1854), V. 592

Barely Possible (1869), V. 646

Bargain Broken = Canterbury Guests

Bargeman of the Thames (1866), V. 646

Bargeman's Secret = Roving Meg

Bargemaster's Daughter (1863), V. 646

Barley Mow (Frith, W., 1892), V. 374

Barmaid (Dance, G., 1891), V. 335

Barmaid's Career = Jenny Vernon

Barmecide (Milner, H. M., 1818), IV. 356

Barnaby Brittle (1781), III. 114, 319

— (1811), IV. 429

Barnaby Rudge (Barnett, C. Z., 1841), IV. 97, 570

— (Phillips, W. and Vining, 1866), V. 523

— (Selby, C. and Melville, C., 1841), IV. 97, 398

— (Stirling, E., 1841), IV. 97, 407, 429, 620

— (1876), V. 646

Barn at Beccles (Hughes, G. and Bickley, A. C., 1891), V. 430

Barn Ball = Wagustur

Barn Burners (Rede, W. L., 1833), IV. 429, 607, 620

Barnes of New York (Collier-Edwards, H., 1888), V. 317

Barnet Fair = Black Legend

Barney Brallaghan (1830), IV. 429

Barney Brallaghan's Courtship (1827), IV. 429

Barney Buntline Ashore (Rogers, W., 1845), IV. 396

Barney Burke (1845), IV. 430

Barney's Mistake (1881), V. 646

— = Dhrame

Barney the Baron (Lover, S., 1857), V. 463, 804

Barn in a Bustle = Swiss Revels

Barnwell, the London Apprentice (1822), IV. 430

Baron (Holcroft, F., 1805), IV. 326

Baron and his Brothers = Three Crumpies

Baron de Trenck (1820), IV. 256, 430, 620

Baroness (Dick, C., 1892), V. 344

Baroness of Bruchsal = Disbanded Officer

Baronet (Sinclair, H., 1893), V. 570

— (Vincent, E. H., 1885), V. 609

— (1840), IV. 430

Baronet Abroad and the Rustic Prima Donna (Horne, F. L., 1864), V. 426

Baronet and the Bandit = Pimple the Pirate

Baronet Bit (1741), II. 366

Baronets (1870), V. 646

Baronet's Wager (Keeble, Mrs, 1869), V. 442

Baron Fitzarden (1845), IV. 620

Baron Golosh (1895), V. 646

Baron Kinkvervankotsdorsprakingatchdern (Andrews, M. P., 1781), III. 8, 204, 233

Baron Munchausen (Fenton, F. and Osman, W. R., 1864), V. 646, 792, 808, 827

— (Lonsdale, M., 1795), III. 319, 391, 398

— (1839), IV. 430

— (1840), IV. 430

Baron of Corvelle (Green, F. and Hanson, E., 1892), V. 392

Baron Rudolph (Howard, B., 1881), V. 428

Baron's Bride = Sylvia

Baron's Daughter (Bowles, E. W. and Phillips, G. R., 1893), V. 271

Barons of Ellenbergh (Weston, F. F., 1808), IV. 418

Barons of Ubaldo = Red Banner

Baron's Wager (Young, Sir C. L., 1881), V. 636

Baron, the Bride and the Battery = Last of the Legends

Baron Trenck (Arnold, S. J., 1830), IV. 256

— (Osbaldistone, W., 1831), IV. 256, 602

— (1899), V. 646

Barrack Room (Bayly, T. H., 1836), IV.
263, 571
Barren Island (1734), II. 366
Barren Land (Byatt, H. and Magnay,
W., 1888), V. 295
Barricade (Holt, C., 1869), V. 424
Barringtons (Fitzgerald, S. J. A. and
Merrifield, J. H., 1884), V. 369
Barrington Geo = Barrington, the
Gentleman Pickpocket
Barrington's Busby (Fraser, J. A.,
1883), V. 372
Barrington, the Gentleman Pickpocket
(Marchant, F., 1862), V. 646, 805, 827
Barrington, the Pick-Pocket (1833), IV.
430
Barrister (Fenn, G. M. and Darnley,
J. H.), V. 365
— (Reynoldson, T. H., 1852) = Home
Truths, V. 542, 693, 813
Barry the Dauntless (Gatward, Hal. and
Thompson, W. T., 1890), V. 377
Bar Sinister = David
Barsissa (Dibdin, C. I. M., 1816), IV.
294
Bars of Gold (Rae, J. and Sidney, T.,
1892), V. 533
Bartholomew Fair (?1668), I. 446
Bartonmere Towers (Barrington, R.,
1893), V. 251
Bartons of Barton Wold (Montgomery,
B. S., 1865), V. 491, 646, 827
Barwise's Book (Craven, H. T., 1870),
V. 329
Bas Bleu (Logan, W. H., 1835), IV. 430,
595, 620
Base Coin = Downward Path
Base Impostor (Wigan, H., 1859), V.
622
Basement to Let = Faith and Hope
Base Metal and Sterling Coin = Crooked
Ways
Bashaw (1801), IV. 430
— (1809), IV. 430
Bashaw and the Bear = Bruno
Bashful Irishman (Lemon, M., 1843),
IV. 344
— (1843), IV. 430
Bashful Lovers (1861), V. 646
Bashful Man (Moncrieff, W. T., 1824),
IV. 359
Bashful Virgin (1760), III. 399

Basil and Barbara, Children of the
Bottle (Pitt, G. D., 1848), IV. 430
Basiliska (1870), V. 646
Basil's Faith (1874), V. 646
Basket Girls of Liverpool (Hazlewood
C. H., 1875), V. 415
Basket-Maker (O'Keeffe, J., 1790), III.
294
— (1831), IV. 430
— = Claudine
Basoche (Harris, Sir A. H. G. and
Oudin, E., 1891), V. 406, 795
Basque Roads (1809), IV. 430
Bassett-Table (Centlivre, Mrs S., 1705),
II. 196, 304
Bastard Brother = Charter
Bastard Child (1768), III. 319
Bastille (Atkyns, S., 1845), IV. 257
— (Dent, J., 1789), III. 19, 34, 54, 254
— (1842), IV. 430
Bastille of Calvados = No. 20
Bat and Ball (Russell, F., 1881), V. 553
Batchelors (1799), III. 63, 319, 399
Bateman (1703), II. 366
Bath (D'Urfey, T., 1701), I. 14; II. 194,
320, 435
Bath Bridge in 1830 = Maiden Lane
Murder
Bathing (Bruton, J., 1842), IV. 272
Bathing Machine (1796), III. 319
Bath Intrigues, II. 366
Bath Road (Poole, J., 1830), IV. 430,
620
Bath Roll (Knight, C. J., 1894), V. 445
Bath Struggle = Dromio the Drinker
Bath Unmask'd (Odingsells, G., 1725),
II, 178, 347
Bath Waters = Hot and Cold
Battered Batavians (Cawdell, J., 1798) =
Down with the Dutch, III. 242, 400
Battle (Villiers, G., 1704), I. 436
Battledore and Shuttlecock (Lee, N.,
1847), IV. 342
Battle Field = (1) Flag; (2) Victories of
Edward the Black Prince
Battle of Agincourt (Milner, H. M.,
1825), IV. 430, 620
— (1834), IV. 430
— = Harry of England
Battle of Aughrim (Ashton, R., 1728), I.
100; II. 262, 295
Battle of Austerlitz (1859), V. 646

Battle of Bannockburn = Robert the Bruce

Battle of Barnet (1845), IV. 430

Battle of Blenheim (Haines, J. T., 1841), IV. 430, 620

Battle of Bosworth Field (1824), IV. 430

— (1827), IV. 90, 430

— = (1) King Richard III; (2) Life and Death of King Richard III; (3) White Rose and the Red Rose

Battle of Bothwell Brig (Calcraft, J. W., 1823), IV. 93, 278

— (Middleton, 1827), IV. 598

— (Townsend, W. T., 1858), V. 646, 821, 827

Battle of Bothwell Brigg (Farley, C. 1820), IV. 93, 310

Battle of Bovines (Mildenhall, T., 1840), IV. 598

Battle of Brunanburgh = Ethelstan

Battle of Chevy Chase (1875), V. 646

Battle of Ching Ho = Chinese War

Battle of Clontarffe = Brian Boroihme, the Victorious

Battle of Cressy = Edward the Black Prince

Battle of Cronstad (1828), IV. 430

Battle of Drumclog = Covenanters

Battle of Eddington (Penn, J., 1792, 1797), III. 297

— = Alfred the Great

Battle of Flodden Field = Marmion

Battle of Garra-muir = Perkin Warbeck

Battle of Hastings (Cumberland, R., 1778), III. 13, 78, 251

— = (1) Invasion of England, by William the Conqueror; (2) King Harold

Battle of Hexham (Colman, G., the Younger, 1789), III. 247, 379; IV. 140

— (1812) IV. 140, 430

Battle of Inkerman (1854), V. 646

Battle of Jersey (1881), V. 646

Battle of Life (Atkyns, S., 1847), IV. 98, 257

— (Dickens, C., Jr., 1873), V. 344

— (Lyon, T. E., 1847), IV. 98, 348

— (Parry, A. W. and Dobb, T., 1894), V. 514

— (Pitt, G. D., 1847), IV. 98, 374

— (Robertson, T. W., 1847), V. 546

Battle of Life (Smith, A. R., 1846), IV. 98, 402

— (Somerset, C. A., 1847), IV. 98, 405

— (Stirling, E., 1847), IV. 98, 408, 613

— (Stocqueler, J. H., 1893), V. 646

— (1847), IV. 98, 430

— = 1870

Battle of Lincoln = King Stephen

Battle of Luncarty (Galloway, G., 1804), IV. 318

Battle of Navarino (1828), IV. 430

Battle of Otterburn = Chevy Chase

Battle of Philippi = Death of Caesar

Battle of Poictiers = Edward the Black Prince

Battle of Pultawa (Raymond, R. J., 1829), IV. 430, 620

— = (1) Charles XII and Peter the Great; (2) Peter the Great

Battle of Salamanca (Dibdin, C. I. M., 1812), IV. 292

Battle of Sedgemoor (Almar, G., 1837), IV. 253

— (1707), II. 366

Battle of Stirling Bridge = Wallace

Battle of Televera (1809), IV. 430

Battle of the Alma (Stocqueler, J. H., 1854), V. 646, 818

— (1856), V. 646

Battle of the Amazons (Wilks, T. E., 1848), IV. 421

Battle of the Bridges = Blood will have Blood

Battle of the Dandies = Half-way House

Battle of the Fairies (1836), IV. 430

Battle of the Greybeards = Humorous Quarrel

Battle of the Heart (Wilkins, J. H., 1865), V. 646, 823, 827

Battle of the Inch = St Valentine's Eve

Battle of the Nile (1799), III. 19, 71, 320

— (1815), IV. 14, 430

Battle of the Poets (Cooke, T., 1730), II. 316

Battle of the Season (Towers, E., 1867), V. 821

Battle of the Sexes (Saunders, J. D., 1898), V. 556

Battle of the World = Slaves of London

Battle of Trafalgar (1806), IV. 430

— (1824), IV. 14, 430

Battle of Vittoria (1813), IV. 431

Battle of Waterloo (Amherst, J. H., 1824), IV. 254, 568
— (1815), IV. 431
— (1825), IV. 431
— (1854), V. 646
Battle of Woman (1851), V. 646
Battle of Worcester (1825), IV. 431
— = King Charles II
Battle of Worcester and the Royal Oak = England's Monarch
Battle Royal (Matthison, A., 1878), V. 481
— (1785), III. 320
Battles of Parnassus and Fall of Bob = Fall of Bob
Battles of the West = Siege of Isca
Battle through Life (Mitchell, W. H., 1890), V. 490
Battle with the World (Courtney, J., 1861), V. 786
Bauble and Co. = Stella
Bauble Shop (Jones, H. A., 1893), V. 440
Baucis and Philemon (1740), II. 366
Bavarian Girl (Suter, W. E., 1869), V. 588
Bawd turn'd Puritan = Bragadocio
Bawdy-House School (1744), II. 366
Bayadère (Deshayes, 1831), IV. 431, 620
— (Horncastle, J. H., 1844), IV. 328, 589
— (1845), IV. 431
Bayaderes = Race for a Rarity
Bayes at Parnassus = Macheath in the Shades
Bayes no Poetaster = Two Queens of Brentford
Bayes's Art of Acting = Meeting of the Company
Bayes's Opera (Odingsells, G., 1730), II. 347
Bayes the Younger = New Rehearsal
Bay of Biscay (+ Rogers, W., 1841), IV. 620
— (Somerset, C. A., 1841), IV. 404
Bayonet (Hart, J. P., 1836), IV. 431, 620
Bays in Chromatics = Music Alamode
Bays in Petticoats = Rehearsal
Bazilette (Fitzsimon, J. F., 1881), V. 369
Bazzard d'Algier (Didelot, 1814), IV. 581
B.B. (Burnand, F. C. and Williams, M., 1860), V. 288, 781
Beacon (Baillie, J., 1812), IV. 258
Beacon Light (Clarance, L., 1891), V. 311

Beacon of Liberty (Bailey, P., 1823), IV. 431, 620
Beacon Tower = Mountain Maid
Beam of Fate = Watch-word
+ Bear (Norton, Mrs Caroline, ?1880)
+ Bear and Forbear (Bell, G., *French*)
Beard and Moustache Movement (1854), V. 646
Bearding the Lion (Fawcett, C. S., 1884), V. 364
Beard's Night (1760), III. 320
Bear-Hunters (Buckstone, J. W., 1825), IV. 272
Béarnaise (Murray, A., 1886), V. 500, 808
Bears, not Beasts (Capel, G., 1880), V. 302
— (Faucit, J. S.), IV. 583
— (Milner, H. M., 1821), IV. 356
— (1823), IV. 431
Bear, the Eagle and the Dolphin = Magic Horn
Bear the worse, and hope for the better = Unfortunate Youth
Beast and the Beauty (Burnand, F. C., 1869), V. 289, 781
Beasts' Burletta = Lions for a Lark
Beata (Fryers, A., 1892), V. 374
Beaten at Last = Man in a Thousand
Beaten by a Shadow (1882), V. 646
Beatrice (Blake, T. G., 1844), IV. 268
Beatrice Maxwell (1896), V. 646
Beatrice of Ferrara (Plunkett, A. H., 1837), IV. 606
Beau Austin (Henley, W. E. and Stevenson, R. L., 1884), V. 61, 187, 417
Beau bedevill'd = Cure for a Coxcomb
Beau Blandish the Rake (Calmour, A. C., 1887), V. 300
Beau Brummel (Jerrold, M. W. B., 1859), V. 436, 800
Beau Defeated (Pix, Mrs M., 1700), II. 171-2, 349, 419, 442
Beau Demolished (1715), II. 366
Beau Ideal (Lover, S., 1835), IV. 347
Beau in the Sudds = Female Parson
Beaujolais the Necromancer = Is She his Daughter?
Beau Lavender (Glennie, G., 1896), V. 382
Beau Metamorphos'd = Happy Lovers

Beau Nash, the King of Bath (Jerrold, D. W., 1834), IV. 332

Beau of the Belles = Dick

Beau outwitted (1788), III. 320

— = Sop in the Pan

Beau's Adventures (Bennet, P., 1733), II. 215, 297

Beau's Duel (Centlivre, Mrs S., 1702) II. 61, 166, 303

Beau! the Belle! and the Blacksmith!!! = Acis and Galatea

Beauties of Canterbury = Oaks

Beauties of the Harem (1854), v. 646

— (1871), v. 827

Beauties of the Poets = Blazing Comet

Beauties Triumph (Duffett, T., ?1675), I. 408

Beautiful Armenia (Ball, E., 1778), III. 235

Beautiful as a Butterfly = Cupid and Psyche

Beautiful Bride and the Bouncing Bachelor (1866), v. 646

Beautiful Duchess (1886), v. 646

Beautiful for Ever (Hay, F., 1868), v. 411

— (Hodgson, G. S., 1868), v. 423 [The two plays may be identical although they were credited to separate authors]

Beautiful Galatea (1882), v. 646

Beautiful Haidee (Byron, H. J., 1863), v. 296

Beautiful Helen of Troy = Helen of Troy up-to-date

Beautiful Insane (McLaren, A., 1824), IV. 352

Beauty and the Bard = Merry Mignon

Beauty and the Beast (Blanchard, E. L., 1869), v. 264

— (Blanchard, E. L. and Greenwood, T. L., 1874), v. 264

— (Brennan, J. C., 1871), v. 274

— (Chambers, T., 1861), v. 783

— (Davey, P., 1897), v. 338

— (Denny, J. T., 1884), v. 342

— (Denny, J. T., 1888), v. 342

— (Green, F. W., 1877), v. 391

— (Hazlewood, C. H., 1874), v. 797

— (James, C. S., 1851), v. 433

— (McArdle, J. F. and Stimson, F. J., 1883), v. 647, 804, 827

Beauty and the Beast (McLelland, H. F., 1892), v. 468

— (Oxenford, J., 1863), v. 510, 809

— (Planché, J. R., 1841), IV. 381

— (Roe, J. E., 1866), v. 814

— (Shaw, W. B., 1860), v. 816

— (Stimson, F. J. and Seymour, F., 1885), v. 818

— (Stratford, W., 1894), v. 585

— (Walden, R., 1879), v. 610

— (Yardley, W. and Harris, Sir A., 1890), v. 634, 825

— (1812, 1819, 1821), VI. 431

— (1854), v. 646

— (1857, 1860), v. 827

— (1875, 1876, 1877, 1879, 1881), v. 646

— (1882, 1884, 1887, 1889), v. 647

— (1891), v. 827

— (1891, 1893, 1894, 1895, 1899), v. 647

— = Azor and Zemira

Beauty and the Bey (Dibdin, T. J., 1820), IV. 431, 620

Beauty and the Brigand (1858), v. 827

Beauty and the Brigands = Fra Diavolo Travestie

Beauty and Virtue (1762), III. 320

Beauty in a Box (Dibdin, T. J., 1825), v. 294

Beauty in Distress (Motteux, P. A., 1698), I. 19, 63, 170, 421

Beauty of Bruges (1842), IV. 431

Beauty of Buttermere = Edward and Susan

Beauty of Ghent (Albert, 1844), IV. 251

Beauty of Lyons = Perourou, the Bellows Mender

Beauty or the Beast (Oxenford, J., 1863), v. 510

Beauty's Awakening (1899), v. 827

Beauty Show (Manley, H., 1899), v. 474

Beauty Stone (Pinero, Sir A. W. and Carr, J. W. C., 1898), v. 525

Beauty's Trials (Fawcett, C. S., 1893), v. 364

Beauty's Triumph = Beauties Triumph

Beauty the Best Advocate = Measure for Measure

Beauty the Conqueror (Sedley, Sir C., 1702), I. 428

Beaux Merchant (?Blanch, J., 1714), II. 261, 299

Beaux Stratagem (Farquhar, G., 1707), II. x, 131, 132, 134, 135, 136, 137, 138, 149, 183, 184, 322, 420, 436; III. 115, 127; IV. 140
— (Lawler, D., 1810), IV. 431, 620
Because of Billy Rudd (Hamilton, C., 1898), v. 401
Becket (Cattermole, R., 1832), IV. 576
— (Tennyson, Alfred Lord, 1879), v. 208, 595
Becky Sharp (Barrie, J. M., 1893), v. 211, 251
Bedding Makes the Bargain = Twice Married and a Maid Still
Bedlam Broke Loose = John Brown
Bed of Roses (Jones, H. A., 1882), v. 439
Bedouin and the Fire-Worshipper = Silver Veil
Bedouins (Irwin, E., 1801), IV. 329
Bedroom Window (Stirling, E., 1848), IV. 409
Beds for Two (Stirling, E., 1843), IV. 407
Bee and the Orange Tree (Planché, J. R., 1845), IV. 382
Beechborough Mystery (Galer, E. J. N. and Mew, J., 1889), v. 375
Beef Tea (Greenbank, H., 1892), v. 392
Bee Hive (Millingen, J. G., 1811), IV. 356, 599
— (1827), IV. 431
Beelzebub on Horseback = Tam o' Shanter
Beelzebub's Belles = Devil's Daughter
Been had (Pleon, H., 1889), v. 528
Beeswing in Port (1855), v. 647
Beethoven (Hein, G., 1879), v. 416
Beethoven's Romance (Raphael, S. A., 1894), v. 535
Before and After Luncheon = Double Courtship
Before and Behind the Curtain = Masks and Faces
Before Breakfast (Peake, R. B., 1826), IV. 370
Before, During and After the French Revolution = Three Generations
Before the Dawn (Byatt, H., 1895), v. 295
Before the Mast (Broughton, F. W., 1884), v. 281
Before the Play = Our Opera

Before the Sun goes Down (Hamilton, C., 1899), v. 401
Beggar (Broughton, F. W., 1889), v. 281
Beggar and the Soldier (1841), IV. 431
— = (1) Assassin of Dijon; (2) Smugglers of Dieppe
Beggar Girl of Lambeth Marsh = Green Mantle
Beggar Marquis (Howe, J. B., 1863), v. 798
Beggar my Neighbour (Morton, T., 1802), IV. 363
— (1870), v. 647
Beggar of Bethnal Green (Knowles, J. S., 1834), IV. 339
Beggar of Brussels (1860), v. 647
Beggar of Cripplegate (Moncrieff, W. T., 1830), IV. 360, 600
Beggar of Crosby Hall = Fool of Finsbury
Beggar on Horseback (O'Keeffe, J., 1785), III. 293
— (Sullivan, R., 1846), IV. 409
Beggar's Banquet (1862), v. 647
Beggar's Bush (1815), IV. 431
— = (1) Merchant of Bruges; (2) Royal Merchant
Beggar's Daughter of Bethnal Green (Knowles, J. S., 1828), IV. 339
Beggar's Grave = Sexton of Stepney
Beggar's Haunt (Blink, G., 1837), IV. 573 [By error, the date is wrongly given in the text as 1847]
Beggars of Flanders = White Hoods
Beggars of London = Seven Dials
Beggars of the Sea = Veva
Beggars of Tivoli = Four Hunchbacks
Beggars of Toulouse (1832), IV. 431
Beggar's Opera (Gay, J., 1728), II. 2, 3, 10, 134, 135, 136, 137, 138, 211, 237, 239-40, 241, 243, 245, 249, 250, 251, 269, 300, 331, 396, 412, 424; III. 116, 191, 192; IV. 1
— (Thompson, E., 1777), III. 116, 311
— (1781), III. 320, 399
— (1781), III. 320
— (1811), IV. 431
Beggar's Opera Burlesqued (1840), IV. 431
Beggar's Opera (parody on) (Hogg, C., 1809, IV. 326
Beggar's Opera Reversed (1781), III. 399

Belle of the Barley Mow (Arnold, H. T., 1867), v. 243

Belle of the Bath (Eliot, A., 1897), v. 356

Belle of the Hotel (1842), IV. 431

Belle of the Season (?Heron, M., 1866), v. 647, 827

— = New Year's Eve

Belle of the West = Wild Violet

Belle Russe (Belasco, D., 1881), v. 255

Belles and Bailiffs = Married and Single

Belles and the Ring (1847), IV. 432

Belles' Association (1780), III. 320

Belle Sauvage = (1) Ko and Zoa; (2) Pocahontas; (3) Wild Girl; (4) Zora

Belles Have at Ye All (1831), IV. 431

Belles of the Kitchen (1869), v. 647

Belles of the Shannon = Garry Owen

Belles of the Village (Foster, H., 1889), v. 371

Belle's Stratagem (Cowley, Mrs H., 1780), III. 165–6, 167, 181, 248, 380; IV. 190

— (Waldron, F. G., 1782) = Imitation, III. 320, 397, 399

— (1781), III. 320

Belles without Beaux (1819) = Young Prude, IV. 432, 620

Belle, the Baron and the Bear Hunter = Daughter of the Danube

Belle Vue (Price, J., 1883), v. 531

— (Quittenden, R., 1877), v. 532

Bell in Campo (Cavendish, M., 1662), I. 396

Belling the Cat (Becher, M., 1886), v. 254

Bell of Belle-Hawke (1873), v. 647

Bell-ringer (Barnett, C. Z., 1834), IV. 259, 570

— (Shirley, A. and Vane, S., 1897), v. 564

Bell-Ringer of Notre Dame (Abel, W. H., 1871), v. 234

Bell-Ringer of St Paul's and his Daughter (Townsend, W. T., 1839), IV. 414

Bells (Lewis, L. D., 1871), v. 149, 459

Bells all gone wrong = Faust Reversed

Bells Bellesqued and the Polish Jew Polished Off (1883), v. 647

Bells in the Storm (Hazlewood, C. H., 1874), v. 415

Bells of Fate (Darbey, E., 1891), v. 356

Bells of Haslemere (Pettitt, H. and Grundy, S., 1887), v. 521

Bells of Notre Dame = Midnight

Bells of Shandon (1863), v. 647

— (1868), v. 647

Bells of the Sledge (Allen, H., 1891), v. 239

Bells of Varnavale (1895), v. 647

Bells that Rung an Old Year Out and a New Year In (1862), v. 647

Belly Wager = Selfe Interest

Belmont and Constance (1841), IV. 432

Belmonti (1830), IV. 432

Below London Bridge (Dowling, R., 1896), v. 349

Belphagor (Wilson, J., ?1675), I. 262, 301, 438

Belphegor (Andrews, M. P., 1778), III. 204, 233

— (Buckingham, L. S., 1856), v. 286

— (Jones, J. W., 1889), v. 441

— (1851), v. 647

Belphegor the Buffoon (Higgie, T. H. and Lacy, T. H., 1851), v. 421, 798

Belphegor the Itinerant (Courtney, J., 1851), v. 326

Belphegor the Mountebank (Webb, C., 1856), v. 647, 823, 827

— (Webster, B. N., 1851), v. 618

Belphegor, the Mountebank to any Amount of Property (Hazlewood, C. H., 1866), v. 647, 796, 827

Belshazzar (Harrison, T., 1727), II. 334

— (Milman, H. H., 1822), IV. 167, 356

— (More, Mrs H., 1782), III. 288

— (1745), II. 390

Belshazzar's Feast (Ball, W., 1834), IV. 569

Belveder (Almar, G., 1831), IV. 82, 252

Ben and Bob, the British Bulldogs = Triumph of the Standard

Ben Block (1835), IV. 432

Ben Bolt (Johnstone, J. B., 1854), v. 438

— (1854), v. 647

Ben Brace (Faucit, J. S., 1836), IV. 432, 583, 620

Ben Bradshaw (Fitzball, E., 1844), IV. 316

Ben Child (Young, Mrs H., 1863) = Swallows' Nest, v. 648, 755, 827, 847

Beneath the Lamps of London = Beggar's Banquet

Beneath the Stars (Ellis, B., 1899), v. 357

Beneath the Surface (Murdoch, J. M., 1873), v. 499

— = Dutch the Diver

Beneath the Three Spires (1876), v. 648

Beneath the Waters (1899), v. 648

Benedetto Mangone (Holl, H., 1836), IV. 432, 620

Benefice (Wild, R., 1689), I. 437

Benefit Night (1844), IV. 432

Benefit of Hanging = Miser Smoked

Benefit of the Doubt (Pinero, Sir A. W., 1895), v. 525, 810

Benevolent Cut-throat (1800), III. 320; IV. 432

Benevolent Israelite = Conrad, the Robber Chief

Benevolent Jew (1821), IV. 432

Benevolent Jew of St Mary Axe = Goodman's Fields in the Olden Time

Benevolent Man (Walker, M. C., 1773), III. 314 [This was first acted Smock Alley, Dublin, 18/2/1773]

Benevolent Planters (Bellamy, T., 1789), III. 236

Benevolent Tar (1823), IV. 432

— = Purse

Benevolent Tars of Old England = Poor Jack

Bengal Tiger (Dance, C., 1837), IV. 288

Ben Hur (?Young, W., 1899), v. 648, 827

Benicia Boy = B.B.

Benighted Monarch = Harry le Roi

Benliel (Travers, W., 1857), v. 648, 821, 827

Benliel, the Son of the Night (1884), v. 648

Ben Lighterware (Rayner, A., 1859) = Foundling of the Sea, v. 648, 812

Ben-my-Chree (Caine, H. and Barrett, W., 1888), v. 299

Ben Nazir, the Saracen (Grattan, T. C., 1827), IV. 320

— (1842), IV. 432

Ben the Boatswain (Wilks, T. E., 1839), IV. 421

Bentivoglio (Masterton, C., 1824), IV. 353

Benvenuto Cellini (Walby, 1853), v. 610

Benyowsky (Kenney, J., 1826), IV. 87, 337

Bequeathed Heart = Gabrielli

Bereaved Wife and Mother (1857), v. 648

Berta (Smart, H., 1855), v. 571

Bertha (Fitzball, E., 1819), IV. 312, 584

— (1851), v. 827

Bertha and Durimel (1821), IV. 432

Bertha Gray (1859), v. 648

Bertha Gray, the Pauper's Child (1851), v. 648

Bertha's Bridal = Kiss

Bertha the Broom Girl (Pitt, G. D., 1845), IV. 373

Bertram (Maturin, C. R., 1816) = Castle of St Aldobrand, IV. 167, 354, 598

Bertrand (Harper, S. B., 1837), IV. 587

Bertrand and Burkenstaff (1834), IV. 432

Bertrand and Matilda = Rival Cavaliers

Bertrand and Suzetta = Marriage of Reason

Bertrand de Courcy (1863), v. 648

Bertulfe, the Provost of Bruges = Provost of Bruges

Beside a Cradle (Latham, G., 1888), v. 449

Beside the Bonny Briar Bush (McArthur, J., 1898), v. 467

Bess (Beringer, Mrs O., 1891), v. 259

Bessie (Brooke, E. H., 1878), v. 276

Bessie Bell and Mary Gray (McLaren, A., 1808), IV. 351

Bess of the Bell (Blake, T. G., 1854), v. 262

Bessy Moore (Hazlewood, C. H., 1860), v. 796

Best Bidder (Andrews, M. P., 1782), III. 233

Best Heart in the World (Moser, J., 1807), IV. 364

Best Intentions (Marshall, P. F. and Purdon, R., 1890), v. 478

Best Man (Lumley, R. R., 1894), v. 465

— (Playfair, G. M. H., 1898), v. 528

Best Man Wins (Melford, M., 1890), v. 484

Best of Husbands (Buckstone, J. B., 1832), IV. 432, 620

Best of Mothers = Medea

Best People (Fairfax, Mrs, 1890), v. 360

Best Room in the House = Grim Griffin Hotel

Best Way (Wigan, H., 1866), v. 622

Be Sure You've Got on Your Own (1880), v. 648

Betha the Betrayer (1881), v. 648

Bethnal Green in the Olden Time = Wilkins the Weaver

Betly (1838), IV. 432

— (1841), IV. 432

Betrayed (Mansell, R., 1886), v. 474

— (1873), v. 648

— = Mary Lister

Betrayed by a Kiss (Saintsbury, H. A., 1891), v. 554

Betrayed Innocence = Lyddy Beale

Betrayer of his Country = Earl of Westmoreland

Betrothal (Boker, G. H., 1853), v. 266, 779

Betrothed (Fitzball, E., 1826), IV. 95, 313

— (1836), IV. 95, 432

— = (1) Betrothal; (2) Minerali

Betrothed Lovers (1881), v. 648

Betsey Baker (Morton, J. M., 1850), v. 495

Betsy (Burnand, F. C., 1879), v. 291

Betsy Baker (Hanray, L., 1895), v. 403

Betsy's Bailiff (Shute, E. A., 1893), v. 565

Betsy's Found (1856), v. 648

Better Angel (Reeve, W., 1868), v. 540

Better Days = Next of Kin

Better Half (Williams, T. J., 1865), v. 625

— (1896), v. 648

Better late than Never (Andrews, M. P. and Reynolds, F., 1790), III. 176, 233

— (Burnand, F. C., 1874), v. 290

— (Davies, W., 1786), III. 253

— (Palmer, E., 1870), v. 511

— = (1) Early Bird; (2) Invitation; (3) Legion of Honour; (4) Look on the Bright Side; (5) Nanette

Better Luck Next Time (Moore, R., 1870), v. 492

Better Man = Darkest Hour

Better Self (1882), v. 648

Better than Gold (East, J. M. and Dodson, E., 1894), v. 353

— = Divorce

Betting Boy (Webb, C., 1852), v. 617

Betting Boy's Career (James, C. S. and Johnstone, J. B., 1852), v. 433

— (1852), v. 648

Betting Boy's Career, from his Home to the Hulks (1852), v. 648

Betting Boy's Career, from the Counting House to the Hulks (1852), v. 648

Betting Boys, from the Counting House to the Hulks (1852), v. 648

Betty (Carey, H., 1732), II. 302, 432

Betty Martin (Robertson, T. W., 1855) = Clockmaker's Hat, v. 546

Between the Acts (Norman, G. T., 1898), v. 505

Between the Lights (Lampard, E. J., 1894), v. 446

Between the Posts = Indécis

Between Two Stools (Gray, L., 1886), v. 390

Betwixt the Cup and the Lip (Lonergan, Mrs E. A., 1896), v. 462

Beulah Spa (Dance, C., 1833), IV. 190, 288

Beverley Bogey (Hingeston-Randolph, M. and Giffard, A., 1897), v. 422

Beware of Jealousy (1891), v. 648

Beware of Man Traps (Younge, A., 1851), v. 637

Beware of the Centenier (1877), v. 648

Bey of Bagdad (Carlton, Charles, 1897), v. 303

Beyond (1894), v. 648

Beyond the Breakers (Vane, S., 1893), v. 606

Bianca (Robson, W. J., 1856), v. 547

— (Shepherd, R., 1772), III. 305

— (1846), IV. 432

Bianca Capello (Thompson, B., 1796), III. 311

Bianca Contarini (Greenwood, T., 1840), IV. 321

Bianca de Molino (Webb, C., 1845), IV. 417

Bianca, the Bravo's Bride (Simpson, J. P., 1860), v. 567

Bianca Visconti (Willis, N. P., 1843), IV. 422

Biarritz (Jerome, J. K. and Ross, A., 1896), v. 436

Bibb and Tucker (Clayton, J., 1873), v. 648, 784, 828

Bibbins and Figgins (Suter, W. E., 1860), V. 648, 818, 828

Bibboo (Somerset, C. A., 1842), IV. 405

— (1839), IV. 432

Bickerstaff's Burying (Centlivre, Mrs S., 1710), II. 168, 210, 305

Bickerstaff's Unburied Dead (1743), II. 215, 366

Bicycle (Bell, Mrs H., 1896), V. 256

Bicycle Belle = Lady Cyclist

Bicycle Girl (Osborne, C., Stuart, E. M. and Seton, H., 1896), V. 508

Biddy O'Neal (Pitt, W. H., 1869), V. 527

Bier Kroeg (Barnett, C. Z., 1830), IV. 259

Bigamy = His Wives

Bigamy, Trigamy and Quadrigamy = Everybody's Husband

Big Bandit (Watson, T. M., 1894), V. 616

Big Blue Bowl (Castles, F., 1888), V. 306

Big-bodied Bill, Big Belzebub's Boy (1850), V. 648

Big Fortune (Bourne, W., 1891), V. 270

Big O and Sir Glory (Cobbett, W., 1825), IV. 281

Bigot (Grove, F. C., 1890), V. 395

Bijou Residence to Let (Van de Velde, Mme, 1889), V. 606

Bilbery of Tilbury (Dauncey, S. and Day, G. D., 1898), V. 337

Bilious Attack = Chamber of Horrors

Bilker Bilk'd (1742), II. 364, 384

Bill Adams the Sailor = Mutineer's Widow

Bill and Me (1883), V. 648

"Bill due Sept. 29th" = Wanted a Partner

Billee Taylor (Stephens, H. P., 1880), V. 580

Billet Doux (1860), V. 648

Billet-master (Ward, W., 1767), III. 317 [By error this appears in III. 317 under W. Wood. The author's name was William Ward]

Billing and Cooing (Oxenford, J., 1865), V. 510

— = Old Turtles

Bill Jones (Amherst, J. H.), IV. 254

Bill of Exchange (Fisher, D., 1879), V. 367

Bill of Fare (Dibdin, C. I. M., 1822), IV. 295

— (Dibdin, T. J., 1822), IV. 303

Bill-Sticker (Jerrold, D. W., 1836), IV. 333, 590

Bill Stickers Beware (1875), V. 648

Bill! the Belle!! and the Bullet!!! = Freischutz

Bill! the Whole Bill!! and Nothing but the Bill!!! = More Reform!

Billy (Cooper, G. and Ross, A., 1898), V. 324

Billy and Mrs Button's Journey = Election

Billy Button's Disaster (1807), IV. 432

Billy Button's Journey to Brentford (Lee, N., 1853), V. 452

Billy Button's Ride to Brentford (1854), V. 648

Billy Doo (Rae, C. M., 1874), V. 532

Billy Duck (Dibdin, C. I. M., 1822), IV. 295

— (Dibdin, C. I. M., 1826), IV. 296

Billy Snivel and Sally Sly (1834), IV. 432

Billy Taylor (Buckstone, J. B., 1829), IV. 273

— (George, G. H., 1871), V. 377

— (Mowbray, T., 1861), V. 807

Billy Taylor, the Gay Young Fellow (1831), IV. 432

Binbian Mine (Praed, Mrs C. and McCarthy, J., 1888), V. 530

Binke's Blues (1884), V. 648

Binks' Photographic Gallery = Dream

Binks the Bagman (Coyne, J. S., 1843), IV. 284, 578

— (1842), IV. 432

Binks the Downy Photographer = Dream

Biorn (Marshall, F. 1877), V. 478

Birdcage Walk (Bennett, H. L. and Tapping, A. B., 1892), V. 258

Bird Catchers (1750), III. 320

Birdcatchers of Whitechapel (1859), V. 648

Bird Fancier = Isn't it a Duck?

Birdie's Nest (1884), V. 648

Bird in a Cage (1786), III. 320

Bird in the Bush = Rossignol

Bird in the Hand worth Two in the Bush (Phillips, F. L., 1857), V. 522, 810

Bird of Paradise (Thompson, A., 1869), V. 597

Bird of Paradise (1800), IV. 432

Bird of Passage (Webster, B. N., 1849), IV. 418

Birds, Beasts and Fishes (Lee, N., 1854), V. 648, 802, 828

Birdseller of Paris = Otto the Outcast

Birds in their little nest agree (Rae, C. M., 1876), V. 532

Bird's Nest (Lindo, F., 1898), V. 460

Birds of a Feather (Hatton, J.), V. 796

— (1796), III. 320

"Birds" of Aristophanes (Planché, J. R., 1846), IV. 382

Birds of Bloomsbury Bower = Bloomers

Birds of Paradise (Jerrold, D., 1835), IV. 432, 620

— = Love Birds

Birds of Prey (Hawkins, Mrs P. L., 1884), V. 410

— (Robertson, T. W.), V. 123, 547

— = Mouth of the Pit

Birds without Feathers (1824), IV. 432

Birmingham Bagsmen = Forty Winks

Birmingham Girl (1844), IV. 432

Birmingham in 1643 = Aston Hall

Birth (Robertson, T. W., 1870), V. 546

Birth and Adventures of Harlequin (1735), II. 366

Birth and Breeding (Jerome, J. K., 1890), V. 436

Birthday (Bancroft, G. P., 1894), V. 248

— (Dibdin, T. J., 1799), III. 122, 256, 383

— (O'Keeffe, J., 1783), III. 293, 393

— (Penny, Mrs A., 1771), III. 297

— (1788), III. 320

— (1799), III. 320

— = (1) Portraits; (2) Parson's Nose; (3) Reconciliation

Birth Day Dinner = Parson's Nose

Birthday Festivities = Merrymaking

Birth-Day Loyalty = Fourth of June

Birthdays (Roberts, G., 1883), V. 544

Birthday Tribute (Sicklemore, R., 1805), IV. 401

Birth-Night (1796), III. 320

Birth of Beauty (Akhurst, W. M., 1872), V. 237

Birth of Hercules (Shirley, W., 1763), III. 306

Birth of Jupiter (Olivari, F., 1797), III. 295

Birth of Merlin, the British Enchanter (1724), II. 378

Birth of the New Year (1860), V. 828

Birth of the Prince of Wales = Caern-arvon Castle

Birth of the Steam Engine (Blanchard, E. L., 1846), IV. 265

Birthplace of Podgers (Hollingshead, J., 1858), V. 424

Birthright (Douglass, J. T., 1894), V. 349

— = Sea-Captain

Birthright of Britons = Magna Charta

Bishop (Field, W. F., 1894), V. 366

Bishop of the Fleet (Clarke, C. A. and Mouillot, F., 1889), V. 312

Biter (Rowe, N., 1704), II. 209, 352

Biter Bit (1731), II. 366, 385

— (1827), IV. 432

— = (1) Big Bandit; (2) Gripe in the Wrong Box; (3) Harlequin Disaffected; (4) Impostor

Biters Bit = (1) Fox and the Wolf; (2) Lynn Wives; (3) South-Sea

Bit of Brummagem = Bowled Out

Bit of Drapery (Hope, P., 1897), V. 426

Bit of Fun (Saxby, A., 1898), V. 557

Bit of Human Nature (Corbett, Mrs G., 1899), V. 324

Bit of Old Chelsea (Beringer, Mrs O., 1897), V. 259

Bit of Scandal = Little Nun

Bit of the Breast (1861), V. 648

Bitter Bargain = Mabel's Life

Bitter Cold (Coates, A., 1863), V. 315, 784

— (1865), V. 648

— (1868), V. 648

Bitter End = Knights of Knavery

Bitter Fruit (Dubourg, A. W., 1873), V. 351

Bitter Lesson (Harris-Burland, J. R. and Weatherley, A., 1896), V. 407

Bitter Love = For Wife and State

Bittern Swamp (1880), V. 648

Bittern's Swamp = Rover's Bride

Bitter Reckoning (Hazlewood, C. H., 1871), V. 414

Bitter Repentance (Samuels, W. R., 1889), V. 555

Bitter Sweet (Kitts, C. S., 1895), V. 445

Bitter Sweets (Parry, A., 1880), V. 514

Bitter Wrong (Lander, G. and Douglass, J. T., 1884), v. 448
— (1896), v. 648
— = In Black and White
Bivouac of Life = White Cuirassier
Bivouac of the Hills (1849), IV. 432
Black Adder (Pitt, G. D., 1850), v. 526
Blackamoor's Head (Thomson, J., 1818), IV. 432, 620
Blackamoor wash'd White (Bate, H., 1776), III. 236
— = Knights of the Post
Black and Blue (1898), v. 649
Black and Red Galleys (1854), v. 649
Black and White (Collins, W. W., 1869), v. 318
— (Melford, M., 1897), v. 484
— (1823), IV. 432
— (1843), IV. 432
— (1851), v. 649
— (1881), v. 649
Black and White Milliners (1788), III. 320
Black Armour (Sicklemore, R., 1813), IV. 611
Black Ball (Darcy, F., 1895), v. 336
Black Band (Young, Mrs W. S., 1861), v. 649, 825, 828
— (1835), IV. 432
— (1862), v. 649
Black Banner (1825), IV. 433
— = Montaldi
Black Banner of Heppenheff = Burgraves
Black Bayaderes (Pitt, G. D., 1847), IV. 375
Black Beard (Cross, J. C., 1798) = Genoese Pirate, III. 250, 380
Blackberries (Melford, M., 1886), v. 484
Blackbirding (Hazlewood, C. H., 1873), v. 414
Black Bishop (Williams, B., 1898), v. 624
Black Boarder (Johnstone, H., 1897), v. 438
Black Book (Simpson, J. P., 1857), v. 567
Black Bottle = Sicilian Hussars
Black Brand of Rome = Royal Crusader
Black Buccaneer (Taylor, T. P., 1841), IV 411, 614

Black Business (Matthison, A., 1878), v. 481
Black but comely (Forrester, S., 1882), v. 371
Black Caesar (Dibdin, C. I. M., 1825), v. 285
Black Captain (Faucit, H. S. and Fisher, W. D., 1867), v. 792
Black Castle (Amherst, J. H., 1801), IV. 253
Black Cat (Rodney, C. M., 1893), v. 548
— (Todhunter, J., 1893), v. 600
Black Cat of Coventry = Ronald Dhu
Black Charger = Brewer of Preston
Black Country (Leslie, H. T., 1867), v. 457
Black Crook (Paulton, J. and Paulton, H., 1872), v. 517
Black Diamonds (Mackay, R. F. and Denbigh, L. S., 1890), v. 470
Black Doctor (Archer, T., 1846), IV. 255
— (Bridgeman, J. V., 1846), IV. 270, 593
Black Domino (À Beckett, G. A., 1838), IV. 83, 250 [See also Queen's Ball]
— (Chorley, H. F., 1861), v. 310, 783
— (Coyne, J. S., 1838), IV. 83, 433
— (Sims, G. R. and Buchanan, R., 1893), v. 569
— (Mathews, C. J., 1838), IV. 83, 354
— (Morton, J. M. and Kenney, J., 1838), IV. 83, 433, 591, 601, 620
— (Webster, B. N., 1846), IV. 418, 616
— (Wilks, T. E., 1838), IV. 83, 420
Black Dove (Gordon-Clifford, E. and H., 1894), v. 385
Black Dwarf (1817), IV. 95, 433
Black Eagle (Almar, G., 1831), IV. 252
— (1841), IV. 433
Blackenberg (Dibdin, C. I. M., 1800), IV. 290
Black Enchanter = Island of Darkness
Black Ey'd Susan (Redgrave, R., 1898), v. 537
Blackeyed Sukey (Cooper, F. F., 1829), IV. 148, 283
Black Eyed Susan (Jerrold, D. W., 1829), IV. 148, 332
— (1829), IV. 433
— (1884), v. 649

43

Black Eyed Susan = (1) All in the Downs; (2) Davy Jones's Locker

Blackeyed Susan at Dunstable (1830), IV. 433

Black Festival (1800), IV. 433

Black Fisherman (Pitt, G. D., 1845), IV. 373

Black Flag (Pettitt, H., 1879), V. 521

Black Flag and the Vow of Vengeance = Elmira, the Female Pirate

Black Flag of Toraldi (1847), IV. 433

Black Forest (Birch, S., 1798) = Albert and Adelaide, III. 320, 378, 399

— = Lost and Found

Black Forester (1831), IV. 433

Black Forest of Istria = Mine

Black Friday (1838), IV. 433

Black Gang Chine = Storm Deed

Black Gentleman (1842), IV. 433

Black God of Love (Graves, J., 1836), IV. 320

Black Gondola (Hazlewood, C. H., 1856), V. 649, 796, 828

— = Tower of Nesle

Black Hand (Fitzball, E., 1834), IV. 433, 621

— (Towers, E., 1864), V. 821

Black Hawks (1893), V. 649

Black Heart = Crime

Black Hearts (Towers, E., 1868), V. 601

Black Helmet = Bavarian Girl

Black Hugh (Rogers, W., 1832), IV. 396

Black Hugh the Outlaw (1836), IV. 433

Black Huntsman of Bohemia = Freischutz

Black Hussar = Statue Steed

Black Inn of the Heath = Coupe Gorge

Black Justice (1897), V. 649

Black King (1830), IV. 433

— (1839), IV. 433

Black Kitten (1894), V. 649

Black Knight (Byrne, J., 1803), IV. 575

Black Knight of Ashton (Stanhope, B., 1874), V. 578

Black Knight of Chelmsford = Tilbury Fort

Black Law of Martinique (1842), IV. 433

Blackleg (Stanhope, B., 1886), V. 578

Black Legend (1837), IV. 433

Black Legend of Rotherhithe (1838), IV. 433

Black Lion of Finsbury (Taylor, T. P., 1839), IV. 411, 614

Blackmail (Dabbs, G. H. R., 1887), V. 332

— (Phillips, W., 1880), V. 523

— (Stanley, H. J., 1896), V. 579

— (1873), V. 649

— = Thumbscrew

Blackmailed Warrior = Athelstane

Blackmailers (Gray, J. and Raffalovitch, A., 1894), V. 390

— = Harvest of Wild Oats

Black Man (Kirkman, F., 1673), I. 418

Blackman and the Blackbird = Negro Slaves

Black Mask (Watson, F. M., 1899), V. 616

Black Monk and the Emperor's Secret = Gunmaker of Moscow

Black Musket (1835), IV. 433

Black Opera (Gay, B., 1847), IV. 318

Black Phantom (1828), IV. 433

Black Pig (Dibdin, C. I. M., 1800), IV. 290

Black Pirate = Roderick of Ravenscliff

Black Prince (Boyle, R., 1667), I. 55, 106–8, 344, 393

— (Farnie, H. B., 1874), V. 362

— (Lindsay, Sir C., 1846), IV. 595

Black Prince in Spain = Peter the Cruel

Black Rainbow (1855), V. 649

Black Reefer = Contraband Captain

Black Robber of the Mountains = Old Swiss Church

Black Rollo (Pitt, C.), V. 810

Black Rover (Searelle, L., 1890), V. 559

Black Seal = With the Colours

Black Sentinel (1840), IV. 621

Black Sheep (Coyne, J. S., 1861), V. 328

— (Raffalovich, A., 1894), V. 533

— (Simpson, J. P. and Yates, E., 1868), V. 567

Blacksmith (Collier, W., 1834), IV. 281

— (Maeder, F., 1892), V. 472

Blacksmith and the Baron = Sons of the Forge

Blacksmith of Antwerp (O'Keeffe, J., 1785), III. 293

— (1816), IV. 433

Blacksmith of Barnet = Irish Girl

Blacksmith of Ghent (Courtney, J., 1848), IV. 284

Blacksmith of Warsaw = Hans of the Iron Hand

Blacksmith's Daughter (Goldsworthy, A., 1888), v. 384, 794

Blacksmith's Daughter and the Mock Marriage = Geoffrey Kurdistan

Blacksmith's Daughter and the Red Hand (Haden, T., 1893), v. 398

Black Somnambulist (1848), IV. 433

Black Spectre = Anna

Black Spider (1831), IV. 433

Black Spirits and White (Dibdin, T. J., 1826), IV. 304

— = Scraps

Black Squire (Stephens, H. P., 1896), v. 580

Black Statue (Hazlewood, C. H., 1874), v. 649, 796, 828

Black Swan at Liverpool (1853), v. 649

Black's White = What's in a Name?

Black Tom of Tyburn (1850), v. 649

Black Tower (1832), IV. 433

— = Montalbert

Black Tower and the Spanish Patriots (1823), IV. 433

Black Tower of Linden (Pitt, C., 1869), v. 526

Black Tribunal = Rinaldo Rinaldini

Black Tulip (Grundy, S., 1899), v. 397

Black Valley (1822), IV. 433

Blackville Derby (1897), v. 649

Black Vulture (Fitzball, E., 1830), IV. 313

Black Walloon = White Wolf

Black Woodsman (Milner, H. M., 1827), IV. 433, 621

Blade Bone (1788), III. 320

Bladud (1777), III. 399

Blaize in Amaze = Conjuror

Blanca Rubea, the Heroine of Padua (1824), IV. 433

Blanche (Sketchley, A., 1870), v. 571

— (1897), v. 649

Blanche and Brunette (1862), v. 649

Blanche de Maletroit (Mason, A. E. W., 1894), v. 480

Blanche de Valmy (Bernard, W. B., 1844), IV. 266

Blanche Dhu, the Spectre Dog (1854), v. 649

Blanche Farneau (Calvert, W., 1890), v. 300

Blanche Heriot (Smith, A. R., 1842), IV. 402

Blanche of Chillon (Paul, H. M.), v. 515

Blanche of Jersey (Peake, R. B., 1837), IV. 370

Blanche of Navarre (James, G. P. R., 1839), IV. 590

Blanche of Nevers (Hyde, W. S., 1863), v. 799

Blanchette (Grein, J. T. and Churchill, M. L., 1898), v. 394

Blanche Westgarth (Lucas, J. T., 1871), v. 464

+ Blank; or, The Tar and the Ticket (Dibdin, C. I. M., R.A., 1797–8)

Blank Cartridge = How to Die for Love

Blarney (Creamer, A., 1875), v. 329

— (Logue, J. D., 1875), v. 462

Blarney Stone (1895), v. 649

— (1898), v. 649

Blasé (1844), IV. 434

Blasé Roué = Ruy Blas

Blaza the Beautiful (Righton, E., 1864), v. 813

+ Blazing Burgee (Bowles, T. G., French)

Blazing Comet (Johnson, S., 1732), II. 268, 340

Bleak House (Burnett, J. P., 1875), v. 80, 292

— (Elphinstone, J. and Neale, F., 1853), v. 80, 358

— (Lander, G., 1876), v. 80, 448

— (Thorne, E., 1876), v. 80, 598

— (1853), v. 649

— (1854), v. 649

— (1892), v. 649

— = No

Bleeding Nun of Lindenburg = Robber's Wife

Bleeding Rose of Normandy = Charlotte Corday

Blessing of Education = Only My Cousin

Blessings of Pxxx and a Scotch Excuse (1763), III. 320 [The last word in the title is 'Excuse', not 'Excise', as in the text]

Blessings of Peace = (1) Farmer Emigrant; (2) Farmer of Labian

Blessings of Two Wives at Once = Thelyphthora

Bletchington House (Craven, H. T., 1846), IV. 285
— (Gaspey, 1836), IV. 434, 621
Blight and Bloom (1855), V. 649
Blighted Bachelors (Lee, N. Jr., 1875), V. 453
— (Williams, H. L., 1881), V. 624
Blighted Being (Taylor, T., 1854), V. 592
Blighted Flower (1851), V. 649
— = (1) Linda di Chamouni; (2) Warrior and his Child
Blighted Home (Howe, J. B., 1864), V. 649
Blighted Hopes (1871), V. 649
Blighted Joys (1852), V. 649
Blighted Love (Masterton, C., 1832), IV. 353
— = Clara Charette
Blighted Moor = Fire-Raiser
Blighted One = Traviata
Blighted Willow (1839), IV. 434
Blight of Ambition (Almar, G., 1832), IV. 568
Blind (1877), V. 649
Blind among Enemies (1885), V. 649
Blind Bargain (Reynolds, F., 1804) = Hear It Out, IV. 391, 607
— = Rejected Addresses
Blind Beggar of Bethnal Green (Dodsley, R., 1741), II. 205, 249, 319, 435
— (Milner, H. M., 1834), IV. 357, 599
— = Injured General
Blind Beggar of Moorfields (1832), IV. 434
Blind Beggars of Burlington Bridge (Clements, A. and Malone, J., 1874), V. 314, 784
Blind Boy (Kenney, J., 1807), IV. 336
— (1899), V. 649
Blind Boy's Murder = Smuggler's Dog
Blind Child of Africa (1851), V. 649
Blind Father (Moncrieff, W. T., 1837), IV. 434, 621
Blind Fiddler (1872), V. 649
Blindfold (Soutar, R., 1882), V. 575
Blind Foundling (Phelps, C. H., 1899), V. 522
Blind Girl (Morton, T., 1801), IV. 363, 601
— = Augusta

Blind Girl of Tessaly = Last Days of Pompeii
Blind Girl's Fortune (1874), V. 649
Blind Girl's Inheritance = Dead Man's Cliff
Blind Girl's Protegée = Lamplighter
Blind Hearts (Collins, C., 1877), V. 317
Blind Justice (Bertrand, E. C., 1886), V. 260
Blind Lady (Howard, Sir R., 1660), I. 214, 414
Blind Love = Hester Gray
Blind Man (Dibdin, C., 1782) = None so Blind as those who won't see, III. 320, 382, 399
Blind Man of the Pyrenees = Cloud of Life
Blindman's Buff (Dibdin, T. J., ?1796, 1802), III. 382; IV. 297, 580
— (1815), IV. 434
Blind Marriage (Francis, F., 1896), V. 372
Blindness (1821), IV. 434
Blindness among Enemies (1878), V. 649
Blind Orphan (1833), IV. 15, 434
Blind Prince = Blindness
Blind Singer (Dabbs, G. H. R., 1898), V. 332
Blind Sister (Lacy, M. R., 1849), IV. 434, 621; V. 649, 801, 828
— (Meritt, P. and Conquest, G., 1874), V. 486
— = Mountain Robber
Blind Wife (Powell, T., 1843), IV. 387
— (1850), V. 649
Blind Wife and the Detective = Stolen Fortune
Blind Witness (Blythe, J. S., 1899), V. 266
— = Bararck Johnson
Blind Witness of Aberdare (1872), V. 649
Blister (1814), IV. 621
Blobb's Holiday (Crozier, C., 1892), V. 331
Blodwin (Parry, J., 1878), V. 514
Blonde or Brunette (Wooler, J. P., 1862), V. 632, 824
Blondin (1861), V. 650
Blondinette Melodists (1873), V. 650
Blondin on the Tight Rope (1873), V. 650

46

Blood demands its Victim (Amherst, J. H., 1828), IV. 254, 568
Blood for Blood = Shade
Bloodhound (1845), IV. 434
Bloodhound of Cuba (Pitt, G. D. 1847), IV. 375
Blood of the Faithful (1898), V. 650
Blood-red Knight (Amherst, J. H., 1810), IV. 253
— (Barrymore, W.), IV. 262
— (Male, G., 1810), IV. 597
Blood Royal (Archer, T., 1843), IV. 254
— (1843), IV. 434
+Blood-spiller; or, The Barber of Bishopsgate and the Fair Maid of Finsbury (C.L. ?1832)
Blood-stained Bandit = Crimson Crimes
Bloodstained Banner (Amherst, J. H.), IV. 254
Blood Stain on the Grass = Bravoes of London
Blood will have Blood (Dibdin, T. J., 1811), IV. 299
— (1813), IV. 434
Blood will tell (1895), V. 650
Bloody Contest between Charles the Twelfth, King of Sweden, and Peter the Great, Czar of Muscovy = Northern Heroes
Bloody Duke (1690), I. 11, 440
Bloody Plot Discovered (1780), III. 320
Bloomer Costume (James, C. S., 1851), V. 433
— (Stirling, E., 1851), V. 584
— (1851), V. 650
Bloomerism (Nightingale, J. H. and Millward, C., 1851), V. 504
Bloomers (Somerset, C. A., 1851), V. 574
Bloomer's Bride (Higgie, T. H., 1851), V. 421
Bloomer Wives = Bloomers
Blossom of Churnington Green (Hoskins, F. R.), V. 427
Blot in the 'Scutcheon (Browning, R., 1843), IV. 178, 273
Blotted Out (James, D. S., 1884), V. 433
Blot upon Humanity = Quadroona
Blower Jones (1881), V. 650
Blow for Blow (Byron, H. J., 1868), V. 114, 297
Blow in the Dark (Townsend, W. T., 1855), V. 602

Blown Up (1895), V. 650
Blue above and the Blue below = Lily Laburnem
Blue Anchor (Pocock, I., 1830), IV. 385
— (1832), IV. 434
— (1844), IV. 434
Blue and Buff (Ward, E. V., 1880), V. 613
Blue Baron (Dibdin, T. J., 1821), IV. 303
Bluebeard (Blanchard, E. L. and Greenwood, T. L., 1879), V. 265
— (Bridgeman, J. V., 1860), V. 275
— (Burnand, F. C., 1883), V. 291, 782
— (Butler, F., 1890), V. 294
— (Byron, H. J., 1871), V. 298, 782
— (Colman, G., the Younger, 1798), III. 27, 32, 51, 61, 98, 104–6, 248, 380
— (Dance, C., 1842), IV. 289
— (Danville, A., 1898), V. 336
— (Gower, Lord F. L., 1841), IV. 320
— (Hazlewood, C. H., 1865) = Harlequin Bluebeard and his Seven Headless Wives, V. 650, 828, 834
— (Lennard, H., 1883), V. 455, 803
— (Lennard, H., 1894), V. 456
— (North, W. S., 1894), V. 505
— (Planché, J. R. and Dance, C., 1839), IV. 381
— (Risque, W. H., 1892), V. 650, 813, 828
— (Woolfe, J. H., 1897), V. 824
— (1791), III. 320, 381, 399
— (1847), IV. 621
— (1858), V. 828
— (1859), V. 828
— (1863, 1864), V. 650
— (1865), V. 651
— (1869), V. 828
— (1870), V. 828
— (1874, 1875, 1876, 1877, 1878, 1879, 1880, 1881, 1882, 1883, 1884, 1885, 1886, 1887, 1888, 1889, 1890, 1892, 1894, 1895, 1896), V. 650
— (1898, 1899), V. 651
— = Barbe Bleue
+Blue Beard; or, Dangerous Curiosity and Justifiable Homicide (Egerton, Lord Francis: printed in *Juvenile Plays for Home Performance* (*French*))
Blue Beard, according to Act of Parliament = Hints to the Curious

Blue Beard and Fat Emma (Green, F. W., 1877), v. 390

Bluebeard and Son (1883), v. 651

Bluebeard, Cinderella and Prince Pretty-step (1872), v. 651

Blue Beard done Brown (Spry, H., 1881), v. 577

Blue Beard from a New Point of Hue (Byron, H. J., 1860), v. 296

Blue Beard, his Blue Chamber (Suter, W. E., 1860), v. 819

Bluebeard in a Black Skin (Williams, M., 1875), v. 625

Bluebeard Re-paired (Bellingham, H., 1866), v. 257, 778

Bluebeard Re-trimmed (1877), v. 651

Blue Beard Re-wived (Douglass, J. T., 1879), v. 348

Bluebeard the Grand Bashaw (Muskerry, W., 1887), v. 501

Bluebeard the Great (1878), v. 651

Bluebeard the Great Bashaw (Arnold, H. T., 1869), v. 243

Bluebeard Trimmed (1895), v. 651

Blue-bells of Scotland (Buchanan, R., 1887), v. 285

Blue Bird of Paradise (Conquest, G. and Spry, H., 1860), v. 651, 785, 817, 828

— = King Charming

Blue Boar (Parker, L. N. and Carson, S. M., 1894), v. 513

Blue Dahlia (Sutcliffe, H. and Bartlett, H., 1898), v. 587

Blue Devils (Colman, G., the Younger, 1798), III. 248, 380

— (1842), IV. 434

— (1862), v. 651

Blue Dwarf (Marchant, F., 1862), v. 651, 805, 828

Blue-eyed Blue Beard, the Masher Pasha (Thorne, G., 1885), v. 598

Blue-eyed Mary (Nantz, F. C., 1835), IV. 434, 621

— (Pitt, G. D., 1835), IV. 373

Blue-eyed Susan (Sims, G. R. and Pettitt, H., 1892), v. 569

Blue-eyed Witch (Hazlewood, C. H., 1869), v. 413

Bluejackets (Stirling, E., 1838), IV. 406

— (1896), v. 651

Blue Jeans (Arthur, J., 1891), v. 244

Blue-legged Lady (Hill, W. J., 1874), v. 421

Blue Man (1834), IV. 434

Blue Monkey (1891), v. 651

Blue Mountain Spirits (1800), v. 424

Blue or Green? (Bell, Mrs H., 1896), v. 256

Blue Ribbon of the Turf (Williams, F., 1867), v. 823

— = Jack o' Lantern

Blue Ribbons (Browne, G. W. and Soden, J. E., 1887), v. 283

Blue Skin (Marchant, F., 1863), v. 651, 828

— (Mildenhall, T., 1846), IV. 598

Blue Stocking = M.P.

Bluff (1888), v. 651

Bluff King Hal (Lee, N. Jr., 1868), v. 453

— (Maddy, J. M., 1848), IV. 434, 621

— (Marchant, F., 1868), v. 475

— (O'Neil, C., 1877), v. 507

— (Spry, H., 1882), v. 577

— (1872), v. 651

— (1876), v. 651

— (1878), v. 651

— (1883), v. 651

Bluff King Hal and the Forest Maid = Herne the Hunter and his Demon Band

Blunderer (Foote, S., 1762), III. 384

Blunders (1898), v. 651

Blunders at Brighton = Irish Mimic

Blunder upon Blunder, yet all's Right at Last = Ephesian Duke

Blunt Tar (1791), III. 320

Blush Rose (D'Arcy, G., 1876), v. 336

— = Banshee's Spell

Blutzherranbhothrum (Marchant, F., 1868), v. 475

Boabdil el Chico (Burnand, F. C., 1866), v. 288

Boa-Constrictor and the Buffalo = Anaconda

Boadacia (Glover, R., 1753), III. 80-1, 265

Boadicea (Bealing, R.), II. 432

— (Dibdin, C. I. M., 1800), IV. 290

— (Hopkinson, A. F., 1888), v. 426

— (Lindsay, Sir C., 1857), v. 804

— = Boadicia

Boadicea Queen of Britain (Hopkins, C., 1697), I. 32, 40, 152, 413

Boadicea Unearthed (Rix, W. F. and Gillett, F. J., 1895), V. 544

Board and Residence (Edwardes, C. T. M., 1870), V. 354

Boarded and Done For = Jenkinses

Boarder (Ryan, R., 1832), IV. 434, 621

Boarding House (Beazley, S., Jr., 1811), IV. 263

Boarding House for 1862 (1862), V. 651

Boarding School (Bernard, W. B., 1841), IV. 266

— (Coffey, C., 1733), I. 275; II. 142, 237, 244, 315

— = Love for Money

Boarding School Ball (1853), V. 651

Boarding School Dissected = Governess

Boarding School Miss (Dibdin, C. I. M., 1816), IV. 294

— (Jodrell, R. P., 1787), III. 277

Boarding School of Montesque = Assurance Company

Boarding School Romps = Boarding-School

Board of Conviviality (1806), IV. 434

Boaster (?1698), I. 446

Boat-builder's Hovel = Negro of Wapping

Boat Builders of Brugen = Crossing the Line

Boatman of Deal = Deal Boatman

Boatmen of the Shannon (Towers, E., 1877), V. 601

Boatswain's Whistle (1859), V. 651

Bob (Marsden, F., 1888), V. 477

Bobbo (Tanner, J. T. and Ross, A., 1895), V. 590

Bob Bradshaw's Dream (Thomas, B. W., 1899), V. 595

Bob Bragshawe (Brown, W., 1876), V. 282

Bob Bretton, the Dead Shot of the Woods (1877), V. 651

Bobby No. 1 (Hodgson, G. S., 1872), V. 423

Bobby's Bride = Constable Jack

Bob Cherry, Rough and Ready (1860), V. 651

Bobinet the Bandit (1815), IV. 434

Bob Lumley's Secret (Pitt, C., 1869), V. 526

Bob Ridley (Lee, N., Jr., 1861), V. 803

Bob Short (Lemon, M., 1840), IV. 344

Bob the Outcast (Lyon, W. F., 1881), V. 465

Boccaccio (Farnie, H. B. and Reece, R., 1882), V. 363, 791

Boccagh (Gomersall, W., 1884), V. 384

Bodack Glas = Waverley

Bodagh of the Boyne = Gramachree Molly

Body in the Boskeen = Ghost Hunter

Bogey (Esmond, H. V., 1895), V. 359

Bogie (1876), V. 651

Bo Girl up-to-date = Romany Lore

Bogle of the Clyde (1836), IV. 434

Bogus Agent (Batho, R., 1895), V. 253

Bogus Bandit (Montague, L. A. D., 1896), V. 491

Bohemia and Belgravia (O'Neil, A., 1872), V. 507

Bohemian (Danvers, G. J. B., 1833), IV. 579

— (Parker, L. N., 1892), V. 513

— (Soane, G., 1817), IV. 403

Bohemian Bandit (Florance, Mrs B. E., 1843), IV. 317

Bohemian Banditti = Trenck the Pandour

Bohemian Gipsy and the Duel at the Willows (Webb, C., 1862), V. 617

Bohemian Girl (Bunn, A., 1843), IV. 276

— (1861), V. 651

Bohemian G'ywl and the Unapproachable Pole (Byron, H. J., 1877), V. 298

Bohemian Miller = Miller and his Men

Bohemian Mother (Ebsworth, J., 1831), IV. 434, 621

— = (1) Infanticide; (2) Rosalie

Bohemians (Farnie, H. B., 1873), V. 361

— (Grist, W. and Pinkerton, P. E., 1897), V. 651, 795, 828

— (Stirling, E., 1843), IV. 407

— (1843), IV. 434

Bohemians of Paris (Barnett, C. Z., 1843), IV. 260

Bohemian's Prophecy = Gold Guitar

Boiling Water (Cross, J., 1885), V. 330

Bold Advertisement (Parker, L. N., 1895), V. 513

Bold Bad Baron (Addison, J., 1889), V. 236

Bold Bucaniers (1826), IV. 434
— = Robinson Crusoe
Bold Buccaneer = Captain Kidd
Bold Dick Turpin (Simpson, J. P., 1878), V. 568
Bold Dragoons (Barnett, M., 1830), IV. 261
Bold Recruit (Stephenson, B. C., 1870), V. 582, 818
Bold Robin Hood (Lee, N., 1848), IV. 434
— (1882), V. 651
Bold Stroke for a Husband (Cowley, Mrs H., 1783), III. 167, 181, 248
— (1862), V. 651
— = Advertisement
Bold Stroke for a Wife (Centlivre, Mrs S., 1718), II. 135, 137, 144, 156, 241, 305, 385, 433; IV. 140
— (1810), IV. 434
— = Guardians Outwitted
Bold Stroke for Dinner = Travelling Incog.
Bold Stroke for Success = Stage Letter
Bolivar (Wills, W. G., 1879), V. 627
Bomb (1894), V. 651
Bombardment and Capture of Canton (Stocqueler, J. H., 1858), V. 651, 818, 828
Bombardment and Capture of St Jean d'Acre = War in Syria
Bombardment of Algiers = Slaves in Barbary
Bombastes Furioso (Rhodes, W. B., 1810), IV. 149, 394
Bombastio Furioso (1889), V. 651
Bombay Brothers = Joker
Bombay to Henley (Parke, W. and Maxwell, C., 1895), V. 512
Bombo the Dwarf (Grover, J. H., 1880), V. 396
Bonafaiso (1804), IV. 434
Bona Fide Travellers (Brough, W., 1854), V. 279
Bonaparte in Egypt (Somerset, C. A., 1852), V. 574
Bond (Gore, Mrs C. G. F., 1824), IV. 319
Bondage (1883), V. 651
Bond and Free = One Shade Deeper
Bondman (Bunn, A., 1846), IV. 277
— (Cumberland, R., 1779), III. 78, 251

Bondman (1719), II. 366
Bondman of Kent = Aylmere
Bondocani (Dibdin, T. J., 1880), IV. 297, 580
Bond of Life (Faucit, H. S., 1870), V. 363
Bond of Love (1854), V. 651
Bondsman (Caine, H., 1892), V. 299
Bond Street, 4 p.m. (Grain, R. C., 1894), V. 388
Bonds Without Judgment (Topham, E., 1787), III, 312
Bonduca (Colman, G., 1778), III. 246
— (Dibdin, C. I. M., 1823), IV. 295
— (Powell, G., 1695), I. 266, 338, 425
Bone for the Lawyers = Will and No Will
Bone of Contention (Harding, C., 1870), V. 403
Boneshaker (1894), V. 651
Bone Squash (1839), IV. 435
Bone Squash Diabolo (Rice, T. D., 1836), IV. 394
Boney Defeated = Peep at the Danube
Bonifacio and Bridgetina (Dibdin, T. J., 1808), IV. 148, 298
Bonnet Builder's Tea Party (Hazlewood, C. H., 1854), V. 412
Bonnie Annie Laurie (Daly, C., 1898), V. 334
Bonnie Babies in the Wood (Craven, T., 1894), V. 329
Bonnie Bo-Peep and Little Boy Blue (Anderton, J., 1893), V. 778
Bonnie Boy Blue (Stephens, V., 1892), V. 581
Bonnie Dundee (Boyd, M., 1881), V. 272
— (Falconer, E., 1863), V. 360
Bonnie Fish Wife (Selby, C., 1858), V. 560
Bonnie Prince Charlie (Exley, C., 1878), V. 359
— (Johnstone, J. B., 1868), V. 438
— (Lowe, W., 1875), V. 464
— (Terriss, T. H., 1889), V. 595
— = Our Bonnie Prince
Bonny Bohemia = Zamet
Bonny Lass of Leith (1793), III. 320
Bon Ton (Garrick, D., 1775), III. 134, 169, 263-4
Boodles (Lee-Bennett, H., 1894), V. 453

Bookmaker (Piggot, J. W., 1889), v. 524

Book of Fate = Captive Princess

Book the Third, Chapter the First = Novel Expedient

Book with the Iron Clasps = Vendetta

Bookworm (Aveling, E. B., 1888), v. 246

Boor's Hut (1820), IV. 435

Bootblack (Jefferson, A., 1897), v. 435

Bootle's Baby (Moss, H., 1888), v. 498, 807

Boot on the Right Leg (1863), v. 651

Boots at the Holly Tree Inn (Webster, B. N., 1856), v. 618

Boots at the Swan (Selby, C., 1842), IV. 398

Bo-Peep (Terry, E., 1863), v. 595

— (1874, 1876, 1894, 1897, 1898, 1899), v. 651

See Little Bo-Peep

Bo-Peep and Boy Blue (1876), v. 652

Borachio the Bandit (Pitt, G. D., 1850), v. 526

Boraldi the Outlaw (Gomersal, E. W., 1862), v. 794

Border Chief = Johnnie Armstrong

Border Chieftains = White Plume

Borderers (Wordsworth, W., 1796), IV. 192-3, 422

Borderer's Son (Coates, A., 1874), v. 652, 784

Border Feuds (1811), IV. 435

Border Heroine (Burnette, C., 1896), v. 293

Border Marriage (Sorrell, W. J., 1856), v. 104, 574

Borders of the Ukraine = True Satisfaction

Borgia (Brown, T., 1874), v. 282

Borgia Ring (Slous, A. R., 1859), v. 571

Born of Hilda (France, E. S., 1878), v. 372

Born to Good Luck (Power, T., 1832), IV. 387

Born to save (Clarke, G. H. and Douglas, L., 1883), v. 312

Born with a Caul (Almar, G., 1850), v. 652, 777, 828

Boro' Bench (1887), v. 652

Borough Elections = M.P. for Puddle-pool

Borough Politics (Marston, J. W., 1846), IV. 353

Borrachio, the Outlaw (1824), IV. 435

Borrowed (Warren, E., 1885), v. 614

Borrowed Feathers (Millingen, J. G., 1836), IV. 356 [Attributed also to M. Barnett]

Borrowed Plumes (Maltby, A., 1866), v. 473

— = Hope of the Family

Borrowing a Husband (Moncrieff, W. T., 1843), IV. 361

Borrowing Boots (Little, A., 1899), v. 461

Boscabel (Springate, H. S., 1880), v. 576

Bos'en and the Middy (1854), v. 652

Bosjesman (1851), v. 652

Bosjesnans (1847), IV. 621

Bosom Friend (1844), IV. 435

Bosom Friends (Wigan, H., 1871), v. 622

Bossu (1863), v. 652

— (1866), v. 652

Bo'sun's Mate (Browne, G. W., 1888), v. 283

Botany Bay (1791), III. 399

Botheration (Oulton, W. C., 1798), III. 185, 296

Both of Them (1889), v. 652

Both Sides of the Question (Salaman, M. C., 1891), v. 555

Both Sides of the Water = Raft

Both Sides of the World (Bailey, 1882), v. 247

Bothwell (Swinburne, A. C., 1874), v. 589

— (Ware, J. R.), v. 614

Bottle (Taylor, T. P., 1847), IV. 411

— (1847), IV. 435

Bottle and the Glass (Barnett, C. Z., 1847), IV. 261

Bottle at Sea = Patriot

Bottle Bane (Pitt, G. D., 1847), IV. 375

Bottle Conjuror Out-done = Amours of Harlequin

Bottle Imp (Conquest, G. and Spry, H., 1865), v. 652, 828

— (Hale, W. P. and Talfourd, F., 1852), v. 398

— (Peake, R. B., 1828), IV. 370

Bottle of Champagne (Fitzball, E., 1832), IV. 314

Bottle of Champagne (1835), IV. 435

Bottle of Smoke (1856), v. 652

Bottles (Squier, C., 1881), v. 577

Bottom the Weaver (Kirkman, F., 1673), I. 418

Boudoir of Burlesque (1844), IV. 435

Bough of Yew = Mary, the Maid of the Inn

Bought (Harvey, F., 1873), v. 408

Boulangère (Farnie, H. B., 1881), v. 362

Bould Soger Boy (Stirling, E., 1848), IV. 409

Boulogne (Burnand, F. C., 1879), v. 291

Bounce (Courtney, J., 1844), IV. 283

— (Maltby, A., 1876), v. 473

— (1874), v. 652

— = While it's to be had

Bouncing Knight (Kirkman, F., 1662), I. 417

Bound Apprentice to a Waterman (1861), v. 652

See Bound 'Prentice to a Waterman

Bounders (Clarke, C. A., 1894), v. 312

Bound for Life (1883), v. 652

Bounding Brigade of the Bakumboilum = Lord Lovel and Lady Nancy Bell

Bound or Free (1873), v. 652

Bound 'Prentice to a Waterman (Campbell, A. V., 1836), IV. 278, 575

See Bound Apprentice to a Waterman

Bounds of the Tiger (1862), v. 652

Bound to Arcadia (1888), v. 652

Bound to keep the Peace = Old Bear

Bound to Succeed (Conquest, G. and Pettitt, H., 1877), v. 321

Bound to the Wheel (1866), v. 652

Bouquet (Diané, 1865), v. 652, 788, 828

— (Towers, E., 1870), v. 601

Bouquet and Three Cards = Maison Rouge

Bouquetière (1852), v. 652

Bourbon League (1762), III. 320, 399

Bourbons and Bonapartists (1837), IV. 435

Bow Bells (Byron, H. J., 1880), v. 115, 299

— (Johnstone, J. B., 1863), v. 652, 828

Bower of Bliss = Venus and Adonis

Bower of Spring (Dibdin, C. I. M., 1803), IV. 291

Bowled Out (Craven, H. T., 1860), v. 328

Bow of Orange Ribbon (Cooper, F. and Jardine, F., 1897), v. 324

Bow-Street Opera (1773), III. 320

Box and Cox (Morton, J. M., 1847), IV. 363

Box and Cox in Caffre Land (1854), v. 652

Box and Cox married and settled (Coyne, J. S., 1852), v. 327

Box B (Grain, R. C., 1893), v. 388

Boxing's the Rage (1789), III. 320

Box-Lobby Challenge (Cumberland, R., 1794), III. 127, 252

Box-Lobby Loungers (Stuart, C., 1787), III. 310, 396

+ Box of Mischief (Peake, S., *French*)

Box, the Fish and the Genii = Three Fishermen

Boy (Law, A., 1894), v. 450

Boy and the Bandits (1838), IV. 435

Boy Bob (1899), v. 652

Boycotted (Salaman, M. C., 1884), v. 555

Boy Detective (Travers, W., 1867), v. 602

Boyhood and Old Age of Mr Yates (1822), IV. 435

Boyhood of Bacchus (Rede, W. L., 1845), IV. 391

Boy in Blue (1862), v. 652

Boy King (1845), IV. 435

Boyne Water (Buckstone, J. B., 1828), IV. 273

Boy of Barcelona = Leon de Val

Boy of Santillane (Macfarren, G., 1827), IV. 102, 350

Boy of the Alps = Amethyst Ring

Boy Pirate (Travers, W., 1864), v. 652, 821, 828

Boys and Girls (Grain, R. C., 1892), v. 388

Boys, Girls and Guardians = Three Times Three

Boy Smuggler (1866), v. 652

Boys of Horsley Down (1827), IV. 435

Boys of Wexford (Matthews, E. C., 1899), v. 481

Boys will be Boys (Mackay, J., 1888), v. 470

Boys Together (Chambers, C. H. and Carr, J. W. C., 1896), v. 307

— (Howell-Poole, W., 1887), v. 429

Boz-i-a-na = Peregrinations of Pickwick "Boz's" Oliver Twist (Greenwood, T., 1838), IV. 97, 321

Brace of Gaol Birds (Melford, M., 1889), v. 484

Brace of Partridges (Ganthony, R., 1897), v. 376

Brace of Uncles (1876), v. 652

Bracewell's Adventures with a Russian Princess (1878), v. 652

Brachman (Dibdin, C. I. M., 1813), IV. 293

Bracken Hollow (Bright, Mrs A., 1878), v. 275

Brag (Wills, W. G., 1879), v. 627

Bragadocio (1691), I. 218, 440

Braganza (Jephson, R., 1775), III. 56, 94–5, 156, 276, 389

Braggadochio (1742), II. 384

Brahman's Curse (1829), IV. 435

Brain Reviver (Barrow, P. J., 1898), v. 252

Brand (Hereford, C. H., 1893), v. 419

Branded (Lee, R., 1881), v. 453

Branded Race (Wooler, J. P., 1858), v. 632

Brand of Cain (Gordon, G. L., 1875), v. 384

Brand of Crime = Walter Lorimer

Brand of Shame = Icebound

Brand of Time and the Mystery of 20 Years = Marianne Duval the Vivandière

Branksome Castle (1811), IV. 435

Brantinghame Hall (Gilbert, W. S., 1888), v. 380

Bras de Fer (Manuel, E., 1875), v. 475

Brass (Rowe, G. F., 1877), v. 552

Bravado (Smale, Mrs T. E., 1889), v. 571

Bravado the Swindler (Travers, W., 1864), v. 822

Brave and the Fair (Bourden, 1816), IV. 435, 621

Brave as a Lion (Douglass, J. T., 1872), v. 348

Brave Cossack (Astley, J., 1807), IV. 435, 569, 621

Brave Coward (Blythe, J. S., 1886), v. 266

Brave Gordons (1898), v. 652

Brave Harry Thorn (Stanley, H. J., 1874), v. 579

Brave Hearts (Comer, G. and Benton, F., 1898), v. 319

— (Matthison, A., 1881), v. 481

Brave Irishman (Sheridan, T., 1737), II. x, 144, 215–16, 355, 444; III. 396

— (1755), III. 396

Bravery and Ingratitude = Jew of Wilna

Brave Scottish Hearts (Hall, K. E., 1873), v. 399

Braving the Storm (Sheen, W. P., 1890), v. 562

— (Woodruffe, A., 1871), v. 631

Bravin's Brow (Fox, J. S., 1863), v. 652, 828

Bravo (Barnett, C. Z., 1833), IV. 97, 259

— (Buckstone, J. B., 1833), IV. 97, 274

— = Red Mask

Bravo and the Venetian Conspirators (1819), IV. 435

Bravoes of Calabria = Black Band

Bravoes of Chiozza = Maid and the Monk

Bravoes of London (Young, Mrs H., 1863), v. 652, 828

Bravo Ix (1854), v. 652

Bravo of Castille = Charles Ganganelli

Bravo of Venice = Rugantino

Bravo Rouse!!! (Pitt, G. D., 1851), v. 526

Bravo's Son (1819), IV. 435

Bravo turn'd Bully (1740), II. 366

Brazen Bust = Hungarian Cottage

Brazen Mask (Dibdin, T. J., 1802), IV. 297, 580

Brazen Nose College (1831), IV. 435

Brazen Water-Tower (1824), IV. 435

Brazilian (Pemberton, M. and Lestocq, W., 1890), v. 518

Brazilian Jack (1834), IV. 435

Brazilian Monkey = Jocko

Breach of Promise (Freund-Lloyd, M., 1891), v. 373

— (Robertson, T. W., 1869), v. 546

— (1841), IV. 435

— (1884), v. 652

— (1892), v. 652

Breach of Promise of Marriage (Rodwell, G. H., 1842), IV. 84, 395, 603, 608

Bread Winner (Calmour, A. C., 1892), V. 300

Break but not bend (Hazlewood, C. H., 1867), V. 413

Breakers Ahead (Haines, J. T., 1837), IV. 322

— = He would be a Sailor

Breakfast Appointment (1862), V. 652

Breakfast for Two (1851), V. 652

Breakfast of Love (1822), IV. 435

Breaking a Butterfly (Jones, H. A. and Herman, H., 1884), V. 439

Breaking it off (Doone, N., 1898), V. 347

— (1899), V. 652

Breaking the Bank = Lady Guide

Breaking the Ice (Thomas, C., 1878), V. 596

— = Holly Branch

Breaking the News (Heathcote, A. M., 1893), V. 415

Breaking the Spell (Farnie, H. B., 1870), V. 361

Break of Morn (1862), V. 652

Bred in the Bone (Lingham, F. T., 1890), V. 460

— (1896), V. 652

Breeze from New York (Raphael, F., 1893), V. 535

Breeze in the Baltic (1801), IV. 435

Breezy Morning (Phillpotts, E., 1891), V. 524

Brenda's Choice (1896), V. 652

Brennus (Maclean, W., 1871), V. 471

— (1832), IV. 435

Bressac (1886), V. 652

Brewer of Preston (Reynoldson, T. H., 1839), IV. 393

— (1876), V. 652

Brewer of Tadcaster (Rodgers, A., 1897), V. 547

Brewing a Bruin (Gee, L., 1873), V. 377

Brian Born (B., J. T., 1879), V. 653

Brian Boroihme (Knowles, J. S., 1811), IV. 170, 338

— (Mara, S. D., 1810), IV. 597

Brian Boroihme, the Victorious (1820), IV. 435

Brian, the Probationer (Hill, I., 1842), IV. 325

Briarly Farm (Conquest, G., 1858), V. 653, 785, 828

Briars and Blossoms (Hazlewood, C. H., 1873), V. 414

Bribery on Both Sides (1784), III. 320

Bric-a-Brac (Coghill, Sir J. J., 1888), V. 316

Bric-a-Brac Will (Fitzgerald, S. J. A. and Moss, H., 1895), V. 369

Brickdustman (1773), III. 399

Bricklayers' Arms (1830), IV. 435

Bridal (Knowles, J. S., 1837), IV. 339

— (Macready, W. C.), IV. 353

— = House of Colberg

Bridal Eve (1847), IV. 435

— = (1) Doom Light; (2) Wedding Eve

Bridal Gift = Bivouac of the Hills

Bridal Night = Conscience

Bridal of Armagnac (Streatfield, T., 1823), IV. 409

Bridal of Beatrix (1859), V. 653

Bridal of Beauty (Blanchard, E. L., 1863), V. 653, 779, 828

Bridal of Death = Red Mantle

Bridal of Flora (Byrne, J., 1816), IV. 435, 621

Bridal of Netherby = Lochinvar

Bridal Phantom (Conquest, G., 1863), V. 653, 828

Bridal Promise (Oxenford, J., 1833), IV. 435, 621

Bridal Ring (Reynolds, F., 1810), IV. 392, 607

— = (1) Bull-Fighter; (2) Mulatto Murderer; (3) Robert the Devil

Bridals (Cavendish, M., 1668), I. 396

Bridals of Messina = John of Procida

Bridal Spectre = (1) Alonzo and Imogine; (2) Alonzo the Brave and the Fair Imogene

Bridal Supper = Witch of Ravensworth

Bridal Three Centuries Back = Ladye of Lambeth

Bridal Tour (Boucicault, D., 1877), V. 269

— (1877), V. 653

Bridal Trip (Mortimer, J., 1876), V. 494

Bridal Wreath (Hazlewood, C. H., 1861), V. 412

Bride (Baillie, J., 1828), IV. 258

— (Bell, A., 1847), IV. 572

— (Korner, 1808), IV. 340

— (Rice, C.), V. 813

Bride and Bridegroom (1828), IV. 435
Bride and No Bride = National Guard
Bride and the Proscribed (1840), IV. 435
Bride at Fifty = Spring and Autumn
Bridegroom from the Sea = Wreck Ashore
Bridegroom of the Wave = Essex Rover
Bride of Abydos (Byron, H. J., 1858), V. 295
— (Dimond, W., 1818), IV. 47, 110, 306
— (1847), IV. 435
Bride of a Day = Barbara
Bride of Albi (Harding, C., 1853), V. 403
Bride of Aldgate (1859), V. 653
Bride of Corsica = Paali
Bride of Everton (1852), V. 828
Bride of Garryowen (1861), V. 653
Bride of Genoa = Valasco
Bride of Golconda (Jones, R. St C., 1852), V. 441
Bride of Lammermoor (Dibdin, T. J., 1819), IV. 94, 302, 436, 581
— (Calcraft, J. W., 1822), IV. 94, 278
— (Moncrieff, W. T., 1819), IV. 94, 436, 621
— (1831), IV. 94, 436
— (1848), IV. 94, 436
— (1863), V. 653
Bride of Love (Buchanan, R., 1890), V. 285
Bride of Ludgate (Jerrold, D. W., 1831), IV. 332
Bride of Messina (Irvine, G., 1837), IV. 329
— (Lockwood, P., 1839), IV. 346
— (Lodge, A., 1841), IV. 346
— (Müller, H., 1887), V. 499
— = John of Procida
Bride of Mexico = Indian Father
Bride of Milton and the Merchant of Gravesend (1859), V. 828
Bride of Munster = Kathleen
Bride of Parma = Carbonari
Bride of Poland (1856), V. 653
Bride of Portugal = Inez
+ Bride of Sicily (Downing, Helen, 4°, 1830)
Bride of Song (Farnie, H. B., 1864), V. 361
Bride of the Battlefield = Strongbow
Bride of the Bleeding Heart (1832), IV. 436
— = Emilie de la Roche

Bride of the Grave = Raven's Nest
Bride of the Isles = Vampyre
Bride of the Nile (1845), IV. 436
Bride of the Prairie (1847), IV. 436
Bride of the Thames = Carpenters of Lambeth
Bride of the Wave (Travers, W., 1867), V. 602
Bride of Two Isles = Bright Days
Bride of Venice = Queen of Cyprus
Bride's Death Sleep (Hazlewood, C. H., 1868), V. 413
Bride's Journey (Courtney, J., 1846), IV. 283
Brides of Florence (Fitzeustace, R., 1824), IV. 584
Brides of Garryowen = Colleen Bawn
Brides of Venice (Bunn, A., 1844), IV. 436
Brides' Tragedy (Beddoes, T. L., 1822), IV. 201–2, 264
Bride, the Bullet and the Bobby = Freischutz
Bridge of Baltaz = Secret Twelve
Bridge of Kehl (Blake, T. G., 1841), IV. 268
Bridge of Notre Dame (Hudson, E. N., 1847), IV. 329
— = Orphans
Bridge of Sighs (Leigh, H. S., 1872), V. 454, 803
— = Bravo
Bridge of Tresino = Forest Oracle
Bridge that carries us safe over (Peake, R. B., 1817), IV. 369
Bridget O'Brien (Lyster, F. and Sheridan, J. F., 1887), V. 466
Bridget's Blunders (Smith, L., 1892), V. 573
Brier Cliff (Morris, G., 1842), IV. 361
Brigadier (Reynoldson, T. H., 1845), IV. 393
Brigand (Douglass, J. T., 1865) = Brigand in a New Suit for Easter, V. 653, 788, 828
— (Osbaldistone, D. W., 1830), IV. 602
Brigand and his Banker (Taylor, T., 1860), V. 593
Brigand and his Son = (1) Bandit of Corsica; (2) Matteo Falcone
Brigand Chief (Planché, J. R., 1829), IV. 378

Brigand Chief = Fra Diavolo

Brigand Chief and the Dog of the Chateau = Diavolo Abruzzi

Brigand Deserter = First Claim

Brigand in a New Suit for Easter (Douglass, J. T., 1865) = Brigand, v. 653, 788, 828

Brigand Marquis = High Road of Life

Brigand Monk and the Dog of Mount St Bernard (1845), IV. 436

Brigand of Albans = Italian Sister

Brigand of Barcelona (1852), v. 653

Brigand of London (Travers, W., 1864), v. 653, 828

Brigand of Savoy = Corse de Leon

Brigands (Gilbert, W. S., 1889), v. 380

— (Leigh, H. S., 1884), v. 454

— = Falscappa

Brigand's Daughter (1845), IV. 436

— = Marinette

Brigand's Doom = Abduction of Bianca

Brigands in the Bud (Mildenhall, T., 1849), IV. 356

Brigands of Ancona (1844; 1845), IV. 436

Brigands of Bluegoria = Joan

Brigands of Calabria (Suter, W. E., 1866), v. 588

— (1831), IV. 621

Brigands of Sicily = Mysterious Hermit

Brigand's Ransom = Birthright

Brigand's Secret (1858), v. 653

Brigand, the Marchese and the Deserter = Perizzi

Briganzio the Brigand (Marshall, F.), v. 805 [A play of this name by F. Hall was printed by French]

Briggate (Bell, C., 1884), v. 255

Bright Beam at Last (Macdermott, G. H., 1872), v. 468

Bright Days (Wheatley, H. and Aldin C. A., 1889), v. 619

Brighter Days in Store (Towers, E., 1867), v. 601

— = Our Lot in Life

Brighter Future (1897), v. 653

Bright Future (Parry, S., 1883), v. 515

Brighthelmstone (Collier, J., 1853), v. 785

Bright Idea (Law, A., 1881), v. 449

Brighton (Howard, B. and Marshall, F., 1870), v. 428

Brighton Cliff (Bew, C., 1831) = White Hawk Lady, IV. 436, 621

Bright Road of Honesty and the Dark Path of Crime = Tom Sheppard

Bright Star of the Morn = Noureddin and the Fair Persian

Brig o' Doon = Tam o' Shanter

Brilliants (1799), III. 320

Brine Oge (Patmore, W. J., 1896), v. 515

Bringing Home the Bride! (Moncrieff, W. T., 1831), IV. 135, 360

Brisket Family (Jerrold, D. J., 1822) = Dolly and the Rat, IV. 436, 621

Bristol Diamonds (Oxenford, J., 1862), v. 510, 809

Bristol Sailor (Bernard, J., 1786), III. 320, 377, 399

Bristol Tar (1792), III. 321

Britain in her Glory = What We Have Been, and What We May Be

Britain's Allies (1813), IV. 436

Britain's Best Bulwarks = Mast and the Ploughshare

Britains Brave Tars!! (O'Keeffe, J., 1797) = All to St Paul's = Our Wooden Walls, III. 321, 393, 399

Britain's Defenders (1797), III. 321

Britain's Genius (Kennedy, R., 1840), IV. 336

Britain's Glory (Benson, 1794), III. 207, 236

— = Naval Volunteers

Britain's Happiness (Motteux, P. A., 1704), II. 346, 441

Britain's Jubilee (Arnold, S. J., 1809), IV. 255

— (Barrett, C. F., 1809), IV. 436, 621

Britains Rejoice = St George's Day

Britannia (Lediard, T., 1732), II. 35, 236, 341

— (Mallet, D., 1755), II. 343; III. 286

— (1734), II. 366

— = Love and Glory

Britannia and Batavia (Lillo, G., 1740), II. 342

Britannia and the Gods in Council (Averay, R., 1756), III. 234

Britannia in full Glory at Spithead = Love and Honour

Britannia, Mistress of the Seas (1895), v. 653

Britannia Rediviva (1746), II. 367

Britannia Rules the Waves = Nelson

Britannia's Relief (1789), III. 321

Britannia's Triumph = Fairy

Britannia Triumphans (1703), II. 447

Britannia Triumphant = (1) Fall of Martinico; (2) Naval Pillar

Britannicus (Boothby, Sir B., 1803), IV. 269

— (Ozell, J., 1714), II. 347

— = Brittanicus

British Admiral and the Seaman's Son (1812), IV. 436

British Amazon = Boadicea

British Amazons (Dibdin, C. I. M., 1803), IV. 291

British and Norman Feuds = Henry I

British at Brussels = Bachelors' Wives

British Beauty (Addison, H. R., 1848), IV. 251

British Born (Meritt, P. and Pettitt, H., 1872), V. 485

British Bravery Triumphant = Point at Herqui

British Brothers (Buchanan, J., 1868), v. 284

British Bull Dogs (Johnstone, J. B., 1868), v. 800

British Captain and the Indian Chief (Simpson, 1822), IV. 401

British Captives = Johnnie Armstrong

British Captives in France = Coronation!!

British Carpenter (McLaren, A., 1808), IV. 351

British Champion = St George and the Dragon

British Courage (1805), IV. 436

British Enchanters (Granville, G., 1706), I. 141; II. 234–5, 333, 437

British Esquimaux = Voyage to the North Pole

British Exile = Earl of Warwick

British Flag of the South American Pirate = Silver Store Island

British Fortitude, and Hibernian Friendship (Cross, J. C., 1794), III. 250

British Freeholder = Eldred

British Glory in Egypt (Astley, P. Jr., 1801), IV. 256

British Gratitude and Hibernian Friendship = British Fortitude and Hibernian Friendship

British Hero (Landeck, B., 1894), v. 447

British Heroes (1808), IV. 436

British Heroine (Jackson, J., 1777), III. 86, 276

— = Bonduca

British Heroism = Death of Captain Faulknor

British Inchanter, and King Arthur, the British Worthy = Merlin

British Intrepidity Triumphant = Northern Fleet

British Kings (Mylne, J., 1790), III. 290

British Legion (Bayly, T. H., 1838), IV. 263

British Liberty = Battle of Eddington

British Lion (1830, 1848), IV. 436

— = Plum Pudding Pantomime

British Loyalty (Moser, J., 1809), IV. 364

— (1789), III. 321

British Officer = Lindor and Clara

British Orphan (Starke, M., 1790), III. 308

British Peasant (1799), III. 321

British Pluck and Yankee Valour = Old World and the New

British Queen (1840), IV. 436

— = (1) Boadicea; (2) Bonduca

British Recruit = To Arms!

British Sailor (1786), III. 321, 377

British Sailor Abroad and at Home (1830), IV. 436

British Sailors in America = French Flogged

British Sailors in 1797 = (1) Mutiny at the Nore; (2) Mutiny of Spithead and the Nore

British Seaman's Fidelity = Faithless Friend

British Seaman's Story = Juan Fernandez

British Seamen at Anchor = Naples Bay

British Slave (Howe, J. B.), v. 428

British Soldier (1805), IV. 436

British Stage (1724), II. 256–7, 367

British Tar in Storm and Sunshine = Afloat and Ashore

British Tars (1859), v. 653

British Tars and Austrian Troops =
Double Defeat

British Tars at Spithead = England's
Glory

British Tars in 1782 = Youthful Days of
William IV

British Tars regaling after Battle =
Vanguard

British Troops Triumphant = Glorious
Queen of Hungary

British Valour Triumphant = Cape St
Vincent

British Vengeance = Slaves in Barbary

British Workman (1894), v. 653

British Worthy = King Arthur

Britomarte (Schofield, W. M., 1866), v.
653, 815, 828

Britomart, the Man-hater (1866), v. 653

Briton (Philips, A., 1722), II. 54, 106,
107, 116, 348

Briton and Boer (1899), v. 653

Briton Chief = Caswallon

Britons Abroad (Davis, H., 1861), v. 787

Britons at Navarino (Milner, H. M.,
1827), IV. 436, 621

Britons in China = Ching-Li-Wang

Britons in the East = Siege of Acre

Britons in the East Indies = Massacre of
Rajahpoor

Britons' Jubilee in Honour of their King
(Cherry, A., 1809), IV. 576

Britons, strike home (Dibdin, C., 1804),
IV. 290

— (Phillips, E., 1739), II. 349, 442

— = Volunteers

Britons to Arms (McLaren, A., 1803),
IV. 350

Brittanicus (D'Oyley, E., 1695), I. 403

Brittany Folk (Frith, W., 1889), v. 373

Brixton Burglary (Sidney, F. W., 1898),
v. 565

Broad Arrow (Holcroft, G., 1885), v.
424

Broadbrim and Co. (1828), IV. 436

Broad but not Long (1814), IV. 436

Broad Grins (1815, 1829), IV. 436

— = Whackham and Windham

Broad Path and the Narrow Way (1899),
v. 653

Broad Road (Marshall, R., 1898), v. 478

Broadsea Cliffs (1835), IV. 436

Brocken Vows = Faust and Loose

Broken Bail (Gordon, G. L., 1878), v.
385

Broken Bonds (Calmour, A. C., 1883),
v. 300

Broken Branch (Du Terreaux, L. H.,
1874), v. 352, 789

— (1888), v. 653

Broken Chain (Haines, J. T., 1839), IV.
587

— (Suter, W. E., 1859), v. 653, 818, 828

— (1838), IV. 436

Broken Coupling (Moonie, J. A., 1890),
v. 491

Broken Faith (1855), v. 653

— = Clouds

Broken Fetters (Thursby, C., 1897), v.
600

— = Convict's Daughter

Broken Gold (Dibdin, C., 1806), IV. 290

Broken Heart (Jerrold, D. W., 1832), IV.
332

— = (1) Agnes de Vere; (2) Beatrice;
(3) Chimes; (4) Destiny; (5) Farmer's
Daughter; (6) Farmer's Daughter of
the Severnside

Broken-Hearted Club (Coyne, J. S.,
1868), v. 328

Broken Hearts (Gilbert, W. S., 1875),
v. 138–9, 140, 145, 380

Broken Home (Wilkins, J. H., 1859), v.
653, 823, 828

Broken Hot Cross Bun = Spectre of
Shooter's Hill

Broken Idol (1874), v. 653

Broken Life = Chris

Broken Lily (Towers, E., 1878), v. 601

— (Willis, A., 1846), IV. 617

Broken Link = Dick's Repentance

Broken Links (Holmes, H., 1882), v. 424

Broken Marriage = Passion's Peril

Broken Melody (Keen, H. and Leader,
J., 1892), v. 442

Broken Off (Phillips, Mrs N., 1892), v.
523

— (1891), v. 653

Broken Pearls (Archer, W. J., 1867), v.
242

Broken Promises (Arnold, S. J., 1825),
IV. 256

Broken Reed = Stepmothers

Broken Sixpence (Thompson, Mrs G.
and Sinclair, K., 1889), v. 597

Broken Spear = Hermann
Broken Spells (Marston, J. W., and
  Wills, W. G., 1872), v. 479
Broken Stock-Jobbers (1720), II. 367
Broken String (Calmour, A. C., 1896),
  v. 300
— (1898), v. 653
Broken Sword (Dimond, W., 1816), IV.
  ' 306
Broken Ties (Simpson, J. P., 1866), v.
  104, 568
— (1874), v. 653
Broken to Harness (Dallas, M., 1883), v.
  332
Broken Toys (Besemeres, J., 1850), v.
  260
Broken Vow = Sixtus V
Broken Vows (Towers, E., 1871), v. 601
Broker bewitch'd (1785?), III. 321
Bronze Horse (Bunn, A., 1836), IV. 83,
  276
— (Fitzball, E., 1835), IV. 83, 315, 584
— (Paul, H. M., 1881), v. 516, 809
— (Soutar, R., 1864), v. 653, 828
— (Soutar, R. and Merion, C., 1871), v.
  575, 817
— (1835), IV. 83, 436
— (1871), v. 653
Bronze Medal (1862), v. 653
Bronze Statue (James, C. S., 1850), v.
  432
Brook (Salsbury, N., 1880), v. 555
Broom (1791), III. 321
Brother against Brother (Harvey, F.,
  1895), v. 409
Brother and Sister (Dimond, W., 1815),
  IV. 306, 581
— (1831), IV. 436
— (1852), v. 653
— = False Marriage
Brother Ben (Morton, J. M., 1840), IV.
  362
Brother Bill and Me (Suter, W. E.,
  1866), v. 588, 819
Brother Bob (Johnstone, J. B., 1853), v.
  438
Brother for Brother (Shirley, A., 1899),
  v. 565
Brother George (Desprez, F., 1892), v.
  343
Brother-in-Law (Card, H., 1817), IV.
  576

Brother Officers (Trevor, L., 1898), v.
  604
Brother of Valencia = Alhamor the
  Moor
Brother Pelican (Rae, A. and Dragnil,
  W. H., 1894), v. 532
Brother Ruin and Brother Sneak (1860),
  v. 653
Brothers (Brockbank, J., 1875), v. 276
— (Byatt, H., 1887), v. 295
— (Coghlan, C. F., 1876), v. 316
— (Cumberland, R., 1769), III. 125, 251
— (Lipthwaite, A. O., 1885), v. 460
— (Sager, R. F., 1897), v. 554
— (Smelt, T. 1843), IV. 436, 621
— (Young, E., 1753), III. 60, 75, 318
— = (1) Richard Markham; (2) Rough
  Rob, the Gipsy Thief of Hangman's
  Hollow; (3) Wolf and the Lamb
Brother Sailors (1855), v. 653
Brother Sam (Oxenford, J., Sothern,
  E. A. and Buckstone, J. B., 1865), v.
  510
Brother's Career = Markham and
  Greenwood
Brother's Crime (Edmonds, E. V.,
  1893), v. 354
Brother's Curse = Petrona
Brother's Destiny and the Early Crime
  = Two Revolutions
Brothers Devoted = Siege of Berwick
Brother's Doom = Ellen Ray
Brothers' Duel (1841), IV. 621
Brothers in Arms (Wilks, T. E., 1838),
  IV. 437, 621
— (1854), v. 653
— (1894), v. 653
— = Corporal
Brothers in Heart = For the King
Brothers in War = Freemason
Brother's Life (1874), v. 653
Brother's Love = (1) Fond Hearts; (2)
  Self-Accusation
Brother's Love and a Sister's Honour =
  Dumb Conscript
Brothers of Coarse = O Gemini
Brothers of Cordova (1826), IV. 437
Brothers of Eden (Rist, R. E., 1885), v.
  544
Brothers of Turin (1831), IV. 437
Brother's Revenge (1854), v. 654
— (1877), v. 653

Brother's Sacrifice (Lemon, M., 1841),
IV. 344
— = Express
Brothers Salacarro = Corsicans
Brother Tom (Buckstone, J. B., 1839),
IV. 275
Brought to Bay (1885), V. 654
— = Buried Alive
Brought to Book (Hay, F., 1875), V.
411
— (Macdermott, G. H. and Pettitt, H.,
1876), V. 468
Brought Together (Mouillot, F., 1894),
V. 498
Brought to Justice (Pettitt, H. and
Meritt, P., 1880), V. 521
Brought to Light (Darbey, E., 1889), V.
336
— (Palmer, T. A., 1868), V. 511
— (Percival, J., 1872), V. 520
— (1876), V. 654
Brought to the Test (1884), V. 654
Brown and the Brahmins (Reece, R.,
1869), V. 537
Brown Devil (Nantz, F. C., 1830), IV.
437, 621
Browne the Martyr (Lucas, J. T.,
1872), V. 464
Browne with an E. (Montague, L. A. D.,
1893), V. 491
Brown Fanny (1834), IV. 437
Brownie of the Brig = All Hallows' Even
Brownies (1894), V. 654
Brown, Jones and Robinson (1838), IV.
437
— (1850), V. 654
— (1866), V. 654
Brown, Jones and Robinson at Brighton
= Where's Brown?
Brown Man (1819; 1820), IV. 437
Brown Man of the Moor = Wizard
Brown's Boarders (1888), V. 654
Brown's Horse (À Beckett, G. A., 1836),
IV. 567
Brown Studies = My Absent Son
Bruce (Davidson, J., 1886), V. 338
Bruin and the Bashaw = Bears not
Beasts
Bruin the Brave (1854), V. 654
Brum (Desprez, F., 1880), V. 343
Brumley's Wife (1863), V. 654
Bruno (1821), IV. 437

Bruno the Black and the Knight
Champion (Dibdin, C. I. M., 1826),
IV. 296
Bruscino = Accidental Son
Brutus (Payne, J. H., 1818), IV. 368
— (1829), IV. 437
— (1854), V. 654
Brutus and Caesar (1866), V. 654
Brutus of Alba (Powell, G., 1696), I.
252, 425
— (Tate, N., 1678), I. 39, 40, 42, 54,
160, 434
Brutus Ultor (Field, M., 1886), V. 366
Bubble (Kirkman, F., 1662), I. 417
Bubble and Squeak (Hay, F., 1871), V.
411
Bubble Reputation (Willing, J. and
Douglass, J., 1885), V. 626
Bubbles (Fawcett, C. S., 1881), V. 364
— (Moser, J., 1808), IV. 364
Bubbles in the Sudds (1887), V. 654
Bubbles of the Day (Jerrold, D. W.,
1842), IV. 185, 333
Bucanier's Bridal = Wreck
Bucaniers of 1660 = Lolonois
Buccaneer (1824), IV. 437
Buccaneers (Pendred, L. St L., 1894), V.
519
— = (1) Captain Kidd; (2) Montbar
Buccaneers of the Arctic Regions =
England Ho!
Buccaneer's Revenge = Rokeby
Buccaneer's Wife (Conquest, G., 1859),
V. 654, 785, 828
Buckaneer and the Little Dear = Zampa
Buckingham (Edwards, J., 1877), V.
355
— (Wills, W. G., 1875), V. 627
— = Favourite of the King
Buckle of Brilliants = Crown Prince
Buckram in Armour = Disappointed
Gallant
Buck's Interlude (1761), III. 321
Buck's Lodge (1790), III. 321
Buckstone's Adventure with a Polish
Princess (Lewes, G. H., 1855), V. 459
Bud and Blossom (Campbell, Lady C.,
1893), V. 301
Budget of Blunders (Greffulhe, 1810),
IV. 321, 437, 586
— (1819), 437
Buffalo Bill (Roberts, G., 1887), V. 545

Buffalo Bill (Stanley, H. J. and Hermann, C., 1887), V. 579

Buffalo Girls (Stirling, E., 1847), IV. 408

Buffalo Hunter of the Death Prairies = White Chief

Buffooning (1887), V. 654

Bugle Call (Parker, L. N. and Bright, A. A., 1899), V. 514, 654

— (1899), V. 654

Bugle Horn = Cumnor

Bugler of the Twentieth (1856), V. 654

Building of the Ship = King of Steel

Built on Sand (Harvey, F., 1886), V. 408

Bull and the Magpie = My Uncle's House

Bull by the Horns (Byron, H. J., 1876), V. 298

Bulldogs, Ahoy! (Daly, B. and Syms, A., 1899), V. 334

Bull-fighter (Almar, G., 1838), IV. 253

— (1855), V. 828

Bull in a China Shop (Mathews, C. J., 1864), V. 480

Bulls and Bears (1715), II. 367

Bull's Head (Beazley, S., Jr., 1818), Saracen's Head removed from Snow Hill, IV. 263, 571

Bully-Huff catch's in a Trap = Boaster

Bulse (Jodrell, R. P., 1787), III. 277

Bumble (Clement, F. A., 1891), V. 314

Bumble's Courtship (Emson, F. E., ?1874), V. 358

Bumbrusher (1786), III. 321

Bumpkin's Dream = St Stephen's Well

Bump of Benevolence (Faucit, J. S., 1841), IV. 311

Bunch of Berries (Blanchard, E. L., 1875), V. 264

Bunch of Keys (Hoyt, C. H. and Gordon, G. L., 1882), V. 429

Bunch of Roses (1897), V. 654

Bunch of Shamrocks (Bateman, F. and Douglass, J. T., 1896), V. 253

Bunch of Violets (Grundy, S., 1894), V. 397

Bundle of Prologues (1777), III. 321

Bungalow (Horner, F. and Wyatt, F., 1889), V. 427

Bungles (De Svertchkoff, A. and Morphew, H., 1892), V. 343

Bunkum Muller (Craven, H. T., 1864), V. 328

Bunthorne's Bride = Patience

Buonaparte (Ripon, J. S., 1803), IV. 394

Buonaparte at the Military School of Brienne = Little Corporal

Buonaparte Burnt Out (1813), IV. 437

Buonaparte in the Dumps = Admiral Nelson's Triumph

Buonaparte's Destiny (1831), IV. 437

Buonaparte's Fatalities (1828), IV. 437

Buonaparte's Invasion of Russia (Amherst, J. H., 1825), IV. 254

Buondelmonte (Woodrooffe, S., 1826), IV. 422

Burch and his Detractors (1875), V. 654

Burden of Guilt = Life for a Life

Burglar Alarm and the Detective Camera (Gannon, J., 1893), V. 375

Burglar and the Bishop (Coghill, Sir J. J., 1893), V. 316

Burglar and the Judge (Philips, F. C. and Brookfield, C. H. E., 1892), V. 522

Burglars (Melford, M., 1885), V. 484

Burglar's Baby (Douglass, J. T. and Williams, C., 1897), V. 349

Burglar's Fate = Struggle for Life

Burgomaster of Sardaam (Reynolds, F., 1818), IV. 392

Burgomaster's Daughter (1863), V. 654

— = Sexton of Cologne

Burgomaster Trick'd = (1) Apollo and Daphne; (2) Daphne and Apollo

Burgraves (Oxberry, W. H.), IV. 602

Burgundy the Bold (1832), IV. 437

Buried Alive (Macpherson, H., 1899), V. 471

— (1874), V. 654

— = (1) Caffres; (2) Cruel Brother; (3) Savage Chieftain; (4) Tom Cobb

Buried Secret = My Lady Hilda

Buried Talent (Parker, L. N., 1886), V. 513

Buried Titan (Leifchild, F., 1859), V. 453

Burlesque Steeplechase (1835), IV. 437

Burletta of Errors (Planché, J. R., 1820), IV. 376, 604

Burley and Morton = Old Mortality

Burlington Arcade (Dance, C., 1838), IV. 289

Burmese = Burmese War

By Special Licence (1895), v. 654
By Special Request (Watson, T. M., 1887), v. 616
By the Deeps Nine (1850), v. 654
By the Hand of Woman = Life's Mistakes
By the King's Command = By Command of the King
By the Midland Sea (McCarthy, J. H., 1892), v. 467
By the Sea (Aveling, E. B., 1887), v. 246
— (1872), v. 654
By this Token (Angus, J. K., 1884), v. 241
Byways of London = Outcast Poor
Byzantium (Poole, R., 1823), IV. 387

Cabal (1763), III. 321
Cabal and Love (Timäus, J. J. K., 1795), III. 63, 321, 397, 399
Cabdriver (Buckstone, J. B., 1830), IV. 575
Cabin Boy (Archer, T., 1846), IV. 255
— (Stirling, E., 1846), IV. 408
— (1836), IV. 437
Cabinet (Dibdin, T. J., 1802), IV. 33, 142, 297
— (1806), IV. 437
Cabinet and Two Wives (Parry, J., 1824) = Two Wives, IV. 368, 603
Cabinet Minister (Pinero, Sir A. W., 1890), v. 525
Cabinet of Bronze = Fairy Lady
Cabinet of Fancy (Stevens, G. A., 1780), III. 309
Cabinet Question (Planché, J. R., 1845), IV. 382
Cabinet Secret (Du Terreaux, L. H., 1872), v. 352
— (1832), IV. 437, 621
— (1856), v. 654
Cabman No. 93 (Williams, T. J., 1867), v. 625
Cabman's Career (1859), v. 654
Cadi (Matthison, A., 1880), v. 481
— (1851), v. 654
Cadi gulled = Tit for Tat
Cadijeh (Jameson, Mrs A., 1825), IV. 590
Cadi's Daughter (Fizball, E., 1851), v. 367

Cadi's Flat = Ocular Misfortunes
Cadmus et Hermione (Quinault, P., 1686), I. 425
Cad of the Buss = Tiger at Large
Cady (1815) = Honesty the Best Policy, v. 437, 621
— = Cady of Bagdad
Cady of Bagdad (Portal, A., 1778), III. 299
Caedmon (Bantock, G., 1892), v. 248
Cælia (Johnson, C., 1732), II. 89, 105, 122, 124, 340
Cælina (Wallace, J., 1802), IV. 416
Caernarvon Castle (Rose, J., 1793), III. 303
Caesar and Clara = Koromantyns
Caesar and Cleopatra (Shaw, G. B., 1899), v. 189, 195, 200, 201, 562
Caesar, Bob and Lucy Neal (1847), IV. 437
Caesar Borgia (Barnett, C. Z., 1831), IV. 259
— (Lee, N., 1679), I. 79, 130, 146, 419
Cæsar in Ægypt (Cibber, C., 1724), II. 15, 70, 71, 103, 312
Caesar's Triumph over the Gauls (1815), IV. 437
Caesar's Wife (1880), v. 654
Caesar the Half-breed = Bloodhound of Cuba
Caesar, the Watch Dog of the Castle (Moncrieff, W. T., 1844), IV. 361
Caffres (Eyre, E. J., 1802), IV. 310
Caffres and Settlers = Cape of Good Hope
Caffre's Vengeance = Olga the Dreaded Witch
Cagliostro (1860), v. 654
Cagliostro the Magician (Clarke, C. A., 1875), v. 311
— = Cagliostro
Cagot (Falconer, E., 1856), v. 360
Cahill Euve Dha Rhug = Red Hand
Caid (1849), IV. 437
Cain (Byron, Lord G. G., 1821), IV. 169, 278
— (1878), v. 655
Cain and Abel (1890), v. 655
Caitiff of Corsica (1807), IV. 437
Caius Gracchus (Joshua, J., 1810), IV. 334
— (Knowles, J. S., 1815), IV. 171, 339

Cambro-Britons (Boaden, J., 1798), III. 238
— (1797), III. 321
Cambyses King of Persia (Settle, E., 1671), I. 40, 55, 66, 83, 116–7, 130, 428
Cameleon (1817), IV. 438
Cameleopard = Giraffe
Camelford (1822), IV. 438
Camelia (1861), v. 655
Camera Obscura (Browne, G. W., 1879), v. 282
Cameronians (Suter, W., 1863), v. 655, 829
Camilla (MacSwiny, O., 1706), II. 32, 58, 79, 227–8, 231, 234, 266, 274–5, 391
Camilla of Camden Town (Stuckey, H. D., 1893), v. 586
Camilla's Husband (Phillips, W., 1862), v. 523
Camilla the Amazon (1817), IV. 438
Camilla, the Wild Flower of the Wilderness (Hillier, A., 1874), v. 421
Camille (Wills, W. G., 1877), v. 627
— (1853), v. 655
— (1883), v. 655
— (1888), v. 655
Camillus and Columna (Powell, T., 1806), IV. 606
Camoens (Tucker, H. St G., 1832), IV. 615
Camp (Sheridan, R. B., 1778), III. 305, 395
— (1825), IV. 438
Campaign (Jephson, R., 1784), III. 277, 389 [This was acted Smock Alley, Dublin, 31/1/1784]
Campaigners (D'Urfey, T., 1698), I. 23, 273, 277–8, 409–10
Campaigning (1879), v. 655
Camp and the Convent (1820), IV. 438
Campanello (1837), IV. 438
Campano (Day, G. D., 1898), v. 340
Camp at Chobham (Lemon, M., 1853), v. 455
Camp at the Olympic (Planché, J. R., 1853), v. 82–3, 110, 117, 527
Camping Out (Howard, B., 1886), v. 428
Camp of Pleasure = Wags
Camp of Silesia (1847), IV. 438

Camp of the Wilderness = Siege of Jerusalem
Camp, the Cottage and the Court = King's Wager
Camp Visitants (Miller, J., 1740), II. 441
Canadian Basket Maker = Iroquois
Canadian War (Hart, J. P.), IV. 587
Canal Boat (1871), v. 655
Canary (Fleming, G., 1899), v. 369
Candida (Shaw, G. B., 1895), v. 189, 195, 204, 562
Candidate (Dent, J., 1782), III. 254
— (McCarthy, J. H., 1884), v. 467
Candidates for Rottenburgh = Election
Can he forgive her? (Calvert, Mrs C., 1891), v. 300
Can Love Kill? (1836), IV. 438
Cannibal (1838), IV. 438
Cannie Soogah (1873), v. 655
Cannon-mouth and Pistol-shot (1828), IV. 438
Canonburg (1834), IV. 438
Canonburg Tower (1831), IV. 438
Canonbury Tower (1857), v. 655
Canon's Daughter = Dione
Cantab (Robertson, T. W., 1861), v. 546
Cantabs (1787), III. 321
Canterbury Guests (Ravenscroft, E., 1694), I. 188, 256, 426
Canterbury Pilgrims (À Beckett, G. A., 1884), v. 234
Can't I do what I like with my own? (1831), IV. 438
Can't Sing Girl (1891), v. 655
Can't ye come out tonight? = Buffalo Girls
Canute's Birthday in Ireland (Buchanan, R., 1868), v. 284
Canute the Great (Field, M., 1887), v. 366
Canvass (1765), III. 321
Cape Mail (Scott, C. W., 1881), v. 558
Cape of Good Hope (Barrymore, W., 1819), IV. 438, 621
Capers (Marriott, F. and Matthews, A. K., 1899), v. 477
— (Stahl, R., 1885), v. 578
Capers and Coronets (Barnett, M., 1854), v. 250
— (Lunn, J., 1835), IV. 348
Capers and Crushers (1847), IV. 621

Capers at Canterbury (Planché, J. R., 1821), IV. 377

Capers of Cupid (1899), V. 655

Cape St Vincent (Sheridan, R. B., 1797), III. 306

Capillary Attraction = Man's Coming

Capital and Labour (Patmore, W. J. and Moss, A. B., 1890), V. 161, 515

— (1895), V. 655

Capital Idea (Arlon, F. and Rushton, A., 1871), V. 243

Capital Joke (De Lara, F., 1889), V. 341

Capital Match (Morton, J. M., 1852), V. 495

— (Parker, W., 1897), V. 514

Capital Pair = Charming Pair

Capitan (Klein, C. H., 1899), V. 445, 801

Capitola (Hazlewood, C. H., 1859), V. 412

Capochio and Dorinna, II. 445

— = Happy Captive

Capochio e Dorinna (1768), III. 321

Caprice (Broughton, F. W., 1889), V. 281

— (McCarthy, J. H., 1892), V. 467

Capriciosa (1880), V. 655

Capricious Beauty (D'Arcy, Major, 1886), V. 336

Capricious Lady (Cooke, W., 1783), III. 248, 380

— (Pye, Mrs J. H., 1771), III. 300

Capricious Lovers (Lloyd, R., 1764), III. 116, 118, 282, 390

— (Odingsells, G., 1725), II. 347; III. 116

Captain (Carlos, Don, 1883), V. 303

— (Field, W. F., 1886), V. 366

— (1677), I. 346, 440

— (1781), III. 321

Captain Bertram (1836), IV. 438

Captain Bertram and Jack Junk (1837), IV. 438

Captain Billy (Greenbank, H., 1891), V. 392

Captain Birchell's Luck (Parker, L. N., 1899), V. 514

— = Chris

Captain Blarney (1898), V. 655

Captain Brassbound's Conversion (Shaw, G. B., 1899), V. 195, 562

Captain Cartouche (1864), V. 655

Captain Charlotte (Stirling, E., 1843), IV. 407

Captain Cook (Faucit, J. S.), IV. 583

Captain Cuttle (Brougham, J., 1880), V. 281, 780

Captain Dreyfuss (Rackow, N., 1898), V. 532

Captain Firebrand (Pitt. C., 1872), V. 655, 810, 829

Captain Fritz (Hamilton, H., 1897), V. 402

Captain Gerald (Archer, W. J., 1867), V. 242

— (Howe, J. B., 1867), V. 428

Captain Hawk in the Coffin Cell = Shadow of Death

Captain is not A-Miss (Wilks, T. E., 1836), IV. 420

Captain Jack (1870), V. 655

Captain Jack, the Little Sheppard, and the Black Sheep, Jonathan Wild (1894), V. 655

Captain J. D. Pitman (1899), V. 655

Captain John Hall, the First Highwayman (1872), V. 655

Captain John Luck (1850), V. 655

Captain John Rock = Tale of the O'Hara Family

Captain Kidd (Abbott, C. H., 1883), V. 233

— (Kummer, C., 1898), V. 446

Captain Leigh, V.C. = Sister Mary

Captain Macheath (Travers, W., 1865), V. 655, 821, 829

Captain MacShane (1802), IV. 438

Captain O'Blunder = Brave Irishman

Captain of the Guard (Wood, F., 1882), V. 630

Captain of the Night Hawk (Jecks, A. E., 1897), V. 435

Captain of the Vulture (Lewis, J. and Falconer, H., 1888), V. 459

— (Vandenhoff, H., 1864), V. 655, 822, 829

— (1863), V. 655

Captain of the Watch (Planché, J. R., 1841), IV. 381

Captain Pop and the Princess Pretty Eyes! = Brown and the Brahmins

Captain pro tem (Lemon, M., 1840) = Captain (Query?), IV. 344, 438, 621

"Captain (Query?)" (Lemon, M., 1840) = Captain pro tem, IV. 344, 438, 621

Captain Ross (1833), IV. 438

Captain Sabertache (Barnett, C. Z., 1845), IV. 260

Captains Daughter (Hodgson, A. H. and Hodgson, A. C., 1890), V. 423

Captain Smith (Berrie, E., 1870), V. 259

Captain Spent's Proposals (Barrow, P. J., 1899), V. 252

Captain Starlight (Mackay, W. J., 1899), V. 471

Captain Stevens (Selby, C., 1832), IV. 397, 437, 621

Captain's Watch (1862), V. 655

Captain Swift (Chambers, C. H., 1888), V. 307

Captain Tarradiddle (1845), IV. 438

Captain Thérèse (Burnand, F. C., 1890), V. 292

Captain Tom Drake (Stephens, W., 1874), V. 581

Captivating Carmen (Byam, M. and Wyke, E. B., 1890), V. 294

Captive (Barrell, M. 1790), III. 91, 235

— (Bickerstaffe, J., 1769), III. 58, 199, 237

— (Lewis, M. G., 1803), IV. 345

Captive Bride = Panthea

Captive Maid = Swindler

Captive Mariner (1804), IV. 438

Captive Monarch (Hey, R., 1794), III. 54, 268

Captive of Silesia = Stella de Rittersdorf

Captive of Spilburg (Hoare, P., 1798), III. 45, 270

Captive Prince (1744), II. 367

Captive Princess (1814), IV. 438

Captives (Gay, J., 1724), II. 29, 31, 32, 111, 264, 331

— (Delap, J., 1786), III. 36, 72, 80, 253

— (1855), V. 829

Captive, the Coffer and the Cocoatina = All at C

Captured (1894), V. 655

Capuchin (Foote, S., 1778), III. 175, 260

Caractacus (Mason, W., 1759, 1764, 1776), III. 221–2, 286

— (Monney, W., 1816), IV. 600

— (Planché, J. R., 1837), IV. 381

— (1808), IV. 438

Caradoc the Great (1727), II. 367

Caravan (Reynolds, F., 1803), IV. 25, 51, 109–10, 391

— (1788), III. 321

— (1791), III. 321

— (1816), IV. 438

Caravansera = Caravan

Carbonari (1845), IV. 438

Card Case (Craven, H. T., 1844), IV. 285

Card Drawer = Murderer's Dream

Card-Drawing (1828; 1829), IV. 439

— (1861), V. 655

Cardillac, the Terror of Paris (1827), IV. 439

Cardinal (Grogan, W. E., 1894), V. 395

Cardinal Beaton (Tennant, W., 1823), IV. 65, 411

Cardinal's Daughter (Townsend, W. T., 1852), V. 602

— = Jewess

Cardinal's Letters (1844), IV. 439

Card Party = (1) High, Low, Jack and the Game; (2) Queen of Hearts

Cards of Invitation (Grain, R. C., 1888), V. 387

"Card! 23 John Street, Adelphi" (Buckstone, J. B., 1826), IV. 273

Career of Crime = Caliph Vathek

Career of the Widow's Son = Third Class and First Class

Careful Servant and the Careless Master (1816), IV. 439

Careless Husband (Cibber, C., 1704), II. 34, 129, 130, 131, 132, 134, 135, 138, 180–1, 183, 184–5, 186, 188, 189, 202, 231, 309, 421, 433

Careless Lovers (Ravenscroft, E., 1673), I. 86, 188, 231, 254, 347, 426

Care Sent to Coventry (1800), IV. 621

Cares of Love (Chaves, A., 1705), II. 10, 171, 209, 306

Carib Chief (Twiss, A., 1819), IV. 415

— (1851), V. 655

Carib Chieftain and the Irish Witch = Vow of Vengeance

Caribee (1827), IV. 439

Cariboo (1842), IV. 439

Caribs = Bold Bucaniers

Carina (Blanchard, E. L. and Bridgman, C., 1888), V. 265

Carl (Wilson, S., 1886), V. 629

Carl Carlsruhe (1840), IV. 439
Carl et Lisbeth (1814), IV. 439
Carline (1831), IV. 439
Carline, the Female Brigand (Stirling, E., 1837), IV. 406
Carlists of La Vendée = Memoirs of the Duchess de Berri
Carlmilham (Fitzball, E., 1835), IV. 314
Carlo (Millingen, J. G., 1837), IV. 439, 621
Carlo Broschi = Ma Part
Carlo Brunari (1856) = Horse of the Cavern, v. 655, 694, 836
Carlo Foscari, the Italian Boy (1861), v. 655
Carlo Leoni (Hazlewood, C. H., 1859), v. 655, 796, 829
Carlos Gangenelli (Pitt, G. D., 1847), IV. 374
Carlowitz and Orloff (1831), IV. 439
Carl's Folly (Greene, C. M., 1891), v. 392
Carl the Clockmaker (Starr, H., 1894), v. 579
Carlyle's Wife (1883), v. 656
Carlyon Sahib (Murray, Sir G., 1899), v. 500
Carl Zeitter and his Bride (1835), IV. 439
Carmelite (Cumberland, R., 1784), III. 49, 78-9, 251
Carmelites (Fitzball, E., 1835), IV. 315
Carmen (Hamilton, H., 1896), v. 402
— (Hersee, H., 1879), v. 419, 797
— (Reece, R., 1879), v. 538
Carmen up-to-date (Sims, G. R. and Pettitt, H., 1890), v. 569
Carnac Sahib (Jones, H. A., 1899), v. 440
Carnation of Carnation Cottage (1862), v. 656
Carnaval de Venise (1821), IV. 439
Carnival (Charke, Mrs C., 1735), II. 306
— (Porter, T. ?1663), I. 219-20, 264, 425
Carnival at Naples (Dimond, W., 1830), IV. 439, 621
Carnival Frolic = One Hour
Carnival of Venice (Tickell, R., 1781), III. 312
— (1824), IV. 439
— (1859), v. 656
Carnival Time (Watson, T. M., 1890), v. 616

Carolan (Victor, H., 1892), v. 608
+ Caroline and Henrietta (*French*)
Caroline's Pupils (Vaun, R. and Atwood, A., 1896), v. 607
Caroona (Ray, E., 1899), v. 535
Carp (Desprez, F., 1886), v. 343
Carpenter (Moreau, 1813), IV. 600
Carpenter of Rouen (Jones, J. S., 1844, 1853), IV. 334; v. 440, 800
Carpenter's Family = Robert Ryland
Carpenters of Lambeth (1847), IV. 439
Carpenters of Paris (Archer, T., 1846), IV. 255
Carpet Bag (Blanchard, E. L., 1869), v. 264
Carpio (Finnamore, J., 1886), v. 367
Carrier and his Dog (1854), v. 656
— = Old Toll House
Carrier of London (Halford, J., 1854), v. 656, 795, 829
Carron Side (Planché, J. R., 1828), IV. 378
Carrot and Pa-snip (Green, F. W., 1872), v. 390
Carry's Breach of Promise (De Frece, M., 1872), v. 341
Carry's Triumph = Carry's Breach of Promise
Carte de Visite (Williams, M. and Burnand, F. C., 1862), v. 624, 824
Cartel at Philadelphia = Seventeen Hundred and Eighty One
Carte over Arm = Roland
Carter of Liverpool (1879), v. 656
Carthusiana (Stephenson, B. C., 1899), v. 582
Carthusian Friar (1793), III. 321
Cartouche (Strauss, F., 1860), v. 656, 818, 829
— (Travers, W., 1859), v. 656, 821, 829
— (1722), III. 367
Cartouche and Co. Ltd. (Newton, H. C., 1892), v. 503
Cartouche, the French Robber (1860), v. 656
Cartouche, the Renowned Robber of France (Travers, W., 1840), IV. 414
Carynthia (Towers, E., 1867), v. 600, 821
Caryswold (Herman, H. and Mackay, J., 1877), v. 419
Casanova (1837), IV. 439

Casco Bay (Bernard, W. B., 1827), IV. 265

Case for Eviction (Smith, S. T., 1882), v. 573

Case for Reflection (Simpson, J. P., 1857), v. 567

Case is Altered = (1) Gaffer's Mistake; (2) Good News! Good News!

Case of Conscience (Oxenford, J., 1857), v. 656, 809, 829

Case of Pickles (Baddeley, G. C., 1871), v. 247

Case of Rebellious Susan (Jones, H. A., 1894), v. 440, 800

Cash for Coronets (Cassilis, I. L. and Morland, F. H., 1894), v. 306

Cash versus Cupid (1862), v. 656

Casimer the Great (Morton, T., 1795) = Zorinski, III. 321, 392, 399

Casino (1780), III. 321

Casket (Fisher, J. B., 1808), IV. 583

— (Lacy, M. R., 1829), IV. 340

+ Casket of Gloriana; or, The Geni and the Black Enchanter (Beverley, H. R.; Tottenham-street, 1819; 8°, 1819 (Songs))

Casket of Jewels (1853), v. 656

Caspar Duverade, the Terror of Spain (1852), v. 656

Casper Hauser (1837), IV. 439

Casper the Doomed (Wilks, T. E., 1841), IV. 439, 621

Cassandra = Virgin Prophetess

Cassilda (1862), v. 656

Cassiope (1866), v. 656

Cassowar (Dibdin, C. I. M., 1807), IV. 292

Cast Adrift (Palgrave, R. and Gover, F., 1882), v. 511

— (1866), v. 656

Cast Aside (Hazlewood, C. H., 1871), v. 414

Castaway (Hazlewood, C. H., 1866), v. 413

Castaways (Smith, S. T., 1885), v. 573

— (1876), v. 656

Castaways, the Wild Men and the Winged Beauty = Pietro Wilkini

Caste (Robertson, T. W., 1867), v. 1, 51, 55, 56, 126, 127–8, 180, 546

Castellan's Oath (Walker, C. E., 1824), IV. 439, 621

Castellan's Son = Old Man of the Mountains

Castilian (Talfourd, F., 1853), v. 590

Castilian Bandit = Phantom Bride

Castilian Honour = (1) Pledge; (2) Valasco

Castilian Minstrel (D'Egville, 1810), IV. 439, 621

Castilian Nobleman = Alvarez

Castilian Nobleman and the Contra-bandista (Oxenford, J., 1835), IV. 367

Casting the Boomerang (Daly, A., 1883), v. 333

Casting Vote (Helmore, W., 1885), v. 416

— = Election

Castle Adamant = Princess Ida

Castle and the Cottage = False Step

Castle Blarneygig (Dibdin, C. I. M., 1812), IV. 293

— = Lady of the Wreck

Castle Botherem (Law, A. and Clarke, H., 1880), v. 449

Castle Burners (Almar, G., 1852), v. 239

Castle Cauldron (Wilks, T. E., 1835), IV. 420

Castle Grim (Reece, R., 1865), v. 537

Castle in the Glen = Mary's Bower

Castlemount Mystery = Slur of Slander

Castle of Andalusia (O'Keeffe, J., 1782), III. 292

— (1817), IV. 439

— = Pedrillo

Castle of Avola (Serres, O., 1805), IV. 610

Castle of Aymon (1844) = Four Sons of Aymon, IV. 439

Castle of Caldora = Sicilian Outlaw

Castle of Como (Searle, C., 1889), v. 559

+ Castle of de Courcy; or, A Bandit's Revenge (Isacson, W. P.; Newmarket, 17/1/1843; manuscript, no. 99 in East Anglian Theatre Exhibition, Norwich, 1952)

Castle of Dunstaffnage = Maid of Lorn

Castle of Eberstein = Serpent Lady

Castle of Ellangowan = Guy Mannering

Castle of Glyndower (Ryley, S. W., 1818) = Castles in the Air, IV. 396, 439, 622

Castle of Lausanne (Reynolds, F., 1805) = Out of Place, IV. 439, 621

Castle of Limburg (1822; 1840), IV. 439

Castle of Lindenbergh = Raymond and Agnes

Castle of Lochleven = Mary Stuart

Castle of Minski = Mines of Poland

Castle of Monte Falcon = Hag of the Lake

Castle of Montval (Whalley, T. S., 1799), III. 315

Castle of Morosino (Loveday, W., 1812), IV. 347

Castle of Olival = Wandering Boys

Castle of Otranto (À Beckett, G. A., 1848), IV. 251

— (Bradwell, W., 1840), IV. 573

— (Siddons, H., 1793) = Sicilian Romance, III. 321, 399

— (1859), V. 656

— = (1) Manfred; (2) Sicilian Romance

Castle of Paluzzi (Raymond, R. J., 1818), IV. 388

Castle of St Aldobrand (Maturin, C. R., 1816) = Bertram, IV. 439, 598, 622

— (1832), IV. 439

Castle of Sorrento (Heartwell, H. and Colman, G., 1799), III. 121, 268

Castle of Steinberg (1831), IV. 439

Castle of Sunderwald = Fire Fiend

Castle of Tarento (1819), IV. 439

Castle of the Forest = Fatal Sisters

Castle of Udolpho (Weston, F. F., 1808), IV. 418

Castle of Valenza (Courtney, J., 1851), V. 326

Castle of Wolfenstein (Thackeray, T. J., 1828), IV. 439, 622

Castle of Wonders (Andrews, M. P., 1786) = Enchanted Castle, III. 321, 377, 399

— (Johnson, 1819), IV. 333, 582, 590

Castles in Spain (Montague, L. A. D.), V. 491

Castles in the Air (Dibdin, C. I. M., 1809), IV. 292

— (Ryley, S. W., 1818) = Castle of Glyndower, IV. 396, 439, 622

— (Rae, C. M., 1879), V. 532

— (Robertson, T. W., 1854), V. 546

— (1832), IV. 439

— = In the Clouds

Castle Sombras (Smith, R. G. and Mansfield, F., 1896), V. 573

Castle Spectre (Lewis, M. G., 1797), III. 50, 52, 62, 72, 98, 99–100, 152, 281; IV. 113

Castle Walstenfurth (1801), IV. 439

Cast of the Lead (1899), V. 656

Cast on the Mercy of the World (Hazlewood, C. H., 1862), V. 412

Cast on the World = Alone in the World

Castruccio (Newbound, E., 1878), V. 502

Casual Acquaintance (Cooke, J. F., 1893), V. 324

Casual Ward (Cave, J. A., 1866), V. 306

Caswallon (Walker, C. E., 1829), IV. 416

Caswallon, the King of Britain (Gandy, E., 1826), IV. 318, 439, 622

Cataclysm = Noah's Flood

Catacombs of St Agnes = Nun

Catalina (Woodville, H., 1892), V. 631

Catalonian Marriage (1763), III. 321

Cat and Dog (Brown, J. R., 1871), V. 282

Cat and the Cherub (Fernald, C. B., 1897), V. 365

Cataract of Amazonia = White Witch

Cataract of Sostenza (1825), IV. 440

Cataract of the Ganges! (Moncrieff, W. T., 1823), IV. 359

Cataract of the Giant's Rock = Pirate Queen

Cataract of the Mountain = Hate

Catarina (Campbell, C., 1844), IV. 83, 440, 622

— (1844), IV. 83, 440

— (1861), V. 656

— (1862), V. 656

— = Crown Jewels

Catch a Weazel (Morton, J. M., 1862), V. 496, 807

Catch Club (1788), III. 321

Catch 'em alive = Bravo Rouse!

Catch 'em alive, oh! (Wild, G., 1851), V. 622

Catch him who can! (Hook, T. E., 1806), IV. 327

Catching a Gander (1854), V. 656

Catching a Governor = Pas de Fascination

Catching a Husband (1862), V. 656

Catching a Mermaid (Coyne, J. S., 1855), V. 327, 786

Catching an Heiress (Selby, C., 1835) IV. 397

71

6-2

Cause of the Greeks = Son of Evin

Cause of the present high Price of Provisions = Inquiry

Causes and Effects = Glass of Water

Caution to Young Ladies = Elopement

Cautious Coxcomb = Sir Salomon

Cavalearyer Costercana (Landeck, B. and Turner, E., 1893), V. 447

Cavalier (McCarthy, J. H., 1894), v. 467

— (Whitehead, D. C., 1836), IV. 419

— = Woodstock

Cavalier in Edinburgh = Woodstock

Cavalier of Wildinghurst = Charles at Tunbridge Wells

Cavaliers (1832), IV. 440

Cavaliers and Roundheads (Pocock, I., 1835), IV. 93, 385

— = Days of Oliver Cromwell

Cavalier, the Count and the Italian = Fair Circassian

Cave of Daroca = Moorish Banditti

Cave of Glenmore = Outlaws

Cave of Hecate (1797), III. 399

Cave of Idra = Heroine of the Cave

Cave of Neptune (Holford, G., 1799), III. 271

Cave of Plunder = Moorish Banditti

Cave of St Cataldo = Mysterious Stranger

Cave of St Robert = Eugene Aram

Cave of Trophonius (Hoare, P., 1791), III. 269, 387

Cavern (Isdell, Sarah, Lady Morgan, 1825), IV. 330, 601

Cavern in the Rock (1804), IV. 440

Cavern of Calabria = Murdered Monk

Cavern of Glotzden = Tower of Zauffen

Caverns of Hoenhelbe = Imperial Victims

C.D.I.T.D. Now Find it Out (1823), IV. 440

Cead Mille Failthe (Murdoch, J. M., 1877), v. 499

Cedar Chest (Almar, G., 1834), IV. 253, 568

Ceinture (1790), III. 322

Celadon and Florimel (Kemble, J. P., 1796), III. 115, 279, 389

Celebrated Case (Arthur, A., 1888), v. 244

— (1890), v. 656

— = Proof

Celeste (1839), IV. 440

Celeste, the French Spy (1831), IV. 440

Celestia (Dalrymple, 1835), IV. 288

Celestial Institute (Sim, E. H., 1896), v. 566

— = Institute Abroad

Celestials (Abbott, C. H. and Houghton, J. W., 1898), v. 233

Celestina (Savage, J., 1708), II. 353

Celia the Gipsy Girl (Galer, E. J. N., 1879), v. 375

Cellar Spectre (1833), IV. 440

— = The Earls of Hammersmith

Cell of Mystery = Iron Tower

Cenci (Shelley, P. B., 1819), IV. 196-7 221, 401

Cenia (1752), III. 61, 322

Census (Brough, W. and Halliday, A., 1861), v. 279

Cent. per Cent. (Pocock, I., 1823), IV. 124, 384 [The entry, IV. 277, under Butler, R. is in error]

Century Gone = St Ann's Well!

Cent Vierges (Grantham, J., 1874), v. 388

Central Figure (Lloyd, H. H., 1897), v. 461

Cephalus and Procris (1730), II. 136, 367, 451

Cephisa (Moser, J., 1804), IV. 364

Cerise & Co. (Musgrave, Mrs H., 1890), v. 500

Certain Age (1851), v. 656

Cervantes Knight = Spanish Gala

C'est l'amour (1820), IV. 440

C'est l'amour, l'amour, l'amour (1828), IV. 440

C'est la vie (Vaun, R., 1898), v. 607

Cestus (Dibdin, C., 1783), III. 256

Cetewayo at Last (1882), v. 656

Cetewayo in South Shields (1882), v. 656

Chachechichochu (Pitt, G. D., 1845), IV. 374

Chaff (1877), v. 656

Chained to Sin and Brought up to Beg (1881), v. 656

Chain Gang (Harcourt, F. C., 1881), v. 403

Chained to the Oar (Byron, H. J., 1873), v. 298

Chain of Events (Lewes, G. H. and Mathews, C. J., 1852), v. 458

Chain of Evidence (1897), v. 656
Chain of Gold (Peake, R. B., 1834), iv. 370
Chain of Guilt (Taylor, T. P., 1836), iv. 411
— = Rosalie
Chain of Roses = Thetis and Peleus
Chains of the Heart (Hoare, P., 1801), iv. 326
— (1835), iv. 440
Chalet (Long, C., 1845), iv. 346
Chalet in the Valley = Madame Berliot's Ball
Chalk and Cheese (Norwood, E., 1888), v. 505
Chalk Farm (1832), iv. 440
Chalk Mark (Francks, F. H. and Tassin, A., 1899), v. 372
Challenge (Milner, H. M. and Planché, J. R., 1834), iv. 380, 599, 605
— (1836), iv. 440
Chamber Comedies (Bell, Mrs H., 1890), v. 255
Chambermaid (Phillips, E., 1730), ii. 349
Chamber-maid turn'd Quaker = Country Innocence
Chamber of Horrors (Wood, A., 1870), v. 630
— (1847), iv. 440
Chamber Practice (Selby, C., 1849), iv. 399
Chambre à coucher = Half an Hour's Courtship
Chameleon (Brough, W., 1852), v. 278
Chamois Hunter (Gibson, C., 1852), v. 378
Champagne (Farnie, H. B. and Reece, R., 1877), v. 362
— (Moore, J., 1848), iv. 440, 622
Champ de Mai (1824), iv. 440
Champ de Mars (1790), iii. 54, 322
Champion Belt (1860), v. 656
Champion Horse and the Saxon Knight = Days of Chivalry
Champion of England (Hazlewood, C. H., 1860), v. 656, 796, 829
Champion of the World (1860), v. 656
Champion's Belt (Travers, W., 1860), v. 821
Champs de Mars = Mythology Run Mad

Chance (Osborne, C., 1869), v. 508
Chance Acquaintance (Denny, W. H., 1894), v. 342
Chance and Change = Faith, Hope and Charity
Chance Interview (Bell, Mrs H., 1889), v. 255
Chancellor of the Exchequer = King and No King
Chance of War (McLaren, A., 1801), iv. 350
— = School for Honour
Chancery Suit (Peake, R. B., 1830), iv. 370
Chances (Garrick, D., 1754), iii. 262
— (Villiers, G., 1667), i. 61–2, 67, 349, 350, 436
Chances of the Cards = Good Luck
Chance the Idiot (Reynolds, E., 1872), v. 541
Chandler's Daughter = (1) Boarding School Miss; (2) Miss Poppy
Chandos (Brooklyn, H., 1882), v. 277
Chang Ching Fow, Cream of Tartar (Martin, W., 1864), v. 479
Change (Pride, F. H. and Palmer, F. G., 1870), v. 531
— (1888), v. 656
Change Alley (Parker, L. N. and Carson, S. M., 1899), v. 514
Changed at Nurse (1821), iv. 440
Changed Heart (Parselle, J., 1860), v. 656, 809, 829
Change for a Sovereign (Wigan, H., 1861), v. 622
— (1855), v. 657
— = (1) Grand Duke; (2) Ulf the Minstrel
Change for Love (Bird, H.), v. 262
Change for the Better (1861), v. 657
Changelings = Court and Country
Change of Air (Manning, E., 1878), v. 474
Change of Crownes (Howard, E., 1667), i. 10, 78, 321, 343, 414
Change of Fortune is the Lot of Life (De Latour, Mlle, 1874), v. 341
Change of Government = Conspiracy
Change of Name (Moore, A., 1867), v. 492, 807
— = Mr Scroggins

Change of System (Paul, H. M., 1860), v. 516

Change Partners (1825) = Turn Hands and Change Partners, IV. 440, 545

Changes (Aylmer, J., 1890), v. 246

— (Proctor, H., 1876), v. 531

— (1843), IV. 440

Changes and Chances (1891), v. 657

Change upon Change (1805), IV. 440

Changing Servants (1836), IV. 440

Changing Years (1896), v. 657

Chaos (Dibdin, C. I. M., 1800), IV. 290

Chaos is come again (Morton, J. M., 1838), IV. 362

Chapel in the Wood = Invisible Witness

Chapel of Miracles = Idiot Queen

Chaperon (Brummel, H., 1899), v. 284

Chaperoned (Harrison, E., 1887), v. 407

Chaplain of the Fleet (1890), v. 657

Chaplain of the Regiment (1849), IV. 440

Chaplet (Mendez, M., 1749), II. 237, 260, 344, 440; III. 287

Chaplet of Innocence = Rose Wreath

Chapter from Don Quixote (Wills, W. G., 1895), v. 628

Chapter of Accidents (Douglass, J. T., 1870), v. 348

— (Lee, S., 1780), III, 120, 281

Character of Solomon Swop (1832), IV. 440

Charade (1852), v. 657

Charcoal Burner (Almar, G., 1832), IV. 252

Charcoal Burner of Charing = Fair Maid of Tottenham Court

Charcoal Burners of the Hartz = Steel Pavilion

Charibel (Green, F. W., 1885), v. 391

Charioteers (1810), IV. 440

Charitable Association (Brooke, H., 1778), III. 240

Charitable Man (Barry, H., 1887), v. 252

Charitable Quixote = Where is She?

+ Charity (Gardner, Mrs S, see *Theatre Notebook*, VII. 1953, 76–9)

— (Gilbert, W. S., 1874), v. 379

— (Hazlewood, C. H., 1862), v. 412

Charity begins at home (Stephenson, B. C. and Scott, C. W., 1872), v. 582

Charity Boy (Cross, J. C., 1796), III. 250, 380

Charity's Cloak (Dauncey, Sylvanus, 1891), v. 337

Charity's Love (Wilkins, J. H., 1854), v. 623

Charlatan (Aylmer, Mrs J., 1889), v. 246

— (Buchanan, R., 1894), v. 285

Charlemagne (Ducrow, A., 1841), IV. 308

— (1838), IV. 74, 440

Charles I (Brewer, E. C., 1828), IV. 270

— (Butler, A. G., 1874), v. 294

— (Flocton, C., 1879), v. 369

— (Mitford, M. R., 1834), IV. 358

— (Wills, W. G., 1872), v. 38, 627

Charles I and Charles II (1899), v. 657

Charles II (À Beckett, G. A., 1872), v. 234

— (Griffith, G., 1867), v. 394

— (Payne, J. H., 1824), IV. 369

— (1842), IV. 440

Charles II and Pretty Nell Gwynne (Soutar, R., 1867), v. 575

Charles VIII of France (Crowne, J., 1671), I. 64, 124, 347, 398–9

Charles XII (Planché, J. R., 1828), IV. 378

Charles XII and Peter the Great (Dibdin, T. J., 1828), IV. 440, 622

Charles at Tunbridge Wells (Forster, J., 1828), IV. 584

Charles Edward Stuart the Pretender in Scotland (Macdonald, 1823), IV. 441, 622

Charles Edward, the Last of the Stuarts (1828), IV. 441

Charles Ganganelli (1847), IV. 441

Charles O'Malley (Somerset, C. A., 1841), IV. 404

— = Galway Go Bragh

Charles O'Malley, the Irish Dragoon (Macarthy, 1843), IV. 349

Charles the Bold (Arnold, S. J., 1815), IV. 82, 256

Charles the Great = Charles the Eighth of France

Charles the Terrible (Faucit, J. S., 1830), IV. 82, 441, 583, 622

— (Raymond, R. J., 1821), IV. 82, 441, 622

Charley over the Water (1831), IV. 441

Chickweed and Groundsel (1884), v. 657

Chicot the Jester (Saintsbury, H. A., 1898), v. 554

Chief of the Arbutzi = Marco Schiarro

Chiefs of Erin = Cormac and Swaran

Chieftain (Burnand, F. C., 1894), v. 292

Chieftain's Banquet (Goff, H., 1824), IV. 585

Chieftain's Daughter = Retribution

Chieftain's Oath (Jerrold, D. W., 1821), IV. 331

Chieftains of Scotia (1809), IV. 441

Chieftains of the Glen = Outlaw's Oath

Chieftains of the Orkney Isles = Cattarans

Chieftain's Vengeance = Kafrali Karabush

Chien du zouave (1856), v. 829

Child has found his Father = Birth of Merlin, the British Enchanter

Childhood's Dreams (Young, Sir C. L., 1881), v. 636

Child Lost (Douglass, J. T.), v. 789

Child of Air (1844), IV. 441

— = Fountain of Zea

Child of a Soldier = Home of the Brave

Child of a Tar = Wapping Old Stairs!

Child of Babylon = Hebrew Son

Child of Chance (Kemble, C., 1812) = Love's Errors, IV. 334, 496, 591, 631

— (Poole, W. H., 1886), v. 529

— (Travers, W., 1860), v. 822

Child of Concealment (Bromley, G. P., 1816), IV. 441, 622

Child of Crime = St Hilda's Cave

Child of Fortune = (1) Emmeline; (2) Ida May, the Kidnapped Child

Child of Love = Lover's Vows

Child of Mistery = Elfrida of Olmutz

Child of Mystery (1821), IV. 441

— = (1) Borrachio, the Outlaw; (2) Monk's Cowl; (3) Pride of the Blood; (4) Zilia

Child of Nature (Inchbald, Mrs E., 1788), III. 121, 144, 275, 388

— (1896), v. 657

— = Amanthis

Child of Science (1881), v. 657

Child of Sorrow = Julia Ackland

Child of the Army = Soldier's Sister

Child of the Desert = (1) Æthiop; (2) Æthiop's Oath; (3) Wild Horse, Mazeppa

Child of the Fire = Flamma

Child of the Foundling Hospital (1856), v. 657

— = Madeleine Dumas

Child of the Hempen Widow = (1) Horsemonger-Lane Joe; (2) Poor Joe of Horsemonger Lane

Child of the Island = Mad Woman through Love

Child of the Storm = Catherine of Russia

Child of the Sun (Brougham, J., 1865), v. 281

Child of the Waves = Life's Trials by Sea and Land

Child of the Wold (Faber, M. A., 1867), v. 790

Child of the Wreck (Planché, J. R., 1837), IV. 381

— = Ida Lee

Children (Hoare, P., 1800), III. 270; IV. 325, 588

Children in the Wood (Blanchard, E. L., 1872), v. 264

— (Blanchard, E. L. and Greenwood, T. L., 1874), v. 264

— (Clay, T. L., 1879), v. 313

— (Douglass, J. T., 1875), v. 348

— (Morton, T., 1793), III. 289

— (Osman, W. R., 1871), v. 508

— (Powell, T., 1805), IV. 387

— (Stirling, E., 1842), IV. 441, 622

— (Suter, W. E., 1860), v. 657, 818, 829

— (1850, 1875, 1876, 1877, 1878), v. 657

Children of Cyprus = Cherry and Fair Star

Children of Kings = Children of the King

Children of Mexico = Black Forester

Children of Mystery = Edwin and Angelina

Children of the Abbey = Fair Words and Foul Deeds

Children of the Alps = Brothers of Turin

Children of the Castle (Fitzball, E., 1857), v. 368

Children of the Earth = Spirit Bride

Chocolate-Makers (Stayley, G., 1759), III. 309

Choice (Cord, D. M., 1887), V. 325
— (McEwan, N., 1893), V. 469
— (Murphy, A., 1765), III. 290
— (1772), III. 322

Choice of Apollo (Potter, J., 1765), III. 299

Choice of Harlequin (1782), III. 322

Choice of Hercules (1753) = Hercules's Choice of Pleasure and Virtue, III. 322

Choknosoff (1871), V. 658

Cholera Morbus (1831), IV. 442

Choleric Count = Otto of Wittelsbach

Choleric Fathers (Holcroft, T., 1785), III. 123, 203, 271, 387

Choleric Man (Cumberland, R., 1774) III. 126, 251

+ Choosing a Bride (*French*)

Choose your own path (1857), V. 829

Chopper's Wedding Morn (Turner, E., 1889), V. 604

Chops of the Channel (Hay, F., 1869), V. 411

Chopsticks and Spikins (Meritt, P., 1873), V. 485

Chorus Girl (1897), V. 658
— = Theatrical Duchess

Chosen for Life (Selby, H. C., 1882), v. 560

Chris (Parker, L. N., 1892), V. 513

Christabelle (À Beckett, G. A., 1872), V. 233

Christening (Buckstone, J. B., 1834), IV. 274
— (1860), V. 658

Christian (Caine, H., 1897), V. 300

Christian and his Comrades = Island

Christian Captives (Bridges, R. S., 1890), V. 275

Christian Hero (Lillo, G., 1735), II. 26, 50, 75, 84, 342

Christians and Moors (1824), IV. 442

Christian's Crime (Mortimer, L. and Wilson, P., 1899), V. 494

Christian's Cross (Oakley, F. and Clay-pole, C., 1897), V. 808

Christian's Cross and Martyr's Crown = Christian's Cross

Christian Slave (1856), V. 658

Christie Johnstone (Reade, C.), V. 812

Christina (Lynwood, P. and Ambient, M., 1887), V. 465

Christine (Broughton, F. W. and Jones, J. W., 1879), V. 281
— (1842), IV. 442
— (1862), V. 658, 829
— = Youthful Queen, Christine of Sweden

Christine of Sweden = Young Queen

Christmas at Brighton (Mathews, C. J., 1820), IV. 354, 597

Christmas Boxes (Mayhew, A. and Edwards, H. S., 1860), V. 483, 806
— (1825), IV. 442
— = New Year's Gift

Christmas Box System = Christmas Boxes

Christmas Capers (1835), IV. 442

Christmas Carol (Barnett, C. Z., 1844), IV. 97, 260
— (Cooper, F. F., 1854), V. 786
— (Stirling, E., 1844), IV. 97, 407, 613
— (Webb, C., 1844), IV. 97, 442, 622
— (1859), V. 658

Christmas Chimes (Williams, A., 1873), V. 624

Christmas Dinner (Taylor, T., 1860), V. 593

Christmas Eve (Cheltnam, C. S., 1870), V. 309
— (Deffell, C. and Browne, M., 1865), V. 341, 788, 842 [Probably = Oracle, below]
— (Fitzball, E., 1860), V. 368, 792
— (1840), IV. 442
— = (1) Oracle; (2) Yule Log

Christmas Gambol = (1) Country 'Squire; (2) Spendthrift; (3) Whim

Christmas Gossips (1812), IV. 442

Christmas Log (1846), IV. 442

Christmas Ordinary (R., W., 1682), I. 440

Christmas Pantomime (Vicars, W. A., 1871), V. 608

Christmas Party (1879), V. 658

Christmas Stocking (À Beckett, G. A. and Hall, K., 1879), V. 234

Christmas Story (Irving, L. S. B., 1893), V. 658, 799, 829
— (1852), V. 658
— = (1) Dot; (2) Holly Tree Inn

Christmas Tale (Garrick, D., 1773), III. 27, 118, 263, 385
— (1817), IV. 442
— =Zapolyta
Christopher Junior=Jedbury Junior
Christopher's Honeymoon (Watson, T. M., 1889), v. 616
Christopher Tadpole (Brown, W., 1877), v. 282
Christ's Passion (Sandys, G., 1687), I. 427
Chronicle of the Life and Death of Jane Shore=Goldsmith's Wife
Chrononhotonthologos (Carey, H., 1734), II. 241, 267–8, 302; IV. 1
Chrystabelle (Falconer, E., 1860), v. 360
Chrystal Cross and Glittering Fountains =Knights of St Albans
Chrystaline (Layton, G. M., 1871), v. 451
Chuck (1736), II. 367
Chuck and Ruck a Roo (1866), v. 658
Chums (Warren, T. G., 1885), v. 615
— (1899), v. 658
— =Ned's Chum
Chuneelah (Campbell, A. V., 1826), IV. 278
Church and Stage (Reynolds, W., 1888), v. 541
Churchwarden (Cassel, H. and Ogden, C., 1886), v. 305
Chymical Counterfeits (1734), II. 367
— =Fate of Narcissus
Ciceley's Secret (Hawkins, Mrs P. L., 1895), v. 410
Cicilia and Clorinda (Killigrew, T. 1664), I. 416
Cicisbea alla Moda (1759), III. 322
Cicisbeo (1837), IV. 622
Cid (Addison, J. and Howell, J. H., 1878), v. 236
— (Neil, R., 1874), v. 501
— (Ozell, J., 1714), II. 347, 442
— (1691), I. 440
— (1802), IV. 442
Cigale (Burnand, F. C., 1890), v. 292, 782
— =Stroller
Cigarette (D'Arcy, G., 1876), v. 336
— (St Leger, E. W., 1892), v. 554, 815

Cinderella (Akhurst, W. M., 1874), v. 237
— (Allan-Fisher, C., 1895), v. 238
— (Allen, O., 1886), v. 239
— (Almar, H., 1831), IV. 252
— (Barwick, E., 1897), v. 252
— (Barwick, E., 1898), v. 252
— (Blanchard, E. L., 1844), IV. 268
— (Blanchard, E. L. and Greenwood, T. L., 1864), v. 263, 779
— (Blanchard, E. L., 1874), v. 264
— (Blanchard, E. L., 1878), v. 265
— (Blanchard, E. L., 1883), v. 265
— (Burnand, F. C., 1885), v. 291
— (Byron, H. J., 1860), v. 296
— (Clair, H. B., 1891), v. 310
— (Daly, B. and East, J. M., 1897), v. 334
— (Douglass, J. T., 1884), v. 349
— (England, A. and Noble, C. R., 1896), v. 358
— (French, H. P., 1889), v. 373
— (French, H. P., 1895), v. 373
— (Green, F. W. and Allen, O., 1883), v. 391
— (Green, F. W. and Clay, T. L., 1879), v. 391
— (Harris, Sir A. H. G., Raleigh, C. and Sturgess, A., 1895), v. 406
— (Hazlewood, C. H., 1872), v. 797
— (Hewson, J. J., 1899), v. 660, 798, 829
— (Jones, F., 1898), v. 439
— (Jones, J. W., 1878), v. 440
— (Lacy, M. R., 1830), IV. 340
— (Leigh, H. S., 1883), v. 454
— (Lemon, H., 1870), v. 454
— (Lennard, H., 1888), v. 455, 803
— (Lennard, H., 1893), v. 456
— (Locke, F., 1892), v. 462
— (Logan, W. H., 1863), v. 804
— (McArdle, J. F., 1875), v. 804
— (McCabe, C. W., 1893), v. 467
— (McLelland, H. F., 1896), v. 468
— (Muskerry, W., 1886), v. 501
— (Rice, C., 1875), v. 542
— (Robertson, T. W., 1892), v. 547
— (Rogers, T. S., 1897), v. 549
— (Rogers, T. S., 1898), v. 549
— (Sturgess, A., Raleigh, C. and Matthews, E. C., 1898), v. 586
— (Summers, W., 1898), v. 587

Cinderella (Taylor, T. and Smith, A., 1845), IV. 411; V. 592, 820
— (Thorne, G., 1893), V. 659, 820, 829
— (Thorne, G., 1896), V. 599
— (Thorne, G., 1897), V. 599
— (Thorne, G. and Clement, W., 1898), V. 599
— (Towers, E., 1881), V. 601
— (Wagner, L., 1886), V. 610
— (Walton, W., 1895), V. 613
+ — (Weston; Bolton, 26/12/1864)
— (Wood, J. H., 1899), V. 660, 824, 829
— (1804, 1809), IV. 442
— (1818), IV. 442, 622
— (1837, 1838, 1848), IV. 422
— (1851, 1852), V. 658
— (1854), V. 829
— (1857), V. 660
— (1858), V. 829
— (1860), V. 660
— (1860), V. 829
— (1865, 1866, 1875, 1876, 1877), V. 658
— (1879) V. 658, 829
— (1880, 1881, 1882, 1883, 1884), V. 658
— (1885, 1887, 1888, 1889, 1890, 1891, 1892), V. 659
— (1893), V. 659, 829
— (1894), V. 659
— (1895, 1896, 1897), V. 659, 829
— (1898), V. 659
— (1899), V. 660
Cinderella and her Cruel Sisters (1861), V. 829
Cinderella and the Fairy Glass Sliper (James, C. S., 1850), V. 433
Cinderella and the Glass Slipper (Spry, H., 1878), V. 577
Cinderella and the Little Glass Slipper (Akhurst, W. M., 1873), V. 237
— (Green, F. W., 1882), V. 391
— (Hall, F., 1882), V. 399
— (1894), V. 660
Cinderella and the Sensation Slipper (Logan, W. H., 1861), V. 804
Cinderella in quite another Pair of Shoes (Green, F. W., 1871), V. 390
Cinderella, Ladybird, Ladybird, fly away home (Henry, R. and Scott, C. W., 1889), V. 418
Cinderella the First (Ward, A. H., 1892), V. 613

Cinderella the Second (Lawrence, S. B., 1893), V. 451
Cinderella, the Sweet Kitchen Belle (Conquest, G. and Spry, H., 1893), V. 322
Cinderella the Younger (Thompson, A., 1871), V. 597, 820
Cinderella up-to-date (R., E. S., 1897), V. 660
Cinder-Ellen, up too late (Leslie, F. and Vincent, W. T., 1891)
+ Cinders (Tinsley, Lily. *French*, 1899)
Cinna's Conspiracy (Cibber, C., 1713), II. 71, 368, 434, 447
Cinq-Mars (Maude, A. and Minton, M., 1883), V. 482
Cinthia and Endimion (D'Urfey, T., 1696), I. 48, 160, 337, 409
Circassian (Broughton, F. W., 1887), V. 281
— (Pratt, S. J., 1781) = Fair Circassian, III. 322, 394, 399
Circassian Bride (Ward, C., 1809), IV. 416
Circassian Chief and the Prophet's Son = Schamyl
Circassian Maid = Broken Chain
Circe (D'Avenant, C., 1677), I. 40, 82 135–6, 348, 357, 400
— = Lady's Triumph
Circle of Loda (Peacock, T. L.), IV. 369
Circlet of Gold (1863), V. 660
Circumstances alter Cases (Ascher, I. F., 1888), V. 244
— (Hoppin, W. J.), V. 426
— (1846), IV. 442
Circumstantial Effie Deans = Great Sensation Trial
Circumstantial Evidence (Barnett, M., 1851), V. 250
— (Carew, R., 1893), V. 303
— = Number Fifty One
Circus Girl = In the Ring
Circusiana (Cross, J. C., 1809), IV. 287
Circus Rider = Fair Equestrienne
Cissy = Love's Devotion
Cissy's Engagement (Lancaster-Wallis, E., 1895), V. 448
Citizen (Murphy, A., 1761), III. 118, 124, 181, 290, 392; IV. 144
— (1819), IV. 442
Citizen of Paris (Arnold, S. J., 1824), IV. 442, 622

Citizen Outwitted = Miraculous Cure

Citizen Pierre (Coghlan, C. F.), v. 316

Citizen Robespierre (Perth, and Condie, 1899), v. 520

Citizen's Daughter (1775), III. 322

— (1847), IV. 622

— = Mark Fresland

Citizen's Wife = Delicate Ground

Citizen turn'd Gentleman (Ravenscroft, E., 1672), I. 76, 83, 188, 254, 347, 348, 425-6

Cits and Sights = Lord Mayor's Day

City Apprentice (1840), IV. 442

City Association (1780), III. 322

City Besieged = Patriots

City Bride (Harris, J., 1696), I. 39, 54, 412

City Customs (1703), II. 368

City Farce (Weddell, Mrs, 1737), II. 363

City Festival = Lord Mayor's Day

City Friends (Collins, C. J., 1855), v. 660, 785, 829

City Games (Rede, W. L., 1833), IV. 607

City Guard (1883), v. 660

City-Heiress (Behn, A., 1682), I. 79, 224, 391

City Intrigue = Why did I marry?

City Lady (Dilke, T., 1697), I. 54, 56, 218, 403

City Madam (Love, J., 1771), III. 283

— (1844), IV. 442

City Match = Schemers

City Merchant (Clinton, J. W., 1841), IV. 577

City Nymph = Tender Husband

City of Pleasure (Sims, G. R., 1895), v. 569

City of Small Trades = Golden Hearts

City of Stars = Valley of Diamonds

City of the Plague (Wilson, J., 1816), IV. 422

City of the Plague and the Great Fire of London (1825), IV. 442

City Outcast (Ellis, B., 1892), v. 357

City Politiques (Crowne, J., 1683), I. 10, 23, 24, 56, 58, 271, 350, 399

City Prison (1861), v. 829

City Ramble (Knipe, C., 1715), II. 341, 375

— (Settle, E., 1711), II. 31, 266, 354

City Rivals (Kenney, J., 1814) = Debtor and Creditor, IV. 443, 622

City Wives = Lesson for Gentlemen

City Wives Confederacy = Confederacy

Ciudad Rodrigo (1812), IV. 443

Civilian (Ryley, S. W., 1789), III. 304, 395

Civilization (Wilkins, J. H., 1852), v. 623, 846

Civil War (Merivale, H. C., 1887), v. 487

Civil War of Poetry (Bolton, G., 1846), IV. 98, 443, 622

Civil Wars between York and Lancaster = Civil Wars in the Reign of King Henry VI

Civil Wars In the Reign of King Henry VI (Cibber, T., 1723), II. 313

Clachan of Aberfoil = Roy's Wife

Claimant (Grattan, H. P., 1871), v. 389

Claimants (Vezin, H., 1891), v. 608

Claire (Bernhardt-Fisher, Mrs, 1887), v. 259

— = Cash for Coronets

Clairval (1877), v. 660

Clairvoyance (1845), IV. 443

Clandestine Marriage (Colman, G. and Garrick, D., 1766), III. 51, 167-9, 182, 246

Clans of Yore = Caledonia

Claperton Chisel (1850), v. 660

Clara (1809), IV. 443

— = Prisoner

Clara Charette (Collier, J. W., 1849), IV. 281

Clara Vere de Vere (Rae-Brown, C., 1888), v. 533

Clare Cottage (James, S., 1888), v. 434

Clarence Clevedon, his Struggles for Life or Death (Stirling, E., 1849), IV. 409

Clari (Payne, J. H. and Planché, J. R., 1823), IV. 377, 605

Claribel's Mystery (Towers, E., 1865), v. 660, 821, 829

Clarice (Browne, G. W. and Roberts, F., 1886), v. 283

Clarice de Clermont (Naden, A. T., 1892), v. 501

Claricilla (Killigrew, T., 1641), I. 416

Clarissa (Buchanan, R., 1890), v. 285

— (Porrett, R., 1788), III. 72, 299

Clarissa Harlowe (?Lacy, T. H. and Courtney, J. or ?Reynoldson, T. H., 1846), IV. 340–1, 393
— (Wills, W. G., 1889), V. 628
— (1831), IV. 443
— (1847), IV. 443
Clarisse (Robertson, T. W., 1855), V. 660, 814, 829
— (Stirling, E., 1845), IV. 408
Clash of Steel (1894), V. 660
Classical Trip = Nicandra
Claude Duval (Bowyer, F. and Payne Nunn, 1894), V. 272
— (Burnand, F. C., 1869), V. 289, 781
— (Haines, J. T., 1841), IV. 323
— (Stephens, H. P., 1881), V. 580
— (Taylor, T. P., 1842), IV. 411
Claude Gower (Lancaster, E. R.), IV. 593
Claudian (Herman, H. and Wills, W. G., 1883), V. 419
Claudia's Choice (Neil, Ross, 1883), V. 502
Claudine (Dibdin, C. I. M., 1803), IV. 291
Claudine of Switzerland = Outcast of Lausanne
Claudio (Thurgood, A. V., 1888), V. 600
Clavidgo (Leftley, F., 1798), III. 63, 322, 390, 399
Clavigo (1847), IV. 443
— (1895), V. 660
Claychester Scandal = Intruders
Clean Sweep = Fluff
Cleanthes (Woodrooffe, S., 1826), IV. 422
Clean Your Boots (Bruton, J., 1858), V. 660, 781, 829
Clear ahead! (Clarke, C. A., 1885), V. 311
Clear Case (À Beckett, G. A., 1835), IV. 249
Clear Conscience (Walter, T. N., 1889), V. 612
Clearing the Toll = Lady Godiva and Peeping Tom of Coventry
Clear the Way (Harcourt, F. C., 1892), V. 403
Cleft Stick (Oxenford, J., 1865), V. 510
Clemence (Ebsworth, J.), IV. 309
Clementina (Kelly, H., 1771), III. 13, 15, 18, 47, 79–80, 278, 389

Clementina (Moncrieffe, E., 1892), V. 491
Clementine (1843), IV. 443
Clemenza (Ainslie, W., 1822), IV. 251
Clench and Wrench (1879), V. 660
Cleomenes (Dryden, J., 1692), I. 79, 145, 407
Cleon (Maltby, A., 1874), V. 473
— (Thom, R. W., 1855), V. 595
Cleone (Dodsley, R., 1758), II. 319; III. 9, 40, 43, 45, 49, 74, 257
Cleonice, Princess of Bithynia (Hoole, J., 1775), III. 59, 83, 197, 272
Cleopatra (Shirley, A., 1889), V. 564
Cléopatre, Reine d'Egypte (Aumer, 1825), IV. 569
Cleora (1736), II. 368
Clergy (1876) = Unequally Sentenced, V. 660, 762, 829, 848
Clergyman's Daughter (Tanner, J. T., 1896), V. 591
Clergyman's Widow and her Orphans = Faith, Hope and Charity
Clerical Error (Jones, H. A., 1879), V. 162, 439
Clerkenwell Election = Law versus Physic
Clerke's Well (1841), IV. 622
Clerk of Clerkenwell (Almar, G., 1834), IV. 253
Clerk of the Weather (Osborne, K. and Hodgson, A. H., 1892), V. 508
Clerkship and Cookery = Fish out of Water
Clever Alice (Thomas, B., 1893), V. 596
Clever Capture (Melford, M., 1890), V. 484
Cleverest Man in China = Shadows on the Water
Cleverest Man in Town = Amorel of Lyonesse
Cleverly Managed (Longmuir, A., 1887), V. 463
Clever People (Rose, E., 1889), V. 550
Clever Sir Jacob (Graves, A. P. and Toft, P., 1873), V. 389
Click Clack (Dibdin, C. I. M., 1804), IV. 291
Clifford Castle (1809), IV. 443
Cliff, Steine, and Level = Humours of Brighton

Climbing Boy (Peake, R. B., 1832), IV. 370

Clinton (Phillips, F. L., 1858), V. 660, 810, 829

Clio (Campbell, B., 1878), V. 301

Clip (1899), V. 660

Cliquot (1892), V. 660

Clito (Grundy, S. and Barrett, W., 1886), V. 396

Cloacina (Man, H., 1775), III. 286

Cloak and the Bonnet (1841), IV. 443

Cloches de Corneville (Farnie, H. B. and Reece, R., 1878), V. 362, 791

Clock-Case (1777), III. 322

Clock has Struck = (1) Demon of the Woods; (2) Wood Daemon

Clock House (Lee, N., 1840), IV. 594

Clock Maker (1892), V. 660

Clockmaker of Bishopgate (1860), V. 660

Clockmaker of Clerkenwell (1860), V. 660

Clockmaker of Mardyk = Old Father Time

Clockmaker's Daughter (1874), V. 660

Clockmaker's Hat (Robertson, T. W., 1855) = Betty Martin, V. 546

— = Sally Smart

Clock on the Stairs (Hazlewood, C. H., 1862), V. 412

Clock Struck Four = Murdered Maid

Clockwork (Reece, R., 1877), V. 538

Clodhopper's Fortune (1872), V. 660

Clodpole's Mistake (1818), IV. 443

Clod, the Bellows Mender = Lady of Lions

Clorinde's Revenge = Leontine

Cloris (Wycombe, M. and Shael, V., 1885), V. 633, 824

Close of the Poll = Humours of an Election

Close Shave (Speight, T. W., 1884), V. 575

— (Thalberg, T. B., 1895), V. 595

— = You mustn't laugh

Close Siege (Dance, G., 1839), IV. 289, 579

Closet Cordial = Married Man

Clotilda (1709), II. 229, 391

Cloud and Sunshine (Anderson, J. R., 1858), V. 240

Cloud and the Silver Lining = Phyllis Thorpe

Cloud King (Cross, J. C., 1806), IV. 286

Cloud of Life (Mead, T., 1859), V. 660, 806, 829

Cloud of Smoke (Squier, C., 1881), V. 577

Clouds (Bowkett, S., 1894), V. 271

— (Percival, A., 1872), V. 519

— (Theobald, L., 1715), II. 359, 444

— (White, J., 1759), III. 315

— (1885), V. 660

Clouds and Sunshine in a Life (Faucquez, A., 1862), V. 363

Clouds of Aristophanes (Cumberland, R., 1797), III. 252

Clouds of Sorrow and Rays of Sunshine = There are Secrets in all Families

Cloven Foot (Mouillot, F. and Steer, J., 1890), V. 498

Clown and the Captain (Dibdin, T. J., 1827) = Turn and Turn, IV. 305, 545 [Originally produced S.W. 26/7/1827]

Clown of China = Whang Fong

Clown's Chronology = April Fools

Clown's Fireside (1809), IV. 443

Clown's Stratagem (1730), II. 368

Clown's Trip to the Moon (1829), IV. 443

Clown turned Beau (1788), III. 322

Club (1891), V. 660

Club Baby (Sterner, L. and Knoblauch, E., 1895), V. 583

Club-men (Kirkman, F., 1662), I. 417

Club Night = Rum Ones

Club of Fortune Hunters (1748), II. 368

Clump and Cudden (Dibdin, C., 1785), III. 256

Cluricanne's Tower (Grover, J. H., 1871), V. 395

Clutch of the Law = Notice to Quit

Clutterbucks (Pocock, I., 1832), IV. 385

Clytemnestra (Galt, J., 1812), IV. 585

Clytie (Hatton, J., 1875), V. 409

Coach Drivers (1766), III. 322

Coal and Coke (Harding, C. and Swanborough, W. H., 1868), V. 403

Coalition (Graves, R., 1793), III. 265, 386

— (Macnally, L., 1783), III. 285

— (1779), III. 322

Coal-ition (Hardman, T. H. and North, H., 1881), V. 403

Coal Mine (Johnstone, J. B., 1867), V. 438, 800

Coals of Fire (Craven, H. T., 1871), v.
148-9, 329
Coast Blockade (Milner, H. M., 1826),
IV. 443, 622
Coastguard (Manning, J. C., 1884), v.
474
Coastguard of the Motherbank = Mark
the Smuggler
Coat of Many Colours (Ryley, M. L.,
1897), v. 554
Cobbler Conjurer (1854), v. 660
Cobbler of Coblentz (Blanchard, E. L.,
1840), IV. 573
Cobbler of Cripplegate = Lucky Stars
Cobbler of Munich (1831), IV. 443
Cobbler's Apprentice of Whitechapel
(Thorne, R. L., 1847), IV. 413
Cobbler's Daughter (Lane, Mrs S.,
1878), v. 448
Cobbler's Hut (Tennant, C., 1841), IV.
614
Cobbler's Luck = Love and Leather
Cobler (Dibdin, C., 1774), III. 119, 202,
254, 381
— (1733), II. 368
Cobler and Lottery Ticket (1787), III.
322
Cobler of Castlebury (Stuart, C., 1779),
III. 310
Cobler of Preston (Bullock, C., 1716),
II. 48, 133, 140, 211-12, 301
— (Johnson, C., 1716), II. 48, 53, 140,
211-12, 339
— (1732), II. 368
Cobler of Preston's Opera = Cobler of
Preston
Cobler's Opera (Ryan, L., 1728), II.
135, 137, 353
Cobler's Stratagem = Matching for
Money
Cobwebs (Wills, C., 1880), v. 626
Cocard et Bicoquet (1888), v. 660
Cock-a-doodle-doo (Millward, C.,
1865), v. 489
Cockney Caliph (Douglass, J. T., 1866),
v. 348
Cockney Farmer = In the Spider's Web
Cockney Gleanings = Home Circuit
Cockney Sportsman = Tithe Sheaf
Cocknies Bit = Country Wedding
Cocknies in California (Coyne, J. S.,
1849), IV. 443, 622

Cock of the Walk = Year in an Hour
Cockorico (1841), IV. 443
Cock Robin and Jenny Wren (Gilling-
ton, C., 1891), v. 381
Cockshott Yeomanry = Our National
Defences
Cocorico (Hazlewood, C. H., 1873), v. 414
Cocq du Village (D'Auberval, 1784), III.
253
Cocum (1882), v. 660
Codrus (Ramsbottom, D., 1774), III.
322, 394
Coelina (Lucas, H., 1795), III. 283
Coercion (Denny, W. H. and Burnside,
T., 1886), v. 342
Cœur de Lion (Cooke, C., 1876), v. 323
— = Richard I
Cœur de Lion Revised, and his Enemies
Corrected (Strachan, J. S., 1870), v. 585
Coffee House (Miller, J., 1738), II. 13,
146, 181, 203, 233, 237, 344, 441
— (1760), III. 322, 399
— = (1) Knavery in all Trades; (2)
Tarugo's Wiles
Coffee-House Politician = (1) Generous
Husband; (2) Rape upon Rape
C[ogglesha]ll Volunteer Corps (1804),
IV. 443
Coiner of Symon's Yat = Grace Clair-
ville
Coiners (Lacy, M. R., 1833), IV. 340, 592
Coiner's Dream (Fitzroy, C. N. T.,
1890), v. 369
Cola's Fury (Burkhead, H., 1645), I. 394
Colberg = House of Colberg
Colin and Susan (1794) = Speechless
Wife, III. 322, 399, 404
Colin's Welcome (O'Keeffe, J., 1770),
III. 292
Collaborators (Chambers, C. H., 1892),
v. 307
— (Kilmarnock, Lord, 1897), v. 444
Collars and Cuffs (French, H. P., 1883),
v. 373
Colleen Bawn (Boucicault, D., 1860), v.
69, 86, 87, 268
— (Byron, H. J. 1870), v. 297
— = Bride of Garryowen
Colleen Bawn settled at last (Brough,
W. and Halliday, A., 1862), v. 279, 780
Colleen Dhas = Ghost Hunter
Colleen Glas (Logue, J. D., 1875), v. 462

College Chums (Kenney, C. H., 1895), v. 443

College Friends (1856), v. 660

+Collegian (Smock Alley, Dublin, 17/4/1776)

Collier Boy (1895), v. 660

Collier's Daughter (Bosworth, H., 1873), v. 267

Collier's Wife (Beverley, H. R., 1869), v. 261

Collision in the Mersey = Cry in the Darkness

Colomba (Hueffer, F., 1883), v. 429

Colomba, the Corsican Sister (1846), IV. 443

Colombe's Birthday (Browning, R., 1844), IV. 272; v. 20, 283

Colombina (1735), II. 368

Colombine Cameron = (1) Harlequin Incendiary; (2) Harlequin Invader

Colombine-Courtezan = Cupid and Psyche

Colombine in her Teens = Harlequin Captain Flash

Colombine Made Happy at Last = Escapes of Harlequin by Sea and Land

Colombine turn'd Elephant = Harlequin in the City

Colonel (Burnand, F. C., 1881), v. 291

— (1830), IV. 443

— (1894), v. 660

Colonel and the Soldier = Martial Law

Colonel Blood (1846), IV. 443

Colonel Bombomb (1893), v. 660

Colonel Gardiner (Barham, F. F., 1823), IV. 569

Colonel Jack (Coates, A., 1863), v. 784

— (Towers, E., 1860), v. 660, 821, 830

Colonel of Hussars = Libertine of Poland

Colonel's Belle (White, R. M., 1846), IV. 419

Colonel's Choice = Three and One

Colonel's Come (Dibdin, C. I. M., 1825), IV. 295

Colonel's Contrivance = Soldier's Stratagem

Colonel Sellers (Twain, Mark, 1874), v. 605

Colonel Split-Tail (1730), II. 368

Colonel's Tactics (1889), v. 660

Colonel's Wife (Reid, B. and Smith, L., 1888), v. 541

Colonel, the Captain and the Corporal = Broken Promises

Colonists (Ravani, E. C., 1895), v. 535

— = America

Colorado Beetle (Minto, W., 1877), v. 490

Coloured Commotion (1852), v. 660

Colour Sergeant (Thomas, B., 1885), v. 184, 595

Columbine (1717), II. 447 [This is evidently the same as Harlequin turn'd Judge, II. 374]

Columbus (Morton, T., 1792), III. 34, 50, 99, 101, 120, 288

— (Thompson, A., 1869), v. 597, 820

Comala (Burrell, Lady S. R., 1793), III. 72, 241

— (1792), III. 322

Comb-seller of Victoria Park = Mysteries of Shoreditch

Come and See (Langsdorff, 1814), IV. 341

Comedy and Tragedy (Gilbert, W. S., 1884), v. 380

— = Tragedy Queen

Comedy and Tragedy of War = Tit for Tat

Comedy Farce (1864), v. 660

Comedy in Embryo = Sir Harry Gaylove

Comedy of 1854 = John Bull

Comedy of Errors (Hull, T., 1779), III. 274

— (Kemble, J. P., 1811), IV. 335

— (Reynolds, F., 1819), IV. 392

— (1762), III. 322

— = Twins

Comedy of Sighs (Todhunter, J., 1894), v. 600

Comedy of Terrors (1855), v. 830

— = Nap

Comedy of Trifles (Beach, W., 1899), v. 253

Come Here (Daly, A., 1876), v. 333

Come if you can (Dibdin, T. J., 1824), IV. 304

Come of Age (1837), IV. 443

+Comet (Dibdin, C. I. M., 1797)

— (Moser, J., 1807), IV. 364

— (1789), III. 322

— (1832), IV. 443

— (1835), IV. 443

87

Completely Successful (1827), IV. 443

Compliment of the Season = Valentine

+Compliments of the Season (Planché, J. R.: *Dicks* (1868, in *Pieces of Pleasantry*)

Composer (Chapman, A., 1891), V. 308

Compromise (Sturmy, J., 1722), II. 178, 358

Compromising Case (Smale, Mrs T. E., 1888), V. 571

Compromising Coat (Grein, J. T. and Jarvis, C. W., 1892), V. 394

Compromising Letters = Who is Sarah?

Comrades (Thomas, B. and Stephenson, B. C., 1882), V. 595

— (1848), IV. 443

Comrades and Friends (Pocock, I., 1831), IV. 385

Comrades in Arms (1894), V. 661

Comrades in Khaki (Brookfield, C. H. E., 1899), V. 277

Comus (Colman, G., 1772), III. 246

— (Dalton, J., 1738), II. 37, 138, 260, 317, 435

— (1815), IV. 443

Concealed Royalty (Carleton, R., 1674), I. 395

Conceited Ladies (Foote, S., 1762), III. 384

Conceited Travellers = Careless Lovers

Conclave del 1774 (1774), III. 322

Condemned (Knowles, E., 1887), V. 445

— (Manning, W., 1878), V. 474

Condemned Duke (1861), V. 661

Condemned House and the Diet of Ratisbon = White Wolf

Condé's Wife (Smibert, T., 1843), IV. 402

Confederacy (Vanbrugh, Sir J., 1705), I. 32; II. 133, 135, 137, 145, 151, 362, 445

— (1827), IV. 443

Confederates (Breval, J., 1717), II. 213, 299

— (Woodville, H., 1897), V. 631

— = Jealousy

Confederate's Daughter (Hazlewood, C. H., 1865), V. 661, 796, 830

Confession (Cumberland, R., 1813), IV. 287

— (Reynoldson, T. H., 1858), V. 661, 813, 830

Confession (Whyte, 1799), III. 316

— (1883), V. 661

— = (1) Ellen; (2) Octavia Bragaldi

Confidence (Boucicault, D., 1848), IV. 270

— (Cantwell, R. F., 1872), V. 302

— (1893), V. 661

Confidential (1894), V. 661

Confidential Clerk (Wilson, S. and Wittman, S., 1886), V. 629

Confined in Vain (Jones, T., 1805), IV. 334

Conflict (Brand, H., 1798), III. 117, 239

Conflagration of Moscow = Buonaparte's Invasion of Russia

Confounded Foreigners (Reynolds, J. H., 1838), IV. 393

Confusion (Derrick, J., 1883), V. 343

— (Moore, F. W., 1876), V. 492

— (1842), IV. 87, 443

Confusion Worse Confounded = Patrician and Parvenu

Congenial Souls (Ryley, J. H., 1878), V. 554

Congress (1878), V. 661

Congress at Paris (Rose, E., 1878), V. 549

Congress of Critics (1783), III. 323

Congress of the Beasts (1748), II. 368

Coningsby (1845), IV. 443

Conjectures (1830), IV. 444

Conjugal Lesson (Danvers, H., 1856), V. 336

Conjurer's Bastard = Devil of a Duke

Conjuror (Andrews, M. P., 1774), III. 232

— (McLaren, A., 1781), III. 284

— (1815), IV. 444

Conjuror's Wife = Legerdemain

Conlath of the Isles (1827), IV. 444

Conn (Green, F. W., 1879), V. 391

Connaught Wife (Ryder, T., 1767), III. 323, 395

Connemara (Chute, J., 1880), V. 310

Connoisseur (Conolly, 1736), II. 159, 160, 316

Con O'Carrolin's Dream = Fairy Circle

Conquered Coquette = Fair Sicilian

Conquered Pride (Mackenzie, R. and Gover, F., 1886), V. 471

Conquering Game (Bernard, W. B., 1832), IV. 265

Conspiracy = (1) Cromwell; (2) Richelieu

Conspiracy against Peter the Great = Natalia and Menzikof

Conspiracy Discovered (1746), II. 368

Conspiracy of Copenhagen = Bertrand and Burkenstaff

Conspiracy of Genoa = Fiesco

Conspiracy of Gowrie (Roscoe, W., 1800), III. 323; IV. 609

Conspiracy of Kamtschatka = Count Benyowsky

Conspiracy of Querini (1837), IV. 622

Conspirator in spite of himself (Coape, H. C., 1852), V. 315

Conspirators (1749), II. 368

— = Bravo and the Venetian Conspirators

Constable Jack (Rodney, S., 1889), V. 548

Constance (Robertson, T. W., 1865), V. 546

Constance Frere (Gough, H. and Edwards, M., 1887), V. 386

Constancy (Barnard, C., 1892), V. 249

— (Hallward, C., 1898), V. 401

Constancy unto Death = Warning Dream

Constant Couple (Carter, J., 1788), III. 242

— (Farquhar, G., 1699), I. 12, 246, 338, 411; II. 147

Constant Couple Rewarded = Emperor of China Grand Volgi

Constant Follower (1866), V. 661

Constantia (Hughes, Mrs A., 1790), III. 274

— (Neale, F., 1852), V. 501

Constantine (Francis, P., 1754), III. 208, 261

— (1898), V. 661

Constantine and Valeria (Dibdin, T. J., 1817), IV. 159, 300

Constantine Paleologus (Baillie, J., 1804), IV. 159, 258

Constantine the Great (Lee, N., 1683), I. 147-8, 419

— = Constantine

Constant Lady = Generous Free-Mason

Constant Lover Rewarded = Mistake

Constant Lovers (Duncan, G., 1798), III. 258

Constant Lovers (1714), II. 368

— (1719), II. 368

— (1734), II. 451

Constant Maid (1787), III. 323

— = Love will finde out the Way

Constant Nymph (1677), I. 101, 138, 440

Constant Quaker (1748), II. 451

Constellations and Cauliflowers (1823), IV. 444

Consul in England = Britons to Arms

Consultation (1705), II. 22, 368

— = Six Physicians

Contempt of Court (Boucicault, D., 1879), V. 269

— (Matthison, A., 1877), V. 481

Contending Brothers (Brooke, H., 1778), III. 240

Contending Colombines = Beggar's Pantomime

Contending Deities (1733), II. 368

Contented Cuckold (Bourne, R., 1692), I. 392

— (1763), III. 323

— = Inconsolables

Contention for the Laurel = Battle of the Poets

Contention of York and Lancaster = Richard, Duke of York

Contested Election (Taylor, T., 1859), V. 593

Contest of Beauty and Virtue (Arne, T. A., 1772), III. 69, 234

Contest of the Aonides = Apollo's Choice

Contraband Captain (Corri, M., 1835), IV. 578

Contrabandist (1847), IV. 444

Contrabandista (Burnand, F. C., 1867), V. 289

Contract (Cobb, J., 1779), III. 243, 379

— (Francklin, T., 1775), III. 118, 261, 385

— (Hiller, H. C., 1887), V. 421

— (Houlton, R., 1782), III. 273 [The date of revival is 19/5/1784]

— (1736), II. 368

— (1899), V. 661

Contract of St Cloud (Blake, T. G., 1846), IV. 268

Contractor (Dabbs, G. H. R., 1887), V. 332

Contradictions (Leigh, A.), v. 453

Contrarieties (1817), IV. 444

Contrariety (Tomlinson, ?1792), III. 312

Contrary Winds (Wood, F., 1882), v. 630

Contrast (Hoadly, J., 1731), II. 337

— (Smith, E., ?1790), III. 308

— (Waldron, F. G., 1775), III. 313, 397

— (Wilton, 1789), III. 316

— (1752), III. 323

Contre Temps (1727), II. 14, 233, 266, 368

Contrivances (Carey, H., 1715), II. 241, 246, 301, 432

— (Lancaster, E. R.), IV. 593

Conundrums (1827), IV. 444

Convenient Distance! = Omnibus!

Convenient Son-in-law (1877), v. 661

Convent (Rannie, J., 1806), III. 300

— (1832), IV. 444

Convent Belle (Bayly, T. H., 1833), IV. 444, 622

Convent Belles = Carmelites

Convent Maid = Kitty

Convent of a Pleasure (Cavendish, M., 1668), I. 396

Convent of St Bartholomew = Agatha

Conversation of a Father with his Children (1792), III. 325

Conversion of England (Creswell, H., 1885), v. 330

Convert (Garnett, C., 1898), v. 376

Converted Twins = Saint Cecily

Converts = (1) Folly of Priest-Craft; (2) Pandora

Convict (Neville, H., 1868), v. 502

— (Sheil, R. L., 1822) = Huguenot, IV. 444, 622

— (Stephenson, C. H., 1868), v. 582

— (1838), IV. 444, 622

Convict Brothers (Mead, T., 1853), v. 483

Convicted = Iron True

Convict of Munich = Genevra, the Scourged One

Convict of Toulon = Prisoner of Toulon

Convict's Career = Only for Life

Convict's Child = Life as it is!

Convict's Daughter (1881), v. 661

Convict's Escape (Marchant, F., 1864), v. 805

Convict's Flight = Blood demands its Victim

Convicts 48 and 49 (1895), v. 661

Convict Ship (1826), IV. 444

Convict's Return (1859), v. 661

Convict Steward = Lisle Wilton

Convict's Vengeance = (1) Chain Gang; (2) Harold Hawk

Convict's Vow = Lawless Witness

Convict's Wife = (1) Marah; (2) On the Track

Convict 33 (1894), v. 661

Cook (1824), IV. 444

Cook and the Secretary (1833), IV. 444

Cooke's Folly (Featherstone, J., 1840), IV. 312

Cookettish Cook (Scarlett, W., 1895), v. 557

Cook in a Stew = Out of his Element

Cooking and Copying = Cupboard and the Cabinet

Cook of Kennington (1846), IV. 444

Cool as a Cucumber (Jerrold, M. W. B., 1851), v. 436

Cooleen Drawn (Dutnall, M. and Johnstone, J. B., 1861), v. 352

Cooper (Arne, T. A., 1772), III. 121, 199, 377, 234

Cooper and Brass (1850), v. 661

Co-operative Movement (Lemon, H., 1868), v. 454

Cooper Deceiv'd (1748), II. 369

Copper and Brass (1850), v. 661

Coquet (Molloy, C., 1718), II. 146, 157, 173, 345, 419, 441; III. 116

— (Storace, S., 1771), III. 310, 396

Coquet at her Wit's End = Impertinent Lovers

Coquet's Surrender (1732), II. 369

Coquette (Dam, H. J. W. and Bingham, G. C., 1899), v. 335, 787

— (Hitchcock, R., 1776), III. 269

— (Mead, T., 1867), v. 483

— (Pattinson, R. E., 1892), v. 515

— (Poel, W., 1892), v. 529

— (Smart, H., 1885), v. 571

— (1761), III. 323

— (1792), III. 323

Coquette Cured = Annie of Edenside

Coquette et les Jaloux (1734), II. 369

Coquettes (Houston, Lady), III. 273

Coquilla (1848), IV. 444

Corsican "Bothers" (Byron, H. J., 1869), v. 297

Corsican Brother-babes-in-the-wood (Sims, G. R., 1881), v. 568

Corsican Brothers (Almar, G., 1852), v. 240

— (Boucicault, D., 1852), v. 84, 86, 267

— (Bradberry, C. S., 1888), v. 272

— (O'Neill, J. R.), v. 808

— (1852), v. 661

— = Vendetta

Corsican Brothers and Co., Limited (Burnand, F. C. and Stephens, H. P., 1880), v. 291

Corsican Conscript = Theodore the Brigand

Corsican Maid (1849), IV. 445

— = Laelia, the Queen of the Hills

Corsican Pirate (Cross, J. C., 1803), IV. 286

Corsicans (Leftly, C.), IV. 343

— (Sala, 1853), v. 555

— (1796), III. 65, 122, 323, 399

Corsican's Revenge = Vendetta

Corsican Vendetta (1897), v. 661

Cortez (Burges, Sir J. B., 1817), IV. 277

— (Helme, E., 1800), IV. 324

— (Planché, J. R., 1823) = Hernando Cortez, IV. 377, 478, 605

— (Wallace, Lady E.), III. 314

Corydon and Cochrania (Pennecuik, A., 1732), II. 348

Cosaque (Grundy, S., 1884), v. 396, 795

Così fan tutte (Browne, M. E., 1890), v. 781

Cosimo (1838), IV. 445, 623

Cosmo de' Medici (Horne, R. H., 1837), IV. 205, 328

Cosmo, Duke of Tuscany (Bird, J., 1822), IV. 199–200, 267

Cossack and No Cossack = Irish Girl

Cossacks (1854), v. 661

Coster Baron (Pleon, H., 1897), v. 528

Coster Girl = Lucky Walker

Coster's Christmas Eve (1897), v. 661

Coster's Holiday = 'Endon Way

Coster's Son (1895), v. 661

Coster Twin Brothers (Hall, F., 1880), v. 399

Cottage (Smith, J., 1796), III. 308

Cottage and the Court (1839), IV. 445

Cottage Festival (Macnally, L., 1796), III. 285

Cottage Foundling (Kean, 1811), IV. 591

Cottage in the Holly (1872), v. 661

Cottage Maid (Sicklemore, R., 1798), III. 307

— (1791), III. 323

Cottage of Love (Oxenford, J., 1845), IV. 367

Cottage of Roses = Gipsy Girl

Cottage of the Cliffs (Rannie, J., 1806), III. 300

Cottage of the Lake (1820), IV. 445

Cottage on the Cliff = Marriage Bells

Cottagers (Brunton, A., i.e. Ross, A., 1788), III. 240, 303

— (Carey, G. S., 1766), III. 197, 242

— (Goodenough, R. J., 1768), III. 265

Cotton Famine (1869), v. 661

Cotton King (Vane, S., 1894), v. 606

Could the Murder? (Dibdin, T. J., 1825) = Black Caesar, IV. 445, 623

Council of Constance = Jewess

Council of Ten (Dibdin, C. I. M., 1811), IV. 292

— (Milner, H. M., 1829), IV. 445, 623

— = Venetian

Council of Three = Red Mask

Counsel for the Defense (1895), v. 661

Counsel's Opinion (Bingham, F., 1898), v. 261

Count Alarcos (Disraeli, B., 1839), IV. 307

Count and his Companions = Lone Chateau

+ Count and the Secretary (*French*)

Count Arezzi (Landor, R. E., 1824), IV. 199, 341

Count Basil (Bailie, J., 1798), III. 224–6, 235; IV. 157

Count Benyowsky (Render, W., 1798), III. 65, 301, 394

— (Thompson, B., 1800), IV. 412

Count Bertram (1823), IV. 445

Count Clermont (Bell, A., 1841), IV. 264

Count d'Alren = Honour

Count de Denia (Hoskins, W. H., IV. 328

Count de Foix (Powell, T., 1842), IV. 387

Count de Villeroi (Haggitt, J., 1794), III. 32, 54, 323, 386

Count Egmont (1848), IV. 445

Country Innocence (Leanerd, J., 1677), I. 264, 269, 410

Country Knight (1675), I. 440

— = Countrey Wit

Country Lass = Mountebank

Country Lasses (Johnson, C., 1715), II. 16, 136, 139–40, 196–7, 211, 339; III. 115–16, 188, 389

Country Mad-Cap in London (1770), III. 323

Country Miss with her Furbeloe = Old Mode & the New

Country Painters (1788), III. 323

Country Poet = Young Hypocrite

Country Quarters (Pocock, I., 1831), IV. 385

Country Revel = Countrey Revell

Country Revels (1732), II. 369

— = (1) Harlequin Restored; (2) Maid of the Mill

Country Squire (Dance, C., 1837), IV. 288, 445 [The play acted at the Olym. is identical with that given at C.G.]

— (Gwinnet, R., 1732), II. 178, 334

— (1859), V. 662

— = Love in a Wood

Country Squire Outwitted = Harlequin turn'd Philosopher

Country-Wake (Doggett, T., 1696), I. 261, 403; II, 434

— (Underwood, T., 1782), III. 313

— = (1) Flora; (2) Hob

Country Wedding (1740), II. 369

— (1749), II. 369

— (1750), III. 323

— = (1) Acis and Galatea; (2) Roger and Joan; (3) Wedding

Country-Wedding and Skimmington = Wedding

Country Wife (Lee, J., 1765), III. 114, 280

— (Wycherley, W., 1675), I. 2, 13, 187, 188, 201, 238, 345, 346, 439; II. 142; III. 45, 114, 163, 170, 205

Country Wit = Countrey Wit

Count's Treasure = Clarice de Clermont

County (Burney, E. and Benham, A., 1892), V. 293

County Concert = Sharps, Flats and Naturals

County Councillor (Graham, H., 1891), V. 386

County Fair (Bernard, C., 1897), V. 259

Coup de combat (1889), V. 662

Coup de Main (McLaren, A., 1783, 1816), III. 284; IV. 351

Coupe Gorge (1836), IV. 445

Couple of Thieves (1865), V. 662

Courage (Gascoigne, H., 1886), V. 376

Courage and Constancy (1766), III. 399

Courage and Liberty = Britannia Rediviva

Courage Rewarded (1798), III. 19, 323

Courier (1851), V. 662

Courier of Lyons (Reade, C., 1854), V. 536

— (Webster, B. N., 1851), V. 618

+ — (acted at Stand. 10/3/1851; printed by *French*)

— (1854), V. 662

— (1891), V. 662

Courier of Strasbourg (1861), V. 662

Courier of the Czar (Marston, H., 1877), V. 478

— (Osborne, C., 1877), V. 508

Course of Comic Lectures = Orators

+ Course of True Love (Emson, F. E., 8°, ?1877)

Court and Camp = Fan-Fan the Tulip

Court and City (Peake, R. B., 1841), IV. 371

Court and Cottage (Taylor, T., 1861), V. 593

Court and Country (1743), II. 369

C[ourt] and Country (1735), II. 262, 369

Court and No Country (1753), III. 323

Court Ball in 1740 (1845), IV. 445

Court Beauties (Planché, J. R., 1835), IV. 380

Court Cards (Simpson, J. P., 1861), V. 567

Court Delinquent (Trueba, J. T. de, 1834), IV. 615

Courtesans (Townley, C., 1760), III. 312

Court Favour (Planché, J. R., 1836), IV. 380

Court Favourites (1847), IV. 445

Court Fool (Burton, W. E., 1833), IV. 80, 277, 575

Court Gallantry = Comical Lovers

Court Gallants (Selby, C., 1863), V. 560

Court Guide (+ Selby, C., 1848), IV. 446; V. 815

Courtiers sent back with their Bribes = Honest Electors

Courting by Mistake (Moncrieff, W. T., 1831), IV. 446, 623

Courting by Proxy = Miss Wright

Courting in the Newspapers = Wives by Advertisement

Court Jester (Mathews, C. J., 1832), IV. 354

Court Lady = Coquet's Surrender

Court Legacy (Manley, Mrs M., 1733), II. 343

Court Masque (Planché, J. R., 1833), IV. 380, 605

Court Medley (1733), II. 369, 372

Courtnay Earl of Devonshire (?1705), II. 369

Court of Alexander (Stevens, G. A., 1770), III. 309

Court of Apollo (1790), III. 323

Court of Augustus Caesar = Gloriana

Court of Babylon = Chaste Susanna

Court of Flora (Woodrooffe, S., 1826), IV. 422

Court of Honour (Lart, J. and Dickinson, C. H., 1897), v. 449

Court of James III = Feudal Times

Court of King Charles and the Cheateries of Mulled Sake = Puritan's Plot

Court of Lions (Gilbert, H. P.,), v. 378

Court of Love = Cupid and Folly

Court of Nassau (Stayley, G., 1753), III. 309

Court of Neptune = Albion

Court of Oberon (Yorke, E., 1831), IV. 422

Court of Old Fritz (Smith, J. F., 1838), IV. 446, 623

Court of Pekin = Wild Islanders

Court of Queen Anne (Moncrieff, W. T., 1834), IV. 446, 600, 623

— = Foreign Affairs

Court of Queen's Bench (1832), IV. 446

Court of St Mary Axe = King, Queen and Knave

Court of Spain (Townsend, W. T., 1839), IV. 414

Court of the Googoos = Buz buz

Court of Tuscany (1822), IV. 446

Court of Vignolia = His Majesty

Court Page = Court Gallants

Courts and Alleys of London (1864), v. 662

Court Scandal (Boucicault, A. and Shillingford, O., 1899), v. 267

Court Secret = Promotion

Courtship (Byron, H. J., 1879), v. 114, 299

Courtship a la Mode (Crauford, D., 1700), II. 27, 28, 154-5, 316

+ Courtship a-la-mode (Bethune, G., 8°, 1831)

Courtship and Congreves = Angels and Lucifers

Courtship and Matrimony in 1712 = Lady Mary Wortley Montague

Courtship of Morrice Buckler (Mason, A. E. W. and Bateman, I., 1897), v. 480

Court, the Prison and the Scaffold (Bell, R., 1874), v. 256

Cousin Adonis (Wooler, J. P., 1865), v. 632

Cousin Campbell's Courtship (Collier, W., 1843), IV. 446, 623

Cousin Charlie (Latimer, K. M., 1889), v. 449

Cousin Cherry (Spicer, H., 1848), IV. 405

Cousin Dick (Prinsep, V., 1879), v. 531

Cousin from Australia (Blackburn, S., 1898), v. 262

Cousin Grace (Dilley, J. J. and Clifton, L., 1884), v. 662, 784, 788, 830

Cousin Jack (Vezin, H., 1891), v. 608

Cousin Johnny (Nisbet, J. C. and Rae, C. M., 1885), v. 504

Cousin Joseph (Oxenford, J., 1835), IV. 446, 623

Cousin Kate (1863), v. 662

— = One of Our Girls

Cousin Lambkin (Morton, J. M., 1842), IV. 362

+ Cousin Letty (*French*)

Cousin Matthew (1848), IV. 446

Cousin Peter (Wilks, T. E., 1841), IV. 421

Cousins (Aideé, H., 1882), v. 236

— (1878), v. 662

— (1893), v. 662

Cousin's Courtship (Collette, M., 1892), v. 317

Cousin Tom (Roberts, G., 1863), v. 544, 814

Couzin Zach (Gardner, H., 1883), v. 376

Covenanters (Dibdin, T. J., 1835), IV. 305
— (1825), IV. 623
— =(1) Battle of Bothwell Brig; (2) Drumclog
Covent Garden Ball (1894), V. 662
Covent Garden Theatre (Macklin, C., 1752), III. 284, 391
Covent-Garden Tragedy (Fielding, H., 1732), II. 265, 325, 436
Coventry Act (Plumptre, J., 1792), III. 298
Covers for Three (1854), V. 662
Coward Conscience (Byrne, C. A. and Wallack, A., 1888), V. 295
Cowardly Foe (Miller, W. F., 1892), V. 489
Cowardy, Cowardy Custard (1836), IV. 446
Cowardy Cowardy Custard ate his Father's Mustard (Thorne, R. L., 1851), V. 599
Cowboy and the Lady (Fitch, C., 1899), V. 367
Cow Doctor (1810), IV. 446
Cox and Box (Burnand, F. C. and Morton, J. M., 1867), V. 289
Coxcombs (Gentleman, F., 1771), III. 112, 264
Coy Shepherdess (Aston, A., 1709), II. 4, 224–5, 295
Cozened Cousins (1850), V. 662
Cozeners (Foote, S., 1774), III. 175, 260
Cozening (Beazley, S., Jr., 1819), IV. 263
Cozy Couple (Lewes, G. H., 1854), V. 106, 458
Cracked Heads (Hay, F. and Clements, A., 1876), V. 411
Cracked Piece of China = Ching-Chow-Hi
Cracker Bon-Bon for Christmas Parties (Brough, R. B., 1852), V. 278
Crack Shot = Red House
Cradle (Mattos, A. T. de, 1893), V. 481
Cradle of Crime = True till Death
Cradle of Steam = Marion Delorme
Craft (Sketchley, A., 1882), V. 571
Craftsman (Mottley, J., 1728), II. 346
Cramond Brig (Murray, W. H., 1826), IV. 365
— (1831), IV. 446
Crank the Clockmaker (1846), IV. 446

Crazed (Phillips, A. R., 1887), V. 522, 810
Crazy Jane (Somerset, C. A., 1827), IV. 304
— (1805), IV. 446
Crazy Old Slippers (1828), IV. 446
Crazy Old Slippers of Bagdad = Bakarak, the Miser
Cream White Woman (Chapman, S. H., 1825), IV. 576
Creatures of Impulse (Gilbert, W. S., 1871), V. 136–7, 379
Credit (À Beckett, G. A., 1844), IV. 250
Credulity (McLaren, A., 1823), IV. 352
Credulous Cuckold = Debauchee
Credulous Don = Impostors
Credulous Husband (1747), II. 369
— (1766), III. 323
Credulous Knight (Millett, 1800), IV. 599
Credulous Man = Quacks
Creeping Shadows (Stanhope, B., 1887), V. 579
Cremation (Height, R., 1879), V. 416
Cremorne (Palmer, T. A., 1876), V. 512
Creole (Brooks, C. W. S., 1847), IV. 105, 271, 574
— (Farnie, H. B. and Reece, R., 1877), V. 362, 813
Creole of St Louis (1862), V. 662
Creole's Daughter = Heart that can feel for another
Creon, the Patriot (Smith, J., 1828), IV. 446, 623
Crëusa, Queen of Athens (Whitehead, W., 1754), III. 71, 315, 398
Crew of the Bright Blue Wave = Union Jack
Crichton (?Ducrow, A. or ?Wilks, T. E., 1837), IV. 308, 446, 623 [There is some doubt about the authorship of this piece: the correct date is 3/7/ 1837]
— (Edgar, R. H., 1871), V. 354
— (1839), IV. 446
Crichton of Clunie (Wilks, T. E.), IV. 421 [where the title is given wrongly as Chrichton]
Cricket Match (+Anderson, J. R., 1850), V. 662
— (Leslie, A., 1870), V. 456

97

Crom-a-boo' (Dibdin, C. I. M., 1825), IV. 296

Cromwell (Duckworth, W., 1870), V. 351

— (Leigh, J. M., 1838), IV. 343

— (Phillips, F. L., 1859), V. 522

— (Richards, A. B., 1847), IV. 394

Cromwell in Scotland = Miller of Fife

Cromwell's Conspiracy (1660), I. 440

Cromwell's Own = Greatest Puritan

Croohove of the Bill-Hook (1828), IV. 446

Crooked Brothers of Damascus = Three Crumps

Crooked Mile (Lemore, C., 1885), V. 455

Crooked Paths (Dawson, L., 1888), V. 339

Crooked Ways (1866), V. 662

— (1875), V. 662

— (1882), V. 662

Croquet (Le Clercq, P., 1868), V. 452

— (Shenton, J., 1877), V. 562

Crosby Ravensworth (Pitt, G. D., 1846), IV. 374

— (1861), V. 662

Cross and the Crescent (Bandmann, D. E., 1876), V. 248

Cross-bow Letter (1854), V. 662

— =(1) Duchess of —!; (2) Miller of Whetstone

Crossed in Love (1880), V. 662

Cross for Valour = Bunch of Shamrocks

Crossing Sweeper (Hood, B., 1893), V. 425

Crossing the Frontier = Flying Colours

Crossing the Line (Almar, G., 1833), IV. 252

Cross of Blood = Armourer of Paris

Cross of Death (Neale, F., 1848), IV. 365

Cross of Gold = Veteran of the Old Guard

Cross of Honour = False Witness

Cross of Olga (Castleton, R. and Gurney, G., 1896), V. 306

+ Cross of St John's (Lucas, W. T., French)

Cross on the Boot = Snow Drift

Cross Partners (1792), III. 118, 323, 386, 388, 399

Cross Purposes (O'Brien, W., 1772), III. 119, 291, 393

— (Parselle, J., 1865), V. 515

Cross Purposes (1878), V. 662

— (1891), V. 662

Cross Roads (Sargent, J., 1885), V. 556

Cross Roads of Life = Scamps of London

Cross Strokes (Niel, C., 1894), V. 504

Crotchet Hall (1852), V. 662

Crotchet Lodge (Hurlstone, T., 1795), III. 275

Crotchets (Hay, F., 1876), V. 411

Crowded House (1877), V. 663

Crowded Houses = Crossing the Line

Crowded Villa (1841), IV. 623

Crown Brilliants (Long, C., 1846), IV. 83, 346

Crown Diamonds (Reynoldson, T. H., 1844), IV. 83, 393

— (1847), IV. 83, 446

Crown for Love (Evelyn, J., 1874), V. 359

Crown Jewels (Fitzball, E., 1846), IV. 83, 317

— =(1) Blood Royal; (2) Catarina; (3) Nigel

Crown of Thorns = Love King

Crown Prince (Wilks, T. E., 1838), IV. 420

— (1848), IV. 466

Cruel Alternative = Woman's Vengeance

Cruel Brother (Travers, W., 1864), V. 663, 830

Cruel Carmen (Jones, J. W., 1880), V. 440

Cruel City (Warden, G. and Jones, J. W., 1896), V. 613

Cruel Corsair and the Marble Maid = Zampa

Cruel Destiny (Carr, W., 1899), V. 304

Cruel Father (Reading, E., 1885), V. 536

Cruel Gift (Centlivre, Mrs S., 1716), II. 74, 80–1, 305

Cruel Heritage = Flash in the Pan

Cruel Husband = Injur'd Love

Cruel Kindness (Crowe, C., 1853), V. 330

Cruel Law (Craven, W. S., 1895), V. 329

Cruel London (Harvey, F., 1887), V. 408

Cruel Test (Hall, R. W., 1881), V. 400

Cruelties of the Dutch = Amboyna

Cruel to be kind (Williams, T. J. and Harris, A. G., 1860), V. 625

Cruelty of the Spaniards in Peru (D'Avenant, Sir W., 1658), I. 29, 60, 286, 401

Cupid and Hymen (Hughes, J., 1735), II. 338

Cupid and Psyche (Burnand, F. C., 1864), v. 288

— (Mason, W.), III. 286

— (Righton, M., 1895), v. 543

— (1714), II. 451

— (1734), II. 136, 369

— (1848), IV. 447

Cupid and the Giant = Fairy of the Fountain

Cupid and the Princess = Amour mouille

Cupid and the Woodcutter (1813), IV. 447

Cupid Astray (1892), v. 663

Cupid from Jewry (Mason, J. A., 1897), v. 480

Cupid in Brighton (Phillips, E., 1848), IV. 372

Cupid in Camp (Vernon, G. C., 1882), v. 608

— (1897), v. 663

Cupid Incog. (Vanderbilt, C., 1888), v. 606

Cupid in Disguise (Fitzball, E., 1825), IV. 313

Cupid in Ermine (Lancaster-Wallis, E., 1899), v. 447

Cupid in London (Rede, W. L., 1835), IV. 390

Cupid in Plush (1869), v. 663

Cupid in Waiting (Jerrold, M. W. B., 1871), v. 436

Cupid of Clerkenwell = Gipsey Daughter

Cupid Pilgrim (1789), III. 324

Cupid's Blunders (Morris, F., 1892), v. 493

Cupid's Coach (1899), v. 663

Cupid's Diplomacy (1840), IV. 447

Cupid's Frolic (Field, W. F., 1889), v. 366

— = Lilliputian Sports

Cupid's Frolics (Macfarren, G., 1831), IV. 597

Cupid's Gift (1795), III. 324

Cupid's Ladder (Buckingham, L. S., 1859), v. 286

Cupid's Messenger (Calmour, A. C., 1884), v. 300

Cupid's Mistake (1898), v. 663

Cupid's Odds and Ends (Lewis, C., 1895), v. 459

Cupid's Revenge (Gentleman, F., 1772), III. 264

Cupid's Triumph (1740), II. 369

Cupid's Vagaries = Sacrifice

Cupid turned Physician (Stafford, J. J., 1831), IV. 447, 623

Cupid Wanderer (1818), IV. 447

Cup of Cold Poison = (1) Romeo and Juliet; (2) Villikins and his Dinah

Cup of Cowld Poison = Loves of Willikind and his Dinah

Cup of Tea (1866), v. 663

Cup of Water (Field, M., 1887), v. 366

Cups and Saucers (Grossmith, G., 1878), v. 395

Cur (Howe, J. B., 1891), v. 428

Curate (Challis, R., 1886), v. 307

— (1888), v. 663

Curate's Daughter (1859), v. 663

— = Life of a Woman

Cure for a Coxcomb (1792), III. 324, 379, 382, 400

Cure for a Mother-in-Law (1885), v. 663

Cure for a Scold (Worsdale, J., 1735), II. 364

— = (1) Merlin's Cave; (2) Whitsun Monday

Cure for Coquettes = Alma Mater

Cure for Covetousness (1733), II. 369

Cure for Coxcombs (1821), IV. 447, 623

Cure for Credulity = Impostors

Cure for Cuckoldom = Rival Queens

Cure for Dotage (1771), III. 324

Cure for Dumbness = Irish Doctor

Cure for Foolery (Jones, E. J. and Brashier, H., 1888), v. 439

Cure for Hysterics = Prescription

Cure for Jealousie (Corye, J., 1699), I. 398; II. 155, 316

+ Cure for Jealousy (Este, William. Smock Alley, Dublin, 13/3/1740)

— = Double Deceit

Cure for Love (Parry, T., 1842), IV. 368

— = (1) Man with the Nose; (2) Modern Receipt

Cure for Romance (Thomson, J., 1819) = Love's Labyrinth, IV. 413, 496, 631

Cure for the Fidgets (Williams, T. J., 1867), v. 625

Cure for the Gout (1859), v. 663

— = Paddy Bull

8

Cure for the Heart-Ache (Morton, T., 1796), III. 142–3, 289
— (1812), IV. 447
Cure of Pride (?1680), II. 441
Curfew (Tobin, J., 1807), IV. 164, 413
Curia (1822), IV. 447
Curio (1892), V. 663
Curiosities of Literature (Boucicault, D., 1842), IV. 447, 573, 623
Curiosity (Clarance, J., 1847), IV. 280
— (Derrick, J., 1886), V. 343
— (Lathom, F., 1801), IV. 341
— (Oulton, W. C., 1786), III. 296
— (1798), III. 64, 324, 400
— (1849), IV. 447
Curiosity Cured (Buckstone, J. B., 1825), IV. 272
Curious Case (Reynoldson, T. H., 1846), IV. 393
Curious Coincidence (1887), V. 663
Curious Cure (1897), V. 663
Curious Curse Curiously Cured = Sir Jack o' Lantern, the Knight of (K)nights
Curious Husband = Amorous Prince
Curious Impertinent = Married Beau
Curious Will = Oakwood Hall
Curling Irons and Capers (1868), V. 663
Current Cash (Clarke, C. A., 1886), V. 311
Current Coin (Cross, J., 1878), V. 330
Curse = (1) Caleb; (2) Pride; (3) Waconsta
Curse Entailed = Basil and Barbara, Children of the Bottle
Curse of Avarice = Treacherous Uncle
Curse of Disobedience (1861), V. 663
Curse of Drink = (1) Assommoir; (2) Intemperance
Curse of Drunkenness = Ten Nights in a Bar-room
Curse of Jealousy = Othello of Private Life
Curse of Kavanagh (Dibdin, C. I. M., 1826), IV. 296
Curse of Kin = Philomel
Curse of Mammon (1839), IV. 447
Curse of St Vallier (1840), IV. 447
— = Francis I
Curse of Scotland = Q. of Diamonds
Curtain Lecture = Recrimination
Curtain Lectures = Mrs Caudle
Cushla-ma-Cree (Levey, J. C., 1873), V. 458

Custom House (Montague, L. A. D., 1892), V. 491
Custom of Dunmow = Flitch of Bacon
Custom of the Country = Bickerstaff's Burying
Custom of the Manor (1766), III. 324
— = Country Lasses
Custom's Fallacy (Grant, J. M., 1805), IV. 320
Customs of the Castle = Cottage Maid
Customs of the Country (1856), V. 663
Cut and come again (Soutar, R., 1879), V. 575
Cut Blooms = Our Lodger
Cut for Partners (Bruton, J., 1844), IV. 272
Cutlet for Two (1848), IV. 447
Cut Miser (Tighe, E., 1788), III. 312
Cut off with a Shilling (Smith, S. T., 1871), V. 573
Cutter of Coleman-street (Cowley, A., 1661), I. 38, 68, 211, 398
Cut your Coat according to your Cloth = Biter Bit
Cybele (Cross, J. C., 1808), IV. 286
Cycling (Chevalier, A., 1888), V. 309
Cyclist (1899), V. 663
Cyclopædia (Hoper, Mrs, 1748), II. 337
Cymbeline (Brooke, H., 1778), III. 57, 240
— (Eccles, 1793), III. 57, 258
— (Garrick, D., 1761), III. 57, 262
— (Hawkins, W., 1759), III. 57, 267
— (Kemble, J. P., 1802), IV. 335
Cymbeline, King of Britain (Marsh, C., 1756), III. 57, 286
Cymbra (Paulton, H., 1883), V. 516
Cymon (Garrick, D., 1766), III. 26, 114, 202, 263, 385
— (1792), III. 324
— (1813), IV. 447
Cymon and Iphigenia (Planché, J. R., 1850), V. 527
— (1790), III. 324
— (1795), III. 324
— (1864), V. 663
Cynick (1731), II. 369
Cynic's Defeat (Thompson, A., 1878), V. 597
Cynthia's Sacrifice (Drew, E., 1893), V. 351
Cyrene (Calmour, A. C., 1890), V. 300

Damp Beds (Parry, T., 1832), IV. 368

Damp Fire (1842), IV. 448

Danaides (Hoguet, 1845), IV. 447, 623

— =Hypermnestra, the Girl of the Period

Dan and Dick (Gough, H. and Edwards, M., 1887), V. 386

Dance of the Shirt (Morton, T., Jr., 1848), IV. 364

Dancing Barber (Selby, C., 1838), IV. 398

Dancing Dervish (Peile, F. K., 1894), V. 518

Dancing Dolls (D'Arcy, G., 1872), V. 787

Dancing Europeans = Difference of Nations

Dancing for Life (Kenney, J., 1834), IV. 337

— =Halt of the Ballet

Dancing Girl (Jones, H. A., 1891), V. 169–70, 187, 440

Dancing Mad =(1) Diable à Quatre; (2) Magic Pipe

Dancing Master (Pemberton, M. and Wellings, M., 1889), V. 518

— (1815), IV. 447

Dancing Master's Ball = Tigers of Paris

Dancing-Master's Lesson (1855), V. 663

Dancing Scotchman (1855), V. 663

Dandelion's Dodges (Williams, T. J., 1867), V. 625

Dandolo (Stirling, E., 1838), IV. 406

Dandy Dan, the Lifeguardsman (Hood, B., 1897), V. 425

Dandy Dick (Pinero, Sir A. W., 1887), V. 175–6, 525

Dandy Dick Turpin (Thorne, G., 1889), V. 598

Dandy Dick Whittington (Sims, G. R., 1895), V. 569

Dandy Drenched = Bride and Bridegroom

Dandy Family and the Ascot Jockies (Moncrieff, W. T., 1818), IV. 358

Dandy Fifth (Sims, G. R., 1898), V. 570

Dane's Dyke (Bright, Mrs A., 1881), V. 275

Danes in the Dumps = Breeze in the Baltic

Danger (Davis, A., 1873), V. 338

Danger (Horncastle, 1879), V. 426

— (Rayner, A., 1868), V. 535

Danger Ahead (1888), V. 663

Danger and Fatality = Alone in the Pirate's Lair

Dangerfield '95 (Dowling, M. T., 1898), V. 349

Danger of Being Wise in a Commonwealth of Fools = Socrates Triumphant

Danger of Presumption = Frankenstein

Danger on the Line (1884), V. 663

— = Railroad of Life

Dangerous (Osborne, C., 1873), V. 508

Dangerous Complaint = I'd be a Butterfly

Dangerous Curiosity and Justifiable Homicide = Bluebeard

Dangerous Friend (Oxenford, J., 1866), V. 510

Dangerous Game (Roberts, Sir R., 1885), V. 545

Dangerous Neighbourhood (1806), IV. 447

Dangerous Path (Reade, C.), V. 812

Dangerous Playthings (1862), V. 663

Dangerous Ruffian (Howells, W. D., 1895), V. 429

Dangerous Women (Scudamore, F. A., 1898), V. 559

Danger Signal (Bryant, E., 1867), V. 284

— = For Life

Dangers of London (Scudamore, F. A., 1890), V. 559

Dangers of Science (Courtney, G. F., 1896), V. 326

Dangers of the Express (1876), V. 663

Dangers of the Gin Palace = Glass

Danicheffs (Shirley, A., 1883), V. 563

Daniel (More, Mrs H., 1782), III. 288

— (Scott, J., 1873), V. 558

Daniel Bartlett (1881), V. 663

— = Deputy Sheriff

Daniel Daisytop's Delight = Dan'l's Delight

Daniel Day and the Faust Child (Johnstone, J. B., 1848), IV. 333

Daniel in the Lion's Den (1793), III. 324

Daniel O'Connell (Levey, J. C., 1880), V. 458

— (Robertson, J., 1882), V. 545

Daniel O'Rourke (1826), IV. 447

Danischeffs (Newry, Lord, 1877), V. 503

Danish Invasion = (1) Alfred the Great; (2) Osburga; (3) Streanshall Abbey

Danish Pirates = Ethelwolf

Danish Wife (Macfarren, G., 1831), IV. 350

Danites (?Howard, B., 1880), V. 664, 830

— (Miller, J., 1877), V. 488

Dan'l Bruce, Blacksmith (Gilbert, W. S. 1876), V. 380

Dan'l's Delight (Armstrong, A., 1893), V. 243

Dan'l Tra-Duced (Clements, A., 1876), V. 314

Dante (Dabbs, G. H. R. and Righton, E., 1890), V. 332

Dan the Outlaw (Robertson, J., 1888), V. 545

Daphne (Huntley, F., 1895), V. 431

Daphne and Amintor (Bickerstaffe, I., 1765), III. 40, 198, 237, 377

Daphne and Apollo (Rich, J., 1726), II. 253, 443

Daphnis (1892), V. 664

Daphnis and Amaryllis (Harris, J., 1762) = Spring, III. 213, 266, 324, 386

Daraxes (Hill, A., 1760), II. 438; III. 268

Darby and Joan (Bellingham, H. and Best, W., 1885), V. 257

— (Rogers, W., 1851), V. 664, 814, 830

— (1801), IV. 447

— (1802), IV. 447

— (1827), IV. 447

Darby Captain = Eunuch

Darby in America (1792), III. 400

Darby Kelly (1843), IV. 623

Darby's Return (Dunlop, 1789), III. 258

Dare-devil (Campbell, A. V., 1835), IV. 278

— (Shirley, A. and Leonard, H., 1894), V. 564

Dare-Devil Dick (1861), V. 664

Dare Devil Max (Brabner, W. A., 1899), V. 272

Daring Brigands = Perilous Cavern

Daring Device (Dancy, A. T., 1879), V. 336

Darius (1784), III. 324

Darius, King of Persia (Crowne, J., 1688), I. 14, 124, 151, 332, 356, 400

Darius, King of Persia = Noble Englishman

Dark Assassin = Maniac

Dark before Dawn (1871), V. 664

— (1875), V. 664

Dark Blue Waters (1862), V. 664

+ Dark Bungalow; or, 'Is his Appointment Pucka?' (Trevelyan, G. O.: 8°, 1869 (in *Ladies in Parliament and other Pieces*: acted privately at the residence of the Lieutenant-Governor of Bengal))

Dark Cloud (Sketchley, A., 1863), V. 570, 816

Dark Continent (Mouillot, F. and Morell, H. H., 1891), V. 498

Dark Days (Carr, J. W. C. and Conway, H., 1885), V. 304

— (1884), V. 664

Dark Deed in the Woods = Jasper Roseblade

Dark Deeds (Fairbairn, Mrs R., 1881), V. 359

Dark Deeds and Doings in London = Shoals and Quicksands

Dark Deeds of a Coal Pit = Collier's Wife

Dark Deeds of Bluegate Fields = Bob Lumley's Secret

Dark Deeds of London (1882), V. 664

Dark Deeds of Night = Ivan the Terrible

Dark Deeds of Old London = Adam Winter, the Fiend of Private Life

Dark Deeds of the Devil's Grip = Fred Frolic

Dark Dens of the City = Red Lamp

Dark Diamond (1832), IV. 448

Dark Doings in the Closet by the Knotting 'em Brothers (Coyne, J. S., 1864), V. 328

Dark Donald, the Idiot of the Cliff (Atkyns, S., 1848), IV. 257

Dark Duel in the Wood = Aurora Floyd

Darkest Hour (Adams-Acton, Mrs, 1895), V. 235

— (1897), V. 664

Darkest London (Stanhope, B., 1891), V. 579

— = My Maggie

Dark Events (1839), IV. 448

Dark Falcon (1846), IV. 448

Dark Glen of Bally Foihl (Stirling, E., 1871), V. 584

Dark Gondola = Tower of Nesle

Dark Hearts = Night Porter

Dark Horse (Garston, C., 1868), v. 376

Dark Hour (St Aubyn, D., 1877), v. 554
— = Break of Morn

Dark Hour before Dawn = Sister's Wrongs

Dark House (1859), v. 664

Darkie that walked in her Sleep = Nigger's Opera

Dark King of the Black Mountains (Hazlewood, C. H., 1866), v. 664, 796, 830

Dark Knight and the Fair Lady = Ah! what a Pity!!!

Dark Lady of Doona (Almar, G., 1840), IV. 568

Darkness Visible (Hook, T. E., 1811) = Four in hand, IV. 328, 463, 589

Dark Night's Bridal (Buchanan, R., 1887), v. 285

Dark Night's Work (Marchant, F., 1865), v. 664, 805, 830
— = Giralda

Dark Page (Breare, W. H., 1885), v. 274

Dark Pandour (1828), IV. 448

Dark Past (Price, F., 1890), v. 530

Dark Secret (Willing, J. and Douglass, J., 1886), v. 626

Dark Shadows and Sunshine = Wild Gipsy Girl

Dark Shadows and Sunshine of Life (Donald, J., 1857), v. 664, 788, 830

Dark Side of London Life = Toilers of the Thames

Dark Side of our Great City = London by Night

Dark Side of the Great Metropolis (Travers, W., 1868), v. 603

Dark Spirit of the Dismal Swamp = Nick of the Woods

Dark's the Hour before the Dawn = Eileen Oge

Dark Turnings in Life = Redemption

Dark Woman (Young, Mrs H., 1861), v. 664, 825, 830

Darnley (Graham, D., 1900), v. 386

Darnley, the Knight of Burgundy (1830), IV. 448

Darthula (Mylne, J., 1790), III. 290

Dash (Lathom, F., 1804), IV. 342

Dash for Freedom (Roy, G., 1884), v. 552

Dashing Dick Turpin (Stanhope, B., 1892), v. 579

Dashing White Sergeant (Barber, J., 1847), IV. 569

Dash of the Day (Lathom, F., 1799), III. 280; IV. 341

Daughter (Bayly, T. H., 1835), IV. 263, 571
— (Knowles, J. S., 1836), IV. 173, 339
— (Pocock, I., 1815) = Magpie or the Maid, IV. 448, 623
— = Sighs

+ Daughter in Law (Seymour, M., French)
— = Vicissitudes

Daughter of Air (1800), IV. 448

Daughter of England (Dundas, H. and Shelley, H., 1896), v. 352

Daughter of Erin = Biddy O'Neal

Daughter of Eve (Meritt, P., 1877), v. 486

Daughter of Fire (Barnett, C. Z., 1845), IV. 260
— = Alina

Daughter of Ghent = Witch of the White Hoods

Daughter of Ishmael = Miriam Gray

Daughter of Midnight (Marchant, F., 1863), v. 664, 830

Daughter of Night (Seaman, W., 1856), v. 664, 815, 830

Daughter of St Mark (Bunn, A., 1844), IV. 276

Daughter of the Air (1831), IV. 448

Daughter of the Danube (Osman, W. R., 1873), v. 508
— (1837), IV. 448
— (1868), v. 664

Daughter of the Deep = Black Fisherman

Daughter of the Million (1899), v. 664

Daughter of the People (Harvey, F., 1891), v. 408
— (1860), v. 664
— (1898), v. 664

Daughter of the Regiment (Archer, T., 1848), IV. 255
— (Davenport, 1848), IV. 448, 623
— (Fitzball, E., 1843), IV. 316, 584
— (Fitzball, E., 1847), IV. 317

Daughter of the Regiment (Weil, O., 1890), v. 619
— (Wigan, H., 1859), v. 622
— (1855), v. 664
— = Fille du Regiment
Daughter of the Stars (Brooks, C. W. S., 1850), v. 277
Daughter of the Tumbrils (Grogan, W. E., 1897), v. 395
Daughter of the Wolf (Travers, W., 1865), v. 822
Daughter of Truth = Truth
Daughters (Warren, T. G. and Edouin, W., 1890), v. 615
Daughter's Courage = Heroine
Daughter's Devotion = Chain of Gold
Daughter's Error = Pride and Patience
Daughter's Honour (Landeck, B. and Shirley, A., 1894), v. 447
Daughters of Babylon (Barrett, W., 1897), v. 251
Daughters of Danaus (Dibdin, T. J., 1821), IV. 303
Daughters of Robert Macaire = Illustrious Chief
Daughters of the Guadalquiver (1858), v. 664
Daughter's Sacrifice (Doone, N., 1888), v. 347
— = (1) Clara Charette; (2) Love's Sacrifice; (3) Riches and Poverty
Daughter's Secret (Peel, G., 1874), v. 518
Daughter's Trial = Henry Dunbar
Daughter's Vow = Nymph of the Grotto
Daughter to Marry (Planché, J. R., 1828), IV. 84, 378
— (1827), IV. 448
— (1837), IV. 448
— = My Daughter, Sir
Dauntless Boy of the Lake = White Spirit
Dauntless Decius, the Doubtful Decemvir = Julius See-Saw
Davenport Brothers & Co. (Pemberton, T. E., 1879), v. 519
Davenport Done (Colomb, 1867), v. 318
Davey Crockett (Dizance, F., 1873), v. 346
David (Parker, L. N. and Carson, S. M., 1892), v. 513

David and Goliath (More, Mrs H., 1782), III. 288
David and his Wives (1894), v. 664
David Copperfield (1870), v. 664
— (1892), v. 664
David Copperfield the Younger of Blunderstone Rookery (1850), v. 664
David e Bersabea (1734), II. 392
David Garrick (Colnaghi, C. P. and Ponsonby, E., 1888), v. 318
— (Robertson, T. W., 1864), v. 123–4, 126, 127, 546
David Hunt (Pitt, G. D., 1845), IV. 374
David Morgan, the Jacobite (1872), v. 664
David Rizzio (Hamilton, R., 1820), IV. 324
David's Lamentation over Saul and Jonathan (Lockman, J., 1736), II. 392, 440
— (1740), II. 392
Davis and Sally Dear (Bruton, J., 1842), IV. 272, 574
Davy Crockett (Murdoch, F. H., 1872), v. 499
— (1875), v. 664
Davy Garrick (1898), v. 664
Davy Jones (Barrymore, W., 1830), IV. 448, 623
Davy Jones's Locker (1812), IV. 448
— (1825), IV. 448
— = Ocean Sylph
Davy Jones, the Merman of the Sea (Dorrington, W., 1858), v. 788
Dawn (Thomas, G. and Oswald, F., 1887), v. 596
Dawning of Peace = Female Volunteer
Dawn of Christianity = For the Cross
Dawn of Hope (Burnette, C. and Cooper, H. B., 1896), v. 293
Dawn of Love (Ross, R., 1885), v. 551
Day after the Fair (Somerset, C. A., 1829), IV. 16, 132, 404
— (1826), IV. 448
Day after the Wedding (Kemble, M. T., 1808), IV. 145, 335
Day after Tomorrow = Old Bachelor
Day and Night (1815), IV. 448
— = Shadowed
Day and Night Adventures of Logic, Tom and Jerry = Life in London

Day and Night Scenes of Tom and
Jerry = Life in Dublin

Day at an Inn (Hook, T. E., 1823), IV.
328, 589

Day at Boulogne (1860), v. 664
— = Master's Rival

Day at Donnybrook (1865), v. 664

Day at Coney Island = Surprises

Day at Dover (1845), IV. 448

Day at Gretna Green = Blacksmith

Day at Rome (Smith, C., 1798), III. 308

Daybreak (Willing, J., 1884), v. 626
— (1895), v. 664

Day by Day = Judgment

Day Dream (Courtney, J., 1846), IV. 283

Day Dreams (Hawthorn, M., 1888), v.
410

— (Leighton, Sir B., 1875), v. 454, 803

— (Swears, H., 1894), v. 589

Daye and Knight (Parke, W., 1895), v.
512

Dayes of Olde (Jarman, F., 1892), v.
434

Day in Algiers = Medicus Borealis

Day in Boulogne (Grain, R. C., 1882),
v. 387

— (Law, A.), v. 450

— (1899), v. 664

Day in France = Master's Rival

Day in High Life (1860), v. 664

Day in Kingsbury Castle (Ashdown,
C. H., 1899), v. 244

Day in London (Cherry, A., 1807), IV.
280

Day in Paris (Selby, C., 1832), IV. 397

— = Lost, Stolen or Strayed

Day in Spain = Masquerade

Day in the Country (1817), IV. 448

Day in the Dockyards = Czar

Day in Turkey (Cowley, Mrs H., 1791),
III. 249

Day in Wales = Cottage Festival

Day near Turin (Maberley, Mrs, 1841),
IV. 349

Day of Atonement (1899), v. 664

Day of Disasters (1860), v. 664, 790

Day of Dupes = Quid pro Quo

Day of Economy = Locked Up

Day of Numa Pompilius = Golden
Shield

Day of Reckoning (Planché, J. R., 1850),
v. 527

Day of Reckoning (1891), v. 664

— (1894), v. 664

Day of Taste (1760), III. 324

Day of Tribute = Kamtchatka

Day's Adventure at Little Snuggleton =
Who's your Hatter?

Days and Knights of the Round Table
= King Arthur

Day's Courtship = Tunbridge-Wells

Day's Fishing (Morton, J. M., 1869), v.
496

Day's Fun (1828), IV. 448

Days of Athens (Ducrow, A., 1831), IV.
307

Days of Charlemagne = Four Sons of
Aymon

Days of Charles II = Whitefriars

Days of Chivalry (1841), IV. 448

Days of Cromwell (Rogers, C. and
Livesey, C., 1896), v. 548

— = Regicide

Days of Edward IV (1835), IV. 448

Days of Ferdinand Cortez = Conquest
of Mexico

Days of Good Queen Bess = Kenilworth

Days of Hogarth (1857), v. 664

Days of Jezebel (Bayne, P., 1872), v. 253

Days of Louis XV (1863), v. 665

— = (1) Armand; (2) Fan-Fan the
Tulip

Days of Old (1797), III. 400

— (1812), IV. 448

Days of Oliver Cromwell (1847), IV. 623

Days of Prince Rupert = Siege of
Liverpool

Days of Queen Bess = (1) Earl of Essex;
(2) Elizabeth and Essex; (3) Kenilworth Castle; (4) Mysterious Freebooter

Days of Terror (Clarke, C. A., 1891), v.
312

— (1896), v. 665

— = (1) Chevalier de Maison Rouge
and Marie Antoinette; (2) Chevalier
of the Moulin Rouge

Days of the Commonwealth = Oliver
Cromwell

Days of the Curfew Bell = William the
Conqueror

Days of the French Revolution = Life's
Revenge

Days of the Plantagenets = Fair Rosamond

Days of the Second Charles = Ye Merrie England

Days of William the Conqueror = Saxon Maid

Days of Yore (Cumberland, R., 1795), III. 106, 252

— = (1) Battle of Hexham; (2) Fairy Records

Day's Pleasure = John Buzzby

Day's Sport (Grain, R. C., 1889), v. 387

Days to come (Dawson, F., 1893), v. 339

Day's Training (1839), IV. 448

Days we live in (McLaren, A., 1805), IV. 351

Day to Day (Clarke, C. A., 1889), v. 312

Day up the River (1829), IV. 448

— = Midgelet

Day well Spent (Oxenford, J., 1836), IV. 367

Day will come (Mackay, W. J., 1892) = The Shadow of the Rope, v. 470

Day Witness = Cross of Death

Deacon (Jones, H. A., 1890), v. 162, 440

Deacon and her Deputy = Scotch Marriage Laws

Deacon Brodie (Stevenson, R. L. and Henley, W. E., 1882), v. 583

Dead (Scott, J., 1891), v. 558

Dead Alive (O'Keeffe, J., 1781), III. 200, 292; IV. 145

— (1819), IV. 448

— = Caliph and the Slave

Dead Alive Again (Collingwood), III. 245

Dead and Buried (1827), IV. 448

Dead and Not Dead (McLaren, A., 1821), IV. 352

Dead and the Living (1855), v. 665

Dead Beat (Conquest, G. and Comer, G., 1885), v. 322

Dead Boxer (1875), v. 665

Dead, Buried and Up Again = Life in an Hotel

Dead Calm (Douglass, J. T., 1868), v. 348

Dead Duchess (Seaman, W., 1856), v. 665, 815, 830

Dead Guest (Peake, R. B., 1834), IV. 370

— (Phillips, F. L., 1863), v. 664, 810, 830

Dead Hand (Travers, W., 1861), v. 665, 821, 830

Dead Hand and the Hour of One = Rightful Heir

Dead Heart (Phillips, W., 1859), v. 523

— (Pollock, W. H., 1889), v. 529

Dead Heat (Cooke, St C., 1891), v. 324

Dead in the Streets = Found Dead in the Streets

Dead Letter (Brabner, W. A., 1891), v. 272

— (Roberts, W., 1873), v. 545

— (1862), v. 665

Deadlock (Cowis, D. and Batson, J. H., 1898), v. 327

Deadlock Mystery = Only a Waif

Deadly Foes (Fiddes, J., 1868), v. 365

Deadly Reports (Simpson, J. P., 1857), v. 567

Deadly Sampson (Akhurst, W. M. and Twigg, J., 1876), v. 237

Deadly Weapons (Lawrence, W., 1884), v. 451

Dead Man's Cliff (1896), v. 665

Dead Man's Gold (Conquest, G. and Spry, H., 1887), v. 322

Dead Man's Hollow (Wardhaugh, M., 1869), v. 614

Dead Man's Point (Burnand, F. C., 1871), v. 290

Dead-Man's Wedding = Hanging and Marriage

Dead Men's Shoes (Milner, H. M., 1829), IV. 357

— (1894), v. 665

Dead Men taken Prisoner = Green Dragon

Dead Men Tell No Tales (1863), v. 665

Dead Mother's Letter = Paul the Showman

Dead o' Night Boys (Branson, W. S., 1874), v. 274

Dead or Alive (Taylor, T., 1872), v. 594

Dead or Not Dead (1829), IV. 448

Dead Past (Fryers, A., 1895), v. 374

— (1884), v. 665

Dead Reckoning (Hazlewood, C. H., 1868), v. 413

— = Jezebel

Dead Secret (Bramwell, E. W., 1877), v. 273

Dead Shot (Buckstone, J. B., 1827), IV. 273

Dead Take In (Wigan, A. S., 1850), V. 621

Dead to the World (Conquest, G. and Pettitt, H., 1875), V. 321

Dead Wife (1838), IV. 448

Dead Witness (Reeve, W., 1863), V. 150, 540

— (1889), V. 665

— = Frozen Stream

Dead Woman's Secret (1861), V. 665, 830

— = (1) Gunsmith of Orleans; (2) Love's Victory

Deadwood Dick (Korrell, P., 1894), V. 446

Deaf and Dumb (Holcroft, T., 1801), IV. 326

— (Thompson, B., 1800), IV. 412

— (1801), IV. 448

Deaf and Dumb Boy = Dumb Boy

Deaf and Dumb Orphan = Julio of Harancour

Deaf as a Post (Poole, J., 1823), IV. 386

Deaf Doctor = Device

Deaf Indeed (Topham, E., 1780), III. 312

Deaf Lover (Pilon, F., 1780), III. 187, 297

Deal Boatman (Burnand, F. C., 1863), V. 288

Dealings with the Firm of Gasup and Harris (1846), IV. 448

Dean of Hazeldene (Dryden, J. P., 1889), V. 351

Dean's Daughter (Grundy, S. and Philips, F. C., 1888), V. 160, 205, 397

Dear Departed (Parke, W., 1890), V. 512

Dearer than Life (Byron, H. J., 1867), V. 297

Dearest Anna Maria (Hatch, P. H., 1851), V. 409

Dearest Elizabeth (Oxenford, J., 1848), IV. 449, 602, 623

Dearest Mama, my Mother-in-Law (Gordon, W., 1860), V. 385

Dear Girls = Lilies

Dear Jack (Giraud, Mrs, 1892), V. 382

Dear Neighbours (Blouet, P., 1885), V. 266

Dear Old Flag (1896), V. 665

Death and Glory = (1) England and Glory; (2) Idle Words

Death and Liberty = Charter

Death and Rachel (Graves, C., 1890) = Rachel, V. 665, 794

Death and the Doctor (Peake, R. B., 1835), IV. 370

Death and the Lady (1851), V. 665

Death at the Stake (James, C. S., 1849), IV. 330

Death by the Law (Towers, E., 1876), V. 601

Death Dealer (1840), IV. 449

Death Doom (1843), IV. 449

Death Fetch (Buckstone, J. B., 1826), IV. 272

— (Milner, H. M., 1826), IV. 449, 623

— (1832), IV. 449

— = Bertha Gray, the Pauper's Child

Death Hand (Taylor, T. P., 1842), IV. 411, 614

Death in the Streets (1864), V. 665

Death Kiss (Seaman, W.), V. 815

Death Light (Almar, G.), IV. 253

Death of Abel (Shoberl, F., 1806), IV. 610

Death of Abercromby (Astley, P., Jr., 1801), IV. 256

Death of Achilles = Rival Father

Death of Adam (Lloyd, R., 1763), III. 61, 282, 390

Death of Alexander the Great = Rival Queens

Death of Bucephalus (Schomberg, R., 1765), III. 304, 395

— = Alexander and Statira

Death of Bucephalus the Great = Rival Favourites

Death of Caesar (1823), IV. 449

Death of Captain Cook (1789), III. 324

Death of Captain Faulknor (1795), III. 324

Death of Christophe, King of Haiti (Amherst, J. H., 1821), IV. 253

+ Death of Darnley (Sotheby, W. in Tragedies, 1814)

Death of David Rizzio (Dibdin, T. J. ? 1795), III. 382

Death of Dido (Booth, B., 1716), II. 259, 299

Death of Dion (Harwood, T., 1787), III. 267

Debauch'd Hypocrite = Trick for Trick
Debauchee (Behn, A., 1677), I. 222, 390
Debauchees = Old Debauchees
Debo-Lear (Hazlewood, C. H., 1864), v.
665, 830
Deborah (Cheltnam, C. S., 1864), v. 309
— (Conquest, G., 1864), v. 665, 830
— (Fielding, H., 1733), II. 326
— (Humphreys, S., 1733), II. 392, 439
— (Mitchell, L. E., 1893), v. 490
Debt (De Pass, E. A., 1872), v. 342
— (1873), v. 665
Debt and the Duel = Husbands and
Wives
Debt of Honour (Broughton, F. W.,
1879), v. 281
— (Colnaghi, G. P., 1891), v. 318
— (Ryves, E.), III. 304
Debtor and Creditor (Kenney, J., 1814)
= City Rivals, IV. 336, 443, 592
Debts of Honour (Poel, W., 1893), v.
665, 811, 830
Debutante (1867), v. 665
— (1893), v. 665
— = First Night
Debutante's Test = Come here
Deceit (Norris, H., 1723), II. 347
Deceitful Steward (1807), IV. 449
Deceived (1882), v. 665
Deceived One = Mary May
Deceiver (McLaren, A., 1816), IV. 351
Deceiver Deceived (Pix, Mrs M., 1697),
I. 225, 266, 424
— (1826), IV. 449
— = Maid or Wife
Deceivers Ever (Salaman, M. C., 1883),
v. 555
December and May (Dimond, W.,
1818), IV. 307
Deception (De Frece, M., 1871), v.
341
— (Longmuir, A., 1889), v. 463, 804
— (?Vaughan, T., 1784), III. 313 [In
The Oracle, 13/2/1796, Vaughan has
a letter disavowing the authorship of
this play]
— (1788), III. 324
— (1835), IV. 449
Deceptions (Cornelys, Mrs T., 1781),
III. 248 [The authoress' Christian
name should be Margaret, not
Teresa]

+ De Chatillon (Hemans, Felicia: in
Works, 8° 1844, vol. IV)
Decided Fix (1860), v. 665
Decision of the Court (1893), v. 665
Decius and Paulina (Theobald, L.,
1718), II. 259–60, 359
Decorum (Bayly, T. H., 1831), IV. 449,
623
Decoy (Eastwood, F., 1883), v. 353
— (Potter, H., 1733), II. 350
Decoy Bird (1892), v. 665
Decoy Duck (1898), v. 665
Decree Nisi (1892), v. 665
Decree of Java = Poison Tree
Deed in the Wood = Aurora Floyd
Deed of Separation (1883), v. 665
Deeds (Freake, Mrs, 1879), v. 372
Deeds and Doings of the Dark House
(1841), IV. 623
Deeds, not Words (Courtney, J., 1855),
v. 326
Deeds of Darkness (1860), v. 665
Deeds of Dreadful Note (Dubois, 1841)
IV. 307
Deed Without a Name (Soutar, R.,
1853), v. 575
— (1824), IV. 449
Deeming (1892), v. 665
Deene Farm (Bateman, A., 1894), v. 253
Deep Deep Sea (Planché, J. R. and
Dance, C., 1833), IV. 380
Deep Shadows (1894), v. 665
Deep Waters (Grundy, S. 1889), v. 397
— (1897), v. 665
Deerfoot (Burnand, F. C., 1861), v. 288
Deer Slayers (Pitt, W. H. and Pitt, C.,
1870), v. 527, 811
Deer Stalker (Lemon, M., 1841), IV.
449, 623
Deer Stealer of 1623 = Waltham Blacks
Defeated (Clay, F., 1881), v. 313
Defeated Widow = Counterfeit Bride-
groom
Defeat of Apollo (1737), II. 370
— = Mirrour
Defeat of Junot = British Heroes
Defeat of the Amazons = Apollo and the
Flying Pegasus
Defeat of the Dutch Fleet by the gallant
Admiral Duncan, on the memorable
Eleventh of October = England's
Glory

Defender of the Faith (Darrell, C., 1897), V. 337

Defend the Sex = Ladies' Champion

Definitive Treaty (O'Keeffe, J.), III. 293

Deformed (Hedderwick, J., 1834), IV. 588

— (Travers, W., 1865), V. 665, 821, 830

— = (1) Castruccio; (2) Dwarf

Deformed of Notre Dame = Esmeralda

Deformed Transformed (Byron, Lord G. G., 1824), IV. 278

— (Ross, R., 1891), V. 551

Degenerate Brother = Fatal Love

Degenerates (Grundy, S., 1899), V. 397

Déguisements = Rose

Déguisements amoureux (1817), IV. 449

Déguisements imprévus (1829), IV. 449

De la Perouse (1825), IV. 449

Delays and Blunders (Reynolds, F., 1802), IV. 391

Delia (Soulbien, F., 1889), V. 574

Delia Harding (Carr, J. W. C., 1895), V. 304

Delicate Attentions (Poole, J., 1836), IV. 387

Delicate Ground (Dance, C., 1849), IV. 125–8, 289

Delights of Dramatic Authorship = How to write an Opera!

Delights of the Diligence (1827), IV. 449

Delights o' London (Mackay, W., Lennard, H. and Gordon, G. L., 1882), V. 470

Delilah (Willing, J., 1880), V. 626

Delinquent (Reynolds, F., 1805), IV. 51, 391

Deliverance of Germany = Arminius

Delivered from Evil (Dix, F., 1899), V. 345

Del Ombra (Mercer, J. A., 1879), V. 485

De l'Orme (1831), IV. 449

Del. Trem. (Banks, W., 1879), V. 248

Deluge (Reade, J. E., 1839), IV. 607

— = Noah's Flood

Delusion (Jameson, R. F., 1813), IV. 330

— (Oxberry, W. H., 1836), IV. 366

— = Monomania

Delusions (Bernard, W. B., 1831), IV. 449, 623

Demented Dragoon and the Terrible Toreador = Cruel Carmen

Demetri the Outcast (1835), IV. 449

Demetrius (Coleridge, S., 1881), V. 784

— (Hoole, J., 1767), III. 387

Demetrius the Impostor (1806), IV. 449

Democrat (Rogers, C., 1893), V. 548

Democratic Rage (Preston, W., 1793), III. 54, 300 [This was acted at Crowstreet, Dublin, 10/6/1793]

Demon (Rubenstein, A., 1888), V. 553, 815

— (1887), V. 665

Demon Arab (Mildenhall, T., 1840), IV. 598

Demon Bracelets (Hazlewood, C. H., 1869), V. 413

Demon Changling = Son of the Desert

Demon Darrell (Cassilis, I. L. and Morland, F. H., 1898), V. 306

Demon Doctor (Towers, E., 1867), V. 600

Demon Duke (1832), IV. 83, 449

Demon Dwarf (Stirling, E., 1842), IV. 450, 623

Demon Father (1832), IV. 83, 450

De Monfort (Baillie, J., 1798), III. 224–5, 235, 367; IV. 59, 157, 158, 257, 591

— (Kemble, J. P.), IV. 591

Demon Gamester = Gold Fiend

Demon Gift (Brougham, J. and Lemon, M., 1840), IV. 271

Demon Horse (1846), IV. 450

Demon Hunter of the Hartzburg = Walpurgis Night

Demon Jockey (1882), V. 665

Demon Knight (1837), IV. 450

Demon Knight and the Baron's Daughter = Enchanted Ring

Demon Lord (1847), IV. 450

Demon Lover (Brougham, J., 1856), V. 281

Demon of Darkness (Travers, W., 1865), V. 665, 821, 830

Demon of Drink = Assommoir

Demon of Jealousy (1830), IV. 450

Demon of Switzerland = Frankenstein

Demon of the Black Forest = Fatal Marksman

Demon of the Cellar (1895), V. 666

Demon of the Crystal Rock = Shadowless Man

Demon of the Desert (Campbell, A. V., 1829), IV. 278

Demon of the Drachenfels (1863), V. 666

Demon of the Drachenfels = Faust

Demon of the Flood = Nerestan, Prince of Persia

Demon of the Ganges (Almar, G., 1834), IV. 253

Demon of the Mystic Dart (1834), IV. 450

Demon of the Night = Nachtteufel

Demon of the Rock = Lazuli

Demon of the Wolf's Glen = Freischutz

Demon of the Woods = Wood Daemon

Demon Oof Bird (Addison, J., 1895), v. 236

Demon Pilot = Phantom Ship

Demon's Bride (Byron, H. J., 1874), v. 298

Demon's Calendar (1844), IV. 450

Demon's Compact = Fairy Page

Demon's Gift (Lemon, M.) [The play cited IV. 595 is apparently The Demon Gift, listed IV. 271]

Demon Seaman = Flying Dutchman

Demon Spider (Simpson, E. G., 1895), v. 567

Demon Statue = Skeleton Hand

Demon's Tribunal (1800), IV. 450

Demon's Trumpet and the Magic Ring (1826), IV. 450

Demon's Victim = Faustus

Demophoon (Hoole, J., 1767), III. 387

Dempster's Doom = Last Key

Denes Rest (Delannoy, B., 1897), v. 341

D'Enghien (Greene, W. A., 1842), IV. 321

Denhams = Crisis

Denham's Folly (Besley, H., 1894), v. 260

Denise (Scott, C. W. and Harris, Sir A., 1895), v. 558

Dennis (Nantz, F. C., 1833), IV. 365

Denouement = Dash

Denounced (Gascoigne, H. and Jefferson, F., 1883), v. 376

Denouncer (1848), IV. 623

— (1860), v. 666

Dentist's Identity = Filumbonum

Deoch and Durass (Dodson, R., 1877), v. 346

Departed not Defunct = Usurer

Dependant (Cumberland, R., 1795), III. 252

Deposing and Death of Queen Gin (1736), II. 370

Depredators = Bravo turn'd Bully

Deputy (Arliss, G., 1897), v. 243

— (Campbell, J. M., 1888), v. 301

— = Roma

Deputy Registrar (Lumley, R. R., 1888), v. 464

Deputy Sheriff (1892), v. 666

De Rayo (1833), IV. 623

Derby Day (Lee, N., Jr., 1867), v. 453, 803

Derby Lost and the Leger Won = Flying Jib by Snapdragon

Derby Winner (Harris, Sir A. H. G., Raleigh, C. and Hamilton, H., 1894), v. 406

Dermot and Kathlane (Byrne, J., 1793), III. 241

Dermot O'Donoghue (Fraser, J. A., 1872), v. 372

Derry Driscoll (Mackenna, S. J. and Aylmer, B., 1877), v. 471

Dervise and the Peri = Black Hand

Descart, the French Buccaneer (Jerrold, D. W., 1828), IV. 331

Descendants of Hugh Myddelton = Student of Blackfriars

Descent of Orpheus into Hell (1661), I. 41, 44, 133, 252

Descent of the Balloon = Mogul Tale

Descent of the Deities = (1) Olympus in an Uproar; (2) Widow of Delphi

Descent of the Heathen Gods (1749), II. 451

Desert (Fitzball, E., 1847), IV. 317

Deserted (Coles, C., 1894), v. 317

— (1879), v. 666

Deserted and Deceived = Cast on the Mercy of the World

Deserted Child = Rosalie

Deserted Daughter (Holcroft, T., 1795) = Tis a Strange World, III. 137, 271; IV. 571

Deserted Mill (1855), v. 666

— = Soldier's Widow

Deserted Mine = Blacksmith's Daughter and the Red Hand

Deserted Mother = Marguerite

Deserted Priory = Malediction

Deserted Tower (Rannie, J., 1806), III. 300

Deserted Village (Cooper, F. F., 1833), IV. 283
— (Saville, Mrs E. F., 1835), IV. 609
Deserted Wife (Faucquez, A., 1873), V. 666, 791, 830
Deserted Wife in Search of a Husband (1849), IV. 450
Deserted Wife of Didcot = Ramblers
Deserter (Dibdin, C., 1773), III. 120, 202, 254, 381
— (1789), III. 324
— (1801), IV. 450
— (1849), IV. 450
Deserter and his Dog = Napoleon Buonaparte
Deserter from Orleans = German Jew
Deserter in a Fix (Soane-Roby, B., 1879), V. 573
Deserter of Dresden = Maid of the Black Rock
Deserter of Moscow = Emperor of Russia
Deserter of Naples (1788), III. 120, 324
— (1789), III. 324
— (1817), IV. 450
Déserteur (1818), IV. 450
Déserteur malgré lui = Carl et Lisbeth
Desert Fiend = Shamacda
Desert Flower (Harris, A. G. and Williams, T. J., 1863), V. 405
Desert Island (Murphy, A., 1760), III. 51, 61, 70, 71, 222, 289
Deserts of Arabia (Reynolds, F., 1806), IV. 391
Deserts of Siberia = Exile
Desmore (1866), V. 666
Desmoro (Archer, W. J., 1866), V. 777
Desolate Island = (1) De la Perouse; (2) Perouse
Desolation (Towers, E., 1865), V. 666, 821, 830
Desperate Adventures of the Baby (Ross, C. H., 1878), V. 551
Desperate Deed (Delannoy, B., 1893), V. 341
Desperate Game (Morton, J. M., 1853), V. 495
Desperate Man (Pond, A. P., 1891), V. 529
Desperate Remedy (Bruce, H. P., 1892), V. 283
— = My Heart's Idol

Desperate Women = Fair Sinners
Desperation (Roy, G. and Reid, B., 1887), V. 552
Despite the World = Voltaire's Wager
Desrues the Deceiver (1833), IV. 450
Destiny (Conquest, G., 1860), V. 666 785, 830
— (Lyon, W. F., 1881), V. 465
— (Towers, E., 1860), V. 666
— (Towers, E., 1869), V. 601, 821
— (1894), V. 666, 830
Destroyed by Drink (Lacy, J. W., 1879), V. 446
Destroyer (1868), V. 666
Destroying Angel (Scudamore, F. A., 1896), V. 559
Destruction of Jerusalem = Titus Caesar
Destruction of Jerusalem by Titus Vespasian (Crowne, J., 1677), I. 40, 83, 124, 151, 346, 350, 399
Destruction of the Bastille (Taylor, T. P., 1844), IV. 411, 614
— (Webster, B. N., 1842), IV. 105-6, 418
— = (1) Paris in an Uproar; (2) Triumph of Liberty
Destruction of the Dockyard = Jack the Painter
Destruction of the Spanish Armada = Golden Days of Good Queen Bess
Destruction of the Turko-Egyptian Fleet = Britons at Navarino
Destruction of the World = Noah's Flood
Destruction of Troy (Banks, J., 1678), I. 54, 66, 67, 120, 125, 165, 389
Detection (1780), III. 324
— (1805), IV. 450
Detective (Hazlewood, C. H., 1863), V. 413, 797
— (Scott, C. W. and Manuel, E., 1875), V. 557
— = Wolves and Waifs
Deuce is in Her (Planché, J. R., 1820), IV. 376
— (Raymond, R. J., 1830), IV. 388
Deuce is in Him (Colman, G., 1763), III. 120, 182, 183, 245, 373
Deuce is in it = Three and the Ace
Deux âges (1817), IV. 450
Deux aveugles (Farnie, H. B., 1871), V. 790

Devils in the Wood (1747), II. 370

Devil's Luck (Conquest, G. and Tinsley, L., 1885), V. 322

— (1888), V. 666

Devil's Mine (Darcy, F., 1894), V. 336

Devil's Mount (Higgie, T. H., 1847), IV. 325

Devil's Opera (Macfarren, G., 1838), IV. 350, 597

Devil's Pills = Pilule du Diable

Devil's Pool (1871), V. 666

Devil's Punch Bowl (1834), IV. 450

— = King's Mail

Devil's Ride to London = More Visitors in Town

Devil's Ring (Rodwell, G. H., 1850), V. 548

Devil's Share (Raymond, C. F. M., 1843), IV. 388

— = (1) Asmodeus; (2) Asmodeus, the Little Demon

Devil's Ship (1832), IV. 450

Devil's Ship and the Pirates of the Charmed Life = Money Diggers

Devil's Son = Robert le Diable

Devil's Three-decker (1853), V. 666

Devil's Violin and the Revolt of the Flowers (Webster, B. N., 1849), IV. 418, 616

Devil's Walk (Moncrieff, W. T., 1830), IV. 450, 623

Devil's Wood = Fratricide

+ Devil to Do (Crow Street, Dublin, 18/3/1779)

Devil to Do about Her = Man's Bewitched

Devil to Pay (Coffey, C. and Mottley, J., 1731), II. 136, 137, 138, 142, 237, 243-4, 315; III. 28, 38

+ — (12°, 1763, Belfast)

— (1845), IV. 450

— = Merry Cobler

Devil turn'd Humourist = Nuns turn'd Libertines

Devil upon Two Sticks (Coffey, C. 1729), II. 134, 244, 315

— (Foote, S., 1768), III. 174-5, 260

Devoted Daughter = Jew and the German

Devoted Son = Murderer

Devotee = Seraphine

Devotion (Boucicault, D. G., 1884), V. 270

— (Cheatham, F. G., 1870), V. 308

— (Lane, Mrs S., 1881), V. 448

— (1884), V. 666

Devotion and Prejudice (Brough, R. B. and Bridgeman, J. V., 1874), V. 278

Dewdrop and Rosebud = Riquet with the Tuft

Dey and a Knight (Somerset, C. A., 1838), IV. 404

— (1843), IV. 450

Dey and the Knight = Zanone

Dhrame (Nugent, J. F., 1876), V. 506

Dhu Blanche = Blanche Dhu

Dhu Colleen of Ballyfoyle = Liberty

Diable à la Chasse = Asgard, the Demon Hunter

Diable à Quatre (1845), IV. 450

— (1846), IV. 450

Diabolus amans (1885), V. 666

Diadeste (Fitzball, E., 1838), IV. 315

Dial of Death (1899), V. 666

Dialogue between a Mother and a Daughter = Female Angler

Diamond and Granle (1894), V. 666

Diamond and the Pearl = Working Man

Diamond and the Snowdrop = Light of Love

Diamond Arrow (Moncrieff, W. T., 1815), IV. 358

Diamond Cavern (1850), V. 666

Diamond cut Diamond (Drayton, H., 1859), V. 666, 789, 830

— (Hook, J. or T. E., 1797), III. 272, 405

— (Murray, W. H., 1838), IV. 365

— (Wallace, Lady E., 1787), III. 121, 314

— = Swindlers

Diamond Deane (Dam, H. J. W., 1891), V. 334

Diamond Gang (Darbey, E., 1892), V. 336

Diamond in the Rough (1895), V. 666

Diamond King (Dawson, F., 1892), V. 339

Diamond Necklace (1891), V. 666

— = Number Ninety Nine

Diamond Queen (Edwards, A., 1889), V. 355

Diamond Ring (Wild, W. J., 1885), V. 622

Dick Whittington and his Cat (Green-wood, T. L., 1852), v. 393, 794
— (Lemon, M., 1842), IV. 344
— (McLelland, H. F., 1894), v. 468
— (Melville, A. and Jones, J. W., 1893), v. 485
— (Milner, H. W., 1823), IV. 451, 623
— (O'Halloran, G. B., 1878), v. 506
— (Richards, J., 1870), v. 542
— (Thorne, G., 1889), v. 598
— (Virgo, J. T. and McCabe, C. W., 1894), v. 609
— (1874, 1875, 1877, 1878, 1881, 1884, 1885, 1891, 1893), v. 668
Dick Whittington and his Cat-astrophe (Horner, J., 1884), v. 427
Dick Whittington and his Good Cat (Green, F. W., 1881), v. 391
Dick Whittington and his King of Pussy Cats (Green, F. W., 1883), v. 391
Dick Whittington and his Wonderful Cat (Lemon, H., 1869), v. 454
— (Marchant, F., 1863), v. 668, 830
Dick Whittington Returned (1881), v. 668
Dick Whittington the Second (1885), v. 668
Dick Wilder (Musgrave, Mrs H., 1891), v. 500
Diddlecombe Farm (Fuller, C. F., 1886), v. 374
Did He Steal It? (Trollope, A., 1869), v. 604
Did I dream it? (Wooler, J. P., 1860), v. 632, 824
Dido (Bridges, T., 1771), III. 240
— (Hoole, J., 1800), III. 387
— (Reed, J., 1767), III. 300
Dido and Aeneas (?D'Urfey, T., 1727), II. 256, 257-8, 320
— (Gildon, C., 1700), II. 332
— (Tate, N., 1689), I. 95, 434
— (1893), v. 668
— = Death of Dido
Dido Done = Æneas
Dido, Queen of Carthage (Hoare, P., 1792), III. 69, 269, 387
Dido, the Celebrated Widow (Burnand, F. C., 1860), v. 288, 781

Did she mean it? (Rennell, C. R., 1871), v. 541
Did You Ever? (Addison, H. R., 1848), IV. 251
Did you ever send your Wife to Camber-well? (Coyne, J. S., 1846), IV. 287
Did you ever take your Wife to Broughty Ferry? (1846), IV. 451
Did you ring? (Houghton, J. W. and Mabson, J. W., 1892), v. 427
Difference of Nations (1733), II. 370
Difference of Opinion (1898), v. 668
Different Husbands = Universal Gallant
Different Widows (Pix, Mrs M., 1703), II. 155, 171, 350
Difficulties of identifying an Irishman = O'Flahertys
Digger's Bride (1859), v. 831
Diggings (1877), v. 668
Dilettanti (Peacock, T. L.), IV. 369
Dillosk Gatherer (Fitzball, E., 1832), IV. 451, 623
Dimity's Dilemma (Salaman, M. C., 1887), v. 555
Dinas Bran (1830), IV. 451
Dine at my Villa (Hoare, P., 1804) = Paragraph, IV. 451, 623
Ding Dong Bell, Pussy's in the Well (Lee, N., Jr., 1866), v. 453
— (Soutar, R., 1866), v. 575
— (1834), IV. 451
Ding Dong Will (1857), v. 666
Dinky Doo (1894), v. 668
Dinner for Nothing (Cheltnam, C. S., 1865), v. 309
Dinner for Six = Who stole the Pocket-book
Dinner for Two (Carton, R. C., 1893), v. 305
Dinner of Madelon (1816), IV. 451 [See also under Sportsman and the Shepherd]
— (1828), IV. 451
Dinner Party (Brewer, G., 1794), III. 239
Dinners and Diners (Grain, R. C., 1891), v. 388
Dinorah (Chorley, H. F., 1859), v. 310, 783
— (Travers, W., 1860), v. 821
— = Little Devil's Share
Dinorah under Difficulties (Brough, W., 1859), v. 279

Dioclesian = Prophetess

Diogenes and his Lantern (Taylor, T., 1849), IV. 411; V. 592

Diogenes in Search of a Contented Man (Pitt, G. D., 1857), V. 668, 810

Dion (Rhodes, G. A., 1806), IV. 393, 608

Dione (Gay, J., 1720), II. 146, 225, 275, 331

— (1733), II. 370

— (1895), V. 668

— (1897), V. 668

Dionysius (1825), IV. 451

Diphilo and Granida (Kirkman, F., 1673), I. 418

Diplomacy (Scott, C. W. and Stephenson, B. C., 1878), V. 557

— (1836), IV. 451

Diplomacy = Dora and Diplunacy

Dirce (1821), IV. 451

Director (Greenbank, H., 1891), V. 392

Directors no Conjurors = Modern Poetasters

Dirty Dick (?Hazlewood, C. H., 1860), V. 668, 796, 831

— (Mildenhall, T., 1842), IV. 598

Disagreeable Surprise (Daniel, G., 1819), IV. 289

— (1798) ? = Saltimbanco, III. 324, 400

— = Saltimbanco

Disappointed Authoress (Wilson, T., 1821), IV. 618

Disappointed Bachelor (Evans, 1812), IV. 583

Disappointed Country Lass = Livery Rake and Country Lass

Disappointed Coxcomb (1765), III. 324

Disappointed Gallant (Thomson, A., 1738), II. 360

Disappointed Marriage = Luckey Chance

Disappointed Villainy (Horde, T., 1775), III. 273

Disappointment (Randal, J., 1732), II. x, 351, 432

— (Southerne, T., 1684), I. 153-4, 240, 264, 350, 432-3

— = Serenade

Disappointments (1810), IV. 451

Disaster (1779), III. 400

Disbanded Officer (Johnstone, J., 1786), III. 50, 61, 122, 277, 389

Discarded Daughter (Raymond, R. J., 1847), IV. 389

Discarded Secretary (Eyre, E. J., 1799), III. 259

Discarded Son (Webster, B. N., 1853), V. 618

Discharge your Tiger (1849), IV. 451

Discontented Man (1804), IV. 451

Discounting a Life (1844), IV. 451

Discovery (Sheridan, Mrs F., 1763), III. 139, 141, 305

— (1810), IV. 451

— = (1) Marciano; (2) Midnight

Discovery of Joseph (Hoole, J., 1800), III. 388

Discreet Princess (Planché, J. R., 1855), V. 527

— (1848), IV. 451

Disengaged (James, H., 1894), V. 433

Disestablishment (1886), V. 668

Disguis'd Lovers = Love's Metamorphosis

Disguise (Jodrell, R. P., 1787), III. 277

Disguised (1897), V. 668

Disguised Nobleman = Romance of a Poor Young Man

Disguises (Haworth, R., 1824), IV. 324

— (Webster, A., 1879), V. 823

— (1817), IV. 451

— = All-Plot

Dish of All Sorts (McLaren, A., 1806), IV. 351

Dish of the Auctioneer's Own Chocolate = Tit for Tat

Dishonourable Affair = Affair of Honour

Dishonour'd Bill = Wildfire Dick

Dishonoured (St John, A., 1896), V. 554

— (1895), V. 668

Dishonoured Bill = House Room

Dishonour's Due = Drummond

Disintegration of Bonaparte = Magic of British Liberty

Disinterested Friend = Patron

Disinterested Love (Hull, T., 1798), III. 113, 274

Disloyal Lover = He's Much to Blame

Dismal Squire = Plotting Lovers

Dismal Swamp = Dominique the Deserter

Disowned (Parry, T., 1851), V. 515

— = Conspiracy

Disputants (1780), III. 324

Doctor Faustus (1662), I. 441
— = Life and Death of Doctor Faustus
Doctor Faustus and the Black Demon
(1823), IV. 451
Doctor Hocus Pocus (Colman, G.,
1814), IV. 282
Doctor in spite of himself (Dixon, G.,
1877), V. 346
— (1871), V. 669
Doctor in the Dumps (1798), III. 400
Doctor Johnson (Trevor, L., 1896), V.
604
Doctor Last in his Chariot (Bicker-
staffe, I. and Foote, S., 1769), III. 117,
237
Doctor Last's Examination (Foote, S.,
1787) = Devil upon Two Sticks, III.
324, 400
Doctor Miracle (1882), V. 669
Doctor of Alcantara = Alcantara
Doctor of Music (1893), V. 669
Doctor Paddy (1884), V. 669
Doctor Poker (1816) = Each for Himself,
IV. 451, 624
Doctor Porter (1887), V. 669
Doctor Sangrado (D'Egville, 1814), IV.
451, 624
Doctors Beware (1897), V. 669
Doctor's Boy (Grant, R., 1877), V. 388
Doctor's Brougham (Manuel, E., 1875),
V. 475
Doctor's Dilemma (Ford, D. M., 1899),
V. 370
— (1893), V. 669
Doctors of Dull-head College (Kirkman,
F., 1662), I. 418
Doctor's Secret (1888), V. 669
Doctor's Shadow (Saintsbury, H. A.,
1896), V. 554
Doctor's Story (Mills, A., 1894), V. 489
Doctor's Ward (Wilton, H., 1899), V.
629
Doctor Syntax and another Doctor
(Dibdin, C. I. M., 1823), IV. 295
Doctor Syntax in London (1823), IV.
451
Doctor the Disease = Mother-in-Law
Doctor, the Miser and the Butcher =
Opiate
Dodge for a Dinner (Palmer, T. A.,
1872), V. 512
Dodges of Cupid (1863), V. 669

Does he love me? (Falconer, E., 1860),
V. 121, 360
Dog and the Duck (Dibdin, T. J., 1816),
IV. 300
Dog and the Shadow = Miss Michael-
mass
Dog Days in Bond Street (Dimond, W.,
1820), IV. 307
Dog Detectives (1879), V. 669
Doge of Duralto (Brough, R. B., 1857),
V. 278
Doge of Venice (Bernard, W. B., 1867),
V. 259
Doge's Daughter = Bianca Contarini
Dog Friend = Victor Hugh
Dog in the Manger = P.U.P.
Dog of Montargis (Barrymore, W.,
1814) = Murder will out, IV. 82, 261,
508, 634
— (Dibdin, T. J., 1814), IV. 82, 299
Dog of the Convent (1831), IV. 451
Dog of the Desert = Avalanche
Dog of the Pyrenees (1845), IV. 451
Dog of the Quarry = Pride of Kildare
Dogs of Australia (1863), V. 669
Dogs of Loch Lomond = Dark Donald,
the Idiot of the Cliff
Dogs of St Bernard (Scott, C. W., 1875),
V. 557
Dogs of the Dark Blue Waters (1859), V.
831
Dogs of the Grange (James, C. S.,
1850), V. 432
Dogs of the Revenue Cutter (1862), V.
669
Dogs of the Wreck = Cherokee Chief
Dogs of Tipple's Farm = Hoxton a
Hundred Years Ago
Doing Banting (Brough, W. and
Halliday, A., 1864), V. 279
Doing for the Best (Lacy, M. R., 1861),
V. 446
Doing my Uncle (Lacy, M. R., 1866),
V. 446
Doings in Bond Street (1842), IV. 624
Doings near Delgany = Mr Smith
Doing the "Hansome" (Harris, A. G.,
1856), V. 405
Doing the Shah (Robinson, N., 1873),
V. 547
Doldrum (O'Keeffe, J., 1796), III.
295

Dollars and Sense (Daly, A., 1883), v.
333
Dolls (Norman, G. T., 1892), v. 505
Doll's House (Archer, W., 1889), v. 187,
242
— (1892), v. 669
Dollusions (Muskerry, W., 1896), v. 501
Dolly (Bannister, J., 1890), v. 248
— (Clarke, H. S., 1892), v. 313
— (1860), v. 669, 831
Dolly and the Rat (Jerrold, D. W.,
1823) = Brisket Family, IV. 331, 436,
590
Dolly's Delusion = May
Dolly's Dilemma (Millward, H., 1887),
v. 489
Dolly's Follies (1884), v. 669
Dolly Varden (Cympson, E., 1889), v.
332
— (Wood, M., 1872), v. 631
Dolores (Lane, Mrs S., 1874), v. 448
Dolph Heyliger = Miser's Will
+ Dombey and Son (Brougham, J.)
[Printed in *Dicks'* series and *French's
American Drama*]
— (Sidney, W., 1849), IV. 611
— (Taylor, T. P., 1847), IV. 98, 411
Domenica (Ellerton, J. H., 1838), IV.
309
Domenico the Vile 'un (Thomas, L.,
1872), v. 596
Domestic Arrangements (1835), IV. 452
Domestic Bliss (1848), IV. 452
— (1869) v. 669
Domestic Diplomacy (Redmond, J.,
1872), v. 537
Domestic Discipline (1855), v. 669
Domestic Economy (Burnand, F. C.,
1890), v. 291
— (Lemon, M., 1849), IV. 345
Domestic Experiment = Mr and Mrs
Muffett
Domestic Hercules (Becher, M., 1870),
v. 254
Domestick Tyrant = Spirit of Contra-
diction
Domestic Mash = Mashing Mamma
Domestic Medicine (Smith, L., 1887),
v. 573
Domestic Tyrant = Temper
Dominicans (Wilson, R. K., 1894), v.
628

Dominique (1831), IV. 452
Dominique the Deserter (Murray, W. H.,
1833), IV. 365
— (1857), v. 669
— (1865), v. 669
Dominique the Possessed (Barnett,
C. Z., 1831), IV. 259
Dominique, the Resolute (1831), IV. 452
Domino (Clarance, L., 1879), v. 310
Domino Noir (1848), IV. 83, 452
Domino of Death = Devilshoof
Domitian, the Roman Actor (1722), II.
370
Don (Merivale, H. C. and Merivale,
Mrs H., 1888), v. 487
— (1854), v. 669
Dona Constanza (Gollmick, A., 1875),
v. 384
Donagh (Rowe, G. F., 1884), v. 552
Donagh's Romance (1883), v. 669
Dona Ignez de Castro (Adamson, J.,
1808), IV. 251
Donald and Peggy (1812), IV. 452
Donald McClean, the Highland Robber
(1820), IV. 452
Don Caesar de Bazan (À Beckett, G. A.
and Lemon, M., 1844), IV. 250
— (Archer, T., 1844), IV. 254
— (Barnett, C. Z., 1844), IV. 260
— (Boucicault, D. and Webster, B.,
1844), IV. 270
— (Saintsbury, H. A., 1899), v. 554
Don Carlos (Bruce, J. W., 1837), IV. 86,
272
— (Cottrell, C. H., 1843), IV. 86, 283
— (Edwardes, C. T. M., 1869), v. 354
— (Noehden, G. H. and Stoddart, J.,
1798), III. 62-3, 291, 392
— (Otway, T., 1676), I. 120, 348, 422
— (Russell, Lord J., 1822), IV. 86, 396
+ — (Symonds, J., 8°, 1898)
— (Thompson, B., 1798), III. 63, 311,
397; IV. 86, 412
— (Towler, J., 1843), IV. 86, 414
— (1798), III. 62, 68, 324
Don Carlos, Prince of Spain (1734), II.
370
Don Cossack in London (1814), IV. 452
— = Hyde Park in an Uproar
Done Brown (Craven, H. T., 1845), IV.
285
Donellan (Innes, P. R., 1899), v. 432

Done for a Hundred = Seth Slope

Done on Both Sides (Morton, J. M., 1847), IV. 363

Done-to-a-Cinderella (Lomax, F., 1881), V. 462

Don Giovanni (Brennan, J. C., 1864), V. 669, 780, 831

— (Brennan, J. C., 1872), V. 274, 780, 831

— (Dibdin, T. J., 1817), IV. 300, 452, 580, 624

— (Dibdin, T. J., 1819), IV. 452, 624

— (Dibdin, T. J., 1826), IV. 304

— = Spectre on Horseback

Don Giovanni in Venice (Reece, R., 1873), V. 537

Don Giovanni, Jr. (1875), V. 669, 831

Don Giovanni, M.P. (1874), V. 669

Don Jerome's Trip to England (1778), III. 324

Don John (Reynolds, F., 1821), IV. 392

— (1734), II. 370

— (1782), III. 325

— = Libertine

Don John of Arragon (1840), IV. 452

Don John of Austria (Gore, Mrs C. G. F., 1836), IV. 319

Don John of Seville (Colona, E., 1876), V. 318

Don Juan (Beazley, S., Jr., 1833), IV. 264

— (Buckstone, J. B., 1830), IV. 273

— (Byron, H. J., 1873), V. 298

— (Delpini, C., 1790), III. 253

— (Tanner, J. T., 1893), V. 590

— (1788), III. 325

— (1790), III. 122, 210, 325

— (1838), IV. 452

— (1844), IV. 624

— (1855), V. 669

— (1858), V. 669

— (1876), V. 669

Don Juan considerably aided (1870), V. 669

Don Juan Junior (Reece, R. and Righton, E., 1880), V. 539

Don Juan's Early Days (Milner, H. M. and Stirling, E., 1837), IV. 357

Don Juan, the Little Gay Deceiver (Spry, H., 1870), V. 576

Don Jumpedo (1749), II. 138, 370

Donkey Races (1826), IV. 452

Donna (Hungerford, Mrs and Phillips, Mrs N., 1892), V. 430

Donna Aurora (1821), IV. 452

Donna Diana (Marston, J. W., 1864), V. 479

Donna Juanita (1880), V. 669

Donna Luiza (Hood, B., 1892), V. 425

Donna Theresa (Wilson, A. J., 1885), V. 628

Donne Cambiate (1812), IV. 452

Donnybrook (Pelzer, J., 1899), V. 518

— (1890) V. 669

Don Pasquale (Reynoldson, T. H., 1843), IV. 393, 452, 608, 624

Don Pedro (Adams, Mrs E., 1892), V. 235

— (Cumberland, R., 1796), III. 62, 79, 252

— (Mitchell, L. E., 1892), V. 490

Don Pedro, King of Castille (Herbert, H. J. G., 1838), IV. 325

Don Pedro the Cruel and Don Manuel the Cobbler (Boaden, C., 1839), IV. 269

Don Quichotte (1809), IV. 452

Don Quixote (Almar, G., 1833), IV. 252, 568

— (D'Urfey, T., 1694–5), I. 21, 83, 265, 276–7, 409; III. 114

— (Hazlewood, C. H., 1867), V. 413

— (Killick, J. M., 1869), V. 444

— (Macfarren, G., 1846), IV. 350

— (Milner, H. T. and Milton, P., 1893), V. 490

— (Paulton, H. and Maltby, A., 1876), V. 516

— (Piguenit, D. J., 1774), III. 297

— (Smith, H. B., 1889), V. 572

— (1818), IV. 452

— = Wild Man of Andalusia

Don Quixote II = Fox Chase

Don Quixote and the Steed Rosinante (Cooke, W., 1857), V. 669, 785, 831

Don Quixote de la Mancha (Poel, W., 1880), V. 811

Don Quixote de la Mancha and the Sleep of a Hundred Years (1852), V. 669

Don Quixote in Barcelona (Moser, J., 1808), IV. 364

Don Quixote in England (Fielding, H., 1734), II. 14, 146, 181, 246, 247, 327, 436; III. 116, 200

Don Quixote in England (1752), III. 325

Don Quixote Junior (Goodman, J. C., and Howson, J., 1879), v. 384

Don Quixote, the Knight of the Wonderful Countenance (1833), IV. 452

Don Quixotte and his Man Sancho Panza (1831), IV. 452

Don Rafaelle (Campbell, A. V., 1845), IV. 278

Don Raymond (1797) = Raymond and Agnes, III. 325, 400

Don Roderic (O'Neil, J. R., 1852), v. 507

Don Sancho (Boyd, Mrs E., 1739), II. 67, 246–7, 299

Don Saverio (Arne, T. A., 1750), II. 236, 295; III. 199, 233

Don Sebastian (Dryden, J., 1689), I. 24, 68, 144–5, 149, 337, 352, 406; III. 58, 199

Don Sebastian, King of Portugal (1823), IV. 452

Don't be Frightened (Morton, J. M., 1839), IV. 452, 624

Don't deceive your Wife (Wilstach, P., 1897), v. 629

Don, the Duck, the Drake and the Invisible Armada = E-liz-abeth

Don't judge by appearances (Morton, J. M., 1855), v. 495

Don't Jump at Conclusions (1895), v. 669

Don't lend your Umbrella (Buckingham, L. S., 1857), v. 286

Don't Mind Me (1872), v. 669

Don't Swear (1853), v. 669

Don't Tell Her Husband (1895), v. 669

Don't you wish you may get it? (Mowbray, 1856), v. 669, 807, 831

Donzella's Oath (1854), v. 669

Doo, Brown and Co. (Rae, C. M., 1886), v. 532

Doom at Midnight = Halvei, the Unknown

Doom'd Child (1832), IV. 452

Doomed (Hodgson, A. H. and Hodgson, A. C., 1890), v. 423

Doomed at Last = Deeming

Doomed Bridge (1856), v. 669

Doomed, Drugged and Drowned at Datchet = Gentle Gertrude

Doomed Entombed = Curiosity

Doomed House (1839), IV. 452

Doomed Knight = Hag of the Storm

Doomed of Dyneley Chase = Will o' the Wisp

Doomed of the Fiend Ship = Black Buccaneer

Doomed One of the Hulk = Phantom Voice

Doomed Son = Black and Red Galleys

Doomed to Darkness (1876), v. 670

Doomed to die = Too late to save

Doomed to Siberia (1897), v. 670

Doomed to Slavery = Wrongs of Twenty Years

Doom Kiss (Pocock, I., 1832), IV. 385

— = Demon Knight

Doom Light (Townsend, W. T., 1845), IV. 414

Doom of Barostein = Ancestress

Doom of Devorgoil (Scott, Sir W., 1830), IV. 194, 397

Doom of Morana (Buckstone, J. B., 1836), IV. 275

Doom of the Daemon Knight = Walpurghi's Eve

Dora (Parker, W. S., 1893), v. 514

— (Reade, C., 1867), v. 536

Dora and Diplunacy (Burnand, F. C., 1878), v. 291

Dora Ingram (Murdoch, J. M., 1885), v. 499

Dora Mayfield (Newbound, E., 1878), v. 502

Dora O'Donovan (Pitt, G. D., 1850), v. 526

Dora's Device (Reece, R., 1871), v. 537

Dora's Dream (Cecil, A., 1873), v. 306

Dora's Love (Chamberlaine, C. W., 1872), v. 307

— (1873), v. 670

Dorastus and Fawnia (1703), II. 370

Dorcas (Paulton, H. and Paulton, E., 1898), v. 517

Do-Re-Mi-Fa (Taylor, J. G., 1873), v. 820

Dorias (Strettle, 1835), IV. 613

Doris (Stephenson, B. C. and Scott, C. W., 1889), v. 582

Dormea, the Lawyer's Daughter (Ward-
haugh, M., 1878), v. 614
Dorothee (1808), IV. 452
Dorothy (Edwards, J., 1877), v. 355
— (Stephenson, B. C. and Scott, C. W.,
1886), v. 582, 818
Dorothy Gray (Nisbet, J. F., 1888), v.
504
Dorothy's Birthday (1884), v. 670
Dorothy's Fortune = St Cupid
Dorothy's Stratagem (Mortimer, J.,
1876), v. 494
Dorothy Vernon (Boulding, J. W.,
1889), v. 270
Dorval (1767), III. 120, 325, 400
Dose in Mistake = Narcotic
Do Shake Hands (Buckingham, L. S.,
1857), v. 286
— (1855), v. 670
Dot (Boucicault, D., 1859), v. 93, 268,
779
Dotheboys Hall (Besemeres, J., 1871),
v. 260
— = Poor Smike
Dotty (Parry, A. and Hugh, E., 1896), v.
514
Double Ambuscade = Kate's Assigna-
tion
Double Amour (1791), III. 325
Double and Quits (Pemberton, T. E.,
1885), v. 519
Double-barrelled Gun Trick = Plague
o' both your Houses
Double-bedded Room (Morton, J. M.,
1843), IV. 362
Double Blunder = Willow Grove
Double Conquest (1873), v. 670
Double Courtship (Rhys, H., 1862), v.
813
Doubleday's Will (1878), v. 670
Double Dealer (Congreve, W., 1693), I.
68, 194, 242, 352, 397; IV. 15
— (Kemble, J. P., 1802), IV. 335
Double Dealing (Suter, W. E.), v.
819
Double Deceit (Popple, W., 1735), II.
144, 200-1, 350; III. 177
Double Deception (Pireau, M. and
Royd, L., 1897), v. 525
— (Richardson, E. 1779), III. 302
Double Defeat (1809), IV. 452
Double Delusions = Clairvoyance

Double Dick (Digges, W., 1875), v. 345
Double Dilemma (Dance, C., 1836), IV.
452, 624
Double Disappointment (Mendez, M.,
1746), II. 344, 440
— = Bachelors' Miseries
Double Disguise (Hook, Mrs J., 1784),
III. 272
— (Murdoch, J., 1783), III. 289
— = Love makes an Irishman
Double Distress (Pix, Mrs M., 1701), II.
31, 74, 97, 160, 349
Double Dose (Shirley, A., 1890), v. 564
Double Dummy (Yates, E. and Harring-
ton, N. H., 1858), v. 635, 825
Double Dummy and Hearts for Trumps
= Lovers at Play
Double Dutchman (1885), v. 670
Double Engagement (1896), v. 670
Double Elopement = Duenna
Double espreuve = Prince troubadour
Double Event (East, J. M., 1891), v. 353
— (Law, A. and Reed, A., 1884), v. 450
— (Towers, E., 1871), v. 601
— (Wilkinson, A., 1891), v. 623
— (1891), v. 670
— = Jockey
Double-faced People (Courtney, J.,
1857), v. 326
Double Faces (Reade, C., 1883), v. 812
Double Falshood (Theobald, L., 1727),
II. 57, 222, 359, 444-5
Double Gallant (Cibber, C., 1707), II.
x, 47, 134, 135, 136, 138, 145, 153,
162, 231, 310, 421, 434; III. 115
Double-Handed Dick (1862), v. 670
Double Imposture = Who's Who?
Double Jealousy (1736), II. 370
Double Life (Elliott, J. C., 1872), v. 356
— (Johnson, E. C., 1892), v. 437
— (Sinclair, L., 1871), v. 570
— (1876), v. 670
— (1897), v. 670
— = Deacon Brodie
Double Lover (1883), v. 670
Double Mark (1805), IV. 452
Double Marriage (Reade, C., 1867), v.
536
— (Serle, T. J., 1848), IV. 400
— (1768), III. 325
— (1855), v. 670
— (1873), v. 670

Double Marriage = (1) Filial Love; (2) Marianne de Lancy; (3) Perplexed Lovers

Double Mistake (Griffith, Mrs E., 1765), III. 58, 114, 153, 266

— (Thompson, F., 1884), v. 597

Double Mistake and Triple Discovery = Family Jars

Double or Quits (Barnett, M., 1831), IV. 452, 624

— (1898), v. 670

Double Perplexity (1796), III. 325

Double Revenge = Spouter

Double Rose (Boulding, J. W., 1882), v. 270

Double Stratagem = Contract

Double Surprize = They would if they could

Double To-do = Confined in Vain

Double Traitor Roasted (1748), II. 370

Double Valet = Hotel

Double X.X. (Dibdin, T. J., 1826), IV. 305

Double Wrong = Hernani

Double Zero (Hurst, J. P., 1883), v. 431

Doubt (Little, J. S., 1889), v. 461

Doubtful Advertisement (1896), v. 670

Doubtful Child = Brazen Water-Tower

Doubtful Hospitality (1880), v. 670

Doubtful Son (Dimond, W., 1810), IV. 306, 581

Doubtful Victory (Oxenford, J., 1858), v. 509

Doubts and Fears (1864), v. 670

+Dougal the Piper (1836), IV. 95 [Apparently this is the play listed under 1852, v. 670]

Douglas (Home, J., 1756), III. 53, 92, 96, 272, 371

— (1818), IV. 452

— (1819), IV. 452

Douglas the Hero = Highland Rivals

Douglas Travestie (Rede, W. L., 1837), IV. 390

Dove and the Serpent (Litchfield, C. and Cook, 1859), v. 670, 785, 804, 831

Dove and the Vulture = White Fairy

Dove Cote (1898), v. 670

Dove Nest Farm = Cross Roads

Doves in a Cage (Jerrold, D. W., 1835), IV. 332

Dowager (Mathews, C. J., 1842), IV. 354

Down among the Coals (Vicars, W. A., 1873), v. 608

Down at Ramsgate (1856), v. 670

Down at Rosherville (1858), v. 670

Down East Bargain (Moncrieff, W. T., 1837), IV. 452, 624

Downfall and Death of King Œdipus (1880), v. 368

Downfall of Alexander the Great = Love and Jealousy

Downfall of Pride (Hazlewood, C. H., 1864), v. 413

Downfall of St Stephens (1784), III. 325

Downfall of Saladin = Black Tower and the Spanish Patriots

Downfall of the Association (1771), III. 325 [The title should be as given here]

Downfall of Tyranny = (1) Brennus; (2) Persian Heroine

Downfal of Bribery (Freeman, M., 1733), II. 237, 251, 329

Downfal of the Pope = Coronation of Queen Elizabeth

Down in a Balloon (Oxenford, J., 1871), v. 510

Down in our Village (Robertson, T. W.), v. 547

Down on his Luck (Douglass, J. T., 1894), v. 349

Down South (1865), v. 670

Down the Area (1823), IV. 452

Down the River (1877), v. 670

Down the Slope (Berg, A. E., 1897), v. 258

Downward Path (Clarke, C. A. and Silva, H. R., 1893), v. 312

— = Man's Enemy

Down with the Dutch (Cawdell, J., 1798) = Battered Batavians, III. 242, 400

Do you call that Nothing? = Trip to Tunbridge

Do you gamble? (Upsher, 1837), IV. 615

Dracula (1897), v. 670

Dragon (Morton, J. M., 1834), IV. 361

Dragoness = Margery

Dragon of Hogue Bie (Draper, J. F., 1871), v. 350

Dragon of Wantley (Blanchard, E. L., 1870), v. 264

Dream of Fate (Barnett, C. Z., 1838), IV. 260

Dream of Life (Watts, W., 1849), IV. 417

— (1861), v. 670

— = Right and Wrong

Dream of Love (Oxenford, J., 1872), v. 510

Dream of Retribution = Paul Zegers

Dream of St Cloud (1797), III. 325

Dream of Scipio (Hoole, J., 1800), III. 387

— (Olivari, F., 1797), III. 295

Dream of the Future (Dance, C., 1837), IV. 288

Dream of the Irish Emigrant (1853), v. 670

Dream of the Past, Present and Future = Christmas Carol

Dream of the Reveller = Whiskey Dream

Dream of the White Boy (1868), v. 670

Dream of Venice = Francesca

Dream of Whitaker's Almanack (1899), v. 670

Dreams = My Lady Clara

Dreams of Delusion (Simpson, J. P., 1862), v. 567

Dreams of the Heart (Reynoldson, T. H., 1847), IV. 393

Dream Spectre (Wilks, T. E., 1843), IV. 421

Dred (Banks, W., 1872), v. 248

— (Phillips, F. L. and Colman, J., 1856), v. 522

— (Suter, W. E., 1856), v. 587, 819

— (1856), v. 670

— (1864), v. 670

— = Dominique the Deserter

Dred, a Tale of the Great Dismal Swamp (1856), v. 670

Dregs (Aveling, E. B., 1889), v. 246

Drenched and Dried (Kerr, J., 1820), IV. 338

Dresden China (Chapin, A. and Oliphant, E. H. C., 1892), v. 308

Dress Coat (Green, F. W., 1876), v. 390

Dress Rehearsal = Opera Buffers

Dr Faust and Miss Marguerite (Martin, R. J. and Hobday, E. A. P., 1885), v. 479

Dr Frankenstein and Hobgoblin of Hoxton = Humgumption

Drifted Apart (Young, Sir C. L., 1882), v. 636

Drifting Clouds (1894), v. 670

Drifting Spar (Gordon, S., 1893), v. 385

Drifting to Seaward = Storm Signal

Drink (Reade, C. and Warner, C., 1879), v. 536, 812

— = Man's Folly

Drink, Poverty and Crime = London Mechanic

Drip, drop, Drip drop (Young, Mrs H., 1863), v. 670, 831

Drive in June (Jones, H. A., 1879), v. 439

Drive Love out at the Door (Rochfort, 1815), IV. 452, 624

Driven from Home (Macdermott, G. H., 1871), v. 468

— (1884), v. 670

— = Fate

Driver and his Dog = Caravan

Dr Jekyll and Mr Hyde (Bandmann, D. E., 1888), v. 248

— (Sullivan, T. R., 1887), v. 586

— (1888), v. 669

Dromio the Drinker (1835), IV. 453

Drones Demolished = Bickerstaff's Unburied Dead

Drooping Flower = Deeds, not Words

Drooping Lily = Amy the Golden

Drop a Tear to her Memory = Richard and Betty

Drop by Drop (Walton, K. A., 1884), v. 612

Dropped In (Boyd, W., 1893), v. 272

Dropping Well of Gedar = Feodora

Dropping Well of Knaresborough = Charcoal Burner

Drop the Curtain (1849), IV. 453

Dross (Braddon, M. E., 1882), v. 273

Drover Boy (1848), IV. 624

Drover's Dog = Cattle-stealers of the Mountain

Drowned Crew = Carlmilham

Drowned for Love (1897), v. 670

Drowned Man's Legacy (Seaman, W., 1872), v. 559

Dr Palgrave (Bryce, L., 1894), v. 284

Dr Quisby (1888), v. 669

Dr Syntax (Creeman, C., 1895), v. 373

Dr Syntax (Planché, J. R., 1820), IV. 376, 604

Dr Syntax the Hypnotist (Busch, W., 1894), v. 294

Drudge, the Prince and the Plated Glass Slipper = Done-to-a-Cinderella

Druid (Capes, J. M., 1879), v. 302

— (Cromwell, T., 1832), IV. 286

— (1815), IV. 624

Druids (1774), III. 325

Druid's Curse = Owen Ivan King of Manko

Druids Elect (1899), v. 670

Druid's Oak (1851), v. 671

Drumclog (1871), v. 671

Drummed Out (1897), v. 671

Drummer (Addison, J., 1716), II. 11, 17, 27, 135, 183, 199, 295, 431

Drummer and the Babies = Military Nurse

Drummond (Poole, S. W., 1870), v. 811

Drum of the Olden Time = Watchmaker of Clerkenwell

Drunkard (Webster, B., the Younger, 1879), v. 618

— (1805), IV. 453

— (1890), v. 671

Drunkard Reclaim'd = Lottery Chance

Drunkard's Children (Johnstone, J. B., 1848), IV. 333

— (Reynoldson, T. H., 1848), IV. 393

— (Taylor, T. P., 1848), IV. 411

— (1848), IV. 453

— (1859), v. 671

— = Life

Drunkard's Doom (Pitt, G. D., 1832), IV. 372

— (1879), v. 671

— = Last Nail

Drunkard's Fate = Bottle Bane

Drunkard's Glass (Morton, T., Jr., 1845), IV. 364, 601

— (1860), v. 671

Drunkard's List (1872), v. 671

Drunkard's Progress = (1) Bottle and the Glass; (2) Our Bottle

Drunkard's Sin = Intemperance

Drunken Cobbler (1819), IV. 453

Drunken News-Writer (1771), III. 325

Drunken Recruit (1821), IV. 453

Drunken Swiss (1793), III. 325

Drury Lane and Park Lane (1879), v. 671

Dryad (1892), v. 671

D.S. = Jack Robinson and his Monkey

D.T. (Callender, E. R., 1879), v. 300

Dublin Adventure = Bashful Irishman

Dublin Bay (Robertson, T. W., 1869), v. 546

Dublin Boy = Andy Blake

Duc d'Olonne (Reynoldson, T. H., 1845), IV. 393, 608

Duchess de la Vaubaliere (Buckstone, J. B., 1837), IV. 275

Duchesse de Guise (1845), IV. 453

Duchesse de la Vallière (Lytton, Lord, 1837), IV. 80, 173, 349

Duchess Eleanour (Chorley, H. F., 1854), v. 310

Duchess of —! (Wilks, T. E., 1842), IV. 617

Duchess of Bayswater and Co. (Heathcote, A. M., 1888), v. 415

Duchess of Coolgardie (Leigh, E. and Clare, C., 1896), v. 454

Duchess of Dijon = French Maid

Duchess of Malfi (Horne, R. H., 1850), v. 426

+ Duchess of Mansfeldt (*French*)

Duchess of Ormond (Banim, J., 1836), IV. 258

Duchess of Padua (Wilde, O. F. O'F.W., 1883), v. 190, 622

Duchess or Nothing (Gordon, W., 1860), v. 385

Duck Hunting (Coyne, J. S., 1862), v. 328

Ducks and Green Pease (Lund, J., 1785), III. 283

Dude and the Dancing Girl (Steele, C. D. and Forward, C. W., 1893), v. 580

Dudley Castle in the Olden Time = King's Secret

Duel (O'Brien, W., 1772), III. 119, 291, 393

— (Peake, R. B., 1823) = My Two Nephews, IV. 369, 509, 603, 634

— (1837), IV. 453

— = Man in the Red Coat

Duel and the Valet = Mysteries of the Wall

Duel d'amour = Battle of Woman

Duel in Richelieu's Time (Boaden, C., 1832), IV. 269

Duel in the Dark (Coyne, J. S., 1852), V. 327

Duel in the Mist = Walter Brand

Duel in the Snow = Christmas Eve

Duelists (McLaren, A., 1811), IV. 351

Duellist (Kenrick, W., 1773), III. 279, 389

Duellists = (1) More Frightened than Hurt; (2) Satisfaction

Duel to the Death = Brother for Brother

Duenna (Pottinger, I., 1776), III. 299

— (Sheridan, R. B., 1775), III. 191, 205, 305

Dugald the Drover (1842), IV. 453

Duke (1837), IV. 453

Duke and No Duke (Tate, N., 1684), I. 257, 349, 434

— (Thurmond, J., 1720), II. 253, 360

— (1758), III. 325

— (1812), IV. 453

Duke and the Demon = Love's Labyrinth

Duke and the Devil (Dibdin, T. J., 1818), IV. 301

— (Dibdin, T. J., 1826), IV. 304

Duke and the Policeman (1830), IV. 453

Duke d'Ormond (Lloyd, C., 1822), IV. 346

Duke for a Day (Dance, G., 1831), IV. 453, 624

— (Neil, R., 1874), V. 501

Duke in Difficulties (Taylor, T., 1861), V. 593

Duke of Florence (1843), IV. 453

Duke of Guise (Dryden, J. and Lee, N., 1682), I. 10, 57, 79, 83, 129, 145-6, 148, 349, 406

Duke of Lerma = Great Favourite

Duke of Lochford (1799), III. 325

Duke of Mantua (Roby, J., 1823), IV. 200-1, 456, 624

Duke of Mercia (Vere, Sir A. de, 1823), IV. 415

Duke of Milan (Cumberland, R., 1779), III. 78, 113, 251

— (1816), IV. 453

Duke of Normandy = Robert the Devil

Duke of Rothsay (Macarthur, S., 1780), III. 283

Duke of Savoy (Reynolds, F., 1817), IV. 392, 607

Duke of Shoreditch (1841), IV. 453

Duke of Swindleton (Burnside, W., 1885), V. 293

Duke's Bequest (Vollaire, H., 1863), V. 822

Duke's Boast (Buckle, H. O., 1889), V. 287

Duke's Coat (1815), IV. 453

— (1824), IV. 453

Duke's Crest = Duke's Daughter

Duke's Daughter (Brougham, J., 1863), V. 280

— (Layton, G. M., 1876), V. 451, 802

— (Robertson, T. W.), V. 547

Duke's Device (Neville, H., 1876), V. 671, 831

Duke's Diversion (Mudie, G., 1892), V. 498

Duke's Double (1857), V. 671

— (1899), V. 671

Duke's Legacy (Calvert, C., 1863), V. 783

Duke's Mistress = Orphan of Paris

Duke's Motto = Duke's Daughter

Duke's Wager (Slous, A. R., 1851), V. 571

— = Duke's Boast

Dulcamara (Gilbert, W. S., 1866), V. 133, 379

Dulce Domum (Dibdin, C. I. M., 1811), IV. 292

Dulverydotty (Adams-Acton, Mrs, 1894), V. 235

Dumaur'alised Trilby (Cheverelles, H., 1895), V. 309

Dumb Bedouin = Arabs of the Desert

Dumb Belle (Bernard, W. B., 1831), IV. 265

Dumb Boy (1821), IV. 453

Dumb Boy and his Horse = Albert and Elmira

Dumb Boy and the Murderer = Torrent of the Valley

Dumb Boy and the Spectre Knight = Homicide

Dumb Boy of Avignon (1841), IV. 453

Dumb Boy of Manchester = Factory Assassin

Dumb Boy of the Mill = Lilly of the Valley

Dumb Boy of Toulon = Ship Launch

Dumb Boy of Vienna = Theodore of Ritzberg

Dumb Brigand (Bernard, W. B., 1832), IV. 453, 624

Dumb Brother = Rock of Arpennaz

Dumb Cake (1787), III. 325

Dumb Carrier Boy and his Pony = Iron Hand

Dumb Conscript (Grattan, H. P., 1835), IV. 320

Dumb Driver (Blake, T. G., 1846), IV. 268

— (1849), IV. 453

Dumb Farce (Thurmond, J., 1719), II. 132, 253, 360

Dumb Girl of Genoa = Maid of Genoa

Dumb Girl of Portici = Masaniello

Dumb Girl of the Inn (1847), IV. 624

— = Mountain Bandit

Dumb Guide of the Tyrol (Blake, T. G., 1837), IV. 267

Dumb Henchman of the Isles = Ivan of the Mask

Dumb Lady (Lacy, J., ?1669), I. 40, 57, 188, 213, 418

Dumb Lady Cured = (1) Irish Doctor; (2) Mock Doctor

Dumb Man of Manchester = Factory Assassin

Dumb Minstrel Boy = Father's Curse

Dumb Norwegian and his Pony of Iceland (1842), IV. 453

Dumb Philosopher = Tipplers

Dumb Princess (Wilde, W. C. K., 1894), V. 623

Dumb Recruit (1840), IV. 453

Dumb Sailor (1854), V. 671

Dumb Sailor Boy = (1) Death Plank; (2) Inchcape Bell

Dumb Savoyard and his Monkey (Thompson, C. P., 1830), IV. 413

Dummerline Castle = Midnight Bell

Dun a Day (1823), IV. 453

Dunbar (Waddie, C., 1899), V. 610

Dundreary a Father (1866), V. 671

Dundreary by Special Train (1862), V. 671

Dundreary in Difficulties = My American Aunt

Dungeon of Death = Prisoner

Dunmow Festival = Spirit of the Haunted Room

Dunoir the Base (Dibdin, C. I. M., 1823), IV. 295

Dunois in the Dark = Giant

Dunstable Actor = Acting Run Mad

Dupe (Sheridan, Mrs F., 1763), III. 305

Dupes of Fancy (Carey, G. S., 1792), III. 242

Duplicate Keys = Prisoner of Lyons

Duplicity (Clift, R., 1871), V. 315

— (Holcroft, T. 1781), III. 134, 141, 270

— (Saker, M. E., 1883), V. 554

— (Turvey, G. F., ?1870), V. 822

— (1893), V. 671

Duprez (1843), IV. 453

Durazzo (Haynes, J., 1838), IV. 324

Durie in Durance = Willie Armstrong

During Her Majesty's Pleasure (Conquest, G. and Pettitt, H., 1877), V. 321

During Supper = Catchwork

During Temporary Sanity (1899), V. 671

During the Dance (Doone, N., 1889), V. 347

Duskie (Thompson, Mrs G. and Sinclair, K., 1893), V. 597

Dust (Grundy, S., 1881), V. 396

Dust in the Eyes (1879), V. 671

Dustman's Belle (Dance, C., 1846), IV. 289

Dustman's Treasure (1866), V. 671

Dutch Alliance (1759), III. 325

Dutch and Scotch Contention (1729), II. 370

Dutch Anna (1864), V. 671

Dutch Cruelties at Amboyna (1672), I. 405, 446

Dutch Girl's Troubles = Christine

Dutch Justice (Pleon, H., 1888), V. 183, 528

Dutch Law (1835), IV. 453

Dutch Lover (Behn, A., 1673), I. 24, 39, 140, 221, 222, 275, 347, 390

Dutch-Man (Bridges, T., 1775), III. 31, 240

Dutchman Outwitted (1746), II. 451

Dutchman's Dream (1835), IV. 453

Dutchmen Tricked (1784), III. 400

Dutch Pirate (1822), IV. 453

Dutch Tea Garden (1788), III. 325

Dutch the Diver (1878), V. 671

Dutiful Deception (1778), III. 325

Duty (Albery, J., 1879), v. 238

— (Bruce, H. P., 1889), v. 283

Duty and Honour = Fugitive

Dux Redux (Rhoades, J., 1887), v. 542

Dwarf (1832), IV. 453

— = Darby and Joan

Dwarf of Naples (Soane, G., 1819), IV. 403

D'ye know me now? (Braham, W. and Wellsey, N., 1872), v. 273

Dying Flower (Rogers, W., 1871), v. 814

Dying for a Kiss (1847), IV. 453

Dying for Love (Morton, J. M., 1858), v. 496

Dying Gift (Phillips, F. L., 1860) = Tramp's Adventure, v. 522, 671, 810, 831

— = (1) Gold Seekers; (2) Minerali

Dying to Live (1859), v. 671

Dyke House (Folkard, H., 1877), v. 370

Each for Himself (1816) = Doctor Poker, IV. 124–5, 453, 624

Each Man his Bird = First of September

Eagle and the Child (1856), v. 671

Eagle Joe (Herman, H., 1892), v. 419

Eagle's Cliff = Mabel Grey

Eagle's Flight = Man in the Moon

Eagle's Haunt (Fitzball, E., 1837), IV. 315

Eagle's Nest = (1) Dillosk Gatherer; (2) Eagle's Haunt

Eagle's Wing (Rimington, C., 1892), v. 543

Earl and the Baron = Bad Neighbours

Earl Goodwin (Yearsley, A., 1789), III. 317, 398

Earl Harold (1837), IV. 454

Earlier Days of Wallace = Marian

Earl of Brecon (Landor, R. E., 1841), IV. 199, 341

Earl of Douglas (1760), III. 325

Earl of Essex (Brooke, H., 1750), III. 85, 240

— (Jones, H., 1751), III. 18, 53, 84–5, 277

— = Unhappy Favourite

Earl of Essex, the Unhappy Favourite (1825), IV. 454

Earl of Gowrie (White, J., 1845), IV. 419

— = James VI

Earl of Leicester (Heath, S., 1843), IV. 324

Earl of Mar Marr'd (Philips, J., 1715), II. 262, 348, 442

Earl of Mulligatawny (Spurr, M. B. and Mayne, W., 1898), v. 577

Earl of Poverty (Almar, G., 1838), IV. 253

Earl of Ross (Munro, C. F., 1823), IV. 454, 624

Earl of Somerset (Lucas, H., 1779), III. 283

Earl of Warwick (Francklin, T., 1766), III. 61, 84, 261, 384

— (Hiffernan, P., 1764), III. 268, 387

— (Tolson, F., 1719), II. 360

Earl of Westmoreland (Brooke, H., 1742), II. 300 [At Smock Alley, Dublin, 13/5/1745, this was acted as "A New Play"]

Earl Olaf's Vow = White Pilgrim

Earl's Daughter (Russell, E. H., 1890), v. 553

Earl's Housekeeper (Seaman, W., 1872), v. 559

Earls of Hammersmith (Poole, J. and Lawler, D., 1811), IV. 386, 594

Earl's Son and the Citizen's Daughter = Curse of Mammon

Early Bird (1892), v. 671

Early Closing (Reach, A. B. and Hamilton, H., 1847), IV. 454, 624

Early Days of King Hal = King Hal's Early Days

Early Days of Richard III = Peerless Pool

Earnest Appeal (Hay, F., 1875), v. 411

Ear-ring (1872), v. 671

Earth, Air, Fire and Water (1848), IV. 454

Earthly Twins (Lewis, T. H., 1896), v. 459

Earthquake (Fitzball, E., 1828), IV. 313, 584

— (1828), IV. 454

Earthquake of Jamaica = Admiral Benbow

Easter Egg (Maynard, W., 1893), v. 483

Easter Fair (1830), IV. 454

Easter Hunting (1821), IV. 454

Easter Monday (1777), III. 325

— (1781), III. 325

Eastern Diplomacy = New Endimion
Eastern Fête = Bashaw
Eastern Treasure = Black and White
Easter Offering (1824), IV. 454
Easter Pastimes (1790), III. 325
East Indian (Lewis, M. G., 1799), III. 117, 122, 152, 281, 390
— (Thomson, A., 1799), III. 122, 312
— (1782), III. 325, 400
— (1812), IV. 454 [By error, this is wrongly equated with Rich and Poor in IV. 595 and 624]
East Lynne (Hardacre, J. P., 1898), v. 403
— (Oxenford, J., 1866), v. 510
— (Palmer, T. A., 1874), v. 148, 512
— (Paulton, J., 1889), v. 517
— (Shelley, H., 1899), v. 562
— (Wilde, L., 1898), v. 622
— (1866, 1869, 1870, 1875, 1883, 1884, 1893, 1896, 1899), v. 671
Eastward Ho = Black Cat
Eastward Hoe (1751), III. 325
Easy Shaving (Burnand, F. C. and Williams, M., 1863), v. 288
Ebb and Flow (Field, W. F., 1888), v. 366
Ebb and Flow of Fortune = High- and Low-Water Bell
Ebon Wand (1832), IV. 454
Ebony Casket (Speight, T. W., 1872), v. 576
Ebu Bekr (1840), IV. 624
Écarté (Newry, Lord, 1870), v. 503
— (1844), IV. 454
Eccentric Guardian (Zimmerman, H., 1885), v. 637
Eccentricities (1814), IV. 454
Eccentricity (McLaren, A., 1826), IV. 352
Eccentric Lover (Cumberland, R., 1798), III. 252
Eccentric Will (1899), v. 671
Echo (Heathcote, A. M., 1893), v. 415
Echo and Narcissus (Graves, R., 1776), III. 265
Echoes of the Night (Grattan, H. P. and Eldred, J., 1884), v. 389
Echoes of the Opera (Grain, R. C., 1893), v. 388
Echo of a Crime = Mighty Hand

Echo of Westminster Bridge (1835), IV. 454
Eclipse (Cross, J. C., 1801), IV. 286
Eclipsing the Son (Hartopp, W. W., 1860), v. 408
Edda (Fitzball, E., 1820), IV. 312
Eddication and Rights = Faith
Eddystone Elf = Monster of the Eddystone
Edelweiss (Broughton, F. W., 1893), v. 282
Edendale (Cheltnam, C. S., 1869), v. 102, 309
Edgar (Hallam, H., 1834), IV. 454, 624
— (Manners, G., 1806), IV. 353
— (Rymer, T., 1877), I. 142, 427
Edgar and Effie (1819), IV. 454
Edgar and Elfrida (Powell, T., ?1792), III. 394
Edgar and Emmeline (Hawkesworth, J., 1761), III. 267
Edgar Harissue (Malcolm, C. H. and Grahame, A., 1898), v. 472
Edgar the Socialist (Bonawitz, J. H., 1892), v. 267
Edict of Charlemagne = Free Knights
Edict of Spain (1859), v. 671
Edict of the Secret Council (Rayner, B. F., 1845), IV. 389
Edinburga (Buchanan, R., 1868), v. 284
Edith (Sidney, W., 1870), v. 566
Editha (Downman, H., 1784), III. 83, 257
Editha's Burglar (Burnett, Mrs F. H. and Townsend, S., 1890), v. 292
— (Clery, E., 1887), v. 313
Edith Lester the Wronged = Old Finsbury
Edith of the Marsh (Blake, T. G., 1840), IV. 268, 573
Edith's Flight (1875), v. 671
Edith the Captive (Towers, E., 1861), v. 671, 821
Edith West (1875), v. 671
Edmond, Orphan of the Castle (1799), III. 72, 325
Edmund Atherton (1853), v. 671
Edmund Kean (Pemberton, T. E., 1895), v. 519
— (Tamplin, H., 1893), v. 590
— (1864), v. 671
— (1871) v. 671

Eight Miles an Hour = Hooking Walker

Eight Pages (1859), v. 672

"£8. 10. 1, if Quite Convenient" (1823), IV. 454

Eighty Years of a Woman's Life = Phoebe Hersel

Eileen Dhu (Gordon, W., 1882), v. 385

Eileen Oge (Falconer, E., 1871), v. 360

Eily O'Connor (Haines, J. T., 1831), IV. 322

— (Wilks, T. E., 1860), v. 623, 823

Eily the Banshee (1835), IV. 454

Eitha and Aidallo (1801), IV. 454

Elaine (Keith, R., 1890), v. 442

Elbow Shakers (Cooper, F. F., 1827), IV. 283

Elder Brother (Anderson, J. R., 1850) v. 777

— (1844), IV. 454

Elder Brutus = Sybil

Elder Miss Blossom (Hendrie, E. and Wood, M., 1897), v. 417

Elders (Man, H., 1780), III. 286

Eldorado (Farnie, H. B., 1874), v. 361

Eldred (Jackson, J., 1773), III. 86, 276

Eleanor's Victory (Johnstone, J. B., 1864), v. 672, 831

— (Oxenford, J., 1865), v. 510

Eleanor the Accursed = Giant's Tomb

Eleanor the Amazon (Rodwell, G. H., 1851), v. 548

Election (Andrews, M. P., 1774), III. 204, 233

— (Baillie, J., 1817), IV. 208, 258

— (Cumberland, R., 1778), III. 251, 381

— (Dibdin, C. I. M., 1826), IV. 296

— (1749), II. 370

— (1784), III. 325

— (1790), III. 325

— (1803), IV. 454

— (1813), IV. 454

— (1818), IV. 454

— = Pasquin

Election at Rottenburgh = Nomination Day

Electioneering (Moncrieff, W. T. 1830), IV. 454, 624

Election Notes (Grain, R. C., 1885), v. 387

Election of the Managers (Colman, G., 1784), III. 247

Election under Difficulties (1865), v. 672

Electra (Francklin, T., 1774), III. 71, 261

— (Shirley, W., 1765), III. 71, 306

— (Theobald, L., 1714), II. 359, 444

— (1714), II. 370, 447

Electra, in a New Electric Light (Talfourd, F., 1859), v. 590

Electric Spark (Bessle, E., 1889), v. 260

— (Pidgin, C. and Blake, C., 1884), v. 524

Electric Telegraph (Somerset, C. A., 1853), v. 574

Electrophobia (Dixon, H. J., 1898), v. 346

Elements (Dibdin, C. I. M., 1818), IV. 294, 454, 580

Elements—Earth, Air, Fire, Water (1837), IV. 455

Elena Uberti (1842), IV. 455

Elephant of Siam (Beazley, S., Jr., 1829), IV. 264

— (1829), IV. 455

Elephants of the Pagoda (1846), IV. 455

— = Rajah of Nagpore

El Escribano (1897), v. 672

Eleven Knots an Hour = Outside Passenger

Eleventh Commandment (Castleton, R., 1899), v. 306

Eleventh Day (1835), IV. 455

Eleventh Hour (Mildenhall, T., 1844), IV. 455, 624

— (Raymond, R. J., 1826), IV. 455, 624

— (Saintsbury, H. A. and Macdonald, R., 1896), v. 554

Eleventh of June (O'Keeffe, J., 1798), III. 295

Elfiana (Simpson, K., 1895), v. 568

Elfie (Boucicault, D., 1871), v. 269

Elfies' Son (1832), IV. 455

Elfinella (Neil, R., 1875), v. 501

Elfin Queen (1835), IV. 455

Elfins of the Ice (1836), IV. 455

Elfin Sprite (1833), IV. 455

Elfin Sprite of the Norwegian Seas = Lord of the Maelstrom

Elfin Tree (Wray, P., 1875), v. 633

Elf-King's Oath = Oberon

Elf of the Flame = Fire Fiend

Elfrid (Dibdin, T. J., 1822), IV. 303, 455, 580, 624

Elfrid (Hill, A., 1710), II. 53, 108-9, 335, 438
Elfrida (Mason, W., 1752, 1772), III. 286
— (1808), IV. 455
— (1834), IV. 455
Elfrida of Olmutz (Dibdin, C. I. M., 1825), IV. 295
El Gambusino (1856), v. 672
El Heyder, the Chief of the Mountains (1857), v. 672
El Hyder (1836), IV. 455
El Hyder, the Chief of the Ghaut Mountains (Barrymore, W., 1818), IV. 262
Eliduke, Count of Yeoloc (Roscoe, W. C., 1846), IV. 609
Elie and Elode (1854), v. 672
Eligible Bachelor (1871), v. 672
Eligible Villa (1869), v. 672, 831
Elijah (Dupuis, T. S., 1789), III. 354, 383
Elise (1862), v. 672
Elisha (Hull, T., 1801), IV. 589
Elisina (Klanert, C. M., 1824), IV. 338
Elisir d'amore (1836), IV. 455
Elixir of Life (Conquest, G., 1873), v. 321
— (Phillips, F. L., 1846), IV. 372
— (1870), v. 672
Elixir of Love (Reynoldson, T. H., 1839), IV. 393, 608
— =Adina
Elixir of Youth (Sims, G. R. and Merrick, L., 1899), v. 570
Eliza (Rolt, R., 1754), III. 303
Eliza and Uncle Tom = Uncle Tom
Elizabeth (1824), IV. 624
— (1828), IV. 455
E-liz-abeth (Burnand, F. C., 1870), v. 289
Elizabeth and Essex (Dibdin, T. J., 1821), IV. 94, 303
Elizabeth Lazarus (Haines, J. T., 1842), IV. 323
Elizabeth of England (Rayner, B. F., 1846), IV. 389
Elizabeth, Queen of England (Williams, T., 1882), v. 625
— (1869), v. 672
Elizabeth Storey (Davis, S., 1868), v. 339
Eliza Fenning (1857), v. 672

Eliza Fenning, the Victim of Circumstances (1855), v. 672
Eliza Holmes (Neale, F., 1845), IV. 365
— (1862), v. 672
Ellaline (1890), v. 672
Ella Rosenberg (Kenney, J., 1807), IV. 117-18, 336
Ella's Love = Midnight Mail
Ellen (Sotheby, W., 1816), IV. 405
— (Wills, W. G., 1879), v. 627
Ellen and Alberto (1812), IV. 455
Ellen and Susan (Pitt, G. D., 1845), IV. 373
— (1863), v. 672
Ellen Mavourneen (Pitt, G. D., 1845), IV. 373
Ellen Porter (Marchant, F., 1864), v. 475
Ellen Ray (1833), IV. 455
Ellen the Bride of Young Lochinvar = Galloping Lover
Ellen Trent (1840), IV. 624
Ellen Wareham (Buckstone, J. B., 1833), IV. 274
— (Burton, W. E., 1834), IV. 277
Ellie Brandon (Price, M., 1868), v. 531
Ellie Forester (Johnstone, J. B., 1857), v. 672, 800, 831
Ellinda (Robertson, Mrs, 1800), III. 302; IV. 394
El Mahdi (1885), v. 672
Elmerick (Lillo, G., 1740), II. 41, 111-12, 342, 440
Elmine (Jones, A. C., 1883), v. 439
Elmira (Stanley, E., 1790), III. 308
— (1781), III. 325
Elmira, the Female Pirate (1865), v. 672
Elodie, the Virgin of the Monastery = Angel of Peace and Pardon
Eloisa (Reynolds, F., 1786), III. 11, 120, 301
Eloise (1839), IV. 455
Eloped = Babes in the Wood
Elopement (Havard, W., 1763), II. 334; III. 267
— (Jones, H. A., 1879), v. 162, 439
— (McLaren, A., 1811), IV. 351
— (1768), III. 325
— (1784), III. 326
— (1826), IV. 455
— = Amateurs and Actors
Elopement Extraordinary (1814), IV. 455

Elopement from the Seraglio = Belmont and Constance

Elopements in High Life (Sullivan, R., 1853), v. 586

Elopement to Rheims = Five Minutes too Late

Eloquence of Silence (1899), v. 672

Elphi Bey (Hamilton, R., 1817), IV. 323

Elsa Dene (Calmour, A. C., 1886), v. 300

Elsa's Hand (May, V., 1893), v. 482

Elsa's Lover: an Idyll of Rheingau (1892), v. 672

Elsdale Hall (Oswin, C. H., 1842), IV. 456, 602, 624 [cited wrongly as Esdale Hall]

Elshie (Gott, H., 1823), IV. 455, 585, 624

Elshie of the Moor = Recluse

Elsie (Broughton, F. W., 1883), v. 281

Elsie Glendinning (Haines, J. T., 1825), IV. 586

Elsie's Rival (Greet, D. A., 1888), v. 393

El Toreador (1855), v. 672

Elves (Selby, C., 1856), v. 560

Elvira (Digby, G., 1662–5), I. 192, 402–3; II. 142; III. 114

— (Mallet, D., 1762), II. 343; III. 286

Elwina (Fitzgerald, M., 1792), III. 259

Elysium (1789), III. 326

Embaras des Richesses (Ozell, J., 1735), II. 347, 442

Embarcation (Franklin, A., 1799), III. 261

Embarcation for Holland = Orange Boven

Embarassed Husband (1785), III. 326

Embarrassed Man (1863), v. 672

Embassy (Planché, J. R. 1841) IV. 381

Emblematical Tribute in Honour of Her Majesty's Nuptials (Macfarren, G., 1840), IV. 350

Emerald Isle (1861), v. 672

Emerald Queen (Travers, W., 1870), v. 603

Emigrant Family (1864), v. 672

Emigrant in London (1795), III. 326

Emigrant Murderer = Martin Rivers

Emigrant Prevented = Live and Hope

Emigrants = Adelaide

Emigrant's Daughter (Raymond, R. J., 1838), IV. 389

Emigrant's Progress (1852), v. 672

Emigrants, the Smuggler and the Bush-ranger = Life of a Labourer

Emigration (Connor, B., 1880), v. 320

— (O'Grady, H., 1883), v. 506

— (1835), IV. 455, 624

— (1836), IV. 455

— (1855), v. 672

Emigration—the Remedy (Stocqueler, J. H., 1848), IV. 455, 624

Emigré's Daughter (1850), v. 672

Emilia (Meilan, M. A., 1771), III. 287

— (1672), I. 441

Emilia Galotti (Holcroft, F., 1805), IV. 326

— (Maty, H., 1786), III. 64, 286

— (Thompson, B., 1800), IV. 412

— (1794), III. 64, 326

Emilie de la Roche (1834), IV. 455

Emily (D'Egville, 1807), IV. 455, 624

— (Hamilton, G., 1877), v. 80, 401

Emily Fitzormond (Denvil, Mrs, 1841), IV. 579

Emir's Edict = Ebu Bekr

Emissary (Dance, G., 1831), IV. 455, 624

Em'ly (1884), v. 672

Emma (Richards, G., 1804), IV. 394

— (1893), v. 672

Emma Hardy (1851), v. 672

Emma the Prude! Ellen the Romp! Eliza the Idiot! = Tria juncta in uno

Emma von Falkenstein = Crusaders

Emma Wingrove (1844), IV. 455

Emmeline (Suter, W. E., 1861), v. 673, 818, 831

— (1816), v. 445

Emmeline of Hungary (Dibdin, T. J., 1826), IV. 304

Emmeline the Female Parricide = Love and Error

Emperor and Galilean (Ray, C., 1876), v. 812

Emperor and his Three Sons = Chinese Sorcerer

Emperor and the Exile = Joseph II

Emperor and the Exiles (1857), v. 673

Emperor and the Page = Night after the Battle

Emperor and the Soldier = Napoleon

Emperor of China Grand Volgi (Chet-wood, W., 1731), II. 306

Emperor of China's Court = Harlequin Invisible

Emperor of Queerumania (1805), IV. 455

Emperor of Russia (1844), IV. 455

Emperor of the Moon (Behn, A., 1687), I. 262, 332, 356, 392; III. 114

— (1777), III. 114, 326

Emperor's Decree (1860), V. 673

Emperor's Gift (1853), V. 831

Emperor's Joke (1836), IV. 455

Emperor's New Clothes (Hood, B., 1897), V. 425

Emperor's Own = San Toy

Emperor's Victim = Celeste

Empirick (Horde, T.), III. 273

Empress and No Empress (McLaren, A., 1810), IV. 351

Empress of Morocco (Duffett, T., 1673), I. 37, 85, 249, 407

— (Settle, E., 1673), I. 33, 37, 49–50, 62, 81, 85, 117, 128, 130, 149, 331, 348, 428

Empty Cottage = Frolics in "Forty-Five"

Empty Khan and the Khurdish Conspirators = Wild Wolf of Tartary

Empty Pocket = English Gentleman

Empty Stocking (Wright, F., 1898), V. 633

Empty Wigwam (1894), V. 673

Enamouring Girdle = Cytherea

Enchanted Arabs = Hundred Battle Steeds

Enchanted Barber (Blanchard, E. L. and Greenwood, T. L., 1877), V. 264

Enchanted Beans (Freeman, C., 1875), V. 372

Enchanted Beauties of the Golden Castle (1846), IV. 455

Enchanted Bell (1844), IV. 455

Enchanted Bird = Magicians

Enchanted Castle (Andrews, M. P., 1786), III. 72, 233, 377

— (Milner, H. M., 1822), IV. 455, 624

— = Mock-Tempest

Enchanted Cavern (1791), III. 400

Enchanted Courser (Croly, G., 1824), IV. 285

Enchanted Dove (1881), V. 673

Enchanted Eyes = Doge of Duralto

Enchanted Fawn (1872), V. 673

Enchanted Fife (1872), V. 673

Enchanted Fire of the Invisible Island (Lewis, M. G., 1824), IV. 456, 624

Enchanted Flute, III. 400

Enchanted Forest (Dance, C., 1847), IV. 289

Enchanted Forth (1861), V. 673

Enchanted Garden (1808), IV. 456

— (1856), V. 673

Enchanted Girdles (Dibdin, T. J., 1825), IV. 304

— (1828), IV. 456

Enchanted Gondola (1846), IV. 456

Enchanted Grove (1831), IV. 456

— (1837), IV. 456

Enchanted Hall (Bradwell, W., 1804), IV. 270

Enchanted Harp (Cross, J. C., 1802), IV. 286

— = Mora's Love

Enchanted Horn (Towers, E., 1860), V. 673, 821, 831

— (1818), IV. 456

— (1836) IV. 456

Enchanted Horse (Smith, A. R. and Taylor, T., 1845), IV. 402; V. 820 [C. L. Kenney was also associated with the writing of this drama]

Enchanted Hull (1805), IV. 456

Enchanted Island (Fawcett, J., 1804), IV. 311, 583

— (1816), IV. 456

— = Tempest

Enchanted Isle (Brough, W. and Brough, R. B., 1848), IV. 151–2, 271

Enchanted Lady = Distressed Knight

Enchanted Lake (Baird, J. F., 1856), V. 673, 831

— (1854), V. 673

— (1868), V. 831

Enchanted Lover (Lower, Sir W., 1658), I. 420

Enchanted Lovers = Brutus of Alba

Enchanted Lute = Rose of the Alhambra

Enchanted Maid (Wyke, E. B., 1882), V. 634

Enchanted Mountain (1897), V. 673

Enchanted Orange Tree (Rogers, T. S., 1880), V. 549

Enchanted Palfrey (1850), V. 673

Enchanted Prince (Douglass, J. T., 1877), V. 348

Enchanted Raven (1841), IV. 456

Enchanted Ring (1836), IV. 456

Enchanted Spell = Mountain Cataract

Enchanted Standard = Alfred the Great

Enchanted Tower (Selby, C., 1848), IV. 399

Enchanted Veil = Fairy Lake

Enchanted Wives (Rice, C., 1853), v. 542

Enchanted Wood (Byron, H. J., 1870), v. 297

— (Francis, 1792), III. 261, 384

— (1785), III. 384

Enchanted Woodman = Fays of the Forest

Enchanter (Garrick, D., 1760), III. 262

— (1828), IV. 456

Enchanter of Stonehenge = Merlin

Enchanters (1806), IV. 456

Enchanter's Slave (Knowles, J., 1850), v. 446

Enchantment (Law, A., 1878), v. 449

— (1812), IV. 140, 456

Enchantress (Bunn, A., 1845), IV. 276, 575

— (Edwards, A. M., 1783), III. 258

Encounter (Kirkman, F., 1662), I. 417

Encounter and Carousal of the Wild Indian (1854), v. 673

End of a Day (Burnett, H., 1891), v. 292

End of June (1846), IV. 456

End of the Tether (Baddeley, G. C.), v. 247

'Endon Way (Brand, O. and Calvert, C., 1898), v. 274

Endora (1871), v. 673

End will come = Step by Step

Endymion (Brough, W., 1860), v. 279

— (1881), v. 673

Enemies (Coghlan, C. F., 1886), v. 316

Enemy (Neville, H., 1879), v. 502

Enemy Note Book (1857), v. 673

Enemy of Man (1899), v. 673

Enemy of the People (Archer, W., 1890), v. 61, 242

Enemy's Camp (Leonard, H., 1894), v. 456

Energy and Force of Love = Beautiful Armenia

Enfant prodigue (1815), IV. 456

Engaged (Gilbert, W. S., 1877), v. 140-1, 380

Engaged to Appear (1879), v. 673

Engagement (Stephenson, B. C., 1890), v. 582

Engelbert (Barnes, J., 1680?), I. 389

Engineer (Bolton, C., 1863), v. 673, 779, 831

Engineering (Matthison, A., 1878), v. 481

England against Italy (1787), III. 326

England and Australia = Give a Dog a Bad Name

England and France in the Days of Chivalry (Stocqueler, J. H., 1855), v. 585

England and Glory (Grafton, S., 1888), v. 386

England expects every Man to do his Duty = Rule Britannia

England Ho! (1878), v. 673

England, Home and Beauty (Bracewell, J., 1882), v. 272

England in 1450 = Sanctuary

England in the Days of Charles II (Wills, W. G., 1877), v. 627

England Invaded = Alfred the Great

England Preserved (Watson, G., 1795), III. 87, 315, 397

England run mad; with particulars of the Stratford Jubilee = Garrick's Vagary

England's Ally = Ransom of Manilla

England's Charter (Barnett, C. Z., 1848), IV. 261

England's Dark Ages = Tower of London

England's Darling (Austin, A., 1896), v. 245

England's Defenders (1895), v. 673

England's Flag (Whyte, H., 1895), v. 621

England's Glory (1706), II. 370

— (1795), III. 326

— (1797), III. 326

— (1894), v. 673

England's Golden Days = Kenilworth

England's Harvest Home and National Steeplechase (1856), v. 673

England's Joy (1795), III. 326

England's King (1827), IV. 456

England's Monarch (1843), IV. 456

England's Pride = Firm as Oak

England's Pride and Glory = Engineer

England, the Anchor and Hope of the World (1828), IV. 456

England, the Home of the Free (Campbell, A., 1874), V. 783
England the Land of Freedom = Dulce Domum
English at Paris (1821), IV. 456
English Born and Scottish Bred (1889), V. 673
English Britons (1763), III. 326
English Chevalier = Coquet
English Etiquette (Oxenford, J., 1840), IV. 367
English Fleet, in 1342 (Dibdin, T. J., 1803), IV. 142, 297
English Frier (Crowne, J., 1690), I. 10, 271, 400
English Gentleman (Byron, H. J., 1870), V. 297
English Hawks and Irish Pigeons (1860), V. 673
English Hearts (Hall, M. and Green, H. 1892), V. 399
English Hearts and Homes = Sons of Toil
English Hermit = Philip Quarll
English Hero and the American Boy = Champion of the World
English in Algeria = Britons Abroad
English, Irish and Scotch = Tricks and Blunders
English King = Harold
English Lawyer (Ravenscroft, E., 1677), I. 255, 426
— = Ignoramus
Englishman from Paris (Murphy, A., 1756), III. 180, 289
Englishman in Germany (1792), III. 326
Englishman in Paris (Foote, S., 1753), III. 172, 259, 383
Englishman in Spain = Hebrew Family
Englishman out of Paris = Reapers
Englishman returned from Paris (Foote, S., 1756), III. 115, 172, 259
Englishman's Fireside = John Bull
Englishman's House is his Castle (Morton, J. M., 1857), V. 496
Englishmen Abroad = Golden Fruit
Englishmen in Bordeaux (1764), III. 326, 400
Englishmen in Corsica = Conscript's Bride
Englishmen in India (Dimond, W., 1827), IV. 307

English Merchant (Colman, G., 1767), III. 12, 119, 140-1, 145, 246, 379
English Monarch = Edgar
English Monsieur (Howard, J., 1663). I. 215, 232, 344, 414
English Nihilist (1883), V. 673
— (1887), V. 673
English Plum-Pudding (1824), IV. 456
English Prince = Edward the Black Prince
English Princess (Caryll, J., 1667), I. 55, 116, 346, 395
English Readings (Cobb, J., 1787), III. 244
English Rogue (Thomson, T., 1668), I. 435
English Rose (Sims, G. R. and Buchanan, R., 1890), V. 569
English Sailors in America (1760), III. 326
English Stage Italianiz'd = Dido and Æneas
English Tar and the Indian Princess = Poccahontas
English Tavern at Berlin (1789), III. 326
English Violet = Mighty Hand
English Volunteer = Courage Rewarded
Englishwoman (Miller, St A., 1894), V. 488
Enjoyment (Selby, C., 1841), IV. 456, 624
Enlisted (1885), V. 673
— (1892), V. 673
— = Chain Gang
Enlisted Shepherds (Hawkins W., 1786), III. 267
Enoch Arden (Matthison, A., 1876), V. 481
Enquire Within (Boucicault, D., 1845), IV. 270
— (Burnand, F. C., 1868), V. 289
Enraged Musician (Colman, G., 1789) = Ut Pictura Poesis, III. 326, 379, 400
— (Raymond, R. J., 1828), IV. 456, 624
En Route (Grain, R. C., 1882), V. 387
— = Bombay to Henley
Ensign (Thompson, B., 1800), III. 122; IV. 412
Ensign of Freedom = Senekos the Greek
Ensnared (Frith, W., 1883), V. 373
En-tail and Ren-tail = Law's Two Tails

Every Cloud has a Silver Lining =
Adrift on the World
Everyday Characters (1805), IV. 457
Every-Day Occurrences (Rhys, H.,
1862), V. 674, 813, 831
Every Dog has his Day = Gelert
Every Inch a Sailor = Ocean of Life
Every Man for Himself (Fairbairn,
Mrs R., 1885), V. 359
Every Man has his Price = Walpole
Every Man his Hobby = Dupes of Fancy
Every Man in his Folly = Connoisseur
Every Man in his Humour (Garrick, D.,
1751), III. 262
— (1725), II. 371
Every One has His Fault (Inchbald,
Mrs E., 1792), III. 145-6, 148, 151,
165, 275
Every One has his Whim = Eccentricity
Every Thing in Season (?1740), II.
451
Every Woman in her Humour (Clive,
C., 1760), III. 243
Eve's Temptation (Bertrand, E. C.,
1888), V. 260
Evicted (1880), V. 674
Eviction (O'Grady, H., 1879), V. 506
Evil Eye (Almar, G.), IV. 273
— (Peake, R. B., 1831), IV. 370
— (1876), V. 674
Evil Genius (Bernard, W. B., 1856), V.
259
— (Collins, W. W., 1885), V. 318
Evil Hands and Honest Hearts (Hazle-
wood, C. H., 1864), V. 674, 831
Evil Life (Warren, F. B., 1898), V. 615
— = Wide World
Evil May Day (Emden, W. S., 1837),
IV. 309
Evil Spirit of a Bit o' Love and a
Revengeful Heart = Mifistifix
Evil Spirits (1775), III. 400
Exalted Cuckold = Farrier Nicked
Example of Justice to Present and
Future Times = Sailor's Opera
Excelsior (Ellis, L., 1887), V. 357
— (1885), V. 674
Exchange Alley (1720), II. 371
Exchange no Robbery (Hook, T. E.,
1820), IV. 328
— = Secretary and the Cook
Excise (1733), II. 371

Exciseman (Knapp, H., 1780), III. 279,
390
Excommunicated Prince (Bedloe, W.,
1679), I. 390
Excursion (1853), V. 674
Excursion Train (McCarthy, J. H. and
Yardley, W., 1885), V. 467
— (1858), V. 674
Execution (1785), III. 326
Executioner (Thackeray, T. J., 1829),
IV. 412
Executioner of Amsterdam = Vanrick of
Voorn
Executioner of Paris = Homme Noir
Executioner's Daughter (Ramsay, A.
and de Cordova, R., 1896), V. 534
Exeter Mail (1828), IV. 457
Exile (Earle, 1804), IV. 582
— (Grover, J. H., 1879), V. 396
— (Reynolds, F., 1808), IV. 51, 391
— = Exiled
Exiled (Clarkson, H., 1877), V. 313
— (Manning, W. and Darbey, E.,
1891), V. 474
Exiled Minister (1820), IV. 457
Exiled Mother = Held at Bay
Exiled Plantagenet = Edict of the Secret
Council
Exile of Erin = Maurice the Outcast
Exile of Genoa (1837), IV. 457
Exile of Siberia (1854), V. 674
— = Elizabeth
Exiles (Rannie, J., 1806), III. 300; IV.
388
— (1894), V. 674
Exile's Daughter = Rosalie
Exiles in Siberia = Frozen Cliff
Exiles of Erin (Buchanan, R., 1881), V.
284
Exiles of Fortune = Icebound
Exiles of France (Hollingsworth, 1840),
IV. 588
Exiles of Kamschatka = Benyowsky
Exiles of Siberia = Russia
Exit by Mistake (Jameson, R. F., 1816),
IV. 330, 590
Ex-Minister (1834), IV. 457
Expectations = My Great Aunt
Expected General (1870), V. 674
Experientia Jocet = Polyphonus
Experiment (Murray, C., 1779), III. 290
— (Stuart, C., 1777), III. 310

Expiation (Manuel, E., 1876), v. 475

Exploits of a Gentleman at Large = Robert Macaire

Exploits of Harlequin = British Stage

Exposition (Brooks, C. W. S., 1851), v. 277

Exposure (1663), I. 441

Express (Masson, A., 1868), v. 480

Expulsion of the Moors = Spaniards

Expulsion of the Tarquins = Lucius Junius Brutus

Exquisite at Fault = Stratagem

Exquisites (De Trueba, J. T., 1831), IV. 457, 624

Extorted Oath = Castle of Paluzzi

Extra Hand (1899), v. 674

Extraordinary Behaviour of Mrs Jallowby (Brooke, C., 1896), v. 276

Extraordinary Version of the Lady of Lyons (1860), v. 674

Extra Turn (1899), v. 674

Extravagant Zealot = Hermon Prince of Chorœa

Extremely Peculiar (1857), v. 674

Extreme Penalty (Holcroft, G., 1886), v. 424

Extremes (Falconer, E., 1858), v. 121, 360

— = De Valencourt

Extremes are Bad = Juvenile Party

Extremes Meet (Field, K., 1877), v. 365

Eye of Light = Hebrew Diamond

Eye-on! (1836), IV. 457

Eyes and No Eyes (Gilbert, W. S., 1875), v. 380

Eyes in the Dark (1866), v. 674

Eyes, Nose and Mouth (Blanchard, E. L., 1847), IV. 269

Eyes Right (Field, K., 1878), v. 674, 792, 831

Eye to Business (Halliday, G. B. and Tardrew, P., 1883), v. 401

Ezio (Humphreys, S., 1732), II. 393, 439

Fabian (1856), v. 674

Fabulist, III. 115, 326

Face at the Window (Warren, F. B., 1897), v. 615

Faces in the Fire (Buckingham, L. S., 1865), v. 286

Face in the Moonlight (Osborne, C., 1871), v. 508

Face to Face (À Beckett, G. A., 1869), v. 233

— (Archer, W. J., 1877), v. 242

— (Hall, C. I., 1872), v. 399

— (Harbourn, A., 1869), v. 403

— (Munns, H. T., 1877), v. 499

— (Stanley, H. J., 1875), v. 579

— = £. s. d.

Facing the Music (Darnley, J. H., 1899), v. 337

Fact and Fancy (1872), v. 674

Factions Citizen = Mr Turbulent

Factory Assassin (Rayner, B. F., 1837), IV. 389

Factory Boy (Haines, J. T., 1840), IV. 323

Factory Girl (Jerrold, D. W., 1832), IV. 332

— (1852), v. 674

Factory Lad (Walker, J., 1832), IV. 416

Factory Strike (Taylor, G. F., 1838), IV. 410, 613

Faddimir (Reed, A., 1889), v. 539

Faded Flowers (À Beckett, A. W., 1872), v. 233

Fadette (Grist, W., 1886), v. 395

Fadette, the Golden Gadfly (Greenwood, P., 1871), v. 393

Fadorougha and the Black Prophet (Stanley, H. J., 1898), v. 579

Faggot-Binder (Foote, S., 1762), III. 384

Faggot Makers (1809), IV. 457

Faigale (Rackow, N., 1898), v. 532

Faint Heart ne'er won Fair Lady (Planché, J. R., 1839), IV. 381

Faint Heart Never Won Fair Lady (1893), v. 674

Faint Heart which did win Fair Lady (Wooler, J. P., 1863), v. 632

Fair (1750), III. 326

Fair American (Pilon, F., 1782), III. 298

— (1771), III. 326 [The date of acting should be 20/5/1771]

Fair and Square (Bell, A. B., 1888), v. 255

Fair Apostate (McDonald, A., 1791), III. 283

Fair Bargain (Harley, G., 1894), v. 404

Fair Bigamist (Burford, U., 1888), v. 287

Fair Brigands = Female Mascaroni

Fair Caledonian = Love and Money

Fair Captive (Haywood, Mrs E., 1721), II. 17, 26, 31, 83–4, 335

Fair Cheating (1814), IV. 457

Fair Circassian (Croxall, S., 1720), II. 223, 317

— (Hazlewood, C. H., 1872), v. 414

— (Pratt, S. J., 1781) = Circassian, III. 299, 393

— = Almoran and Hamet

Fair Conquest (Drinkwater, A. E., 1887), v. 351

Fair Crusader (1815), IV. 457, 636

Fair Deceivers (Church, C., 1893), v. 310

Fair Deserter (1816), IV. 457

Fair Encounter (Rae, C. M., 1875), v. 532

Fair Equestrienne (Russell, E. H., 1890), v. 553

Fair Example (Estcourt, R., 1703), II. 133, 145, 183, 194–5, 320, 435

Fair Exchange (Williams, M., 1860), v. 624, 824

— (1865), v. 674

Fairfair the Tulip and the Camp at Coen = Days of Louis XV

Fair Fame (Day, J. T., 1884), v. 340

Fair Foundling = Patie and Peggie

Fair France (Digges, W., 1874), v. 345

Fair Fugitive = Coffee-House

Fair Fugitives (Porter, A. M., 1803), IV. 387, 606

Fair Gabrielle (Planché, J. R., 1822) = Henri Quatre, IV. 377, 477, 604, 628

Fair Game (Dudley, Sir H. B., 1813), IV. 308

Fair Geraldine = Count Tremolio [By error on IV. 628 The Fair Geraldine is given for The Fair Gabrielle]

Fair Greek = Irene

Fair Helen (Amcotts, V.), v. 240

Fair Hypocrite (1745), II. 451

— = Maiden Queen

Fairies (?Garrick, D., 1755), III. 111, 262, 385

— = Falls of Clyde

Fairies' Festival on Shakespeare's Birthday (Falconer, E., 1864), v. 360

Fairies' Frolic (Shield, H., 1863), v. 816

Fairies' Haunt (1856), v. 674

Fairies' Home (1840), IV. 625

Fairies of the Rhine = Alva

Fairies of the Silver Mine = Demon Arab

Fairies' Revels (Fawcett, J., 1802), IV. 311

Fair Inconstant = Elfrid

Fair Intriguers (1835), IV. 457

Fair Lady (1807), IV. 457

Fairleigh's Birthright (Peel, G., 1878), v. 518

Fair Libertine = Rival Widows

Fair Lilias (Young, Mrs H., 1865), v. 674, 825, 831

Fairlop Fair (Dibdin, C. I. M., 1812), IV. 293

Fair Lunatick (1749), II. 451

Fairly Caught (Day, G. D., 1892), v. 339

Fairly Foiled (Allen, O., 1871), v. 239

Fairly Hit and Fairly Missed (Martin, J.), IV. 597

Fairly in for't = Plants and Planets

Fairly Puzzled (Brand, O., 1884), v. 273

Fairly Taken In = Personation

Fairly Won (1873), v. 674

Fair Maid of Clifton (Goodyer, F. R., 1872), v. 384

Fair Maid of Islington = Canonburg Tower

Fair Maid of Kent = Windsor Castle [The plays listed III. 297 and 400 are probably identical]

Fair Maid of Perth (Webb, C., 1845), IV. 95, 417

— (1828), IV. 95, 457

— = St Valentine's Eve

Fair Maid of the West = Unnatural Parents

Fair Maid of Tottenham Court (1840), IV. 457

Fair Maid of York = Ivanhoe

Fair Mendicant and the Spirit of the Rock = Fatherless Fanny

Fair of Saint-Germain (Ozell, J., 1718), II. 347, 420, 442

Fair Old Maid of 1725 = Countess of Lilliput

Fair One with the Golden Locks (Conquest, G. and Spry, H., 1891), v. 322

— (Millward, C., 1877), v. 674, 807, 831

— (Planché, J. R., 1843), IV. 382, 605

— (1867, 1879, 1887, 1894), v. 674

Fair One with the Locks of Gold (Conquest, G. and Spry, H., 1861), v. 674, 817, 831

Fair on the Ice = Yahrmanka nal Dhu

Fair Orphan (Stevens, G. A., 1771), III. 326, 396, 400

Fair Parricide (1752), III. 326

Fair Penitent (Kemble, J. P., 1814), IV. 335

— (Rowe, N., 1703), II. 57, 58, 59, 70, 99–100, 352, 443

— (1813), IV. 457

Fair Persian = Noureddin

Fair Peruvian (1786) = Peruvian, III. 326, 400, 403

Fair Play (Reynolds, F., 1808) = Begone Dull Care, IV. 457, 625

— = Scarlet Sins

Fair Play's a Jewel = Heart of Hearts

Fair Pretender (Simpson, J. P., 1865), v. 567

Fair Princess (Bernard, F., 1886), v. 259

Fair Quaker (Thompson, E., 1773), III. 116, 311, 397

— (1812), IV. 140, 457

Fair Quaker of Deal (Shadwell, C., 1710), II. 9, 42, 53, 132, 133, 136, 176, 354; III. 116, 397; IV. 140

Fair Refugee (1784), III. 327, 400

Fair Rivals (Hewitt, J., 1729), II. 335

Fair Rosamond (Akhurst, W. M., 1873), v. 237

— (Burnand, F. C., 1862), v. 288

— (Ellis, B., 1893), v. 357

— (Faucit, J. S., 1821), IV. 311

— (Field, M., 1884), v. 366

— (Godwin, E. W., 1886), v. 383

— (James, C. S., 1847), IV. 330

— (Lee, N., Jr., 1860), v. 803

— (Upton, 1801), IV. 415

— (1734), II. 371

— (1813), IV. 457

Fair Rosamond (1860), v. 675

Fair Rosamond, according to the History of England (Taylor, T. P., 1838), IV. 411

Fair Rosamond's Bower (Langbridge, F.), v. 448

Fair Rosamund (Barnett, C. Z., 1837), IV. 260

Fair Sicilian (Albert, 1834), IV. 567

Fair Sinner (Appleton, G. W., 1885), v. 241

Fair Sinners (Paget, 1881), v. 511

Fair Slave (1806), IV. 457

Fair Star (Smith, A. R. and Oxenford, J., 1844), IV. 402

Fair Sylvia (1869), v. 675

Fair Take-in = Martha

Fair Venetian (1776), III. 327

Fair Winds for Foul Ways = Captain John Luck

Fair Women and Brave Men (Tharp, T. A., 1897), v. 595

Fair Words and Foul Deeds (Travers, W., 1868), v. 603

Fairy (1801), IV. 457

— (1804), IV. 457

— (1861), v. 675

Fairy and the Fawn (Rice, C., 1852), v. 542

Fairy and the Golden Dove (Stirling, E., 1858), v. 818

Fairy Ball = Milliners

Fairy Benison (Bishop, S., 1796), III. 238

Fairy Birds of the Forest = Children of the Wood

Fairy Blue and Fairy Red (Dibdin, T. J., 1825), IV. 304

Fairy Call = Appel des Fées

Fairy Circle (Grattan, H. P., 1857), v. 675, 794, 831

Fairy Court (Gentleman, F., 1761), III. 264

Fairy Elves of the Fourth Estate (Frost, F., 1856) = Tit, Tat Toe, v. 675, 793, 831, 835

Fairy Favour (Hull, T., 1766), III. 274

— (1790), III. 327

Fairy Favours (1797) = Fairy Festival, III. 327, 400

Fairy Fawn (1872), v. 831

Fairy Fern Flower (1856), v. 675

Fairy Festival (1797) = Fairy Favours,
 III. 327, 400
Fairy Friendship = Queen Mab
Fairy Genesta (1892), V. 675
Fairy Gift = Alzora and Nerine
Fairy Glen (Brand, O., 1884), V. 273
Fairy Gnomes of the Golden Caves
 (1844), IV. 457
Fairy-Hill (Mansell, W., 1784), III. 213,
 217, 286
Fairy Lady (Wilks, T. E., 1844), IV.
 421
Fairy Lake (Lee, A., 1839), IV. 342
— (Selby, C., 1839), IV. 398, 610
— (1839), IV. 458
— = (1) Magic Minstrel; (2) Swan and
 Edgar
Fairy Land (Merion, C., 1872), V. 485
+ — (Paxton, A., *French*)
— (1809), IV. 458
Fairy Legends (1818), IV. 458
Fairy Madge (Trevelyan, C., 1891), V.
 603
Fairy Man = Poul a Dhoil
Fairy Oak (Coape, H. C., 1845), IV.
 577
Fairy of the Coral Grot (1857), V. 675
Fairy of the Fountain (1813), IV. 458
Fairy of the Lake (Thelwall, J., 1801),
 III. 311; IV. 412
Fairy of the Lakes = Kate Kearney
Fairy of the North Star (1819), IV. 458
Fairy of the Oak (1811), IV. 458
Fairy of the Silver Mine = Gnome King
Fairy Page (Harris, A. G., 1852), V. 675,
 795, 832
Fairy Pool of the Giant Mountain =
 Steel Hand and his Nine Thieves
Fairy Prince (Colman, G., 1771), III.
 27, 112, 212, 246, 379
Fairy-Queen (Settle, E., 1692), I. 12,
 38, 39, 135, 160-1, 352, 429
— (1711), II. 371
— (1730), II. 371
Fairy Queen of the Golden Starlight
 (1877), V. 675
Fairy Records = Fairy Legends
Fairy Reformed = Erl King's Daughter
Fairy Ring (1869), V. 675
— (1886), V. 675
Fairy Roses = (1) Prince Amabel; (2)
 Turko the Terrible

Fairy's Fantasy (1795), III. 327
Fairy's Father (Cheltnam, C. S., 1862),
 V. 309
Fairy Slipper (Albert, 1834), IV. 567
Fairy's Post Box (Simpson, J. P., 1885),
 V. 568
Fairy's Revenge = Prince Camaralza-
 man
Fairy Tale (Colman, G. and Garrick,
 D., 1761), III. 111, 245-6
— (1848), IV. 458
— (1860), V. 675
Fairy Tale of the Home = Cricket on the
 Hearth
Fairy Tales of Mother Goose (1855), V.
 675
Fairy Tempter = Banshee's Spell
Faith (Lart, J., 1884), V. 449
— (Wills, F., 1884), V. 627
— (1879), V. 675
— (1887), V. 675
Faith and Falsehood (Rede, W. L.,
 1834) = Sunshine and Shade, IV. 390,
 539, 640
Faith and Hope (Rodway, J., 1886), V.
 548
— (1848), IV. 458
Faithful and True = Angels
Faithful Bride of Granada (Taverner,
 W., 1704), II. 79, 358
Faithful Country Maid = Village Wed-
 ding
Faithful Couple (1722), II. 371
— = Mangora, King of the Timbusians
Faithful General (1706), II. 371, 447
Faithful Genius (?1660-1700), I. 441
Faithful Guide = Mountains of Modena
Faithful Heart (Palgrave, R., 1875), V.
 511
— = Laura
Faithful Infidel = Turkish Lovers
Faithful Irishman = (1) Committee; (2)
 Teague; (3) What News from Bantry
 Bay; (4) Widow and no Widow
Faithful Irishwoman (Clive, C., 1765),
 III. 243
Faithful James (Stephenson, B. C.,
 1889), V. 582
Faithful Lover = Laura
Faithfull Shepheard = Pastor Fido
Faithful Pair (Maxwell, J., 1740), II.
 343

Faithful Shepherd (Grove, W., 1782),
III. 70, 266, 327, 386

+— (Sheridan, T., Smock Alley, Dublin, 31/1/1740) [This is probably a
revised version of the following: if so,
that was by T. Sheridan]

— (1736), II. 224, 371, 447

— = Pastor Fido

Faithful to the End = Denounced

Faithful under Peril = Faith under Peril

Faithful unto Death (Newbound, E.,
1876), v. 502

— (Robson, E. M. and Compton, E.,
1881), v. 547

Faithful Virgins (?1663), I. 441

Faith, Hope and Charity (Blanchard,
E. L., 1845), IV. 268

— (Hazlewood, C. H., 1863) = Widow
and Orphans, v. 675, 768, 796, 832,
850

Faith in Love (1862), v. 675

Faithless Cosen german = Jugurtha

Faithless Favourites = Elfrida

Faithless Friend (Amherst, J. H., 1821),
IV. 253

Faithless Wife (Lane, Mrs S., 1876), v.
448

Faith's Fraud (Landor, R. E., 1841), IV.
199, 341

Faith's Reward (1885), v. 675

Faith Triumphant = Esther

Faith under Peril (Abel, W. H., 1873),
v. 1, 235

Falcon (Tennyson, Alfred Lord, 1879),
v. 594

Falka (Farnie, H. B., 1883), v. 363

Falka's Baby = Brother Pelican

Fallen among Thieves (Harvey, F.,
1890), v. 408

— (Morton, W. E., 1888), v. 497

Fallen Spirit (1836), IV. 458

Fallen Star (Lee, N., Jr., 1859), v. 675,
802, 832

— (Young, Mrs H., 1864), v. 675, 832

Fall from the Cliff = Minna

Falling out of Lovers is the Renewing of
Love (1710), II. 371

Falling Star (1855), v. 675

Fall of Algiers (Walker, C. E., 1825), IV.
145, 416

Fall of Angels = State of Innocence

Fall of Arabi = Egyptian War

Fall of a Shattered Flower = Old Old
Story

Fall of Badajoz (1812), IV. 458

Fall of Bob (Kelly, J., 1736), II. 340, 440

Fall of Bob, alias Gin = Fall of Bob

Fall of Caius Martius Coriolanus =
Ingratitude of a Common-Wealth

Fall of Carthage (Joshua, J., 1810), IV.
334

— (Watkins, W., 1801), IV. 417

Fall of Clyde (1858), v. 675

Fall of Constantina = Victoire

Fall of Delhi (1857), v. 675

— = Veemah Kareeda

Fall of Desmond = Rebellion Defeated

Fall of Egypt (Hawkesworth, J., 1774),
III. 355, 386

Fall of Essex (Warmington, G., 1842),
IV. 616

— = Envious Statesman

Fall of Fair Rosamond (1821), IV. 458

— (1832), IV. 458

Fall of Gollo = Sophy of Brabant

Fall of Jerusalem (Milman, H. H.,
1820), IV. 167, 336

— = Wars of the Jews

Fall of Khartoum (Stanley, H. J., 1885),
v. 579

— (1885), v. 675

Fall of Man = State of Innocence

Fall of Martinico (1794), III. 327

Fall of Missolonghi (Amherst, J. H.),
IV. 254

— = Greek Renegade [This, listed at
IV. 469, may = the above]

Fall of Monsieur St Ruth = Battle of
Aughrim

Fall of Montevideo (1807), IV. 458

Fall of Mortimer (Robinson-Morris,
M., 1806), IV. 394

— (1731), II. 371

Fall of Otranto = Corsair's Son

Fall of Palmyra = Zenobia

Fall of Pantomime = Harlequin Student

Fall of Phaeton (Pritchard, 1736), II.
136, 256, 350

— (1733), II. 371

Fall of Portugal (Wolcot, J., 1808), III.
316; IV. 458

Fall of Pride = (1) Downfall of Pride;
(2) Edith

Fall of Public Spirit (1757), III. 327

Fall of Rizzio (1795), III. 327

Fall of Robespierre (Coleridge, S. T. and Southey, R., 1794), III. 54, 245

Fall of Rosamond = Henry II

Fall of Saguntum (Frowde, P., 1727), II. 21, 28, 29, 31, 92, 329

Fall of Sebastopol (1855), v. 675

Fall of Siam = Fatal Vision

Fall of Tarquin (Hunt, W., 1713), II. 338

— = Brutus

Fall of the Avalanche (Conquest, G. and Suter, W. E., 1865), v. 675, 785, 818, 832

Fall of the Curtain = Domino

Fall of the Decemvirs = (1) Virginia; (2) Virginius

Fall of the Earl of Essex (Ralph, J., 1731), II. 350

Fall of the French Monarchy (Bartholomew, J., 1794), III. 54, 245

Fall of the Inquisition = Fatal Brand

Fall of the Leaf (Carlton, R. C., 1893), v. 305

— (1852), v. 675

Fall of the Mogul (Maurice, T., 1806), III. 286; IV. 354

Fall of Theodore = Conquest of Magdala

Fall of the Sea Robbers = French Expedition

Fall of Tunis = Bellamira

Falls of Clyde (Black, J., 1806), IV. 458, 625

— (Soane, G., 1817), IV. 403

— (1827), IV. 458

Falsacappa (Leigh, H. S., 1871), v. 454, 803

False Accusation (Fuller, F., 1874), v. 374

— (1818), IV. 458

— (1828), IV. 458

— = (1) Flirt; (2) Home once more; (3) Monte d'Or

False Accusations (1874), v. 675

— = False Accusation

False Alarm (Young, A. W., 1872), v. 635

— (1871), v. 675

False Alarms (Kenney, J., 1807), IV. 336

— = Love gives the Alarm

False Alarum = British Peasant

False and Constant (Lunn, J., 1829), IV. 348

False and Fair = Captain Gerald

False and True (Moultru, 1798), III. 289

— (1806), IV. 458

— (1864), v. 675

— = Love

False and True Heir and the Brigand of Palermo = Disputed Title

False Appearances (Conway, H. S., 1788), III. 121, 248, 380

— (1807), IV. 458

False Beacon = Sea Devil

False Bride = Merchant of Paisley

False Cards (Creamer, A., 1873), v. 329

False Colours (Fitzball, E., 1837), IV. 315

— (Morris, E., 1793), III. 21, 138, 288

— (Pass, G. F., 1881), v. 515

— = Little Laundress

False Conclusions (Long, C., 1845), IV. 346

False Concord (Townley, J., 1764), III. 169, 312

False Count (Behn, A., 1681), I. 188, 191, 261–2, 391; III. 114

False Delicacies (1803), IV. 458

False Delicacy (Kelly, H. and Garrick, D., 1768), III. 45, 130, 155, 157, 278, 389

— (Thompson, B., 1800), IV. 412

False Demetrius (Cumberland, R., 1813), IV. 287

False Dervise (Dibdin, C.), IV. 290

False Earl (1863), v. 675

False Evidence (Miller, W. F., 1891), v. 489

— (1889), v. 675

— = Honest Criminal

False Friend (Cross, J. C., 1806), IV. 287

— (Howlett, S., 1893), v. 429

— (Kemble, J. P., 1789), III. 115, 278

— (Pix, Mrs M., 1699), I. 424; II. 96–7

— (Vanbrugh, Sir J., 1702), II. 135, 136, 150–1, 221, 361, 419, 445; III. 115

— (1720), II. 451

— (1803), IV. 458

— = Constant Lovers

False Friendship (1829), IV. 458

False Glitter (Harvey, F., 1875), v. 408

False Guardians Outwitted (Goodall, W., 1740), II. 333

False Hands and Faithful Hearts (Towers, E., 1867), v. 600

False Hearts (Carter, A., 1886), v. 305

False Heire and Formal Curate (Kirkman, F., 1662), I. 417

False Impressions (Cumberland, R., 1797), III. 51, 129, 252

False Jewels = Catarina

False Key (Almar, G., 1831), IV. 252

False Knight = Woodman's Horse

False Light (Blake, T. G., 1847), IV. 268

False Lights (Bannister, T. B., 1886), v. 248

Falsely Accused (Carlyle, R., 1897), v. 303

— (Griffiths, J. C., 1876), v. 394

— = Waiting for the Verdict

Falsely Judged (Granville, H. S., 1880), v. 388

False Marriage (1828), IV. 458

False Mother (Hazlewood, C. H., 1865), v. 413, 797

False Mother and the Parent Guardian = Violet's Perils

False Mr Pope (Peake, R. B., 1845), IV. 371

False One Fitted = Female Fop

False Penitent (1805), IV. 458

False Position = (1) Patronage; (2) Trevanion

False Pride (Fairbairn, Mrs R., 1883), v. 359

— = Victor and Hortense

False Prophet of the Sudan = El Mahdi

False Relique = Excommunicated Prince

False Report = Mistakes

False Shame (Marshall, F., 1872), v. 478

— (1799), III. 65, 327, 400

— (1801), IV. 458

False Step (Matthison, A., 1878), v. 481

— (1859), v. 675

False Steps (Vanneck, F., 1886), v. 607

False Tiberinus = Agrippa King of Alba

False Triumph (1712), II. 371

False Visions (Parry, J., 1846), IV. 368, 458, 625

False Witness (Shirley, A. and Gally, M., 1890), v. 564

Falstaff (Kingston, W. B., 1896), v. 801

— = Purse

Falstaff in Pantomime = Shakespeare's Choice Spirits

Falstaff's Wedding (Kenrick, W., 1766), III. 279, 389

Fame (Osborn, H., 1850), IV. 602; v. 808

— (Rae, C. M., 1877), v. 532

— (1737), II. 371

Familiar Friend (Lemon, M., 1840), IV. 343

Families Supplied (Cuthbert, E., 1882), v. 331

Famille Laffarge = Accusation

Family Arrangements (Long, C., 1846), IV. 347

Family Compact (Rose, J., 1792), III. 303

Family Concert = Students of Jena

Family Distress (1799), III. 400

— = Self-Immolation

Family Failing (Oxenford, J., 1856), v. 509, 809

— (1896), v. 675

Family Fast (1866), v. 675

Family Feud = Vendetta

Family Feuds = Sons

Family Fix (Shelley, H., 1897), v. 562

Family Fool (Melford, M., 1882), v. 484

Family Friends (1872), v. 675

Family Genius's = London out of Town

Family Ghost (Brunton, A., 1881), v. 284

Family Honour (Marshall, F., 1878), v. 478

Family Jars (Lunn, J., 1822), IV. 348

Family Jars Mended (1839), IV. 458

Family Legend (Baillie, J., 1810), IV. 159–61, 258

Family Likeness (1839), IV. 458

Family Man (1842), IV. 458

Family Masquerading = March of Intelleck

Family Matter (Compton, C. G. and Hockley, A. G., 1894), v. 319

Family Novelette (Nesbit, E. and Barron, O., 1894), v. 502

Family of Anglade = (1) Accusation; (2) Portfolio

Family of Genius (1826), IV. 458

Family Party (Davidge, W. P., 1842), IV. 289

Family Party (Grain, R. C., 1889), v. 387

— (Oxenford, J., 1849), IV. 367

— (1789), III. 189, 327

— (1835), IV. 458

Family Peculiarities (1835), IV. 458

Family Picture (1781), III. 120, 327

— (1822), IV. 458

— = Sailor's Chest

Family Pictures (Stirling, E., 1849), IV. 409

Family Politics (1814), IV. 458, 635

Family Pride (Murray, G., 1862), v. 500

— (Sullivan, R., 1847), IV. 409

Family Propensities = Master's Rival

Family Punch-Bowl = Jack in the Green

Family Quarrel = Nobleman

Family Quarrels (Dibdin, T. J., 1802), IV. 52, 297

Family Relations (1850), v. 675

Family Secret (Falconer, E., 1860), v. 360

— (Leslie, H. T., 1861), v. 457

— = Troubled Waters

Family Secrets (Brough, W., 1853) = How to make Home happy, v. 279, 675, 832

Family Ties (Burnand, F. C., 1877), v. 290

— (1856), v. 832

Family Treacheries (Muir, J. F., 1846), IV. 365

Family Treason (1861), v. 675

Family Troubles = Old Phil Hardy

Family Tutor = Trip to the Ball

Family Will (1888), v. 675

Famine (O'Grady, H., 1886), v. 506

Famous Beauty (Stanley, H. J., 1892), v. 579

Famous Trojan Horse = Siege of Troy

Fanatic (Day, J. T., 1897), v. 340

Fanatic of Aleppo = Klebir in Egypt

Fanchette (Levey, W. C., 1864), v. 675, 832

— (Bateman, Mrs H. L., 1871), v. 253

— (Weil, O., 1894), v. 619

Fanchonette the Cricket (1871), v. 676

Fanchon the Cricket (Schuler, F., 1863), v. 815

— (1862), v. 676

Fanchon the Grasshopper (1867), v. 676

Fancourt's Folly (Findon, B. W., 1894), v. 366

Fancy Ball (Wardroper, H., 1889), v. 614

— (1832), IV. 625

Fancy'd Queen (Drury, R., 1733), II. 319

Fancy Dress Ball (Grain, R. C., 1892), v. 388

Fancy Fair (Lumley, R. R., 1892), v. 464

Fancy Land (Fuller, C. F., 1884), v. 374

Fancy's Friends = World as it Runs

Fancy's Opera (1823), IV. 458

Fancy's Sketch (Planché, J. R., 1819), IV. 376

Fan-Fan the Tulip (Suter, W. E., 1863), v. 588

Fannette (Johnstone, J. B., 1868), v. 438

Fanny (Sims, G. R. and Raleigh, C., 1895), v. 569

Fanny Lear (1885), v. 676

Fanny's Flirtations (Miller, W. F. and Havard, P., 1887), v. 489

Fanny Sims, Mistress of Arts (Coyne, J. S., 1838), IV. 458, 625

Fanny Wild, the Thief-taker's Daughter (Blake, T. G., 1851), v. 262

Fanny Wyndham (1862), v. 676

Fans and Fandangas (1865), v. 676

Fans and Fandangoes = Spanish Dancers

Fantisticuff (1871), v. 676

Far Away = Hawthorne

Far away where Angels dwell (Hazlewood, C. H., 1869), v. 414

Farce upon Segmoor Fight = Battle

Farce Writer (Pocock, I., 1815), IV. 384, 606

Farewel Folly (Motteux, P. A., 1705), II. x, 5, 38, 45, 50, 129, 209-10, 346, 441

Farewell and Return (?1739), II. 371

Farewell of the Fairies (Reece, R., 1867), v. 812

Farfadets (1881), v. 676

Farfaletta (1866), v. 676

Far, far at Sea = Mary's Dream

Far from the madding Crowd (Hardy, T. and Carr, J. W. C., 1882), v. 404

Farinelli (Barnett, C. Z., 1839), IV. 260

Farinelli in Madrid = Queen of Spain

Farm by the Sea (Wedmore, F., 1889), v. 619

Farmer (O'Keeffe, J., 1787) = Ups and Downs, III. 200, 293, 393

Farmer and his Wife = Village Story

Farmer and Pheasant (Thompson, C. P., 1836) = Poachers and Petticoats = Pheasant Shooting, IV. 614, 458, 625

Farmer Deceived (1779), III. 400

Farmer Disappointed = Harlequin Executed

Farmer Emigrant (1847), IV. 459

Farmer Hayseed (Pleon, H., 1889), v. 528

Farmer in Distress = Disaster

Farmer of Inglefield Forest (Hazlewood, C. H., 1859), v. 676, 796, 832

Farmer of Inglewood Forest (Rogers, W., 1846), IV. 396

Farmer of Labian (1825), IV. 459

Farmer of Lyons (1858), v. 676

Farmer on the Coast = Ship-Wreck

Farmer's Boy (Dibdin, C. I. M., 1809), IV. 292

— (1808), IV. 459

Farmer's Bride (1840), IV. 625

Farmer's Daughter (Pitt, G. D., 1845), IV. 374

— (1837), IV. 459

— = (1) Flitting Day; (2) Ring

Farmer's Daughter of the Severnside (Raymond, R. J., 1831), IV. 389

— = Broken Heart

Farmer's Dream = Mark Lawrence

Farmer's Gun (1834), IV. 459

Farmer's Journey to London (1769), III. 327

Farmer's Knife (1827), IV. 459

Farmer's Return from London (Garrick, D., 1762), III. 263

Farmer's Son (1733), II. 371

— (1835), IV. 459

— = Golden Glove

Farmer's Sons = Veteran Soldier

Farmer's Story (Bernard, W. B., 1836), IV. 266

Farmer's Wife (Dibdin, C. I. M., 1814), IV. 293, 580

Farm House (Kemble, J. P., 1789), III. 51, 116, 188, 278, 389

Farmhouse Story (1803), IV. 459

Farm of Senange = Henriette

Farm of Sterwick (1823), IV. 459

Farnley (Davies, B., 1894), v. 338

Far Off (Moncrieff, W. T., 1842), IV. 361

Faro Table (Tobin, J., 1816), IV. 164, 413

— (1789), III. 115, 327, 400

Farrago (1882), v. 676

Farriar Made Physician = Dumb Lady

Farrier Nicked (1734), II. 371

Farthing Rushlight (Oulton, W. C., 1810), IV. 366

Fascinating Fellows (Palmer, T. A., 1876), v. 512

Fascinating Individual (Danvers, H., 1856), v. 336, 787

Fascination (Jay, H. and Buchanan, R., 1888), v. 435

— (Merion, C., 1871), v. 806

Fashion (McLaren, A., 1802), IV. 350

— (Mowatt, A. C. O., 1850), v. 498

— (Stephens, W., 1869), v. 581

— (1884), v. 676

Fashionable Amusement = Sailor and Soldier

Fashionable Arrivals (Lemon, M., 1840), IV. 344, 595

Fashionable Beauty (Moore, G. and Glover, J. M., 1885), v. 492

Fashionable Crop quizzed (1792), III. 327

Fashionable Fallacy (1865), v. 676

Fashionable Friends (Walpole, H., 1802), III. 314; IV. 416

Fashionable Intelligence (Fendall, P., 1894), v. 364

— = World of Fashion

Fashionable Lady (Ralph, J., 1730), II. 267, 350

Fashionable Levities (Macnally, L., 1785), III. 14, 31, 49, 170, 285

Fashionable Life (Murray, A., 1845), IV. 365

Fashionable Lover (Cumberland, R., 1772), III. 126, 251

— (1706), II. 141, 177, 371

Fashionable Playfolks = Marriage by Comedy

Fashionable Recluse = Labyrinth Farm

Fashionable Wife (1782), III. 400 [A play of the same name was acted at the Haymarket, 6/5/1782]

Fashion and Famine (1855), v. 676

— (1857), v. 676

Fashion and Feeling = Steward
Fashion and Passion = Frou-Frou
Fashion Displayed (Burton, P., 1770),
III. 241
Fashion's Fools (Dibdin, C. I. M.,
1809), IV. 292
Fast and Slow (Lunn, J., 1827), IV, 348
Fast Asleep (Abbott, C. H., 1892)
= Opiate, V. 233
— (Birch, S., 1797), III. 238, 378
Fast Coach (Soutar, J., Jr. and Claridge,
C. J., Jr., 1851), V. 574, 817
— (Soutar, R., 1873), V. 575
Fast Family (Webster, B., the Younger,
1866), V. 618
Fast Friend (Herbert, F. H., 1877), V.
418
Fast Friends (Barrett, F., 1884), V.
250
— (Henry, R., 1878), V. 417
Fast Friends up a Tree (Anderson,
J. R., 1864), V. 676, 777, 832
Fast Life (O'Grady, H., 1896), V. 506
— = Follies of the Day
Fast Life and Noble Life = Pace that
Kills
Fast Mail (Carter, L. J., 1891), V. 305
Fast Man (1848), IV. 459
Fast Married Men (1863), V. 676
Fast Train! (Maddox, J. M., 1853), V.
472
Fatal Accusation (1825), IV. 459
— = Italians
Fatal Armour = Dark Pandour
Fatal Attachment (1831), IV. 459
Fatal Beauty (Fysher, G., 1892), V.
375
Fatal Birth-Day = Valentia
Fatal Brand (Pitt, G. D., 1850), V. 526
— = Prisoner of France
Fatal Bridge = Blood-red Knight
Fatal Card (Chambers, C. H. and
Stephenson, B. C., 1894), V. 307
Fatal Chest = Mistletoe Bough
Fatal Choice = St Valentine's Day
Fatal Clock = Wood Demon
Fatal Conquest = Florazene
Fatal Constancy (Jacob, Sir H., 1723),
II. 53, 91, 338
— (Whitehead, W., 1754), III. 80, 315
Fatal Coral Bank = Wreck of the
Leander Frigate

Fatal Curiosity (Colman, G., 1782), III.
59, 247, 379
— (Lillo, G., 1736), II. 64, 115, 121-4,
342, 440; III. 59
— = (1) Blue Beard; (2) Shipwreck
Fatal Deed = Midnight Spectre
Fatal Discovery (Home, J., 1769), III.
18, 28, 72, 93, 272
— (1698), I. 24, 66, 170, 441
Fatal Divorce = Phæton
Fatal Dowry (Knowles, J. S., 1825), IV.
339
— (Sheil, R. L., 1840), IV. 610
Fatal Duel of the Glacis (1832), IV. 459
Fatal Elopement (1799), III. 327
Fatal Embarrassment = Labyrinth
Fatal Error (Victor, B., 1776), III. 58, 90,
313
— (1833), IV. 459
— = Florence
Fatal Experiment (Dibdin, T. J., 1826),
IV. 305
Fatal Extravagance (Hill, A., 1721), II.
53, 70, 109, 115, 118-19, 120, 123,
336, 438; III. 59
Fatal Falsehood (More, Mrs H., 1779),
III. 91, 97, 288
Fatal Falshood (Hewitt, J., 1734), II. 26,
115, 122, 335
Fatal Fire Damp = Life of a Miner
Fatal Floodgate (1834), IV. 459
— = Xaia of China
Fatal Friendship (Trotter, C., 1698), I.
57, 435
Fatal Gift (1876), V. 676
Fatal Glen = Meg Murnock
Fatal Gridiron = Jewess
Fatal Inconstancy (Phillips, R., 1701),
II. 349
Fatal Interview (Hull, T., 1782), III. 72,
86, 90, 274
Fatal Island (Dibdin, T. J., 1817), IV.
300
Fatal Island and the Hour of Four
(1824), IV. 459
Fatality (Boaden, C., 1829), IV. 269
— (Cameron, K., 1898), V. 301
— (1859), V. 676
— (1887), V. 676
Fatal Jealousie (Payne, H. N., 1672), I.
69, 83, 136, 347, 423
Fatal Keepsake = Military Execution

Fate of a Matricide = Wrecker's Son

Fate of Calais (Dibdin, T. J., 1820), IV. 302

Fate of Capua (Southerne, T., 1700), II. 355

Fate of Charles the Bold = Solitary of Mount Savage

Fate of Corsica (1732), II. 371

Fate of Derwentwater (Rothery, W. G., 1865), V. 814

Fate of Disobedience = False Friend

Fate of Forgery (Seaman, W., 1862), V. 815

Fate of Frankenstein = (1) Man and the Monster; (2) Presumption

Fate of Margaret = Faust

Fate of Mary Edmonstone = Mary Edmonstone

Fate of Milan (1724), II. 371

Fate of Narcissus (1748), II. 371

Fate of Patriotism = Count de Villeroi

Fate of Pha'ton = Son of the Sun

Fate of Pizarro = Peruvian Heroes

Fate of Polypheme = Minerva and Ulysses

Fate of Sparta (Cowley, Mrs H., 1788), III. 83, 249

Fate of Taranto = Conquest of Taranto

Fate of the Bushranger = Faith and Falsehood

Fate of the Falcon = Burnt at Sea

Fate of the Fancy Lad = Apprentice's Opera

Fate of the Gambler (1834), IV. 459

Fate of the House of Rookwood = Richard Turpin

Fate of the Lily of St Leonard's = Whistler

Fate of the Macdonalds = (1) Glencoe; (2) Massacre of Glencoe

Fate of the Raven of Rheinfeldt = Burgundy the Bold

Fate of the Widow's Son = Military Punishment

Fate of Troy = Virgin Prophetess

Fate of Tyranny = Grecian Heroine

Fate of Villany (Walker, T., 1730), II. 222-3, 363 [This was acted Smock Alley, Dublin, as Love and Loyalty, 24/5/1744]

Fate of Walsingham = Ticket Porter

Fate of War (Selby, C., 1836), IV. 398

Fates (Eyre, E. J., 1813), IV. 310

— (1819), IV. 459

Fates and Furies (Densmore, G. B., 1877), V. 342

Fate's Decree (Williamson, H. W., 1883), V. 626

Fate's Victim = Destroyer

Father (1770), III. 120, 327

Father and Daughter (Moncrieff, W. T., 1829), IV. 359

— = (1) Juggler; (2) Lear of Private Life; (3) Rosalie

Father and his Children (Reynolds, F., 1817), IV. 392

Father and Son (Fitzball, E., 1825), IV. 313, 584

— (1814), IV. 459, 636

— = (1) Alvarez; (2) Calas; (3) Exiled Minister

Father and Sons = Fatality

Father and the Son (1823)? = Murderer, IV. 625

Father Avenged (Hunt, L., 1828), IV. 329

Father Buonaparte (Hudson, C., 1891), V, 429

"Father, come home." = Ten Nights in a Bar-room

Father Girard the Sorcerer (1732), II. 371, 425

Father in search of his Child = Lost Child

Fatherland (Labouchere, H., 1878), V. 446

Fatherless Fanny (1834), IV. 459

Father Luke and Darby (Dibdin, C. I. M., 1819), IV. 294

Father Matthias (Selby, C., revised, 1849), IV. 459

Father, Mother and Son = Jack Royal

Father Murderer (1834), IV. 459

Father of a Family (1756), III. 122, 327

Father outwitted (1784), III. 123, 327

Fathers (Fielding, H., 1778), II. 329; III. 383

Fathers and Sons = Mysteries of Paris

Father Satan (Spiers, H. F., 1896), V. 576

Father's Crime (Serle, T. J., 1835), IV. 459, 625

Father's Curse (1820), IV. 459

—— (1830), IV. 460

Father's Curse (1833), IV. 460
— (1836), IV. 460
— = Note Forger
Father's Dream = Old Adam
Father's Grave = Rescue of the Orphans
Father's Guilt (1823), IV. 460
Father's Legacy = Wild Flower of the Prairie
Father's Love = (1) Home; (2) Story of the Heart
Father's Love and a Mother's Care = Beggar's Petition
Father's Oath (Gould, F., 1892), v. 386
Father's Plea (Mayhew, E., 1834), IV. 460, 625
Father's Ransom and the False Key = Pilot's Son
Father's Revenge (Howard, F., 1783), III. 273
— = Stolen Birthright
Father's Sacrifice (Selby, C., 1837), IV. 398
— (Varty, W. R., 1887), v. 607
Father's Sin (Smith, H. B., 1886), v. 572
— (1896), v. 676
Father's Tragedy (Field, M., 1885), v. 366
Fathoms Deep (Cleve, J. B., 1883), v. 314
Fatinitza (Leigh, H. S., 1876), v. 454, 803
Faubourg St Germain (Reade, C., 1859), v. 536
Faugh a Ballagh = '99
Faulkner (Godwin, W., 1807), IV. 19, 319
Faults on Both Sides = Compromise
Faust (Bernard, W. B., 1866), v. 259
— (Bernays, L. J., 1839), IV. 86, 266
— ('Beta', 1895), v. 779
— (Birch, J., 1839), IV. 86, 267
— (Birds, J. A., 1880, 1889), v. 779
— (Blackie, J. S., 1834), IV. 86, 267
— (Bowen, C. H., 1878), v. 779
— (Brooks, C. T., 1856, 1857), v. 780
— (Chorley, H. F., 1864), v. 310, 784
— (Clarke, W. B., 1865), v. 784
— (Colquhoun, W. H., 1878), v. 785
— (Duckett, Sir G. F., 1845), IV. 86, 307
— (Filmore, L., 1841), IV. 86, 312
— (Galvan, J., 1860), v. 793
Faust (Gower, Lord F. L., 1823), IV. 86, 320
— (Grant, J. W., 1867), v. 794
— (Grattan, H. P., 1842), IV. 86, 320

— (Gurney, A. T., 1842), IV. 86, 322, 397
— (Hayward, A., 1833), IV. 86, 324
— (Hazlewood, C. H., 1867), v. 413
— (Hills, J., 1840), IV. 86, 325
— (Huth, A. H., 1889), v. 799
— (James, C. S., 1849), IV. 330
— (Knox, C. H., 1847), IV. 86, 340
— (Lefevre, Sir G., 1841), IV. 86, 343
— (Macdonald, W. B., 1838), IV. 86, 349, 596
— (Martin, Sir T., 1865, 1886), v. 806
— (Paul, C. K., 1873), v. 809
— (Swanwick, A., 1850), v. 819
— (Syme, D., 1834), IV. 86, 410
— (Talbot, R., 1835), IV. 86, 410
+ — (Taylor, Arthur, 8° 1838)
— (Taylor, R., 1871, 1872), v. 820
— (Webb, T. E. 1880), v. 823
— (Wills, W. G., 1885), v. 627, 824
— (1838), IV. 86, 460
— (1861, 1863, 1886, 1891, 1894) v. 676
Faust and Co. (Gordon, G. L., 1886), v. 385
Faust and Loose (Burnand, F. C., 1886), v. 291
Faust and Margaret (Boucicault, D., 1854), v. 268, 779
— (Markwell, W. R.), v. 477
Faust and Marguerite (Burnand, F. C., 1864), v. 288
— (Daly, B. and Somerset, C. W., 1899), v. 334
— (Halford, J., 1854), v. 398 [The entry in IV. 323 should be deleted]
— (Halford, J., 1866), v. 398
— (Robertson, T. W., 1854), v. 546
— (1854, 1855, 1866, 1881), v. 676
Faust and Mephistopheles (1854), v. 676
Faust and the Fair Imogene = Alonzo the Brave
Faust in a Fog (Reece, R., 1870), v. 537
Faustine (Young, Sir C. L., 1880), v. 636
— (1887), v. 676
Faustine's Love (Stanhope, W., 1889), v. 579
Faust in Forty Minutes (Locke, F., 1885), v. 462
Faust in Three Flashes (Blood, J. J., 1884), v. 265
Faust Reversed (Bruce, H. P., 1888), v. 283

Female Adventurer (1790), III. 118, 327

Female Advocates (Taverner, W., 1713), II. 210, 358

Female Angler (Houlton, R., 1783), III. 273

Female Archer (1767), III. 327

Female Archers = Kenneth, King of Scots

Female Bandit = Fillebrande

Female Barbarism (Hancock, E. L., 1890), V. 402

Female Bluebeard (Dillon, C., 1845), IV. 305

— (1845), IV. 460

— (1862), V. 677

— = Devil's Mount

Female Buccaniers = Pauline the Pirate

Female Captain = (1) Black Eagle; (2) Contract

Female Cavaliers (Dunlop, Mrs, 1834), IV. 460, 625

Female Chevalier (Colman, G., 1778), III. 116, 246

Female Constancy = Laugh when you can

Female Contest = Rose

Female Courage (1809), IV. 460

Female Crusoe = Hannah Hewitt

Female Curiosity = (1) Blue-Beard; (2) Clock-Case

Female Detective (1865), V. 677

Female Dramatist (Colman, G., the Younger, 1782), III. 262, 379 [It would appear that this play definitely belongs to Colman and not to Mrs Gardner]

Female Duellist (1793), III. 112, 327

Female Enthusiast (1744), II. 372

Female Fop (Sandford, 1723), II. 353

Female Fortune Hunters = (1) Belle's Stratagem; (2) Imitation

Female Fortune-Teller (Johnson, C., 1726), II. 51, 142, 157, 339

Female Freebooter (Dibdin, C. I. M., 1823), IV. 295

Female Freemason (1831), IV. 460

Female Gamester (Howard, G. E., 1782), III. 273

Female Government (Dibdin, T. J., 1834), IV. 305

Female Heroism (West, M., 1804), IV. 418

— = (1) North Briton; (2) Russian Daughter

Female Hussar (1802), IV. 460

Female Iago (Goldsmith, W. H., 1872), V. 383

Female Innocence (1732), II. 372

Female Intrepidity = Heroic Sergeant

Female Jacobin-Club (Siber, J. C., 1801), IV. 87, 401

Female Jockey (Dimond, W.), IV. 581

Female Judas = Lady Satan

Female Lancers (1833), IV. 460

Female Macbeth = Elfrida

Female Mascaroni (Somerset, C. A., 1831), IV. 404

Female Matchmakers = Sharpers

Female Officer (Brooke, H., 1740), III. 240

— (Kemble, J. P., 1778), III. 278

Female Orators (1780), III. 327

— = Belles' Association

Female Parliament (1754), III. 327

Female Parricide (Crane, E., 1761), III. 249

Female Parson (Coffey, C., 1730), II. 237, 243, 315

Female Patriots = Spanish Heroine

Female Pedant (Horde, T., 1782), III. 273

Female Pirate (Stewart, D., 1870), V. 583

Female Politician = (1) Fate of Corsica; (2) Rival Priests

Female Politics (1841), IV. 460

Female Prelate (Settle, E., 1679), I. 37, 40, 79, 148-9, 428-9

Female Pursuit (1790), III. 328

Female Rake (Dorman, J., 1736), II. 160, 247, 372, 435

Female Rebellion (?Burkhead, H., ?1660), I. 394

Female Robinson Crusoes of America = Three Fast Men

Females Beware! (McLaren, A., 1820), IV. 352

Female Sentinel (1829), IV. 460

Female Serenaders = Buffalo Girls

Female Society = Baronet

Female Soldier (1789), III. 328

Female Spy and the Chief of Ten = Master Passion

Female Tournament (1849), IV. 460

Female Travellers = Colonel

Female Travelling Companion = Mutual Expense

Female Vertuoso's (Wright, T., 1693), I. 12, 13, 188, 260, 438

— = No Fools like Wits

Female Victor = Witty Combat

Female Volunteer (Halloran, L. H., 1801), IV. 323

— (Oxberry, W. H., 1833), IV. 460, 602, 625

Female Volunteers (1859), V. 677

— = Saw ye Bony coming?

Female Warriour = Friendship Improv'd

Female Waterman's Society (Worrell, 1840), IV. 460 [This is the same as The Ran-Dan Club, see IV. 618]

Female Wits (?1697), I. 250, 441

Feminine Strategy (Adams, C., 1893), V. 235

Femme Sentinelle (Barnett, Miss, 1832), IV. 460, 625

Femme Soldat = Colonel's Come

Fencing Master (Smith, H. B., 1892), V. 572

Fénelon (Merry, R., 1795), III. 287

Fenian (O'Grady, H., 1888), V. 506

Feniza (?1660–1700), I. 441

Fennel (Jerome, J. K., 1888), V. 436

Feodora (Pitt, G. D., 1845), IV. 373

Ferdinand, Count Fathom (Dibdin, T. J., 1818), IV. 96, 301

Ferdinand Lassalle (1893), V. 677

Ferdinando (Parke, W., 1886), V. 512

Ferdinand of Spain (1813), IV. 460

Ferguson (1837), IV. 460

Fernande (Edwardes, H. S., 1870), V. 43, 355

Fern Light = Wreck at Sea

Ferry and the Mill (Pocock, I., 1833), IV. 385

Ferry Girl (Downshire, Dowager Marchioness of, 1890), V. 350

Ferryman (Landor, R. E., 1841), IV. 199, 341

Ferryman of the Lone Hut (Taylor, T. P., 1843), IV. 411, 614

Ferryman's Daughter (Johnson, H. T. and Cordingley, C., 1891), V. 437

— = Old Father Thames

Ferry of the Guiers (1823), IV. 460

Festa di Ballo (1864), V. 677

Festival (1733), II. 372

Festival of Bacchus (Byrne, J., 1802), IV. 460, 625

Festival of Fancy (1805), IV. 460

Festival of Peace (1856) = Triumph of Peace, V. 677, 760, 848

Festival of Roses = Felix

Festival of the Fauns = Sylvan Statue

Festival of the Rose = Who kissed Jeannette

Festive Cottagers (1823), IV. 460

Fetches (Falconer, E., 1861), V. 360

Fête à Lisbon (1856), V. 832

Fête at Rosherville = Out on the Sly

Fête at Seville (1865), V. 677

Fête au serail = Marchand d'esclaves

Fête Champêtre (1843), IV. 460

— = Carron Side

Fête dansante (1856), V. 832

Fete-day and the Fall = Robespierre

Fête du Village (Hullin, 1820), IV. 589

Fête in Andalusia (1855), V. 677

Fête Napolitaine (1852), V. 677

Fête of Nations (1855), V. 677

Fête of Terpsichore (Albert, 1844), IV. 567

Fête of the Hermitage = Lestocq

Fête orientale (1853), V. 832

Fêtes de Memphis = Enfant prodigue

Fettered (Phillips, W., 1869), V. 523

Fettered at Last (1881), V. 677

Fettered Freedom (Kenne, M. and Stephenson, C. H., 1887), V. 442

Fettered Lives (Whyte, H., 1893), V. 621

— (1893), V. 677

Fetters (Burnley, J., 1875), V. 293

Fetters of Passion (Warwick, H. S. and Holderness, C. T., 1894), V. 615

Feudal Lady (1831), IV. 460

Feudal Times (Colman, G., the Younger, 1799), III. 248

— (White, J., 1847), IV. 419

Feuds of Loch Lomond = Ratheil Sullivan

Few More Passages in the Life of the Renowned and Illustrious Robert Macaire = Jacques Strop

F.F.F. (Bracewell, J., 1882), v. 272

Fiammina (1872), v. 677

Fiat of the Gods (Outram, L. S., 1891), v. 509

Fibbing for a Friend = Peter Jenkyns

Fibs (Tylar, W., 1882), v. 605

Fickle Fair One = Fortune's Task

Fickle Fatima (Robertson, W. G., 1892), v. 547

Fickle Fortune (Steele, C. D., 1890), v. 580

Fickle Shepherdess (1703), II. 141, 224, 372

Fiction and Reality = Tea-Room

Fiddler's Wife = O'Jupiter

Fidelio (Browne, M. E., 1891), v. 781

— (Phillips, M., 1837), IV. 372

— (1845), IV. 461

Fidelity (1884), v. 677

Fidget's First Floor = F.F.F.

Field against the Favourite (1855), v. 677

— = Derby Day

Field of Death = Sacred Trust

Field of Forty Footsteps (Farren, W., 1830), IV. 311

— (1858), v. 677

Field of Terror (Fitzball, E., 1852), v. 368

— = Black Spider

Field of the Cloth of Gold (Brough, W., 1868), v. 117, 280

— (Scott, S., 1869), v. 558

— (1831), IV. 461

— = Darnley, the Knight of Burgundy

Fiend (1842), IV. 461

Fiend at Fault (Edwards, H. S. and Taylor, W., 1894), v. 355

Fiend Father (Lacy, M. R., 1832), IV. 83, 461, 625

Fiend King (1838), IV. 461

Fiend of Ferrara = Lucrece Borgia

Fiend of Fleet Street = String of Pearls

Fiend of the Drachenfels (1852), v. 677

Fiend of the Fated Valley = Land of Enchantment

Fiend of the Fountain = Student's Dream

Fiend of the Volcano = Faust

Fiend of the Watch (1830), IV. 461

Fiend of the Whirlpool = Kerim the Pearl Diver

Fiend's Mountain (1855) = Adventurer, v. 638, 677, 832

Fiery Coursers of the Sun = Jupiter's Decree and the Fall of Phaethon

Fiery Furnace = Fiery Ordeal

Fiery Ordeal (Hazleton, F., 1862), v. 677, 796, 832

— (1894), v. 677

Fiery Parisienne (1898), v. 677

Fiesco (Anderson, J. R., 1850), v. 740

— (Noehden, G. H. and Stoddart, J., 1796), III. 63, 291, 392

— (Planché, J. R., 1850), v. 527

— (1841), IV. 86, 461

Fiesko (Daguilar, Sir G. C., 1832), IV. 86, 287

Fif (McArdle, J. F., 1882), v. 467

Fi, Fi (1845), IV. 461

1588 (Upton, 1804), IV. 415

Fifteen Minutes Grace (Goodman, W., 1894), v. 384

Fifteenth Carbineers (1834), IV. 461

Fifteenth Century (Fuller, C. F., 1883), v. 374

Fifteenth of October (Leterrier, E. and Vanloo, A., 1875), v. 457

Fifteen Years of a British Seaman's Life (1830), IV. 461

— (1859), v. 677

Fifteen Years of a Drunkard's Life! (Jerrold, D. W., 1828), IV. 331

Fifteen Years of a Soldier's Life (1848), IV. 461

Fifteen Years of Labour Lost (Amherst, J. H.), IV. 254

Fifteen Years of Prosperity and Adversity = London Tradesman's Life

Fifth of November (Bridel, E. P., 1807), IV. 574

— (Cox, R. D., 1854), v. 327

— (Rhodes, G. A., 1830), IV. 393

— = Guy Fawkes

Fifty Fafty, the Tyneside Mystery (Freeman, C., 1882), v. 373

Fifty Millions of Money = All for Gold

50 to 1 against him = Betting Boy's Career, from the Counting House to the Hulks

Fifty Weddings = Daughters of Danaus

Fifty Years After (Alberg, A., 1888), v. 237

Fifty Years Ago = Frank Heartwell

Fifty Years below the Sea (1833), IV. 461

Figaro (1816), IV. 461

— (1841), IV. 461

Figaro in London (À Beckett, G. A., 1834), IV. 249

Fig for Invasion = (1) Britain's Defenders; (2) Times

Fig for the French (1782), III. 400

Fig for the Invasion = Old England for Ever!

Fig Hall (Dibdin, C. I. M., 1818), IV. 294

Fight against Fate (Grattan, H. P. and Dawson, F., 1885), v. 389

— = Gasman

Fight at Dame Europa's School (Ferneyhaugh, G. F., 1871), v. 365

Fight for Freedom (Landeck, B. and Shirley, A., 1894), v. 447

— = Schneider

Fight for Honour (Harvey, F., 1892), v. 408

Fight for Life (Dillon, C., 1895), v. 677, 832

— (Clarke, H. S. and Du Terreaux, L. H. F., 1876), v. 312

Fight for the Beacon = Shark of the Atlantic

Fight for the Queen's Colours = Zulu War

Fighting by Proxy (Kenney, J., 1833), IV. 337

Fighting Fortune (Scudamore, F. A., 1881), v. 558

Fighting Forty-First (Hazlewood, C. H., 1876), v. 415

Fight of Marson Moor = Cavaliers

Fight of St Crispin's Day = Battle of Agincourt

Fight of the Sempach = Arnold of Winkelreid

Fight with Fate (1864), v. 677

— = Destiny

Figlia di Boby (Pratesi, G., 1898), v. 530

Figure of Fun (Dibdin, C. I. M., 1825), IV. 296

— (Stirling, E., 1821), IV. 406

— (Stirling, E., 1851), v. 584

— = Bloomer Costume

Filial Duty (McLaren, A., 1819), IV. 93, 352

Filial Love (Dibdin, C. I. M., 1825), IV. 296

— (1800), IV. 461

Filial Piety = (1) Honest Criminal; (2) Insolvent

Fillebrande (Dibdin, C. I. M., 1822), IV. 295

Fille de Mme Angot (Byron, H. J., 1873), v. 298, 782

— (Du Terreaux, L. H., 1874), v. 352, 789

— (Farnie, H. B., 1873), v. 361, 790

— (Lee, N., Jr., 1874), v. 453

— (1893), v. 677

Fille de Roland (1893), v. 677

Fille du Prefet (1878), v. 677

Fille du Regiment (1858), v. 677

Fille du tambour major (Farnie, H. B., 1880), v. 362, 791

Fille mal gardée (Conquest, Mrs G., 1858), v. 785

Fille mal Gardu = Honi soit qui mal y pence

Fillip on the Nose (Fitzball, E., 1831), IV. 314

Filumbonum (1899), v. 677

Financeering = Templar's Tricks

Financier (1771), III. 328, 347, 401

Fine Feathers (Byron, H. S., 1873), v. 115, 298

Fine Feathers make Fine Birds = Major's Dilemma

Fine Lady's Airs (Baker, T., 1708), II. 130, 159–60, 175–6, 297

Fine Lady's Frolic (1777), III. 391

Fine Old British Veterans (Pitt, G. D., 1848), IV. 375

Finesse (Gifford, Countess of, 1863), v. 378

— (1881), v. 677

Finesse de l'epée = Don Quixote

Fingal (1813), IV. 461, 625

— (1881), v. 677

Finger of Fate = Utopia

Finger Post = Five Miles Off

Fin Maccoul (Boucicault, D., 1874), v. 269

Finnegan's Fortune (Art, H., 1897), v. 244

Fire Alarm (Graham, R. G., 1893), v. 387

First Love (Cumberland, R., 1795), III. 128–9, 252

— (Edwardes, C., 1841), IV. 582

— (Phillips, E. and Wigan, A. S., 1839), IV. 604

— (Pocock, I., 1828), IV. 461

— (Suter, W. E., 1863), V. 588

— (Travers, W., 1859), V. 821

— (1866), V. 678

— = Bourbons and Bonapartists

First Love and False Hearts (1856), V. 678

First Mate (Henry, R., 1888), V. 418

First Night (Maddox, J. M., 1853), V. 472

— (Parry, T., 1834), IV. 368

— (Saintsbury, H. A., 1899), V. 554

— (Wigan, A. S., 1849), IV. 419, 461, 617, 625

— (1888), V. 678

First Night of a New Piece = Broad but not Long

First Night of my Wedding (1848), IV. 461

First Night's Lodging (McLaren, A., ?1800), III. 284; IV. 350

First of April (Boaden, C., 1830), IV. 369

— (McLaren, A., 1802), IV. 350

— = (1) My Beaux; (2) My Uncle's Card

First of August = Waterman

First of May (Hill, I., 1829), IV. 325

— (Young, A., 1849), IV. 423

First of October (1899), V. 678

— = Fair Game

First of November = Our Town

First of September (Oliphant, R., 1789), III. 328, 393, 401

— (Oxberry, W. H. and Phillips, F. L., 1839), IV. 366

— = Shooter's Hill

First Printer (Taylor, T. and Reade, C., 1856), V. 592

First Rehearsal (Cottell, L., 1892), V. 325

First Step (Heinemann, W., 1895), V. 416

First Violin (Bowkett, S., 1899), V. 271

Fish and the Ring (Amherst, J. H.), IV. 254

Fisher Girl (Hannan, C., 1890), V. 402

Fisherman (Tobin, J., 1819) = Fisherman's Hut, IV. 413, 461, 614, 625

Fisherman and the Genie (Blanchard, E. L., 1856), V. 263, 779

— = Enchanted Lake

Fisherman a Prince = Rise and Fall of Massaniello

Fisherman caught = Bathing Machine

Fisherman of Algiers = Abdellac the Terrible

Fisherman of the Lake = Lost Child

Fisherman of the Thames = Queen of the Thames

Fisherman's Daughter (Garvice, C., 1881), V. 376

— (Ward, M. A., 1892), V. 613

— (1843), IV. 461

— = Found at Sea

Fisherman's Hut (Tobin, J., 1819) = Fisherman, IV. 413, 461, 614, 625

— = Knight of the Black Plume

Fishermen (Stanfield, J. F., 1786), III. 308

Fisher's Prize = Maxey's Money

Fisher's Story = Dead Calm

Fishguard in an Uproar = Cambro-Britons

Fish in the Ring (Neale, F., 1848), IV. 366

Fish-o'-Man of Naples = Masaniello

Fish out of Water (Lunn, J., 1823), IV. 348

— = Changed at Nurse

Fists (1895), V. 678

Fit of Heroics (1880), V. 678

Fit of the Blues (1873), V. 678

Fits and Starts (Jones, J. W. and Browne, G. W., 1885), V. 441

Fitzpatricks (Moncrieff, W. T., 1838), IV. 462, 625

FitzSmythe of FitzSmythe Hall (Morton, J. M., 1860), V. 496

Five Brothers = Wolf Rock

Five Days Fête of Pekin = Chinese Wonders

Five Degrees of Crime (Rede, W. L., 1833), IV. 389

Five Hours at Brighton = (1) Boarding House; (2) My New Boarding House

Five Hundred Francs (Browne, E. M., 1885), V. 283

Five Hundred Pounds (1821), IV. 462

Flying Dutchman (Jerrold, D. W., 1839), IV. 332
— (Reece, R., 1883), V. 539
— (1869), V. 678
— (1877), V. 678
Flying Dutchwoman (1827), IV. 462
Flying Fish (1835), IV. 462
Flying from Justice (Melford, M., 1890), V. 484
Flying Indians = Peter Wilkins
Flying Island of Laputa (1806), IV. 462
Flying Jib by Snapdragon (1867), V. 678
Flying Scud (Boucicault, D., 1866), V. 269
Flying Visit (Grain, R. C. and Law, A., 1880), V. 387
— (Greet, D. V., 1889), V. 393
Fly in the Honey = Happy Pair
F.M. Julius Caesar (Burnand, F. C., 1870), V. 289
Foam of the Sea (1899), V. 678
Fog Family = Boarding School Miss
Fog Fiend and the Fairy Fanakin = Bargemaster's Daughter
Fogged (1882), V. 679
Foggerty's Fairy (Gilbert, W. S., 1881), V. 380
Foiled (Alberton, J. R., 1891), V. 237
— (Buckland, W., 1890), V. 286
— (Williamson, H. W., 1882), V. 626
— = Mate
Foiled at Last = Aileen
Foire de Batavia (1803), IV. 462
Foire de Smirne (D'Auberval, 1792), III. 253
Folded Page (Greet, D. V., 1891), V. 393
Folds of the Flag (1896), V. 679
Folle Farine (Avondale, W., 1884), V. 246
Follet (1725), II. 372
Follies of a Day (Holcroft, T., 1784), III. 119, 270–1, 387; IV. 140
— (Kemble, J. P., 1811), IV. 335
— (1812), IV. 140, 462
— = Bloomerism
Follies of a Night (Planché, J. R., 1842), IV. 382
— (1787), III. 328
— = April Fool
Follies of Fashion (Butler, R., 1829), IV. 277
— = Ton

Follies of the Day (Grattan, H. P. and Eldred, J., 1882), V. 389
Follower of the Family = Katty O'Shiel
Following the Ladies (1855), V. 679
Follow my Leader (Maxwell, H. B., 1899), V. 482
— (Thomson, J., 1843), IV. 413
— = Playing First Fiddle
Follow the Drum (Challis, R., 1888), V. 307
Follow the Leader (Rae, C. M., 1873), V. 153, 532
— (1868), V. 679
Folly (1862), V. 679
Folly and Friendship (Planché, Mrs J. R., 1837), IV. 462, 625
Folly as it Flies (Reynolds, F., 1801), IV. 391
— (1828), IV. 462
Folly Exposed (McLaren, A., 1820), IV. 352
— = How to grow wise
Folly Fête (Galer, E. J. N., 1865), V. 679, 793, 832
— = May Queen
Folly, Love and Marriage = Rake and his Pupil
Folly of Age (Ingram, A., 1894), V. 431
— (1797), III. 328
Folly of Priest-Craft (1690), I. 441
Folly Reclaim'd = City Lady
Folly's Fortunes (1899), V. 679
Fond Cuckold = (1) Fair Hypocrite; (2) Maiden Queen
Fond Hearts (Evanson, F., 1889), V. 359
Fond Hearts Blighted = Dying Flower
Fond Husband (D'Urfey, T., 1677), I. 26, 273, 308, 349, 351, 408
— (?1723), I. 408
Fond Lady = Amorous Old-woman
Fondlewife and Letitia (1767), III. 114, 328
Fond Uncle (Miller, H., 1843), IV. 356
Fontainebleau (O'Keeffe, J., 1784), III. 293
— (1814), IV. 462
Fontainville Abbey (1824), IV. 462
Fontainville Forest (Boaden, J., 1794), III. 18, 33, 60, 72, 98, 103–4, 238
Food for Gossip (1855), V. 679
Food for Mirth (McLaren, A., 1821), IV. 352

Fool (Topham, E., 1785), III. 40, 47, 186, 312

Fool and his Money (Byron, H. J., 1878), v. 298

Fooled by Fortune (Walton, H., 1874), v. 612

Fool in Fashion = Love's Last Shift

Fool Made Wise (Johnson, S., 1741), II. 340, 439-40

Fool of Finsbury (Pitt, G. D., 1842), IV. 604

Fool of Fortune = King's Favourite

Fool of the Family (Hume, F., 1896), v. 430

— (1860), v. 679

— (1876), v. 679

Fools (McCord, T. D., 1885), v. 468

+ Fool's Cap (Dibdin, C. I. M., R.A., 1798)

Fool's Errand = First of April

Fool's Expectation (1698), I. 441

Fool's Fidelity (Capel, G., 1887), v. 302

Fools Have Fortune (?1680), I. 441

Fool's Mate (Broughton, F. W., 1889), v. 281

Fools of Fashion (Lathom, F., 1802), IV. 462, 625

Fool's Opera (Aston, A., 1731), II. 246, 296

Fool's Paradise (Grundy, S., 1887), v. 205, 396

— (Meritt, P. and Maltby, A.), v. 486

Fool's Preferment (D'Urfey, T., 1688), I. 275, 409

Fool's Revenge (Taylor, T., 1859), v. 98, 593, 820

Fool's Tragedy = Death's Jest Book

Fool's Trick (Votieri, A., 1891), v. 609

Fool Turn'd Critick (D'Urfey, T., 1676), I. 16, 17, 43, 273, 346, 408

Football (1886), v. 679

Football King (Gray, G., 1896), v. 390

Foote, Shuter and Weston in the Shades = Peep into Elysium

Footlights (Shenton, J., 1872), v. 562

— (1880), v. 679

Footman (1732), II. 372

Footman turn'd Gentleman (1717), II. 372

Footmarks in the Snow (Towers, E., 1867), v. 600

Footprints in the Sand = Pyramids

Fop's Fortune = Love Makes a Man

For a Child's Sake (Herman, H. and Turner, M., 1899), v. 419, 797

For a Life (McCloskey, J., 1886), v. 468

For an Old Debt (Buckley, F. R. and Panting, J. H., 1895), v. 286

For a Woman's Honour (Herbert, F. H., 1899), v. 418

For Better, for Worse (Braddon, M. E., 1890), v. 273

— (Farren, F., 1891), v. 363

— (Maltby, A., 1870), v. 473

Forbidden Fruit (Abbotts, F. M., 1869), v. 233

— (Boucicault, D., 1876), v. 269

— (1850) = What will my Aunt say? v. 679, 766, 832, 849

Forbidden Love (Digges, W., 1877), v. 345

For Bonnie Prince Charlie (Clarke, J. J., 1897), v. 313

For Bonnie Scotland (Stevens, E., 1897), v. 583

Forc'd Inconstancy = Fatal Love

Forc'd Marriage (Behn, A., 1670), I. 55, 101, 140, 267, 390

Forc'd Vallour (Kirkman, F., 1662), I. 417

Forced from Home (Wills, W. G., 1880), v. 627

— (1882), v. 679

Forced Marriage (Armstrong, J., 1770), III. 233

— (Cooke, Mrs T. P., 1842), IV. 282

— (Faucquez, A., 1861) = Willow Marsh, v. 679, 791, 832, 850

— (Foote, S., 1762), III. 384

+ — (8°, 1834)

— = (1) Dona Costanza; (2) Exiled

Forced to Crime = Travers' Secret

Force of Calumny (Plumptre, A., 1799), III. 65, 298, 393

Force of Conscience (Dibdin, T. J., 1819), IV. 302

— = Ravens

Force of Credulity = Fortunate Youth

Force of Fashion (Mackenzie, H., 1789), III. 284

Force of Friendship (Johnson, C., 1710), II. 105, 116, 339, 439

— (Sheil, R. L., 1821) = Damon and Pythias, IV. 462

Force of Friendship = Dionysius

Force of Love (Tighe, E., 1786), III. 59, 312

— = (1) Perjur'd Devotee; (2) Theodosius

Force of Nature (Thackeray, T. J., 1830), IV. 412

— = (1) Thirteen Years' Labour Lost; (2) Wild Boy of Bohemia

Force of Ridicule (Holcroft, T., 1796), III. 271

Force of Superstition = Credulity

For Charity's Sake (Bowyer, F. and Hedgecock, W. H., 1893), V. 271

— (Fawcett, C. S., 1891), V. 364

For Claudia's Sake (Lloyd, M. F., 1891), V. 461

For Country's Sake (1894), V. 679

For Cuba's Freedom (1898), V. 679

For Dear Life (Muskerry, W., 1873), V. 501

Ford Frivolous (Wyke, E. B., 1880), V. 633

Forecastle Fun (1798), III. 328

Foreign Affairs (Webster, B. N., 1841), IV. 418

Foreign Airs and Native Graces (Moncrieff, W. T., 1839), IV. 361

Foreign Policy (Doyle, Sir A. C., 1893), V. 350

Foreign Prince (1839), IV. 462

— = Irish Nigger

Foreman of the Works (Fenn, G. M., 1886), V. 365

For England (Vane, S., 1893), V. 606

— = Send her Victorious

For England, Ho! (Pocock, I., 1813), IV. 115, 384

— (1818), IV. 462

For England's Glory (1898), V. 679

For England's Sake (Lindley, H., 1889), V. 459

Forest Bandit = Anchorite

Forest Bride (1890), V. 679

Forester (Bayley, J., 1798), III. 111, 236

Forester King (Howard, J., 1892), V. 428

Forester of Savoy (1829), IV. 462

Foresters (Atkyns, S., 1849), IV. 257

— (Dibdin, C. I. M., 1826), IV. 296

— (Plumptre, B., 1799), III. 63, 298, 394

— (Serle, T. J., 1838), IV. 400

Forester's Daughter (Masters, W. C., 1867), V. 480

— = Aloyse

Forester's Fate = Robin Hood

Foresters, Robin Hood and Maid Marian (Tennyson, Alfred Lord, 1892), V. 595

Forest Fiend = Kapschou

Forest Flower = Sylvia

Forest Foundling = Maniac Mother

Forest Keeper (Holl, H., 1860), V. 424

Forest Knight (Scott, J. M., 1813), IV. 462, 625

— (1824), IV. 462

Forest Maiden and the Moorish Page (Tully, J. H., 1847), IV. 414

Forest of Ardennes (Wade, T., 1833), IV. 415

Forest of Blarney = Cat of Kilkenny

Forest of Bondy = Dog of Montargis

Forest of Cercotte = Ravens of Orleans

Forest of Friuli = Serbelloni

Forest of Hermanstadt (Dibdin, T. J., 1808), IV. 298

Forest of Monte-Scarpini = Bobinet the Bandit

Forest of Palms = Sacred Standard and the Chinese Prince

Forest of Picardy = Child of Concealment

Forest of Rosenwald = Travellers Benighted

Forest of St Ange = Convict

Forest of Saint Euphemia = Brigands of Calabria

Forest of St Vallier = Two Farmers

Forest of Segovia = Pedro the Devil

Forest of Unterwald = Laurette

Forest Oracle (Campbell, A. V., 1829), IV. 76, 101, 103, 112, 278

Forest Princess (Barnes, C. M. S., 1844), IV. 259

Forest Queen = Una and the Lions

Forest Rose and the Yankee Ploughboy (Woodworth, S., 1851), V. 631

Forest Savage (1825), IV. 462

Forest Tangle = Dux Redux

Forêt aux aventures = Zelis

Forêt Enchantée (1802), IV. 462

Forêt noire (1792), III. 328

For Ever (Meritt, P. and Conquest, G., 1882), V. 486

For Ever and Ever = Prodigal Parson

For Ever Mine (Stevens and Logan, 1889), v. 583

Forewarned is Forearmed = Won by a Head

For Family Fame (McDonald, B. P., 1895), v. 468

For Further Particulars Enquire Within = Bill of Fare

Forged Cheques (Darbey, E., 1882), v. 336

Forge in the Forest = Robber's Sister

Forge Master (Wood, G. W., 1884), v. 630

Forger (Roberts, G., 1886), v. 544

— (1884), v. 679

Forger and his Victim (Pitt, C., 1856), v. 679, 810, 832

Forgery (Buckstone, J. B., 1832), IV. 274

— (Carne-Ross, J., 1888), v. 303

— (Self, C. S., 1899), v. 560

— (1814), IV. 463, 635

— (1824), IV. 463

— (1828), IV. 463

— = Billet-Master

Forgery in Love = Twin Sisters

Forges of Kanzell = Illustrious Traveller

Forget and Forgive (Besemeres, J., 1874), v. 260

— (Conquest, G., 1861), v. 679, 785, 832

— (Kenney, J., 1827), IV. 337

— (Lindoe, 1794), III. 390; IV. 346

— (McLaren, A., 1814), IV. 351

— = Reapers

Forget me not! (Dibdin, C. I. M., 1817), IV. 294

— (Merivale, H. C. and Grove, F. C., 1879), v. 487

Forget-me-not (1876), v. 679

— = (1) Man's Talisman—Gold; (2) Three to One

Forgive and Forget (Dance, C., 1838), IV. 463

— (1835), IV. 463

Forgiven (Albery, J., 1872), v. 237

— (Cave, R. H., 1873), v. 306

— (1878), v. 679

— (1899), v. 679

Forgiveness (Carr, J. W. C., 1891), v. 304

Forgive us our Trespasses (Hope, N., 1896), v. 426

For Gold (Galer, E. J. N., 1882), v. 375

For Good or Evil (Macdonnell, Mrs A. J., 1894), v. 468

Forgotten (Moore, F. F., 1889), v. 492

Forgotten Trust = Wind and Wave

For Hearts and Home (1888), v. 679

For Her Child's Sake (Young, Sir C. L., 1880), v. 636

For Her Sake (Aveling, E. B., 1888), v. 246

— (1886), v. 679

For Himself Alone (Kingston, H., 1888), v. 444

For His Life = His Natural Life

For Honour's Sake (Hazlewood, C. H., 1873), v. 414

For King and Country (Leathes, E., 1883), v. 451

For Lack of Gold ("Maia", 1880), v. 472

For Life (Coghlan, C. F., 1880), v. 316

— (1871), v. 679

— (1878), v. 679

For Life through Thick and Thin (Taylor, J. G., 1868), v. 591

Forlorn Hope (Hazlewood, C. H., 1871), v. 414

— (Scott, C. W. and Coward, J. M., 1896), v. 558

For Love (Robertson, T. W., 1867), v. 546

For Love and Liberty (1888), v. 679

For Love of Prim (Phillpotts, E., 1899), v. 524

For Love or Money (Halliday, A., 1870), v. 401

+ — (Nichol, C. J. S., 8°, Bedford, n.d.)

For Love's Sake (Stephens, L. E. B., 1882), v. 581

For Mildred's Sake (Steele, C. D., 1895), v. 580

Formosa (Boucicault, D., 1869), v. 269

For Old Sake's Sake (Grange, A. D., 1898), v. 388

For Old Virginia (Herman, H., 1891), v. 419

For Papa's Sake (Spurr, M. B., 1896), v. 577

For Queen and Country (Ashley, Mrs J. B., 1890), v. 245

— = Absent-minded Beggar

Forsaken (Marchant, F., 1869), v. 475

Forsaken Daughter = Selima de Gray

For Sale (Douglass, J. T., 1869), v. 348

Forte Thieves, played piano (Smith, B., 1889), v. 572

For the Benefit of the Playful Crocodile (Buckingham, L. S., 1854), v. 679, 781, 832

For the Cause (1895), v. 679

For the Colours (Brabner, W. A., 1899), v. 272

For the Cross (Soden, J. E., 1898), v. 573

For the Crown (Davidson, J., 1896), v. 338

For the Czar (Sykes, P. H. T., 1896), v. 589

For the Honour of the Family (1897), v. 679

For the Honour of the House (1894), v. 679

— (1895), v. 679

For the King (Howard, W. and Pease, S., 1899), v. 428

For the King's Sake (Hale, Mrs C., 1897), v. 398

For the Old Love's Sake (Rogers, T. S. and Kimm, H., 1884), v. 549

For the People = Lady Godiva

For the Queen (1883), v. 679

For the Sake of a Name (Pilmore, F. and Holland, J., 1888), v. 524

For the Sake of a Woman (1895), v. 679

For the Sake of the Duchess (Dawson, F., 1899), v. 339

Fortress (Hook, T. E., 1807), iv. 82, 327

— (Stocqueler, J. H., 1848), iv. 409

Fortress and the Mine = Zamoski

Fortress of Astracan = Almazaide

Fortress of Ganzbrough (1845), iv. 463

Fortress of Kingratz = Signal Fire

Fortress of Magdeburg = Baron Trenck

Fortress of Paluzzi (1822), iv. 463

Fortress of Pressburg (1822), iv. 463

Fortress of Rotzberg (Bounden, J., 1818), iv. 573

Fortress of St Jacques = Fidelio

Fortunate Departure (1810), iv. 463

Fortunate Isles (Planché, J. R., 1840), iv. 381, 605

Fortunate Irishman = Ups and Downs of Life

Fortunate Peasant (Victor, B., 1776), iii. 118, 313

Fortunate Prince (1734), ii. 372

Fortunate Sailor (Morison, D.), iii. 288

Fortunate Slave = Paul

Fortunate Tar = Thomas and Susan

Fortunate Tars (Oulton, W. C., 1810), v. 356

Fortunate Youth (1818), iv. 463

Fortunatus (1866), v. 832

Fortunatus and his Sons (1819), iv. 463

Fortune (Albery, J., 1873), v. 777

Fortune Hunter (Bernard, W. B., 1846), iv. 463, 625

— (Gilbert, W. S., 1897), v. 381

— = Noble Pedlar

Fortune-Hunters (Carlisle, J., 1689), i. 218, 279, 395

— (Dibdin, C., 1789), iii. 256

— (Hewlett, 1812) = Love and Impudence, iv. 325, 495, 588, 631

— (Macklin, C., 1750), ii. 342

— = Double Disappointment

Fortune-Hunters rightly served = Match Maker Fitted

Fortune in her Wits (Johnson, C., 1705), ii. 339, 439

Fortune Mends (Holcroft, F., 1805), iv. 326

Fortune of War (Kenney, J., 1815), iv. 336

— (Philips, F. C., 1896), v. 522

— = (1) Farewell and Return; (2) Josephine

Fortunes and Vicissitudes of a Bohemian Girl = Arline

Fortune's Changes = Beggar's Haunt

Fortune's Favourite (1813), iv. 463

Fortune's Fool (Hamilton, H., 1895), v. 402

— (Harbury, C., 1890), v. 403

— (Reynolds, F., 1796), iii. 133, 301

Fortune's Frolic (Allingham, J. T., 1799), iii. 188, 232; iv. 140

— (1812), iv. 140, 463

— = Frolics of Fortune

Fortune's Frolics (1806), iv. 463

Fortune's Gift (1810), iv. 463

Fortunes of an Irish Peasant = Ballanasloe Boy

Fortunes of Nigel (Fitzball, E., 1822), IV. 93, 312, 584
— = (1) George Heriot; (2) King Jamie
Fortunes of Smike (Stirling, E., 1840), IV. 97, 407
Fortunes of War = Soldier's Orphan
Fortune's Task (Horne, J., 1684), I. 413
Fortune's Toy = Tom Cobb
Fortune's Tricks in Forty Six (1747), II. 372
Fortune's Wheel (1793), III. 328
Fortune-Teller (Dibdin, C. I. M., 1814), IV. 293
— (Travers, W., 1860), V. 679, 821, 832
— (1808), IV. 463
Fortune Tellers (Hardham, J., ?1750), III. 266
— (1740), II. 372
Fortune-teller's Frolic = Soldier's Return
Fortunio (Planché, J. R., 1843), IV. 382
Fortunio and Harlequin (1815), IV. 463
Fortunio and his Gifted Servants (1846), IV. 463
Fortunio and his Seven Magic Men = Lady Belle Belle
Fortunio and the Seven Gifted Men (1820), IV. 463
Forty and Fifty (Bayly, T. H., 1836), IV. 263, 571
Forty Five = Waverley
Forty Robbers (1892), V. 679
Forty Thieves (Barrett, O. and Osman, W. R., 1882), V. 250
— (Blanchard, E. L., 1876), V. 264, 779
— (Blanchard, E. L., 1886), V. 265, 779
— (Blood, J. J., 1890), V. 680, 779, 832
— (Byam, M. and Melville, A., 1890), V. 294
— (Colman, G., the Younger, 1806), IV. 282, 577
— (Conquest, G., 1857), V. 320
— (Douglass, J. T., 1864), V. 679, 788, 832
— (Jones, J. W., 1885), V. 680, 800, 832
— (Lee, N., 1846), IV. 342
— (Lennard, H., 1891), V. 455
— (Locke, F. and Hemming, J. W., 1896), V. 462
— (Pemberton, T. E. and Hewson, J. J., 1887), V. 810
— (Reece, R., 1880), V. 538

Forty Thieves (Rogers, C., 1896), V. 548
— (Sturgess, A. and Collins, A., 1898), V. 586
— (Weemore, 1879), V. 619
— (1812, 1821, 1835), IV. 463
— (1856), V. 679
— (1858), V. 832
— (1859, 1860), V. 679, 832
— (1869), V. 680
— (1874, 1875, 1877), V. 679
— (1879, 1880, 1881, 1884, 1885, 1887, 1888, 1890, 1893, 1894, 1895, 1896, 1897, 1898, 1899), V. 680
Forty Thieves and the Court Barber (Green, F. W., 1875), V. 390
Forty Thieves and their Wonderful Cave (Conquest, G. and Spry, H., 1888), V. 322
Forty Thieves Limited (1891), V. 680
Forty Thieves up-to-date (Keast, G. V., 1890), V. 442
Forty Winks (Farnie, H. B., 1872), V. 361, 790
— (Roberts, G., 1862), V. 544
— (1835), IV. 463
Forty Years Ago = Sailor's Wife
For Valour (Fawcett, C. S., 1891), V. 364
Forward to the Front (Rowe, G. F., 1888), V. 552
For Wife and State (Lancaster-Wallis, E. and Boulding, J. W., 1883), V. 447
Foscari (Mitford, M. R., 1826), IV. 176, 357
Foster Brother = Eily O'Connor
Foster Brothers (Burnand, F. C. and Hall, K., 1865), V. 288
— (1830), IV. 463
Foster Brother's Revenge = Black Tower of Linden
Foster Sister = (1) Clarisse; (2) Ernestine
Foster Sisters = Bella-go-faugh
Foster Sisters of Wicklow (1882), V. 680
Foster Son (1855), V. 680
Foulahs (Barrymore, W., 1823), IV. 262
Foulah Son = Negro's Curse
Foul Anchor (1830), IV. 463
Foul Deeds will Rise (Arnold, S. J., 1804), IV. 255, 569
Foul Play (Boucicault, D. and Reade, C., 1868), V. 269, 812

Foul Weather (Somerset, C. W., 1881), v. 574

Foul Weather Jack = (1) Life Boat; (2) Mary Marsden

Found (Haywell, F., 1869), v. 412

— (Stein, F. J., 1888), v. 580

Found at Last (Wise, A. B., 1899), v. 629

Found at Sea (Chetham, T. G., 1863), v. 680, 833

Found Brummy (Maltby, A., 1874), v. 473

Found Dead in the Streets (Waldron, W. R., 1869), v. 611

Found Drowned (Rowe, G. F., 1870), v. 552

— (Townsend, W. T., 1865), v. 680, 821, 833

Found Dying (Wardhaugh, M., 1877), v. 614

Found Dying in the Streets (Wardhaugh, M., 1870), v. 614

Foundered Fortune (Morton, W. E., 1890), v. 497

Found in a Four-wheeler (Williams, T. J., 1866), v. 625

Found in Exile (Galer, E. J. N., 1888), v. 375

Found in London (Baldie, D., 1879), v. 247

Foundling (Lestocq, W. and Robson, E. M., 1894), v. 457

— (Moore, E., 1748), II. 137, 184, 206–7, 345, 423, 441

— (1881), v. 680

— = (1) Tom Jones; (2) Walter

Foundling of Fortune (Cheatham, F. G., 1867), v. 308

Foundling of Notre Dame (Banks, W., 1876), v. 248

Foundling of the Forest (Dimond, W., 1809), IV. 306, 581

Foundling of the Sea (Rayner, A., 1859) = Ben Lighterware, v. 812

Foundling of the Streets = Female Detective

Foundling Prince and the Vizier's Daughter = Beauty in a Box

Foundlings (Buckstone, J. B., 1852), v. 287

— (Lewis, L. D., 1881), v. 459

Foundlings of Notre Dame = Julie de Launay

Found £100 (1847), IV. 463

Found Out (Hewson, J. J., 1888), v. 420

Found out at home = Peter Piper

Foundry of Kanzel = Hoorn, the Scourge of Norway

Fountain of Beauty (Kingdom, J. M., 1853), v. 444

Fountain of Life (1886), v. 680

Fountain of Zea (Coyne, J. S., 1848), IV. 285

Four and Twenty Hours in Algiers = Dey and a Knight

Four Brothers = Castle of Aymon

Four by Honours (1879), v. 680

— = Reprobate

Four Cousins (Mayhew, A. and Edwards, H. S., 1871), v. 483

Four Gates (1813), IV. 463

Four Hunchbacks (Gott, H., 1825), IV. 585

£452. 12. 6. (1874), v. 680

Four in Hand (Hook, T. E., 1811) = Darkness Visible, IV. 463

Four Inside (1824), IV. 463

Four Kings (Hazlewood, C. H., 1873), v. 414

Four Knaves and the Pack (Towers, E., 1865), v. 680, 821, 833

Four-leaved Shamrock (Travers, W., 1863), v. 680, 833

— = Rogue Riley

Four Legged Fortune = Flying Scud

Four Legs and Two Legs (Dibdin, T. J., 1826), IV. 304

Four Legs better than Two = Bears not Beasts

Four Little Girls (Craven, W. S., 1897), v. 329

Four Lovers (Coyne, J. S., 1836), IV. 284

Four Mowbrays (1851), v. 680

Four O'Clock Tea (1887), v. 680

Four Phantoms = Ye Legende

Four Quarters of the Globe (1850), v. 680

Four Quarters of the World (1791), III. 328, 381, 401

Four Score Years Ago = London Actor

Four Seasons (Motteux, P. A., 1699), I. 421; II. 345

— (1859), v. 680

Four Sisters (Bernard, W. B., 1832), IV. 265

— (1833), IV. 463

Four Sons of Aymon (Fitzball, E., 1850), V. 367

— (1844) = Castle of Aymon, IV. 463

Four Stages of Life (1862), V. 680

Fourteen Days (Byron, H. J., 1882), V. 299

Four Thieves = Pestilence of Marseilles

Fourth of June (1792), III. 328

— = British Sailor

Four Valiant Brothers = Quatres Fils d'Hemons

Four Wishes = Bee and the Orange Tree

Fowl Play (Burnand, F. C., 1868), V. 289

Fox and Geese (Dibdin, C. I. M., 1802), IV. 290

— (1823), IV. 464

Fox and the Goose (Webster, B. N. and Boucicault, D., 1844), IV. 418, 616

Fox and the Grapes (Lee, N., 1855), V. 681, 802, 833

Fox and the Wolf (1839), IV. 464

Fox and Wolf (1898), V. 681

Fox Chase (Boucicault, D., 1853), V. 268

Fox Glove (Dyall, C., 1883), V. 353

Fox Hunt = Fox Chase

Foxonian Charity = Bankrupt

Fox trap't = Raree Show

Fox Uncas'd (1733), II. 372

Fox versus Goose (Brough, W. and Stockton, J. D., 1869), v. 280

Fra Angelo (Russell, W. C., 1865), V. 553

Fra Diavolo (Lacy, M. R., 1831), IV. 340, 592

— (1830), IV. 464

— (1831), IV. 464

— (1857), V. 681

Fra Diavolo the Second (Denny, J. T., 1882), V. 342

Fra Diavolo Travestie (Byron, H. J., 1858), V. 295

Fragment (Hannan, C., 1894), V. 402

Frailty (Harris, Sir A. H. G. and Merritt, P., 1893), V. 406

France (1822), IV. 464

— = Paris

France and Algeria = Veteran and his Son

France and Austria (1859), V. 681

France as it was (1795), III. 328

France in an Uproar = Royal Fugitives

Francesca (Falconer, E., 1859), V. 360

Francesca da Rimini = Francesca

Francesca Doria (Morris, V., 1849), IV. 464, 625

Francesco di Rimini (Williams, T. J.), V. 824

Francillon (1897), V. 681

Francis Beaumont (Kennedy, C. R., 1860), V. 443

Francis I (Kemble, F. A., 1832), IV. 335

— (McKinlan, 1838), IV. 464, 625

— (Slous, F. L., 1843), IV. 402

Francois the Radical (McCarthy, J. H., 1885), V. 467, 804

Franco-Prussian War (Elphinstone, J., 1872), V. 358

Frank Charington's Return (Norman, G. T., 1897), V. 505

Frankenstein (Brough, W. and Brough, R. B., 1849), IV. 96, 271

— (Henry, R., 1887), V. 417

— (Milner, H. M., 1823), IV. 96, 356

— (1823), IV. 96, 464

Frankfort Lottery = Barber Baron

Frank Fox Phipps, Esq. (Selby, C., 1834), IV. 397

Frank Heartwell (Taylor, T. P., 1848), IV. 411

— (1854), V. 681

Frank-in-Steam (1824), IV. 464

Franklin (Brougham, J., 1868), V. 281

Frankly Feminine (1897), V. 681

Frank the Fool (Wilks, T. E., 1843), IV. 617

Frank the Ploughman (Rogers, W., 1849, 1859), IV. 396; V. 681, 814, 833

Frank Wildeye (1848), IV. 464

— (1861), V. 681

Frantick Stock-Jobber = Female Advocates

Fra Rupert (Landor, W. S., 1841), IV. 199, 341

Frasquita (1893), V. 681

Fraternal Friendship = Step-mother

Fraternization (1855), V. 681

Fratricide (1840), IV. 464

— = Murder will out

Fraud and its Victims (Coyne, J. S., 1857) = Victims of Fraud, v. 327

Freaks and Follies (Rodwell, G. H., 1827), IV. 395

Freaks at Aboukir Bay = Petticoat Service

Freaks in an Attic (Webb, C., 1841), IV. 464, 625

Freaks of Fortune = Y.Y.

Freaks of Love = Men and Women

Freaks of the Passions = Arcadia

Freda (Bussy, B. F. and Blackmore, W. T., 1887), v. 294

Freddy's Client (1896), v. 681

Frederick and Voltaire (Dibdin, T. J., 1821), IV. 303

Frederick, Duke of Brunswick-Lunenburgh (Haywood, Mrs E., 1729), II. 58, 74, 104, 335, 438

Frederick of Bavaria (Milner, H. M., 1822), IV. 464, 625

— (1822), IV. 464

Frederick of Prussia (Selby, C., 1837), IV. 398, 464, 610, 625

Frederick the Great (Arnold, S. J., 1814), IV. 256

— (Maddox, F. M., 1824), IV. 353

Frederick the Great and the Deserter (1821), IV. 464

Fred Frolic, his Life and Adventures (Pitt, C., 1868), v. 526

Fredolfo (Maturin, C. R., 1819), IV. 167, 354

Fred Walters, a Grimsby Fishing Apprentice (Stuart, B., 1877), v. 585

Free and Easy (Arnold, S. J., 1816), IV. 256

— = Arbitration

Free Archers of the New Forest = Deer Slayers

Freebooter = Buonaparte

Freebooters (Napier, H., 1827), IV. 464, 601, 625

Freebooter's Boy = Sea Devil

Freebooters of the Desert = Arab

Freebooters of Vienna (Milner, H. M., 1824), IV. 464, 625

Freedom (Rowe, G. F. and Harris, Sir A., 1883), v. 552

Freedom and Slavery (Morton, T., 1816) = Slave, IV. 464, 626

Freeholder (Moser, J., 1810), IV. 364

Free Judges = Herman and Halstein

Free Knights (Reynolds, F., 1810), IV. 52, 391

Free Labour = Put Yourself in his Place

Free Lance (Horsman, C., 1869), v. 427

Freemason (Hart, J. P., 1839), IV. 324

— (Smith, J. F., 1843), IV. 611

— (1854), v. 681

Freemen and Slaves (Ball, W., 1838), IV. 258

Free Nigger of New York (1840), IV. 464

Free Pardon (Philips, F. C. and Merrick, L., 1897), v. 522

— (1893), v. 681

Free Trader = False Colours

Free-traders of Piedmont = Strozzi

Freezing a Mother-in-Law (Pemberton, T. E., 1879), v. 519

— (1887), v. 681

Freischutz (Almar, G.), IV. 253

— (Amherst, J. H., 1824), IV. 87, 254, 568

— (Burnand, F. C., 1866), v. 289

— (Byron, H. J., 1866), v. 296

— (Douglass, J. T., 1866), v. 348

— (Fitzball, E., 1824), IV. 87, 312

— (Kerr, J., 1824), IV. 592

— (Logan, W. M., 1824), IV. 367, 596, 603

— (Oxenford, J., 1866), v. 681, 809, 833

— (Planché, J. R. + with Washington Irving), 1824), IV. 87, 377

— (Soane, G., 1824), IV. 87, 403

— (1824), IV. 87, 88, 464

— (1828), IV. 464

Freischutz Travestie (1824) = Fryshot, IV. 88, 464, 626

French Beau = Deceiver Deceived

French Company (À Beckett, G. A., 1835), IV. 249

French Conjurer (Porter, T., 1677), I. 253, 425

French Coronation = Ramsbottoms at Rheims

French Doctor Outwitted (1743), II. 372

French Exhibition (Hay, F., 1867), v. 411

French Expedition (1830), IV. 464

French Faith (1786), III. 328

French Flogged (Stevens, G. A., 1760), III. 309

French Forest (1803), IV. 464

Friend of the Family (Dixon, B. H., 1894), v. 346
— (Siddons, H., 1810), IV. 401, 611
— =(1) Atlantic Jack; (2) Swamp Hall
Friend of the People (Rowsell, M. C. and Saintsbury, H. A., 1893), v. 552
Friend or Foe (Wright, F., 1891), v. 633
Friends (Meilan, M. A., 1771), III. 287
— (Parker, A. D., 1887), v. 513
+ — (Seymour, M., *French*)
— (1872), v. 681
— (1884), v. 681
— = Benevolent Planters
Friends and Foes (Roberts, T., 1858), v. 545
Friends and Neighbours (Bayly, T. H., 1839), IV. 263
Friends and their Shadows = Man with the Red Beard
Friends at Court (Taylor, T., 1845), IV. 465; v. 820
— = Cattarina
Friends at Sea and Foes on Shore = Sailor's Sheet-Anchor
Friendship (Reece, R., 1873), v. 537
Friendship à la Mode (1766), III. 115, 328
Friendship Improv'd (Hopkins, C., 1699), I. 413
Friendship in Fashion (Otway, T., 1678), I. 258, 349, 422
— (1829), IV. 465
Friendship, Love and Duty (Siddons, H., 1813), IV. 465, 611, 626
Friendship, Love and Truth (Leslie, H. T., 1868), v. 457
Friendship's Test (Dibdin, C. I. M., 1826), IV. 296
Friends in Need = Pedlar
Friends, Lovers and Enemies = Blanche and Brunette
Friends or Foes (Wigan, H., 1862), v. 622
— (1886), v. 681
Friend Waggles (Morton, J. M., 1850), v. 495
Frightened Ghost (1835), IV. 465
Frightened to Death (Oulton, W. C., 1817), IV. 366
Frightful Accident (Higgie, T. H., 1860), v. 421
Frightful Frost (1879), v. 681

Frightful Hair (Burnand, F. C., 1868), v. 289, 781
Frightful Murder in Hoxton (1857), v. 681
Frightful Tragedy in Willow Walk (1859), v. 681
Frilled Petticoats (Lyne, L. C., 1871), v. 465
Fringe of Society (Wyndham, Sir C. and Moore, J., 1892), v. 681, 807, 825, 833
Fritz, Our German Cousin (Halliday, A., 1872), v. 401
Fritz's Folly (Starr, H., 1896), v. 579
Fritz's Wager (1888), v. 681
Fritz the Outlaw (1813), IV. 465
— (1838), IV. 465
Frivoli (Beatty-Kingston, W., 1886), v. 254
Frivolity (Leopolds, 1895), v. 456
— (Melford, M., 1883), v. 484
Frog (Aveling, E. B., 1893), v. 246
Froggie goes to Eaton (Ambient, M., 1892), v. 240
Froggy would a-wooing go (Green, F. W., 1874), v. 681, 794, 833
Frog he would a-wooing go (Allen, O., 1875), v. 239
— (Cave, J. A., 1877), v. 306
— (Hall, F., 1884), v. 399
— (1876), v. 681
— (1880), v. 681
Frogs (Dunster, C., 1785), III. 258
Frogs and Bulls (Wilmot, Mrs B., 1838), IV. 618
Frog that would a-wooing go (1876), v. 681
Frog, the Tortoise and the Sapajou = King of the Hills
Frog who would a-wooing go (Muskerry, W., 1887), v. 501
Frolic (Brown, J., 1783), III. 240
— (Dibdin, C., 1804), IV. 290
Frolic in Bagdad = Little Hunch-Back
Frolick (Polwhele, E., 1671), I. 424
— (1786), III. 328, 401
Frolicks in France (Kenney, J., 1828), IV. 337
Frolicksome Lasses (1747), II. 372
Frolics in Bagdad = Hunchback
Frolics in "Forty-Five" (?Peake, R. B., 1836), IV. 465, 626

Frolics in France (1856), v. 681
Frolics of an Hour (1795), III. 328
Frolics of Fancy = Match for a Widow
Frolics of Fortune (1835), IV. 465
Frolics of Puck = Robin Goodfellow
Frolics of the Fairies (?À Beckett, G. A.,
 1834), IV. 465, 626
— (Rede, W. L., 1841), IV. 390
Frolicsome Fanny (Calmour, A. C.,
 1897), v. 300
Frolique (Farnie, H. B. and Byron,
 H. J., 1882), v. 363
From Bad to Worse (Holcroft, F.,
 1805), IV. 326
From Beneath the Deep (Abel, W. H.,
 1876) v. 235
From Cross to Crown = Christian's
 Cross
From Fatherland to the Far West =
 Heinrich
From Father to Son (À Beckett,
 A. W. and Simpson, J. P., 1882),
 v. 233
From Grave to Gay (Webster, B., the
 Younger, 1867), v. 618
From Gulf to Gulf (Smith, H. J., 1892),
 v. 572
From Information Received = John
 Wopps
From Life to Death (1875), v. 681
From London to Paris (Raleigh, C. and
 Harris, Sir A., 1892), v. 533
From Nine till Ten = Ninth Hour
From Scotland Yard (Douglass, J. T.
 and Bateman, F., 1897), v. 349
— (1897), v. 681
From Shore to Shore (Edwin, P., 1891),
 v. 356
— (England, A. and Noble, C. R.,
 1892), v. 358
From Start to Finish = Kildare
From Stem to Stern (Hay, F., 1876), v.
 411
From the Jaws of Death (Patmore,
 W. J., 1893), v. 515
From the Vanished Past (Holton, F.,
 1888), v. 424
From Village to Court (Morton, J. M.,
 1854), v. 495
+ Frontello and Dorinda (Lumley,
 George, 4°, 1737 (Newcastle))
Frontier Life (1895), v. 681

Frost and Thaw (Holman, J. G., 1812)
 = Adolphus Count Zelmar, IV. 327,
 424, 589
Frost at the Heart = Two Winters
Frost Fair (1814), IV. 465
Frost of Life (Wilkins, J. H., 1856), v.
 623
Frou-Frou (Achurch, J. and Charring-
 ton, C., 1886), v. 235
— (Carr, J. W. C., 1881), v. 304
— (Daly, A., 1870), v. 333
— (Edwards, H. S., 1870), v. 355
— (Webster, B., the Younger, 1870), v.
 618
— (1870), v. 681
— (1887), v. 681
— (1894), v. 681
Frozen Cliff (1827), IV. 465
Frozen Deep (Collins, W. W., 1857), v.
 318, 785
Frozen Gift = Kolaf
Frozen Hand = Ice Witch
Frozen Hands (1831), IV. 465
Frozen Lake (Planché, J. R., 1824), IV.
 84, 377
— (1824), IV. 84, 465
Frozen Mountain (1809), IV. 465
Frozen Regions (1822), IV. 465
Frozen Ships and the Hermit of the
 Sea-bound Bay = Sea Lion
Frozen Stream (Coates, A., 1872), v.
 315
Fruitless Precaution = Spanish Barber
Fruitless Revenge = Unhappy Kindness
Fruits of a Single Error = Adelgitha
Fruits of a Single Lie = Victim of False-
 hood
Fruits of Bad Advice = Ten Years of a
 Woman's Life
Fruits of Geneva = Teresa Tomkins
Fryer Bacon and Fryer Bungay (1711),
 II. 372
Fryshot (1825) = Freischutz Travestie,
 IV. 88, 465
Fugitive (Craven, T., 1887), v. 329
— (O'Keeffe, J., 1790), III. 294
— (Richardson, J., 1792), III. 13, 112,
 139-40, 196, 302
— (Shapter, T. 1790), III. 305, 307 [The
 author's name is Shapter, not
 Shrapter]
— (1850), v. 681

Fugitive Baron = Love and Agility
Fugitives (Conquest, G., 1858), v. 681, 785, 833
— (Roberts, W., 1791), III. 302
— (1778), III. 328
Fugitives and their Faithful Steed = Revolt in the East
Fugitive Slave = Uncle Tom's Cabin
Fugitives of Derrinane = Poor Parisheen
Fugitive's Pearls = Volcano of Italy
Fugitives' Wedding = Forgery
Fugitive Tree (1857), v. 681
Fulham Waterman Defeated = Country Wedding
Full Moon (1891), v. 681
Full Particulars of that Affair at Finchley (1861), v. 681
+ Full Private Perkins; or, He Wiped away a Tear (Byron, H. J.: *Dicks* (in *Sensation Dramas*))
Fulvius Valens (Serle, T. J., 1823), IV. 399
Fun (Kenrick, W., 1752), III. 279
Fun Alive = St Bartholomew
Fun and Fright (?Rodwell, T. G., 1819), IV. 465, 626
Fun and Frolic (1799), III. 328
Fun and Harmony = Board of Conviviality
Funeral (Steele, Sir R., 1701), II. 35, 129, 130, 131, 134, 137, 140, 183, 191, 230, 356
Funeral a la Mode = Funeral
Funeral Pile (1821), IV. 465
— = (1) Gallic Gratitude; (2) Orlando and Seraphina
Fun for the Gallery = Scraps
Fun in a Fog (1871), v. 681
Fun in a Japanese Tea House (1898), v. 682
Funnibone's Fix (Williams, A., 1880), v. 624
+ Funny Facts and Foolish Fancies (Paxton, A., *French*)
Funny World (Grain, R. C., 1894), v. 388
Fun on an Island (1895), v. 682
Fun on the Bristol (1882), v. 682
Fun on the Rhine = Our Goblins
Furibond (1807), IV. 465, 626
Furioso (1836), IV. 465
Furioso the Terrible (1862), v. 682

Furnished Apartments (Hay, F., 1860), v. 411
Furor of Friendship (Dibdin, C. I. M., 1822) = Manslaughter by Moonlight, IV. 295, 500
Fuss about Nothing (1862), v. 682
Future Mrs Ransome (1894), v. 682
Future Mrs Skillimore (Craven, S., 1897), v. 329

Gaberlunzie (Black, L., 1839), IV. 572
Gaberlunzie Man (Ballantyne, J., 1858), v. 247
— (Rede, W. L., 1836), IV. 390
Gabriel Grub the Sexton (Furtado, C., 1880), v. 375
Gabriella (Byrne, C. A., 1893), v. 295, 782
Gabrielle (Hodges, F. S., 1884), v. 423
— (1835), IV. 465
Gabrielle de Belleisle (1840), IV. 465
Gabrielle the Girondist (1854), v. 682
Gabrielli (Peake, R. B., 1847), IV. 371
Gabriel's Plot (1871), v. 682
Gabriel's Trust (Calmour, A. C., 1891), v. 300
Gadfly (Shaw, G. B., 1898), v. 562
+ Gaffer Grey's Legacy (*French*)
Gaffer Jarge (Ramsay, A., 1896), v. 534
Gaffer's Mistake (Dibdin, T. J., 1795), III. 328, 382, 401; IV. 297, 580
Gaia = Léonore
Gaiété (Eldred, J. and Aylen, H., 1874), v. 356
Gaiety Girl (Hall, O., 1893), v. 11, 399
Gain (Sargent, H., 1880), v. 556
— (1885), v. 682
Galatea (Schwab, F. A., 1887), v. 682, 833
— (Stephens, H. P., 1883), v. 580
— (1831), IV. 465
Galatea of Oregon (1895), v. 682
Gale Breezeley (Johnstone, J. B., 1845), IV. 333
Galician Fête (1855), v. 682
Gallantee Showman (Jerrold, D. W., 1837), IV. 333, 590
Gallant in the Closet = Coquettes
Gallant Moriscoes (1795), III. 328
Gallant Peasants (1767), III. 328
Gallantry (Penley, S., 1820), IV. 465, 626

Gallant Tom (Prest, T. P.), v. 811
Gallant Twenty First = Soldier's Son
Gallery of St Nicholas (Bow, C., 1832),
    IV. 465, 572, 626
Galley Slave (Campbell, B., 1879), v.
    301
Galley Slaves (1859), v. 682
Gallic Freedom (1789), III. 328
Gallic Gratitude (Dodd, J. S., 1772),
    III. 119, 257, 383
Galligantus (1758), III. 328, 401
Gallopade (1833), IV. 465
— = Horse and Foot
Galloping Lover (1815), IV. 465
Gallop to Gretna Green = Giovanni in
    the Country
Galvanic Ring (1845), IV. 465
Galway Go Bragh (Falconer, E., 1865),
    v. 360
Galway Practice in 1790 = Irish Attorney
Gambia (1832), IV. 465
Gambler (Boudling, J. W., 1891), v. 270
Gamblers (1823), IV. 465, 466, 626
Gambler's Dupe (1863), v. 682
Gambler's Fate (Milner, H. M., 1827),
    IV. 357
Gambler's Life in London (Campbell,
    A. V., 1828), IV. 278, 466, 575, 626
Gambler's Secret = Queen of Spades
Gambler's Wife (Courtney, J., 1853), v.
    326
— (1858), v. 682
— (1883), v. 682
— = For a Child's Sake
Gambols (1788), III. 329
Game (Henry, R., 1888), v. 417
Game and Game (Blanchard, E. L.,
    1843), IV. 268
Game at Commerce (Dibdin, C.), III.
    256
Game at Golf = St Andrew's Festival
Gamecock of the Wilderness (Rede,
    W. L., 1845), IV. 390
Game for Anything (1886), v. 682
Gamekeeper (Macpherson, H. and
    Marryat, F., 1898), v. 472
Gamekeeper of Quarry Dell (1866), v.
    682
Gamekeeper's Gun (Wilks, T. E.,
    1840), IV. 617
Gamekeeper's Wife (Hodgson, A. H.
    and Hodgson, A. C., 1890), v. 423

Game of Cards (Carlyon, F., 1898), v.
    303
— (1882), v. 682
Game of Chess (1858), v. 682
— = Ambitious Slave
Game of Dominoes (Reece, R., 1867),
    v. 537
Game of Fortune = Rose's Victory
Game of Hearts = Love's Trial
Game of Life (Brougham, J., 1853), v.
    280
— (Grattan, H. P. and Vollaire, H.,
    1863), v. 794
— (Howell-Poole, W., 1887), v. 429
Game of Life and Death (1856), v. 682
Game of Life for the Odd Trick = Four
    Knaves and the Pack
Game of Romps (Morton, J. M., 1855),
    v. 495
Game of Speculation (Lewes, G. H.,
    1851), v. 458
Gamester (Centlivre, Mrs S., 1705), II.
    9, 130, 133, 145, 157, 183, 195, 196,
    303, 433; III. 115, 134
— (Kemble, J. P., 1814), IV. 335
— (Moore, E. and Garrick, D., 1753),
    III. 88–9, 288, 370, 392
— (1813), IV. 466
Gamester Father (1837), IV. 466
Gamester of Metz (March, C., 1897), v.
    475
Gamester of Milan (Serle, T. J., 1834),
    IV. 399
Gamesters (Garrick, D., 1757), III. 58,
    113, 262
Gamester's Doom = Invisible Witness
Gamester's Son (1848), IV. 466
Gamester, the Seducer and the Mur-
    derer = Benevolent Jew
Gaming Table (À Beckett, G. A., 1834),
    IV. 466, 626
Gammer Gurton (1832), IV. 466
Gammon (Mortimer, J., 1882), v. 494
Gander Hall (Franklin, A., 1799), III.
    261
Ganem, the Slave of Love (Talfourd, F.,
    1852), v. 590
Ganger's Daughter = Permit
Ganymede and Galatea (1872), v. 833
Gaoler's Daughter = Brighter Days in
    Store
Garcia (Tomlins, F. G., 1849), IV. 413

Garde Nationale (Boucicault, D., 1850), v. 267
— = International Visits
Gardener of Versailles (1854), v. 682
Gardener's Wedding (1740), II. 372
Garden of Life = Weeds and Flowers
Garden Party (Jones, H. A., 1880), v. 439
— (Morton, J. M., 1877), v. 496
Garibaldi (Cooper, F. F., 1860), v. 682, 786, 833
— (Taylor, T., 1859), v. 593
Garibaldi Excursionists (Byron, H. J., 1860), v. 111, 296
Garibaldi in Sicily (Sawyer, W., 1867), v. 557, 815
Garibaldi's Englishmen (1859), v. 682
Garibaldi the Italian Liberator = Garibaldi
Garland (Hook, T. E., 1805) = Soldier's Return, IV. 466
— (1765), III. 329
Garland of Love (1815), IV. 466
Garland of Truth = Integrity
Garnet King = Corporal's Daughter
Garret Angel (Webb, C., 1867), v. 617
— (1860), v. 682
Garrick (Daly, A., 1874), v. 333
— (Muskerry, W., 1886), v. 501
Garrick and his Double (Dibdin, T. J., 1825), IV. 304
Garrick Fever (Planché, J. R., 1839), IV. 381
Garrick in the Shades (1779), III. 329
Garrick's Sacrifice (Lindo, F. and Young, Sir C. L., 1897), v. 460
Garrick's Vagary (1769), III. 329
Garrick the Actor (1890), v. 682
Garry Owen (Levey, J. C., 1877), v. 458
Gasconado the Great (Worsdale, J., 1759), III. 317
Gascon Adventurer = Fiend's Mountain
Gascons (Muskerry, W., 1876), v. 501
Gas in Burlesque Meter = Oxygen
Gasman (Bradford, H., 1873), v. 273
Gaspard Hauser (1838), IV. 466
Gaspardo the Gondolier (Almar, G., 1838), IV. 253
Gaston Boissier (Courtney, W. L., 1893), v. 326
+ Gaston de Foix (Mitford, E. L. in Poems, 1869)

Gaston Phoebus (Buchanan, R., 1868), v. 284
Gathering = Lord of the Isles
Gathering of the Clans (Dibdin, C. I. M., 1818), IV. 294
— (1895), v. 682
— = (1) Bonnie Dundee; (2) Lord of the Isles; (3) Montrose
Gaul, King of Ragah (Hawkes, W. R., 1813), IV. 466
Gaul versus Lavater = Knobs and Noses
Gauntlet (Braekstad, H. L., 1890), v. 780
— (Edwards, O. and Hawtrey, G. P., 1894), v. 355, 789
— (1799), III. 62, 329
Gavotte (Bell, M., 1890), v. 256
Gawyim Honor (Jones, M. E. M., 1844), IV. 591
Gay Boulogne = J.P.
Gay Cavalier (Cuthbert, E., 1879), v. 331
Gay Chaperon (Howlett, S., 1894), v. 429
Gay City (Sims, G. R., 1881), v. 568
— (1871), v. 682
Gay Deceiver (Mortimer, J., 1879), v. 494
Gay Deceivers (Colman, G., the Younger, 1804), IV. 282, 577
Gay Goddess = Juno
Gay Gracer of Three Wives (1845), IV. 466
Gay Grisette (Dance, G., 1898), v. 335
Gay Husband (Allerton, 1886), v. 239
Gay Lord Quex (Pinero, Sir A. W., 1899), v. 525, 810
Gay Lothario (Calmour, A. C., 1891), v. 300
Gay Musketeers (Eldred, J. and Paulton, H., 1870), v. 356
Gay Parisienne (Dance, G., 1894), v. 335
Gay Photographer (1896), v. 682
Gay Widow (Burnand, F. C., 1894), v. 292
Gay Widower (Mayer, S., 1892), v. 482
Gay Young Fellow = Billy Taylor
Gazette Extraordinary (Holman, J. G., 1811), IV. 327
Gazza Ladra (1835), IV. 466
Geisha (Hall, O., 1896), v. 400
Gelert (Balsilio, D., 1896), v. 247

Gellert the Faithful Dog=Llewellyn, Prince of Wales

Gemea (Newbound, E., 1880), v. 502

Gemini (Peake, R. B., 1838), IV. 371

Gemma of the Isles (1859), v. 682

Gem of a Girl (Le Queux, W. T., 1886), v. 456

Gems of Ould Ireland=Agra-ma-chree

General and the Jesuit=Lalli Tollendal

General Cashier'd (1712), II. 50, 262, 372

General Election (1868), v. 682

General Elliot in 1782=Siege of Gibraltar

Generall (Boyle, R., 1662), I. 85, 100, 106–10, 393

General Lover (Moss, T., 1749), II. 345

General Tom Thumb (Dillon, C., 1844), IV. 305

Générosité d'Alexandre=Apelles et Campaspe

Generous Artifice (Foote, S., 1762), III. 384

Generous Attachment (Smythe, G., 1796), III. 308

Generous Brother=She Lives

Generous Chief (Norval, J., 1792), III. 291

Generous Choice (Manning, F., 1700), II. 50, 170, 343

Generous Conqueror (Higgons, B., 1701), II. 335

Generous Counterfeit (Davies, W., 1786), III. 253

Generous Enemies (Corye, J., 1671), I. 98, 225, 398

Generous Farmer (1821), IV. 466

Generous Fortune Hunter=Honour Rewarded

Generous Free-Mason (Chetwood, W., 1730), II. 237, 241–2, 306

Generous Friends=Hymeneal Party

Generous Husband (Johnson, C., 1711), II. 49, 146, 169, 339, 439

Generous Impostor (O'Beirne, T. L., 1780), III. 118, 291, 392

Generous Lover (O'Keeffe, J.), III. 292

Generous Lovers=(1) Orphans; (2) St Stephen's Green

Generous Mistris=Disappointed Marriage

Generous Moor (Linnecar, R., 1789), III. 282

Generous Portugal=Island Princess

Generous Portuguese=Island Princess

Generous Quaker=Three Fives

Generous Refusal=Portsmouth Heiress

Generous Revenge=Ambitious Slave

Generous Rivals (1773), III. 329

Generous Sailor=Fair Lunatick

Generous Tars=Dairy Maids

+ Generous Turk (Dibdin, C. I. M., R.A., 1798)

— (1790), III. 329

— =(1) Captive Mariner; (2) Turk

Geneva Cross (Rowe, G. F., 1874), v. 552

Geneviève (Barnett, C. Z., 1843), IV. 466, 626

— (Boucicault, D., 1853), v. 86, 267

— (Braddon, M. E., 1874), v. 273

— (Conquest, G., 1872), v. 320, 785

— (West, B., 1824), IV. 466, 626

— (1861), v. 682

— (1865), v. 682

Geneviève de Brabant (Farnie, H. B., 1871), v. 361, 790

— (1839), IV. 466

Genevieve (Fearns) (Albery, J.), v. 777

Genevieve, the Maid of Switzerland (Baron-Wilson, Mrs C., 1834), IV. 261

Genevra, the Scourged One (1846), IV. 466

Geni and the Black Enchanter=Casket of Gloriana

Génie du Globe (Barnett, M. B., 1847), IV. 570

Genie of the Oak=Fairlop Fair

Genii (Becket, A., 1814), IV. 264, 635

— (Woodward, H., 1752), III. 209, 317

Genii Horsemen of the Air=Spectre Monarch and his Phantom Steed

Genii of Paloguam (Leclercq, 1822), IV. 466, 626

Genii of the Deep (1799), III. 329

Genii of the Elements=Talisman

Genii of the Lake (1821), IV. 466

Genii of the Ring (Hendrie, E., 1882), v. 417

Genii's Tomb (1803), IV. 466

Genius (Williamson, H. W., 1881), v. 626

— (1899), v. 682

Genius of Glasgow (1792), III. 329

Genius of Ireland (Macaulay, J., 1784), III. 283

Genius of Liverpool (Harpley, T., 1789), III. 266

Genius of Nonsense (Colman, G., 1780), III. 210, 247, 379

Genius of the Ring = Bride of Golconda

Genius Wanted (1831), IV. 466

Genoese Conspiracy = Fiesco

Genoese Pirate (Cross, J. C., 1798) = Black Beard, III. 250, 380

Genoveva (Vance, L., 1893), V. 606

Gentle Amy Robsart = Kenilworth

Gentle Gertrude (Pemberton, T. E., 1881, +4°, 1880 (Birmingham) as Gentle Gertrude of the Infamous Red Lyon Inn, or Drugged and Drowned in Digbeth), V. 519

Gentle Ivy (Fryers, A., 1894), V. 374

Gentle Juliet = Modern Juliet

Gentleman (Steele, Sir R.), II. 444

Gentleman and the Upstart (Ranger, E., 1848), IV. 606

Gentleman Citizen (Foote, S., 1762), III. 384

Gentleman-Cully (Johnson, C., 1701), II. 21, 169, 339, 422

Gentleman Dancing-Master (Wycherley, W., 1672), I. 13, 75, 188, 192, 238, 438; III. 114, 198

Gentleman Gardener (Wilder, J., 1751), III. 316

— (1749), II. 138, 372

Gentleman in Black (Gilbert, W. S., 1870), V. 379

— (Lemon, M., 1840), IV. 344

— (Rede, W. L., 1842), IV. 607

— = (1) Dominique the Deserter; (2) Grave Subject

Gentleman in Difficulties (Bayly, T. H., 1835), IV. 262, 571

Gentleman in Paris = Discounting a Life

Gentleman in White (1866), V. 682

Gentleman Jack (Mouillot, F., 1888), V. 498

— (Vincent, C. T. and Brady, W., 1894) V. 609

— (1850), V. 682

Gentleman Jim (Walkes, W. R., 1893), V. 611

Gentleman Joe (Wilks, T. E., 1838), IV. 420

— (1838), IV. 466

Gentleman Joe, the Hansom Cabby (Hood, B., 1895), V. 425

Gentleman Opposite (Buckingham, L. S., 1854), V. 682, 781, 833

Gentleman Quack = Justice Busy

Gentleman Rover (1827), IV. 466

Gentleman's Son = Lancers

Gentleman Whip (Paull, H. M., 1894), V. 516

Gentleman with a Bee in his Bonnet = Slightly Touched

Gentlemen of the Night = Under the Lamps

Gentlemen, we can do without you = Ladies at Home

Gentle Nelly (1871), V. 682

Gentle Revenge = Treble Lover

Gentle Savage = Pocahontas

Gentle Shepherd (Bethune, G., 1817), IV. 267

— (McLaren, A., 1811), IV. 351

— (Ramsay, A., 1725), II. 250, 350, 443; III. 117

— (Tickell, R., 1781), III. 117, 312

— (Turner, Mrs M., 1790), III. 117, 313

— (Vanderstop, C., 1777), III. 117, 313

— (Wood, W., ?1785), III. 117, 317

— = Patie and Roger

Gentle Thieves (1877), V. 682

Gentoo's Daughter = Brahman's Curse

Genuine Grub-Street Opera = Welsh Opera

Geoffrey Dunstan (1828), IV. 466

Geoffrey Kurdistan (Pitt, G. D., 1845), IV. 373

George (James, W., 1895), V. 434

George III, the Father of his People (Macfarren, G., 1824) = Life and Reign of George III, IV. 349, 492, 597, 631

George a Green (1775), III. 113, 329

George and the Crocodile (1834), IV. 466

George Barnwell (1811), IV. 466

— (1844), IV. 466

— = London Merchant

George Barrington (Taylor, T. P., 1844), IV. 19, 411

— = Night Birds

George Cameron (Mitchell, L. E., 1891), V. 490

George Dandin (1747), III. 145, 372, 447
George Darville (Boucicault, D., 1857), v. 268
George de Barnwell (Byron, H. J., 1862), v. 296
George Geith (Reeve, W., 1877), v. 540
George Heriot (Murray, W. H., 1823), IV. 93, 365, 601
— (Ryder, C., 1823), IV. 93, 396
— = Fortunes of Nigel
George's Natal Day (1780), III. 329
Georgette (1854), v. 682
George Vernet (Conquest, G., 1855), v. 682
Georgey Barnwell (1833), IV. 466
Georgey Porgey Pudding and Pie (Douglass, J., 1857), v. 348
Georgian Princess (Craven, E., 1799) = Princess of Georgia, III. 329, 380, 401
Georgians (Wilson, C. J. S., 1875), v. 628
Gerald (Marston, J. W., 1842), IV. 353
Geralda = British Heroine [This appears in the newspapers also as Gerilda]
Geraldi Duval, the Bandit of Bohemia (Walker, C. E., 1821), IV. 416
Geraldine (À Beckett, G. A., 1843), IV. 466, 567, 626
— (Bateman, Mrs H. L., 1865), v. 253
— (1887), v. 682
Geraldine's Ordeal (Bannister, T. B., 1871), v. 248
+ Gerald of Kildare (Bibby, T., 12°, 1854, Dublin)
Gerard the Pedlar = Leontine
Gerilda = Geralda
German Baron (1784), III. 401
German Blunder (Greffulhe, 1809) = Is He a Prince? IV. 467, 626
German Forest = Natural Son
German Hotel (Holcroft, T., 1790), III. 7, 122, 134–5, 271, 387
Germanicus (Bernel, G., 1817), IV. 266
— (1775), III. 329
— (1817), IV. 467
German Jew (Tilbury, W. H., 1830), IV. 467, 626
German Patrol (1830), IV. 467
German Princess (Holden, J., 1664), I. 220, 413
Germans and French (Douglass, J. T., 1871), v. 348
German Silver (1895), v. 682

German Silvery King (Burnot, W., 1883), v. 293
Gertie's Garter (Southern, E. H., 1883), v. 574
Gertrude (Collins, M. T., 1848), IV. 577
— (Richardson, S., 1810), IV. 394
Gertrude and Beatrice (Stephens, G., 1839), IV. 406
Gertrude of Elsinore (1836), IV. 467
Gertrude's Cherries (Jerrold, D. W., 1842), IV. 129, 333
Gertrude's Money Box (Lemon, H., 1869), v. 454
Gerty (1881), v. 683
Gervaise Skinner (Jerrold, D. W., 1830), IV. 332
Gervase Skinner (1831), IV. 467
G.G. = Mistake
Gheber (Dibdin, C. I. M., 1818), IV. 294
Ghebirs of the Desert = Lalla Rookh
Ghetto (Fernald, C. B., 1899), v. 683, 792, 833
Ghillie Callum (1895), v. 683
Ghost (James, H. and others, 1899), v. 799
— (1767), III. 115, 329
— (1892), v. 683
Ghost Hunter (Banim, J., 1833), IV. 258
— (Conquest, G., 1862), v. 683, 785, 833
— (1856), v. 683
Ghost in Spite of Himself (1866), v. 683
— = Spectre Bridegroom
Ghost no Conjurer = All up at Stockwell
Ghost of a Hamper of Wine = (1) Manslaughter by Moonlight; (2) Furor of Friendship
Ghost of an Idea (Heathcote, A. M., 1892), v. 415
Ghost of an old Fiddle = Music hath Charms
Ghost of Cock Lane (1862), v. 683
Ghost of the Back Drawing Room = Jane Jenkins
Ghost of the Past (Darrell, C., 1899), v. 337
Ghosts (Archer, W., 1891), v. 187, 242
— (Holden, J., 1665), I. 413
— (1886), v. 683
Ghost's Advice = Leave the House
Ghosts and Apprehensions = All a Fetch
Ghost's Bargain = Haunted Man

Ghost Seer = Bannockburn

Ghosts of Tom and Jerry (Dibdin, C. I. M., 1823), IV. 295

Ghost Story (Serle, T. J., 1836), IV. 400

Ghost's Tower = Seven Maids of Munich

Ghost! The Ghost! = Awful Rise in Spirits

Ghost with the Golden Casket = Wreckers of the Craig Foot

Gian Ben Gian and the Elixir = Loadstone of the Earth

Giant (Webb, C., 1839), IV. 467, 626

Giant and the Dwarf (Addison, J., 1896), V. 236

Giant Defeated (1789), III. 329

Giant Horse (1833), IV. 467

Giant of Palestine (1838), IV. 467

Giant of the Mountains (Addison, J., 1894), V. 236

— (Marchant, F., 1869), V. 476

Giant's Castle (1839), IV. 467

Giant's Causeway (1829), IV. 467

— (1844), IV. 467

Giant Spectre = Prophecy

Giant Staircase = Council of Ten

Giant's Tomb (1858), V. 683

Giaour (1897), V. 683

Gibbet and the Rampart = Just in Time

Gibbet Law of Halifax = Dennis

Gibbet of Hounslow = Young Highwayman

Gibbet of Mont Faucon = Dagger and the Cross

Gibraltar (Dennis, J., 1705), II. 16, 129, 210, 318

— (Houlton, R., 1783), III. 273

— (Murray, A., 1881), V. 499

Giddy Galatea (Edlin, H., 1895), V. 354

Giddy Girl (1899), V. 683

Giddy Godiva (Newton, H. C., 1883), V. 503

Giddy Major General (1898), V. 683

Giddy Miss Carmen (Lester, S., 1894), V. 457

Gideon Giles the Roper (Pitt, G. D., 1845), IV. 374

Gideon's Ghost (1860), V. 683

Gifted Lady (Buchanan, R., 1891), V. 285

Gift of Mammon = Devil's Ducat

Gift of Venus (1895), V. 683

Gifts of Immortality = Tempter

Gilbert the Idiot (1859), V. 683

Gil Blas (Bates, 1788), III. 329, 377

— (Moore, E., 1751), III. 7, 288, 392

— (1823), IV. 467

— = Boy of Santillane

Gil Blas and the Robbers of Asturia = Boy of Santillane

Gil Blas at 17, 25, 52 (Macfarren, G., 1822), IV. 349 [There is doubt about the authorship of this play. It is attributed as well to R. B. Peake, while Thomas Hood's daughter said it was by her father and J. H. Reynolds, see *University of Texas Studies in English* (1951), p. 187]

Gil Blas de Santillane (1821), IV. 467

Gilded Age = Colonel Sellers

Gilded Crime (1884), V. 683

Gilded Love (Yeldham, Major, 1888), V. 635

Gilded Youth (Young, Sir C. L., 1872), V. 149, 635

Gilderoy (Murray, W. H., 1827), IV. 365

Gilderoy, the Bonnie Boy (Barrymore, W., 1822), IV. 262

Gillette (Clarke, H. S., 1883), V. 313, 784

Gillian the Gipsey (Blake, T. G., 1846), IV. 268

Gin (Roberts, G., 1880), V. 544

Gin and Water (1854), V. 683

Gingerbread Nut (1790), III. 329

Gin versus Water (1854), V. 683

Giorno Felice (Scott, J. M., 1812), IV. 609

Giovanna of Naples (Landor, W. S., 1839), IV. 199, 341

Giovanni in Botany (1822), IV. 467

Giovanni in Ireland (Moncrieff, W. T., 1821), IV. 467, 626

— (1821), IV. 467

Giovanni in London (Moncrieff, W. T., 1817), IV. 358, 600

Giovanni in the Country (1820), IV. 467

Giovanni Redivivus (Cooper, F. F., 1864), V. 786

Giovanni, the Vampire (Planché, J. R., 1821), IV. 376

Gipsey and the Gentle Goat = Esmeralda

Gipsey and the Stolen Child = Justice

Gipsey Belle = Gideon Giles the Roper
Gipsey Daughter (1824), IV. 467
Gipsey Farmer (Johnstone, J. B., 1845), IV. 333
Gipsey Norris = Gipsey Twins
Gipsey of Milan (1844), IV. 467
Gipsey's Prophecy = (1) Guilt; (2) Guy Mannering
Gipsey's Revenge = Retribution
Gipsey's Romance (Johnstone, J. B., 1852), V. 438
Gipsey's Vengeance = Troubadour
Gipsey Twins (Pitt, G. D., 1847), IV. 375
Gipsies (Dibdin, C., 1778), III. 118, 203, 255
— (Hood, B., 1890), V. 425
— (Moser, J., 1807), IV. 364
Gipsies of Castile = Elie and Elode
Gypsie's Stratagem = Minstrels of Provence
Gipsy = Zingara
Gipsy and the Showman (Rogers, W., 1855), V. 683, 814, 833
Gipsy Boy (1855), V. 683
Gipsy Bride (Taylor, T. P., 1845), IV. 411
Gipsy Dumb Boy (Dobbs, J., 1823), IV. 467, 626
Gipsy Earl (Sims, G. R., 1898), V. 570
Gipsy Gabriel (Parke, W. and Hogarth, W., 1887), V. 512
Gipsy George the Outcast = Willow Grove
Gipsy Girl (1815), IV. 467
— (1863), V. 683
Gipsy Girl and the Guilty Conscience = Wayside Wiolets
Gipsy Girl of Granada (Travers, W., 1861), V. 683, 821, 833
Gipsy Girl of Madrid (1859), V. 683
Gipsy Girl of Notre Dame = Quasimodo
Gipsy Girl of Paris = Notre Dame
Gipsy Jack (Moncrieff, W. T., 1831) = Napoleon of Humble Life, IV. 360, 510
Gipsy King (Bosworth, J., 1837), IV. 269
— (1861), V. 683
Gipsy Mother = Raphelina
Gipsy of Ashburnham Dell = Linishee Lovel
Gipsy of Derncleuch (Jerrold, D. W., 1821), IV. 93, 331

Gipsy of Paris = Gipsy Twins
Gipsy Outcast = Poacher Bill
Gipsy Prince (Moore, T., 1801), IV. 361
Gipsy Princess (Bingham, F., 1895), V. 261
— (1899), V. 683
Gipsy Queen (1854), V. 683
— (1893), V. 683
— = Camp of Silesia
Gipsy Romance = Withered Oak
Gipsy's Bride (Young, Mrs H., 1863), V. 825
Gipsy Showman (Rogers, W., 1861) = Gipsy and the Showman, V. 683, 833 [where, by error, Travers is given for Rogers]
Gipsy's Prophecy = Knights of the Road
Gipsy's Revenge = Mother's Dream
Gipsy's Secret = Pet Heiress
Gipsy's Vengeance (Jefferys, C., 1856), V. 435, 800
— = (1) Mabel; (2) Woman's Love
Gipsy's Warning (Linley, G. and Peake, R. B., 1838), IV. 346
Gipsy Twins (1861), V. 683
Giraffe (1827), IV. 467
Giralda (Baildon, A., 1876), V. 247
— (Boucicault, D., 1850), V. 267
— (Davidson, Mrs, 1850), V. 338
— (Kingdom, J. M.), V. 444
— (Webster, B. N., 1850), V. 106, 618
— (Welstead, H., 1850), V. 619
Giraldi = Ruffian Boy
Girl Graduate (Rose, E., 1886), V. 550
Girl he left behind him (Sims, G. R., 1881), V. 568
— = On the Rink
Girl I left behind me (Belasco, D. and Fyles, F., 1893), V. 255
— (Oxenford, J., 1864), V. 683, 809
Girl in Style (Scawen, J., 1786), III. 304
Girl of Erin = Norah
Girl of my Heart = Savourneen Deelish
Girl of the Lips = Arrah-No-Brogue
Girl of Today = Kittens
Girl o' my Heart (Leonard, H., 1896), V. 456
Girls and Boys (Pinero, Sir A. W., 1882), V. 525
Girl's Freak (Feltheimer, L. and Dixey, K., 1899), V. 364

Girls of Chelsea Reach = Boys of Horsley Down

Girls of the Period (Burnand, F. C., 1869), v. 289

Girl's Romance = Rescued

Girl that was sent to Coventry = Giddy Godiva

Giroflé Giroflá (O'Neil, C. and Clarke, C., 1874), v. 507

Girouette (Reece, R., 1889), v. 539, 813

Gisela (Holroyd, J. J., 1839), IV. 327

Giselle (Byron, H. J., 1871), v. 298

— (Moncrieff, W. T., 1841), IV. 101, 103, 113, 361

— (1843), IV. 467

— (1846), IV. 467

— = Wilis

Giselle and the Phantom Night Dancers (Fenton, F. and Osman, W. R., 1863), v. 683, 833

Gisippus (Griffin, G., 1842), IV. 321

Gismonda (1895), v. 683

Gis, the Armourer of Tyre (Selby, C., 1859), v. 560

Gitana (Moreton, F. L., 1895), v. 493

— (Towers, E., 1876), v. 601

Gitama's Love = Manola

Gitanilla (Wilson, J. C., 1860), v. 628

Gitano Boy (Reynoldson, T. H., 1866) = True at Last, v. 683, 813, 833

Gitta la ballerina (1865), v. 683

Give a Dog a Bad Name (Lewes, G. H., 1854), v. 458

— (Lewis, L. D., 1876), v. 459

— (1866), v. 683

Give a Man Luck = New Way to get Married

Give and Take (Pryce-Jenkins, T. J., 1894), v. 531

Give me my Wife (Suter, W. E., 1859), v. 587

Give Them their Way = Children

Gladiator (Bird, R. M., 1836), IV. 267

— (1786), III. 401

Gladiator of Ravenna (Charlton, W. H., 1861), v. 783

— (Martin, Sir T., 1885), v. 806

— (Vericour, de, 1859), v. 608

Gladiators (Bannister, T. B., 1893), v. 248 [The entry in IV. 258 is in error and should be deleted]

Glad Tidings (Willing, J. and Stainforth, F., 1883), v. 626

Gladys (Law, A., 1886), v. 450

Glamour (Farnie, H. B. and Murray, A., 1886), v. 363

Glance at a Court = Madame du Barry

Glasgow in 1300 (1855), v. 683

Glashen Glora (Dodson, R., 1875), v. 346

Glass (1847), IV. 467

Glass Door (Ebsworth, J., 1837), IV. 308

Glass Houses (Broughton, F. W., 1881), v. 281

Glass of Fashion (Grundy, S. and Sims, G. R., 1883), v. 396

Glass of Water (Suter, W. E., 1863), v. 588

Glass too much = (1) Challenge; (2) Truth

Glaucus (Traill, F. T., 1865), v. 602, 821

Glazier (Dibdin, T. J., ?1796), III. 383

Glazier's Conspiracy = Illumination

Gleam in the Darkness (1899), v. 683

Gleam of Hope (1866), v. 683

Gleam of Sunshine = Wanderer

Gleaner (Moser, J., 1809), IV. 364

Gleaners (1809), IV. 467

— (1811), IV. 467

— (1857), v. 683

Glenarvon (1819), IV. 467

Glencoe (Talfourd, T. N., 1840), IV. 48, 64, 79, 177-8, 410

Glendelough (Gurney, E., 1891), v. 398

Glendwyr of Snowdon (1849), IV. 467

Glen Girl (Blake, T. G.), IV. 573

Glider (1895), v. 683

Glimpse of Paradise (Dilley, J. J., 1887), v. 345

Glimpse of the World (Howlett, S., 1895), v. 429

Glin Gath (Meritt, P., 1872), v. 148, 485

Glitter (À Beckett, G. A., 1868), v. 233

Glittering Gem (Rennell, C. R., 1874), v. 541

Gloaming and the Mirk (1869), v. 684

Globe (1881), v. 684

Gloriana (Lee, N., 1676), I. 14, 67, 96, 123-4, 126, 128, 129, 148, 419

— (Mortimer, J., 1891), v. 494

Glorie Aston (Dawson, F., 1898), v. 339

Glories of England in 1356 = Edward the Black Prince

Glorious Bit of Fun (1857), v. 684

Glorious First of August = (1) Aboukir Bay; (2) Mouth of the Nile

Glorious First of June (Sheridan, R. B. and Cobb, J., 1794), III. 306

Glorious Princess (1747), II. 372

Glorious Queen of Hungary (1743), II. 372, 452

Glorious Revolution, 5th November, 1688 (Lee, F., 1821), IV. 342

Glory (Grattan, H. P., 1873), v. 389

Glory's Resurrection (Settle, E., 1698), v. 429

Glo'stershire Squire = Country 'Squire

Gloucestershire Story = Lock and Key

Glove and Fan (1857), v. 684

Glow-worm (Isla, Count de la, 1884), v. 432

Gnome (Wewitzer, R., 1788), III. 315

Gnome Fly (Conquest, G. and Spry, H., 1869), v. 320

— (1838), IV. 467

Gnome King (Brough, W., 1868), v. 280

— (Reynolds, F., 1819), IV. 468, 607, 626

— (1823), IV. 467

— (1838), IV. 467

Gnome Lamp = Field of Terror

Gnome of the Gold Mines = (1) Mirror of Fate; (2) Slave of Wealth

Gnome of the Hartsberg = Berta

Gnomes and Fairies (Dibdin, C. I. M., 1816), IV. 298

+ Goal (Jones, H. A., 8°, 1898 (priv.))

Goatherd of the Mountain = Octavian

Goat-herd's Oath = Worga

Go Bang (Ross, A., 1894), v. 551

Goblin Bat (Bowyer, F., 1886), v. 271

Goblin Mine = Fairy Fern Flower

Goblin of the Chest = Trooper's Horn

Goblin Tale = Chimes

God-daughter = Atonement

Goddess of El Dorado = Naida

Goddess of Morni = Aurora

Goddess of the Moon = Diana

Godefroi and Yolande (Irving, L. S. B., 1894), v. 684, 799, 833

Godfather's Legacy = Two Sisters

Godfrida (+ J. Davidson, 8°, 1898), v. 684

Godiva (Hale, W. P. and Talfourd, F., 1851), v. 398

God of War (Whitlock, C., 1898), v. 621

Godolphin (Hope, 1843), IV. 589

Godolphin Arabian (1845), IV. 468

Godolphins (1860), v. 684

Godolphin, the Lion of the North (Thompson, B., 1813), IV. 413

Godpapa (Philips, F. C. and Brookfield, C. H. E., 1891), v. 522

Gods as they were and not as they ought to have been = Venus

God save the Queen (Palgrave, R. and Gover, F., 1886), v. 511

Gods grown old = Thespis

Goetz of Berlichingen, With the Iron Hand (Scott, Sir W., 1799), III. 63, 304; IV. 193

Gog and Magog (Dibdin, T. J., 1822), IV. 303

— = Pindar of Wakefield

Goggin's Gingham (Wigan, H., 1863), v. 622

Going it (Morton, J. M. and Vicars, W. A., 1885), v. 497

Going on the Stage (Henry, Mrs R., 1895), v. 417

Going out a-shooting = First of September

Going over to Rome = Innocents Abroad

Going the Pace (Shirley, A. and Landeck, B., 1898), v. 565

Going to Chobham (Hazlewood, C. H., 1853), v. 412

Going to Cremorne (Courtney, J., 1852), v. 326

Going to Execution (1822), IV. 468

Going to my Uncle's (1833), IV. 468

Going to see the Fireworks (1856), v. 684

Going to the Bad (Taylor, T., 1858), v. 593

Going to the Derby (Morton, J. M., 1848), IV. 363

Going to the Dogs (Brough, W. and Halliday, A., 1865), v. 280

Gold (Reade, C., 1853), v. 535

— (1851), v. 684

— (1880), v. 684

+ Gold and Guilt; or, The True Ring of the Genuine Metal (Byron, H. J.: *Dicks* (in *Sensation Dramas*))

Gold and Silver (1886), v. 684
Gold Craze (Thomas, B., 1889), v. 596
Gold Curse (Stirling, E., 1847), IV. 409
— = Fiend
Gold Diggings of Australia (1853), v. 684, 824
Gold Dreamer = Black King
Gold Dust (De Lara, G., 1887), v. 341
— (Rymer, J., 1878), v. 554
Golden Age (Byatt, H., 1897), v. 295
Golden Apple (Silvester, F., 1891), v. 566
Golden Arrow (Pitt, G. D., 1845), IV. 373
Golden Axe (Barrymore, W., 1823), IV. 468, 570, 626
— (Dibdin, T. J., 1817), IV. 300
Golden Bait (Lunn, H. C., 1891), v. 465
Golden Band (Herman, H. and Wills, F., 1887), v. 419
Golden Barrier (1887), v. 684
Golden Bell (1845), IV. 468
Golden Bond (1893), v. 684
Golden Bough (Scott, D., 1887), v. 558
Golden Branch (Planché, J. R., 1847), IV. 382; v. 44
Golden Bubble = Aesop
Golden Calf (Coveney, G. H., 1883), v. 326
— (Jerrold, D. W., 1832), IV. 332
Golden Cask (O'Neill, A., 1866), v. 507
Golden Chance (Miller, St A., 1891), v. 488
Golden Cornet (Wilks, T. E., 1834), IV. 420
Golden Cross (Jackson, J. P., 1878), v. 432, 799
Golden Daggers (Yates, E., 1862), v. 635
— (1877), v. 684
Golden Days (Jeffrey, P. S. and Shore, W. T., 1893), v. 436
Golden Days of England's Elizabeth = Kenilworth
Golden Days of Good Queen Bess (1826), IV. 468
— = (1) Kenilworth; (2) Life and Adventures of Will Shakespeare
Golden Days of Queen Bess = Spanish Armada
Golden Dream (Brougham, J., 1864), v. 684, 780, 833

Golden Dream (1799), III. 329
— (1805), IV. 468
— (1812), IV. 468
— (1889), v. 684
Golden Dustman (Farnie, H. B., 1866), v. 361
Golden Evidence = (1) Heir from the Ocean; (2) Ocean Knight
Golden Farmer (Cross, J. C., 1802), IV. 286
— (Webster, B. N., 1832), IV. 417
— (1821), IV. 468
Golden Fetter = Fettered
Golden Fetters = Man
Golden Fleece (Planché, J. R., 1845), IV. 382, 605
Golden-footed Steed (1847), IV. 468
Golden Fortune = Run to Earth
Golden Fox (Wilks, T. E., 1840), IV. 617
Golden Fruit (Pettitt, H., 1873), v. 520
Golden Glove (Lake, J., 1815), IV. 341
Golden Goblin (Marryat, F., 1888), v. 477
Golden Goddess = Merry Madcap
Golden Goose (1828), IV. 468
Golden Gulch (1879), v. 684
Goldenhair the Good (Byron, H. J., 1862), v. 296
Golden Harvest (Bellamy, G., 1868), v. 256
— (Jarman, F., 1890), v. 434
Golden Hatch (1885), v. 684
Golden Heart (1852), v. 684
Golden Hearts (Roy, G., 1892), v. 552
— (1862), v. 684
Golden Key = (1) Gladys; (2) Necromancer
Golden King (1899), v. 684
Golden Ladder (Dims, G. R. and Barrett, W., 1887), v. 569
Golden Leek (Wade, F. E., 1891), v. 610
Golden Lily (Pitt, G. D., 1845), IV. 374
Golden Lining (1883), v. 684
Golden Net = Venus and Mars
Golden Nugget (1853), v. 684
Golden Pheasant = One Thousand Napoleons
Golden Pippin (O'Hara, K., 1772), III. 195, 208, 291
— (O'Neill, J. R.), v. 808
Golden Plough (Meritt, P., 1877), v. 486

Golden Plume (Howells, C. E., 1880), v. 429

Golden Ring (Sims, G. R., 1883), v. 569

— (1883), v. 684

Golden Serpent (Walter, T. N., 1897), v. 612

Golden Shield (1836), IV. 468

Golden Sorrow (Drinkwater, A. E., 1891), v. 351

Golden Test (1887), v. 684

Golden Web (Stephenson, B. C. and Corder, F., 1893), v. 582

Golden Wedding (Cole, J. P., 1899), v. 316

— (Groves, C. and Phillpotts, E., 1898), v. 810

— (Sketchley, A., 1885), v. 684, 816, 833

Golden Witness (Pitt, G. D., 1850), v. 526

Golden Wreath (Albery, J., 1878), v. 684, 777, 833

Gold Fields of Australia (1853), v. 684

Gold Fiend (Townsend, W. T., 1850), v. 602

Gold Fiend of Australia = Gold Fiend

Gold Fiend of the Black Forest (1859), v. 684

Goldfinch (Hoskins, F. R., 1851), v. 427

Gold Finders of Australia (1853), v. 684

Goldfish (Mattos, A. T. de, 1892), v. 481

Gold Goblin = Heart of Old Ireland and the Lepreghaun

Gold Guitar (Wilks, T. E., 1843), IV. 617

Golding's Debt = Friendship

Gold is Nothing—Happiness is All (Levey, J. C., 1868), v. 458

Gold Mine (Matthews, B. and Jessop, G. H., 1889), v. 480

— (Stirling, E., 1854), v. 584

Gold Regions of Australia (Johnstone, J. B., 1853), v. 438

Gold Seekers (Grattan, H. P., 1839), IV. 320

— (1838), IV. 468

Gold Seekers of Alasca (1842), IV. 468

Gold Seekers of Carpentara = New Fortune

Gold Slave (Barclay, T. G., 1886), v. 248

Goldsmith (Holcroft, F., 1827), IV. 326

Goldsmith of Frankfort (Haines, J. T.), IV. 587

Goldsmith of Grenoble = Mount St Bernard

Goldsmith's Daughter = Julie Ledru

Goldsmiths Jubilee (Jordan, T., 1674), I. 416

Goldsmiths of Clerkenwell = Pledge

Goldsmith's Wife (1889), v. 684

Gombeen's Gold (1891), v. 684

Gommoch (O'Grady, H., 1877), v. 506

Gondibert and Birtha (Thompson, W., 1751), III. 312

Gondolier (1815), IV. 636

Gondoliers (Gilbert, W. S., 1889), v. 145, 380

— (1751), III. 329

Gone Away (Righton, E. and Stow, D., 1886), v. 543

Gone to Texas (Oxenford, J., 1844), IV. 468, 626

Gonsalve de Cordoue (1816), IV. 468

Gonsalvo (1822), IV. 626

Gonsalvo de Cordova (Cross, J. C., 1802), IV. 286

Gonzaga (Solly, H., 1877), v. 574

— (1814), IV. 468, 636

Gonzalo (Fortescue, 1821), IV. 317

Gonzalo, the Traitor (Roscoe, T., 1820), IV. 609

+ Gonzalvo of Cordova (Wilmot, Mrs B., 8°, 1821)

Good and Bad (1792), III. 329

— = Hearts, Hearts, Hearts

Good and Evil = Forger

Good as Gold (Hazlewood, C. H., 1869), v. 413

— (Monk, M., 1883), v. 491

— (1877), v. 684

Good Business (Hervey, R. K., 1887), v. 420

Good-bye (Bourchier, A., 1889), v. 270

— (Hicks, Sir S., 1893), v. 420

— (Johnson, H. T., 1896), v. 437

Goodbye Sweetheart (1894), v. 684

Good Cast for a Piece = Freischutz

Good Conduct Prize = Jane Annie

Good Fairy of St Helen's (Brockbank, J., 1872), v. 276

Good for Both (Kennedy, J., 1887), v. 443

Good for Evil = (1) Home Truths; (2) Little Bidette; (3) Reconciled

Good for Nothing (Buckstone, J. B., 1851), v. 107, 287

— (Lemon, M., 1841), IV. 344

— (Yates, E. and Harrington, N. H., 1858), v. 635

Good Fortune (Coghlan, C. F., 1880), v. 316

Good Friday that came on Saturday = Jack Robinson Crusoe

Good Gracious! (Hawtrey, G. P., 1885), v. 410

Good Hearts (1858), v. 684

Good Husbands make Good Wives (Buckstone, J. B., 1835), IV. 274

Good King Arthur = Merry Mr Merlin

Good-looking Fellow (Almar, G., 1834), IV. 253

— (Kenney, J. and Bunn, A., 1834), IV. 337

Good Luck (Burnett, J. P., 1885), v. 292

— (1878), v. 684

— = Glorie Aston

Good Luck at Last = (1) Richmond Wells; (2) Virtue's Escape; (3) Virtuous Wife

Goodman's Fields in the Olden Time (1831), IV. 468

Good Morning, Mr Smith (1861), v. 684

Good Name (Stocqueler, J. H., 1845), IV. 468, 626

Good Natur'd Man (Goldsmith, O., 1768), III. 45, 130, 157-9, 162, 265, 386

— = Fathers

Good News (Byron, H. J., 1872), v. 298

Good News for British Tars (1790), III. 329

Good News! Good News! (McLaren, A., 1814), IV. 351

Good Night, Signor Pantalon (Somerset, C. A., 1852), v. 574

— (1851), v. 684

Good Night's Rest (Gore, Mrs C. G. F., 1837), IV. 319

Good Old Barnes of New York (Burnot, W., 1888), v. 293

Good Old Cause = Roundheads

Good Old Queen Bess (Lewin, W., 1891), v. 459

Good Old Times (Caine, H. and Barrett, W., 1889), v. 299

Good or Evil (1885), v. 684

Good out of Evil = (1) Vagabonds; (2) Sid

Good Queen Bess (Collins, C. J., 1856), v. 684, 785, 833

— (Trevor, H. and Trevor, L., 1895), v. 603

— (1861), v. 684

Good Run for it (Bridgeman, J. V., 1854), v. 274

Good Samaritan (1892), v. 685

Good Shepherd (1898), v. 685

Good Sovereign and the Bad Yellow Boy = Yellow Dwarf

Good Time = Shipped by the Light of the Moon

Good Time Coming (1851), v. 685

Good Times of Queen Bess = Northern Inn

Good Turn (Broughton, F. W., 1880), v. 281

Good Woman in the Wood (Planché, J. R., 1852), v. 527

Goody Goose (Hazlewood, C. H., 1858), v. 412

Goody Two Shoes (Blanchard, E. L., 1862), v. 263

— (Clarance, L., 1877), v. 310

— (Dibdin, C. I. M., 1803), IV. 291

— (Dibdin, T. J., 1820), IV. 302

— (1878, 1879, 1884, 1887, 1889, 1890, 1891, 1895, 1899), v. 685

Goody Two Shoes and her Queen Anne's Farthing (Strachan, J. S., 1872), v. 585

Goose and the Golden Eggs (Draper, J. F., 1869), v. 350

Goose Chase = Fox versus Goose

Goose Fair (Goodyer, F. R., 1874), v. 384

Goose Green = Pop!

Goose with the Golden Eggs (Mayhew, A. and Edwards, H. S., 1859), v. 482

Goosey Goosey Gander (Hazlewood, C. H., 1860), v. 685, 796, 833

— (1832), IV. 468

Gordian Knot Unty'd (1690), I. 442

Gordon Gray (1811), IV. 468

Gordon Highlanders = Our British Empire

Gordons to the Front = Ladder of Life

Gordon the Gypsey (Peake, R. B., 1822), IV. 468, 626

Gore (1889), V. 685

Gorilla Hunt in the Forest of Gabon (Hazlewood, C. H., 1863), V. 685, 796, 833

Gorillas (Marchant, F., 1869), V. 805

Gorilla Warfare = Sugar and Spice

Gortz of Berlingen, with the Iron Hand (Lawrence, R., 1799), III. 63, 280, 390

Gosling the Great (Keating, Miss, 1860), V. 685, 800

Gospel Shop (Hill, R., ?1770), III. 269

Gossip (Fitch, C. and Dietrichstein, L., 1895), V. 367

— (Harris, A. G. and Williams, T. J., 1859), V. 405

— (1831), IV. 468

Go straight (Outram, L. S., 1894), V. 509

Gotham Election (Centlivre, Mrs S., 1715), II. 20, 211, 305

Gotham in Alarm ("Odd Fellow", 1816), IV. 602

Gothmund the Cruel (Dibdin, C. I. M., 1804), IV. 291

Go-to-bed Tom (Morton, T., Jr., 1852), V. 497

Go to Putney (Lemon, H., 1868), V. 454

Gout = Tragopodagra

Governess (Belot, A., 1886), V. 257

— (1785), III. 329

— = Duenna

Governor (1793), III. 329

Governor of Barcelona (1711), II. 373

Governor of Kentucky (1896), V. 685

Governor's Wife (Mildenhall, T., 1845), IV. 355, 598

Governour of Cyprus (Oldmixon, J., 1703), II. 26, 30, 53, 105–6, 160, 347, 442

Gowrie Conspiracy (Wilson, J. M., 1828), IV. 618

Gowrie Plot = James VI

Go Wyn Wyn Wyn = Taffy's Triumph

Grace (Dutch, J. S., 1880), V. 352

Grace Challoner (Barnett, C. Z., 1845), IV. 260

Grace Clairville (Lewis, A., 1843), IV. 345

Grace Darling (Bosworth, J., 1838), IV. 573

Grace Darling = Wreck at Sea

Grace Darrell (James, R., 1896), V. 433

Grace Gayton (1846), IV. 468

Grace Holden (Cheltnam, C. S., 1869), V. 309

Grace Huntley (Holl, H., 1833), IV. 326

Grace Mary (Jones, H. A., 1895), V. 440

— (1899), V. 685

Grace Rivers (Lee, N., 1844), IV. 468, 626

Grace Royal (Meritt, P., 1876), V. 486

Graces (Dibdin, C., 1782), III. 256

Graciosa and Percinet (Planché, J. R., 1844), IV. 382

Graciosa the Fair (Roberts, J. F., 1807), IV. 394

Graeme (1824), IV. 468

Gra-Gal-Machree (Connor, B., 1876), V. 320

Graham, the Regent of Scotland (1827), IV. 468

Gramachree Molly (1844), IV. 468

Granada taken and done for = Court of Lions

Granby Enticed from Elysium (Watson, W., 1782), III. 315

Grandad's Darling (Gurney, E.), V. 398

Grand Army (1838), IV. 468

Grand Baby Show (1856), V. 685

Grand Caravan and the Saddler of Cairo = Peacock's Feather

Grand Duchess (Brookfield, C. H. E., 1897), V. 277

Grand Duchess of Gerolstein (Kenney, C. L., 1867), V. 443, 801

— (1871), V. 685

Grand Duke (Gilbert, W. S., 1896), V. 381

— (Gordon, G. L., 1886), V. 385

— = Prima Donna

Grand Duke of Camberwell (Akhurst, W. M., 1876), V. 237

Grande Doctresse = Lucrezia Borgia, M.D.

Grandfather's Clock (Baron, J., 1883), V. 250

— (Bertrand, E. C., 1879), V. 260

Grandfather's Little Nell (1870), V. 685

Grandfather's Secret (1885), V. 685

+ Grandfather's Story (French)

Grandfather Whitehead (Lemon, M., 1842), IV. 344

Grand Junction Canal (Dibdin, C. I. M., 1801), IV. 290

Grand Master of Malta = Corsican Pirate

Grand Mogul (Farnie, H. B., 1884), V. 363, 791

Grandmother Browning (À Beckett, G. A., 1844), IV. 250

Grandmother Grizzle (Buckstone, J. B., 1851), V. 287

Grandmother's Gown = Lord Dolly

Grandmother's Pet (1844), IV. 468

Grand National (Elphinstone, J., 1869), V. 358

Grandpapa (1825), IV. 468

Grandpapa's Promise (Corcoran, L., 1887), V. 325

Grandpa's Birthday (1895), V. 685

Grand Sabre, the Traitor (1829), IV. 468

Grand Secret; A Tale of 1642 = Lord Mayor's Fool

Grandsire (Woodhouse, W. A., 1889), V. 631

Grand Tour (1821), IV. 468

Grand Venetian Carnival (1821), IV. 469

Granna Waile and the Bridal Eve (Archer, W. J., 1874), V. 242

Grape Girl of Madrid (1850), V. 685

Grapeshot (Field, W. F., 1889), V. 366

Grasping a Shadow (Craven, T., 1885), V. 329

Grasshopper (Hollingshead, J., 1877), V. 424

— (Webster, B., the Younger, 1867), V. 618

Grass Widow (Fane, F., 1898), V. 361

Grass Widows (Whittaker, J. H. G., 1879), V. 621

Grateful (Towers, F., 1877), V. 602

Grateful Fair (Smart, C., ?1747), II. 355

Grateful Father (Pemberton, T. E., 1878), V. 519

Grateful Lion (1793), III. 401

Gratitude (Hazlewood, C. H., 1859), V. 685, 796, 833

— (Pitt, W. H., 1869), V. 527

Grau-a-Aille (1891), V. 685

Grave (1802), IV. 469

Grave Charge (1896), V. 685

Grave-makers (Kirkman, F., 1662), I. 417

Graven Image (Cheatham, T., 1862), V. 685, 783, 833

Grave of the Forsaken = Adeline

Grave on the Sands = Eyes in the Dark

Grave Subject (1828), IV. 469

Gray Ladye of Fernlea (Towers, E., 1867), V. 600

Gray Lady of Fernlea (Hazlewood, C. H., 1867), V. 413

Gray Mare (Webster, B., the Younger, 1863), V. 618

Great Alexander (1828), IV. 469

Great Bank Robbery (Darbey, E., 1896), V. 336

Great Bastard = Royal Cuckold

Great Bear and the Two Kings = Toolooloo and Woolooloo

Great Bed of Ware (Glover, E., 1852), V. 382

Great Caesar (Grossmith, G., Jr. and Rubens, P., 1899), V. 395

Great Casimir (Leigh, H. S., 1879), V. 454, 803

Great Catch (Aidé, H., 1883), V. 236

Great Cigar = Page 21

Great City (Halliday, A., 1867), V. 400

Great Comet (Dick, C., 1896), V. 344

Great Demonstration (Zangwill, I. and Cowen, L., 1892), V. 637

Great Devil (Dibdin, C. I. M., 1801), IV. 290

Great Diamond Robbery (Alfriend, E. M. and Wheeler, A. C., 1898) = Heart of Fire, V. 238, 691

— (Delannoy, B. and Waldron, W. R., 1892), V. 341

Great Dismal Swamp = Dred

Great Divorce Case (Scott, C. W., 1876), V. 557

Greatest Puritan (1899), V. 685

Great Exhibition of 1851 (Webb, C., 1851), V. 617

Great Expectations (Gilbert, W. S., 1871), V. 379

— (1892), V. 685

Great Favourite (Howard, Sir R., 1668), I. 137–8, 415

Great Felicidad (Paull, H. M., 1887), V. 516

Great Fire of London (Pitt, G. D., 1861), V. 810

Great Gentleman in the Little Parlour (Dibdin, T. J., 1825), IV. 304

Great Globe (Stewart, J. O., 1889), v. 584

Great Gun Trick (Le Ross, C., 1855), v. 456

Great Horse of Greece = Siege of Troy

Great Illusion (Bell, Mrs H., 1895), v. 256

Great Metropolis (Burnand, F. C., 1874), v. 290

— (Terriss, W., 1892), v. 595

— (1845), IV. 469

Great Mogul (Oxenford, E., 1881), v. 509

Great Muddleborough Election = Blue and Buff

Great News from France = Whimsicality

Great Night (1860), v. 685

Great Pearl Case (Courte, S. X., 1894), v. 325

Great Percentage = Upstairs and Downstairs

+ Great Pickwick Case (Pollitt, R., 8°, 1884, Manchester)

Great Pink Pearl (Carton, R. C. and Raleigh, C., 1885), v. 305

Great Ruby (Raleigh, C. and Hamilton, H., 1898), v. 534

Great Russian Bear (Morton, T., Jr., 1859), v. 497

Great Secret (1885), v. 685

Great Sensation (Lee, S., 1862), v. 685, 803, 833

Great Sensation Trial (Brough, W., 1863), v. 279

Great Separation (1876), v. 685

Great Steeplechase (1844), IV. 469

Great Strike (1866), v. 685

— = Work and Wages

Great Success (Hewson, J. J., 1884), v. 420

Great Taykin (Law, A., 1885), v. 450

Great Temptation (Shirley, A., 1899), v. 565

— (1874), v. 685

Great Temptations = Great Temptation

Great Tichborne Case (Mackay, W., 1872), v. 471

Great Tom-Tom (Stanhope, B., 1886), v. 578

Great Tyrant (1861), v. 685

Great Unknown (Daly, A., 1889), v. 333

— (Stirling, E., 1840), IV. 469, 626

Great Unknown (1823), IV. 469

Great Unpaid (Horner, F., 1893), v. 427

Great Wall of China (1876), v. 685

Great Wealth (1885), v. 685

Great World of London (Lander, G. and Melville, W., 1898), v. 448

— (1893), v. 686

Grecian Amazon = Massacre of Cyprus

Grecian Daughter (Kemble, J. P., 1815), IV. 335

— (Murphy, A., 1772), III. 29, 31, 52, 53, 76, 290

— (1813), IV. 469

Grecian Heroine (D'Urfey, T., 1718), II. 320

— = Tyrant of Syracuse

Gredel (1884), v. 686

Greed for Gold = Mystery

Greed of Gold (Silva, H. R., 1894), v. 566

Greek Amazon (1833), IV. 469

Greek Boy (Lover, S., 1840), IV. 347

Greek Brigands (Meadows, L., 1870), v. 483

Greek Brothers (Pitt, G. D., 1844), IV. 373

Greek Captive (1844), IV. 469

Greek Family (Raymond, R. J., 1829), IV. 388

— = Suliote

Greek Girl (1862), v. 686

Greek Hero and the Jewish Maid = Hebrew Tribe of Rome

Greek Pirates of the Gulph = Corsair

Greek Renegade (1845), IV. 469

Greeks and the Turks (1821), IV. 469

Greeks at Brixton = Treadmill

Greek Slave (Fitzball, E., 1851), v. 368

— (Hall, O., 1898), v. 400

— (1791), III. 112–13, 329

Greek Soprano (1897), v. 686

Green Bushes (Buckstone, J. B., 1845), IV. 275

Green Business = Stock Exchange

Green Dragon (Moncrieff, W. T., 1819), IV. 358

— (1828), IV. 469

Green Enchantress (Sharp, E., 1898), v. 561

Greene's Tu Quoque (D'Avenant, Sir W., 1667), I. 401

Green-eyed = Jealous of the Past

Green-eyed Monster (Planché, J. R., 1828), IV. 378

— (Pocock, I., 1811), IV. 383

Green Gosling (1828), IV. 469

+ Green Grow the Rushes, Oh! or, The Squireen, the Informer and the Illicit Distiller (Byron, H. J.: *Dicks* (in *Sensation Dramas*))

Green Hills of Shannon = My Poor Dog Tray

Green Hills of Surrey (Courtney, J., 1849), IV. 284

Green Hills of the Far West (Wilkins, J. H.), IV. 420

Green in France (1823), IV. 469

Green Isle of the Sea (1874), V. 686

Green Lanes and Blue Waters (1861), V. 686

Green Lanes of England (Conquest, G. and Pettitt, H., 1878), V. 321

Greenleaf and Redburg, the Forest Twins = Gold Finders of Australia

Greenleaf the Graceful (Osman, W. R., 1872), V. 508

Green Man (Jones, R., 1818), IV. 334

Green Mantle (1837), IV. 469

Green Old Age (Reece, R., 1874), V. 538

Green Rider = De Bassenvelt

Green Room (Finney, 1783), III. 259

— (Kenney, J., 1826), IV. 337

— (1821), IV. 626

— (1825), IV. 459

Green-Room Controversy = Rivals

Green Room Scene (Monro, T., 1795), III. 392

Greenwich Fair (1831), IV. 469

Greenwich Park (Mountfort, W., 1691), I. 38, 69, 279, 421

Greenwich Pensioner (Cheltnam, C. S., 1869), V. 309

— (1830), IV. 469

— (1832), IV. 469

Greenwich Railway (1835), IV. 469

Gregarach, the Highland Watchword (Barrymore, W., 1821), IV. 93, 469, 626

Gregory VII (Horne, R. H., 1840), IV. 328

Grelley's Money (Ross, E., 1882), V. 551

Grenadier (Bayly, H., 1831), IV. 469, 626

— (O'Keeffe, J.), III. 294

Grenadier (1788), III. 329

— = Brigadier

Grenadier Guard = Holstein Hussar

Gr[envi]lle Agonistes (Hale, 1807), IV. 587

Greshamite = Harlequin-Hydaspes

Gretchen (Gilbert, W. S., 1879), V. 380

Gretna Blacksmith = Scotch Lovers

Gretna Green (Beazley, S., Jr., 1822), IV. 264

— (Ford, T. M., 1889), V. 370

— (Stuart, C., 1783) = New Gretna Green, III. 310, 403

— = Trip to Gretna

Grey Doublet (Lemon, M., 1838), IV. 343

Grey Man of Tottenham Cross = Seven Sisters

Grey Mare (Sims, G. R. and Raleigh, C., 1892), V. 569

Grey Mare's Better Horse (1795), III. 329

Grey Mare the Better Horse = Welsh Opera

Grey Parrot (Jacobs, W. W. and Rock, C., 1899), V. 432, 799

Grey the Collier (Soane, G., 1820), IV. 469, 626

Grief A-la-mode = Funeral

Grierson's Way (Esmond, H. V., 1899), V. 358

Grieving's a Folly (Leigh, R., 1809), IV. 343

Grif (Lestocq, W., 1891), V. 457

— (Towers, F., 1877), V. 602

Griffith Gaunt (Reade, C., 1871), V. 536

Griffith Murdoch (Spier, M. H., 1893), V. 576

Grimaldi (Bailey, W., 1822), IV. 257

— (Murray, G. and Hipkins, T. H., 1861), V. 422

— = Life of an Actress

Grimalkin (Rodwell, G. H., 1828), IV. 395

Grimalkin the Great (Blanchard, E. L., 1868), V. 264

— (Buckstone, J. B., 1830), IV. 469, 626

Grim Goblin (Conquest, G. and Spry, H., 1876), V. 321

Grim Grey Woman = Elfin Sprite

Grim Griffin Hotel (Oxenford, J., 1867), V. 510

Grim Look Out (1877), V. 686

Grimshaw, Bagshaw and Bradshaw (Morton, J. M., 1851), v. 495

Grimstone Grange (À Beckett, G. A., 1879), v. 234, 777

Grimthorpe Case (1894), v. 686

Grim Will, the Collier of Croydon (1825), IV. 469

"Grin" Bushes (Byron, H. J., 1864), v. 296

Gringoire (Bessle, E. and Basing, S. H., 1890), v. 260

— (Stephenson, B. C., 1899), v. 582

— (Wills, W. G., 1885), v. 627

— (1879), v. 686

— (1892), v. 686

Gringoire the Ballad Monger = Pity

Grip (1871), v. 686

Gripe in the Wrong Box (1831), IV. 469

Grip of Iron = Stranglers of Paris

Griselda (Anstruther, R. A., 1841), IV. 254

— (Arnold, Sir E., 1856), v. 243

— (Braddon, M. E., 1873), v. 273

— (1844), IV. 469

Griseldis (Sieg, W., 1871), v. 816

Griselides (1893), v. 686

Grist to the Mill (Planché, J. R., 1844), IV. 382

Grizzel Jamphray (Ellenden, 1846), IV. 309

Grove (Oldmixon, J., 1700), II. 233, 347

Groves of Blarney (Hall, Mrs A. M., 1838), IV. 323

Grub-Street Opera = Welsh Opera

Grumbler (Goldsmith, O., 1773), III. 265, 386

— (Sedley, Sir C., 1719), I. 428; III. 114

— (1754), III. 114, 330

Grump's Menage (1876), v. 686

Grunt and Gaby = Mrs Mullins

Guarded by Honour (Stanley, H. J., 1885), v. 579

Guard House (Dance, G., 1835), IV. 469, 626

Guardian (Cowley, A., 1650), I. 398

— (Garrick, D. 1759), III. 119, 262, 385

Guardian Angel (Brooks, C. W. S., 1849), IV. 271

Guardian Out-witted (Arne, T. A., 1764), III. 199, 233

— = Venetial Nuptials

Guardians (1808), IV. 469

— = (1) Faro Table; (2) Man of Taste

Guardians off their Guard (1840), IV. 469

Guardians Outwitted (1823) = Assumptions, IV. 469, 626

Guardians overreached in their own Humour (1742), II. 384

Guardian Spirit (O'Neil, J. R., 1853), v. 507

Guardian Storks = Ida

Guardian Sylph (Selby, C., 1835), IV. 397

Guardroom Slave (1841), IV. 469

Guards = Mirabel

Guardsman (Sims, G. R. and Raleigh, C., 1892), v. 569

Gubbins stands for the Council (1889), v. 686

Gude Man of Ballangeich (1849), IV. 469

Gudeman of Ballangrich = Cramond Brig

Gudgeons (Carson, S. M. and Parker, L. N., 1893), v. 304

Gudgeons and Sharks (Poole, J., 1827), IV. 386

Guerilla Boy and the Spectre Sister = Zitella

Guerilla Chief (1826), IV. 469

Guerilla Chief and his Daughters (1827), IV. 470

Guerillas (Atkyns, S., 1848), IV. 257

Guide of the Tyrol (?Blake, T. G., 1838), IV. 470, 626

Guiding Star (Elkington, C., 1899), v. 356

— (Suter, W. E., 1868), v. 588

Guiding Star of Virtue = Lamplighter

Guido and Imilda (Moore, R., 1869), v. 492

Guido Fawkes (Stirling, E., 1840), IV. 407

Guido Ferrandi = Duchess of Padua

Guidone (Smith, W., 1846), IV. 612

Guillaume Tell (Bunn, A., 1838), IV. 276

Guilt (Frye, W. E., 1819), IV. 318

— (Gillies, R. P., 1819), IV. 319

Guilt Discovered = Father's Curse

Guilt its own Punishment = Fatal Curiosity

Guy Fawkes (Douglass, J. T., 1870), v. 348, 789
— (Macfarren, G., 1822), IV. 349
— (Smith, A. R., 1849), IV. 402
— (Taylor, T., Smith, A. R., Hale, W. P., Draper, E. and Smith, A., 1855), v. 592
— (1793), III. 330
— (1860), v. 833
Guy Fawkes, A Gingerbread Tragedy (1821), IV. 470, 626
Guy Fawkes Day (Burnand, F. C., 1852), v. 287
Guy Fawkes Esq. (Leslie, F. and Clark, H. F., 1890), v. 456
Guy Mannering (Reece, R., 1866), v. 537
— (Terry, D. and Scott, Sir W., 1816), IV. 93, 411
Guzman (Boyle, R., 1669), I. 39, 257, 393
Gwenllian (Andrews, E., 1841), IV. 568
Gwilty Governess and the Downey Doctor (Layton, G. M., 1876), v. 451
Gwinett Bremmel (1834), IV. 470
Gwinnet the Accused = Sea-side Story
Gwyneth Vaughan (Lemon, M., 1840) IV. 343, 595
Gwynne's Oath (Wheatcroft, N., 1888), v. 619
Gycia (Morris, Sir L., 1886), v. 493
Gypsy = Leo
Gypsy Father (Norton, Mrs E. B., 1831), IV. 602
Gypsy Jack (Bedford, H., 1899), v. 255

Hackles of Hackle Hall (Oxberry, W. H., 1834), IV. 602
Hackney Coachman = Number One!
Hackney Coachman of the Barrier St Denis = Old Chateau
Haddon Hall (Grundy, S., 1892), v. 397
Hafed the Gheber (1824), IV. 470
Hag and the Emperor = Xo Fi
Hagar, the Outcast Jewess (1869), v. 686
Hag of the Glen (1819), IV. 470
— = Meg Murnoch
Hag of the Hollow = Night in a Church-yard
Hag of the Lake (1812), IV. 470
Hag of the Rapids = Maid of Canada
Hag of the Storm (1833), IV. 470

Hag's Haunt = Witch of the Whirlpool
Hags of Mischief (1806), IV. 470
Hail Fellow, well met (Pratt, S. J., 1805), IV. 388
— (1792), III. 330, 401
Hainault Forest = Henault Forest
Hakon Jarl (Chapman, J., 1875), v. 783
Half a Loaf better than no Bread—A Night in the Workhouse = Nobody's Son
Half an Hour after Supper (1789), III. 330
Half an Hour in England, without Cozening (1819), IV. 470
Half an Hour in France = Cozening
Half an Hour in the Highlands = (1) Dead and Not Dead; (2) Food for Mirth
Half an Hour's Courtship (Planché, J. R., 1821), IV. 376
Half an Hour with the Original Lyceum Wizard = Great Gun Trick
Half Caste (Robertson, T. W., 1856), v. 123, 546
Half-crown Diamonds (Reece, R., 1875), v. 538, 812
Half-mast High (Craven, T., 1893), v. 329
Half Pay Officer (1819), IV. 470
Half-Pay Officers (Molloy, C., 1720), II. 142, 214, 345
Halfpenny Club (1857), v. 686
Half Seas Over (Mark, Mrs, 1882), v. 476
Half-way House (McLaren, A., 1818), IV. 351
— (Sims, G. R., 1881), v. 568
Halidon Hill (Scott, Sir W., 1822), IV. 193-4, 397
Hall of Augusta (1793), III. 330
Hall of Fate = Wizard Priest
Hall of Mischief (1814), IV. 470
Hall of Silence = Tarempon and Serinda
Hall of Torture = Geneviève de Brabant
Hallowe'en (Cross, J. C., 1799), III. 250, 251
— (1821), IV. 470
— (1859), v. 686
— (1877), v. 686
Hallow Fair (Woods, W., 1784), III. 398
Hallowmas Eve (Almar, G., 1832), IV. 252

Hall Porter (Lover, S., 1839), IV. 347

Halls of my Fathers = Regicide

Hall, the Workshop and the Farm = Adam Bede

Hal o' the Wynd (Rae, L., 1874), V. 533

Halt! = Sentinel

Hal, the Highwayman (Paull, H. M., 1894), v. 516

Halt of the Ballet (1854), v. 686

Halt of the Caravan (1822), IV. 470

Halvei, the Unknown (Wilks, T. E., 1843), IV. 421

Halves (Doyle, Sir A. C., 1899), v. 350

Hamet and Zelina (1854), v. 686

Hamilton of Bothwell Haugh (Slous, A. R., 1855), v. 571

Hamilton's Excursion to America and Panstereoragma of Passing Events (1878), v. 686

Hamlet (D'Avenant, Sir W., 1661), I. 401

— (Garrick, D., 1772), III. 57, 263

— (Kemble, J. P., 1802), IV. 335

— (Murphy, A., 1772), III. 290

— (Talfourd, F., 1849), IV. 410

— (1838), IV. 470

Hamlet, according to Act of Parliament (1853), v. 833

Hamlet à la mode (Gordon, G. L. and Anson, G. W., 1876), v. 384

Hamlet Prince of Denmark (Milner, H. M., 1828), IV. 470, 626

Hamlet the Dane (Beckington, C., 1847), IV. 264

Hamlet the Hysterical (Snow, W. R., 1874), v. 686, 817, 833

Hamlet Travestie (Barton, 1853), v. 252

— (Poole, J., 1811), IV. 386

Hamlet, whether he will or no (Booth, G., 1879), v. 267

Hammock (1888), v. 686

Hampden (Maclaurin, J., 1799), III. 285

Hampshire Hog (Melford, M., 1899), v. 484

Hampstead-Heath (Baker, T., 1705), II. 22, 175, 297

Hand and Glove (Meritt, P. and Conquest, G., 1874), v. 486

Hand and Heart (Yardley, W. and Stephens, H. P., 1886), v. 634

Hand and the Heart = Auld Robin Gray

Hand and Word = Yamun Dhuv

Handcuffs (Stockton, E. and Hudson, E. V., 1893), v. 585

Handfast (Hamilton, H. and Quinton, M., 1887), v. 401

Hand-in-Hand (Darbey, E., 1889), v. 336

Hand of Cards (Stirling, E., 1846, 1857), IV. 408; v. 686, 833

Hand of Elmsley (Lemain, B., 1877), v. 454

Hand of Fate (Shirley, A., 1884), v. 563

Hand of Fire (James, C. S., 1849), IV. 330

Hand of Justice (Goldberg, M., 1891), v. 383

Hand of Providence (Warren, T. G., 1897), v. 615

Hand of the Prisoner = Glorie Aston

Hand of Time (Glendinning, J., 1897), v. 382

Hands Across the Sea (Pettitt, H., 1888), v. 521

Handsell Penny (Selby, C., 1841), IV. 470, 626

— (1844), IV. 470

Hands of Destiny = Too Late

Handsome Apology (Longmuir, A., 1888), v. 463

Handsome Hernani (Byron, H. J., 1879), v. 299

Handsome Housemaid = Piety in Pattens

Handsome Husband (Planché, Mrs J. R., 1836), v. 373

Handsome is that Handsome does (Ribton-Turner, C. J., 1888), v. 542

— (Taylor, T., 1870), v. 594

Handsome Jack (Howe, J. B., 1861), v. 428

Hand that governs all = Turned out to starve

Handy and Dandy = Right Man in the Right Place

Handy Andy (Floyd, W. R., 1860), v. 369

Handy Pandy Sugar and Candy, Which hand will you have (1858), v. 686

Hanged Man (Conquest, G., 1862), v. 687, 785, 833

Hanging and Marriage (Carey, H., 1722), II. 42, 52, 302, 432

Hān Koong Tsew (Davis, Sir J. F., 1829), IV. 579

Hannah (Smart, C., 1764), III. 356, 396

Hannah Hewitt (Dibdin, C., 1798), III. 256, 382

Hannele (Archer, W., 1894), v. 242

Hannibal (Nichol, J., 1873), v. 504
— (Shore, L., 1898), v. 565
— (1861), v. 687

Hannibal in Bithynia (Knight, H. G., 1839), IV. 592

Hannibal's Overthrow = Sophonisba

Hans, an Alsatian (1880), v. 687

Hans Anderson's Fairy Tales (Hood, B., 1897), v. 798

Hansel and Gretel (Bache, C., 1894), v. 687, 778, 833

Hans Ketzler's Close Shave = Enchanted Barber

Hans of Iceland (Fitzball, E., 1825, 1841), IV. 316, 470, 627

Hans of the Iron Hand (1832), IV. 470

Hansom Cab (1888), v. 687

Hans the Boatman (Greene, C. M., 1887), v. 392

Hans von Stein (Fitzball, E., 1851), v. 367

Hap (1882), v. 687

Happier Days (Scotti, S., 1886), v. 558

Happiest Day of my Life (Buckstone, J. B., 1829), IV. 273

Happiest Man Alive (Bernard, W. B., 1840), IV. 266

Happiness (1880), v. 687

Happiness at Home (Hazlewood, C. H., 1871), v. 414

Happiness at Last = Rover

Happiness of Colombine = Harlequin's Distress

Happy African = Irishman in London

Happy Africans (1796), III. 391

Happy Arcadia (Gilbert, W. S., 1872), v. 379

Happy at Last (1805), IV. 470

Happy Bungalow (Law, A., 1877), v. 449

Happy Captive (Theobald, L., 1741), II. 359, 399, 445

Happy Change = Late Revolution

Happy Constancy (Jacob, H., 1738), II. 205, 338

Happy Converts = Pilgrims

Happy Counterplot = Celadon and Florimel

Happy Cruise (Cuthbert, E., 1873), v. 331

Happy Day (Henry, R., 1886), v. 417
— = Giorno Felice

Happy Disguise (Oulton, W. C., 1784), III. 295

Happy Fair One = Love's Triumph

Happy Family (Dance, C., 1848), IV. 289
— (Taylor, J. G., 1873), v. 687, 820, 834
— (Thompson, B., 1799), III. 311, 397; IV. 412

Happy-go-lucky (Hazleton, F., 1875), v. 412
— (Pemberton, T. E., 1884), v. 519

Happy-go-lucky, True-love and Forget-me-not (Spry, H., 1882), v. 577

Happy Hamstead (Desprez, F., 1876), v. 343

Happy Hero (1746), II. 373

Happy Hours (1862), v. 687

Happy Island = Enchantress

Happy Land (Gilbert, W. S. and À. Beckett, G. A., 1873), v. 379

Happy Life (Parker, L. N., 1897), v. 513

Happy Lovers (Ward, H., 1736), II. 363, 446

Happy Man (Lover, S., 1839), IV. 347

Happy Manager (O'Neil, J. R., 1852), v. 507

Happy Marriage (1727), II. 373
— = Orphan

Happy Medium (Pemberton, T. E., 1875), v. 519
— = Planchette

Happy Miller just arriv'd = All Alive and Merry

Happy New Year (Law, A., 1882) = Strange Host, v. 450, 687, 802

Happy Nuptials (1733), II. 373

Happy Pair (Smith, S. T., 1868), v. 152-3, 573
— = Indian Merchant

Happy Prescription (Hayley, W., 1784), III. 226-7, 267, 386

Happy Recess = Fugitive

Happy Relief = Soldier's Widow

Happy Resentment = Mistakes

Happy Result (1865), v. 687

Happy Return (+Dubois, M., 1828), IV. 470

— (Law, A., 1883), v. 450

— =Come of Age

Happy Returns (Horner, F., 1892), v. 427

Happy Thought (Edgar, H. T., 1895), v. 354

Happy Valley (Lee, H., 1880), v. 452

— =(1) Rasselas; (2) Rasselas Prince of Abyssinia

Happy Village (Rayner, E., 1894), v. 535

— (1870), v. 834

Haps and Hazards (Wilkins, J. H., 1849), IV. 419

Harbour Lights (Sims, G. R. and Pettitt, H., 1885), v. 184, 569

Harbour Master's Secret (1868), v. 687

Hard as Iron (1881), v. 687

Hard Case (Dawe, W. C., 1893), v. 339

Hard Frost (1833), IV. 470

Hard Hands and Happy Hearts (Palmer, T. A., 1869), v. 512

Hard Hearts (Charleson, A. J. and Wilmot, C., 1886), v. 308

Hard Hit (Jones, H. A., 1887), v. 439

Hard Lines (Comer, G., 1883), v. 319

— (Dickinson, C. H., 1887), v. 344

Hard Struggle (Marston, J. W., 1858), v. 103, 479

Hard Times (Cooper, F. F., 1854), v. 687, 786, 834

— (1866), v. 687

Hard Times in Manchester = Belle Vue

Hard Up (Righton, E., 1883), v. 543

Hare and Hounds (Grundy, S., 1883), v. 396

Harem (1865), v. 687

Harlequin (Marshall, E., 1862), v. 477

Harlequin, a Butler, a Pimp, a Minister of State, Generalissimo, and Lord High Admiral = Dido and Aeneas

Harlequin Achilles (Dibdin, C. I. M., 1822), IV. 295, 470, 580, 627

Harlequinade (Bantock, G., 1899), v. 248

Harlequin a Director = Magician

Harlequin Aladdin (1860), v. 687

Harlequin Aladdin and the Wonderful Lamp (Douglass, J. T., 1871), v. 348

+Harlequin Alchymist (Dibdin, C. I. M.; S.W., 1800)

Harlequin Alfred the Great (Lee, N., 1850), v. 452, 802

Harlequin Ali Baba (O'Neil, J. R., 1852), v. 507

Harlequin Ali Baba and the Forty Thieves (Greenwood, T. L., 1854), v. 794

Harlequin Amulet (+Powell, C., 1800), IV. 470

— (1780), III. 330

Harlequin and Æsop (Dibdin, C. I. M., 1805), IV. 291, 580

Harlequin and a Happy New Year (1846) = Harlequin and the Happy New Year, IV. 470, 473, 627

Harlequin and Asmodeus (Farley, C., 1810) = Harlequin Zambullo, IV. 471, 583, 627

Harlequin and Beauty and the Beast (Greenwood, T. L., 1857) = Harlequin Beauty and the Beast, v. 393, 794, 834

Harlequin and Bluebeard (Dibdin, C. I. M., 1811), IV. 292

Harlequin and Bluff King Hal (Hall, F., 1879), v. 399

Harlequin and Buttercups and Daisies (1850), v. 687

Harlequin and Cinderella (Courtney, J., 1860), v. 687, 786, 834

— (Greenwood, T., 1841), IV. 471

— (1820), IV. 471

Harlequin and Cock Robin (1827), IV. 471

Harlequin and Cupid (1829), IV. 471

Harlequin and Don Quixote (1813), IV. 471

Harlequin and Don Quixotte (1819), IV. 471

Harlequin and Duke Humphrey's Dinner (1841), IV. 471

Harlequin and Fair Rosamond (1838), IV. 471

Harlequin and Fancy (Dibdin, T. J., 1815), IV. 300

Harlequin and Faustus (1793), III. 209, 330

Harlequin and Flora (1810), IV. 471

Harlequin and Fortunio (1815), IV. 471

Harlequin and Friar Bacon (Farley, C., 1820), IV. 154, 310

Harlequin and Georgey Barnwell (Younge, H., 1836), IV. 471, 627

Harlequin Fortunatus (Woodward, H., 1753), III. 209, 317
— (1793), III. 401
Harlequin Fortune Teller (1748), II. 451
— = Frolicksome Lasses
Harlequin Fortunio and his Horse Comrade (Lee, N., 1852), V. 452
Harlequin Foundling (1784), III. 401
Harlequin Freemason (Dibdin, C., 1780), III. 255
Harlequin Friar Bacon (Frost, F., 1863), V. 793
Harlequin from the Moon (1775), III. 401
Harlequin Fun (1866), V. 688
Harlequin Genius (1850), V. 688
Harlequin Georgy Porgy (Lee, N., 1840), IV. 594
Harlequin Gladiator (1725), II. 373
Harlequin Golden Farmer (1846), IV. 474
Harlequin Goody Two Shoes (Towers, E., 1864), V. 688, 821, 834
Harlequin Graceful (1877), V. 688
Harlequin Grammar (Lee, N., 1843), IV. 342
Harlequin Grand Vol-Gi (1740), II. 451
— = Cephalus and Procris
Harlequin Green Beetle (Johnstone, J. B., 1858), V. 688, 800, 834
Harlequin Greenlander (Dibdin, C. I. M., 1802), IV. 290
Harlequin Gulliver (Morton, J. M., 1861), V. 496
— (1817), IV. 474
— (1845), IV. 474
— (1852), V. 689, 834
Harlequin Gulliver and his Wife (1864), V. 689
Harlequin Guy Faux (Conquest, G. and Spry, H., 1858), V. 689, 785, 817, 834
Harlequin Guy Fawkes (1835), IV. 474
— (1867), V. 689
Harlequin Handy (1827), IV. 474
Harlequin Hans and the Golden Goose (Greenwood, T. L. and Blanchard, E. L., 1859), V. 689, 779, 794, 834
Harlequin Happy (1740), II. 373
— (1745), II. 373
— = Dutchman Outwitted
Harlequin Happy and Poor Pierot Married (1728), II. 134, 373

Harlequin Happy-go-Lucky and the Babes in the Wood (1883), V. 689
Harlequin Harper (Dibdin, T. J., 1813), IV. 299
Harlequin Hermit (1739), II. 373
Harlequin Hero (1795), III. 401
Harlequin Hey Diddle Diddle the Cat and the Fiddle (Suter, W. E., 1861), V. 689, 818, 834
Harlequin Hey-diddle-diddle the Cat and the Fiddle and the Cow that jumped over the Moon (Dutnall, M., 1861), V. 689, 789, 834
Harlequin High flyer (Dibdin, C. I. M., 1808), IV. 292
Harlequin Hoax (Dibdin, T. J., 1814), IV. 10, 78, 153, 299
Harlequin Hogarth (Morton, J. M. and Lee, N., 1851), V. 495, 807
Harlequin Hop o' my Thumb (Marchant, F., 1872), V. 476
Harlequin-Horace (1731), II. 256, 258
Harlequin Horner (1816), IV. 474
Harlequin Hudibras (Blanchard, E. L., 1852), V. 20, 263
Harlequin Humbug and the Shams of London (Buckingham, L. S., 1857) = Magic Mistletoe, V. 689, 714, 781, 834
Harlequin Humming Top (Blanchard, E. L. and Lee, N., 1853), V. 263
Harlequin Humpty Dumpty = Harlequin King Humpty Dumpty
Harlequin Humpty Dumpty and Dame Trot and her Cat (Greenwood, T. L. and Arnold, H. T., 1868), V. 393, 778
Harlequin Hunchback (1837), IV. 627
Harlequin Hurlothrumbo (Smith, L., 1848), IV. 611
Harlequin Hyacinth (1827), IV. 474
Harlequin-Hydaspes (Aubert, Mrs, 1719), II. 33, 133, 296
Harlequin Incendiary (1746), II. 253, 373
Harlequin in Egypt (1804), IV. 474
Harlequin in his Element (Dibdin, T. J., 1807), IV. 298
Harlequin in Ireland (1792), III. 330
+ Harlequin in Malabar (Dibdin, C. I. M.; R.A., 1798)
Harlequin in Scotland (1807), IV. 474
Harlequin in the City (1734), II. 373
Harlequin in the Moon (1799), III. 401

Harlequin's Whim = (1) As You Like It; (2) Tithonus and Aurora

Harlequin Tam o' Shanter (1851), V. 690

Harlequin Tam o'Shanter and his Steed Meg (Lee, N., 1843), IV. 476, 627

Harlequin Teague (O'Keeffe, J., 1782), III. 210, 292

Harlequin Tee-to-Tum (1847), IV. 627

Harlequin the Knight of the Silver Shield (1863), V. 690

Harlequin the Man in the Moon (1741), II. 374

Harlequin the Phantom of a Day (Dibdin, C., 1783), III. 256

Harlequin the Queen of Spades and the Fairy the Fawn (1852), V. 690

Harlequin Tit, Tat, Toe (Frost, F., 1856) = Fairy Elves of the Fourth Estate = Tit, Tat, Toe, V. 374, 675, 690, 793, 835

Harlequin Tom Moody (Lee, N., Jr., 1859), V. 690, 835

Harlequin Tom the Piper's Son Stole a Pig (1820), IV. 476

Harlequin Tom the Piper's Son who stole the Pig and away he run (George, G. H., 1869), V. 377

Harlequin Tom, Tom, the Piper's Son, Pope Joan and Little Bo-Peep (Greenwood, T. L., 1865), V. 690, 794, 835

Harlequin Tom Tucker (Blanchard, E. L. and Greenwood, T. L., 1863), V. 263

Harlequin Touchstone (1789), III. 331

Harlequin Toy Horse (1858), V. 690

Harlequin trapped by Colombine = Robbers

Harlequin Traveller (1782), III. 401

— (1832), IV. 476

Harlequin Triumphant = (1) Defeat of Apollo; (2) Mirrour; (3) Punch's Defeat

Harlequin True Blue and Queen Britannia (1858), V. 690

Harlequin turn'd Cook (1746), II. 374

Harlequin turn'd Dancing-Master (1730), II. 374

Harlequin turn'd Enchanter by Magic Art = Fairy Queen

Harlequin turn'd Fryar = Ship Launching

Harlequin turn'd Judge (Weaver, J., 1717), II. 132, 252, 374, 446

— = Columbine

Harlequin turn'd Philosopher (1739), II. 374

Harlequin turn'd Tapster = Guinguette

Harlequin Uncle Tom (Neale, F., 1852), V. 501

Harlequin Valentine and Orson (Conquest, G. and Spry, H., 1859), V. 690, 785, 817, 835

— (1861, 1866), V. 690

Harlequin Vulcan and Venus (1829), IV. 476

Harlequin Warrior (1801), IV. 476

Harlequin White Cat (Morton, J. M., 1857), V. 496

Harlequin Whittington (1814), IV. 476

Harlequin Whittington and his Cat (Douglass, J. T., 1885), V. 349

Harlequin Wild Man (Dibdin, C. I. M., 1814), IV. 293 [This is the same as Rival Genii, see IV. 527]

Harlequin William the Conqueror and King Vice of the Silent City (1856), V. 690

Harlequin Worm Doctor = Chymical Counterfeits

Harlequin Yorkshireman (1833), IV. 476

Harlequin Zambullo (Farley, C., 1810) = Harlequin and Asmodeus, IV. 476, 627

Harlot's Progress (Cibber, T., 1733), II. 28, 136, 254, 314

— (1730), II. 451

— = Decoy

Harmonious Discords (1873), V. 690

Harmony = Harmony Restored

Harmony Hall (Lunn, J., 1836), IV. 476, 627

Harmony Restored (Jones, H. A., 1879), V. 162, 439, 800

Harold (Boyce, T., 1786), III. 239

— (Bussy, F. M., 1892), V. 294

— (Dew, D., 1820), IV. 290

— (Hopkins, T., 1843), IV. 589

— (Malet, Sir E., 1895), V. 472, 805

— (Nance, A., 1875), V. 501

— (Tennyson, Alfred Lord, 1877), V. 208, 594

Harold Hawk (Selby, C., 1858), V. 560

Harold the Renegade (1823), IV. 476

Harold the Saxon (Boulding, J. W., 1897), v. 270

Haroun Alompra (1824), IV. 627

Haroun Alraschid (Dibdin, T. J., 1813), IV. 299, 580

Harper's Daughter (Lewis, M. G., 1803), IV. 345

Harper's Son and the Duke's Daughter (Dibdin, T. J., 1810), IV. 298

Harp of Altenberg (1833), IV. 476

Harpooner (1833), IV. 476

Harpooner of Fish Hook Bay = Gwinett Bremmel

Harry Bluff (1840), IV. 627

Harry Carley (1862), v. 690

Harry Hawser (1858), v. 690

Harry le Roi (1834), IV. 476

— = Forest Knight

Harry le Roy (Pocock, I., 1813), IV. 383, 606

Harry of England (Greenwood, T., 1842), IV. 476, 627

Harry's Disguise (1868), v. 690

Harsh Step-Father = Taking the Veil

Hartford-Bridge (Pearce, W., 1792), III. 26, 29, 297

Hartley Manor (Farmer, E., 1849), IV. 311

Harvest (Hamilton, H., 1886), v. 401

Harvest Frolic = Gleaners

Harvest Home (Bennett, G., 1808), IV. 476, 627

— (Dibdin, C., 1787), III. 203, 256

— (Parry, T., 1848), IV. 368

— (1801), IV. 476

— (1811), IV. 476

— = (1) Autumn Sheaves; (2) Generous Father; (3) Great Steeplechase

Harvest of Crime (Randford, M., 1897), v. 534

— (1897), v. 690

Harvest of Hate (Withers, F. and Eglington, H., 1899), v. 630

Harvest of Sin (1891), v. 690

Harvest of Wild Oats (Bartlett, H., 1897), v. 252

Harvest Queen (1838), IV. 476

Harvest Storm (Hazlewood, C. H., 1862), v. 796

Harvey's Portrait—Twelve for One Shilling (Sorrell, W. J., 1869), v. 574

Has anybody seen Mr Brown? (Legg, J., 1860), v. 690, 803, 835

Haska (Spicer, H., 1877), v. 576

Hassan and Lara (1829), IV. 476

Hassan Pacha (1837), IV. 476

Haste (Wood, C., 1879), v. 630

Haste to the Wedding (Gilbert, W. S., 1892), v. 381

— (Sorrell, W. J., 1873), v. 574

— (1804), IV. 476

Hasty Conclusion (Planché, Mrs J. R., 1838), IV. 383

Hasty Conclusions (Dance, C., 1844), IV. 289

— (1891), v. 690

Hasty Wedding (Shadwell, C., 1717), II. 354

Hate (West, B., 1824), IV. 476, 627

Hate and Love (1836), IV. 476

Hated Race = Alfonso and Claudina

Hatred (1880), v. 690

Haunted Abbey Ruin = Owl Sisters

Haunted Castle (Oulton, W. C., 1783), III. 295

Haunted Chamber (1821), IV. 476

— (1823), IV. 476

— = (1) Barney the Baron; (2) Black Spirits and White

Haunted for Ever (Howe, J. B., 1880), v. 428

Haunted Glen (Webber, H. and Davis, M., 1888), v. 617

Haunted Grange = Heart and the Key

Haunted Grove (Dubois, Lady D., 1773), III. 258

Haunted Hall (Pitt, G. D., 1847), IV. 375

Haunted Head (1836), IV. 476

Haunted House (1847), IV. 627

— = (1) Drummer; (2) Stolen Will

Haunted House at Lodore (Jefferys, C. A., 1895), v. 435

Haunted Houses (Byron, H. J., 1872), v. 298

Haunted Hulk (Fitzball, E., 1831), IV. 313

— (Haines, J. T., 1824), IV. 322

— (1832), IV. 476

Haunted Hut = Rival Brothers

Haunted Inn (Peake, R. B., 1828), IV. 370

— (1832), IV. 476

Haunted Lives (Jones, J. W., 1884), v. 441

Haunted Man (Dircks, R., 1863), v. 345

— (Robertson, T. W., 1849), IV. 608; v. 546

— (Stirling, E., 1848), IV. 98, 476, 627

— (1848), IV. 98, 477

— (1849), IV. 98, 477

Haunted Manor = Incendiaries

Haunted Mill (Wooler, J. P., 1865), v. 632

Haunted Priory = De Raye

Haunted Tower (Cobb, J., 1789), III. 244

— = Fire Raiser

Haunted Village (Young, 1800), III. 318; IV. 423

— (1792), III. 331

— (1809), IV. 477

— (1811), IV. 477

Haunts of the Hunted Down = Night and Day

Have at All (Williams, J., 1694), I. 437

Haven of Content (Watson, T. M., 1896), v. 616

Haven of Rest (Walker, M., 1868), v. 611

Have you seen my Sister? = Where is Eliza?

Hawaia (Thompson, A., 1880), v. 597

Hawkes Nest (Mackay, J., 1878), v. 470

Hawk's Grip (Don, L., 1887), v. 347

Hawk's Nest = Wheel of Fortune

Hawkwood Hall (Royd, L., 1895), v. 552

Hawser Trunnion on Horseback = Peregrine Pickle

Hawthorne (1882), v. 690

Haydee (Soane, G., 1848), IV. 84, 404

— (1848), IV. 84, 477

Haymakers (James, C. S., 1849), IV. 330

Haymaking (Allwood, 1877), v. 239

Hazard (Burnett, H., 1891), v. 292

Hazard of the Die (Jerrold, D. W., 1835), IV. 332

— = Blue Beard

Hazel Kirke (Mackaye, J. S., 1880), v. 471

Hazelwood Hall (Bloomfield, R., 1823), IV. 269

"H.B." (Peake, R. B., 1839), IV. 371

Headless Horseman (Hazlewood, C. H., 1868), v. 413

Headless Man (Burnand, F. C., 1889), v. 291

— (1857), v. 691

+ Headless Woman (Serle, T. J., ?1837)

Head of a Clan (Horne, F. L., 1875), v. 691, 798, 835

Head of a Lawyer = Marianne, the Child of Charity

Head of the Family (Emden, W. S., 1859), v. 358, 790

Head of the Pole (Law, A., 1882), 450

Head or Heart (Chapman, A., 1890), v. 308

Head Professor (1871), v. 691

Head Quarters (1853), v. 835

Heads and Blockheads (1819), IV. 477

Heads and Hearts (Burslem, C., 1877), v. 293

Heads and Tails (1843), IV. 477

Heads and Tales = Our Family Legend

Heads, Hands and Hearts = Strike

Head's in Peril (1851), v. 691

Headsman (Almar, G., 1831) = Headsman of Vienna, IV. 477, 627

— (Smith, A. R., 1849), IV. 402

— = Mount St Bernard

Headsman of Vienna (Almar, G.) = Headsman, IV. 253, 477, 627

Headsman's Axe (Macdermott, G. H., 1870), v. 468

Headsman's Bond = Hinko

Heads or Tails (Simpson, J. P., 1854), v. 567

Heads versus Pockets (1826), IV. 477

Health to the Rich and Work to the Poor (McLaren, A., 1817), IV. 351

Hear Both Sides (Holcroft, T., 1803), IV. 326

Hear Him Out = Hear It Out

Hearing is Believing (1835), IV. 477

Hear It Out (Reynolds, F., 1804) = Blind Bargain, IV. 391, 477 [By error, this appears in the text as Hear Him Out]

Heart (1848), IV. 477

Heart and the Key (1848), IV. 477

— = Death Secret

Heart and the World (Marston, J. W., 1847), IV. 353

— (1858), v. 691

Heart for Heart = Cagot

Heartless = Puck

Heart of a Brother (1871), v. 691

Heart of a Father = Jew of Lubeck

Heart of a Hero = Saved from the Scaffold

Heart of an Irishman (1854), v. 691

Heart of a Queen = Mary Tudor

Heart of a Sailor (1861), v. 691

Heart of a Soldier = Frederick the Great

Heart of a True Blue = White Nun

Heart of a Woman = Ups and Downs

Heart of Fire (Alfriend, E. M. and Wheeler, A. C., 1897), v. 238, 691

Heart of Gold (Jerrold, D., 1854), v. 69, 800

Heart of Hearts (Jones, H. A., 1887), v. 439

Heart of Hours = Esperance

Heart of London! (Moncrieff, W. T., 1830), IV. 360

Heart of Maryland (Belasco, D., 1895), v. 255

Heart of Midlothian (Dibdin, T. J., 1819), IV. 39, 93, 301, 477, 580

— (Dimond, W., 1819), IV. 93, 307

— (Montague and Jervis, 1819), IV. 93, 361

— (Murray, W. H., 1824), IV. 93, 365

— (Osman, W. R., 1863), v. 691, 835

— (Rafter, 1849), IV. 93, 388

— (Terry, D., 1819), IV. 93, 412

— (1862), v. 691

— = (1) Filial Duty; (2) Trial of Effie Deans

Heart of Old Ireland and the Lepreghaun (Litchfield, C., 1859), v. 691, 804, 835

Heart Repose (Irvine, Mrs M. C., 1867), v. 432

Hearts (Bertie, J. C., 1874), v. 259

— (Bruce, H. P., 1891), v. 283

— = Sailor and his Lass

Hearts against Diamonds and the Struggle of Life = Frost of Life

Hearts and Actresses = Lilies

Hearts and Diamonds (Jerrold, D. W., 1835), IV. 332

Hearts and Hampers (Clarke, M., 1881), v. 313

Hearts and Hands (Taylor, T., 1865), v. 593

Hearts and Homes (Barnett, C. Z., 1848), IV. 261

Hearts and Homes (Browne, G. W., 1876), v. 282

— (1886), v. 691

— = Life's Seasons

Hearts are Trumps (Lawrence, W., 1879), v. 451

— (Lemon, M., 1849), IV. 345

— (Raleigh, C., 1899), v. 534

— (1857), v. 691

— (1889), v. 691

Hearts at Fault (Courtney, J., 1850), IV. 284

Heart's Delight (Halliday, A., 1873), v. 401

Heart's Devotion = First Love

Heartsease (Mortimer, J., 1875), v. 494, 807

Hearts, Hearts, Hearts (Hazlewood, C. H., 1868), v. 413

Hearts of Gold (Darbey, E., 1888), v. 336

— (1892), v. 691

Hearts of Iron (Almar, G., 1845), IV. 253

Hearts of Oak (Allingham, J. T., 1803), IV. 252

— (Jones, H. A., 1879), v. 162-3, 439

— (Stevens, G. A., 1762), III. 309

Hearts of the West (Cassidy, J. R., 1896), v. 305

Heart's Ordeal (Courtney, J., 1863), v. 691

— = Day Dream

Hearts or Diamonds (Cassilis, I. L., 1891), v. 306

Heart's Secret = Deserted Wife

Hearts that Love us (Archer, W. J., 1862), v. 691, 778, 835

Heart's Trials (1849), IV. 477

Heart Strings and Fiddle Strings (Fisher, D., 1865), v. 367

Heart's Victory (Mead, T., 1858), v. 691, 806, 835

Heart Test = Heart

Heart that can feel for another (Rogers, W., 1836), IV. 396

— (1850), v. 691

Heart Wreck = (1) Alvarez; (2) Signet Ring

Heathen Goddess (1894), v. 691

Heathen Martyr (Adams, G., 1746), II. 294

Heather Field (Martyn, E., 1899), v. 479

Heather Flower = Snapdragon
Heautontimoroumenos (1777), III. 331
Heaven and Earth (Byron, Lord G. G., 1824), IV. 278
Heaven and Hell (Gazul, C., 1825), IV. 318
Heaven defend the Right = Trial by Battle
Heaven points to the Murderer = France
"Heaven send we may all be alive this day three months" = Croaking
Heavy Fathers (Hilton, B. H., 1879), V. 422
Hebrew (Soane, G., 1820), IV. 93, 403
— (1852), V. 691
Hebrew Diamond (Hazlewood, C. H., 1865), V. 691, 796, 835
Hebrew Dramas (Tennant, W., 1845), IV. 411
Hebrew Family (1825), IV. 477
Hebrew Husband (Pitt, G. D., 1833), IV. 372
Hebrew Maiden (1841), IV. 477
— (1869), V. 691
Hebrew Patriarch (1822), IV. 477
Hebrew Queen = Jew of Aragon
Hebrew Son (1852), V. 691
Hebrew's Sacrifice (1852), V. 691
Hebrew Tribe of Rome (1852), V. 691
Hebrew Twins (Lucas, W. J., 1847), IV. 477, 627
Hecate's Prophecy (1758), III. 331
He couldn't say No = Vincent Veriphleet
Hector (Galt, J., 1814), IV. 318, 636
— (Mangin, E., 1810), IV. 353
— (Shepherd, R., 1770), III. 305
Hector's Retribution (Panting, J. H., 1881), V. 512
Hecuba (Delap, J., 1761), III. 80, 253
— (Morell, T., 1749), II. 345
— (West, R., 1726), II. 13, 90–1, 364
Hecuba à la mode (Metcalfe, C., 1893), V. 488
Hedda Gabler (Gosse, Sir E. and Archer, W., 1891), V. 187, 386, 778
Hedge Carpenter (Hazlewood, C. H., 1870), V. 414
Heigho for a Husband (Waldron, F. G., 1793), III. 314
Heights of Alma = Soldier's Wife
Heinrich (Cross, J., 1876), V. 330

Heir at Law (Colman, G., the Younger, 1797), III. 248
— (1816), IV. 477
Heiress (Burgoyne, J., 1786), III. 47, 120, 152, 241
— (Cavendish, W., 1669), I. 90, 344, 396
— (Mozeen, T., 1759), III. 289
+ — (Seymour, M., *French*)
— = Stolen Heiress
Heiress and the Orphan = Quarter of a Million of Money
Heiress Hunting (Bucknall, E., 1882), V. 286
Heiress of Arragon (1863), V. 691
Heiress of Bruges (Selby, C., 1834), IV. 397
Heiress of Cardigan (1840), IV. 477
Heiress of Daventry (Brabner, W. A., 1899), V. 272
Heiress of Hazledene (Darbey, E., 1893), V. 336
Heiress of Maes-y-Felin (Ward, A. H., 1893), V. 613
Heiress of Munster (1855), V. 691
Heiress of Strathearn (Pinkerton, J., 1813), IV. 477, 604, 627
Heir from the Ocean (1871), V. 691
Heir in his Old Age = Laon-Sing-Urh
Heir of Arundel = Minstrel
Heir of Ashmore (Courtney, J., 1849), IV. 284
Heir of Crowshall = Dick Tarleton
Heir of Ellangowan (Bolton, C., 1863), V. 691, 835
Heir of Fernside = Ladder across the Street
Heir of Glen Allen = Antiquary
Heir of Innes (1822), IV. 628
Heir of Linn (Waddie, C., 1899), V. 610
Heir of Lynne (Neil, R., 1877), V. 501
Heir of Melford Castle (1861), V. 691
Heir of Milnwood = (1) Cameronians; (2) Old Mortality
Heir of Morocco (Settle, E., 1682), I. 101, 149, 429
Heir of Mowbray = Wandering Tribe
Heir of Rookwood = Turpin's Ride to York
Heir of Roselva = Mysterious Marriage
Heir of Valvoni = Cataract of Sostenza
Heir of Villeroy (1835), IV. 477

Henry II (Ireland, S. W. H., 1799), III. 276

— (Whightwick, G., 1851), V. 823

Henry III (1840), IV. 628

Henry III of France (Shipman, T., 1672), I. 116, 432

Henry IV (Kemble, J. P., 1815), IV. 335

Henry IV, Sequel of (Betterton, T., 1707), II. 298

Henry V (Boyle, R., 1664), I. 9, 66, 107–8, 393

— (Kemble, J. P., 1806), IV. 335

— (Macready, W. C., 1839), IV. 352

— (1830), IV. 477

Henry VI, the First Part (Crowne, J., 1681), I. 10, 79, 173, 399

Henry VI, the Second Part = Misery of Civil War

Henry VII (Chenevix, R., 1812), IV. 279

Henry VIII and Anne Bullen (1732), II. 374

Henry VIII and Francis I = Field of the Cloth of Gold

Henry and Almeria (Birrell, A., 1802), IV. 195, 267

Henry and Edwy = Secret Castle

Henry and Emma (Arne, T. A., 1749), II. 138, 374, 431, 447

— (Bate, H., 1774), III. 235

Henry and Louisa (1797), III. 331

Henry and Mary (1817), IV. 477

Henry and Rosa (1819), IV. 478

Henry and Rosamond (Hawkins, W., 1749), II. 335, 438

Henry de Fleurville (1820), IV. 478

Henry Dunbar (Taylor, T., 1865), V. 593

Henry Esmond (Pemberton, T. E., 1897), V. 519

Henry, Lord Darnley (Brown, R., 1823), IV. 574

Henry of Richmond (Edison, J. S., 1857), V. 354

Henry of Transtamare (1805), IV. 478

Henry's Entertainment (1828), IV. 478

Henry's Table-Talk (1825), IV. 478

— (1826), IV. 478

Henwitchers (Fitzgerald, P., 1878), V. 369

He of the Red Hand = Red Hand

Heraclius (1664), I. 98, 442

Heraclius, Emperor of the East (Carlell, L., 1664), I. 50, 98, 395

Her Advocate (Frith, W., 1895), V. 374

Her Apron Strings (Hood, B., 1897), V. 425

Her Atonement (1885), V. 691

Her Birthday (Young, Sir C. L., 1884), V. 636

— (Young, G., 1899), V. 636

Her Cousin Frank (Capel, G., 1879), V. 302

Hercules (Motteux, P. A., 1697), I. 263, 421

— (1749), II. 394

Hercules and Omphale (Brough, W., 1864), V. 280

— (1746), II. 374

— (1794), III. 331

Hercules, King of Clubs (Cooper, F. F., 1836), IV. 283

Hercules's Choice of Pleasure and Virtue (1753), III. 399

Her Dearest Foe (Lindley, H., 1894), V. 459

Hereditary Honours (Lancaster, E. R. and Oxberry, W. H.), IV. 593

Heredity = Gifted Lady

Here He Is Again = Pedro Lobo

Here's Another Guy Mannering (Burnand, F. C., 1874), V. 290

Here, There and Everywhere (1785), III. 331

— = Tourist

Here we are (Dibdin, T. J., 1825), IV. 304

Her Father (Rose, E. and Douglass, J. T., 1889), V. 550

Her Father's Friend (Rudall, H. A., 1896), V. 553

Her Father's Sin (1889), V. 691

Her First Appearance (Russell, E. H., 1890), V. 553

Her First Ball (Cutler, J., 1899), V. 332

Her First Engagement (Swan, M., 1894), V. 588

Her First Night = (1) Debutante; (2) First Night

Her Guardian (Brown, J. R., 1895), V. 282

Her Hero = Sensualist

Her Ladyship (Fenn, G. M., 1889), V. 365

Heroine (Phillips, R., 1819), IV. 372

Heroine of Cambria (Hayley, W., 1811), IV. 588

Heroine of China = Zingina

Heroine of Glencoe (Marsh, C. H., 1899), V. 477

Heroine of Love (Robertson, 1778), III. 302

Heroine of Padua = Montrezar

Heroine of the Cave (Hiffernan, P., 1774), III. 268

Heroine of Yucatan = Aggression

Heroines of Switzerland = Sisters

Her Only Failing (1864), V. 692

Hero of an Hour (Summers, K., 1869), V. 587

Hero of England = Edward the Black Prince

Hero of Heroes (Whitbread, J. W., 1889), V. 620

Hero of Jerusalem (Fineman, S. H., 1896), V. 367

Hero of Romance (Marston, J. W., 1868), V. 479

Hero of Switzerland = William Tell

Hero of the Arctic Regions = Captain Ross

Hero of the Drama (1860), V. 692

Hero of the North (Dimond, W., 1803), IV. 306

Hero, the Champion and the Murderer = Mountain Monarch

Her Own Enemy = Only a Woman

Her Own Rival (Broughton, F. W. and Lawrence, S. B., 1889), V. 281

Her Own Witness (Dabbs, G. H. R., 1889), V. 332

Her Release (Edlin, H., 1892), V. 354

Her Retaliation (Vorzanzer, C., 1889), V. 609

Her Royal Highness (Hood, B., 1898), V. 425

— (1852), V. 692

Her Second Love = Passion's Power

Her Secret (Courtney, G. F., 1897), V. 326

Her Sin = My Partner

Her Talisman (Scott, F., 1896), V. 558

Hertford (Eastwood, F., 1880), V. 353

Hertfordshire Tragedy (Milner, H. M., 1824), IV. 478, 628

Her True Colours (Brabner, W. A., 1891), V. 272

Her Trustee (Blood, J. J., 1887), V. 266

Her Uncle (1886), V. 692

Her Vengeance (1895), V. 692

Her Wedding Day (De Banzie, E. T., 1895), V. 340

Her World against a Lie (Marryat, F. and Neville, G. F., 1880), V. 477

He's a Lunatic (Dale, F., 1867), V. 332

He's coming via Slumborough (Burnand, F. C., 1874), V. 290

He's Here Again (1828), IV. 478

He's Much to Blame (Holcroft, T., 1798), III. 120, 121, 271, 387

He's no Conjuror (Harding, C. T., 1829), IV. 478, 628

— = Legerdemain

He's not a-miss (Dance, C., 1832), IV. 478, 628

He's so nervous (De Frece, M., 1872), V. 341

Hester (1893), V. 692

Hester Gray (Reece, R. and Farnie, H. B., 1877), V. 538

Hester Prynne (Hatton, J., 1876), V. 409

Hester's Legacy (1892), V. 692

Hester's Mystery (Pinero, Sir A. W., 1880), V. 524

He stoops to win (Bridgman, C., 1891), V. 275

+He that will not when he may (Gardner, H., French)

Heureuse ruse = Lindorf et Rosalie

Hewie the Witless (1854), V. 692

He Wiped away a Tear = Full Private Perkins

He with the Hump (1846), IV. 478

He would be a Bohemian (Garton, W. R., 1870), V. 376

He would be an Actor (Mathews, C. J., 1836), IV. 354, 478, 598, 628

He Would Be a Player (1810), IV. 478

— That's the Manager

He would be a Sailor (Hazlewood, C. H., 1868), V. 413

— = Coming Up, Sir!

He Would be a Soldier (Pilon, F., 1786), III. 40, 43, 298

+He Would be in Love (Crow Street, Dublin, 1/5/1795)

He Wou'd if he Cou'd (Bickerstaffe, I., 1771), III. 199, 237, 378

Hewson Reduc'd (1661), I. 442

Hexen am Rhein (Stirling, E., 1841), IV. 613

Hey Diddle Diddle (Blanchard, E. L., 1855), V. 263

Hezekiah, King of Judah (Allen, 1798), III. 54, 232

Hibernia Freed (Phillips, W., 1722), II. 26, 107, 349

Hibernian Hag and the Chief of Kildare = O'Donnell the Red

Hibernia's Triumph (1748), II. 374

Hic et Ubique (Head, R., 1663), I. 413

Hickedy Pickedy my Black Hen (1857), V. 692

Hickerty Pickerty (1833), IV. 478

Hickety Pickety, the Black Hen (1834), IV. 478

Hickory Dickory Dock (Hazlewood, C. H., 1863), V. 692, 835

Hidden (Wyke, E. B., 1888), V. 634

Hidden Crime (Pitt, C., 1871), V. 692, 810, 835

Hidden Enemy (Gray, A., 1887), V. 390

Hidden Foe (Cassilis, I. L., 1892), V. 306

Hidden Gold (Bertrand, E. C. and Gould, F., 1882), V. 260

Hidden Hand (Taylor, T., 1864), V. 98, 593

— = Masked Mother

Hidden Light (Conquest, G., 1861), V. 692, 785, 835

Hidden Past (Edmonds, E. V., 1896), V. 354

Hidden Terror (Melford, M., 1891), V. 484

Hidden Treasure (Parry, T. and Oxenford, J., 1871), V. 515

— = (1) Hedge Carpenter; (2) Hollow Way; (3) Idiot of the Mill; (4) Marietta; (5) Past and Present; (6) Rock of Sculls

Hidden Worth (Sedger, H., 1886), V. 560

Hide and Seek (Lunn, J., 1824), IV. 348, 596

— (?Lunn, J., 1830), IV. 478, 628

— (1789), III. 331 [This is attributed to William Walter in *The Town and Country Magazine*, Feb. 1789]

Hide and Seek (1833), IV. 478

High and Low, Rich and Poor = 1874

High- and Low-Water Bell (1855), V. 692

High Art (1883), V. 692

High Crime and Low Crime = (1) Money and Misery; (2) Starved to Death

Highdays and Holidays = Ingratitude

Highdays and Holydays from Tyburn to Whitechapel = London

Highest Bidder (1898), V. 692

Highgate Mystery = Over the Garden Wall

Highgate Tunnel (Smith, T., 1812), IV. 403

High Jinks (1886), V. 692

Highland Cateran (Murray, W. H., 1837), IV. 478, 628

Highland Chiefs (McLaren, A., 1815), IV. 351

Highland Drover (McLaren, A., 1795), III. 284, 391

— (McLaren, A., 1805), IV. 351

Highlander Bit = Harlequin turn'd Dancing-Master

Highlanders (Bruce, E., 1872), V. 283

Highlander's Return = Caledonian Laurels

Highland Fair (Mitchell, J., 1731), II. 250, 345

Highland Fling (Dilley, J. J., 1879), V. 345

Highland Funeral (McLaren, A., 1819), IV. 352

— = Private Theatre

Highland Hearts (Gordon, H. C., 1889), V. 385

Highland Jessie Brown (1858), V. 692

Highland Laddie = Hooley and Fairly

Highland Lassie = Lowland Lassie in London

Highland Legacy (Thomas, B., 1888), V. 596

Highland Reel (O'Keeffe, J., 1788), III. 294

Highland Revenge = Kelpie's Cave

Highland Rivals (1822), IV. 478

Highland Robbers (McLaren, A., 1817), IV. 351

— = Edgar and Effie

Highland Wedding (McLaren, A., 1819), IV. 352

His Highness (Houghton, J. W. and Tate, A., 1893), v. 427
His Highness (Hurst, B., 1894), v. 431
— (1832), IV. 479
His Holiday (1894), v. 692
His Hydropathic Highness = Belle of the Bath
His Journey to London = Robin Bullcalf's Readings
His Landlady (Mudie, G., 1892), v. 498
His Last Chance (Harraden, H., 1890), v. 404
— (1896), v. 692
His Last Cruise (Gunton, R. T., 1893), v. 397
His Last Legs (Bernard, W. B., 1839), IV. 266
His Last Stake (Webster, J. P., 1888), v. 618
His Last Victory (Phillips, W., 1862), v. 523
His Little Dodge (McCarthy, J. H., 1896), v. 467
His Little Mania (1890), v. 692
His Lordship (Barczinski,A.,1890),v. 249
His Lordship's Birthday (Raphael, F. and Lauri, E., 1894), v. 535
His Majestie's Entertainment (Ogilby, J., 1661), I. 422
His Majesty (Burnand, F. C. and Lehmann, R. C., 1897), v. 292
His Majesty's Musketeers = Three Musketeers
His Masterpiece (Vane, S., 1898), v. 606
His Mother (Day, G. D., 1891), v. 339
His Mother's Ransom (1891), v. 692
His Natural Life (1886), v. 692
— (1896), v. 692
His Nephew (1896), v. 693
His New French Cook (1899), v. 693
His Novice (Spicer, H., 1878), v. 576
His Only Coat (1882), v. 693
His other I (Outram, L. S. and Brown, W. H., 1898), v. 509
His Own Enemy (Dillon, C., 1898), v. 345
— (Meadow, A., 1873), v. 483
His Own Guest (Ayres, A. and Blake, P., 1883), v. 247
His Own Wife (1894), v. 693
His Relations (Saintsbury, H. A., 1896), v. 554
His Romance (Milton, M., 1888), v. 490

His Satanic Majesty (Marlow, F. and Barron, H., 1899), v. 477
His Second Wife (Hope, V., 1892), v. 425
His Son-in-Law (Giveen, R. F., 1896), v. 382
— (Watson, W. G. and Rodman, A., 1890), v. 616
His Success (Grogan, W. E., 1895), v. 395
His Toast (Heathcote, A. M., 1889), v. 415
Historical Register, For the Year 1736 (Fielding, H., 1737), II. 7, 18, 68, 126–7, 261, 328, 434, 436; III. 116; v. 142–3
History and Her-story in a Modern Milo-metre = Antony and Cleopatra
History of a Crime = Dead Man's Gold
History of a Flag (1860), v. 693
History of a Rough Gem = King of Diamonds
History of Bacon in Virginia = Widdow Ranter
His Treasures (Kingsley, E., 1897), v. 444
His Wife (Jones, H. A., 1881), v. 162, 439
His Wife's Little Bill (Henning, A., 1894), v. 417
His Wives (Cleveland, E. A., 1894), v. 314
— (Warren, T. G., 1888), v. 615
His Word, his Bond = Winning Defeat
His Worship the Cully = Braggadochio
Hit him, he has no friends (Yates, E. and Harrington, N. H., 1860), v. 635
Hit if you like it = Success
Hit or Miss (Burnand, F. C., 1868), v. 289, 781
— (Milton, A., 1883), v. 490
— (Pocock, I., 1810), IV. 144, 383
Hive of Life: Its Drones and Workers (Calvert, C., 1862), v. 693, 783, 836
H.M.S. Missfire (Drury, W. O., 1894), v. 351
H.M.S. Pinafore (Gilbert, W. S., 1878), v. 143–4, 380
Hoax (1810), IV. 479
— (1826), IV. 479
Hoaxer (1814), IV. 479
Hoaxing (1824), IV. 479

Hob (Cibber, C., 1711), II. 132, 133, 250, 311, 434
— = Flora
Hobbies (Stephens, H. P. and Yardley, W., 1885), v. 580
Hobbs, Dodds and Stubbs (Webster, B. N., 1840), IV. 417
Hobby-Horse (Pinero, Sir A. W., 1888), v. 176, 177, 525
— (Thompson, E., 1766), III. 311
Hobby Horses (1789), III. 331
Hob in the Well = Flora
Hobson's Choice (Oulton, W. C., 1787), III. 296
— (Summers, K., 1895), v. 587
Hob's Wedding (Leigh, J., 1720), II. 341
Hocus Pocus, IV. 479
Hoddy Toddy, all Head and no Body (1851), v. 693
Hodge Podge (1781), III. 331
Hofer (Fitzball, E., 1830) = Andreas Hofer, IV. 584
— (Planché, J. R., 1830), IV. 379
Hogarth's Apprentices (1821), IV. 479
— (1848), IV. 479
Hogarth's Mirror (1847), IV. 628
Hogmanay (Sidney, F. W., 1896), v. 565
Hokee Pokee (Conquest, G. and Spry, H., 1878), v. 321
Hokey Pokey Wankey Fum (1836), IV. 479
Hold Fast (1885), v. 693
Holding the Mirror (Howell-Poole, W., 1885), v. 429
Hold your Tongue (Planché, J. R., 1849), IV. 129, 383
Hole in the Wall (Poole, J., 1813), IV. 386
— = Secret
Holidays (Eyre, E. J., 1813), IV. 479, 628
— = Juvenile Friendship
Holiday Time (Lathom, F., 1799), III. 280; IV. 341, 342
Hollow Tree = Raykisnah the Outcast
Hollow under the Hill = Saul the Servant
Hollow Way (Moncrieff, W. T., 1828), IV. 479, 628
Holly Branch (Thomas, C., 1891), v. 596
Holly Bush Hall (Mordaunt, J., 1860), v. 693, 807, 836

Holly Bush Hall (Seaman, W., 1860), v. 693, 815, 836
— (Suter, W. E., 1860), v. 587, 819
— (1866), v. 693
Holly Lodge (1855), v. 693
Holly Tree Inn (Beringer, Mrs O., 1891), v. 259
— (Johnstone, J. B., 1856), v. 693, 800, 836
Holofernes (?1664), I. 446
Holyrood (Bell, S., 1896), v. 256
Holstein Hussar (Pitt, G. D., 1838), IV. 373
Homage to Flora (1860), v. 693, 836
Homburg (Hatton, J., 1893), v. 409
Home (Robertson, T. W., 1869), v. 546
— (1880), v. 693
Home Affairs (1879), v. 693
Home Again (Fitzball, E., 1844), IV. 316
— (Jones, H. A., 1881), v. 162, 439
— (Marston, H., 1877), v. 478
Home and Happiness = Paris and Pleasure
Home and the Homeless = Alone in the World
Home and the Love of Yore = Home Chimes
Home Chimes (Arthur, A., 1888), v. 244
Home Circle (1850), v. 693
Home Circuit (Mathews, C. J., 1827), IV. 354
Home Coming (Cosham, E., 1892), v. 325
Home Diplomacy (1867), v. 693
Home Feud (Frith, W., 1890), v. 374
Home for a Holiday (Gordon, W., 1860), v. 385, 794
Home for Home (Lee, R., 1879), v. 453
Home for the Holidays (Moncrieff, W. T., 1828), IV. 359 [This was printed 8°, 1828 as Old Heads on Young Shoulders, and evidently is an earlier version of the play listed under that title IV. 360]
Home from War (1855), v. 693
Home in the Heart (Conquest, G., 1861), v. 693, 785, 836
Home in the Mountains = Indian Queen
Home in the West (1853), v. 693
Home is Home After All = King's Coin
Homeless (Murray, J. K. and Comer, G., 1893), v. 500

Home of our Adoption (1892), v. 693

Home of the Brave (1832), IV. 479

Home once more (Crauford, A. L., 1885), v. 328

Home, Out and Home (Squires, J., 1862), v. 817

Home Phantasies (1879), v. 693

Home Plays (Blake, T. G.), v. 262

Home Rule (Brady, E. J., 1880), v. 273

— (Taylor, J. G., 1877), v. 591

Home Rule Bill (1893), v. 693

Home Ruler = Tight Rein

Home Secretary (Carton, R. C., 1895), v. 305

Home Service = Nice Young Ladies

Homespun (Calmour, A. C., 1884), v. 300

Homestead Story (1861), v. 693

Home Sweet Home (Farjeon, E., 1876), v. 361

— (Somerset, C. A., 1829), IV. 404

— (Swears, H., 1895), v. 589

— = Swiss Family

Home Truths (Reynoldson, T. H., 1852) = Barrister, v. 542, 693, 813, 836

—(1858), v. 693

Homeward Bound (Bertie, J. C., 1874), v. 259

— (1833), IV. 479

— (1838), IV. 479

— (1882), v. 693

— (1885), v. 693

Homewreck (Coyne, J. S. and Denis, J., 1869), v. 328

— (1851), v. 693

Homicide (Baillie, J., 1836), IV. 258

— (1824), IV. 479

Homme blasé = Used Up

Homme Noir (1839), IV. 479

Homoeopathy (1837), IV. 479

Honest Attorney (Emden, W. S., 1855), v. 693, 790, 836

Honest Cheats (Coyne, J. S., 1836), IV. 284

Honest Criminal (Astley, P., Jr., 1808), IV. 257

— (1778), III. 331

Honest Electors (1733), II. 375

Honest Farmer (Berguin, M., 1791), III. 236

Honest Frauds (Lunn, J., 1830), IV. 348

Honest Hearts = Go Straight

Honest Irishman = Brave Irishman

Honest Israelite = Little Aaron

Honest Jew of Frankfort = Rise of the Rothschilds

Honest John (Hazlewood, C. H., 1875), v. 415

Honest Labour (Marchant, F., 1870), v. 476

Honest Lawyer = Honest Attorney

Honest Living (Lawrence, W., 1891), v. 451

Honest Man (Pettitt, H., 1878), v. 521

— = John of the Forge

Honest Man's Fortune (1849), IV. 479

Honest Men of Taunton = Downfal of Bribery

Honest Munsterman = Connaught Wife

Honest Soldier (Colls, J. H., 1805), III. 245; IV. 281

Honest Tar and the Wicked First Luff = H.M.S. Missfire

Honest Thieves (Knight, T., 1797), III. 114, 280; IV. 479, 592, 628

Honest Welchman (Dibdin, T. J., 1827), IV. 305

— = Journey to Bristol

Honest Welshman = St David's Day

Honest Wife = Intriguing Widow

Honesty (Spicer, H., 1845), IV. 405

— (Young, M., 1897), v. 636

— (1872), v. 693

Honesty in Distress (Ward, E., 1708), II. 363

Honesty is the Best Policy (1791), III. 331

— = Good Hearts

Honest Yorkshire-Man (Carey, H., 1735), II. 43, 137, 233, 302, 432-3

Honesty the Best Policy (Lemon, M., 1849), IV. 345

— (1815) = Cady, IV. 479, 628

— (1865), v. 693

— (1879), v. 693

— (1898), v. 693

— = (1) Heir of Vironi; (2) Power of Gold; (3) Tantara-Rara, Rogues All; (4) Tricks of London; (5) World as it goes

Honeydove's Troubles (Reece, R., 1867), v. 537, 812

Honey Moon (Linley, W., 1796), III. 281, 390

Honey Moon (Tobin, J., 1805), IV. 164, 413

— (1812), IV. 479

Honeymoon Hints (George, G. H., 1852), V. 377

Honeymoon in Eclipse (Moore, G., 1888), V. 492

Honeymoon Scruple (Jerrold, D. W., 1845), IV. 333

Honeymoon Tragedy (Clifford, Mrs W. K., 1896), V. 314

Hong Puf (1821), IV. 479

Honi Soit (1886) = Modern Godiva, v. 693, 720, 836, 841

Honi soit qui mal y pence (1799), III. 331

Honor Bright (Towers, E., 1870), v. 601

Honour (Barrymore, M., 1881), v. 252

— (Cromwell, T., 1819), IV. 479, 628

— (Levey, J. C., 1871), v. 458

— (Reed, R. L., 1876), v. 540

— (1870), v. 693

Honourable Herbert (Chambers, C. H., 1891), v. 307

Honourable John (Mouillot, F., James, C. and Malyon, E. J., 1898), v. 498, 799, 805, 807

Honourable Member (Gattie, A. W., 1896), v. 377

Honour Among Thieves (Hannan, C., 1895), v. 402

— (Towers, E., 1877), v. 601

— = Desperate Game

Honour and Arms (1863), v. 693

Honour and Industry = Labour Question

Honour and Shame (1849), IV. 479

Honour before Titles (Reade, C., 1852), v. 536

Honour before Wealth (Edwards, P., 1861), v. 356

— (1885), v. 693

— = Reflection

Honour Bright (Grahame, R. and De Banzie, E. T., 1897), v. 387

Honour, Love and Friendship = Dread Sentence

Honour of a Castilian = Hernani

Honour of the House (Holderness, C. T. and Warwick, H. S., 1893), v. 424

— (Lewis, H. H., 1895), v. 459

Honour of the House (1857), v. 693

— = Radical

Honour or Love (Newton, H. C., 1898), v. 503

Honour Rewarded (Dalton, J., 1775), III. 253

Honours (Vane, F., 1879), v. 606

Honours and Tricks (Brooks, C. W. S., 1846), IV. 271

Honours Divided (Burrow, C. K. and Benington, W., 1895), v. 293

Honours of War (1793), III. 331

Honour's Price (Murdoch, J. M., 1884), v. 499

Honour's Test = Prisoners of the Ball

Honour thy Father (Clarke, C. A. and Silva, H. R., 1898), v. 312

— (1896), v. 693

Honour to the Brave = (1) Festival of Peace; (2) Triumph of Peace

Hooded Bridegroom (1848), IV. 479

Hoodman Blind (Jones, H. A. and Barrett, W., 1885), v. 439

Hook and Eye (Norwood, E., 1887), v. 505

Hooker and Snooker (1851), v. 693

Hooking Walker (1821), IV. 479

Hook or Crook (1878), v. 693

Hooley and Fairly (1789), III. 331

Hoop of Gold (Murdoch, J. M., 1878), v. 499

Hoops into Spinning Wheels (Blanch, J., 1725), II. 261, 299

Hoorn, the Scourge of Norway (1830), IV. 479

Hop (1791), III. 331

Hope (Law, A., 1882), v. 450

— (Saunders, R., 1895), v. 556

Hope Deferred (1885), v. 693

Hopeless Passion (Morton, J. M., 1851), v. 495

Hope of Britain (1802), IV. 479 [This is evidently an earlier version of The Twelfth of August, see IV. 546]

Hope of the Family (Coyne, J. S., 1853), v. 327

Hopes and Fears (1854), v. 693

— (1864), v. 693

Hope's Answer (Edwards, M. and Gough, H., 1886), v. 355

Hop o' my Thumb (Green, F. W., 1876), v. 390

Hop o' my Thumb (Green, F. W., 1880), v. 391
— (Green, F. W., 1881), v. 391
— (Smith, A. R., 1846), IV. 402, 611
— (1854, 1877), v. 693
Hop o' my Thumb and his Brothers (1831), IV. 479
Hop o' my Thumb and his Eleven Brothers (Blanchard, E. L., 1864), v. 263, 779
Hop o' my Thumb and the Giant Ogre of the Seven Leagued Boots (1863), v. 694
Hop Pickers (1849), IV. 479
— (1861), v. 694
Hop Pickers and Gipsies (Hazlewood, C. H., 1869), v. 413
Hops! and Steps! (1811), IV. 479
Hops without Malt (1823), IV. 479
Horace (Cotton, C., 1671), I. 98, 398
— (Philips, K. and Denham, Sir J., 1668), I. 98, 344, 423
+Horace at the University of Athens (Trevelyan, G. O.: 8°, 1869 (in *Ladies in Parliament and other Pieces*; apparently acted privately at Cambridge))
Horatia (1845), IV. 479
Horatii (1846), IV. 628
Horatii and Curatii (Macfarren, G., 1820), IV. 349
Hornet's Nest (Byron, H. J., 1878), v. 299
— (Gordon, G. L., 1876), v. 384
Horn of Plenty (Ascher, G., 1897), v. 244
Horns and Hounds = Is it a Wedding?
Horns of a Dilemma = Ernani
Horoscope = Pong Wong
Horrid Barbarian = Our Geordie
Horrification (Dibdin, C. I. M., 1825), IV. 295
Horrors (1885), v. 694
Horrors of an Assault = Victim of St Vincent
Horrors of Extravagance = Prodigal
Horrors of Intemperance = Profligates
Horrors of 1720 = Plague of Marseilles
Horrors of Slavery = Uncle Tom's Cabin
Horrors of the Bastile (1835), IV. 479
Horrors of the Bastile = Tale of Two Cities

Horrors of the Forest = Stop Thief!
Horrors of the French Revolution = Reign of Terror
Horrors of the Press-gang = Paul Periwinkle
Horrors of War (1827), IV. 480
— (1831), IV. 479
— = (1) Siege of Sebastopol; (2) Soldier's Progress
Horse and Foot (1834), IV. 480
— = Gallopade
Horse and the Murderer = (1) Black Legend; (2) Kentucky Rifle
Horse and the Ostler = Black Legend of Rotherhithe
Horse and the Widow (Dibdin, T. J., 1799), III. 122, 189, 256, 383
Horse Banditti = (1) Gil Blas de Santillane; (2) Voorn the Tiger
Horse Banditti and their Forty Steeds (1830), IV. 480
Horse Dealer of Vienna (1860), v. 694
Horseman (1893), v. 694
Horsemonger-lane Joe (Travers, W., 1861) = Poor Joe of Horsemonger-lane, v. 734, 843
Horse of the Arab Chief = Moors of Spain
Horse of the Cavern (1856) = Carlo Brunari, v. 655, 694, 836
Horse of the Disinherited = Battle of Blenheim
Horse of the Elements = Prince of Cyprus
Horse Poisoner = James Lawson
Horseshoe (1860), v. 694
— (1898), v. 694
Horse to be Sold (1861), v. 694
Hortensia (1815), IV. 480, 636
Horton Towers (1895), v. 694
Hospital for Fools (Miller, J., 1739), II. 13, 145, 237, 344, 437, 441
Hot and Cold (Dibdin, T. J., 1826), IV. 304
— (1850), v. 694
Hot Boiled Beans and the Very Good Butter (1834), IV. 480
Hot Codlings (1822), IV. 480
Hotel (Jephson, R., 1783), III. 122, 277, 389
— (Vaughan, T., 1776), III. 185-6, 313
Hotel Charges (Selby, C., 1853), v. 560

Hot Night = Kindred Souls

Hot Potatoe (1885), v. 694

Hot Potatoes = Cousin Johnny

Hottentot Venus (1810), IV. 480

Hot Water (Farnie, H. B., 1876), v. 362

Hot Weather (1846), IV. 480

Houp-la! (Warren, T. G., 1891), v. 615

— (1885), v. 694

Houp La! Tra, la, la! (Dunstan, H. M., 1886), v. 352

Hour and a Half in Paris = Retaliation

Hour at Ipswich Station (Harvey, F., 1874), v. 408

Hour at Rugby Junction (1873), v. 694

Hour at the Carnival = Hour in Venice

Hour at Weybridge = Spirit of the Grotto

Hour before Marriage (1772), III. 332

— = Man of Two Thousand

Hour in Seville (Selby, C., 1858), v. 560

Hour in Venice (1859), v. 694

Hour of Midnight = Deception

Hour of One = Amazon's Oath

Hour of Retribution, see St Aubert

Hour of Retribution (1821), IV. 480

— (1846), IV. 480

— = St Aubert

Hour of Triumph (1896), v. 694

Hour of Twelve (1836), IV. 480

Hour's Romance = Where's Brown?

Hour with Napoleon (Webb, C., 1844) = One Hour with Napoleon, IV. 480, 628

House Besieged = Mad Monarch

House Boat (Williamson, H. W., 1886), v. 626

Housebreaker (Rogers, T. S., 1892), v. 549

— (1897), v. 694

Housebreaker of the Last Century = Jack Sheppard

House Burners = Incendiary

House Divided (Haines, J. T., 1836), IV. 322, 586

— = (1) Lord Marple's Daughter; (2) Uncle Oliver

House Dog (Higgie, T. H., 1845), IV. 325

Housefull of Rebels (1895), v. 694

Household Fairy (Talfourd, F., 1859), v. 590

Household Gods = Junius Brutus

Household Picture under Two Lights = Wife's Portrait

Household Words (Bourne, W., 1884), v. 270

— (1858), v. 694

Household Words, All the Year Round (1859), v. 694

House in a Hurry = All Bedevil'd

House in Thames Street (Dorrell, A., 1885), v. 347

House in the Forest = Old Heads on Young Shoulders

House in the Valley (Conquest, G., 1860), v. 694, 785, 836

Housekeeper (Jerrold, D. W., 1833), IV. 332

Housekeeper's Elopement = Marriage by Licence

House of Aspen (Scott, Sir W., 1829), IV. 194, 397

House of Atreus and the House of Laius (Smith, J., 1818), IV. 611

House of Cards (Grundy, S., 1891), v. 397

House of Colberg (Serle, T. J., 1832), IV. 399

House of Commons = Westminster

House of Darnley (Lytton, Baron, 1877), v. 466

House of Dives (1893), v. 694

House of Ladies (Lemon, M., 1840), IV. 344

House of Lies (Hannan, C., 1892), v. 402

House of Lords (Greenbank, H., 1894), v. 392

House of McOuld = Life's Mistakes

House of Morville (Lake, J., 1812), IV. 341

House of Mystery (Harvey, F., 1898), v. 409

House of Sleep (Warwick, H. S., 1897), v. 615

House on the Bridge (Johnstone, J. B., 1852), v. 438

House on the Bridge of Notre Dame (Douglass, J. T., 1861), v. 694, 788, 836

— (Hazlewood, C. H., 1861), v. 412

— (Lacy, M. R., 1861), v. 694, 801

— = Gipsy Twins

House on the Cliff = Royal Pardon

House on the Heath (1857), v. 694
House on the Marsh (Warden, F., 1885), v. 613
— (Willoughby, H., 1885), v. 626
— (Wood, G. M., 1885), v. 630
House or the Home? (Taylor, T., 1859), v. 185, 593
House out at Windows (Kenney, J., 1817), IV. 337
House out of Windows (Brough, W., 1852), v. 278
House Room (Peake, R. B., 1836), IV. 370
Houses of Campbell and Maclean = John of Lorne and Helen of Argyle
Houses of York and Lancaster = Days of Old
House that Jack built (Chambers, T., 1862), v. 783
— (Fox, G., 1821), IV. 317
— (Keating, Miss, 1859), v. 801
— (Mackay, J., 1878), v. 470
— (Newton, H. C., 1894), v. 503
— (1859), v. 694
— (1860), v. 836
— (1864), v. 694
— (1871), v. 836
— (1877, 1878, 1880, 1881, 1889, 1890), v. 694
— (1897), v. 836
— (1898), v. 694
House that Jack built in 1851 (Greenwood, T. L., 1850) = Harlequin and the House that Jack built in 1851, v. 393, 687, 794, 834
House to be Sold (Baylis, J., 1804), IV. 262
— (Cobb, J., 1802), IV. 145, 281
House to Let (1859), v. 694
House Tyrant = Spirit of Contradiction
House upon the Heath = All in One Night
House versus the Home = House or the Home?
House-warming (Dibdin, T. J., 1816), IV. 300, 480, 580, 628
Hovel (1797), III. 332
Howard Howard (Arthur, A., 1888), v. 244
How does he love me? (1876), v. 694
How do you manage? (Bayly, T. H., 1835), IV. 262, 571

How Dreams come true (Todhunter, J., 1890), v. 600
How Fair the World Is! (1843), IV. 480
How happy could I be with either! (Dibdin, T. J., 1807) = Two Faces under a Hood, IV. 480
How I found Crusoe (Thompson, A., 1872), v. 597
How I tamed Mrs Cruiser (1858), v. 694
How it's to be done (Buckingham, L. S., 1857), v. 694, 781, 836
Howlet's Haunt (1832), IV. 480
How London lives (Field, M. and Shirley, A., 1897), v. 365
How Many More Wives? = Family Man
How many were Bavarians = "Buy a Broom?"
How many Wives has he? (1832), IV. 480
How Money's Made (Warren, F. B., 1899), v. 615
How Remarkable! = Whang Fong
Howse the Informer (1897), v. 694
How shall we get rid of him? = Giovanni, the Vampire
How she loves him! (Boucicault, D., 1863), v. 268
How Silver was tricked (1899), v. 694
How's that, Umpire? (Bidwell, H., 1880), v. 261
How stout you're getting (Morton, J. M., 1855), v. 495
How's your poor Feet? (1862), v. 694
How's your Uncle? (Wilks, T. E., 1855), v. 623, 823
How the Average became the Abnormal = Average Man
How the Duchess convinced the Princess (1899), v. 694
How Time Flies (Elphinstone, J., 1869), v. 358
How to Act (Albery, J., Vezin, H. and Wills, W. G., 1865) = Doctor Davy, v. 237, 694
How to be happy though married = Woman Tamer
How to Buy a Horse without Money = Speculation
How to choose a Husband = Lottie's Love
How to come at Her = Comet
How to Cook a Biffin = Hotel Charges

How to Die for Love (1812) = Blank Cartridge, IV. 87, 480

How to Dish up a Farce = Dramatic Cookery

How to Draw a Long Bow = Love's Vagaries

How to Drive a Tandem = She's not to be Managed

How to Furnish a House without Money = Wager

How to Gain Consent = Fun and Fright

How to gain Five Thousand Pounds = Peter Proteus

How to get a Freehold = Right of Common

How to get a Place = Place Hunters

How to get married (1795), III. 332

How to get off (+ Dance, C., 1834), IV. 480

How to get out of a Mess (1824), IV. 480

How to get rich = Railroad for Ever

How to get your Money = Green-eyed Monster

How to give a Rout = Advantages of Lying

How to Grow Rich (Reynolds, F., 1793), III. 16, 132, 301

How to grow wise (McLaren, A., 1808), IV. 351

How to kill him (Robson, F., 1873), V. 547

How to Live without Money (1830), IV. 14, 480

How to Make a Will = Watching a Body

How to make Home happy (Brough, W., 1853) = Family Secrets, V. 279, 675, 780, 832

How Tom proposed (1897), V. 695

How to Pay Rent without Money = (1) I.O.U. £7. 16s. 6d.; (2) Quarter Day

How to Pay the Rent (Power, T., 1840), IV. 387

How to Pay your Taxes (1820), IV. 480

How to Raise the Wind = (1) Dead and Buried; (2) Raising the Wind

How to Raise your Salary = Actor in Distress

How to rule a Husband = School of Reform

How to settle Accounts with your Laundress (Coyne, J. S., 1847), IV. 14, 122, 285

How to Shave the Governor = Fast Friends up a Tree

How to take up a Bill (Moncrieff, W. T., 1833), IV. 143, 360, 600

How to Tame a Woman = Shrew

How to Tease and How to Please (1810), IV. 480

How to touch the Ladies' Hearts = Tender Chord

How to Win a Wager (Otley, 1874), V. 508

How to write an Opera! (Dibdin, T. J., 1818), IV. 301

How we live in the World of London (Johnstone, J. B., 1856), V. 695, 800, 836

How we spent Christmas Day in '69 (Pitt, H. M., 1870), V. 526

How Will It End? (West, Mrs J.), III. 315

— (1809), IV. 480

— = (1) Baronets; (2) Begone Dull Care

How will they get out of it? (Sketchley, A., 1864), V. 571

Hoxton a Hundred Years Ago (Atkyns, S., 1845), IV. 257

Hubby (Sherburn, H. A., 1884), V. 563

Hubby's Jealousy = Kiss in the Dark

Hubert's Pride (Fraser, J. A., 1872), V. 372

Hubert, the Bowyer's Son (Stewart, D., 1874), V. 583

Hudibras (1730), II. 375

Hudibrasso (1741), II. 375

Hue and Cry (Brady, E. J., 1883), V. 273

— (Cross, J. C., 1797) = Escape into Prison, III. 332, 380, 401

— (Inchbald, Mrs E., 1791), III. 275, 388

— (Shirley, A. and Landeck, B., 1897), V. 564

— = Yours or Mine?

Hue and Cry after Honesty = Diogenes and his Lantern

Hue and Cry to Change Alley = Chimæra

Hue and Dye (Hay, F., 1869), V. 411

Hugenot (Meryon, E., 1876), V. 488

Hugenot Captain (Phillips, W., 1866), V. 523

+ Hugger Mugger (Clarke, H. S., *French*)

Hugh the Gipsey (Barnett, C. Z., 1844), IV. 260

Hugh Weston's Mill (1880), V. 695

Hugo Bambino (1824), IV. 480

Hugo the Dane (Lighterness, W. B.), IV. 595

Huguenot (Sheil, R. L., 1822) = Convict, IV. 401, 444, 610

Huguenots (Howe, J. B., 1873), V. 428

— (Russell, H., 1849), IV. 83, 480, 628

— (Wilkins, J. H., 1851), V. 695, 823, 836

— (1832), IV. 83, 480

— (1836), IV. 83, 480

— (1857), V. 695

Huguenots under Louis XV = Paul Rabaut

Hull Fair (1774), III. 402

Human Hearts = Stolen from Home

Humanity (Locksley, C., 1881), V. 462

— (Marston, H. and Rae, L., 1882), V. 478

Human Nature (Harris, A. G. and Williams, T. J., 1867), V. 405

— (Pettitt, H. and Harris, Sir A., 1885), V. 185, 521

Human Spider (Lyle, K., 1898), V. 465

Human Sport (Fryers, A., 1895), V. 374

Humble Origin = Victim of Delusion

Humbug (Burnand, F. C., 1867), V. 289

— (Jones, H. A., 1881), V. 439

— (Silvester, H., 1845), IV. 480, 628

— (1827), IV. 480

— (1885), V. 695

Humbugs of the Hour (À Beckett, G. A., 1844), IV. 250

Humfrey, Duke of Gloucester (Philips, A., 1723), II. 54, 106, 348

Humgumption (1823), IV. 480

Humorists (Shadwell, T., 1670), I. 24, 204, 236, 430

Humorous Cuckold = Merry Masqueraders

Humorous Lieutenant (Reynolds, F., 1817), IV. 392, 607

Humorous Lovers (Cavendish, W., 1667), I. 215, 346, 396

Humorous Quarrel (Pottinger, I., 1761), III. 299

Humourist (Cobb, J., 1784), III. 244

Humourists (1754), III. 332

Humour of Bumpkin (Kirkman, F., 1662), I. 417

Humour of Hobbinal (Kirkman, F., 1662), I. 417

Humour of John Swabber (Kirkman, F., 1662), I. 417

Humour of Simpleton (Kirkman, F., 1662), I. 417

Humour of the Age (Baker, T., 1701), II. 174–5, 181, 296, 432

Humours and Passions = School of Shakespeare

Humours of an Election (Coyne, J. S., 1837), IV. 480, 628

— (Pilon, F., 1780), III. 298

Humours of an Inn = Rider

Humours of an Irish Court of Justice (1750), III. 332

Humours of Bluff King Hal = Beggar of Cripplegate

Humours of Brighton (Cross, J. C., 1792), III. 249

Humours of Covent-Garden = Rival Milliners

Humours of Dublin = Hic et Ubique

Humours of Dugald = Bonny Lass of Leith

Humours of Elections = Gotham Election

Humours of Exchange Alley = (1) It should have come sooner; (2) Stock-Jobbers

Humours of Gil Blas (1788), III. 332

Humours of Greenock Fair (McLaren, A., 1788), III. 284

Humours of Harlequin (1729), II. 375

Humours of Harry Humbug = Intriguing Footman

Humours of John Bull (Oswald, J., 1789), III. 295

Humours of King Henry VIII and the Merry Cobler (1797), III. 332

Humours of May Day (1787), III. 332

Humours of Monsieur Galliard (Kirkman, F., 1662), I. 417–18

Humours of Oxford (Miller, J., 1730), II. 177, 203, 344

Humours of Portsmouth (1760), III. 332

Humours of Purgatory (Griffin, B., 1716), II. 142, 212, 333, 375, 447

Humours of St Andrews = Students

Humours of Sancho Panza = Don Quixote, the Knight of the Wonderful Countenance

Humours of Teague = Irish Evidence

Humours of the Army (Shadwell, C., 1713), II. 53, 145, 176, 354, 444; III. 116

Humours of the Compter (1717), II. 375
— = City Ramble

Humours of the Court (Bridges, R. S., 1893), V. 275
— (1732), II. 18–19, 251, 375

Humours of the Fair = Mountebank

Humours of the Forc'd Physician (1732), II. 375

Humours of the Forth = Easter Monday

Humours of the Green Room = Critic anticipated

Humours of the Militia = Hen-Peck'd Captain

Humours of the Navy (1830), IV. 480
— = (1) Fair Quaker; (2) Fair Quaker of Deal

Humours of the Road (1738), II. 375

Humours of the Times (McLaren, A., 1799), III. 284

Humours of the Town (1748), II. 375

Humours of the Turf = Newmarket

Humours of Wapping (1703), II. 375
— = (1) Constant Quaker; (2) Sailor's Wedding

Humours of Whist (1743), II. 262, 375
— = Polite Gamester

Humours of York = Northern Heiress

Humpback (Rede, W. L., 1832), IV. 480, 628
— (1843), IV. 480

Hump-backed Lover (Mathews, C. J., 1835), IV. 354, 597

Humphrey Clinker (Dibdin, T. J., 1818), IV. 96, 301

Humpty Dumpty (Harris, Sir A. H. G. and Nichols, H., 1891), V. 406
— (Jones, J. W., 1890), V. 801
— (Seaman, W., 1864), V. 815
— (1832), IV. 480
— (1875, 1876, 1882, 1883), V. 695
— (1892), V. 836
— (1898), V. 695

Humpty Dumpty Crook-a-back Dick and Jane Shore (1857), V. 836

Hunchback (Knowles, J. S., 1832), IV. 172, 339
— (1820), IV. 481
— (1831), IV. 481

Hunchback and his Horse Beelzebub (1832), IV. 481

Hunchback and the Sutler (Lewis, A.), IV. 595

Hunchback back again (Burnand, F. C., 1878), V. 291

Hunchback Doctor (1866), V. 695

Hunchbacked Brothers of Bagdad (1826), IV. 481

Hunchback of Notre Dame = (1) Bell-ringer; (2) Esmerelda

Hunchback of Paris = Duke's Daughter

Hunchback's Love = Bell-Ringer of Notre Dame

Hundred Days of Buonaparte = Champ de Mai

Hundred Eyes (1820), IV. 481

Hundred Thousand Pounds (Byron, H. J., 1866), V. 297

Hundredth Victim of the Shark's Cliff = Sightless Tyrant of Persia

Hundred Years Ago (Aveling, E. B., 1892), V. 246
— = (1) Barrington; (2) Green Bushes; (3) Life and Adventures of George Barrington

Hungarian Cottage (Kemble, C., 1813), IV. 334 [The entry on IV. 481 refers to the same play]

Hunger (Raymond, W., 1869), V. 535
— (1858), V. 695
— (1860), V. 696

Huniades (Brand, H., 1791), III. 239 [This was acted Norwich, 7/4/1791]

Hunt after Happiness = Abou Hassan

Hunted by the Law = Iron Maiden

Hunted Down (Bennett, G. W., 1881), V. 258
— (1883), V. 695
— = Two Lives of Mary Leigh

Hunted Down by Fate (1883), V. 695

Hunted Tailor's Journey to Brentford (1813), IV. 481

Hunted to Death (Cooper, H., 1867), V. 324
— = Convict

Hunted to Death by a Woman = Old Sarum

Hunter (1729), II. 375
Hunter and his Dogs = Borachio the Bandit
Hunter Chief = Haroun Alompra
Hunter of the Alps (Dimond, W., 1804), IV. 306
— (1813), IV. 481
Hunter's Bride (Brougham, J., 1841), IV. 272
— (1844), IV. 481
Hunters of Moldavia = Queen of Poland
Hunters of the Pyrenees = Fatal Ravine
Hunt for a Husband (Wooler, J. P., 1864), V. 632
Hunting a Fox (Trievnor, J. W., 1878), V. 604
— (1881), V. 695
Hunting an Heiress = Heiress Hunting
Hunting a Turtle (Selby, C.,1835), IV. 397
Hunting a Widow (1860), V. 695
Huntingdon Divertisement (1678), I. 442
Huntingdon the Disinherited = Forester King
Huntress of Arlingford = Maid Marian
Huntsman and the Spy = Bell-Ringer of St Paul's and his Daughter
Hunt the Slipper (Knapp, H., 1784), III. 279
— (Locke, F., 1887), V. 462
Huon of Bordeaux = Oberon
Hurlothrumbo (Johnson, S., 1729), II. 58, 255, 258, 268, 340
Hurly Burly (Cobb, J. and King, T., 1785), III. 244
— (Hendricks, H., 1884), V. 417
— (1792), III. 332
— (1885), V. 695
Huron Chief (Wilkins, J. H. and Anderson, J. R., 1860), V. 846
Hurricanes = Truth
Husband (À Beckett, G. A.,1844), IV. 250
— (Donne, C. E. and Burnand, F. C.), V. 782, 788
Husband and Wife (Philips, F. C. and Fendall, P., 1891), V. 522
Husband at Sight (Buckstone, J. B., 1830), IV. 273
— = Short Notice
Husband his Own Cuckold (Dryden, J., Jr., 1696), I. 28, 262, 407
Husband in Clover (Merivale, H. C., 1873), V. 487

Husband of an Hour (Falconer, E., 1857), V. 360
Husband of my Heart (Selby, C., 1850), V. 560
Husband of my Wife (1849), IV. 481
Husband on Trial (Suter, W. E., 1853), V. 587
Husbands and Wives (Pocock, I., 1817), IV. 384
Husbands, Beware! (Falconer, E., 1859), V. 360
— (1831), IV. 481
Husband's Confession = Lost Wife
Husband's Cure = Wife's Relief
Husband's First Journey = Bringing Home the Bride!
Husband's Humiliation (Hughes, A., 1896), V. 430
Husband's Mistake (1830), IV. 84, 481
Husbands Reformed = Double Marriage
Husbands Revenge = Bussy D'Ambois
Husband's Sacrifice = St Marc
Husband's Vengeance (Fitzball, E., 1857), V. 368
— = Frederick of Bavaria
Husbands, Wives and Lovers = Pic Nic
Husband! the King! and the Court Favourite! = Maria Padilla
Husband to Order (Morton, J. M., 1859), V. 496
Husband Wanted (Barnett, M., 1832), IV. 481, 628
Hush (Kenney, J., 1836), IV. 338
— (1872), V. 695
Hush-a-bye Baby on the Tree-top (Millward, C. and Gilbert, W. S., 1866), V. 489
— (1856), V. 695
Hush Money (Keith, H., 1892), V. 442
— (Dance, G., 1833), IV. 288, 579
Hussar (1821), IV. 481
Hussars (Wilson, Mrs C. B., 1831) = Petticoat Colonel = Venus in Arms, IV. 481, 628
Hussars of Hesse (Pitt, G. D., 1846), IV. 374
Hustings (1818), IV. 481
— (1847), IV. 628
Hut of La Vendée = Midnight Attack
Hut of Sarona = Alerame, the Knight of the Lion

Hut of the Danube = Fortress of Pressburg
Hut of the Red Mountains (Milner, H. M., 1827), IV. 357
Hut of Valais (1843), IV. 481
Huzza for Lisbon = Spain and Portugal
Huzza for Old England (1782), III. 332
— = Little Ben and Little Bob
Hydaspes = Idaspe Fedele
Hyde Park in an Uproar (Eyre, E. J., 1813), IV. 310
Hyder Ali (Buckstone, J. B., 1831), IV. 26, 481, 628
— (Bunn, A., 1831), IV. 481, 628
— (1832), IV. 481
Hydra, the Moon and the Daffodil (1830), IV. 481
Hydropathics (1898), V. 695
Hydropathy (Boyce, W., 1892), V. 272
Hydrophobia (Herbert, J., 1820), IV. 325
+ Hyldemoer, the Witch of the Elder-Tree (Rose, E.; R. Polytechnic, 1878; 8° [1878])
Hymen (Allen, 1764), III. 232
Hymeneal Party (1789), III. 332
Hymen's Muster Roll (Long, C., 1847), IV. 347
— (1860), V. 695
Hymen's Triumph (1737), II. 375
Hymen wins (Field, W. F., 1890), V. 366
Hypatia (Ogilvie, G. S., 1893), V. 506
Hypermnestra (Owen, R., 1703), II. 347, 442
Hypermnestra, the Girl of the Period (Sikes, F., 1869), V. 566
Hypnotist (McCullough, B., 1895), V. 468
— = Suggestion
Hypochondriac (Mathews, C. J., 1821), IV. 354, 597
— (1718), II, 133, 375, 447; III. 188
— (1825), IV. 481
— = Robust Invalid
Hypocondriac (Franklin, A., 1785), III. 261 [This was first acted Smock Alley, Dublin, 28/12/1784]
— (1771), III. 402
Hypocrisie Alamode = Stage-Beaux toss'd in a Blanket
Hypocrite (Bickerstaffe, I., 1768), III. 115, 237
— (Shadwell, T., ?1670), I. 430
— (1819), IV. 481, 628

Hypolita, Queen of the Amazons (1819), IV. 481
Hyram Balthazar (1856), V. 695

I am here = Blache of Nevers
I and my Double (Oxenford, J., 1835), IV. 367
I beg you wouldn't mention it (Suter, W. E., 1857), V. 695, 818, 836
I believe you, my busy = Red Rover
Ibrahim (Pix, M., 1696), I. 75, 424
Ibrahim the Illustrious Bassa (Settle, E., 1676), I. 86, 96, 118, 129, 428
Ibsen Christmas (Gibson, H., 1897), V. 378
Ibsen's Ghost (Barrie, J. M., 1891), V. 211, 251, 778
Icebound (Cooke, F., 1892), V. 324
Ice Fiend of the Alps = Mont Blanc
Ice King (1843), IV. 481
Iceland King (1835), IV. 481
Ice Sea and the Monster Whale of Greenland = Harpooner
Ice Witch (Buckstone, J. B., 1831), IV. 273
— (1860), V. 836
Içi on (ne) parle (pas) français (1891), V. 695
Ici on parle français (Williams, T. J., 1859), V. 625
I couldn't help it (Oxenford, J., 1862), V. 510, 809
Ida (Simpson, J. P., 1865), V. 567
Ida and Carelia = Sisters
+ Ida de Galis; a Tragedy of Powis Castle (Morgan, R. W., 8°, 1851)
Ida Lee (Young, Mrs H., 1863), V. 695, 836
Idalia (Roberts, G., 1867), V. 544
Ida May (Young, H., 1855), V. 695, 825, 836
Ida May, the Kidnapped Child (1857), V. 695
Ida of the Cottage (Soane, G., 1819) = Self-Sacrifice, IV. 481, 628
Idaspe Fedele (1710), II. 32, 34, 229, 394
I'd be a Butterfly (1868), V. 695
Ideal Husband (Wilde, O. F. O'F. W., 1895), V. 190, 192, 622
Idealist (1897), V. 695
Ideal King = Fancy Land
Idela (Simeon, Y. F., 1802), IV. 401

I did it for the best=Our Cousin German

I Dine with my Mother (Levey, R. M., 1871), v. 458

— (McLachlan, C., 1886), v. 471

Idiot and the Twin Brother=Fate and its Wonders

Idiot Boy (Oxenford, J., 1838), IV. 367

Idiot Heir (1819), IV. 481

Idiot of One-Tree Lane=Jared Swool

Idiot of the Island=Sea Lion's Den

Idiot of the Mill (Stirling, E., 1848), IV. 409

— (1859), v. 836

Idiot of the Mountain (Lee, N., Jr. and Travers, W., 1862), v. 695, 802, 836

— (Suter, W. E., 1861), v. 588

Idiot Queen (Milner, H. M., 1835), IV. 357

Idiot Son=Tower of Lochlain

Idiot, the Roue and the Miser=Lost Inheritance

Idiot Witness (Haines, J. T., 1823), IV. 322

Idle Apprentice (Marchant, F., 1865), v. 695, 805, 836

— =Jack Sheppard

Idle Jack (1883), v. 695

Idleness the Root of Evil (Suter, W. E., 1864), v. 819

Idle 'Prentice (Farnie, H. B., 1870), v. 361

Idler (Chambers, C. H., 1890), v. 187, 307

Idle Words (Fraser, J. A., 1896), v. 372

Idol (Wyndham, Sir C., 1878), v. 634

Idolaters (Hazlewood, C. H., 1862), v. 695, 796, 836

Idol of an Hour (Collingham, G. G., 1899)=Sappho, v. 317, 746, 785, 846

Idol of the King=Launcelot the Lovely

Idol's Birthday (Oxenford, J., 1838), IV. 481, 628

Idol's Eye=Indian Mutiny

Idols of the Heart (Steer, J., 1890), v. 580

Iduna (Conway, H., 1889), v. 323

— (Wilkinson, T. F., 1846), IV. 617

Idyll of New Year's Eve (Filippi, R., 1890), v. 366

Idyll of Seven Dials=Idyll of New Year's Eve

Idyll of the Closing Century (Burney, E., 1896), v. 293

If I had a Thousand a Year (Morton, J. M., 1867), v. 496

If it takes Place=When it takes Place

If I were rich (Stainforth, F., 1881), v. 578

If the Cap fits (Harrington, N. H. and Yates, E., 1859), v. 404

If the Cap fits ye, wear it=Latin, Love and War

If you don't—=Pay me

Ignacio (Maes, F., 1845), IV. 353

Ignatius (1781), III. 332

Ignes de Castro (Musgrave, T. M., 1825), IV. 365

— (Thompson, B., 1800), IV. 412

Ignoramus (Codrington, R., 1662), I. 354, 397

— (Parkhurst, F., 1662), I. 423

— (1736), II. 375

I hope I don't intrude=Mr Paul Pry

Iky le Noir (1877), v. 695

Ildamor and Zulem (1811), IV. 481

Iliad=Siege of Troy

I'll be your Second (Rodwell, G. H., 1831), IV. 395

Ill-gotten Gains (1898), v. 695

+Ill-Natured Man (8°, 1773)

I'll not have a Wife (Selby, C., 1838), IV. 398

I'll see you right (Crauford, J. R., 1878), v. 328

"I'll sleep on it"=(1) Victor Dene; (2) Victorine

I'll Stay where I am (1823)="I won't go!", IV. 481

I'll tell your Wife (Webster, N. S., 1855), v. 619

— (1855), v. 695

I'll tell you What (Inchbald, Mrs E., 1785), III. 145, 148, 150, 165, 275

Ill-treated Il Trovatore (Byron, H. J., 1863), v. 296

Illuminated Lake=Prince

Illumination (Pilon, F., 1779), III. 297

Illuminé=Urania

Illusion (Arnold, S. J., 1813), IV. 481, 628

— (Le Clercq, P., 1890), v. 452

In and out of a Punt (Esmond, H. V., 1896), v. 359

In and out of Place (Johnson, G. D., 1857), v. 695, 800, 836

In and out of Service (Douglass, J. T., 1869), v. 348

In and Out of Tune (Lawler, D., 1808), IV. 280, 342

In Another Man's Castle (Lundin, C., 1898), v. 465

Ina of Sigiswold = Ina

In a Telegraph Office (Bell, Mrs H., 1893), v. 256

In a Terrible Storm (1897), v. 695

In Black and White (Bertrand, W. C., 1880), v. 260

Inca (1819), IV. 481

In Camp (Vokes, V., 1883), v. 609

Incarcerated Victim of the Bastille = Tale of Two Cities

In Carnival Time (1890), v. 695

Incas (Thelwall, J.), III. 101, 311

Incas of Peru (1790), III. 332

Incendiaries (1859), v. 695

Incendiary (1834), IV. 481

Incestuous Marriage = Arsinoe

In Chancery (Pinero, Sir A. W., 1884), v. 525

In Charge (Cassel, H. and Duckworth, H. C., 1888), v. 305

— (1885), v. 695

Inchavogue (Cahill, W. B., 1873), v. 299

Inchcape Bell (Fitzball, E., 1828), IV. 313

In Chrysanthemum Land (Moore, H. T., 1899), v. 492

Inch Verra = Verdict of the World

Incidents of the War of 1871 = Germans and French

Incog. (?Lennox, Lord W. or Keep, W. A., 1817), IV. 345, 428, 591, 595

— = (1) Gabrielle; (2) Tom, Dick and Harry

Incognita (Burnand, F. C., 1892), v. 292

— (Rose, E., 1879), v. 550

Incognito (Aidé, H., 1888), v. 236

— (Antonini, Mlle, 1881), v. 241

"Incog!" What's in a Name (1829), IV. 481

Incompatibility of Temper (Suter, W. E.), v. 588

Inconsolables (1738), II. 375

Inconstant (Farquhar, G., 1702), I. 183; II. 135, 140, 148, 321, 435

Inconstant Villager (1814), IV. 481

Incorrigibles (1882), v. 696

Incorruptible = Citizen Robespierre

In Cupid's Court (Watson, T. M., 1885), v. 616

In Danger (Lestocq, W. and Creswell, H., 1887), v. 457

In Darker London (1894), v. 696

In Days of Old (Rose, E., 1899), v. 211, 550

In Deadly Peril (Collier, H., 1890), v. 317

Indécis (Bell, Mrs H., 1887), v. 255

Independence (Allingham, J. T., 1809) = Trustee, IV. 252, 545, 568, 641

— = Uncle Jonathan

Independent Patriot (Lynch, F., 1737), II. 68, 205, 233, 342

India in 1857 (1857), v. 696

Indian (Fenwick, J., 1800), IV. 312

Indiana (Farnie, H. B., 1886), v. 363

Indian Captive (1796), III. 332

Indian Chief (Williams, J.), III. 316

Indian Chief's Revenge = Magawiska

Indian Emperour (Dryden, J., 1665), I. 26, 36, 96, 99, 111–13, 126, 227, 234, 315, 343, 344, 345, 404; IV. 102

Indian Empress (1731), II. 375

Indian Exiles (Thompson, B., 1800), IV. 412

Indian Father (1822), IV. 481

Indian Girl (1837), IV. 482

Indian Hunters = Inscription

Indian Lovers = Nabob

Indian Maid (1823), IV. 482

— (1850), v. 696

Indian Merchant (1748), II. 451–2

Indian Mutiny (Daventry, G., 1887), v. 338

Indian Nuptials (Rochfort, 1815), IV. 482, 629

Indian Pirate's Vessel = Koeuba

Indian Prince (Perry, T. G., 1897), v. 520

Indian Princess = Pocahontas

Indian Puzzle (À Beckett, G. A.) v. 234

Indian Queen (Howard, Sir R. and Dryden, J., 1664), I. 35, 36, 39, 49, 50, 81, 83, 96, 107, 110–12, 125, 337, 354, 414

Innocents all abroad (Clarke, A. C., 1886), v. 311

Innocent Sins (Macfarren, G., 1836), IV. 350

Innocent Theft = Timon in Love

Innocent Usurper (Banks, J., 1694), I. 10, 79, 129, 167–8, 389

Inn of Death (1847), IV. 482

Inn of Glendery = Maid of Moffat Dale

Inn of Terracina = Fra Diavolo

Inn of the Three Olive Trees = Two Fathers

Inn on the Heath = Chain of Guilt

Inns and Outs = Prisoner of Rochelle

Ino (Spedding, J. J., 1869), v. 575

Inoculation (Gattie, A. W., 1892), v. 377

Inoculator (Carey, G. S., 1766), III. 242

In Olden Days (Hodgson, A. H. and Hodgson, A. C., 1890), v. 423

In Old Kentucky (Shirley, A., 1894), v. 564

In Old Madrid (Kirke, F. and Clifford, W. T., 1897), v. 445

In One Day (Fell, T. and Tompkins, G., 1896), v. 364

In One Short Year (1889), v. 696

In Place or Out of Place (1857), v. 696

In Possession (Becher, M., 1871), v. 254

— (Reece, R., 1871), v. 537

In Pursuit of a Wife (Courtney, J., 1840), IV. 482, 629

+ In Quarantine (Ware, J. R., *Dicks*)

Inquiry (1785), III. 332

Inquisition (Philips, J., 1717), II. 262, 348

— (Upton, 1880), IV. 415

Inquisition of 1650 (1816), IV. 482

Inquisitor (Andrews, J. P. and Pye, H. J., 1798), III. 64, 232

— (Holcroft, T., 1798), III. 271

— = Lupone

Ins and Outs (Lemon, M., 1840), IV. 344, 595

— = Too Late for Dinner

Inscription (Scott, J. M., 1814), IV. 482, 629

In Search of a Father (Erskine, W. and Stuart, A., 1898), v. 358

In Search of an Engagement = In Want of an Engagement

In Search of a Wife (1828), IV. 482

Inseparables = Gamblers

In Sight of St Paul' (Vane, S., 1896), v. 606

Insignificants (Bacon, P., 1757), III. 235

In Slavery's Days (1898), v. 696

Insolvent (Hill, A., 1758), II. 438; III. 113, 268

In Spite of All (Anderson, G., 1898), v. 240

In Spite of Society (Dickinson, C. H., 1898), v. 344

In Statu Quo! (Dance, G., 1835), IV. 482, 629

Institute Abroad (Stalman, A. and Cargill, G. B., 1897), v. 578

Institution of the Garter (Garrick, D., 1771), III. 263

Institution of the Order of the Garter (West, G., 1742), II. 364

In Strict Confidence (Heriot, P., 1893), v. 419

Instrument of Torture (1844), IV. 482

In Summer Days (Blatchford, R., 1891), v. 265

In Sunny Spain (Dearlove, W. H. and Woodroffe, P., 1896), v. 340

Insurance Money (Righton, E., 1894), v. 543

Insured at Lloyd's (Palmer, T. A., 1870), v. 512

Insuring his Life (Brierley, B., 1875), v. 275

In Taunton Vale = Taunton Vale

Integrity (1801), IV. 482

Integrity Proved = Integrity

Intemperance (Hazleton, F., 1879), v. 412

— (1879), v. 696

Interesting Case (1899), v. 696

Interior Cabinet laid open = Junto

Interlude (Clifford, Mrs W. K. and Pollock, W. H., 1893), v. 314

International Dog Show (1863), v. 696

International of 1862 (1862), v. 696

International Visits (Addison, H. R., 1850), v. 235

Interrupted Harmony = Quartette

Interrupted Honeymoon (Peile, F. K. 1898), v. 518

Interrupted Sacrifice (1826), IV. 482 [This seems to be the same as The Oracle, IV. 515]

Interrupted Wedding (1885), v. 696

Invitation à la Mode (1791), III. 332

Invitation to the Nigger Ball = Somebody's in the House with Dinah

Invulnerable = Infernal Secret

In Want of an Engagement (Ganthony, N., 1891), V. 375

In Want of a Wife (Toplis, G. A., 1885), V. 600

Iolanthe (Gilbert, W. S., 1882), V. 144, 380

— (Wills, W. G., 1880), V. 627

Ion (Cooper, F. F., 1836), IV. 283

— (Talfourd, T. N., 1836), IV. 177, 410

— (1890), V. 696

I.O.U. (Grover, J. H., 1879), V. 396

— (Hawtrey, G. P., 1887), V. 410

— (1832), IV. 482

— (1873), V. 696

— = Shylock and Co.

I.O.U. £7. 16s. 6d. (1831), IV. 482

Iphigenia (Dennis, J., 1699), I. 402; II. 18, 63, 85, 317

— (Hull, T., 1778), III. 86, 274

Iphigenia at Delphi (Gurney, A. T., 1855), V. 397

Iphigenia in Aulis (Calcraft, J. W., 1846), IV. 575

— (Wodhull, M., 1786), III. 316

— (1768), III. 332

— = Achilles

Iphigenia in Tauris (Swanwick, C., 1850), V. 819

— (1840), IV. 482

Iphigenia of Tauris (Taylor, W., 1793), III. 63, 311, 396

Iran Safferi (1854), V. 696

I promise to pay = Call again to-morrow

Ireland (Thompson, C. P., 1831), IV. 482, 629

Ireland as it is (Amherst, J. H.), IV. 254, 568; V. 836

— (1856), V. 696, 836

Ireland as it was = Ireland as it is

Ireland by Night and Day = Norah

Ireland in 1798 = White Boys

Ireland Preserv'd (Michelburne, J., 1705), II. 344

Irena (1664), I. 442

Irene (Farnie, H. B., 1880), V. 362, 791

— (Goring, C., 1708), II. 80, 333

Irene (Johnson, S., 1749), I. 142; II. 59, 94–5, 340, 417; IV. 213

Irene, the Greek Girl of Janina (1859), V. 696

Irish Absentee (Hyde, J. W., 1838), IV. 590

— (Macarthy, 1836), IV. 596

Irish Ambassador (Kenney, J., 1831), IV. 337

Irish Aristocracy (1884), V. 697

— (1886), V. 697

Irish Assurance and Yankee Modesty (Williams, Mrs B., 1856), V. 624

Irish Astrologer = Meet me by Moonlight

Irish Attorney (Bernard, W. B., 1840), IV. 266

Irish Baronet (1847), IV. 482

Irish Barrister (1838), IV. 483

— = Barber Barrister

Irish Belle (1873), V. 697

Irish Boy = Andy Blake

Irish Boy and the Gipsy Girl = Carlo Leoni

Irish Brigade = King O'Neil

Irish Cake (1788), III. 332

Irish Chief = (1) Patriot King; (2) Sir Arthur

+ Irish Courtship; or, The Lasses of Leixlip (Dibdin, C. I. M., R.A., 1797–8)

Irish Crispin (1818), IV. 483

Irish Darby in Doncaster (1792), III. 402

Irish Darby in Leeds (1792), III. 402

Irish Diamond (1850), V. 697

— = Andy Blake

Irish Diploma = Irish Doctor

Irish Doctor (Wood, G. A. F., 1844), IV. 422

Irish Dragoon (Selby, C., 1845), IV. 399

Irish Elopement (1887), V. 697

Irish Emigrant (1860), V. 697 [This apparently was Temptation: or, The Irish Emigrant, by J. Brougham, printed in *French's American Theatre*]

Irish Engagement (Watts, W., 1848), IV. 417, 616

— (1857), V. 697

Irish Evidence (?1682), I. 446

Irish Expedition = Royal Voyage

Irish Eyes (Douglas, Sir G., 1889), V. 347

Irish Fidelity = (1) Aileen Asthore; (2) Round Tower

Irish Fine Lady (Macklin, C., 1767), III. 284

Irish Footman (Clements, A., 1872), V. 314

Irish Gentleman (Murray, D. C. and Shine, J. L., 1897), V. 500

— (Raymond, R. J., 1834), IV. 483, 629

Irish Girl (McLaren, A., 1813), IV. 351

— (Ryan, R., 1830), IV. 483, 629

— (1819), IV. 483

Irish Heiress (Boucicault, D., 1842), IV. 269

— (1832), IV. 483

Irish Hospitality (Shadwell, C., 1717), II. 183, 354 [This was acted Smock Alley, Dublin, late in 1717]

— (1766), III. 332

Irish Immigrant (Brougham, J., 1854), V. 280

Irish Intrigue (Doyle, T. F., 1873), V. 350

Irish Legacy (Arnold, S. J., 1797) = Legacy, III. 234, 377

Irish Life (Creamer, A. and Downey, L. T., 1888), V. 330

Irish Lion (Buckstone, J. B., 1838), IV. 275, 575

Irish Loyalty (1821), IV. 483

Irishman (Whitbread, J. W., 1889), V. 620

Irishman Bothered = Mistake upon Mistake

Irishman in all his Glory = Sprig of Shillelah

Irishman in Bagdad = Ninth Statue

Irishman in Distress = Committee

Irishman in England = Phantoms

Irishman in France = British Carpenter

Irishman in India = Surooz Seeing

Irishman in Italy (1813), IV. 483

— = False and True

Irishman in London (Macready, W., 1792), III. 285, 391

Irishman in Naples (1822), IV. 483

Irishman in Spain (Stuart, C., 1791), III. 310, 396

Irishman in Turkey = Middle Dish

Irishman in Windsor (1826), IV. 483

Irishman's Dream (1839), IV. 483

Irishman's Fortune (1830), IV. 483

Irishman's Fortune = Born to Good Luck

Irishman's Frolics = Money at a Pinch

Irishman's Heart (Levey, J. C., 1879), V. 458

Irishman's Home (1833), IV. 483

— (1875), V. 697

Irishman's Love = Teddy O'Connor

Irishman's Policy (Richardson, H., 1875), V. 543

Irish Mimic (O'Keeffe, J., 1795) = Lounge at Brighton, III. 294, 393

Irish Minstrel (Court, F. H., 1867), V. 697, 786, 836

— (1889), V. 697

Irish Molly (+Pitt, G. D., 1845), IV. 483 [This is the same as The Primrose of Ireland, see IV. 374]

Irish Nieces = All at Home

Irish Nigger (Rede, W. L., 1841), IV. 483, 629

Irish Patriot = Pike O'Callaghan

Irish Poleander (1823), IV. 483

Irish Post (Planché, J. R., 1846), IV. 382

Irish Priest (Ellis, B., 1890), V. 357

Irish Promotion (1791), III. 332 [A newspaper notice declares this was by "Counsellor Shannon"]

Irish Reapers (1818), IV. 483

Irish Sharebroker = Railway Mania

Irish Tar (Oulton, W. C., 1797), III. 296

Irish Taylors (1791), III. 332

Irish Tiger (Morton, J. M., 1846), IV. 362

Irish Traveller = False Friendship

Irish Tutor (Butler, R., 1822), IV. 277, 575

Irish Valet = More Blunders than One

Irish Wedding = Dermot and Kathlane

Irish Widow (Garrick, D., 1772), III. 117, 263

— (1821), IV. 483

Irish Wife (1832), IV. 483

Irish Witch (Amherst, J. H.), IV. 254

Irishwoman (Clarke, Lady O., 1819), IV. 280

Irma (Bonawitz, J. H., 1885), V. 267, 779

Irmengarda (Beatty-Kingston, W., 1892), V. 254

Iron Arm (Suter, W. E., 1857), V. 697, 818, 836

Iron before Gold (Osborne, C., 1872), v. 508

Iron Casket (1868), v. 697

— = Hans of Iceland

Iron Chain (1895), v. 697

Iron Chest (Colman, G., the Younger, 1796), III. 41, 43, 72, 104–5, 247–8, 367

— (1811), IV. 483

Ironclad Warriors and the Little Tug of War = Ulysses

Iron Clasp (Townsend, W. T., 1862), v. 697, 821

Iron Collar (Amherst, J. H., 1832), IV. 254

— = Death by the Law

Iron Gates (Henderson, J., 1883), v. 416

Iron Grave = Waiting for Death

Iron Grip (James, C. S., 1849), IV. 330

Iron Hand (Haines, J. T., 1841), IV. 323, 483, 629

Iron Hand and Velvet Glove = Secret Society

Iron Hands (Pitt, H. M., 1873), v. 526

Iron Heart (1830), IV. 483

Iron Latch Farm (Mackay, H., 1865), v. 697, 805, 836

Iron Maiden (Wilkinson, M. and Hallatt, W. H., 1896), v. 623

Iron Mask = Queen's Secret

Iron Masque = Island of St Marguerite

Iron Master (Pinero, Sir A. W., 1884), v. 525

Iron Master of Samarkand by Oxus = Timour the Tartar

Iron Road (1899), v. 697

Iron Statue (1868), v. 697

Iron Tower (Astley, P., Jr., 1801), IV. 256

Iron True (Sennett, T., 1886), v. 561

Iroquis (1820), IV. 483

— (1823), IV. 483

Irregular Rum 'un = F.M. Julius Caesar

Irresistibles (Moncrieff, W. T., 1828), IV. 359

— (1857), v. 697

Irvingmania (1877), v. 697

Isaac Abroad (Plowman, T. F., 1878), v. 528

Isaac Comnenus (Taylor, H., 1827), IV. 410

Isaac of York (Plowman, T. F., 1871), v. 528

— = (1) Isaac Abroad; (2) Ivanhoe

Isaac the Jew of York = Ivanhoe

Isabel (Cape, F., 1874), v. 302

Isabel Bertrand (1846), IV. 483

Isabel D'Arville (1895), v. 697

Isabella (Garrick, D., 1757), III. 58, 262

— (Kemble, J. P., 1814), IV. 335

Isabelle (Buckstone, J. B., 1834), IV. 274

Isabelle de Montral (1834), IV. 483

Isabel that was a Belle = East Lynne

Isalda (Horner, F., 1890), v. 427

Isaure (Webster, B. N., 1832), IV. 483, 616, 629

— (1833), IV. 483

Is Brown at Home? (De Frece, M., 1873), v. 341

Is he a Christian? (Connynghame, F. L. and Price, F., 1898), v. 320

Is He Alive? (1818), IV. 483

Is He a Prince? (Greffulhe, 1809) = German Blunder, IV. 321, 467, 586, 626

Is He Dead? (1847), IV. 629

Is He Jealous? (Beazley, S., Jr., 1816), IV. 263, 571

— (1820), IV. 483

Is his Appointment Pucka? = Dark Bungalow

Ishnabrogue (1891), v. 697

Isidore and Merida (Dimond, W., 1827), IV. 483, 629

Is it a Spectre? = Dunoir the Base

Is it a Wedding? (1800), IV. 483

Is it a Woman? (Abbott, W., 1833), IV. 483, 629

Is it He or his Brother = Twins

Is it the King? (Greenwood, T. L., 1861), v. 697, 836

Island (Jerrold, D. W., 1823), IV. 331, 483, 590, 629

Island Ape = (1) Bibboo; (2) Juan Fernandez

Islanders (Byrne, O., 1816), IV. 483, 629

— (Dibdin, C., 1780), III. 119, 255, 381

Island Home (Calvert, C., 1861), v. 697, 783, 837

Island Nymph (Barrez, 1846), IV. 483

Island of Bachelors (Reece, R., 1874), v. 538, 812

Island of Calypso = Telemachus
Island of Darkness (1815), IV. 484
Island of Jewels (Planché, J. R., 1849), IV. 383, 605
Island of Nowpartickeler Folley = Girls of the Period
Island of Owhyhee = Captain Cook
Island of St Marguerite (St John, J., 1789), III. 304, 395
Island of Silver Store (1858), V. 697
Island of Slaves (Clive, C., 1761), III. 118, 243, 379
Island of Trances and the Land of Flowers (1852), V. 697
Island of Tranquil Delights = Invisible Prince
Island Princess (Motteux, P. A., 1699), I. 55, 426; II. 29–30, 132, 134, 345
— (Tate, N., 1687), I. 338, 434
— (1669), I. 40, 344, 345, 351, 442
Island Queens (Banks, J., 1684), I. 53, 79, 166–7, 389
Is Law Justice? = Iron Maiden
Isle of Love = St Helena
Isle of Mull (McLaren, A., 1820), IV. 352
Isle of Palms (Wilson, 1812), IV. 422
Isle of St Tropez (Williams, M. and Burnand, F. C., 1860), V. 624, 824
Isle of the Genii = Storm
Isle of Utopia (St Clare, G., 1892), V. 554
Is Life worth living? (Scudamore, F. A., 1887), V. 559
Islington (Osman, W. R., 1867), V. 508
Islington in Olden Time = Clerke's Well
Islington in the Olden Time = St John's Priory
Islington Spa = Spleen
Islington Stage = Double X.X.
Is Madame at Home? (Bell, M., 1887), V. 256
Is Marriage a Failure? (Collier, H. and Dudley, F. H., 1888), V. 317
Isn't it a Duck? (Barnett, M., 1849), IV. 484, 629
Isofel (Lawrence, E., 1887), V. 451
Isolate and the Ape (Dibdin, C. I. M., 1826), IV. 296
Isolda (Richards, A. B., 1848), IV. 394

Isoline of Bavaria = Bavarian Girl
Israel in Egypt (1739), II. 394
Israelites (Smollett, T. G., 1785), III. 308
Israelites in Egypt (Lacy, M. R., 1833), IV. 484, 629
Is she a Woman? (Collier, W., 1835), IV. 281
Is she guilty? (Faucquez, A., 1877), V. 364
Is she his Daughter? (Murray, G. and Hipkins, T. H., 1861), V. 798, 808
Is She his Wife? (Dickens, C., 1837), IV. 146–7, 305
Is She Mad? = Delusion
Italian Boys (1833), IV. 484
Italian Bravo (1861), V. 697
Italian Brigand = Nameless
Italian Captain (1847), IV. 629
Italian Conspiracy = Patriot
Italian Flower Girl (1817), IV. 484
Italian Foresters = Minstrel
Italian Gamester (Barrett, C. F., 1810), IV. 484
— = Wife and Mistress
Italian Husband (Eyre, E. J., 1812) = Look at Home, IV. 484, 629
— (Lewis, E., 1754), III. 281
— (Ravenscroft, E., 1697), I. 169–70, 426
— (1795), III. 332
Italian Jealousy (1729), II. 376
Italian Love = Ravenna
Italian Lover (Phillips, F. L., 1846), IV. 372
— = Julia
Italian Monk (Boaden, J., 1797), III. 72, 238
Italian Nuptials = Corsair
Italian Patriot = Patriot
Italian Romance (Darwin, P., 1889), V. 337
Italians (Bucke, C., 1819), IV. 68, 78, 200, 272
Italian Shadows (1720), II. 376
Italians in Algiers (1844), IV. 484, 629
Italian Sister (1829), IV. 484
Italian's Revenge = Hunted Down
Italian Traitors (1830), IV. 484
Italian Villagers (Hoare, P., 1797), III. 197, 270
Italian Wanderers = Minstrel Boy

Italian Wife (Dibdin, T. J., 1816), IV. 300
— (Doubleday, T., 1823), IV. 582
— (1817), IV. 484
— (1855), V. 697
— (1858), V. 697
— = Fazio
It Cannot Be = Sir Courtly Nice
It is all a Farce = Modern Comedy
It is a long lane that has no turning = Released Convict
It is Fate = Sensualist
It is Justice (Zech, M., 1890), V. 637
It is never too late to learn (1864), V. 697
It is the Devil! = Dominique
It might have been worse = My Lord and my Lady
It must be true, 'twas in the papers (1862), V. 697
It never rains but it pours (Meritt, P., 1877), V. 486
— (1862), V. 697
It runs in the Family (1855), V. 697
It's All a Mistake (Farrell, J., 1819), IV. 311
— = (1) Newspaper Blunders; (2) Q.E.D.
It's all through the Lad (1885), V. 697
It's All Very Well Mr Ferguson, But You Don't Sleep Here (Suter, W., 1837), IV. 613
It's a Long Lane that has no Turning (Suter, W. E., 1860), V. 819 [This is presumably the original form of The Test of Truth, see v. 588]
It's an Ill Wind that blows Nobody Good (Oxenford, J., 1860), V. 697, 809, 837
It's better late than never = Better late than never
It's Fifty Years Since = Irish Attorney
It Should have come Sooner (Hawling, F., 1723), II. 335
Its Mother's Pet (1848), IV. 629
It's never too late to mend (Reade, C., 1864), V. 110, 536
— (Young, H., 1860), V. 825
— (1861), V. 837
It's never too late to repent (Lewis, G., 1875), V. 459

It's only my Aunt (Bartholomew, Mrs A. C. V., 1849), IV. 484, 571
It's Only Round the Corner = Harmony Restored
It's Two to One = No Misses
It's Well if it Takes = More Ways than One
It was a Dream (Field, J., 1890), V. 697, 792, 837
It was Right at the Last (Horde, T., 1787), III. 115, 273
Ivan (Sotheby, W., 1816), IV. 405
Ivan Daniloff (Planché, Mrs J. R., 1835), IV. 383
Ivan de Bessenvelt (Phillips, F. L., 1845), IV. 372
Ivanhoe (Beazley, S., Jr., 1820), IV. 93, 264
— (Bunn, A., 1820), IV. 93, 484, 629
— (Calcraft, J. W., 1823), IV. 93, 278
— (Cooper, F. F., 1859) = Lists of Ashby, V. 80, 697, 786, 837
— (Cowie, R., 1875), V. 80, 327
— (Dibdin, T. J., 1820), IV. 93, 302
— (Edgar, R. H., 1871), V. 80, 354
— (Jones, R.), IV. 93, 591
— (Moncrieff, W. T., 1820), IV. 93, 358, 484, 600, 629
— (Murray, W. H., 1824), IV. 93, 345
— (Stevens, E., 1896), V. 80, 583
— (Sturgis, J., 1891), V. 80, 586
— (Suter, W. E., 1863), V. 80, 697, 837
— (1820) IV. 93, 484
— (1872), V. 80, 697
Ivanhoe in accordance with the Spirit of the Times (Byron, H. J., 1862), V. 80, 296
Ivanhoe settled and Rebecca righted = Isaac Abroad
Ivan of the Mask (Lynch, T. J., 1826), IV. 484, 629
Ivan the Armourer = Czarina
Ivan the Terrible (1866), V. 697
Ivar (1785), III. 332
I've beat all three (Douglass, J. T., 1861), V. 697, 788, 837
I've been roaming = Scapegrace
I've eaten my Friend (Bridgeman, J. V., 1851), V. 274
I've left my Place = I've lost my Place
I've lost my Place (1833), IV. 484
I've quite forgot = Green Dragon

Iver and Hengo (Rees, T. D., 1795),
    III. 301
Ivers Dean (Young, Sir C. L. and
    Howard, B., 1877), IV. 635
I've seen a Harem = Morocco Bound
I've taken a House (Grain, R. C., 1889),
    V. 387
I've written to Browne (Williams, T. J.,
    1859), V. 625
Ivor (Hitchener, W. H., 1808), IV. 325
Ivory Tablets (1898), V. 697
Ivy (Melford, M., 1887), V. 484
— (1894), V. 697
Ivy Hall (Oxenford, J., 1859), V. 509
+ Ivy Hall, Richmond (Emson, F. E.,
    8°, 1873)
Iwan (Fitzball, E., 1823), IV. 484, 629
Iwanowna (Dibdin, C. I. M., 1816), IV.
    294
"I want my Ma" = Sham Captain
I will be a Duchess (Buckstone, J. B.,
    1839), IV. 275
I will have an Uncle (Dance, C., 1836),
    IV. 484, 629
I will have a Wife! (Planché, J. R.,
    1823), IV. 377
I will if you will (Bruton, J., 1860), V.
    284
I wish you may get it (1825), IV. 484
I won't go! (1823) = I'll stay where I
    am, IV. 484, 629
Ixion (Burnand, F. C., 1863), V. 69, 288
— (Ravenscroft, E., 1697), I. 426
Ixion Rewheeled (Burnand, F. C.,
    1874), V. 290
Izaak Walton (Dance, C., 1839), IV. 289

Jabez North = Dark Deeds
Jacintha (1821), IV. 484
Jack (Beckett, Mrs H., 1886), V. 254
— (Rogerson, H., 1898), V. 549
— (1879), V. 697
— (1882), V. 697
— (1884), V. 697
Jackal (Aveling, E. B., 1889), V. 246
— = Only Way
Jack and his Nine Wives (1840), IV. 484
Jack and Jack's Brother (Johnstone,
    J. B., 1855), V. 438
— = Gipsey Farmer
Jack and Jill (Blanchard, E. L., 1854),
    V. 263, 779

Jack and Jill (Blanchard, E. L., 1872),
    V. 264
— (Clements, A. and Soutar, R., 1874),
    V. 314
— (Conquest, G. and Spry, H., 1898),
    V. 323
— (Green, F. W., 1876), V. 390
— (Green, F. W., 1879), V. 391
— ("Marcus", 1882), V. 476
— (Wade, W., 1893), V. 698, 822, 837
— (1812), IV. 484
— (1854), V. 698
— (1876, 1878), V. 697
— (1878, 1879, 1883, 1884, 1889, 1893,
    1897), V. 698
— = (1) Seaweed Hall; (2) Toto and
    Sata
Jack and Jill and the Sleeping Beauty
    (Soutar, R., 1868), V. 575
Jack and Jill and the Well on the Hill
    (Conquest, G. and Spry, H., 1883),
    V. 322
Jack and Jill Up-to-date (1899), V. 698
Jack and the Beanstalk (Blanchard,
    E. L., 1844), IV. 268
— (Blanchard, E. L., 1859), V. 698, 779,
    837
— (Conquest, G. and Spry, H., 1886),
    V. 322
— (Dibdin, C. I. M. 1819), IV. 294
— (Green, F. W., 1873), V. 390
— (Green, F. W., 1875), V. 390
— (Green, F. W., 1878), V. 391
— (Green, F. W., 1884), V. 391
— (Green, F. W. and Clay, T. L.,
    1880), V. 391
— (Hersee, H. and Lennard, H., 1887),
    V. 420
+ — (Hodson, W., printed in *Juvenile
    Plays for Home Performance*
    (*French*))
— (Lennard, H., 1884), V. 455
— (Lennard, H., 1893), V. 456
— (McLelland, H. F., 1893), V. 468
— (McLelland, H. F., 1897), V. 468
— (Millward, C., 1872), V. 489
— (Millward, C., 1877), V. 489
— (Nichols, H. and Harris, Sir A.,
    1889), V. 504
— (Thorne, G., 1893), V. 599
— (Thorne, G. and Palmer, F. G.,
    1886), V. 598

Jack Sheppard, the Housebreaker (Moncrieff, W. T., 1825), IV. 359

Jackson's Boy (Greet, D. V., 1891), v. 393

Jack Spaniard caught in a Trap = Harlequin's Frolics

Jack Spaniard Hit = Harlequin Happy

Jack Sprat, the Three Blind Mice, Big A Little a, Bouncer's B, The Cat's in the Cupboard and She can't See (Greenwood, T. L., 1864) = Harlequin Jack Sprat, 1864), v. 689, 699, 835, 837

Jack's Return (1895), v. 699

Jack's Return from Canton (1858), v. 699

Jack Stedfast (Pitt, C., 1869), v. 526

Jack's the Boy (1897), v. 699

Jack's the Lad = Garland of Love

Jack Straw King Munkey Punkey (1865), v. 699

Jack Straw's Castle (1835), IV. 485

Jack Tar = (1) Great Temptation; (2) River of Life

Jack the Giant Killer (Allen, O., 1885), v. 239

— (Blanchard, E. L., 1853), v. 699, 779, 837

— (Byron, H. J., 1859), v. 295

— (Byron, H. J., 1878), v. 299

— (Dibdin, C. I. M., 1803), IV. 290, 485, 580, 629

— (Douglass, T. J., 1869), v. 699, 788, 837

— (Green, F. W., 1875), v. 390

— (Green, F. W. and Didcot, H. J., 1882), v. 391

— (Hall, F., 1878), v. 399

— (Roe, J. E., 1865), v. 814

— (Rogers, T. S., 1897), v. 549

— (Soutar, R., 1879), v. 575

— (Tully, J., 1882), v. 699, 822, 837

— (1730), II. 376

— (1810, 1846), IV. 485

— (1847), IV. 629

— (1853, 1859), v. 699

— (1860, 1861), v. 837

— (1861, 1869), v. 699

— (1869), v. 837

— (1872, 1874, 1875, 1876, 1878, 1879, 1880, 1881, 1882, 1883, 1884, 1895), v. 699

Jack the Giant Killer and the Butterfly Queen (French, H. P., 1887), v. 373

Jack the Giant Killer, Jack and the Beanstalk, Merry Jill, and the Gnome Fairies of Number Nip (Lemon, H., 1869), v. 454

Jack the Gyant Queller (Brooke, H., 1749), II. 300

Jack the Painter (1840), IV. 629

Jack, the Pretty Princess, the Wicked Ogre, and the Seven Champions of Christendom (1893), v. 699

Jack, the Tale of a Tramp (1877), v. 699

Jack Union and his Dog Quid (1854), v. 699

Jack the Valiant (Marchant, F., 1877), v. 476

Jack White's Trial (Parr, F. C. W., 1883), v. 514

Jacky Jingle (Lee, N., 1841), IV. 594

Jacob Faithful (Haines, J. T., 1834), IV. 322

— (Pitt, G. D., 1834), IV. 485, 629

— (1841), IV. 485

Jacobi (Hanray, L., 1895), v. 403

Jacobite (Planché, J. R., 1847), IV. 180, 382, 605

Jacobite and the Man of Warsman = Pride and its Fall

Jacobites in 1745 = Jack's Alive

Jacob's Ramble (1796) = Ramble to Bath, III. 332, 402, 404

Jacqueline (Harvey, F., 1874), v. 408

Jacqueline Doucette (1855), v. 699

Jacques Strop (Selby, C., 1838), IV. 398

Jagger's Trust (1899), v. 699

Jailor's Daughter = Letter Box

Jaloux Puni (Egville, J. d', 1793), III. 258

James I of Scotland (1837), IV. 485

— = Regicide

James III (Woodley, W., 1825), IV. 618

James III, King of Scotland (1820), IV. 485

James VI (White, J., 1845, 1852), v. 620

James Crichton of Clunie and Catherine de Medicis (1838), IV. 485

James Stuart, King of the Commons (1864), v. 699

James Lawson (Pitt, G. D., 1841), IV. 604

Jamie and Bess (Shirrefs, A., 1787), III. 307

Jamie of Aberdeen (1815), IV. 485

Jan Ben Jan (Dibdin, C. I. M., 1807), IV. 291

Janderkins (1874), V. 699

Jane (Nichols, H. and Lestocq, W., 1890), V. 504

Jane Annie (Barrie, J. M. and Doyle, A. C., 1893), V. 251

Jane Eyre (Brougham, J., 1848), IV. 272
— (Brougham, J., 1856), V. 80, 281
— (Paul, T. H., 1879), V. 80, 516
— (Wills, W. G., 1882), V. 80, 627
— (1877), V. 699
— = Poor Relations

Jane Jenkins (À Beckett, G. A., 1844), IV. 250

Jane Lomax (Stirling, E., 1839), IV. 406

Jane of Flanders (1801), IV. 485

Jane of Liverpool (1862), V. 837

Jane of Pentonville (Dibdin, T. J., ?1796), III. 382

Jane of Primrose Hill = Brothers' Duel

Jane of the Hatchet (Almar, G., 1840), IV. 253
— (1877), V. 699

Jane Paul (Fitzball, E., 1842), IV. 316

Jane Seton (Nicholson, S., 1870), V. 504
— (1878), V. 699

Jane Shore (Boulding, J. W. and Palgrave, R., 1885), V. 270
— (Jones, J. W., 1880), V. 440
— (Kemble, J. P., 1815), IV. 335
— (Rowe, N., 1714), II. 51, 57, 58, 59, 61, 70, 100–1, 352, 443
— (Wills, W. G., 1875), V. 627
— (1833), IV. 485
— (1894), V. 699
— (1895), V. 700

Jane, the Licensed Victualler's Daughter (Hart, J. P.), IV. 588

Janet O'Brien (Robinson, N., 1869), V. 547

Janet Pride (Boucicault, D., 1854), V. 268

Janet's Ruse (1872), V. 700

Japanese Girl (Fryers, A., 1897), V. 374

Japanese Idyll (1897), V. 700

Japanese Lamp (Dorisi, L., 1897), V. 347

Japanese Wife = Adzuma

Japhet in Search of a Father (Pitt, G. D., 1845), IV. 374

Japs (Paulton, H. and Tedde, M., 1885), V. 517

Jared Swool (Lancaster, E. R., 1843), IV. 593

Jarvis, the Honest Man (Pitt, G. D., 1846), IV. 374, 485, 604, 629
— (1854), V. 700

Jason (Glover, R., 1799), III. 265

Jason and Medæa (1747), II. 376

Jason and Medea (1791), III. 402
— (1878), V. 700

Jason et Medea (Wooler, J. P., 1851), V. 632

Jason in Colchis, and Medea in Corinth = Golden Fleece

Jasper Langton = Duel in the Dark

Jasper Roseblade (1859), V. 700

Jasper's Revenge (Miller, W. F., 1891), V. 489

Jasper's Uncle (1895), V. 700

Jaunty Jane Shore (Henry, R., 1894), V. 418

Java (Dibdin, T. J., 1812), IV. 299

Jealous Bridegroom = Forc'd Marriage

Jealous Clown (Gataker, T., 1730), II. 26, 237, 245, 330

Jealous Doctor (Rich, J., 1717), II. 133, 253, 376, 443

Jealous Farmer Deceiv'd (1739), II. 376

Jealous Husband (1732), II. 376
— (1777), III. 113–14, 333
— (1839), IV. 485
— = Lost Lover

Jealous Husband Outwitted (1732), II. 376

Jealous Husbands = Rambling Justice

Jealous in Honour (Broke, B., 1893), V. 276

Jealous Lover cured (1788), III. 333

Jealous Mistake (Fitzgerald, S. J. A., 1899), V. 369

Jealous Moth = Butterfly Ball

Jealous of the Past (Chandos, A., 1885), V. 307

Jealous on All Sides (Beazley, S., Jr., 1818), IV. 263

Jealous Queen = (1) Sultana; (2) Vanquish'd Love

Jealous Taylor (1731), II. 376

Jealous Wife (Colman, G., 1761), III. 51, 167–8, 182, 183, 210, 245
Jealousy (Dearlove, W. H., 1891), v. 340
— (Reade, C., 1878), v. 536
— (Shannon, C. and Shannon, F. S., 1838), IV. 400
— (1851), v. 700
— = Countess and the Dancer
Jealousy Deceived (1730), II. 376
Jealous Yeoman Defeated = Harlequin's Contrivances
Jealousy Out-witted = Troubadours
Jeames (Burnand, F. C., 1878), v. 291
Jeames the Railroad Footman (1845), IV. 485
Jean (Coveney, G. H., 1878), v. 326
— (1882), v. 700
Jean de Paris (Arnold, S. J., 1814), IV. 256, 569
— (1830), IV. 485
Jean Hennuyer (1773), III. 333
Jeanie Deans (Bennett, J., 1894), v. 258
Jean Mayeux (De la Bretesche, B., 1894), v. 341
Jeanne Dubarry (Herman, H., 1875), v. 419
Jeanne, Jeannette and Jeanneton (Reece, R., 1881), v. 539, 813
Jeannette (1898), v. 700
Jeannette and Jeannot (Stirling, E., 1848), IV. 409
Jeannette et Jeannot (1848), IV. 485
Jeannette's Wedding (Buckingham, L. S. and Harris, A. G., 1861), v. 286, 781
Jeannie Deans (Hazlewood, C. H., 1862), v. 700, 796, 837
— (1863), v. 700
Jeannie of Midlothian (1863), v. 700
Jean the Disgraced = Roger-le-Honte
Jedbury Junior (Ryley, M. L., 1895), v. 554
Jeffery the Seaman (1830), IV. 485
Jeffreys (Spicer, H., 1846) = Judge Jeffreys, IV. 405, 485, 629
Jehu (1779), III. 333
Jemmy for Ever (Dibdin, T. J., 1827), IV. 305
Jenkinses (Planché, J. R., 1830), IV. 379
Jenkins Love-Course (Kirkman, F., 1662), I. 417

Jenny Foster, the Sailor's Child (Hazlewood, C. H., 1855), v. 412
Jenny Jones (Cooper, F. F., 1838), IV. 283
Jenny Lind (1847), IV. 485
Jenny Lind at Last (Reach, A. B., 1847), IV. 485, 629
Jenny Lind in New York = More Ethiopians
Jenny l'ouvrière (1854), v. 700
Jenny's Whim (O'Keeffe, J., 1794), III. 294
Jenny the Barber (Barrett, W., 1891), v. 250
Jenny Vernon (Young, Mrs H., 1862), v. 825
Jenny Wren (1880), v. 700
Jephtha (Edison, J. S., 1863), v. 354
— (Free, J., 1752), III. 357, 384
— (Hoadly, B., 1737), II. 395, 439
— (Salmon, Mrs, 1846), IV. 609
Jephthah's Daughter (Wilson, Mrs A., 1783), III. 316
Jephtha's Rash Vow, I. 446; II. 376
Jephtha's Vow (Lacy, T. H.), IV. 593
Jericho Jack, the Foremast Man (Wilkins, J. H., 1861), v. 700, 823, 837
Jerry Abershaw (Hazlewood, C. H., 1855), v. 700, 796, 837
— (Lee, N., 1844), IV. 594
Jerry and a Sunbeam (Hamilton, C., 1898), v. 401
Jerry Builder (Melford, M., 1892), v. 484
— (1899), v. 700
Jerry-Builder Solness (Bell, Mrs H., 1893), v. 79, 256
Jerry's Wagers (Haywell, F., 1874), v. 412
Jersey Girl (Pitt, G. D., 1835), IV. 372
Jerusalem Delivered = Crusaders
Jesmond Dene (1892), v. 700
Jess (Lawrence, E. and Bisgood, J. J., 1890), v. 451
— (1887), v. 700
Jessamy's Courtship (Hazlewood, C. H., 1875), v. 415
Jesse James, the Bandit King (1895), v. 700
Jessie Ashton (Sawyer, W., 1863), v. 557
— (Young, Mrs H., 1862), v. 700, 825, 837

251

Jew's Daughter (Stirling, E., 1857), v. 584
— = Ivanhoe
Jew's Eye (Lane-Fox, F., 1889), v. 448
Jew's Revenge (Duncan, J., 1844), IV. 308
Jews' Revolt = Hebrew Husband
Jew, the Gamester, the Seducer, the Murderer and the Thief = Scenes in London
Jezebel (Boucicault, D., 1870), v. 269
Jezebel's Husband (Dale, B., 1893), v. 332
Jibbenainosay (Rayner, R., 1858), v. 700, 812, 837
Jilt (Boucicault, D., 1885), v. 269
Jilted (Maltby, A., 1877), v. 473
Jilt in all Humours = Intrigues at Versailles
Jim along Josey (1840), IV. 485
Jim Crow in his new Place (Taylor, T. P., 1838), IV. 411
Jim Crow's Visit to Chobham (1853), v. 700
Jim Drags, the Drayman (Hay, F., 1870), v. 411
Jimmy Watt (Boucicault, D., 1890), v. 269
Jim, the Penman (Young, Sir C. L., 1886), v. 149–50, 636
Jingle (Albery, J., 1878), v. 238
Jinks among the Breakers = Lucette's Husband
Jinks the Gent (1849), IV. 485
+ Jinks, the Man that can't help it! (C. L. 13/2/1843; *Cattermole*)
Jo (Cheatham, F. G., 1864), v. 701, 783, 837
— = Bleak House
J.O. (1862), v. 700
Joan (Martin, R. J., 1890), v. 479
— (Reade, C., 1878), v. 536
Joan Lowrie (1878), v. 700
Joanna of Montfaucon (Cumberland, R., 1800), III. 52, 65, 106–7, 252; IV. 87, 287
— (Geisweiler, M., 1799), III. 65, 264, 385
Joanna of Surinam (Cross, J. C., 1804), IV. 286
Joan of Arc (Brough, W., 1869), v. 280
— (Clarke, C. A., 1871), v. 311
— (Clarke, C. A., 1891), v. 312
— (Cross, J. C., 1798), III. 250, 380

Joan of Arc (Fitzball, E., 1822), IV. 312, 485, 584, 629
— (Fitzball, E., 1837), IV. 315
— (Henderson, J., 1896), v. 416
— (Innes, G. W., 1890), v. 432
— (Mildenhall, T., 1847), IV. 356
— (Shine, J. L. and Ross, A., 1891), v. 563
— (Taylor, T., 1871), v. 594, 820
— (Villiers, E., 1871), v. 608
— (1832), IV. 485
Joan of Arc, Maid of Orleans (1826), IV. 486
Joan of Arc, the Maid of Orleans (Serle, T. J., 1837), IV. 400
Joan of the Hatchet (1844), IV. 629
Job Fox, the Yankee Valet (Peake, R. B., 1836), IV. 486
Jockey (Bousfield, F., 1894), v. 270
Jockey and Jenny (1806), IV. 486
Jockey and the Three Witches = Tempest
Jockey Club (Sanger, G., 1892), v. 555
— (Stirling, E., 1846), IV. 408
Jockey's Stratagem (1843), IV. 486
— = In to Win
Jocko (Dibdin, T. J., 1825), IV. 304
— (Planché, J. R., 1825), IV. 26, 149, 378
Jocko, the Brazilian Ape (Ebsworth, J., 1825), IV. 582
Joconde (Moncrieff, W. T., 1816), IV. 358, 600
— (Santley, 1876), v. 555
— (1818), IV. 486
Jocrisse the Juggler (Robertson, T. W., 1861), v. 546
Joe and Nolly Stubbs (1876), v. 700
Joe Miller (Lee, N., 1857), v. 700, 802, 837
— (1833), IV. 486
Joe Miller and his Men (À Beckett, G. A., 1844), IV. 250
Joe Sterling (Hazlewood, C. H., 1870), v. 414
Joe the Miner (Thomas, B. W., 1893), v. 595
Joe the Waif (Rhoyds, H., 1876), v. 542
John Adams (Moncrieff, W. T., 1816), IV. 486, 629
John-a-Dreams (Chambers, C. H., 1894), v. 307

John and Angelina (Lathair, H., 1890), v. 449

John Anderson my Jo (1839), IV. 486
— = Old Church Porch

John and Jeannette (Machale, L., 1885), v. 469

John Aylmer's Dream (Burbey, E. J., 1886), v. 287

John Baliol (Tennant, W., 1828), IV. 411

John Brown (1823), IV. 486
— (1826), IV. 486

John Bull (Boucicault, D., 1872), v. 269
— (Colman, G., the Younger, 1803), IV. 52, 184, 282
— (Lacy, T. H., 1854), v. 802

John Bull Abroad (Grain, R. C., 1888), v. 387

John Bull and Buonaparte (Cross, J. C., 1803), IV. 286

John Bull and the Rural Police = Prometheus Britannicus

John Bull and the Wet Quaker = Irishman in Windsor

John Bull in France (1811), IV. 486

John Bull in his Dotage = Jubilee

John Bull's Dilemma (1885), v. 700

John Bull Triumphant = Reform

John Buzzby (Kenney, J., 1822), IV. 337

John Cade of Asliford (1850), v. 700

John Chetwynd's Wife = Dr Chetwynd

John Churchill, Duke of Marlborough (1820), IV. 630

John Darrell's Dream (France, E. S.), v. 792

John Dobbs (Morton, J. M., 1849), IV. 363

John du Bart (Pocock, I., 1815), IV. 384

John Duddlestone, the Breeches Maker of Bristol (1837), IV. 486

John, Earl of Gowrie (Brown, R., 1825), IV. 574

John Felton (1850), v. 700

John Gabriel Borkman (Archer, W., 1897), v. 242
— (1896), v. 700

John Gilpin (1815), IV. 486, 630
— (1817), IV. 486, 630

John Grant's Daughter and the Flaming Hand = Blacksmith's Daughter and the Red Hand

John Heriot, Yeoman (1887), v. 700

John Howard, the Philanthropist = Convict Ship

John Jasper's Wife (Harvey, F., 1876), v. 408

John Johnson (Pitt, G. D., 1835), IV. 373

John Jones (Buckstone, J. B., 1831), IV. 274

John Lester, Parson (Knight, R. and Foster, L., 1892), v. 445

John Marchmont's Legacy (1866), v. 700

John Martin's Secret (Vane, S., 1895), v. 606

Johnnie Armstrong (Cross, J. C., 1803), IV. 486, 630
— (1822), IV. 486

Johnnie Fa (1842), IV. 630

Johnny Gilpin (1823), IV. 486

Johnny Gilpin's Ride to Edmonton (Lee, N., Jr., 1861), v. 700, 802, 837

Johnny Newcomes at Epping = Easter Hunting

John o' Armhall (1828), IV. 630

John of Calais (Dibdin, T. J., ?1796), III. 382

John of Leyden (1849), IV. 486

John of Lorne and Helen of Argyle (1824), IV. 486

John of Paris (Pocock, I., 1814), IV. 144, 384

John of Procida (Knowles, J. S., 1840), IV. 339

John of the Forge (1850), v. 700

John Overy, the Miser (Jerrold, D. W., 1829), IV. 331

John Savile of Haysted (White, J., 1847), IV. 419

John Smith (Hancock, W., 1862), v. 402
— (Law, A., 1889), v. 450

John Stafford (Townsend, W. T. or Bosworth, J., 1835), IV. 414, 573

John Thurgood, Farmer (Byatt, H., 1893), v. 295

John Wharton (Fielding, H., 1868), v. 366

John Wilson (1865), v. 700

John Woodvil (Lamb, C., 1802), IV. 194-5, 341

John Wopps (Suter, W. E., 1860), v. 588

Joint Household (Bell, Mrs H., 1891), v. 255

Joke = Sixty-third Letter

Joker (Tennyson, M. H., 1894), v. 595

Joke's a Joke (Hook, T. E., 1830), IV. 486, 630

Joking Girl = Aunt Chimpanzee

Jolie Parfumeuse (Kenny, C. L., 1875), v. 801

Jolliboy's Woes (Fawcett, C. S., 1878), v. 364

Jolly Beggars (Burns, R., 1823), IV. 277

Jolly Boy Blue (1893), v. 701

Jolly Crew (1799), III. 333

Jolly Dick the Lamplighter = Life's a Lottery

Jolly Dogs of London (Hazlewood, C. H., 1866), v. 701, 796, 837

Jolly Jack (1850), v. 701

Jolly Jock (1899), v. 837

Jolly Joe (Hazlewood, C. H., 1868), v. 413

Jolly King Christmas (Marchant, F., 1863), v. 701, 837

Jolly Miller (1861), v. 701

Jolly Miller of Stratford (Giovanelli, A., 1869), v. 382

Jolly Miller of the Dee (Millward, C., 1864), v. 807

Jolly Young Waterman = Alice Lowrie

Jonathan (Barber, J., 1845), IV. 259

Jonathan Bradford (Fitzball, E., 1833), IV. 36, 120, 314

— (1835), IV. 486

Jonathan Dobson, the Congress Trooper (1831), IV. 486

Jonathan in England (Peake, R. B., 1824), IV. 369

Jonathan Oldakre (Wilson, J. C.), v. 824

Jonathan Wild (James, C. S., 1848), IV. 330

— (Young, H., 1886), v. 636

— (Young, Mrs H., 1868), v. 636

Jonathan without a David (Foster, L., 1894), v. 371

Jones (Shirley, A. and Landeck, B., 1891), v. 564

Jones and Co. (Burleigh, F., 1893), v. 781

Jones and Co., Matrimonial Agents (Bingham, F., 1893), v. 261

Jones's Aunt = Prodigal Father

Jones's Notes (Tabrar, J., 1886), v. 589

Jones the Avenger (Talfourd, F., 1856), v. 701, 819, 837

Jonnie Armstrong (Dibdin, C. I. M., 1812), IV. 292

Jonny Gilpin (1808), IV. 486

Joseph (1745), II. 395

Joseph II (1830), IV. 486

Joseph and his Brethren (Howard, H. L., 1824), IV. 589

— (Miller, J., 1744), II. 395

— (Wells, C. J., 1824), IV. 202-3, 418

Joseph Andrews (Pratt, S. J., 1778), III. 299

Joseph Chavigny (Phillips, W., 1856), v. 523

Joseph Gombert (1860), v. 701

Josephine (Buckstone, J. B., 1844), IV. 275

Josephine, the Child of the Regiment (Buckstone, J. B., 1858), v. 287

Joseph's Luck (1897), v. 701

Joseph sold by his Brethren (1789), III. 333

Joseph's Sweetheart (Buchanan, R., 1888), v. 285

Joshua (Morell, T., 1747), II. 395, 441

Joshua Haggard (Young, J., 1879), v. 636

Josiah's Dream (Rogers, C., 1896), v. 548

Jo, the Waif (1881), v. 701

Jour de Fête (1856), v. 837

Journey of Adventure = I've lost my Place

Journey of Love = Knight of the Eagle Crest

Journey's End (Newte, H. C. W., 1891), v. 503

Journeys End in Lovers Meeting (Hobbes, J. O., 1894), v. 422

Journey to Bristol (Hippisley, J., ?1730), II. 337

Journey to London (Vanbrugh, Sir J., 1728), II. 15, 152, 190, 363

— = Provok'd Husband

Journey to Paris (1860), v. 701

Jo versus Jo (Green, F. W. and Allen, O., 1876), v. 390

Jovial Coopers (1759), III. 402

Jovial Crew (Concanen, M., Rooke, E. and Yonge, Sir W., 1731), II. 142, 237, 247, 376, 434, 446

Julie (1898), v. 701

Julie de Launay (1860), v. 701

Julie de Moin (Barnett, C. Z., 1849), IV. 261

Julie Ledru (1846), IV. 486

Juliet by Proxy (1899), v. 701

Juliette (1860), v. 701

Julio of Harancour (1819), IV. 486

Julio Romano (Bucke, C., 1830), IV. 272

Julius Caesar (D'Avenant, Sir W. and Dryden, J., ?1676), I. 173, 402

— (Kemble, J. P., 1812), IV. 335

— (Sheffield, J., 1722), II. 355

— (1818), IV. 90, 486

+ Julius Caesar, The Rum Un (Emson, F. E., 8°, ?1877)

Julius See-Saw (Pitt, H. M., 1869), v. 526

Julius Sterne = Old Jew

Jumbo Jim (1838), IV. 486

Jump a Little Wagtail (Johnstone, J. B., 1868), v. 438

Jumper = Sam Patch

Jumping at Conclusions (Homrigh, A. Von, 1892), v. 425

Jungle Death = Lion Conqueror

Junior Partner (Naden, A. T., 1890), v. 501

— (Russ, S., 1887), v. 553

— = Fate and Fortune

Juniper Jack (Hallett, Mrs, 1845), IV. 587 [see also 323, where the play is entered wrongly under Mrs A. M. Hall]

Junius Brutus (Lytton, Baron, 1885), v. 466

Juno (1896), v. 701

Juno, by Jove! = Caught Courting

Junto (1778), III. 333

Jupiter and Alcmena (Dibdin, C., 1781), III. 113, 255

— (1750), III. 333

Jupiter and Europa (Rich, J., 1723), II. 253, 376, 443

Jupiter and Io (1735), II. 376

Jupiter and Juno (Rede, W. L., 1835), IV. 607

Jupiter Chuff (1865), v. 701

Jupiter, Juno and Mercury (Fielding, H., 1743), II. 328

Jupiter L.L.D. (1894), v. 701

Jupiter's Decree and the Fall of Phaethon (Suter, W. E., 1853), v. 587

Jura (1868), v. 701

Juror (1718), II. 376

Juror Murderer = Cry of Blood

Just as Well (+ Manners, J. Hartley, Kensington Town Hall, 20/1/1899, French), v. 701

Just Broke Up = Holidays

Justice (Dening, Mrs C., 1893), v. 342

— (Doran, J., 1824), IV. 581

— (Faucit, J. S., 1820), IV. 311

— (1853), v. 701

— (1892), v. 701

— (1893), v. 701

— = Law, not Justice

Justice and Quackery (1822), IV. 486

Justice at Fault = Guilty or Not Guilty

Justice at Last (Roberts, G., 1894), v. 545

— (1884), v. 701

Justice Busy (Crowne, J., 1699), I. 400

Justice Caught in his Own Trap = Rape upon Rape

Justice Nell (Soutar, J. F. and Harwood, R., 1899), v. 575

Justice Triumphant (1747), II. 376

— = Elmerick

Justifiable Homicide (1884), v. 701

Justina (McCarthy, D. F., 1848), IV. 596

Justinio (1820), IV. 487

Just in Time (Anderson, C., 1897), v. 240

— (Burnand, F. C., 1884), v. 291

— (Hurlstone, T., 1792), III. 274

— (1862), v. 701

— = One too many

Justizia (Bennett, G. J., 1848), IV. 265

Just like a Woman (Dubourg, A. W., 1879), v. 351

Just like Roger (Webster, B., the Younger, 1872), v. 618

Just my Luck (Maltby, A., 1852), v. 473

— (Maltby, A., 1877), v. 473

Just One Word (1873), v. 701

Just Retribution (Bayne, R., 1893), v. 253

Juvenile Dramatist (1801), IV. 487

Juvenile Friendship (McLaren, A., 1822), IV. 352

— (1802), IV. 487

Juvenile Indiscretion = Emily

Juvenile Party (1852), v. 701

Kindred (Capadose, H., 1837), IV. 87, 279, 487, 576, 630

Kindred Souls (Manning, W., 1884), V. 474

Kind to a Fault (Brough, W., 1867), V. 280

King Ahasuerus and Queen Esther (Kirkman, F., 1673), I. 418

+ King Alfred (Egerton, Lord Francis: printed in *Juvenile Plays for Home Performance* (*French*))

King Alfred the Great (Blanchard, E. L., 1846), IV. 269

King and Artist (Mowbray, L. and Pollock, W. H., 1897), V. 498

King and his Crown (1835), IV. 487

King and I (Morton J. M., 1845), IV. 362

King and No King (1733), II. 377

— (1821), IV. 487

King and Rebel (Vellère, Dr, 1873), V. 607

King and Subject = Earl of Warwick

King and the Actor (1833), IV. 487

King and the Actress = Nell Gwynne

King and the Angel (Neil, Ross, 1874), V. 501

King and the Carpenter (Lawrance, F., 1838), IV. 594

King and the Cobbler (1791), III. 333

— (1810), IV. 487

King and the Cobler = Friend at Court

King and the Comedian = Frederick of Prussia

King and the Commoner (Langford, J. A., 1870), V. 448

King and the Countess (Poel, W., 1890), V. 702, 811, 838

King and the Czar = Battle of Pultawa

King and the Deserter = Frederick the Great

King and the Duke (Jameson, R. F., 1814), IV. 330

— (Pocock, I., 1839), IV. 385

King and the Freebooter (?Wilks, T. E., 1837), IV. 487, 630 [In IV. 630 this is attributed to J. C. Wills, but it appears to be the same as Lord Darnley, by T. E. Wilks: *see* IV. 420]

King and the Miller of Mansfield (Dodsley, R., 1737), II. 136, 137, 138, 204–5, 249, 318

King and the Piper (1847), IV. 488

King and the Poet = Frederick and Voltaire

King and the Protector = Charles I

King and Titi (1737), II. 447

King Arthur (Brough, W., 1863), V. 279, 780

— (Carr, J. W. C., 1895), V. 304

— (Dryden, J., 1691), I. 135, 159–60, 267, 338, 352, 407

— (Earle, A. W. and Sim, E. H., 1895), V. 353

— (Garrick, D., 1770), III. 58, 263

— (1840), IV. 630

King Arthur and the Knights of the Round Table (Pocock, I., 1834), IV. 92, 385

King at Rheims (1825), IV. 488

King Bewildered = Forest Knight

King Bladud, Founder of Bath (1711), II. 366

King Bluebottle (1846), IV. 488

King Bluster-Bubble and the Demon Ogre (Somerset, C. A., 1857), V. 702, 817

King Caesar (Cross, J. C., 1801), IV. 286

King cannot Err (Cooke, A. M. E., 1762), III. 248

King Capital (1866), V. 702

King Charles (1851), V. 702

King Charles I (Gurney, A. T., 1846), IV. 322; V. 397

— (Havard, W., 1737), II. 16, 21, 26, 70, 113, 232, 334

— = Royal Martyr, King Charles I

King Charles II (Longland, J., 1872), V. 463

— (Ryan, D. L., 1849), IV. 396 [where wrongly ascribed to M. D. Ryan]

— (1821), IV. 488

King Charles II's Merry Days = Rochester

King Charles at Brighthelmstone = Royal Escape

King Charles at Tunbridge Wells = Killigrew

King Charles in the Royal Oak = (1) Battle of Worcester; (2) Waggery in Wapping

King Charming (Planché, J. R., 1850), V. 527

King Chess (1865), V. 702

King Christmas (Planché, J. R., 1871), v. 528

King Coal and his Merry Men = Good Fairy of St Helen's

King Coffee (Elphinstone, J., 1874), v. 358

— (1873), v. 702

King Comet and Prince Quicksilver (Lee, N., Jr., 1858), v. 702, 802, 838

King Crib (1856), v. 702

King Diamond (Young, E., 1864), v. 825

Kingdom of the Birds = Wonders in the Sun

King Dreams (1894), v. 702

King Edgar and Alfreda (Ravenscroft, E., 1677), I. 54, 101, 255, 426

+King Edward II (Grindrod, C., 8°, 1883)

King Edward III (Bancroft, J., 1690), I. 168, 352, 357, 388

King Edward VI (Gregg, T. D., 1857), v. 394

King Egbert, King of Kent and Monarch of England (1719), II. 370

King Emerald (Lee, N., 1852), v. 452

+King Eric and the Outlaws (Chapman, J. F., 12°, 1843) [Translated from a play by B. S. Ingemann]

King Flame and Queen Pearly-drop (Lee, N., Jr., 1865), v. 452

King Foo (Adams, E., 1873), v. 235

King for a Day (Smith, V., 1893), v. 573, 817

King Galistan (1898), v. 703

King George's Shilling (Stirling, E., 1879), v. 584

King Glumpus (Barrow, J., 1837), IV. 570

King Hal and Herne the Hunter = Rose of Windsor

King Hal's Early Days (1837), IV. 488

King Hal the Bluff (Lee, N., Jr., 1862), v. 803

King Harold (Haines, J. T., 1839), IV. 323

+King Henry I (Grindrod, C., 8°, 1883)

+King Henry II (Grindrod, C., 8°, 1883)

King Henry III (Edison, J. S., 1840), IV. 582

+— (Grindrod, C., 8°, 1883)

King Henry III (Helps, Sir A., 1843), IV. 588

— = England Preserved

King Henry IV (Betterton, T., 1700), II. 297

— (Valpy, R., 1801), IV. 415

King Henry IV of France (Beckingham, C., 1719), II. 27–8, 90, 297

King Henry V (Hill, A., 1723), II. 30, 109, 336, 438

— (Kemble, J. P., 1789), III. 278, 389

King Henry VI = Roses

King Henry VII (Macklin, C., 1746), II. 342, 440

King Henry VIII (Kemble, J. P., 1804), IV. 335

King Henry VIII and the Cobbler (1812), IV. 488, 630

King Incog. (À Beckett, G. A., 1834), IV. 249, 567

King Indigo (Burnand, F. C., 1877), v. 290, 782

King in Dublin = Irish Loyalty

King in the Country (Waldron, F. G., 1789), III. 314

— = Loyal Salopian

King James I (Buchanan, R., 1868), v. 284

King James I and his Times = Fortunes of Nigel

+King James I of Scotland (Erskine, D.; 12°, 1827 (Kelso))

+— (Grindrod, C., 8°, 1883)

King James II (Whitehead, J. C., 1828), IV. 419

King James and the Piper (Duggan, J., 1847), IV. 308

King Jamie (1849), IV. 488

— (1879), v. 703

King Jamie's Frolic = Lancashire Witches

King John (Kemble, J. P., 1800), IV. 335

— (Valpy, R., 1800), III. 313; IV. 415

— (1749), II. 452

— (1823), IV. 488

King John with the Benefit of the Act (À Beckett, G. A., 1837), IV. 249, 567

King Jupiter and the Freaks of the Graces (1856), v. 703

King Klondyke (Addison, J., 1898), v. 236

King Solomon's Wisdom (Kirkman, F., 1673), I. 418

King's Outcast (Mackay, W. G., 1899), v. 470

King's Pardon = Buried Alive

King's Password (Campbell, Mrs V., 1900), v. 301

King's Pleasure (Thompson, A., 1870), v. 597, 820

King's Pledge (Charles, G. F., 1870), v. 308

King's Proxy (Arnold, S. J., 1815), IV. 256

King's Ransom (Archer, T., 1843), IV. 254

King's Rival (Taylor, T. and Reade, C., 1854), v. 99–100, 592

King's Seal (Kenney, J. and Gore, Mrs, 1835), IV. 337

King's Secret (Hazlewood, C. H., 1878), v. 415

King Stephen (Paynter, D. W., 1822), IV. 369

— (1835), IV. 488

King's Sweetheart = Regina, B. A.

King's Wager (Wilks, T. E., 1837), IV. 17, 420

— = (1) Cottage and the Court; (2) Golden Cornet

King's Watch = Hearts of Iron

King's Word (Addison, H. R., 1835), IV. 251

King Teapot the Great (Suter, W. E., 1857), v. 703, 819, 838

King, the Princess and the Genie = Fountain of Beauty

King, the Ring and the Giddy Young Thing (Reeves, G., 1882), v. 540

King, the Tailor and the Mischievous F = Carrot and Pa-snip

King Thrushbeard (Talfourd, F., 1859), v. 590

King Trickee (Addison, J., 1887), v. 236

King Victor and King Charles (Browning, R., 1842), IV. 272

King William's Happy Deliverance (?1740), II. 452

Kinsmen of Naples (Bunn, A., 1821), IV. 444

Kirkauld's Point (1839), IV. 488

Kirk-o-Field (Thompson, R. H., 1895), v. 598

Kirk Sessions Confounded = Planters of the Vineyard

Kismet (Jones, J. W., 1888), v. 441

Kiss (Clarke, S., 1811) = Perplexed Husband, IV. 280, 576

— (Collier, W., 1842), IV. 488, 630

— (Gray, J., 1892), v. 390

Kiss Accepted and Returned (Ayres, J., 1744), II. 296

Kiss and Be Friends (1816), IV. 488

Kiss and the Rose (Moncrieff, W. T., 1827), IV. 135, 359

Kiss for a Kingdom (1899), v. 703

Kiss from the Bride = Corporal's Wedding

Kissi-Kissi (Burnand, F. C., 1873), v. 290, 781

Kissing Cup Race (Rae-Brown, C., 1891), v. 533

Kissing goes by Favour (Stirling, E., 1847), IV. 408

Kissing Kissing (1873), v. 703

Kiss in the Dark (Buckstone, J. B., 1840), IV. 275

Kiss in the Ring (1818), IV. 488

Kiss Me Quick (1896) = Trip to Klondyke, v. 703, 759, 838, 848

Kiss of Delilah (Grant, G. and Lisle, J., 1896), v. 388

Kiss o' the Blarney = Irishman's Heart

Kitchen (1832), IV. 488

Kitchen Belles (1869), v. 704

Kitchen Girl (East, J. M., 1899) = Spouse Trap, v. 353, 754, 789, 847

Kitchen Love (Courtneidge, R., 1888), v. 326

Kitchen Rehearsal (1880), v. 704

Kitchen Sylph (Buckstone, J. B., 1834), IV. 488, 630

Kitchen Tragedy (Barwick, E., 1887), v. 252

Kith and Kin (1879), v. 704

Kithogue = Hue and Cry

Kit Marlowe (Courtney, W. L., 1890), v. 326

Kittens (Lyster, F., 1887), v. 466

Kitty (Parke, W. and Parker, H., 1897), v. 512

— (1891), v. 704

— (1894), v. 704

Kitty Clive (Moore, F. F., 1895), v. 492

Klebir in Egypt (Dibdin, C. I. M., 1825), IV. 295

Klepht of the Evil Eye = Demetri the Outcast

Kleptomania (Melford, M., 1888), v. 484

Klondyke Nugget (Cody, S. J., 1898), v. 315

Klondyke Rush (Fielding, H., 1898), v. 366

Klondyke the Golden (1897), v. 704

Knapsack (1884), v. 704

Knave of Clubs = Card-Drawing

Knave of Diamonds (Henry, S. C., 1896), v. 418

Knave of Hearts = Baccarat

Knave of Hearts and the Companions of Crime = Rocambole

Knave of Spades (1895), v. 704

Knave or Not? (Holcroft, T., 1798), III. 99, 122, 137, 271, 387

Knavery in all Trades (1664), I. 442

Knaves and Fools (Reynolds, W., 1899), v. 541

Knaves of Knaves Acre = Sixteen String Jack

Knaves Overtrumped = Heads versus Pockets

Knife, Fork and Spoon (Lee, N., 1850), v. 452

Knight against Rook (Dove, O. and Lefebre, J. G., 1893), v. 349

Knight and his Page (Dibdin, C. I. M., 1826), IV. 296

Knight and the Naiads = Nymph of the Lurleyburg

Knight and the Sprite (À Beckett, G. A. and Lemon, G., 1844), IV. 250

Knight and the Water-Lily (1854), v. 704

Knight and the Wood Daemon = One O'Clock!

Knight Errant (Barrington, R., 1894), v. 251

Knight for a Day = Patrick the Foreigner

(K)night in Armour (Burnot, W. and Bruce, H. P., 1895), v. 293

+ Knight in a Wood (Smock Alley, Dublin, 5/5/1772)

Knight of Arva (Boucicault, D., 1848), IV. 270

Knight of Burgundy = Field of the Cloth of Gold

Knight of Malta (1783), III. 113, 333

Knight of Rhodes (Burges, Sir J. B., 1817), IV. 276

Knight of Snowdoun (Morton, T., 1811), IV. 92, 363

— (1823), IV. 92, 489

Knight of the Black Plume (1814), IV. 489

Knight of the Bloody Hand = Valvoni

Knight of the Boots (1817), IV. 489

Knight of the Couch Leopard = King Richard Cœur de Lion

Knight of the Doleful Countenance = Dox Quixote

Knight of the Dragon and the Queen of Beauty (Stirling, E., 1839), IV. 406

Knight of the Eagle Crest (1849), IV. 489

Knight of the Garter (Wilson, S., 1882), v. 628

Knight of the Hermitage = Bonifacio and Bridgetina

Knight of the Road (French, W. P., 1891), v. 373

— (Russell, E. H., 1892), v. 553

Knight of the Sepulchre (Almar, G., 1840), IV. 568

Knight of Wharley = Husband's Vengeance

Knights (Foote, S., 1749), III. 172, 259, 403

Knight's Lodging (1898), v. 704

Knights of Castile = Poisoned Goblet

Knights of Knavery (1895), v. 704

Knights of Merry England = Ivanhoe

Knights of Rhodes (Dibdin, T. J., 1820), IV. 302

Knights of St Albans (Taylor, T. P., 1837), IV. 411

Knights of St George (1805), IV. 489

Knights of St John (Almar, G., 1833), IV. 252

Knights of Sicily = Ocean Fiend

Knights of the Cross (Beazley, S., Jr., 1826), IV. 95, 264

Knights of the Garter (1805), IV. 489

Knights of the Green Baize = Way of the Wicked

Knights of the Last = Daisy

Knights of the Lion (Dibdin, T. J., 1818), IV. 301

Knights of the Oven = Royal Baker

Knights of the Post (1797), III. 118, 333

— = System of Lavater

Knights of the Road (Travers, W., 1868), v. 603
Knights of the Round Table (Planché, J. R., 1854), v. 527
— = King Arthur
Knights of the Sun (1802), IV. 489
Knights of Villeroy (1817), IV. 489
Knights Templar = Ivanhoe
Knights Templars = Maid of Judah
Knight Templar = Ivanhoe
Knight, the Giant and the Castle of Manchester = Lancashire Witches
Knight, the Lady and the Lake = Mountain Dhu
Knobs and Noses (1820), IV. 489
Knotting 'em Brothers = Dark Doings in the Closet by the Knotting 'em Brothers, v. 328
Knowing ones taken in (1797), III. 333
Knowledge (Ogilvie, G. S., 1883), v. 704, 808, 838
Known to the Police (Douglass, J. T., 1897), v. 349
Know Whom you Marry = Keep your Temper
Know Your Own Mind (Murphy, A., 1777), III. 118, 164, 290
Ko and Zoa (Dibdin, C. I. M., 1802), IV. 290
Koeuba (Fitzball, E., 1824), IV. 489, 630
Koffee Kan Brothers (1897), v. 704
Kohal Cave (Rede, W. L., 1838), IV. 390
Koh-i-noor (Rice, C.), v. 813
Kolaf (Akhurst, W. M., 1876), v. 237
Kompact, the Kick and the Kombat = New Edition of the Corsican Brothers
Kongo Kolo (1811), IV. 489
Koranzo's Feast (Hayes, 1811), IV. 324
Korastikam Prince of Assassins (1821), IV. 489
Koromantyns (1808), IV. 489
Kosciusko (1840), IV. 489
Kouli Khan (Dibdin, T. J., 1818), IV. 301
Ku-Klux-Klan (Macdermott, G. H. and Major, H. A., 1873), v. 468
Kynge Lear and Hys Faythefull Foole (Marchant, F., 1860), v. 704, 805

La Ba Kan (Roe, J. E., 1869), v. 548
Labour Leader (1895), v. 704
Labour of Love (Broughton, F. W., 1875), v. 281

Labour of Love (Newte, H. C. W., 1897), v. 503
Labour Question (1861), v. 704
Labyrinth (Stratford, A., 1795), III. 333, 396, 402
— (1664), I. 442
— (1797), III. 333
Labyrinth Farm (1812), IV. 489
Labyrinth of Crete = Theseus and Ariadne
Labyrinth of Death = Wreck and Rescue
Labyrinth of Love = Trip to Marseilles
Labyrinths of Life = Haunted Houses
Lacemakers of Lisle = Lessons of Life
Ladder across the Street (1848), IV. 489
Ladder of Life (Rogers, C. and Boyne, W., 1898), v. 548
— (1884), v. 704
— = (1) Jack in the Water; (2) Pride shall have a Fall; (3) Ups and Downs
Ladder of Love (Bayly, T. H., 1837), IV. 263
Ladder of Wealth (Orchard, J. R., 1899), v. 507
Lad from the Country (Morton, J. M., 1863), v. 496
Ladies a la Mode = Damoiselles a la Mode
Ladies among themselves = Belles without Beaux
Ladies at Court (1832), IV. 630
Ladies at Home (Millingen, J. G., 1819), IV. 356, 599
Ladies' Battle (Reade, C., 1851), v. 535
— (Robertson, T. W., 1851), v. 546
— (1891), v. 704
Ladies Beware (1847), IV. 489
— (1858), v. 704
Ladies' Champion (Gwindon, H., 1868), v. 398
Ladies' Chance (1894), v. 704
Ladies' Club (Lemon, M., 1840), IV. 343, 595
Ladies Distress = Banditti
Ladies Doctor = Self-Enamoured
Ladies Friendship = Lying Lover
Ladies Frolick (Love, J., 1770), III. 113, 283, 391
Ladies Idol (Law, A., 1895), v. 450
+ Ladies in Parliament (Trevelyan, G. O., 8°, 1869 (apparently acted privately at Cambridge))

Ladies' Matrimonial Club (1840), IV. 489

Ladies of St Cyr (1869), V. 704

Ladies of the Convent (Suter, W. E., 1853), V. 587

Ladies of the Court = How's your Uncle

Ladies of the Palace (1735), II. 377

Ladies' Pet = Paul Clifford

Ladies Philosophy = Refusal

Ladies' Privilege = Leap Year

Ladies Ridiculed = Two Pence

Ladies Seminary (Wilks, T. E., 1841), IV. 421

Ladies' Stratagem (Hitchcock, R., 1775), III. 269

Ladies' Subscription (Cleland, J., 1755), III. 243

Ladies' Temperance Club (1869), V. 704

Ladies Visiting-Day (Burnaby, W., 1701), II. 50, 142, 153, 162, 301

Ladle (Dibdin, C., 1773), III. 254

Lad of the Hills = Wicklow Gold Mines

Lad of the Village (Burton, E. G., 1850), V. 294

Ladrone's Daughter = Paula Lazaro

Lads of the Hills = Wicklow Gold Mines

Lads of the Village = Jemmy for Ever

Lady and Gentleman in a peculiarly perplexing Predicament (Selby, C., 1841), IV. 398

Lady and the Convict (1841), IV. 489

Lady and the Devil (Dimond, W., 1820), IV. 307

Lady and the Lawyer = Irish Poleander

Lady and the Lawyers (De Vere, F., 1857), V. 343

Lady and the Magistrate (Sharp, T., 1897), V. 561

Lady Anne's Well (Travers, W., 1868), V. 603

Lady at Dover (1848), IV. 489

Lady Audley's Secret (Hazlewood, C. H., 1863), V. 415, 797

— (Roberts, G., 1863), V. 544

— (Suter, W. E., 1863), V. 588

Lady Aurora (Woodward, F. W. and Woodward, J. W., 1894), V. 631

Lady Barbara's Birthday (Barker, 1872), V. 249

Lady Barter (Coghlan, C. F., 1891), V. 316

Lady Belle Belle (Byron, H. J., 1863), V. 296, 782

Lady Bird (Boucicault, D., 1862), V. 268

Lady-Bird Bower (Webb, C.), IV. 616

Lady Bookie (Hallward, C., 1898), V. 401

Lady Bountiful (Pinero, Sir A. W., 1891), V. 179, 187, 525

Lady Browne's Diary (Bell, M., 1892), V. 256

Lady Burglar (Malyon, E. J. and James, C., 1897) = In a Fit of Abstraction, V. 473, 695, 805

Lady by Birth (Smythies, W. G., 1893), V. 573

Lady Cameleon = Traviata

Lady Caprice (Jones, H. A., 1880), V. 439

Lady Clancarty (Taylor, T., 1874), V. 98, 594

Lady Clara Vere de Vere (1888), V. 704

Lady Clare (Buchanan, R., 1883), V. 284

Lady Clerk (Hurst, C., 1899), V. 431

Lady Contemplation (Cavendish, M., 1662), I. 396

Lady Cyclist (Miller, St A., 1897), V. 488

Lady Daisy (Dent, B., 1896), V. 342

Lady D'Arcy (Hilton, B. H., 1870), V. 422

Lady Deadlock's Secret (Simpson, J. P., 1874), V. 568

Lady Deane (Wilmot, A. A., 1887), V. 628

Lady Delmar (1891), V. 704

Lady Detective = Bilbery of Tilbury

Lady Di's Visit (Thursby, C., 1897), V. 600

Lady Dorothy's Scheme (Walton, T., 1895), V. 613

Ladye Bird Bower (Somerset, C. A., 1858), V. 574

Ladye-Bird, fly away home (Neale, F., 1853), V. 501

Lady Elizabeth = 'Twixt Axe and Crown

Ladye of Lambethe (Wilks, T. E., 1839), IV. 421

Lady Flora (Coghlan, C. F., 1875), V. 316

Lady Fortune (Thomas, C., 1887), V. 596

Lady from the Sea (Aveling, E. M., 1891), V. 187, 246

Lady Gladys (Buchanan, R., 1894), v. 285

Lady Godiva (Akhurst, W. M., 1871), v. 236

— (Grattan, H. P., 1885), v. 389

— (Muskerry, W., 1889), v. 501

— (Robson, F., 1873), v. 547

— (1851), v. 704

— (1877), v. 704

— (1894), v. 704

Lady Godiva and Peeping Tom (Ridgway, J., 1846), iv. 394

— (Spry, H., 1875), v. 576

Lady Godiva and Peeping Tom of Coventry (Lee, N., 1848), iv. 343

— (1846, 1848), iv. 489

Lady Godiva, the Bare-back Rider (1896), v. 704

Lady Guide (1891), v. 704

Lady Hatton (Pitt, G. D., 1850), v. 704, 810, 838

— (1883), v. 704

Lady Hatton and the Mystery of the Bleeding Heart = Suicide's Tree

Lady Henrietta (St George and Mazilier, 1844), iv. 489, 630

Lady in Black (Somerset, C. A., 1848), iv. 405

— (Young, H., 1860), v. 825

— (1859), v. 704

Lady in Difficulties (Planché, J. R., 1849), iv. 383

— (1835), iv. 489

Lady in Fashion = Woman's Wit

Lady in her Sleep (Dibdin, T. J., 1828), iv. 305

Lady in Search of an Heiress (Leigh, A.), v. 453

Lady Interviewer (Swears, H., 1896), v. 589

Lady Isabel (Kempe, A., 1873), v. 442

Lady Jane Gray (Rowe, N., 1715), ii. 18, 58, 101-2, 353, 443; iii. 85

Lady Jane Grey (Hazlewood, C. H., 1874), v. 415

— (Neil, R., 1871), v. 501

— (Poel, W., 1885), v. 529, 811

— (1875), v. 704

Lady Jemima (Grant, N., 1888), v. 388

Lady Journalist (Zangwill, I., 1893), v. 637

Lady Judge (1894), v. 704

Lady Killer (Chevalier, A. and Mackintosh, W., 1885), v. 309

— (Fawcett, C. S., 1893), v. 364

— (Jerrold, D., 1831), iv. 489, 630

— = Gay Lothario

Lady Lady's Maid = Military Manœuvre

Lady Laura's Arcadia (Broughton, F. W., 1897), v. 282

Lady Lawyer (Lynch, G. D., 1897), v. 465

Lady Legislators = Mrs Speaker

Lady Lillian (Towers, E., 1880), v. 601

— (1885), v. 704

Lady Lovington (Villars, G., 1888), v. 608

Lady Macbeth (Galt, J., 1812), iv. 585

Lady Mary Wortley Montague (1839), iv. 489

"Lady May" = Dream of an Irish Emigrant

Lady of Bayonne (Macgowan, W. S., 1897), v. 469

Lady of Belleisle (Gully, J. M., 1839), iv. 321

Lady of Buccleuch = Border Feuds

Lady of Kildare (1872), v. 704

Lady of Lions (Dowling, M. G., 1838), iv. 489, 630

Lady of Longford (Harris, Sir A. H. G. and Weatherley, F. E., 1894), v. 406

Lady of Lyons (Byron, H. S., 1858), iv. 175; v. 295

— (Lytton, Lord, 1838), iv. 63, 173-5, 349, 596

— (Younge, W., 1879), v. 637

Lady of Lyons Married and Claude Unsettled (Reece, R., 1884), iv. 175; v. 539

Lady of Lyons married and settled (Merivale, H. C., 1878), iv. 175; v. 487

Lady of Munster (1860), v. 704

— = Perfection

Lady of Nuremberg = Broken Chain

Lady of Ostend (Burnand, F. C., 1899), v. 292

Lady of Quality (Burnett, Mrs F. H. and Townsend, S., 1896), v. 292

Lady of St Tropez (1845), iv. 489

— (1846), iv. 489

— (1857), v. 704

— = Privateer

Lady of the Camelias (1852), V. 704, 838

— (1858), V. 704

Lady of the Haystack (1862), V. 704

Lady of the Lake (Dibdin, T. J., 1810), IV. 92, 298, 580

— (Eyre, E. J., 1811), IV. 92, 310

— (Lemon, M., 1843), IV. 92, 345, 489, 630

— (Pitt, W. H., 1872), V. 811

— (Taylor, R. W., 1862), V. 704, 819, 838

— (Tully, J. H., 1843), IV. 92, 414

— (Webb, C., 1871), V. 617

Lady of the Lake and the Knight of Snowdoun (1827), IV. 92, 489

Lady of the Lake—Plaid in a Tartan (Reece, R., 1866), V. 537

Lady of the Lane (Byron, H. J., 1872), V. 298

Lady of the Locket (Hamilton, H., 1885), V. 401

Lady of the Lone House = Second to None

Lady of the Louvre (Oxberry, W. H., 1839), IV. 489, 602

Lady of the Manor (Kenrick, W., 1778), III. 116, 279, 389

Lady of the Mill (1862), V. 704

Lady of the Rock (Holcroft, T., 1805), IV. 326

— = Family Legend

Lady of the Tower (1811), IV. 490

Lady of the Willow (1844), IV. 490

Lady of the Wreck (1817), IV. 490

— = Castle Blarneygig

Lady on the Rock = Isle of Mull

Lady or the Tiger (Rosenfeld, S., 1888), V. 550

Lady Pentweazel in Town (1787), III. 333

Lady Philosopher (Hughes, H., 1898), V. 430

Lady Satan (Sheen, W. P., 1896), V. 562

Lady's Choice (Hiffernan, P., 1759), III. 268

Lady's Dream (Jefferson, G., 1822), IV. 331

Lady's Hobby Horse = Black Pig

Lady's Last Stake (Cibber, C., 1707), II. 5, 11, 27, 38, 50, 134, 162, 183, 184, 185–6, 189, 233, 310, 434; III. 42

Lady Slavey (Dance, G., 1893), V. 335

Lady's Lecture (Cibber, C., 1748), II. 313

Lady's Maid (Hamilton, H., 1893), V. 402

Lady's Oath (Reade, C.), V. 812

Lady's Opera (1781), III. 399

Lady's Revenge (Popple, W., 1734), II. 13, 184, 200–1, 350

— = Love and Levity

Lady's Satisfaction = Injur'd Love

Lady's Triumph (Settle, E., 1718), II. 6, 234, 354, 359

— (Theobald, L., 1718), II. 260, 359

Lady Tartuffe (1853), V. 704

Lady Volunteers (Phelps, S., 1896), V. 522

— (1867), V. 704

Lady Windermere's Fan (Wilde, O. F. O'F. W., 1892), V. 187, 190–2, 622

Lady Wrangler (Hicks, Sir S., 1898), V. 421

Laelia, the Queen of the Hills (Wilkins, J. H., 1858), V. 823

Laffarge (Coyne, J. S., 1840), IV. 490, 630

Laggard in Love (Lennard, H., 1893), V. 456

Laid up in Port (Higgie, T. H., 1846), IV. 325

Laird in Disguise = Jamie and Bess

Laird, the Daftie and the Highland Maiden = McAllister McVitty McNab

Laird, the Lady and the Lover = Lucia di Lammermoor

Laitière suisse = Natalie

Lakers (Plumptre, J., 1798), III. 298

Lake of Geneva = Out of Place

Lake of Lausanne = Out of Place

Lake of Lugano (1827), IV. 490

Lake of the Apennines = Black Eagle

Lake of the Grotto = Council of Ten

Lakes of Killarney (1855), V. 705

Lakmé (1885), V. 705

Lalla Rookh (Amcotts, V., 1868), V. 240

— (Brough, W., 1857), V. 279

— (Hall, F., 1879), V. 399

— (Lennard, H., 1884), V. 455, 803

Lalla Rookh (O'Sullivan, M., 1818), IV.
366
— (Rayner, B. F., 1836), IV. 389
Lalli Tollendal (1839), IV. 490
Lambeth in Olden Times = Edith of the
Marsh
Lambeth in the Olden Time = Old
House on the Thames
Lambton Worm (Roxby, S., 1848), IV.
396
— (1877), V. 705
Lame Common-wealth (Kirkman, F.,
1662), I. 417
Lamed for Life (Marston, J. W., 1871),
V. 479
Lame Excuse (Hay, F., 1869), V. 411
Lame Lover (Foote, S., 1770), III. 174,
260
Lamp and the Scamp = Aladdin
Lamplighter (Davis, S., 1855), V. 787
— (Dickens, C., 1879), IV. 209–10, 305
— (1854), V. 705
Lancashire Lass (Byron, H. J., 1867), V.
114, 297
Lancashire Life (Towers, E., 1875), V.
601
Lancashire Sailor (Thomas, B., 1891), V.
596
Lancashire Weaver Lad (Brierley, B.,
1877), V. 275
Lancashire Witches (Dibdin, C., 1783),
III. 256
— (Fitzball, E., 1848), IV. 317
— (Fitzball, E., 1858), V. 368
— (Gunton, R. T., 1879), V. 397, 795
— (Pitt, G. D., 1847), IV. 375
— (Shadwell, T., 1681), I. 8, 10, 79, 90,
132, 207, 337, 431
— (1810), IV. 490
Lancelot the Lovely (Henry, R., 1889),
V. 418
Lancer = Long Cloth
Lancers (Payne, J. H., 1827), IV. 369
— (Vernon, L., 1853), V. 107, 608
Land Ahead (Fenn, G. M., 1878), V.
365
Land and Love (Dubourg, A. W.,
1884), V. 351
Land and Sea (Blake, T. G.), IV. 573
Land and the People (Moss, A. B. and
Patmore, W. J., 1893), V. 497
Land and Wave = Life of the Brave

Landed from China = My Wife's Lodg-
ings
Landgartha (Barnes, J., 1683), I. 389
Landgrave's Leap (1819), IV. 490
Landlady (Aveling, E. B., 1889), V. 246
— (Kirkman, F., 1662), I. 418
— (1888), V. 705
— = Pothooks
Landlord (Hall, W. J. C., 1886), V. 400
Landlord and Tenant (1847), IV. 490
Landlord Bit = Merry Sailors
Landlord in Jeopardy! = Jealous on All
Sides
Landlord outwitted = Who pays the
Rent?
Landlord's Dilemma (1895), V. 705
Land of Diamonds (Coen, L., 1884), V.
316
Land of Enchantment (1846), IV. 490
Land of Gold (Lander, G., 1888), V. 448
Land of Heart's Desire (Yeats, W. B.,
1894), V. 635
Land of Khem = Snefern the Second
Land of Luna = Celestia
Land of Nod (Chevalier, A., 1897), V.
309
Land of Pie (Bunner, H. C., 1899), V.
287
Land of Promise = Christian's Crime
Land of Simplicity (Dibdin, C.), IV. 290
Land of the Living (Harvey, F., 1889),
V. 408
Land Rats and Water Rats (Phillips,
W., 1868), V. 523
Land Sharks and Sea Gulls (Edwards,
1841), IV. 309
Land Storm (1819), IV. 490
Land we live in (Holt, F. L., 1804), IV.
30, 327
— (1791), III. 333
— = Hall of Augusta
Langamo's Cave (1844), IV. 490
Language of Flowers (Wooler, J. P.,
1852), V. 705, 824
— = Bouquet
Lansdown Castle (Cunningham, A. C.,
1893), V. 331
Lantern Light (D'Arcy, G. and Ross,
C. H., 1873), V. 336
Laoeudaimonos (1789), III. 333
Laon-Seng-Urh (Davis, J. F., 1817), VI.
579

La-Peyrouse (Plumptre, A., 1799), III.
65, 298, 393
— (Thompson, B., 1799), III. 65, 311,
397
— (1781), III. 333
Lapidary of Leyden (1840), IV. 490
+Laplander (Smock Alley, Dublin,
21/3/1772)
Laplanders (1788), III. 333
Lapland Fairy (1812), IV. 490
Lapland Witch (Lancaster, E. R.), IV.
593
Lapse of 20 Years = Gambler's Fate
Lara (Bass, C., 1827), IV. 262
— (Oxenford, J., 1865), v. 705, 809, 838
Larboard Fin (1837), IV. 490
Large as Life (1890), v. 705
Larkin's Love Letters (Williams, T. J.,
1866), v. 625
Lark in the Temple (1866), v. 705
Larks (Jones, J. W., 1886), v. 441
Larks in a Cage (1863), v. 705
Larks in London = Larks
Larks of Logic, Tom and Jerry = Life in
London
Larks with a Libretto = Trovatore
Lashed to the Helm (Hazlewood, C. H.,
1864), v. 705, 838
La! Somnambula! (Byron, H. J., 1865),
v. 297
Lasses of Leixlip = Irish Courtship
Lass of Gowrie (1839), IV. 490
— (1853), v. 705
— = Rose Graham
Lass of Richmond Hill (Trevor, H.,
1893), v. 603
Lass of the Lakes = Helvetic Liberty
Lass o' Moorside = Puck
Lass that Loved a Carpenter (1879), v.
705
Lass that loved a Sailor (Clarance, L.,
1883), v. 310
— (Doone, N., 1893), v. 347
— = H.M.S. Pinafore
Lass that Loves a Sailor = Ruth
Last Act (Leigh, E. M., 1899), v. 453
— (1814), IV. 490, 635
Last Appeal (1859), v. 705
— = Alice May
Last Call (Charles, H. and Greigg,
H. J. S., 1895), v. 308
Last Cause (1868), v. 705

Last Century = Great Metropolis
Last Chance (Sims, G. R., 1885), v. 185,
569
Last Chapter (Broadhurst, G. H., 1899),
v. 276
Last Chime of Midnight (France, E. S.),
v. 792
Last Chord (1879), v. 705
Last Command = My Comrade
Last Crime = Golden Farmer
Last Cruise of the Vampire = Coast-
guard
Last Crusade (Vyse, B., 1850), v. 609
Last Day (Godwin, G., Jr., 1840), IV.
490, 585, 630
Last Days of Napoleon Buonaparte
(1828), IV. 490
Last Days of Nelson = Trafalgar
Last Days of Pompeii (Buckstone, J. B.,
1834), IV. 97, 274
— (Fitzball, E., 1835), IV. 97, 314
— (Oxenford, J., 1872), v. 510
Last Deed of Garboni = Maid of Velitri
Last Dread Penalty (1897), v. 705
Last Edition of Ivanhoe (Brough, R. B.
and Brough, W., 1850), v. 277
Last Express (Abel, W. H., 1871), v. 234
Last Glass (1851), v. 705
Last Guerilla Chief (1826), IV. 490
Last Hope (Abel, W. H., 1873), v. 235
— (Oxenford, J., 1859), v. 509
Last Hour (1811), IV. 630
— = (1) Love's Rescue; (2) Midnight
Bell
Lasting Love (Newbound, E., 1878), v.
502
Last Key (1834), IV. 490
Last Kiss (Stirling, E., 1846), IV. 408
Last Leaf of the Tree = Light of Other
Days
Last Life (Palmer, T. A., 1874), v. 512
Last Lily (Scott, C. W., 1886), v. 558
Last Link in the Chain = (1) Babbi's
Son; (2) Wager
Last Link of Love (Hazlewood, C. H.,
1867), v. 413
— (1845), IV. 490
Last Link of the Chain = (1) Whitsun
Eve; (2) Whitsuntide
Last Mail (1836), IV. 490
Last Man (Pitt, G. D., 1833), IV. 373,
604

Last Man (1845), IV. 490
— = Miser of Eltham Green
Last Man on Earth (Stephens, V., 1897), V. 581
Last Moment (Travers, W., 1867), V. 602
— (1875), V. 705
Last Nail (Pitt, G. D., 1833), IV. 372, 604
Last New Year's Gift = Artificial Flower Maker
Last Night and the Last Morning (1860), V. 705
Last of his Race = (1) Gamester's Son; (2) King Maker
Last of Lord Nelson's Agamemnon = Ben Brace
Last of the Barons (Du Terreaux, L. H., 1872), V. 352
— (1845), IV. 490
— = (1) Hit or Miss; (2) Battle of Barnet
Last of the Bravoes (Oxenford, J., 1845), IV. 367
Last of the Burnings = Two Fishermen of Lynn
Last of the Caesars = Constantine and Valeria
Last of the Cavaliers = Bonnie Dundee
Last of the Cobbler = Rienzi Reinstated
Last of the Decemviri = Death of Virginia
Last of the Doges = Dandolo
Last of the Doomed Race = Kiddle-a-wink
Last of the Fairies (Fitzball, E., 1852), V. 368
Last of the Family (Cumberland, R., 1797), III. 252
Last of the Greeks (Howard, F., 1828), IV. 329
Last of the Latouches (Ellis, Mrs R. and Rennell, C. R., 1877), V. 357
Last of the Legends (À Beckett, G. A., 1873), V. 147–8, 234
Last of the Lotteries (1847), IV. 630
Last of the Mohicans = Uncas
Last of the Moors of Granada = Mendicant's Revenge
Last of the Murdakes (1830), IV. 490
Last of the Paladins (Reece, R., 1868), V. 537

Last of the Pigtails (Selby, C., 1858), V. 560
Last of the Race (Sanger, G., 1871), V. 555
Last of the Romans (1830), IV. 490
Last of the Stuarts = Prince Charlie
Last of the Vendeans = Carline
Last of the Wampanoags = Metamora
Last of the Welsh Bards (1873), V. 705
Last on the Programme (Ganthony, N., 1892), V. 375
Last Overture (1892), V. 705
Last Prince of Abyssinia and the True British Seaman = Blind Child of Africa
Last Resource (1886), V. 705
Last Sacrifice (1874), V. 705
Last Shift (McLaren, A., 1814), IV. 351
Last Shilling (Faucit, J. S., 1844) = Lost Shilling (IV. 311, 495, 631
— = Spendthrift
Last Slave (1867), V. 705
Last Straw (Dickinson, C. H., 1888), V. 344
— (1892), V. 705
Last Stroke of Midnight (Guiver, J., 1879), V. 397
Last Temptation (Sykes, P. H. T., 1897), V. 589
Last Train (Forshaw, F., 1898), V. 371
Last Voyage of Captain Cook = Floating Kingdom
Last Whistle (Addison, H. R., 1835), IV. 490, 630
Last Witch = Jackeydora
Last Witness (1840), IV. 630
Last Word (Daly, A., 1890), V. 333
Last Words = Conrad
Latch Key (Stirling, E., 1855), V. 705, 818, 838
Late Lamented (Horner, F., 1891), V. 427
— (Taylor, T., 1859), V. 593
Late Love (Outram, L. S., 1886), V. 509
Late Mr Castello (Grundy, S., 1895), V. 206, 397
Late Mr M. = Procrastination
Late Ralph Johnson (Edwards, H. S., 1872), V. 355
Late Revolution (1690), I. 442
Late Sir Benjamin (Young, Sir C. L., 1882), V. 636

Lawyers and their Clients (1815), IV. 491

Lawyer's Clerk = Lottery Ticket

Lawyer's Feast (Ralph, J., 1743), II. 140, 350

Lawyer's Fortune (Grimstone, W., 1705), II. 334

Lawyer's Panic (Dent, J., 1785), III. 254

Lawyer, the Jew and the Yorkshireman (Dibdin, T. J., 1825), IV. 304

Laycock of Langleyside (1866), V. 705

Lay Figure (1894), V. 705

Laying a Ghost (1843), IV. 491

Layo'ers for Meddlers (1823), IV. 491

Lay of a Lady (1899), V. 706

Lazaria the Greek (1823), IV. 491

Lazinetta and Other Drawing-Room Plays (Blanchard, E. L., 1883), V. 265

Lazuli (1831), IV. 491

Lazy Dick of Leadenhall = Old Bogie

Lazy Life (Shirley, A., 1882), V. 563

Leader of Men (Ward, C. E. D., 1895), V. 613

Leading Lady (Morton, M., 1896), V. 497

Leading Strings (Troughton, A. C., 1857), V. 604

— (1854), V. 706

Leaf from the Captain's Log Book = Bound to Succeed

Leaf in the Life of our American Cousin (1871), V. 706

Leaguers of Austria = Avenger

Leah (1864), V. 706

— (1868), V. 706

Leah: A Hearty Joke in a Cab Age (Routledge, W., 1869), V. 552

Leah and Nathan (Courtney, J., 1848), IV. 284

Leah the Forsaken = Leah, the Jewish Maiden

Leah the Jewess of Constantine = Leah and Nathan

Leah, the Jewish Maiden (Daly, A., 1862), V. 333

Leander and Hero (Horde, T., 1769), III. 272, 333

Leander and Leonora (Byrne, J., 1814), IV. 491, 630

Leap for Liberty (1862), V. 706

Leap for Life (Vane, S., 1898), V. 607

— (1861), V. 706

— — = Dick Fly-by-night and Dare-devil Dan

Leap from the Log = Lively Nancy

Leap in the Dark (1850), V. 607

Leap of Death = Wounded Horse

Leap Year (Buckstone, J. B., 1850), V. 106-7, 287

— (Kerr, F., 1892), V. 443

Leap Year's Comedy (Kenyon, J. R., 1899), V. 443

Learned Lady (Oliphant, R., 1789), III. 295

Learned Lions (1831), IV. 491

Lear of Cripplegate = Sharp Practice

Lear of Private Life (Moncrieff, W. T., 1820), IV. 91, 358

Leatherlungos the Great (Cheltnam, C. S., 1872), V. 118, 309

Leathern Bottle (1884), V. 706

Leave it to me (Hazlewood, C. H. and Williams, A., 1870), V. 414

— (1877), V. 706

Leavenworth Case (1885), V. 706

Leaves of Shamrock (Sullivan, J. P., 1891), V. 586

Leave the House (1828), IV. 491

Lecture on Heads (Pilon, F., ?1780), III. 393

Led Astray (Boucicault, D., 1873), V. 269

Leeds Fair (1775), III. 402

Leeds Merchant (Wallis, G., 1776), III. 314

Lefevre (Barnett, M., 1839), IV. 491, 630

Left Alone (Young, Mrs H., 1864), V. 706, 825, 838

Left-handed Marriages (Hazlewood, C. H., 1864), V. 706, 838

Left in a Cab (Stirling, E., 1851), V. 584

+ Left the Stage (*French*)

Left to her Fate = Disinherited

Left to Himself (1868), V. 706

Left Wing = Genius Wanted

Legacy (Allingham, J. T., 1806) = Romantic Lover, IV. 252, 491

— (Arnold, S. J., 1797) = Irish Legacy, III. 333, 377, 402

— (Foote, S., 1762), III. 384

— (Godfrey, W. P., 1879), V. 383

— (Lindo, F., 1894), V. 460

— (1810), IV. 491

Legacy Hunting (Smith, J. F., 1840), IV. 491, 630

Libertine Destroyed = (1) Don John; (2) Libertine

Libertine Lord, and the Damsel of Daisy Farm = Village Virtue

Libertine Lovers (Blacket, 1811), IV. 267

Libertine of Paris (Lighterness, W. B.), IV. 595

Libertine of Poland (Fitzball, E., 1830), IV. 492, 630

Libertine Reclaimed = (1) Giovanni in London; (2) Prodigal Son

Libertine's Bet (Reade, C., 1857), V. 536

Libertine's Lesson (Fitzball, E., 1827), IV. 313

Libertine's Remorse = Soldier's Vow

Libertine's Ship (1854), V. 706

— = Margaret's Ghost

Libertine's Wager Lost = Gabrielle de Belleisle

Libertine Tam'd = Doating Lovers

Libertine Transported = Giovanni in Botany

Liberty (Clarke, C. A., 1890), V. 312

— (Richardson, H., 1876), V. 543

Liberty Asserted (Dennis, J., 1704), II. 63, 86, 318

Liberty Chastised (Carey, G. S., 1768), III. 242

Liberty Hall (Carton, R. C., 1892), V. 305

— (Dibdin, C., 1785), III. 116, 203, 256

— (1807), IV. 492

Liberty Regain'd = Fatal Necessity

Liberty Vanquished = Triumphs of the Sons of Baliol

Librarian (Douglas, G. R., 1885), V. 347

Licensed Victualler's Daughter = Jane of Liverpool

Lick at the Town (Woodward, H., 1751), III. 317, 398

Lidiana (1885), V. 706

Lie for a Life = Morays

Lie of the Day (O'Keeffe, J., 1796), III. 295

— = Toy

Lie upon Lie (Scott, J. M., 1818) = Two Spanish Valets, IV. 492, 631

Lieutenant's Daughters = Home Again

Life (Barrs, H., 1894), V. 252

— (Brockbank, J., 1873), V. 276

— (Palmer, B., 1846), IV. 367

Life (Reynolds, F., 1800), IV. 391

— (1848), IV. 492

Life among the Lowly = Uncle Tom's Cabin

Life among the Slaves and Pirates of the Mississippi = Maum Guinea

Life and Adventures of a Suffolk Girl = Margaret Catchpole, the Female Horse-stealer

Life and Adventures of General Anderson = Marjory Gilzean

Life and Adventures of George Barrington (Young, Mrs H., 1862), V. 706, 825, 838

Life and Adventures of Will Shakespeare, the Poacher, the Player and the Poet (Saville, H. F., 1864), V. 706, 791, 815, 838

Life and Almost Death of Joan of Arc (1847), IV. 631

Life and Death of a Drunkard (1858), V. 706

Life and Death of Chatterton (March, M. G., 1885), V. 475

Life and Death of Common-Sense (1782), III. 116, 333

— = Pasquin

Life and Death of Doctor Faustus (Mountfort, W., 1685), I. 252, 260, 421

Life and Death of Guy Fawkes (Somerset, C. A., 1851), V. 574

Life and Death of Jack Sheppard (1860), V. 706

Life and Death of Jane Shore = Royal Mistress

Life and Death of Jo (Price, E., 1876), V. 530

Life and Death of King Richard II (1834), IV. 90, 492

— = Wat Tyler and Jack Straw

Life and Death of King Richard III (1813), IV. 90, 492

— = Battle of Bosworth Field

Life and Death of Little Nell = Old Curiosity Shop

Life and Death of Miss Rump (1660), I. 441

Life and Death of Pantaloon (Delpini, 1806), IV. 579

Life and Death of Sir William Wallace (Lamb, T., 1866), V. 446

Life and Death of Sweeny Tod = String of Pearls

Life and Death of Tom Moody = Royal Foxhunt

Life and Death of Tom Thumb = Tom Thumb

Life and Death of Uncle Tom = Christian Slave

Life and Honour = Blanche Farreau

Life and Love in These Times = Under the Gaslight

Life and Reign of George III = George III, IV. 359, 492, 631

Life and Struggles of a Working Man (1853), V. 706

Life as it is (Blake, T. G., 1839), IV. 268, 573

— (Blake, T. G., 1852), V. 262

Life as we find it in 1850 = Tricks and Trials

Life at the East End of London (Lee, N., Jr., 1864), V. 803

Life below the Earth = Coal Mine

Life Boat (Blake, T. G., 1850), V. 707, 779, 838

— (1887), V. 707

Life Buoy (Hoskins, F. R., 1869), V. 427

Life Chase (Courtney, J., 1852) = Marriage Day, V. 326, 716, 786, 840

— (Oxenford, J. and Wigan, H., 1869), V. 510

Life, Death, and Renovation of Tom Thumb (1785), III. 334

Life, Death and Restoration of the High Mettled Racer (Dibdin, T. J., 1815) = High Mettled Racer, IV. 492, 631

Life down South (Cantwell, R. F., 1874), V. 302

Life Epitomised = Lyric Novelist

Life for a Life (Baring, S. and Beaumont, W., 1899), V. 249

— (Hazlewood, C. H., 1860), V. 412

— (Travers, W., 1860) = Reprieve, V. 707, 740, 821, 838, 845

Life for Life (Marston, J. W., 1869), V. 479

— = (1) Comrades and Friends; (2) Humanity

Life for Love = Bolivar

Life for the Czar (1888), V. 707

Lifeguardsman (1849) = Little Guardsman, IV. 492, 631

Life in All Shapes (1857), V. 707

Life in America (1836), IV. 492

Life in a Mirror = Dash of the Day

Life in an Hotel (1823), IV. 492

Life in Australia, from Our Own Correspondent (Phillips, Mrs A., 1853), V. 522

Life in Death = Innocent

Life in Dublin (Egan, P., 1839), IV. 492, 582, 631

Life in Edinburgh = Writer's Clerk

Life in England and California = Land of Gold

Life in Galway = O'Dowd

Life in Glasgow = Speculation

Life in Ireland = Florence Macarthy

Life in Lambeth (Osman, W. R., 1864), V. 707, 808, 838

Life in Little = Yorkshire School

Life in London (Dibdin, C. I. M., 1821), IV. 96, 295

— (1821), IV. 492

— = (1) Diamond King; (2) Hunger; (3) Key of the Streets; (4) Tom and Jerry; (5) Tom, Jerry and Logic

Life in London as it was and is = What will become of him?

Life in Louisiana = Octoroon

Life in New Orleans = Slave Hunter and the Half Caste

Life in New York (1848), IV. 492

— = Fashion

Life in Olympus (Mowbray, T., 1860), V. 807

Life in Oxford = Peter Priggins

Life in Paris (1822), IV. 492

Life in Russia = Living Death

Life in Santa Lucia = Elise

Life in 1796 = Incorrigibles

Life in the Black Country = Old Grimey

Life in the Clouds (Brougham, J., 1840), IV. 272

Life in the Coal Pits (Levey, J. C., 1867), V. 458

Life in the Cotton Fields = Down South

Life in the Diggings = In for a Dig

Life in the Far Wild West = Mexican Bill

Life in the Golden Gulch = Danites

Life in the Merry Greenwood = Gipsey Norris
Life in the Mine = Pit's Mouth
Life in the Rail = Hooker and Snooker
Life in the Ranks = Whipping Post
Life in the Streets = Islington
Life in the Sunny South (1857), v. 707
Life in the Temple = Chamber Practice
Life in the Trenches (1855), v. 707
Life in the Wild West = Buffalo Bill
Life, its Morn and Sunset (Hazlewood, C. H., 1872), v. 414
Life Lost = Lost Life
Life, Love and Fortune = London Vice and London Virtue
Life of a Beggar (Travers, W., 1857), v. 707, 821, 838
Life of a Betting Boy (1852), v. 707
Life of a Cabman = George Pernet
Life of a Gamester = Thirty Years
Life of a Labourer (Atkyns, S., 1848), IV. 257
Life of a Member of Parliament = Blight of Ambition
Life of a Mill Girl (1884), v. 707
Life of a Miner (Faucquez, A., 1862), v. 707, 839
Life of an Actor (Peake, R. B., 1824), IV. 370
Life of an Actress (Boucicault, D., 1855), v. 268
— (Suter, W. E., 1853) = Violette la Grande, v. 587, 764, 819, 849
Life of an Ape = Brazilian Jack
Life of an Emigrant = (1) Gold Diggings of Australia; (2) New World
Life of a Pickpocket = George Barrington
Life of a Policeman = Willie the Wanderer
Life of a Pottery Lass (Walters, F., 1869), v. 612
Life of a Sailor = Nelson
Life of a Shingler (Hall, C. I., 1870), v. 399
Life of a Ship from her Cradle to her Grave (Townsend, W. T., 1847), IV. 414
Life of a Slaver = Under the Line
Life of a Soldier (Pitt, G. D., 1848), IV. 604
— (1861), v. 707

Life of a Soldier = (1) Horrors of War; (2) Standard of England
Life of a Street Boy = London
Life of a Thames Waterman = Jacob Faithful
Life of a Tradesman's Daughter = Two Homes
Life of a Vagrant = Moneylender
Life of a Weaver (Hazlewood, C. H., 1859), v. 412
Life of a Woman (Haines, J. T., 1840), IV. 323, 587
Life of Guilt (1851), v. 707
Life of James Dawson (1841), IV. 631
Life of King Ahasuerus (1719), II. 376
Life of King Henry VIII = Queen Catherine and Cardinal Wolsey
Life of Man and Horse = Favourite of the Derby
Life of Ned Cantor (1855), v. 707
Life of Pleasure (Harris, Sir A. H. G. and Pettitt, H., 1893), v. 406
Life of Spritsail Jack = Blue Anchor
Life of the Brave (1844), IV. 492
Life of William Shakespeare = Shakespeare's Early Days
Life on the Board = Gentleman Jack
Life on the Mississippi = Conrad and Lizette
Life on the Ocean (1868), v. 707
Life on the Ocean and the Land = Boy Pirate
Life on the Ocean Wave (1849), IV. 492
Life on the Road = Captain Macheath
Life on the Turf = Chase
Life on the Western Border = Si Slocum
Life or Death (Harvey, F., 1886), v. 408
Life Policy (Davis, H., 1894), v. 339
Life Preserver (1876), v. 707
Life Race (Evelyn, J., 1872), v. 359
Life Raft (Townsend, W. T.), v. 707, 821, 839
— (1845), IV. 492
Life's a Dream = Such Stuff as Dreams are made of
Life's a Jest = Ridicule
Life's a Lottery (Rede, W. L., 1842), IV. 390
Life's Battle (Comer, G., 1891), v. 319
— (Faucit, H. S., 1878), v. 363
Life's Battle for Gold = Gratitude

Life's Bondage (Byrton, H., 1890), v. 299

— = Redeemed

Life's Campaign = British Soldier

Life's Chances = Vendetta

Life's Cloud and Sunshine = Hewie the Witless

Life's Debt (Graham, J. F., 1887), v. 387

Life's Devotion (Abel, W. H., 1870), v. 234

Life's Faults and Follies = Seven Poor Travellers

Life's Harvest (Shute, E. A., 1891), v. 565

Life's Highway (Dillon, C., 1844), IV. 305

— (1857), v. 707

Life's Ladder (1885), v. 707

Life's Luck (1848), IV. 492

Life's Magic (1854), v. 707

Life's Mistakes (Edwards, J. C., 1885), v. 355

Life's Morning (Webb, C.), IV. 616

Life's Mysteries and Woman's Devotion (1856), v. 707

Life's Parting Ways (Gilbert-Gilmer, J., 1893), v. 381

Life's Peril (Stanley, H. J., 1874), v. 579

Life's Pilot = Home in the Heart

Life's Ransom (Marston, J. W., 1857), v. 479

Life's Repentance = Paid in Full

Life's Revenge (Farjeon, B. L., 1865), v. 790

— (Howard, W., 1897), v. 428

— (Suter, W. E., 1858), v. 587, 819

Life's Sacrifice = Valjean

Life's Sarcasm (Macdonnell, Mrs A. J., 1898), v. 468

Life's Seasons (1852), v. 707

Life's Shadows = No Pain, no Gain

Life Signal (Hazlewood, C. H., 1867), v. 413

Life's Thorny Path and the Orphan's Highborn Husband = Castaway

Life's Trial (Bernard, W. B., 1857), v. 259

Life's Trials = Leoline

Life's Trials by Sea and Land (Hazlewood, C. H., 1856), v. 707, 796, 839

Life's Troubles (1866), v. 707

Life's Vagaries (O'Keeffe, J., 1795), III. 176, 294

Life's Victory (Don, L., 1885), v. 347

Life Task (1862), v. 707

Life, Trial and Execution of the Wretched Homicide Rush (Rice, C., 1860), v. 813

Life Underground = Light in the Dark

Life we Lead (Mackay, R. F. and Denbigh, L. S., 1892), v. 470

Life Without a Mask = Soldier's Opera

Light (Callender, E. R., 1882), v. 300

— (Dalton, L., 1893), v. 333

— (Flaxman, A. J., 1877), v. 369

— (1898), v. 707

Light Ahead (Leonard, H., 1891), v. 456

Light and Dark (Wardhaugh, M., 1871), v. 614

Light and Shade (Broughton, F. W., 1877), v. 281

— (Pitt, G. D., 1848), IV. 492, 631

Light and Shadow (Slous, A. R., 1864), v. 571

Light as Air (1870), v. 707

Light at Last (Patmore, W. J., 1890), v. 515

— (1874), v. 707

Light behind the Cloud (1861), v. 707

Light Dragoons (1847), IV. 492

Lighterman of the Bankside (Courtney, J., 1848), IV. 284

Light Fantastic (Byron, H. J., 1880), v. 299

Lighthouse (Collins, W. W., 1857), v. 318

— (Levey, J. C., 1871), v. 458

— (Soane, G., 1842), IV. 612

Lighthouse Keepers = Monster of the Eddystone

Lighthouse on the Carn Ruth = Dead Man's Point

Lighthouse on the Crimson Rock (1883), v. 707

Light in the Dark (Sidney, W., 1867), v. 566

— (1883), v. 707

Lightning Flash (Shirley, A., 1891), v. 564

Lightning's Flash (Hazlewood, C. H., 1871), v. 414

— = Innocence

Light o' Day (McCullough, B., 1888), v. 468

Light of Asia (Beatty-Kingston, W., 1892), v. 254

Light of his Eyes (Bellingham, H. and Best, W., 1895), v. 257

Light of Love (Young, Mrs H., 1867), v. 636

— =(1) Angel's Visit; (2) Blanche

Light of Other Days (Meller, R., 1889), v. 485

— (Taylor, T. P., 1837), IV. 411

Light of Pengarth (Cassilis, I. L., 1891), v. 306

Light of the Isles (Allen, O., 1876), v. 239

Lights and Shades of Virtue and Vice= Mechanic

Lights and Shadows=Road of Life

Lights and Shadows in a Young Girl's Path=Nearly Lost

Lights and Shadows of Life=Dissolving Views

Lights and Shadows of London Life= Guinea Gold

Lights and Shadows of Pit Life=Black Diamonds

Lights and Shadows of the World we live in=Maximums and Speciments of William Muggins

Lights of Home (Buchanan, R. and Sims, G. R., 1892), v. 285

Lights of Liberty=Power of the Press

Lights of the Age (1899), v. 707

Lights o' London (Sims, G. R., 1881), v. 568

Light that failed (Thorpe, C., 1891), v. 599

Light Troop of St James's (1847), IV. 492

Like and Unlike (Langford, and Sorrell, W. J., 1856), v. 448

Like Father, like Son (Behn, A., 1682), I. 391

— (Raymond, R. J. or Kenney, J., 1840), IV. 389, 592, 606

— (1801), IV. 492

— (1876), v. 707

Like Master, Like Man (Ryder, T., 1766), III. 115, 303

— =(1) Jacintha; (2) Lover's Quarrels; (3) Wrangling Lovers

Likeness (1849), IV. 492

Like to Like (1701), II. 377

Lilia (1886), v. 707

Lilian Gervais (Barnett, M., 1853), v. 250

Lilian Locke, the Widow of the Mill= Last Glass

Lilian, the Show Girl (Soane, G., 1836), IV. 404

Lilies (Paulton, H., 1884), v. 517

+ Lilies that Fester (Poel, W.: St George's Hall, 9/7/1897; N.Y. 1906. Adapted from *Arden of Feversham*)

Liline and Valentin (Layton, G. M., 1875), v. 451, 802

Lilla (Planché, J. R., 1825), IV. 378

Lilla the Lost One (Hazlewood, C. H.), v. 797

Lillian Trafford (Bronson, W. S., 1864), v. 707, 780, 839

Lilliput (Fisher, F. G., 1817), IV. 492, 583, 631

— (Garrick, D., 1756), III. 262

Lilliputian Camp (1767), III. 334

Lilliputian Sports (1802), IV. 492

Lilliput Island (1810), IV. 492

Lilly Dawson (Atkyns, S., 1847), IV. 257

— (Stirling, E., 1847), IV. 408

Lilly Laburnem (Pitt, G. D., 1848), IV. 375

Lilly of the Valley (1844), IV. 493

Lily (Darbey, E., 1878), v. 336

— (Delille, H. A., 1888), v. 342

Lily and the Rose=Protector at Houghall

Lily Dale (Delafield, J. H., 1869), v. 341

Lily Lyle=Workman

Lily of Devon=Amy the Skipper's Daughter

Lily of Killarney (Oxenford, J. and Boucicault, D., 1862), v. 510, 809

Lily of Léoville (Rémo, F. and Murray, A., 1886), v. 541

Lily of Limerick=Dora O'Donovan

Lily of Lismore=Row of Ballynavogue

Lily of Pontsarn (1893), v. 707

Lily of St Clarens=Laurette

Lily of St Leonard's=(1) Effie Deans; (2) Heart of Midlothian; (3) Jeannie Deans

Lily of Snowdon=Welsh Wolf

Lily of the Desert (Stirling, E., 1849), IV. 409

Lily of the Field (Hannan, C., 1896), v. 403

Lily of the Village = Blue-eyed Mary

Lily's Love (Abel, W. H., 1872), v. 234

Limbs of the Law (1879), v. 707

Limerick Boy (Pilgrim, J., 1865), v. 524

Lime Tree Chateau (1857), v. 707

Limited = Skittles Limited

Limited Liability (Naden, A. T., 1888), v. 501

+ Lina and Gertrude (*French*)

Linco's Travels (Garrick, D., 1767), III. 263

Linda di Chamouni (Edwardes, C. T. M., 1869), v. 354

— (Linley, G., 1851), v. 460

Linda Grey (Young, Sir C. L., 1885), v. 636

Lindamira (Foote, S., 1805) = First Act of Taste, III. 260, 384

— (1821), IV. 493

Linda of Chamouni (Thompson, A., 1869), v. 597, 820

Linda of Chamouny (Ryan, M. D., 1848), IV. 493, 631

Lindlove's Abbey (1877), v. 707

Lindor and Clara (Fennell, J., 1790), III. 259

Lindorf et Rosalie (1813), IV. 493

Linen Draper (Brown, J. R. and Thornthwaite, J. F., 1890), v. 282

Linen-draper's Tour = Jonny Gilpin

Line of Fate (Hewson, J. J., 1894), v. 420

Line of March = Bagshot-Heath Camp

Lines to an Old Ban-ditty = Utter Perversion of the Brigand

Lingo in a New School = Fig Hall

Lingo's Opinions on Men and Manners (Edwin, J., 1787), III. 383

Lingo's Wedding (1784), III. 334

Line of Life (Sidney, W. and Grattan, H. P., 1871), v. 566

Linishee Lovel (1828), IV. 493

Link by Link (Hay, F. and Fenton, F., 1870), v. 411

Linked by Love = Thad

Link of Love (Colville, W. F., 1882), v. 319

Link o' Gold (Capel, G., 1882), v. 302;

Linnet's Lark (Hay, F., 1878), v. 411

Lion and the Mouse = (1) Only a Waif; (2) Stolen Kisses

Lion and the Tiger = Mr Pep

Lion and the Unicorn (Higgie, T. H., 1851), v. 421

Lion and the Unicorn were fighting for the Crown (Byron, H. J., 1864), v. 296, 782

Lion at Bay (Phillips, W., 1869), v. 523

Lion Brothers of the Burning Zaara = Aslar and Ozines

+ Lion Chief; or, The African Horseman (Farrell, J.; Roy. 10/1820)

Lion Conqueror (Townsend, W. T., 1860), v. 707, 821, 839

Lionel and Clarissa (Bickerstaffe, I., 1768), III. 198–9, 237

Lionel Prince of Saxony = White Eagle

Lioness of the North (Selby, C., 1845), v. 389

Lioness of the Sea = Female Pirate

Lion Hunters of the Burning Zaara = Aslar and Ozines

Lion King (1840), IV. 493

— (1842), IV. 493

— (1851), v. 707

Lion Limb (Pitt, C., 1867), v. 525

Lion of England (Clifton, 1825), IV. 576

Lion of England and the Eagle of France (1855) = United Service, v. 707, 762, 839

Lion of the Desert (1840), IV. 493

Lion of the Jungle (Johnstone, J. B., 1844), IV. 333

Lion Queen (1852), v. 707

Lion Queen and the Lawyer's Clerk = Mysteries of Old Father Thames

Lion's Den (1871), v. 708

— (1882), v. 708

Lions for a Lark (1838), IV. 493

Lion's Heart (Shirley, A. and Landeck, B., 1892), v. 564

Lion Slayer (Williams, T. J., 1860), v. 625

Lion's Love (Conquest, G., 1866), v. 707, 839

Lion's Mouth (Thompson, A., 1867), v. 597

Lions of Mysore = Hyder Ali

Lion's Tail and the Naughty Boy who wagged it (Reece, R., 1877), v. 538

Lirenda's Misery = Cola's Fury

Lisbeth of the Tyrol (1845), IV. 493

Lisbon (1811), IV. 493

Lischen and Fritzchen (1869), v. 839

Lisette (1831), IV. 493

— (1873), v. 708

Lisle Wilton (1849), IV. 493

Listeners hear no good of themselves = Figure of Fun

Lists of Ashby (Cooper, F. F., 1837) = Ivanhoe, IV. 94, 493, 631, 697, 837

Lita (Conway, A. G., 1888), v. 323

Literary Dustman (Rogers, W., 1840), IV. 609

Literary Nephew (Seed, H., 1868), v. 560

Litigants (Ozell, J., 1715), II. 347, 442

Litigious Suitor Defeated (1742), II. 172, 384

Little Aaron (1810), IV. 493

Little Alexander the Great = Rival Queens

Little Amy Robsart (1887), v. 708

Little Amy Robsart from a Comic Point of View (1872), v. 708

Little and Good = Quite Out of the Common

Little Back Parlour (Stirling, E., 1839), IV. 406

Little Baronet (Hoffman, M. H., 1897), v. 423

Little Beauty and the Great Beast = Bella Donna

Little Ben and Little Bob (1795) = Poor Sailor, III. 334, 402, 403

Little Ben Bolt (Keene, E., 1879), v. 442

— (1876), v. 708

Little Bidette (Pitt, G. D., 1850), v. 526

Little Billie Carlyle (Harbon, W. J., 1881), v. 403

Little Bill that was taken up = Latest Edition of Black-eyed Susan

Little Blind Earl (1898), v. 708

Little Blue Bottle (Baddeley, G. C., 1873), v. 247

Little Bob and Little Ben = Poor Sailor

Little Bo-Peep (Buckstone, J. B., 1854), v. 287, 781

— (Glover, E., 1854), v. 382

— (Henderson, J., 1892), v. 416

— (Locke, F., 1892), v. 708, 804, 839

Little Bo-peep (Paulton, H. and Paulton, J., 1875), v. 516

— (Woolfe, J. H., 1894), v. 708, 839

— (1857, 1860), v. 839

— (1865), v. 708

— (1873), v. 839

— (1875, 1876, 1877, 1878, 1879, 1880, 1881), v. 708

— (1881), v. 839

— (1882, 1883, 1884, 1887, 1890, 1891), v. 708

— (1892), v. 839

— (1892, 1894, 1896, 1898), v. 708

Little Bo-Peep! Boy Blue! (Stainforth, F., 1880), v. 578

Little Bo-Peep, Little Boy Blue and the Little Old Woman that lived in a Shoe (Younge, W., 1881), v. 637, 825

Little Bo-Peep, Little Red Riding Hood and Hop o' my Thumb (Harris, Sir A. H. G. and Jones, J. W., 1892), v. 406

Little Bo-Peep who lost her Sheep (McCabe, F., 1867), v. 467

— (Marchant, F., 1875), v. 476

Little Bo Peep, who lost her Sheep, and Humpty Dumpty (Marchant, F., 1871), v. 476

Little Boy Blue (Watts, F. J., 1875), v. 616

— (1863), v. 839

— (1877, 1880), v. 708

Little Boy Blue and Red Riding Hood (1894), v. 708

Little Boy Blue, come blow your Horn (Merion, C., 1874), v. 485

Little Bright Eyes (1860), v. 708

Little Buonaparte and his Warhorse = King of Rome

Little Busy Bee (Hazlewood, C. H., 1864), v. 708, 839

Little Captive (1828), IV. 493

Little Captive King (1852), v. 708

Little Carmen (Murray, A., 1884), v. 499

Little Chang (Burnand, F. C., 1872), v. 290

Little Change (Grundy, S., 1872), v. 205, 396

Little Chap, Curly and Brown (Rix, W. J. and Gillett, F. J., 1895), v. 544

Little Christopher Columbus (Sims, G. R. and Raleigh, C., 1893), v. 569

Little Cinderella (Jones, J. W., 1887), v. 441

Little Claude and the Big Lady of Lyons (Field, W. F., 1892), v. 366

Little Claus and Big Claus (Hood, B., 1897), v. 425

Little Comedies (Sturgis, J., 1882), v. 818

Little Coquette (Barry, J. L., 1899), v. 252

Little Corporal (Buckstone, J. B., 1831), IV. 493, 631

Little Cricket (Mortimer, J., 1878), v. 494

Little Culprit (Atwood, A. and Vaun, R., 1897), v. 245

Little Daisy (Williams, T. J., 1863), v. 625

Little Dawson (1847), IV. 493

Little Demon (Halford, J., 1855), v. 708, 795, 839

Little Demon's Treasure = Little Devil's Share

Little Devil (Webster, B. N., 1843), IV. 418

Little Devil's Share (1860), v. 708
— = Asmodeus, the Little Demon

Little Dick Whittington (Byron, H. J., 1866), v. 782
— (1894), v. 708

Little Dicky Dilver with his Stick of Silver (Blanchard, E. L. and Greenwood, T. L., 1871), v. 264

Little Dinner (Grain, R. C., 1884), v. 387

Little Doctor Faust (Byron, H. J., 1877), v. 298

Little Don Caesar de Bazan (Byron, H. J., 1876), v. 298

Little Don Giovanni (Byron, H. J., 1865), v. 297

Little Don Quixote (1882), v. 708

Little Dorothy (Thorne, R., 1863), v. 709, 839

Little Dorrit (Cooper, F. F., 1856), v. 709, 786, 839

Little Duchess (Marshall, F. W. and Mouillot, F., 1898), v. 478
— (1861), v. 708

Little Duck and the Great Quack = Dulcamara

Little Duke (Scott, C. W. and Stephenson, B. C., 1878), v. 557
— (1841), IV. 493

Little 18-Carat (Dawtrey, R. A., 1885), v. 339

Little Emily (Halliday, A., 1869), v. 80, 401
— = (1) Emily; (2) Poor Em'ly

Little Em'ly's Trials (Brooke, E. H., 1871), v. 80, 276

Little Eyolf (Archer, W., 1896), v. 242

Little Fanny's Love = Scotch Ghost

Little Fibs (Berrie, E., 1869), v. 259

Little Flirting = I will be a Duchess

Little Flutter (Clarke, H. S., 1892), v. 313

Little Foster Brother (1877), v. 709

Little Fra Diavolo (1881), v. 709
— = Young Fra Diavolo

Little Freeholder (Hailes, Lord, 1790), III. 185, 266

Little French Doctor = Morgue

Little French Lawyer (Booth, Mrs, 1778), III. 113, 239
— (1749), II. 140, 377, 447

Little Game of Nap = Rip Van Winkle

Little Genius (Harris, Sir A. H. G. and Sturgess, A., 1896), v. 406

Little Gentleman (1867), v. 709

Little Gerty = Uncle True

Little Gil Blas (Farnie, H. B., 1870), v. 361

Little Gipsies (Dibdin, C. I. M., 1804), IV. 291

Little Gipsy (Lemon, M., 1841), IV. 344
— (1888), v. 709
— = May-Day

+Little Girl who Tells Fibs (*French*)

Little Giselle, the Dancing Belle (Hazlewood, H. C., Jr., 1867), v. 415

Little Glass Man and the Fiend of the "Pinkiknoll" = Peter Monk's Dream of the Marble Heart

Little Goody Two Shoes (Blanchard, E. L. and Greenwood, T. L., 1872), v. 264
— (Blanchard, E. L., 1876), v. 264
— (Filippi, R., 1888), v. 366
— (Green, F. W., 1871), v. 794
— (1829), IV. 493
— (1875, 1877, 1878, 1899), v. 709

Little Guardsman (1849) = Lifeguardsman, IV. 493, 631

Little Gulliver's Travels to the North
Pole (1876), V. 709

Little Hand and Muckle Gold (1889),
V. 709

Little Hermit (Trimmer, Mrs S., 1788),
III. 313

Little Hunch-Back (O'Keeffe, J., 1789),
III. 294

— (1839), IV. 493

— = Hunchback

Little Innocent (Townsend, W. T.,
1843), IV. 493, 631

Little Intruder = Shadows on the Blind

Little Jack and the Big Beanstalk
(Lloyd, A., 1887), V. 461

Little Jack Carpenter (1875), V. 709

Little Jack Frost (1883), V. 709

Little Jack Horner (Allen, O., 1876), V.
239

— (Blanchard, E. L., 1857), V. 263, 779

— (Clay, T. L. and Allen, O., 1881), V.
313

— (Stainforth, F., 1879), V. 578

— (1870, 1880, 1893), V. 709

Little Jack Horner and his Christmas
Pie (1858), V. 839

Little Jack Shepherd (Stephens, H. P.
and Yardley, W.), V. 580

Little Jack the Giant Killer (1871,
1875), V. 709

Little Jessie (Darâle, F., 1891), V. 336

— (1892), V. 709

Little Jim, the Collier's Son = Black
Country

Little Jockey (Dimond, W., 1831), IV.
307

Little Joey (1845), IV. 493

Little John and the Giants = Jack the
Gyant Queller

Little Johnny Horner (1896), V. 709

Little King (1861), V. 709

Little King Charles (1883), V. 709

Little King Pippin (Blanchard, E. L.,
1865), V. 264

Little Lady Loo = Jealousy

Little Lalla Rookh (Denny, J. T., 1885),
V. 342

Little Laundress (Peake, R. B., 1837),
IV. 493, 631

— (1856), V. 709

Little Lohengrin (Bowyer, F., 1884), V.
271

Little Lord Fauntleroy (Seebohm,
E. V., 1888), V. 560

Little Madcap (Cheltnam, C. S., 1846),
IV. 279

— (1884), V. 709

Little Man in Green = Young Man in
Green

Little Mary Plowden (1896), V. 709

Little Milliner = Mam'zelle

Little Minister (Barrie, J. M., 1897), V.
211, 251

Little Misery and a Little Mischief =
Cheap Bargain

Little Miss Beauty (1884), V. 709

Little Miss Cute (Vincent, C. T., 1894),
V. 609

Little Miss Muffet = Mulberry Bush

Little Miss Muffett and Little Boy Blue
(Buckstone, J. B., 1861), V. 287

Little Miss Nobody (Graham, H.,
1898), V. 386

Little Miss Wallflower (1895), V. 709

Little Mistake (1894), V. 709

Little Mother (Morton, J. M., 1870), V.
496

Little Mouse who built a House in a
Christmas Cake (Hazlewood, C. H.,
1860) = Harlequin and the Little
Mouse, V. 709, 834, 839

Little Mr Faust (Leslie, A., 1894), V. 456

Little Ned (1844), IV. 493

Little Nell = Nell

Little Nelly (Wood, M., 1872), V. 631

Little Nobody (Righton, M., 1890), V.
543

Little Nun (Craven, H. T., 1847), IV.
285

Little of Everything = Dead and the
Living

Little Offspring (1843), IV. 493

Little Offsprings (Peake, R. B. or
Percy, T. 1828), IV. 371, 603, 604

Little Old Man (1897), V. 709

Little Old Woman and her Pig (Lee,
N., 1841), IV. 493, 631

Little One (Ayres, A., 1885), V. 247

Little Orphan of the House of Chao
(Percy, T., 1763), III. 297

Little Orpheus and his Lute = (1)
Eurydice; (2) Pluto

Little Paul (Stephens, W., 1871), v. 581

Little Peggy's Love (1796), III. 334

Little Pest (Richardson, H., 1875), v. 543

Little Pet and the Great Passion = King Thrushbeard

Little Piece to Draw = Blister

Little Pigs (1830), IV. 493

Little Pilgrim (Wills, W. G., 1886), v. 627

Little Pleasure (Dance, C., 1834), IV. 288

Little Prince Poppet (1871), v. 709

Little Princess who was lost at Sea = Orange Tree and the Humble Bee

Little Prince's Tower = Dragon of Hogue Bie

Little Puss in Boots (Reece, R., 1873), v. 538

Little Ragamuffin (1868), v. 709

Little Ray of Sunshine (Ambient, M. and Heriot, W., 1898), v. 240

Little Rebel (Coyne, J. S., 1861), v. 328

Little Red Cross (Gower, J., 1885), v. 386

Little Red Man (Buckstone, J. B., 1832), IV. 274, 493, 574, 631

Little Red Riding Hat = Rose d'Amour

Little Red Riding Hood (À Beckett, G. A., 1843), IV. 250

— (Allen, O. and Tabrar, J., 1884), v. 239

— (Ashcroft, T., 1873), v. 244

— (Barry, J. L., 1897), v. 252

— (Blanchard, E. L., 1877), v. 264

— (Bridgeman, J. V. and Edwards, H. S., 1858), v. 709, 780, 789, 839

— (Buckingham, L. S., 1861), v. 286

— (Cheatham, F. G., 1867), v. 308

— (Clay, T. L., 1878), v. 313

— (Douglass, J. T., 1882), v. 348

— (Doyle, T. F., 1880), v. 710, 789, 839

— (Green, F. W., 1883), v. 391, 710, 794

— (Henry, A., 1874), v. 709, 797, 839

— (Hewson, J. J., 1897), v. 710, 798, 839

— (Keating, Miss, 1858), v. 801

— (Locke, F., 1893), v. 710, 804

— (Millward, C., 1857), v. 807

— (Moreton, R., 1897), v. 493

— (Muskerry, W., 1892), v. 501

Little Red Riding Hood (Parker, C. S., 1891), v. 513

— (Planché, J. R., 1832), IV. 605

— (Reeve, W., 1860), v. 813, 839

— (Taylor, T., 1851), v. 592, 820

— (1811, 1812), IV. 493

— (1854), v. 710

— (1857, 1859, 1860), v. 839

— (1871), v. 710

— (1873), v. 839

— (1875, 1876, 1877), v. 709

— (1879, 1880, 1881, 1882, 1883, 1884, 1885, 1886, 1887, 1889, 1891, 1892, 1894, 1895, 1896, 1897), v. 710

Little Red Riding Hood and Baron von Wolf (Keating, Miss, 1858), v. 801

Little Red Riding Hood and Harlequin Blue Boy (Robinson, N., 1868), v. 814

Little Red Riding Hood and Little Bo-Peep (1881), v. 710

Little Red Riding Hood and Little Miss Muffet (1881), v. 710

Little Red Riding Hood and the Wolf (Reynoldson, T. H., 1844), IV. 393, 608

Little Red Riding Hood, Harlequin Boy Blue, the Fiend Wolf and the Butterfly Fairies of the Fuchsia Grove (1862), v. 710

Little Robin Hood (Reece, R., 1871), v. 537, 812

— (Reece, R., 1882), v. 539

Little Robinson Crusoe (David, D. S., 1885), v. 433

Little Savage (Morton, J. M., 1858), v. 496

Little Sentinel (Williams, J. T., 1863), v. 625

Little Sins and Pretty Sinners (Selby, C., 1836), IV. 398

Little Snow White (Millward, C., 1871), v. 489

Little Squire (Greet, D. V. and Sedger, H., 1894), v. 393

Littlest Girl (Hilliard, R., 1896), v. 421

Little Stowaway (Emery, C. P., 1894), v. 358

Little Stranger (Derrick, J., 1881), v. 710, 788, 839

Little Strawbonnetmaker (1849), IV. 493

— (1857), v. 710

Little Sunbeam (Wylde, Mrs H., 1892), v. 634

Little Sutler (1858), v. 710

Little Thumb and the Ogre (1807), IV. 493, 631

Little Tiger (Blake, T. G.), IV. 573

Little Toddlekins (Mathews, C. J., 1852), v. 480

Little Tom Bowling (Simpson, F., 1889), v. 567

Little Tommy Tucker (1845), IV. 493

Little Tom Tittlemouse and the Eleven Dancing Princesses (Greenwood, P. and Arnold, H. T., 1870), v. 393

Little Tom Tucker (Akhurst, W. M., 1876), v. 237

— (Clarance, L., 1877), v. 310

— (Ward, 1864), v. 822

— (1878), v. 710

Little Tom Tucker sang for his Supper (1859), v. 710

Little Tom Tucker, who sang for his Supper (Green, F. W. and Allen, O., 1877), v. 391

Little Tom Tug (Burnand, F. C., 1873), v. 290

Little too Late = Too Late for Dinner

Littletop's Christmas Party (1866), v. 710

Little Trader = Prize

Little Treasure (Buckstone, J. B., 1862), v. 287

— (Harris, A. G., 1855), v. 405

Little Vagrant (Moule, F. and Avery, E. W., 1897), v. 498

Little Viscount (Vezin, H., 1884), v. 608

Little Vixen (Capel, G., 1884), v. 302

Little Vixens (Neville, G. F., 1878), v. 502

Little Widow (Jarman, F., 1891), v. 434

Little Wonder (Jones, J. W., 1874), v. 440

— = Pizarro, the Great Tyrant

Little Youth (1881), v. 710

Live and Hope (McLaren, A., 1817), IV. 351

Live Lumber (1796), III. 334

Lively Boy (1895), v. 710

Lively Hal (Yabsley, A. G., 1893), v. 634

Lively Honeymoon (Stuart-Smith, E., 1897), v. 586

Lively Nancy (Taylor, T. P., 1838), IV. 614

Liverpool in 1796 (1812), IV. 494

Liverpool in the Olden Time = Bride of Everton

Liverpool Merchant = (1) Gold Curse; (2) Two Friends

Liverpool Prize (Pilon, F., 1779), III. 297

Liverpool Welcome = Elopement

Livery Rake = Livery Rake and Country Lass

Livery Rake and Country Lass (Phillips, E., 1733), II. 247–8, 349

Livery Rake Trapped = Livery Rake and Country Lass

Living at Ease (Sketchley, A., 1870), v. 571

Living Dead = Miriam Gray

Living Death (1891), v. 710

Living for Appearances = London Pride

Living for Love (1849), IV. 494

Living in Glass Houses (Courtney, J., 1851), v. 326

Living in London (Jameson, R. F., 1815), IV. 183, 330

Living Lie (Dickens, F., 1883), v. 344

— = Won by a Neck

Living Models (Walton, G., 1898), v. 612

Living or Dead (Stephens, W., 1886), v. 581

Living Skeleton (Jerrold, D. W., 1825), IV. 332

Livingstone's Son = Hilda's Inheritance

Living too fast (Troughton, A. C., 1854), v. 604

Living Will = Dead

Liz (Matthison, A. and Hatton, J., 1877), v. 481

Lizer's New Lodger (Kingsley, E., 1897), v. 444

Lizzie Leigh (Waldron, W. R., 1863), v. 610

Lizzie Lyle = Flower Makers and Heart Breakers

Lizzie Shrie, the Brave Lass o' Halt-wistle (1868), v. 711

Lizzie Stone (1868), v. 711

Llewellyn, Prince of Wales (Cherry, A., and Dibdin, T. J., 1813), IV. 280

Llewelyn the Great = Cambrian Hero

London Barber (1875), v. 711

London Beaux and Bath Belles (1848), IV. 631

London, Birmingham and Bristol = Railroad Trip

London Bridge a Hundred and Fifty Years Ago (McNab, J., 1873), v. 471

London by Day and Night = (1) Bootblack; (2) Jessie Ashton

London by Gaslight (Hazlewood, Miss, 1868), v. 415

London by Night (Selby, C., 1845), IV. 399

— (Selby, C., 1868), v. 560

— (1899), v. 711

— = Cruel City

London Carrier (1835), IV. 494

London Characters (Jerrold, D. W., 1825), IV. 331

London Chimes (1897), v. 711

London Cuckolds (Ravenscroft, E., 1681), I. 74, 79, 188, 255, 308, 349, 426

London Day by Day (Sims, G. R. and Pettitt, H., 1889), v. 569

+ Londoner in Dublin (Crow Street, Dublin, 10/5/1779)

London Fog (Lemon, M., 1851), v. 455

London Frolics in 1638 = Merchant's Wedding

London Gentleman (Howard, E., 1667), I. 414

London Hermit (O'Keeffe, J., 1793), III. 294

— (1810), IV. 494

— (1822), IV. 494

London Highways and Byways (1864), v. 711

London in 1840 = Cripple of the Clink

London in 1814 = Hard Frost

London in Exhibition Time = Good Time Coming

London in 1444 = Widow of Cornhill

London in its Splendor (Jordan, T., 1673), I. 416

London in Luster (Jordan, T., 1679), I. 416

London in 1724 = Jack Sheppard, the Housebreaker

London in 1664 = Queen of Bohemia

London in the Days of Charles II = Queen of Bohemia

London in the Last Century = Law of the Land

London in the Reign of George II = Felix Heron

London in 1370 = Dick Whittington and his Cat

London Labour and London Poor (Elphinstone, J., 1854), v. 711, 790, 840

London Lady (1848), IV. 494

London Life (Clark, T. G., 1881), v. 311

London Lions (1838), IV. 494

London, Liverpool and Bristol = Wanted, a Wife

London Love = £20,000

London Manners at a Country Mansion (1823), IV. 494

London Mechanic (1859), v. 840

London Merchant (Lillo, G., 1731), II. 2, 59, 61, 115, 119, 120-2, 124, 248, 341, 418, 440; III. 88

— = George Barnwell

London Merchant Tailor = George Barnwell

London Mystery (Bourne, W., 1895), v. 270

London out of Town (McLaren, A., 1809), IV. 351

London 'Prentice (?Clive, C., 1754), III. 334, 378, 402

— = Distressed Beauty

London Prentice's Glory = Amurath, the Great Emperor of the Turks

London Pride (Gordon, G. L. and Mackay, J., 1882), v. 385

— (Kenney, J., 1859), v. 443

London Raree Show = Day of Taste

London's Anniversary Festival (Taubman, M., 1688), I. 435

London's Annual Triumph (Taubman, M., 1685), I. 435

London Scamps = Modern Bohemians

London Sensation = Stolen Bonds

London's Glory (Jordan, T., 1680), I. 416

— (Tatham, J., 1660), I. 434

London's Great Jubilee (Taubman, M., 1689), I. 435

London's Joy (Jordan, T., 1681), I. 416

London's Light o' Love = Power and the Glory

London's Poor (1899), v. 711

London's Resurrection to Joy and Triumph (Jordan, T., 1671), I. 415

London's Royal Triumph (Jordan, T., 1684), I. 416

London Stars (1821), IV. 494

London Streets (Monk, M., 1899), v. 491

London's Triumph (Bulteel, J., 1656), I. 394

— (Tatham, J., 1662), I. 434

— (Taubman, M., 1687), I. 435

London's Triumphs (Jordan, T., 1676), I. 416

— (Jordan, T., 1677), I. 416

— (Tatham, J., 1664), I. 434

London's Tryumphs (Tatham, J., 1661), I. 434

London's Yearly Jubilee (Taubman, M., 1686), I. 435

London Tradesman's Life (1831), IV. 494

London trip'd down to Bath = Casino

London Triumphant (Jordan, T., 1672), I. 40, 415

London Vice and London Virtue (Saville, H., 1861), v. 711, 791, 840

Lone Chamber of the Silent Highway = Lucky Horseshoe

Lone Chateau (1851), v. 711

Lone Farm = Adèle

Lone House = Lone Hut

Lone House of Marylebone = Shore Devil

Lone House on the Bridge = Bohemian Gipsy and the Duel at the Willows

Lone House on the Heath (1834), IV. 494

Lone Hut (Raymond, R. J., 1842), IV. 389, 606

Lone Hut of Limehouse Creek (1832), IV. 494

Lone Hut of the Swamp = Bandit Host

Lonely Fisherman of Bagdad = Zebroni, the Fire King

Lonely Lighthouse (1835), IV. 494

Lonely Man of Shiraz (Jerrold, D. W., 1829), IV. 332

Lonely Man of the Ocean (Blake, T. G., 1847), IV. 268

Lone Star (1856), v. 711

Long Age (1882), v. 711

Long Ago (À Beckett, A. W., 1882), v. 233

Long Beard, Lord of Londano (Stirling, E., 1847), IV. 408

Long Cloth (Dibdin, T. J., 1828), IV. 305

Long Engagement (1892), v. 711

— = Vol. III

Long Finn (Bernard, W. B., 1832), IV. 265

— (Bernard, W. B., 1833), IV. 494

Long Interview (1896), v. 711

Longinus (Jones, J., 1827), IV. 333

Long Live the Queen (Brady, E. J., 1887), v. 273

Long Lost Brother (1899), v. 711

Long-lost Brothers = Cox and Box

Long Odds (Dibdin, C., 1783), III. 256

— (Edwardes, C. T. M., 1883), v. 354

Long Pack (1879), v. 711

Long Rifle (1831), IV. 494

Long Stories = We Fly by Night

Long Strike (Boucicault, D., 1866), v. 268

Long-threatened French Invasion = Test of Union and Loyalty

Loo and the Party who took Miss (Farnie, H. B., 1874), v. 361

Looey Napoleong (Robinson, N., 1868), v. 547

Look at Home (Dance, C., 1833), IV. 494

— (Eyre, E. J., 1812) = Italian Husband, IV. 310, 484, 629

Look Before You Leap (Lovell, G. W., 1846), IV. 347

— (Robson, H., 1788), III. 120, 302

— (Worgan, T. D., 1808), IV. 422

— (1822), IV. 494

— (1829), IV. 494

— = (1) Fancy's Sketch; (2) New Marriage Act; (3) Uncle and Nephew

Look on the Bright Side (1866), v. 711

Lookout and the Rescue (1862), v. 711

Look out for Squalls = Harry Bluff

Look to your Luggage (Clarance, J., 1847), IV. 280

Loose Cash (Oxenford, J., 1837), IV. 494, 631

Loose Fish (1852), v. 711

Loose Tiles (Hurst, J. P., 1885), v. 431

Loquacity = Invisible Girl

Lord Alingford (Grogan, W. E., 1895), v. 395

Loretta: A Tale of Seville (Bunn, A., 1846), IV. 276, 575 [By an error, this is wrongly duplicated as Lucetta, IV. 497, and Toretta, IV. 543]

Lorna Doone (1897), v. 711

Lorraine (Grogan, W. E., 1898), v. 395

Lorris and Fedora (1883), v. 711

Lose No Time (Skeffington, L. St G., 1813), IV. 402

Losing Hazard (Hurst, B., 1892), v. 431

Loss of the Alceste (1832), IV. 495

Loss of the Eurydice = Beneath the Surface

Loss of the Monarch (1848), v. 846

Loss of the Royal George (Barnett, C. Z., 1835), IV. 259

— (1840), IV. 260

Lost (Thiboust, L., 1871), v. 595

— (Wyndham, Sir C., 1874), v. 634

Lost and Found (Faucquez, A., 1862), v. 711, 791, 840

— (March, M. G., 1870), v. 475

— (Masters, M. K., 1811), IV. 353, 569

— (Wilson, J. C., 1872), v. 628

— = (1) Maniac; (2) Our Village; (3) Romantic Lover

Lost and Won (Lemon, M., 1841), IV. 344, 595

— (Spicer, H., 1840), IV. 405

Lost a Sovereign (Addison, H. R., 1848), IV. 495, 631

Lost at Sea (Boucicault, D. and Byron, H. J., 1869), v. 269

Lost Bag (Poel, W., 1883), v. 811

Lost Bride of Garryowen (?Horsman, C., 1862), v. 711, 798, 840

Lost by a Head (Collins, M. T., 1850), IV. 577

— (1876), v. 711

Lost by Drink = D.T.

Lost Cause = Bonnie Dundee

Lost Child (Suter, W. E., 1863), v. 588

— (1818), IV. 495

— (1833), IV. 495

— = Bereaved Wife and Mother

Lost Child of the Manor = Agatha

Lost Children = Woman and her Master

Lost Daughter = Hop Pickers and Gipsies

Lost Diamond = Hebrew Maiden

Lost Diamonds (Stirling, E., 1849), IV. 409

Lost Discharge (Mann, C. P., 1873), v. 474

Lost Earl = Captain Starlight

Lost Eden (Hills, Miss H., 1897), v. 422

Lost Emily (Murray, G., 1870), v. 500

Lost Em'ly (Wood, M., 1873), v. 631

Lost for Ever (Nicholson, G. A., 1869), v. 504

Lost for Gold (Illingworth, J. H., 1885), v. 431

Lost for Love = Fif

Lost Fortune (Faucquez, A., 1865), v. 792

— (1865), v. 711

Lost Heir (Henderson, T. B., 1868), v. 417

— (Price, E., 1872), v. 530

— = Dangers of the Express

Lost Heir of Macclesfield (Dakin, T. M., 1875), v. 332

Lost Heir of Maningdale Manor = Edith the Captive

Lost Heir Restored = Simon

Lost Heir Stand = Handy Andy

Lost Husband (Reade, C., 1852), v. 535

— (1862), v. 712

— (1884), v. 712

Lost Inheritance (1864), v. 712

Lost in London (Phillips, W., 1867), v. 523

Lost in New York (Grover, L., 1896), v. 37, 396

Lost in the Snow (Marchant, F., 1864), v. 475

— (1864), v. 712

— = Scarlet Letter

Lost Jewels = (1) Intrigue; (2) Three Secrets

Lost Lady Lillian = Lady Lillian

Lost Lady of Lynne (Willoughby, A., 1883), v. 626

Lost Legion (Locke, W. J., 1898), v. 462

Lost Letter (1843), IV. 495

— (1860), v. 712

Lost Life (Moncrieff, W. T., 1821), IV. 359, 600

— (Walford, H. L., 1870), v. 611

Lost Likeness = Lefevre

Lost Love (Murdoch, J. M., 1879), v. 499

Lost Lover (Manley, M., 1696), I. 75, 225, 420

Lost One Found = Claimant

Lost Overture (1892), v. 712
Lost Paradise (De Mille, H. C., 1892), v. 342
Lost Pleiad = All for Love
Lost Prince (Rendell, H. W., 1895), v. 541
Lost Regalia = (1) Babil and Bijou; (2) Intimidad
Lost Rosabel (Travers, W., 1864), v. 822
Lost Sheep (Parker, W. and Shirley, A., 1891), v. 514
Lost Shepherdess = Parthenia
Lost Shilling (Faucit, J. S., 1844) = Last Shilling, iv. 495, 631
Lost Ship (Townsend, W. T., 1843), iv. 414
— (1857), v. 712
Lost Ship and the Wild Flower of Mexico = Thirst of Gold
Lost Sisters (Reade, C.), v. 812
Lost Son (1831), iv. 495
— = Luke the Labourer
Lost Son Found (1855), v. 712
Lost, Stolen or Strayed (Goodwin, J. C., 1897), v. 384
Lost £30,000 (1856), v. 712
Lost Thread (Bell, Mrs H., 1890), v. 255
Lost to Life (Horner, J., 1884), v. 427
Lost to the World (Hunter, Mrs T., 1892), v. 431
Lost Treasure = Stratagems
Lost Wager = Midnight Hour
Lost Wife (Hazlewood, C. H., 1871), v. 150, 414
— = Genevieve
Lost Will (1864), v. 712
— = Roger O'Hare
Lost Witness (Pettitt, H. and Merritt, P., 1880), v. 521
Lota (Jarman, F., 1892), v. 434
Lot 49 (Fisher, W. J., 1888), v. 367
Lothair, Batti, Batti and Shah Dee Doo (Green, F. W. and Soutar, R., 1873), v. 390
Lot No. 1 (Lee, N., Jr., 1874), v. 453
Lottery (Fielding, H., 1732), ii. 138, 237, 245, 324, 436
— (1728), ii. 377
Lottery Chance (McLaren, A., 1803), iv. 350
Lottery of Life (1899), v. 712
— = Win and Wear

Lottery of Love = Raffle for an Elephant
Lottery Prize = Pedantic Apothecary Quizzed
Lottery Ticket (Beazley, S., Jr., 1826), iv. 264, 571
Lottie (1884), v. 712
Lottie's Love (Davis, A., 1868), v. 338
Lotus Land (1879), v. 712
Louis XI (Boucicault, D., 1855), v. 86, 268
— (Coupland, J. A., 1889), v. 786
— (Markwell, W. R., 1853), v. 102, 477
— (Pitt, H. M., 1869), v. 526
Louis XIV (1855), v. 712
Louis XVI (Dear, P. J., 1895), v. 340
— = Fall of the French Monarchy
Louisa (1867), v. 712
Louisa Meller, the Musician's Daughter (1853), v. 712
Louis and Antoinette (Hunter, G. M., 1794), iii. 274
Louisa of Lombardy (Cross, J. C., 1803), iv. 286
Louis Chaumont (1828), iv. 495
Louise (Bernard, W. B., 1843), iv. 84, 266
— (Leigh L., 1838), iv. 343 [This is attributed to H. Hall, as Louise; or, The White Scarf, printed by W. Strange]
Louise de Lignarolles (Pardoe, Miss, 1838), iv. 495, 631
Louisiana (Douglas, J. T., 1861), v. 788
Louisiana Creole (1891), v. 712
Louis in the Elysian Fields (Holcroft, T., 1789), iii. 271
Louis the Unfortunate = Democratic Rage
Lounge at Brighton (O'Keeffe, J., 1795) = Irish Mimic, iii. 334, 393, 402
Loup-garcon of the Odenwald = Man-Wolf
Love (Knowles, J. S., 1839), iv. 339
— (Lester, G., 1876), v. 457
— (1877), v. 712
Love a Bo-Peep (1829), iv. 496
Love against Money = Maid of St Aubin's
Love against the World = Woman
Love à la Militaire (Hort, 1841), iv. 328
Love A-la-Mode (Macklin, C., 1759), iii. 183-4, 284, 391

Love A-la-Mode (Southland, T., ?1663), I. 189, 233, 433
— (1875), V. 712
— =Amour A-la-Mode
Love among the Mermaids = Knight and the Water-Lily
Love among the Roses (Beazley, S., 1822), IV. 495, 631
— =Enchanted Island
Love and a Bottle (Farquhar, G., 1698), I. 6, 23, 62, 411; II. 147
Love and a Bumper (1718), II. 377
Love and a Fate (1860), V. 712
Love and Agility (1830), IV. 495
Love and Ambition (Darcy, J., 1731), II. 81, 317
Love and Anatomy (1828), IV. 495
Love and Art (Wilmot, A. A., 1889), V. 628
Love and Charity (Lemon, M., 1838), IV. 343
Love and Chastity (1854), V. 712
Love and Crime (Kingdom, J. M., 1858), V. 712, 801
— (1844), IV. 495
Love and Danger = Knights of the Sun
Love and Dentistry (Swears, H., 1893), V. 589
— (1891), V. 712
Love and Duty (Pitt, G. D., 1850), V. 526
— (Slade, J., 1756), III. 307
— (Sturmy, J., 1722), II. 90, 358
— (1895), V. 712
— =(1) Cid; (2) Eunice; (3) Respectability
Love and Empire = Abra-Mule
Love and Enchantment = Calypso
Love and Error (Pitt, G. D., 1851), V. 526
Love and Fame = Sultan
Love and Fear = Crisis
Love and Folly (1739), II. 395
— (1865), V. 712
Love and Fortune (Planché, J. R., 1859), V. 527
Love and Friendship (1723), II. 377
— (1745), II. 377, 447
— (1746), II. 377
— (1754), III. 334
— =(1) Alexander; (2) Epaulette; (3) Lord Ullin's Daughter; (4) Ormasdes

Love and Fright = Cholera Morbus
Love and Gratitude = Noyades
Love and Glory (Phillips, T., 1734), II. 349
Love and Gout (Jameson, R. F., 1814) = Turns and Returns, IV. 330, 590
Love and Halfpence (Poel, W., 1888), V. 529
+ Love and Hate (Mitford, E. L., in Poems, 1869)
— (Wigan, H., 1869), V. 622
— (1875), V. 712
— = King's Advocate
Love and Hatred = Dorothee
Love and Honour (Carpenter, J. E., 1855), V. 95–6, 129–31, 303
— (Clarke, C., 1875), V. 151, 311
— (Delamayne, T., 1742), II. 223, 317
— (1753), III. 334
— (1794), III. 334
— =(1) French in Algiers; (2) Half Pay Officer; (3) Nellie's Trials
Love and Hunger (Morton, J. M., 1859), V. 496
Love and Impudence (Hewlett, 1812) = Fortune Hunters, IV. 495, 631
Love and Indiscretion = Only Six Hours More
Love and Innocence (1789), III. 334
Love and Jealousy (1733), II. 377
— (1846), IV. 495
— =(1) Secret Springs; (2) Tracey Castle; (3) Orphans; (4) Valiant Clara
Love and Jollity = Tars on Shore
Love and Larceny = Claude Duval
Love and Laudanum (Baynes, 1818), IV. 571
— (1865), V. 712
Love and Laugh (Moncrieff, W. T., 1842), IV. 600
— =All at Coventry
Love and Laurel (1829), IV. 495
Love and Law (Edgeworth, M., 1817), IV. 209, 309
— (Latimer, F., 1891), V. 449
— =Transformation
Love and Leather (1835), IV. 495
Love and Levity (1835), IV. 495
Love and Liberty (Johnson, C., 1709), II. 63, 70, 105, 339

Love and Liberty = (1) American Slaves; (2) Bondman; (3) Scanderbeg

Love and Life (Taylor, T. and Merritt, P., 1878), v. 594

Love and Lottery = Rival Serjeants

Love and Love's Vision = Agnes of Bavaria

Love and Loyalty (McDonald, A., 1791), III. 283

— (Robson, W. J., 1854), v. 547

— (1795), III. 334

— = (1) Captive Prince; (2) Fate of Villany; (3) Gascons; (4) Irish Poleander

Love and Lucre (1860), v. 712

Love and Madness (Waldron, F. G., 1795), III. 113, 314, 397

— (1811), IV. 495

— = (1) Amy; (2) Charlotte and Werther

Love and Magic (1802), IV. 495

— = Enchanter

Love and Mercy = (1) Hussar; (2) Young Huzzar

Love and Money (Benson, 1795), III. 207, 236

— (Reade, C. and Pettitt, H., 1882), v. 536

— (1795), III. 334

Love and Murder (Barnett, M., 1851), v. 250

— (Brougham, J., 1861), v. 280

— (Buckstone, J. B., 1837), IV. 275

Love and Mystery (Haines, J. T., 1832) = Mystification, IV. 322, 509, 587, 634

— = Strolling Players

Love and Nature (Berkeley, G. M., 1789), III. 236

Love and Passion = Cora

Love and Politics (Johnson, H. T., 1888), v. 437

Love and Poverty (1817), IV. 495

Love and Pride = Lady of Lyons

Love and Reason (Lacy, M. R., 1827), IV. 340

Love and Revenge (Settle, E., 1674), I. 40, 205, 348, 428

— (1729), II. 377

Love and Riches Reconcil'd (1699), I. 412

Love and Stratagem (Brand, O. and Linging, E. W., 1886), v. 273

Love and the Chase (1819), IV. 495

Love and the Lancet (1817), IV. 495

Love and the Law (Millward, H., 1886), v. 489

Love and the Slave-Trade (1828), IV. 495

Love and the Toothache (1816), IV. 495

Love and Transformation = Soldier's Stratagem

Love and Treason = Sailor and his Lass

Love and Valour (1779), III. 113, 334

Love and Wambles = My Old Woman

Love and War (Jephson, R., 1787), III. 277

— (Lemon, M., 1842), IV. 344

— (Olde, B. and Young Sir W. L., 1895), v. 507

— (1897), v. 712

— = Estelle Dumas

Love and War in Yankyland = Coup-de-Main

Love and Wine (1754), III. 334

Love Apple (1874), v. 712

Love at a Loss (Trotter, Mrs C., 1700), II. 176–7, 361

Love at a Venture (Centlivre, Mrs S., 1706), II. 4, 142, 145, 162, 186, 304

— (1782), III. 334

Love at Fault = Widow Bewitched

Love at First Sight (Craufurd, D., 1704), II. 154, 316, 434

— (Jocelyn, J. K. J., 1889), v. 437

— (King, T., 1763), III. 279

— (Yarrow, J., 1742), II. 364

— = Princesse

Love at Home (Dauncey, S., 1891), v. 337

Love, Avarice and Repentance = Orphans

Love Awake and the Guard Asleep = Patrick's Return

Love Betray'd (Burnaby, W., 1703), II. 27, 50, 140, 153, 195, 301, 432

Love beyond Price = Cupid from Jewry

Love Bird (Edwardes, C. T. M., 1872), v. 354

Love Birds (1844), IV. 496

— (1883), v. 712

Love brooks no jesting (Whitaker, John, Jr., 1882), v. 620

Love by Lantern Light (Barnett, M., 1862), v. 250

Love can move the Heart of a Stone = Sculptor

Love Charm (Planché, J. R., 1831), IV. 29, 84, 379

Love-Chase (Knowles, J. S., 1837), IV. 339

Love Conquers (Townley, A. H., 1889), V. 602

Love conquers all (Cowdroy, W., 1786), III. 334, 380, 402

— = Faigale

Love created Madness = Hydrophobia

Loved and Deceived = Cheap Jack

Loved and Lost (Hatton, J. and Matthison, A., 1879), V. 409

Love, Debt and Fun (1826), IV. 496

Love Despised (1668), I. 442

Love Distracted Maid = Nina

Love Extempore (Kenney, J., 1841), IV. 338

Love Finds the Way (Hull, T., 1777), III. 274

Love for Love (Congreve, W., 1695), I. 64, 69, 73, 240, 242, 308, 398; III. 161, 168

Love for Money (D'Urfey, T., 1690), I. 273, 275–6, 409; II. 142; III. 114

Love, Fun and Fighting = Galway Go Bragh

Love Game (Browne, G. W., 1885), V. 283

Love Gift (Stirling, E., 1843), IV. 613

— (1859), V. 712

Love gives the Alarm (Holman, J. G., 1804), IV. 327, 589

Love has turned her Head = Nina

Love, Hatred and Revenge (Dibdin, T. J., 1816), IV. 300

— = (1) Bella Ridstone; (2) Farmer's Bride

Love, Honour and Friendship = Warrior's Faith

Love, Honour and Interest (Galt, J., 1814), IV. 318, 636

Love, Honour and Obey (1860), V. 712

Love in a Bag (1810), IV. 496

Love in a Blaze (Atkinson, J., 1799), III. 234

Love in a Bustle = Robin and Marion

Love in a Camp = Patrick in Prussia

Love in a Chest (Johnson, C., 1710), II. 131, 212, 339, 439

Love in a China Cupboard (1881), V. 712

Love in a Convent (Craven, E., 1805), III. 249; IV. 285

Love in a Cottage (Bayly, T. H., 1835), IV. 496, 631

— (Waker, J., 1785), III. 313, 397

— (1836), IV. 496

— = Lubin and Laura

Love in a Dale = Country Wedding

Love in a Flat (Lounde, S., 1899), V. 463

Love in a Fog = Jo

Love in a Forest (Johnson, C., 1723), II. 140, 157, 339

Love in a Frame = Paquita

Love in a Furze Bush = Miller's Holiday

Love in a Garden = Pets of the Parterre

Love in a Hollow Tree = Lawyer's Fortune

Love in a Hurry (Aston, A., 1709), II. 295

Love in a Labyrinth (1746), II. 377

— = Tutor for the Beaus

Love in Algiers (1843), IV. 496

Love in all Corners (1858), V. 712

Love in all its Horrors = Leonora

Love in All Shapes (1739), II. 377

Love in a Maze (Boucicault, D., 1851), V. 267

Love in a Meadow = Happy Disguise

Love in America = Black Festival

Love in a Mist (Cunningham, J., 1747), II. 50, 216, 317

— (Parker, L. N., 1891), V. 513

— (1881), V. 712

— = Jamie of Aberdeen

Love in a Mystery (Horde, T., 1786), III. 273

Love in and Love out of Fashion = Amorous Orontus

Love in an Orchard (1805), IV. 496

Love in a Nunnery = Assignation

Love in a Puddle (1750–1800), III. 334

Love in a Riddle (Cibber, C., 1729), II. 15, 134, 232, 250, 313, 434

Love in Arms = Cicilia and Clorinda

Love in a Sack (Griffin, B., 1715), II. 212, 333

— (Smith, 1838), IV. 611

— (1844), IV. 496

Love in a Snowstorm = Wheedling

Love in a Tub (Degville, 1809), IV. 496, 631

Love's Test (Edwards, J., 1874), V. 355

Love's the Physician = Quacks

Love's Trial (Moore, H. W., 1882), V. 492

— (1846), IV. 631

— (1857), V. 713

Love's Trials (Pratt, S. J., 1805), IV. 388

Love's Trickery (Bridgman, C., 1889), V. 275

Love's Triumph (Cooke, E., 1678), I. 125, 398

— (Motteux, P. A., 1708), II. 229, 395

— (Planché, J. R., 1862), V. 528

— (1718), II. 377

— (1866), V. 713

— = Fleurs de Lys

Love Suits = Lawyers and their Clients

Love's Vagaries (Vaughan, T., 1776, 1791), III. 313

— (1823), IV. 497

— = Tho' Strange 'Tis True

Love's Victim (Gildon, C., 1701), II. 28, 30, 31, 67, 76, 116, 332

— = Charlotte and Werther

Love's Victory (Chamberlayne, W., 1658), I. 396

— (Hyde, G., 1825), IV. 329

— (1846), IV. 497

Love's Weathercock = Way of the Wind

Love's Young Dream (Bright, E., 1891), V. 276

— (Buckingham, L. S., 1864), V. 286

— = Moreen and Sham Van Voght

Love Test (Johnstone, J. B., 1859), V. 713, 800, 840

— (Lisle, W., 1872), V. 152, 460

— = Amilie

Love Tests (Amcotts, V.), V. 240

Love that blooms for ever = Marriage not Divorce

Love that Kills (Brandon, J., 1888), V. 274

— (1868), V. 713

— = Jewess and Christian

Love that lasts (Harvey, F., 1881), V. 408

Love that wins = Karl

Love the best Contriver = Friendly Rivals

Love the Cause and Cure of Grief (Cooke, T., 1743), II. 115, 123, 316

Love the Cure of all Woes = Mournful Nuptials

Love the Leveller (1704), II. 188, 221, 377

— = Dora Mayfield

Love the Magician (Rae, J. and Sidney, T., 1892), V. 533

Love Trap (Moss, H., 1883), V. 498

Love Triumphant (Bellamy, D., 1722), II. 235, 297

— (Dryden, J., 1694), I. 83, 93, 145, 407

— (1788), III. 334

Love under a Lamppost = Wooing a Widow

Love unto Death = Sacrifice

Love versus Science (Lonergan, Mrs E. A., 1896), V. 462

Love, War and Victory = King of the Assassins

Love, War, Physic and Latin = Student

Love will finde out the Way (1661), I. 443

Love will find out the Way = Rencontre

Love wins (Clarke, H. S. and Du Terreaux, L. H. F., 1873), V. 312

Love wins the Day (Finlayson, 1865), V. 713, 792, 840

— (Towers, E., 1879), V. 601

Love Wisely = Setting of the Sun

Love without Interest (Pinkethman, W., 1699), I. 424; II. 377

Love, Youth and Folly = Youth, Love and Folly

Loving and Scheming (Walker, G. R., 1874), V. 611

Loving Cup (Halliday, A., 1868), V. 401

Loving Enemies (Maidwell, L., 1680), I. 217, 420

Loving Hearts and Buried Diamonds (Neville, G. F., 1870), V. 502

Loving Legacy (Sidney, F. W., 1895), V. 565

Loving not wisely but too well = Cast Aside

Loving Woman (Peake, R. B., 1849), IV. 497, 631

Lowina of Tobolskoi (1817), IV. 497

Lowland Lassie (Rannie, J., 1806) = Lowland Lassie in London, III. 300; IV. 388

Lowland Lassie in London (Rannie, J., 1803) = Lowland Lassie, III. 300; IV. 388

Lowland Romp (1810), IV. 497

Low Life above Stairs (1759), III. 334

Low Life below Stairs (1867), V. 713

Lowther Arcade (Brooks, C. W. S., 1854), V. 277

— (1845), IV. 497

Low Water (Pinero, Sir A. W., 1884), V. 525

Loyal (Johnson, H. T., 1894), V. 437

Loyal and Generous Free-Mason (1731), II. 377

Loyal Bandeau (O'Keeffe, J.), III. 294

Loyal Brother (Southerne, T., 1682), I. 79, 99, 101, 129, 153, 432

Loyal Citizens (Kirkman, F., 1662), I. 417

Loyal Effusion (Dibdin, C., 1794), III. 256

Loyal Favourite = Ambitious Statesman

Loyal General (Tate, N., 1679), I. 172, 434

Loyal Love (Neil, R., 1887), V. 502

— = Reparation

Loyal Lovers (Garrick, C., 1885), V. 376

Loyal Peasants (Straycock, J., 1804), IV. 409

Loyal Salopian (Colls, J. H., 1795), III. 245

Loyal Shepherds (Goodwin, T. 1779), III. 265

Loyal Soldier = French Village surrender'd

+ Loyal Subject (Gardner, Mrs S., see *Theatre Notebook*, VII. 1953, 76–81)

— (Sheridan, T., 1741), III. 306

Loyal Tar = Maid of Liverpool

Loyal to the Last (Pemberton, T. E., 1896), V. 519

Loyal Traitor (1899), V. 713

Loyalty (Charnock, J., 1810), IV. 279

— (Lyste, H. P., 1876), V. 465

— (1845), IV. 497

— (1882), V. 713

— (1887), V. 713

Loyalty or Love (Field, M., 1885), V. 366

Loyal Volunteers = Volunteers

£. s. d. (À Beckett, A. W., 1872), V. 233

— (1844), IV. 497

— (1889), V. 713

Lubin and Laura (1817), IV. 497

Lubin Log's Journey to London (1820), IV. 497

Lubly Rosa, Sambo don't come = White Rose of the Plantation

Lucetta [At IV. 497 this appears in error for Loretta: see IV. 276]

Lucette's Husband (1894), V. 713

Lucette's Legacy (Wyke, E. B., 1884), V. 634

Lucia di Lammermoor (Byron, H. J., 1865), V. 297

— (1843), IV. 497

— (1844), IV. 497

Lucifer Match = Devil in Six

Lucifer Matches (1856), V. 713

Lucifer's Match = Sorrowful Satan

Lucifer, Son of the Morning (Castleton, R., 1898), V. 306

Lucille (Bernard, W. B., 1836), IV. 265

— (1851), V. 713

Lucina's Rape (Wilmot, J., ?1679), I. 437

Lucinda (Jenner, C., 1770), III. 276

Lucius Catiline, the Roman Traitor (Milner, H. M., 1827), IV. 497, 631

Lucius Junius Brutus (Downman, H., 1779), III. 83, 257

— (Duncombe, W., 1734), II. 63, 71, 72, 94, 320, 435

— (Lee, N., 1680), I. 10, 55, 79, 96, 147, 419; II. 71, 437

Lucius, the First Christian King of Britain (Manley, Mrs M., 1717), II. 28, 31, 50, 79, 116, 343

Luck (Levey, J. C., 1869), V. 458

— (Templar, C., 1879), V. 594

Luckey Chance (Behn, A., 1686), I. 193, 267–8, 391; III. 114, 177

Luck in the Lottery (1829), IV. 497

Lucknow Rescued = Highland Jessie Brown

Luck of Life (Murray, J. K., 1898), V. 500

Luck's All (Wigan, A. S., 1845), IV. 419

— = Fools Have Fortune

Lucky Amour = Sir Giddy Whim

Lucky and Unlucky Days = Charming Polly

Lucky Bag (Willard, Mrs E. S., 1893), V. 623

Lucky Bag of Life = Quits

Lucky Bob (1849), IV. 497

Lucky Discovery (Arthur, J., 1737), II. 53, 137, 248–9, 295

Lucky Dog (Sapte, Walter, Jr., 1892), V. 556

Lucky Escape (Cheltnam, C. S., 1861), v. 309
— (Dupret, 1800), IV. 582
— (Linnecar, R., 1789), III. 282
— (Robinson, M., 1778), III. 302
Lucky Extravagant = Sham Lawyer
Lucky Friday (Wigan, A. S., 1852), v. 621
Lucky Girl (Fitzgerald, S. J. A., 1889), v. 369
Lucky Hit (Appleyard, C., 1872), v. 242
— (Paul, H. M., 1866), v. 516, 809
— (Stirling, E., 1836), IV. 406
— (Stirling, E., 1858), v. 584, 818
Lucky Hits = Random Shots
Lucky Horseshoe (1842), IV. 497
— (1846), IV. 497
— = (1) Dobbin's Horse; (2) Woman's Trials
Lucky Jemmy (1855), v. 713
Lucky Lovers (1773), III. 334
+ Lucky Mistake (Terson, Thomas, Smock Alley, Dublin, 27/4/1772)
— = Jealous Clown
Lucky Prodigal (1715), II. 377
Lucky Recovery = Love and Friendship
Lucky Return (1787), III. 334
Lucky Shilling (Willing, J. and Douglass, J., 1888), v. 626
Lucky Star (Brookfield, C. H. E., 1899), v. 277, 780
— (Comer, G. and Matthews, E. C., 1887), v. 319
Lucky Stars (Dance, G., 1842), IV. 289, 579
Lucky Stone (1877), v. 713
Lucky Walker (1895), v. 713
Lucky Waterman (1820), IV. 497
Lucky Younger Brother = Beau Defeated
Lucre against Love = Conquest of Cupid
Lucrece Borgia (Almar, G., 1833), IV. 252
— (1832), IV. 497
Lucretia (Dallas, R. C., 1797), III. 253
Lucretia Borgia, the Poisoner (1858), v. 713
Lucrezia Borgia (Belton, F., 1871), v. 257
— (French, S., 1867), v. 373
— (Reade, C.), v. 812

Lucrezia Borgia (Weston, J. M., 1843), IV. 80, 419
— (Young, W., 1847), IV. 80, 618
Lucrezia Borgia at Home and All Abroad (Buckingham, L. S., 1860), v. 286
Lucrezia Borgia, M.D., (Byron, H. J., 1868), v. 297
Lucy (Jones, H., ?1780), III. 277
Lucy Brandon (Buchanan, R., 1882), v. 284
Lucy Did-Lub-Him-More! (1857), v. 840
Lucy Hatton (1863), v. 713
Lucy Lisle (Pitt, G. D., 1841), IV. 604
Lucy Neal (1847), IV. 497
Lucy of Lammermoor (Oxberry, W. H., 1848), IV. 367
— (1863), v. 713
Lucy Wentworth, the Village-born Beauty (Priest, 1857), v. 531
Ludolph the Fiend of Germany (1823), IV. 497
Lugarto the Mulatto (O'Bryan, C., 1850), v. 506, 808
Luggage per Rail (Russell, F., 1882), v. 553
Luisa Miller (Jefferys, C., 1858), v. 800
Luke Somerton (Soane, G., 1836), IV. 497, 631
Luke Sommerton (Rogers, W., 1845), IV. 396
Luke the Labourer (Buckstone, J. B., 1826), IV. 38, 116–17, 214, 273, 574
Luna (1892), v. 713
Lunacy Commission (Anderton, J., 1876), v. 241
Lunatic (Barrow, P. J., 1898), v. 252
Lunatic Asylum (1832), IV. 497
Lunatick (1705), II. 45, 210, 377
Lundy (1840), IV. 497
Lun's Ghost (1782), III. 334
Lupone (Gordon, A., 1731), II. 333
Lured to London (Patmore, W. J. and Moss, A. B., 1889), v. 515
Lured to Ruin = Hero of Heroes
Lurette (Desprez, F. and Murray, A., 1883) = Belle Lurette, v. 343, 788, 827
Luria (Browning, R., 1846), IV. 272
Lurline (Amcotts, V., 1860), v. 240
— (Fitzball, E., 1860), v. 368
— (Pitt, G. D., 1834), IV. 372, 604

Lurline (Reece, R. and Farnie, H. B., 1886), v. 539
— (1874), v. 713
— (1881), v. 713
Lyar (Foote, S., 1762), III. 117, 173–4, 260, 384
— (1763), III. 334
— = Mistaken Beauty
Lycidas (Jackson, W., 1767), III. 276
— (1762), III. 334
Lyddy Beale (Hazlewood, C. H., 1861), v. 713, 796, 840
Lying Dutchman (Green, F. W. and Swanborough, W. H., 1876), v. 390
Lying in Ordinary (Peake, R. B., 1838), IV. 371
Lying Lover (Steele, Sir R., 1703), I. 263; II. 129, 183, 191–2, 193, 356, 444
Lying made Easy (1826), IV. 497
Lying Valet (Garrick, D., 1741), II. 138, 329, 437
Lynce and Pollidore (1781), III. 334
Lynch Law (Pettitt, H., 1874), v. 520
— (1854), v. 713
— (1881), v. 713
Lynn Wives (1838), IV. 497
Lyons Mail = Courier of Lyons
Lyrical Lover (Clarke, H. S., 1881), v. 313
Lyric Novelist (Cherry, A., 1804), IV. 279

Mabel (Fox, G. D., 1891), v. 371
— (Hay, F., 1880), v. 411
— (Reynoldson, T. H., 1840), IV. 497, 632
Mabel Connell (1845), IV. 497
Mabel Gray (1844), IV. 497
Mabel Lake (Hazlewood, C. H., 1873), v. 414
Mabel's Curse (Hall, Mrs A. M., 1837), IV. 323
Mabel's Life (Byron, H. J., 1872), v. 298
Mabel's Secret (Ferneyhaugh, G. F., 1870), v. 365
Mabel's Twins = Those Terrible Twins
Mabel's Two Birthdays = Ebony Casket
Mabel the Forsaken (Lloyd, H., 1869), v. 461
Mabel the Maniac = Whitefeet
Mabel Whyte, the Maid of Stratford (1851), v. 713

Mab's Mangle (1883), v. 713
Macaire (Fox, G. D., 1887), v. 371
— (Henley, W. E. and Stevenson, R. L., 1885), v. 417
+ McAllister McVitty McNab; or, The Laird, the Daftie and the Highland Maiden (Byron, H. J.: *Dicks* (in *Sensation Dramas*))
Macaroni (Hitchcock, R., 1773), III. 269
Macbeth (D'Avenant, Sir W., 1673), I. 37, 59, 133, 134, 172, 401–2
— (Kemble, J. P., 1794), III. 278, 389
— (Lee, J., 1753), III. 57, 280
— (Macready, W. C., 1837), IV. 352
— (Rowe, H., 1799), III. 395
— (1857), v. 713
— (1889), v. 713
Macbeth according to Act of Parliament (Hodson, G., 1853), v. 423
Macbeth Modernized (Bell, R., 1838), IV. 91, 264
Macbeth Mystified (Mason, W. H. and Rae, J. E., 1869), v. 480
Macbeth Travestie (Malone, 1853), v. 805
— (Talfourd, F., 1850), IV. 91, 410
— (1813), IV. 91, 497
— (1842), IV. 91, 497
MacCarthy More (Lover, S., 1861), v. 463
Macfarlane's Will (Mackay, J., 1881), v. 470
McGreggors (1825), IV. 632
MacHaggis (Jerome, J. K. and Phillpotts, E., 1897), v. 436
Macheath in the Shades (1735), II. 377
Macheath turn'd Pyrate (1737), II. 447
Macintosh and Co. (Kenney, J., 1838), IV. 338
McKenna's Flirtation (Selden, E., 1892), v. 560
McTavish (1896), v. 713
Mad (Dearlove, W. H., 1893), v. 340
— (Rose, E., 1880), v. 550
Mad Actor (1825), IV. 497
Madame (Coghlan, C. F.), v. 316
— (Tanner, J. T., 1895), v. 590
Madame Angot (Desprez, F., 1875), v. 343, 788
Madame Berliot's Ball (Burnand, F. C., 1863), v. 288

Madame Cartouche (Edwards, H. S., 1891), v. 335, 789
Madame de Moray's Secret = Guiltless
Madame de Raimont (Henry, R., 1883), v. 417
Madame du Barry (Poole, J., 1831), IV. 497, 632
Madame Favart (Farnie, H. B., 1879), v. 362, 791
Madame l'Archiduc (Farnie, H. B., 1876), v. 362, 790
Madame Midas, the Gold Queen (Beck, P. and Hume, F., 1888), v. 254
Madame Morensky (1896), v. 713
Madame Pompadour's Pearl (Wilks, T. E., 1840), IV. 617
Madame Rose = Gibraltar
Madame Sans-Gene (Carr, J. W. C., 1897), v. 304
Madam Fickle (D'Urfey, T., 1676), I. 24, 43, 273, 348, 408
Madam Laffarge (1841), IV. 497
Madam Scaite in the Seraglio = Odd Fish
Mad as a Hatter (Marshall, F., 1863), v. 478
— (Thorp, A. C., 1872), v. 599
Mad as a March Hare (1837), IV. 479
— (1857), v. 713
— (1879), v. 713
Madcap (Aveling, E. B., 1890), v. 246
— (Reece, R. and Farnie, H. B., 1878), v. 538
— = Lowland Romp
Madcap Madge (Stephens, L. E. B., 1895), v. 581
Madcap Midge (Fawcett, C. S., 1889), v. 364
Madcap Prince (Allen, A. M., 1894), v. 238
— (Buchanan, R., 1874), v. 284
— (1884), v. 713
Mad Captain (Drury, R., 1733), II. 247, 319
— (Stevens, G. A., 1769), III. 334, 396
Madcap Violet (Stockton, E., 1882), v. 584
Mad Couple = All Mistaken
Mad Crime (1895), v. 713
Maddalen (Galt, J., 1812), IV. 585
Madeira (Adams, H., 1875), v. 235
Madelaine (1843), IV. 498

Madelaine = Daughter of the Regiment
Madeleine (Mortimer, J., 1873), v. 494
— (1841), IV. 632
— (1851), v. 713
Madeleine Dumas (1856), v. 714
Madeline (Bedingfield, R., 1847), IV. 264
— (Cooke, C., 1874), v. 323
— (Kingdom, J. M.), v. 444
— (1837), IV. 498
Madeline Martel (Harvey, F., 1882), v. 408
Madeline Morel (Bandmann, D. E., 1878), v. 248
Madelon (Peake, R. B., 1844), IV. 371
Mademoiselle de Belle Isle (Kemble, F. A., 1864), v. 442
Mademoiselle de Lira (Thompson, Mrs G. and Sinclair, K., 1890), v. 597
Mademoiselle Fifi (1898), v. 714
+ Mademoiselle Squallino (Featherstone, J. L., French)
Mad for Love = Maypole
Mad-Fred (Dutnall, M., 1863), v. 714, 840
Madge (Rogers, F., 1888), v. 548
— (Wade, F. and Austin, H., 1890), v. 610
Madge's Adventure (1874), v. 714
Madge Wildfire (Stirling, E., 1868), v. 584
Mad Girl of St Martin's = Pirate Smuggler
Mad Guardian (Dibdin, T. J., 1794), III. 256, 382
Mad House (Baker, R., 1737), II. 296
— (Oulton, W. C., 1784), III. 296 [The date of production should be 1/5/ 1784]
Mad Inventor (1895), v. 714
Mad Lover (1701), II. 447
Mad Lovers (1738), II. 378
— = Blazing Comet
Madman (Walker, G. R., 1881), v. 611
— (1770), III. 334
Mad, Marred and Married = Our M.D.
Mad Marriage (Harvey, F., 1884), v. 408
Mad Match (Moss, H., 1887), v. 498
Mad Meg (Burnette, C., 1885), v. 293
Mad Monarch (1834), IV. 498
Mad Mother and her Lost Son (1884), v. 714

Magic Minstrel (Dibdin, C. I. M., 1808), IV. 292
— = Oberon
Magic Mirror (À Beckett, G. A., 1843), IV. 250, 567
— = Ninth Statue
Magic Mistletoe (Buckingham, L. S., 1856) = Harlequin Humbug, v. 689, 714, 781, 834, 840
Magic Moonstone (1899), v. 714
Magic Mule (Marchant, F., 1878), v. 476
Magic Oak (Bennett, J., 1793), III. 377
— (Farley, C. and Dibdin, T. J., 1799), III. 335, 383, 402; IV. 310, 583
Magic of British Liberty (Cherry, A., 1803), IV. 498, 632
Magic of Life (Courtney, J., 1851), v. 326
Magic of Orosmanes (1785), III. 335
Magic Opal (Law, A., 1893), v. 450
Magic Pagoda (Astley, P., Jr., 1808), IV. 257
Magic Pearl (Fitzball, E., 1873), v. 368
Magic Picture (Bate, H., 1783), III. 32, 33, 113, 236
Magic Pipe (1810), IV. 498
— (1833), IV. 498
— = Harlequin Orpheus
Magic Pipe and the Fatal I.O.U. = Innocentinez
Magic Purse and Wishing Cap = Fortunatus and his Sons
Magic Ring (Brand, O., 1886), v. 274
— = Magic Opal
Magic Rose (1871), v. 714
— = (1) Azor and Zemira; (2) Beauty and the Beast; (3) Cloud King; (4) Enchanter's Slave; (5) Guardian Sylph; (6) Man in the Moon
Magic Shield (1896), v. 714
Magic Star (1807), IV. 632
Magic Sword (1807), IV. 498
Magic Thimble = Cymbra
Magic Toys (Oxenford, J., 1859), v. 509
Magic Urn (1808), IV. 498
Magic Veil = Fairy Lake
Magic Well (1804), IV. 498
Magic Whisper (Hazlewood, C. H., 1870), v. 414
Magic Wishing Cap (Hazlewood, C. H., 1865), v. 714, 796, 840

Magic Wishing Cap = Fortunatus
Magic Witch = Rothomago
Magic World (1787), III. 335
— (1807), IV. 498
— (1810), IV. 498
Magic Zone = Olympic Frailties
Magistrate (Pinero, Sir A. W., 1885), v. 174–5, 525
— (1808), IV. 498
Magloire = Jocrisse the Juggler
Magna Charta (Faucit, J. S., 1840), IV. 498, 583, 632
— (1823), IV. 498
— (1888), v. 714
— = Runnymede
Magnet (Dalton, L., 1893), v. 333
— (Dubois, Lady D., 1771), III. 258
Mago and Dado (Lonsdale, M., 1794), III. 282, 401
Magpie (Dibdin, T. J., 1815), IV. 299, 580
Magpie and Thimble (Smelt, T., 1877), v. 571
Magpie or the Maid (Pocock, I., 1815) = Daughter, IV. 33, 115, 148, 384, 448, 606, 623
Mahatma (Montague, L. A. D., 1894), v. 491
Mahdi (1894), v. 714
Mahmoud (Hoare, P., 1796), III. 270
Mahogany Polka = Spirit Rappings and Table Moving
Mahomet and Irene = Irene
Mahomet the Impostor (Miller, J., 1744), II. 66, 72–3, 111, 345, 441
Maid and the Magpie (Byron, H. J., 1858), v. 295
— (James, S., 1848), IV. 330
— (Lee, N., 1844), IV. 342
— (1846), IV. 498
— (1852), v. 714
Maid and the Magpye (Arnold, S. J., 1815), IV. 256
Maid and the Mandarin = Chinese Junk
Maid and the Mirror (Pitt, G. D., 1847), IV. 375
Maid and the Monarch = Priscella
Maid and the Monk (1840), IV. 632
Maid and the Monkey = Miss Esmeralda
Maid and the Monster = Perseus and Andromeda

Maid of Moscow = Iwanowna

Maid of Munster = Kathleen

Maid of Normandy (Barrett, J. C., 1853), v. 250

— (Eyre, E. J., 1794), III. 54, 259

Maid of Norway (Waddie, J., 1859), v. 822

Maid of Orleans (Bethune, J. E. D., 1835), IV. 86, 267

— (Egestorff, G. H. C., 1836), IV. 86, 309

— (Ireland, S. W. H., 1822), IV. 329

— (Lucas, N. J., 1841), IV. 86, 347

— (Peter, W., 1843), IV. 371

— (Salvin, H., 1824), IV. 396

— (Swanwick, A., 1843), IV. 86, 409

— (Thompson, H., 1845), IV. 86, 413

— (Turner, E. S. and Turner, F. J., 1842), IV. 86, 415

— = Joan of Arc

Maid of Palaiseau (Fitzball, E., 1838), IV. 315

— = (1) Magpie; (2) Ninetta

Maid of Paris = Victorine

Maid of Portugal = Inquisition

Maid of Prague (1837), IV. 632

Maid of St Aubin's (Skea, J., 1870), v. 570

Maid of Saragossa (Barnett, C. Z., 1845), IV. 499, 632

— (Dillon, C., 1843), IV. 581

Maid of Saxony (Morris, G., 1842), IV. 361

Maid of Snowdon (Kertland, W., 1833), IV. 592

Maid of Switzerland (Wilson, Mrs C. B. + Qns. 16/1/1832), IV. 618

— = Mariette

Maid of the Alder Well = Claude Gower

Maid of the Alps (1895), v. 714

Maid of the Cherry-tree Garden of Bermondsey = Simon the Tanner

Maid of the Cottage = Self-Sacrifice

Maid of the Forest (Milner, H. M., 1823), IV. 499, 632

Maid of the Fountain = Rival Tinkers

Maid of the Glen (?Male, G., 1810), IV. 499, 632

Maid of the Inn = Poor Mary

Maid of the Mill (Bickerstaffe, I., 1765), III. 47, 198, 237, 377

— (1750), III. 335

Maid of the Ness (1893), v. 714

Maid of the Oaks (Burgoyne, J., 1774), III. 27, 201, 241

— (Fitzball, E., 1830), IV. 313

Maid of the Rock = Maria

Maid of the Tyrol = Theresa

Maid of the Vale (1775), III. 122, 335, 402

Maid of the Warpath = Pioneers of America

Maid of Tokio (1898), v. 714

Maid of Velitri (Courtney, J., 1849), IV. 284

Maid of Venice (Dibdin, C. I. M., 1825), IV. 296

Maid of Warsaw (1846), IV. 499

Maid of Yesterday (Campbell, Mrs V., 1896), v. 301

Maid or Wife (Levius, B., 1821), IV. 144, 345

Maid o' the Mill (Carter, B., 1897), v. 305

Maids (Wild, J., 1812), IV. 419

Maids and Bachelors (Skeffington, L. St G., 1806), IV. 402

— (Westmacott, C. M., 1824), IV. 499, 632

Maids and Matrons (Morris, R. G., 1892), v. 494

Maids Beware of Moonshine! = Three Vampires

Maids Last Prayer (Southerne, T., 1693), I. 241, 433

Maid's Murder = Mary Livingstone

Maids of Honour (Kenney, C. L., 1875), v. 443

Maids of Honour and the Night Demon (1839), IV. 499

Maids of Merrie England = School of (He)Arts

Maids of Moscow (1874), v. 714

Maids of St Michael (Pitt, G. D., 1845), IV. 373

Maid's Philosophy = Venus and Adonis

Maid's Tragedy Altered (Waller, E., 1690), I. 437

Maid, the Amazon and the Martyr = Joan of Arc

Maid, the Marriage and the Malediction = Miss Leer

Maid the Mistress (O'Keeffe, J., 1783), III. 123, 200, 293

Maid the Mistress (Taverner, W., 1708), III. 141, 170–1, 232, 358; III. 116
— =(1) He Wou'd if He Cou'd; (2) Serva Padrona
Maid, the Murder and the Mystery = Gamekeeper's Gun
Maid, Wife and Widow =(1) Paradox; (2) Ruth of Rosedale; (3) 'Tis She
Maid with the Milking Pail (Buckstone, J. B., 1846), IV. 275
Maid with the Parasol = Cat in the Larder
Mail-Coach Passengers (Jameson, R. F., 1816), IV. 330
Main Chance (Farnie, H. B., 1873), v. 361
Maine Liquor Law = Teetotal Family
Main Hope (Comer, G., 1885), v. 319
Main-top Night Watch = Homeward Bound
Maintop Watch (1868), v. 714
Maison à Vendre (1840), IV. 499
Maison de Santé (Pitt, C., 1860), v. 810
Maison Rouge (1849), IV. 499
Maison Rustique = Country House
Maitre de chapelle (1845), IV. 499
Majesty Misled (1734), II. 378
Major (Jones, J. McL., 1890), v. 440
— (Melford, M., 1882), v. 484
— (1893), v. 714
Major and Miner (Ellis, W., 1881), v. 357
Major and Minor (Dance, G., 1835), IV. 499, 632
— = White Lies
Major Baggs (Lloyd, A., 1878), v. 461
Major Domo (1844), IV. 499
Major Hope = Hope
Major Marie Annie (Newbound, E., 1880), v. 502
Major Proposes (Milner, H. T., 1884), v. 490
Major Raymond (Havard, P., 1896), v. 410
Majors and Minors = Dramatic Committee
Major's Daughter (Bridgeman, J. V., 1849), IV. 499 [+L.C.]; v. 780
Major's Dilemma (1894), v. 714
Major, the Miner and the Cock-a-doodle-do = Olympic Games
Make a Noise Tom (1718), II. 378

Makebeliefs (Grein, J. T., 1892), v. 394
Make the best of it (Oxenford, J., 1851), v. 509
Make yourself at home (Maltby, A., 1875), v. 473
Make your Wills (Mayhew, E. and Smith, G., 1836), IV. 354
Making it pleasant (Clement, W., 1887), v. 314
Malade imaginaire (Wright, J.), I. 438
Maladetta (1863), v. 714
Malaeska (1866), v. 714
Malak the Jew (1830), IV. 499
Malala (1871), v. 714, 840
Malcolm (Roberts, R., 1779), III. 302
Male and Female Serenaders (Wilson, G., 1847), IV. 422
Male Coquette (Garrick, D., 1757) = Modern Fine Gentleman, III. 262
Male Curiosity = Sir Peter Pry
Malediction (1830), IV. 499
— = Rigoletti
Malediction of the Dead = Moyra
Malice (1898), v. 714
Maliel the Avenger = Retributive Justice
Mall (?Dover, J., 1674), I. 233, 241, 262, 403
Malt and Hops = Brewer of Preston
Maltster's Daughter = Rye House Plot!
Malvesi the Deformed = Dwarf
Malvina (Macfarren, G., 1826), IV. 349
— (1786), III. 335
Malvina and Calmar = Chieftains of Scotia
Malvoli (1849), IV. 499
Mamamouchi = Citizen turn'd Gentleman
Ma mie Rosette (Dance, G., 1892), v. 335
Mamma (Chippendale, Mrs M. J., 1876), v. 310
— (Grundy, S., 1888), v. 397
Mamma's Opinions (Poel, W., 1893), v. 714, 811, 840
Mammon (Grundy, S., 1877), v. 396
Mammon and Gammon (Talfourd, F., 1848), IV. 499, 632
Mam'zelle (Gill, W., 1894), v. 381
Mam'zelle Nitouche (1884), v. 714
Man (Glyn, H. A., 1874), v. 382
— (Pettitt, H., 1873), v. 520
— (1856), v. 715

Man about Town (Bernard, W. B., 1836), IV. 265
— (Mee, H., 1897), V. 483
— (Stange, S., 1899), V. 578
Management (Lunn, J., 1828), IV. 348
— (Reynolds, F., 1799), III. 301
Manager (Burnand, F. C., 1882), V. 291
— (1834), IV. 499
— = Impresario
Manager an Actor in spite of himself (Bonnor, C., 1784), III. 121, 239, 378
— = Transformation
Manager and his Friends = Mr Buckstone at Home
Manager at a Nonplus = Wanted an Actor
Manager at Home (1852), V. 715
Manageress in a Fix = Please to Remember the Grotto
Manager Hoax'd = Opening Night
Manager in Affliction (1795), III. 335
Manager in Distress (Colman, G., 1780), III. 210–11, 247
Manager in his Slippers = Rejected Addresses Received
Manager in Love (1870), V. 715
Manager in Perplexities (1862), V. 715
Manager in Prosperity (1820), IV. 499
Managers (1768), III. 335
Manager's Daughter (Lancaster, E. R., 1837), IV. 499, 593, 632
Manager's Last Kick = Quadrupeds
Managers Manag'd = Author's Triumph
Manager's Night = Spoiled Children
Manager's Room (1852), V. 715
Manager's Son = Country Actors
Manager Worried = Smock Alley Secrets
Managing Director = No. 13
Managing Mama = New Men and Old Acres
Man and a Brother = Worcester Sauce
Man and her Master = Jack Ram
Man and his Brother (1872), V. 715
Man and his Makers (Barrett, W. and Parker, L. N., 1899), V. 251
Man and his Master (1883), V. 715
— (1894), V. 715
Man and Metal (1894), V. 715
Man and Money (1860), V. 715
Man and the Maid = Trick for Trick

Man and the Marquis (Dibdin, T. J., 1825), IV. 304
Man and the Monkey (1815), IV. 148, 499
— = Animal Sympathy
Man and the Monster (Milner, H. M., 1827), IV. 499, 632
— = Frankenstein
Man and the Shadow (1866). V. 715
Man and the Spirit (Hazlewood, C. H., 1881), V. 415
Man and the Tiger = P.P.
Man and the Woman (Buchanan, R., 1889), V. 285
Man and Wife (Arnold, S. J., 1809), IV. 255
— (Collins, W. W., 1873), V. 318
— (Colman, G., 1769), III. 45, 118, 183, 246
— (James, D. S., 1885), V. 433
— (Stephenson, C. H., 1870), V. 582
Man and Wife before Marriage = Who's at Home?
Man and Woman (De Mille, H. C. and Belasco, D., 1893), V. 342
— (1883), V. 715
Man at the Wheel = Ixion
Man Cat (1871), V. 715
Manchester Friends = Love in his Dotage
Manchester Girl = False Glitter
Manchester Man's Million = Grelley's Money
Manchester Marriage (Cheatham, F. G., 1859), V. 715, 783, 840
Mandarin (1789), III. 335
— (1811), IV. 499
— (1896), V. 715
Mandarin's Daughter = Willow-Pattern Plate
Mandarin's Ghost (1897), V. 715
Mandingo Warriors = Kongo Kolo
Mandrill (1830), IV. 499
Mandrin (Mathews, C. J., 1835), IV. 354
— (1864), V. 715
Manette (Reynoldson, T. H., 1846), IV. 393, 537 [Manette and A Speaking Likeness are identical]
Man for the Ladies (Jerrold, D. W., 1836), IV. 333
— = Peter the Beauty

Manfred (Byron, Lord G. G., 1817), IV. 169, 277
— (1803), IV. 499
— (1841), IV. 499
Man-Fred (À Beckett, G. A., 1834), IV. 249
Manfredi (1834), IV. 499
Manfredoni (1821), IV. 499
Man from Borneo (1898), v. 715
Mangora, King of the Timbusians (Moore, Sir T., 1717), II. 49, 106, 345
Man-Hater (Foote, S., 1762), III. 384
— (1771), III. 402
— = Britomarte
Man his Own Master (1816), IV. 499
Manhood (Hewson, J. J., 1888), v. 420
— (Pitt, C. I., 1876), v. 526
Man Hunter (Jarman, F., 1891), v. 434
Maniac (Arnold, S. J., 1810), IV. 255, 569
— (Dibdin, C. I. M., 1818), IV. 294
— (1823), IV. 499
Maniac Bride = Lady of the Lake
Maniac Father and the Triumph of Love = Paul the Rover
Maniac Jew = Hyram Balthazar
Maniac Lover (1866), v. 715
Maniac Maid (Roberdeau, J. P., 1804), 394
Maniac Mother (1823), IV. 499
Maniac of the Alps = Isaure
Maniac of the Cave = Love and Madness
Maniac of the Pyrenees (Shipp, J., 1829), IV. 610
Maniac of the Sierra Morena (1830), IV. 499
Maniac of the Torrent = Switzer's Curse
Maniac, the Mystery and the Malediction = Veiled Prophet of Korassan
Man in a Thousand (Burnette, C., 1890), v. 293
Man in Black (Williams, H. E., 1897), v. 624
Man in Brown = Robber of Epping Forest
Man in Grey (Howe, J. B., 1863), v. 715, 840
Man in Love (Rassindyll, E., 1895), v. 535
Man in Mourning for Himself (Peake, R. B., 1816), IV. 499, 632

Man in Possession (Albery, J., 1876), v. 237
— (Overton, R., 1892), v. 509
— = Lot No. 1
Man in Search of a Sensation = Blasé
Man in the Camlet Cloak = Conjectures
Man in the Cleft = Glin Gath
Man in the Cloak (Marchant, F., 1870), v. 476
Man in the House (Melford, M., 1884), v. 484
Man in the Iron Mask (Goldberg, M., 1899), v. 383
— (Lucas, W. J., 1832), IV. 499, 632
— (Perth, and Condie, 1899), v. 520
— (Serle, T. J., 1832), IV. 399, 610
— (1860), v. 715
Man in the Macintosh = Glass Door
Man in the Moon (Addison, J., 1892), v. 236
— (Astley, P., Jr., 1808), IV. 257
— (Barrymore, W., 1826), IV. 499, 632
— (Blanchard, E. L., 1871), v. 264
— (Brewer, G., 1799), III. 239
— (McLaren, A., 1815), IV. 351
— (Merion, C., 1873), v. 485
— (Phillips, R., 1817), IV. 372
— (Powell, G., 1697), I. 425
— (Vandeightone, 1847), IV. 499, 632
— (1816), IV. 499
— (1875, 1877), v. 715
— (1879), IV. 840
— = Woman of Dreams
Man in the Red Coat (1829), IV. 499
Man in the Street (Parker, L. N., 1894), v. 513
Man in the Ulster (Manuel, E., 1874), v. 475
Man is not perfect, nor Woman neither (Webster, B., the Younger, 1867), v. 618
Mankind (Conquest, G. and Merritt, P., 1881), v. 322
Man like himself (1785), III. 335
Manlius Capitolinus (Ozell, J., 1719), II. 347, 442
Man loaded with Mischief (Marchant, F., 1870), v. 476
Man Milliner (O'Keeffe, J., 1787), III. 293

Man Milliner (1821), IV. 500
Manners and Customs of America (1857), V. 715
Manners make the Man = Love is Blind
Man o' Airlie (Wills, W. G., 1867), V. 627
Manoeuvre = Blind Man
Manoeuvres of Jane (Jones, H. A., 1898), V. 440
Manoeuvring (Planché, J. R. and Dance, C., 1829), IV. 84, 378, 605
— (1814), IV. 635
— = Two make a Pair
Man of Business (Cobb, J., 1809) = Sudden Arrivals, IV. 500, 632
— (Colman, G., 1774), III. 119, 123, 141, 246
— (Olaf, W. and Chapman, W., 1887), 507
Man of Bus'ness = Love in the Dark
Man of Crime = Quadroona
Man of Destiny (Shaw, G. B., 1897), V. 189, 195, 203-4, 562
Man of Enterprise (Shillito, C., 1789), III. 188-9, 306
Man of Family (Jenner, C., 1771), III. 120, 276, 388
Man of Few Words = Joe Miller
Man of Forty (Frith, W., 1898), V. 374
— (Poel, W., 1880), V. 529, 811
Man of Genius = William March
Man of Honour (Davies, W., 1786), III. 253
— (Lynch, F.), II. 342
— = Brittanicus
Man of Iron (1885), V. 715
Man of Law (Webster, B. N., 1851), V. 618
Man of Many Friends (Coyne, J. S., 1855), V. 327
Man of Mile End (1834), IV. 500
Man of Mode (Etherege, Sir G., 1676), I. 43, 60, 188, 198, 236, 348, 410
Man of My Choice = Guardians
Man of Mystery (1826), IV. 500 [and see note under Fatal Precept]
— (1870), V. 715
Man of Newmarket (Howard, E., 1678), I. 52, 214, 414
Man of No Principle (Brownson, J. H., 1895), V. 283

Man of Parts (Jackman, I., 1785), III. 276 [This was acted as A Trip to London, Smock Alley, Dublin, 2/12/1785]
Man of Quality (Hollingshead, J., 1870), V. 424
— (Lee, J., 1773), III. 280
Man of Reason (Kelly, H., 1776) = Reasonable Lover, III. 131, 278, 389
Man of Stratagems = Clinton
Man of Straw = My Grandfather's Will
Man of Taste (Miller, J., 1735), II. 135, 144, 164-5, 203, 344; III. 116
— (1752), III. 116, 335
Man of Ten Thousand (Holcroft, T., 1795), III. 271
Man of the Black Forest (1820), IV. 500
Man of the Day = Well-born Workman
Man of the Family (Jenner, C., 1771), III. 276
Man of the Mill (1765), III. 335
Man of the People (Branson, W. S., 1879), V. 274
Man of the Red Chateau = Chevalier of the Moulin Rouge
Man of the Red Mansion (Rice, C., 1851), V. 715, 813, 840
Man of the Wood, the Fair Maniac and the Dumb Brother and Sister (1823), IV. 500
Man of the World (Goldman, L. B., 1894), V. 383
— (Macklin, C., 1781), III. 19, 140, 284, 391
Man of Two Lives (Bernard, W. B., 1869), V. 259
— (Thompson, L., 1879), V. 598
Man of Two Masters (1858), V. 715
— = Jonathan
Man of Two Thousand (1821), IV. 500
Man of War (Bosworth, J., 1838), IV. 573
Manola (Farnie, H. B., 1882), V. 362, 791
— (Lucas, Sergeant, 1872), V. 464
Manon (Bennett, J., 1885), V. 258
Man on the Rock = Prometheus
Manor House of Mont Louvier = Marie
Man or Wife = Castle of Limburg
Man-o'-War's Man (Dellow, H. and Livesey, C., 1894), V. 342

Man o' War's Man and the Privateer =
Lost Ship
Man Proposes (Grundy, S., 1878), V.
396
Man's a Man for a' that (1891), V. 715
Man's Ambition = Secret Crime
Man's an Ass (Jerrold, D. W., 1835), IV.
332
Man's Bewitch'd (Centlivre, Mrs S.,
1709), II. 131, 145, 167, 305
— (1738), II. 378, 385; III. 115
Man's Coming (1850), V. 715
Man's Enemy (Longden, C. H. and
Hudson, E. V., 1897), V. 463
Man's Evil Spirit (1859), V. 715
Man's Folly (1879), V. 715
Man's Hate and Woman's Friendship =
Persecution
Mans Heart his greatest Enemy =
Traitor to Himself
Man she loved = Devil's Luck
Man's Inhumanity = Self
Mansion of Terrors (Bellingham, H.,
1852), V. 257
Manslaughter by Moonlight (+ Dibdin,
C. I. M., 1822) = Furor of Friendship,
IV. 500
Manslayer (Dibdin, C. I. M., 1825), IV.
296
Man's Love (Grein, J. T. and Jarvis,
C. W., 1895), V. 394
Man's Mercy (Pitt, W. H., 1874), V. 527
— = In the Holly
Man's Shadow = Roger-la-Honte
Man's Talisman—Gold (Newbound,
E., 1877), V. 502
Man's the Master (D'Avenant, Sir W.,
1668), I. 11, 13, 26, 33, 191, 247-8,
347, 348, 401; III. 114
— (Woodward, H., 1775), III. 114, 317
Manteaux Noirs (Parke, W. and
Paulton, H., 1882), V. 512, 809
Man that follows the Ladies (Paull,
H. M., 1856), V. 516
Man that hesitates (Godfrey, G. W.,
1887), V. 383
Man, the Spirit and the Moral = Grape
Girl of Madrid
Man to Man (Bourne, W., 1884), V.
270
Man too hard for the Master = Love
without Interest

Man Trap (Hatch, P. H., 1849), IV. 500,
632
— (McLaren, A., 1816), IV. 351
Mantuan Revels (Chenevix, R., 1812),
IV. 279
Manuel (Maturin, C. R., 1817), IV. 167,
354
Manuel of Spain (Phillips, R., 1859), V.
715, 810, 840
Manumission = Native Land
Manuscript (Cooke, W., 1809), IV. 283
— (Lucas, W., 1809), IV. 347
Man who couldn't die (1895), V. 715
Man who "couldn't help it" = Perils of
Pippins
Man who wasn't (Ransom, H. A. V.,
1895), V. 534
Man with a Past (1895), V. 715
— (1899), V. 715
Man without a Head (Wooler, J. P.,
1845), IV. 500, 632
Man without a Shirt = Adam Bluff
Man with the Carpet Bag (À Beckett,
G. A., 1834), IV. 249, 567
— (1834), IV. 500
Man with the Hump and the Belle of
Notre Dame = Quasimodo, the De-
formed
Man with the Iron Hand = Tom Cringle
Man with the Iron Heart = Fatal
Shadow
Man with the Nose (1837), IV. 500
Man with the Pigeons (Douglass, J. T.),
V. 789
Man with the Red Beard (Wilkins,
J. H., 1852), V. 623
Man with Three Coats = Strange Legacy
Man with Three Wives! (Rae, C. M.,
1886), V. 532
Man with Two Wives (Waldron, F. G.,
1798), III. 314
Man-Wolf (Moncrieff, W. T., 1831),
IV. 500, 632
Manxman (Barrett, W., 1894), V. 251
Many a Slip between the Cup and the
Lip = Mervyn Clitheroe
Many a Slip 'twixt Cup and Lip =
Tantalus
Many Happy Returns (À Beckett, G. A.
and Scott, C., 1881), V. 234
Many Sides to a Character = Not as bad
as we seem

Ma Part (Horncastle, J. H., 1846), IV. 328

Mara (Sapte, Walter, Jr., 1889), v. 556

Marble Arch (Rose, E. and Garroway, A. J., 1881), v. 550

Marble Bride (Hazlewood, C. H., 1857), v. 412

Marble Heart (Selby, C., 1854), v. 97, 560

Marble King (James, C. S., 1851), v. 433

Marble Lover (1854), v. 715

Marble Maiden (Layton, G. M., 1873), v. 451

— (Stocqueler, J. H., 1846), IV. 500, 632

— (1845), IV. 500, 632

— (1866), v. 715

Marble Statue (1856), v. 715

— (1883), v. 715

Marcelia (Boothby, F., 1669), I. 140, 392

Marcella (Hayley, W., 1789), III. 227, 267, 386

Marcelle (1879), v. 715

Marcelline (Selby, C., 1839), IV. 398 +Marcellus and Julia (8°, 1788)

Marchand d'esclaves (1819), IV. 500

Marches Day (Finlayson, J., 1814), IV. 583

— (1771), III. 335

March Hare Hunt (Moore, F. F., 1877), v. 492

Marchioness de Brinvilliers (1846), IV. 500

Marchioness of Brinvillion (1862), v. 715

March of Crime = Oscar the Bandit

March of Intelleck (Macfarren, G., 1827), IV. 350

March of Intellect = Adelphi Academy

March on Magdala (Warrington, F., 1870), v. 615

March Winds and April Showers (1860), v. 715

Marciano (Clark, W., 1662), I. 397

Marcoretti (Kingdom, J. M., 1853), v. 444

Marco Schiarra (1860), v. 715

Marco Sciarro (Dillon, C., 1844), IV. 581

— (1840), IV. 632

Marco Spada (Simpson, J. P., 1853), v. 567

Marcus Brutus (Sheffield, J., 1722), II. 355

Marcus Manlius (Colombine, D. E., 1837), IV. 577

Marcus Tullius Cicero (Patsall), III. 296

Marden Grange (1869), v. 715

Mardo (Frayne, F. J., 1883), v. 372

Mareschal de Logis = Veteran

Mare's Nest (Hamilton, H., 1887), v. 401

— (Mouillot, F., 1889), v. 498

Marforio (1736), II. 378

Margaret Byng (Philips, F. C. and Fendall, P., 1891), v. 522

Margaret Catchpole (Stirling, E., 1845), IV. 407

— (1845), IV. 500

Margaret Catchpole, the Female Horse-stealer (1845), IV. 500

Margaret Maddison (Pitt, G. D., 1846), IV. 374

Margaret of Anjou (Jerningham, E., 1777), III. 84, 277

— (Wilson, J. M., 1829), IV. 500, 618, 632

Margaret of Regensburg (1837), IV. 500

Margaret's Ghost (Fitzball, E., 1833), IV. 500, 584

Margate (White, B., 1895), v. 620

Margate Milkmaid = Pyramus and Thisbe

Margate Sands (Hancock, W., 1864), v. 402

— = New Brighton Sands

Margery (Carey, H., 1738), II. 137, 266–7, 303, 433

Margery Daw (Morton, J. M., 1861), v. 496

— = Ballad Singer

Margery's Lovers (Matthews, B., 1884), v. 480

Margot (Manuel, E., 1875), v. 475

— (1879), v. 715

Marguerite (Halford, J., 1856), v. 398

— (Pede, T., 1873), v. 518

— (Reade, C.), v. 812

— (1821), IV. 500

Marguerite's Colours (Archer, T., 1847), IV. 190, 255

Marguerite's Mangle = Faust

Maria (Davidson, A., III. 253, 381

Maria (Meighan, J., 1890), v. 483

Mariage Night (Cary, H., 1663), I. 136, 395

Mariamne (Fenton, E., 1723), II. 6, 43, 58, 72, 110, 264, 323, 436; III. 78
— (Waller, W., 1839), IV. 615

Marian (Arnold, W. N., 1825), IV. 569
— (Brooke, F., 1788), III. 240
— (Cooke, C., 1870), v. 323

Mariana (Graham, J., 1897), v. 387

Marian and the Knight Templar = Marian

Marianne de Lancy (1854), v. 840

Marianne Duval the Vivandière (Phillips, L., 1851), v. 523, 810

Marianne, the Child of Charity (Pitt, G. D., 1844), IV. 373

Marian of the Grange = Marian

Maria Padilla (Barnett, C. Z., 1841), IV. 260

Maria Stuarda (Williams, T. J.), v. 824

Marie (Addison, H. R., 1836), IV. 251
— (Barnett, C. Z., 1843), IV. 260
— (Carte, R. D., 1871), v. 305
— (1855), v. 715

Marie Antoinette (Simpson, J. P., 1868), v. 568
— (Yarnold, E., 1835), IV. 422
— (1858), v. 716

Marie de Chamouni (Wilton, F., 1848), IV. 618
— (1843) = Marie, the Pearl of Chamouni, IV. 632

Marie de Courcelles (Holford, Mrs, 1878), v. 424

Marie de Meranie (1864), v. 716

Marie de Rohan (1862), v. 716

Marie de Roux (1860), v. 716

Marie de Rudney = Nun

Marie Ducange (Bernard, W. B., 1841), IV. 266

Marie Jeanne (Bandmann, D. E., 1879), v. 248

Marie Mignot = Ambition

Marie Stuart (1876), v. 716

Marie, the Foundling of the Lake (1849), IV. 500

Marie, the Pearl of Chamouni (1843) = Marie de Chamouni, IV. 500, 632

Marietta (?Raymond, E. M. or C. F. M., 1843), IV. 500, 632 [There is some

doubt about this play: it is attributed to E. M. Raymond, but a Mariette of the same year is given to C. F. M. Raymond]

Marietta = Mariette's Wedding

Mariette (?Raymond, C. F. M., 1843), IV. 388 [see also under Marietta]
— (1821), v. 490

Mariette Duval (Barnett, C. Z., 1839), IV. 260

Mariette's Wedding (Morton, W. E. and Millars, H., 1882), v. 497

Marigold (Matthison, A., 1879), v. 481

Marigold Farm (Sapte, Walter, Jr., 1893), v. 556

Marina (Coleman, J., 1888), v. 316
— (Lillo, G., 1738), II. 70, 141, 223, 342, 440

Mariner and his Monkey = Phillip IV

Mariner and the Delowar (1854), v. 716

Mariners (Birch, S., 1793), III. 238

Mariner's Compass (Leslie, H. T., 1865), v. 457

Mariner's Daughter (1866), v. 716
— = White Squall

Mariner's Dream (Barnett, C. Z., 1838), IV. 260

Mariners of England (Buchanan, R. and Jay, H., 1897), v. 285

Mariner's Sister = Minute Gun at Sea

Marinette (Stonehouse, J., 1843), IV. 409
— (1853), v. 716

Marino Faliero (Byron, Lord G. G., 1821), IV. 169, 220, 278
— (Swinburne, A. C., 1885), v. 589

Marion (Ellis, W. and Greenwood, P., 1898), v. 357

Marion Delorme (Davey, R., 1887), v. 338, 787
— (1859), v. 716

Marionettes (Reece, R. and McArdle, J. F., 1879), v. 539
— (1876), v. 716

Marion Hazleton (Courtney, J., 1848), IV. 284
— (1854), v. 716

Marishka (Zalewska, W., 1891), v. 637

Maritana (Fitzball, E., 1845), IV. 316

Maritta (1899), v. 716

Marjolaine (Edwards, H. S., 1877), v. 355

Mary Livingstone (Pitt, G. D., 1846), IV. 374

Mary, Mary Quite Contrary (1845), IV. 501

— (1860), V. 839

Mary, Mary, Quite Contrary, how does your Garden grow? (1859), V. 717

Mary May (1856), V. 717

Mary Melvyn (Fitzball, E., 1843), IV. 316

Mary of Manchester (Stirling, E., 1847), IV. 408

Mary of Scotland = Abbot

Mary of the Lighthouse (1861), V. 717

Mary Pennington, Spinster (Walkes, W. R., 1896), V. 612

Mary Price (Hazlewood, C. H., 1853), V. 717, 796, 840

— (1852), V. 717

Mary Queen of Scots (Boulding, J. W., 1873), V. 270

— (Deverell, Mrs M., 1792), III. 85, 254

— (Francklin, T., 1737), III. 261

— (Murray, W. H., 1825), IV. 94, 365

— (St John, J., 1789), III. 85, 304

— (Thompson, R. H., 1894), V. 598

— (Wills, W. G., 1874), V. 627

Mary's Bower (Brown, R., 1811), IV. 574

Mary's Devotion (Frere, C., 1898), V. 373

Mary's Dream (Townsend, W. T., 1837), IV. 414

Mary's Holiday (Vandervell, W. F., 1879), V. 606

Mary's Secret (Matthison, A., 1876), V. 481

Mary Stewart, Queen of Scots (Grahame, J., 1801), IV. 195, 501, 633

Mary Stuart (Gibbons, Mrs A., 1838), IV. 585

— (Haynes, J., 1840), IV. 324

— (Macaulay, Miss, 1823), IV. 596

— (Mellish, J. C., 1801), IV. 86, 355

— (Percival, E. L., 1839), IV. 86, 371

— (Peter, W., 1841), IV. 86, 371

— (Salvin, H., 1824), IV. 86, 396

— (Swinburne, A. C., 1881), V. 589

— (Trelawney, A., 1838), IV. 86, 414

— (Wingfield, L., 1880), V. 629

— (1833), IV. 86, 501

— (1839), IV. 82, 501

— (1850), V. 717

Mary Stuart (1866), V. 717

— = Mary, Queen of Scots

Mary Stuart, Queen of Scotland (1819), IV. 501

Mary Stuart, the Child of Misfortune (1893), V. 717

Mary, the Maid of the Inn (Scott, J. M., 1809), IV. 501, 633

— (1857), V. 717

Mary Tudor (Dickinson, A., 1876), V. 344

— (Gregg, T. D., 1858), V. 394

— (Stirling, E., 1849), IV. 613

— (Vere, A. de, 1847), IV. 415

— (1835), IV. 501

+ Mary Tudor (Duvard, P., 8°, 1844 (Northallerton))

Mary Turner (Burnand, F. C., 1867), V. 289

Mary Warner (Taylor, T., 1869), V. 593

Mary White (1842) = Mary White, the Charity Girl, IV. 501, 633

Mary White, the Charity Girl (1840) = Mary White, IV. 501, 633

Marzovan, the Apostate (1830), IV. 501

Masaniello (Brough, R. B., 1857), V. 278

— (Kenney, J., 1829), IV. 83, 337, 592

— (Levius, B., 1829), IV. 83, 345

— (Milner, H. M., 1829), IV. 83, 357, 599

— (1829) IV. 83, 501

— (1886), V. 717

Masaniello, the Fisherman of Naples (Soane, G., 1825), IV. 403, 612

— (1826), IV. 501

Mascotte (Farnie, H. B. and Reece, R., 1881), V. 362, 791

Mashing Highwayman = Dandy Dick Turpin

Mashing Mamma (Park, T., 1888), V. 512

Mask and the Surgeon = Huguenots

Mask'd Friend (1796), III. 135, 335

Masked (1870), V. 717

Masked Ball (Fitch, C., 1892), V. 367

— (1850), V. 717

— = (1) Black Domino; (2) Gustavus III; (3) Gustavus of Sweden; (4) Woman's the Devil

Masked Battery (1834), IV. 502

Masked Man (1866), V. 717

Masked Mother (Calvert, C., 1859), v. 783

Masked Mother and the Hidden Hand = Capitola

Masked Rider = Wife's Revenge

Mask of Bronze (1860), v. 717

Mask of Death (Ford, H., 1897), v. 370

Mask of Guilt (Vane, S., 1894), v. 606

Mask of Love (Osborne, C., 1877), v. 508

Masks and Faces (Taylor, T. and Reade, C., 1852), v. 68, 105, 150, 592, 820

— (1856), v. 717

Ma's Mistake (Parker, W., 1895), v. 514

Ma's Old Bean (Hill, H., 1888), v. 421

Mason (1899), v. 717

Mason and the Locksmith (1879), v. 717

Mason of Buda (Planché, J. R., 1828), IV. 378

Masonry (Dibdin, T. J., 1821), IV. 303

Masque for the Marriage of the Prince of Wales (Gretton, J., 1795), III. 386

Masque for Valentinian (Fane, Sir F., 1684), I. 410

Masque of Hymen = Royal Nuptials

Masque of the Deities (Thurmond, J., 1723), II. 360

Masquerade (Galt, J., 1814), IV. 318, 635

— (Griffin, B., 1717), II. 212, 333

— (Johnson, C., 1719), II. 132, 142, 144, 156-7, 175, 183, 339

— (1795), III. 335, 402

— (1820), IV. 502

— = Cent per Cent

Masquerade Ball (Ward, H. R., 1846), IV. 416

Masquerade Frolic = Fair Intriguers

Masqueraders (Jones, H. A., 1894), v. 166-7, 189, 440

— = (1) Love a Bo-Peep; (2) Oh! this Love

Massacre of Abergavenny (Furness, J. R., 1897), v. 375

Massacre of Cyprus (Milner, H. M., 1823), IV. 502, 633

Massacre of English Tourists by the Aravaniteakai = Greek Brigands

Massacre of Glencoe (1856), v. 717

Massacre of Jerusalem = Warrior Kings

Massacre of Paris (Lee, N., 1689), I. 148, 352, 420

— = Paris

Massacre of Paris on the 27th, 28th and 29th of July = French Revolution

Massacre of Rajahpoor (Milner, H. M., 1826), IV. 502, 633

Massacre of St Bartholomew = (1) Carpenter of Rouen; (2) Huguenots; (3) Jean Hennuyer, Bishop of Lisieux

Massacre of the Greeks = Siege of Missolonghi

Massacre of the Huguenots = Lady of the Louvre

Massacre of the 28th = Paris

Massacres of 1576 = Huguenots

Massaniello = Rise and Fall of Massaniello

Massaroni (Moreton, F. L., 1894), v. 493

Masse-en-yell-oh (Paulton, H. and Tedde, M., 1886), v. 517

Mass Unmask'd = Antichristian Opera

Mast and the Ploughshare (1804) = Ship and the Plough, IV. 502, 633

Master (Ogilvie, G. S., 1898), v. 506

Master Alfred (Combe, J., 1876), v. 319

Master and Man (Sims, G. R. and Pettitt, H., 1889), v. 569

— = Married Bachelor

Master Bell Blue (1860), v. 717

Master Builder (Archer, W. and Gosse, E., 1893), v. 242

Master Clarke (Serle, T. J., 1840), IV. 400, 610

Master Humphrey and His Clock = Tables Turned

Master Humphrey's Clock (Cooper, F. F., 1840), IV. 283

Master Jones's Birthday (Morton, J. M., 1868), v. 496

Master Key (1821) = Two Wives!, IV. 502

— = Love among the Roses

Master of Hope (Hawkins, L., 1898), v. 410

Master of Ravenswood (Simpson, J. P., 1865), v. 567

Master of the Forge (Bernard, C., 1884), v. 778

Master of the Situation (Hannan, C., 1899), v. 403

Master Passion (Falconer, E., 1859), v. 360

— (Phillips, Mrs A., 1852), v. 522

Matrimonial Masquerading = Snapping Turtles

Matrimonial Noose (Spier, M. H., 1885), v. 576

— = (1) Next-door Neighbours; (2) Queen Ellinor

Matrimonial Perplexity = What a Corporation!

Matrimonial Prospectuses (Simpson, J. P., 1852), v. 567

Matrimonial Trouble (Cavendish, M., 1662), I. 396

Matrimonio segreto (Grist, W., 1877), v. 795

Matrimony (Cameron, C., 1886), v. 300

— (Derby, C., 1844), IV. 290

— (Kenney, J., 1804) = Two Prisoners, IV. 144, 336, 547, 592, 641

— (Norman, G. P., 1893), v. 505

— (1798), III. 335

— (1812), IV. 502

— (1883), v. 717

Matrimony and Magic = Taming a Tartar

+ Matrimony by Advertisement (Emson, F. E., 8°, n.d.)

+ Matrimony Displayed (Smock Alley, Dublin, 24/4/1740)

Matron of Palermo = Sicilian Mother

Matteo Falcone (Oxberry, W. H., 1836), IV. 366

Matteo Falconi (Mayhew, E., 1834), IV. 502, 633

Matter of Doubt (Rodwell, G. H., 1823), IV. 502, 633

Matter of Right (1849), IV. 502

Matthew Hopkins (1829), IV. 502

Maud = Maud's Peril

Maude Muller (1883), v. 717

Maudlin, the Merchant's Daughter of Bristol (1729), II. 378

Maud's Peril (Phillips, W., 1867), v. 70-1, 523

Maum Guinea (1862), v. 717

Maureen na Laveen (Cooke, F., 1873), v. 323

Maurice (Dibdin, C. I. M., 1822), IV. 295

— (Dibdin, C. I. M., 1825), IV. 296

Maurice the Outcast (1834), IV. 502

Maurice the Woodcutter (Somerset, C. A., 1829), IV. 404, 612

Maurice the Woodcutter (?Somerset, C. A., 1835), IV. 502, 633

— (1854), v. 717

Mausoleum (Hayley, W., 1784), III. 267

Maxey's Money (1893), v. 717

Maximian (Burrell, Lady S. R., 1800), III. 60, 241; IV. 277

Maximums and Speciments of William Muggins (Selby, C., 1842), IV. 502, 633

May (Reece, R., 1874), v. 538

May and December (Grundy, S. and Mackay, J., 1882), v. 396

— (Miller, W. F., 1890), v. 489

— (1832), IV. 502

— (1835), IV. 502

— (1858), v. 840

— (1865), v. 717

— (1875), v. 717

— = Old Man's Darling

May Blossom (?Belasco, D., 1884), v. 717, 840

— = Thunderbolt

May Brierley = Six Years After

May-Day (Garrick, D., 1775), III. 202, 264

— = Fairy-Hill

May-Day Wedding = Sailor's Prize

May Dudley (Marchant, F., 1863), v. 717, 840

Mayfair (Pinero, Sir A. W., 1885), v. 185, 525

Mayfair and Ragfair (Mackay, J., 1878), v. 470

Mayflower (Moore, F. F., 1892), v. 492

— (Parker, L. N., 1899), v. 514

May Marsden (1846), IV. 502

May Meetings (Nowell, H. and Wynne, H., 1894), v. 506

May Morning (Norman, G. T., 1895), v. 505

— (1850), IV. 502

May Myrtle (1875), v. 717

Mayoralty of Trueborough = Contrast

Mayor and the Monkey (Coyne, J. S., 1838), IV. 502, 633

Mayor and the Three Coffins = Misconception

Mayor Deceived = Harvest Home

Mayor in a Hamper = Peeping Tom

Mayor of Garratt (1810), IV. 502

— (1837), IV. 502

Mayor of Garret (Foote, S., 1763), III. 114, 260
Mayor Outwitted = Hoaxing
Mayor's Dilemma = Well Played
Maypole (Wade, C. B. and Elliot, S., 1887), V. 610
May Queen (Buckstone, J. B., 1828), IV. 273
— (Buckstone, J. B., 1843), IV. 502
— (1871), V. 717
— (1874), V. 718
— (1883), V. 717
— (1893), V. 718
— (1898), V. 718
— = (1) Folly Fête; (2) Concealed Royalty; (3) Sylvia
May 17th, 1076 = Gallery of St Nicholas
May Tempest (1883), V. 718
Maze of Life (1882), V. 718
Mazeppa (Burnand, F. C., 1885), V. 291
— (Byron, H. J., 1859), V. 295
— (Milner, H. M., 1823), IV. 357, 502, 633
— (Newton, H. C., 1882), V. 718, 808, 841
— (1851), V. 718
— (1866), V. 718
— (1880), V. 718
— (1883), V. 718
— (1888), V. 718
— (1893), V. 718
Maze, the Maiden and the Monarch = Fair Rosamond
Mazourka (Byron, H. J., 1864), V. 296
— (1835), IV. 502
M.D. (Barri, O., 1879), V. 251
— (Lee, N., Jr., 1874), V. 453
— (Paulton, H. and Tedde, M., 1888), V. 517
M.E. = Post House
+ Meadows of St Gervais (Ware, J. R., Dicks)
Meadow Sweet (Prevost, C. M., 1890), V. 530
Mean Advantage (Dircks, R., 1863), V. 345
— (Hart, F. and Herbert, G., 1897), V. 407
Me and Myself (1834), IV. 633
Measure for Measure (Gildon, C., 1700), II. 67, 71, 220, 332, 437
— (Kemble, J. P., 1803), IV. 335

Mechanic (Clair, G., 1859), V. 718, 784, 841
— (Lindo, F., 1889), V. 460
Mechanical Babes in the Wood (1882), V. 718
Mechanical Partner (Redmond, J., 1873), V. 537
Mechanical Toy (Taylor, M., 1870), V. 591
Mechanic's Wife (1883), V. 718
— = Downfall of Pride
Medæa (Johnson, C., 1730), II. 89, 264, 339
Medal of Death (Towers, E., 1866), V. 718, 821, 841
Meddle and Muddle (Bellingham, H. and Best, W., 1887), V. 257
Medea (Brough, R. B., 1856), V. 278
— (Glover, R., 1761), III. 71, 81, 265
— (Heron, M., 1861), V. 419
— (Sherburne, Sir E., 1648), I. 432
— (Stillingfleet, B., 1765), III. 309
— (Webster, A., 1867), V. 617
— (Williams, T. J., 1856), V. 625
— (1876), V. 718
— (1883), V. 718
Medea and Jason (1781), III. 336
Medea in Corinth (Heraud, J. A., 1857), V. 418
— (Wills, W. G., 1872), V. 627
Medea's Kettle (1792), III. 336
Medecine for the Million = Humbug
Medecin Malgre Lui = Love's Contrivance
Media (1853), V. 718
Mediaeval Strike = Simon the Smith
Medical Man (Gilbert, W. S., 1872), V. 379
Medical Student (Frances, B. and Laeland, H. J., 1893), V. 372
Medician Brutus = Italian Traitors
Medicine Man (Traill, H. D. and Hichens, R. S., 1891), V. 602
Medico (Lane, F., 1894), V. 448
Medicus Borealis (1816), IV. 502
Medium (Brown, J. R., 1899), V. 282
Medlars = King and Titi
Medley (1765), III. 336
— (1778), III. 336
Medley Lovers = Benevolent Man
Medley of Lovers = Miss in her Teens

Mercantile Lovers (Wallis, G., 1775), III. 314

Mercedes (Wood, F., 1896), v. 630

Mercer of Ludgate (Barnett, C. Z., 1847), IV. 261

Merchant (Colman, G., 1769), III. 246

Merchant and his Clerks (Coyne, J. S., 1842), IV. 284

Merchant and the Mendicant (Rice, C., 1858), v. 542, 813

Merchant of Bruges (Kinnaird, D. J. W., 1815), IV. 338

Merchant of Brussels = Widow's Son

Merchant of Guadeloupe (Wallace, J., 1802), IV. 416

Merchant of London (Serle, T. J., 1832), IV. 399

Merchant of Paisley (1870), v. 718

Merchant of Venice (Blanchard, E. L., 1843), IV. 268

— (Kemble, J. P., 1814), IV. 335

— (Talfourd, F., 1849), IV. 410

— (Valpy, R., 1802), IV. 415

— (1896), v. 718

— = Shylock

Merchant Prince of Cornville (1896), v. 718

Merchant's Clerk (Pitt, G. D., 1847), IV. 375

Merchant's Daughter (Barnett, C. Z., 1839), IV. 260

— (1884), v. 718

— = (1) Clarisse; (2) Grace Rivers; (3) Jarvis the Honest Man

Merchant's Daughter of Toulon (Thomas, Mrs E., 1856), v. 596

Merchant's Honour (1858), v. 718, 841

Merchant's Steed of Syracuse (1840), IV. 503

Merchant's Venture (Moore, R., 1868), v. 492

Merchant's Vow = Canonburg

Merchant's Wedding (Planché, J. R., 1828), IV. 378

Merchant's Wife of Havre = Two Clerks

Merciful Soul (1899), v. 718

Merciless Marauder = Alaric and Eliza

Merciless World = Light Ahead

Mercury Harlequin (Woodward, H., 1756), III. 209, 317

Mercury Harlequin in Ireland (1763), III. 336

Mercy (Goodwin, 1879), v. 384

Mercy Dodd = Presumptive Evidence

Mercy's Choice (1871), v. 718

Mercy to the Penitent = Babes of the Castle

Mere Blind (Villiers, E., 1871), v. 822

Mere Child (Marston, J. W., 1866), v. 479

Merely Acting (Ashlyn, Q., 1898), v. 245

Merely Players (1882), v. 718

— (1898), v. 718

Mere Question of Time (Malyon, E. J. and James, C., 1897), v. 473

Mere Scratch (1883), v. 718

Merit and Justice = Scales of Justice

Merit before Money = Choice

Merit is its own Reward = Honesty

Meritorious Maiden and the Millicious Milliner = Little Ben Bolt

Merlin (Giffard, W., 1736), II. 332

— (Theobald, L., 1734), II. 359

— (1767), III. 336

Merlin in Labour = Hint to the Theatres

Merlin in Love (Hill, A., 1760), II. 254–5, 438; III. 268

Merlin's Cave (1750), III. 336

— (1788), III. 336

— (1814), IV. 503

— = Royal Chace

Merlin's Mount (Dibdin, T. J., 1825), IV. 304

Mermaid (Dibdin, C. I. M., 1815), IV. 293

— (Franklin, A., 1792), III. 268

— (Galt, J., 1814), IV. 318, 636

— (Heath, S., 1887), v. 415

— (Walter, T. N., 1898), v. 612

— (1804), IV. 503

— (1822), IV. 503

Mermaiden's Well (+ Calcraft, J. W., 1828), IV. 94, 503

Mermaids (Mackay, W. G., 1897), v. 470

Mermaid's Well = Bride of Lammermuir

Meroflède (Collingham, G. G., 1892), v. 317

Merope (Arnold, M., 1858), v. 244

— (Ayre, W., 1740), II. 73, 95, 296, 432

— (Hill, A., 1749), II. 59, 73, 110, 336, 418, 438

Merope (Jeffreys, G., 1731), II. 31, 65, 73, 95, 338, 439

— (Theobald, J., 1744), II. 358, 444

Merrie Days of Shakespeare and Queen Bess = Angel of Islington

Merrie England (Webb, G., 1877), v. 617

Merrie Family (Field, W. F., 1886), v. 366

Merrie Men of Hoxton = Red Lance

Merrie Prince Hal (Thomas, W., 1891), v. 596

Merrifield's Ghost (Paull, H. M., 1895), v. 516

Merry Andrew (?1668), I. 447

Merry Archers = Sherwood Forest

Merry Blacksmith (Dunbar, E. C., 1893), v. 352

Merry Cheat = Whim

Merry Christmas (Law, A., 1880), v. 449

— (Scott, C. W. and Stephenson, B. C., 1897), v. 558

— = Sir Roger de Coverly

Merry Cobbler = Detection

Merry Cobler (Coffey, C., 1735), II. 237, 244, 315

Merry Counterfeit (1762), III. 114, 336

Merry Cuckold = City Bride

Merry Day at Greenwich = All the World's a Fair

Merry Days of Old England = Kenilworth

Merry Dell (1888), v. 718

Merry Duchess (Sims, G. R., 1883), v. 568

Merry Forester = Merry Sherwood

Merry-Go-Round (Fitch, C. and Peile, K., 1898), v. 367

— (Hicks, Sir S., 1899), v. 421

Merry Lasses = Love in the Grove

Merry London Cuckolds = Unlucky Lovers

Merry Madcap (Stephens, or Stevens, V., 1896), v. 581

Merry Maidens (1831), IV. 503

Merry Major Muddle = Village Venus

Merry making (Perry, J., 1867), v. 520

— (1787), III. 336

Merryman and his Maid = Yeomen of the Guard

Merry Marchioness (McCabe, C. W., 1897), v. 467

Merry Margate (Grundy, S., 1889), v. 397

Merry Masqueraders (Aubin, Mrs, 1730), II. 296

Merry Meeting (Lestocq, W., 1887), v. 457

Merry Men of Englewood = Foresters

Merry Men of Kent (1789), III. 336

Merry Midnight Mistake (Ogborne, D., 1765), III. 291

Merry Mignon (Jones, J. W., 1882), v. 440

Merry Milkmaid of Islington (1680), I. 443

Merry Miller (Sadler, T., 1766), III. 304

Merry Millers (1854), v. 718

Merry Monarch = (1) Charles II; (2) Lucky Star

Merry Monk (Duré, M. and Bell, M., 1897), v. 352

Merry Monte Carlo (1894), v. 718

Merry Mourners (O'Keeffe, J., 1791) = Modern Antiques, III. 336, 393, 402

Merry Mr Merlin (Patterson, E. H. and Grattan, H., 1895), v. 515

Merry Muddling World (1893), v. 718

Merry Outlaws of Sherwood = Robin Hood

Merry Piper of Nuremberg (Willard, Mrs E. S., 1893), v. 623

Merry Pranks (1704), II. 378

Merry Sailors (1707), II. 378

Merry Sell (Sallenger, W., 1888), v. 555

Merry Shepherd = Rural Love

Merry Sherwood (O'Keeffe, J., 1795), III. 294, 393

Merry Swain = Rival Nymphs

Merry Terry (1841), IV. 503

Merry Throwster (1731), II. 378

Merry Wags of Warwickshire (Curling, H., 1854), v. 331

Merry War (Reece, R., 1882), v. 539, 813

Merry Widow (Buckingham, L. S., 1863), v. 286

Merry Wives of Barbican (1831), IV. 503

Merry Wives of Broad Street (Shadwell, C., 1713), II. 354

Merry Wives of Madrid (1829), IV. 503

Merry Wives of Windsor (Hersee, H., 1878), v. 797

Merry Wives of Windsor (Kemble, J.
P., 1797), III. 279, 389; IV. 335
— (Reynolds, F., 1824), IV. 392
— (1812), IV. 140, 503
— (1850), V. 718
Merry Woodcutters = Sabotiers
Merry Zingara (Gilbert, W. S., 1868), V.
379
Mervyn Clitheroe (Conquest, G., 1859),
V. 718, 785, 841
Mesmeric Mystery (Osman, W. R.,
1867), V. 508
Mesmerism (Clyde, C., 1890), V. 315
Mesmerism versus Galvanism (Beswick,
G., 1845), IV. 267
Mesmerist (Conquest, G. and Robin-
son, H., 1879), V. 321
— (Jarman, F., 1890), V. 434
Message from Mars (Ganthony, R.,
1899), V. 376
Message from the Dead = Wrath
Message from the Sea (?Collins, W. W.,
1861), IV. 318, 785
— (1869), V. 718
— (1873), V. 718
Message of Mercy (1898), V. 718
Messalina (Blackburn, V., 1899), V.
262
Messene Freed (Preston, W., 1792), III.
300
Messiah (1742), II. 396
Metamora (Stone, J. A., 1845), IV. 503,
633
Metamorphoses (Dibdin, C., 1775), III.
117, 254
— (1867), V. 718
Metamorphoses of Harlequin (1740), II.
378
Metamorphosis (Corye, J., 1704), II.
141, 145, 208, 231, 316
— (Jackson, W., 1783), III. 276
— (1723), II. 378
Metamorphosis of the Beggar's Opera
(1730), II. 378
Metaphysical Muddle (Moss, H., 1882),
V. 497
Meted Out! (Vellère, Dr, 1873), V.
607
Metempsychosis (Bernard, W. B.,
1832), IV. 265
— (Fonblanque, A., 1853), V. 370
— = Puss

Meteor (Gent, 1809), IV. 319 [The
sub-title should be "but a Bright
One", not "for a Bright One"]
Methinks I see my Father (Mathews,
C. J., 1837), IV. 503, 633
— (1849), IV. 503, 633
Methodism Display'd (Este, 1744), II.
447–8
Methodist (Pottinger, I., 1761), III. 299
— (1823), IV. 503
Methodist Preachers (1775), III. 336
Mexican Bandit (Young, Mrs H., 1863),
V. 719, 841
Mexican Bill (Stanhope, B., 1887), V.
579
Mexican's Watchword = War Woolf of
Tlascala
Mexico (1895), V. 719
Mezzetin Outwitted = Restoration of
Harlequin
Miami (Hollingshead, J., 1893), V. 424
Micawber (Collette, C., 1881), V. 784
Michael and Christine (Kerr, J., 1849),
IV. 84, 503, 592, 633
Michael and his Lost Angel (Jones,
H. A., 1896), V. 162, 168–9, 172, 189,
440
Michael Cange, the Porter of the
Abbaye (1832), IV. 503
Michael Ceno (1854), V. 719
Michael Dane's Grandson (Cassilis,
I. L., 1896), V. 306
Michael Earle, the Maniac Lover
(Wilks, T. E., 1839), IV. 421
Michael Howe, the Terror of Van
Dieman's Land (1821), IV. 503
Michaelmas Day (Vaile, 1851), V. 606
Michael Scott the Wizard = Anster Fair
Michael Strogoff (Byron, H. J., 1881), V.
299
Michel Perrin (Younge, A., 1850), V.
719, 825, 841
Michigan Chief = Rifle-Shot
Midas (O'Hara, K., 1762), III. 195, 291
— (1827), IV. 503
Mid-day Murder = Red Barn
Middle Dish (Oulton, W. C., 1804), IV.
366, 602
— (1815), IV. 503
Middleman (Jones, H. A., 1889), V.439
Middle Temple (Peake, R. B., 1829), IV.
370

Middy Ashore (Bernard, W. B., 1836), IV. 265

Midge (Martin, R. J. and Burnett, J. P., 1879), V. 479

Midgelet (Benson, E., 1893), V. 258

Midnight (Furrell, J. W. and Stafford, E. C., 1888), V. 375

— (Shirley, A. and Landeck, B., 1892), V. 564

— (1832), IV. 503

Midnight Adventure = Have at All

Midnight Adventures of Three Spaniards = Bashaw

Midnight Angel (?Douglass, J. T., 1861), V. 788

— (1861), V. 719

— = Angel of Midnight

Midnight Assassin = Fatal Prediction

Midnight Assembly = Cavern in the Rock

Midnight Attack (1824), IV. 503

Midnight Bell (1809), IV. 503

— (1813), IV. 503

— = Mogul Tale

Midnight Crime = Old Ferry House

Midnight Hour (Inchbald, Mrs E., 1787), III. 121, 144, 184, 275, 388

— (1848), IV. 633

— = Wager

Midnight Journey = Juanita the Devoted

Midnight London Express = Self

Midnight Mail (Melford, M., 1877), V. 484

Midnight Marriage (Osborne, C., 1883), V. 508

— = (1) Master of the Forge; (2) Withered Daisies

Midnight Murder (1835), IV. 503

Midnight Revelation = Fatal Letter

Midnight Revelry (1818), IV. 503

Midnight Shriek (Payn, D., 1896), V. 517

Midnight's Intrigues (?1677), I. 391, 443

Midnight Spectre (1861), V. 719

Midnight, the Thirteenth Chime (Barnett, C. Z., 1845), IV. 260

Midnight Torch (Barnett, C. Z., 1846), V. 251

Midnight Trust = Baby

Midnight Wanderers (Pearce, W., 1793), III. 203-4, 297

Midnight Watch (Morton, J. M., 1848), IV. 363

— (Townsend, W. T., 1846), IV. 414

Midocean (Hoffman, M. H., 1889), V. 423

Midst Shot and Shell (Howard, B., 1899), V. 428

Midshipman Easy (Oxenford, J., 1836) = Mr Midshipman Easy, IV. 367, 603

Midsummer Day (Frith, W., 1892), V. 374

Midsummer Eve (Kaye, A., 1893), V. 442

Midsummer Jest (1894), V. 719

Midsummer Night (Rumsey, M. C., 1854), V. 553

Midsummer Night's Dream (Garrick, D., 1763), III. 263

— (Reynolds, F., 1816), IV. 392

— (1833), IV. 503

Midsummer Night's Dream (not Shakespeare's) = O'Flannigan and the Fairies

Midsummer-Night's Nightmare = Vision of Venus

Midsummer Night's Scream = Nap

Midsummer's Eve (Yelland, W. H., 1861), V. 719, 825, 841

Midsummer's Madness (French, W. P., 1892), V. 373

Mifistifix (1870), V. 719

Might and Right (Scudamore, F. A., 1881), V. 558

— (1852), V. 719, 841

Might of Right (Brougham, J., 1864), V. 281, 780

Mighty Dollar (Woolf, B. E., 1875), V. 632

Mighty Error (Outram, L. S., 1891), V. 509

Mighty Hand (Shelley, H., 1899), V. 562

Mighty Motive (Williams, B., 1899), V. 624

Mignon (Matthison, A., 1880), V. 806

— (1886), V. 719

Mignonette (Brand, O., 1889), V. 274

Mikado (Gilbert, W. S., 1885), V. 144-5, 380

Mike (Pletts, M., 1876), V. 528

Milady (Brand, O., 1885), V. 273

Milanese Peasant Girl = Clari

Mildred's Choice = Waters

Millions of Money (Melville, A., 1886), v. 485

Mill of Aldervon (1829), IV. 504

Mill of Austerlitz = Treasure Seeker

Mill of Bagdad (1834), IV. 504

— = Barber

Mill of Berezina (Pitt, G. D., 1835), IV. 373

Mill of Glaris = Red Riven

Mill of Keben (1831), IV. 504

— = Siege of Montgatz

Mill of Marimount = Stanislaus of Poland

Mill of St Aldervon = Two Galley Slaves

Mill of the Happy Valley (Hazlewood, C. H., 1870), v. 797

Mill of the Lake (1827), IV. 504

Mill of the Loire = Soldier's Widow

Mill of the Pyrenees (Webb, C., 1836), IV. 504, 616

Millo' Taftie Annie (1888), v. 719

Mills of God (Overton, R., 1892), v. 509

Mills of the Eternal = Master of Hope

Milly, the Collier's Wife = Lost for Ever

Milo of Brittany = Wood Wolf of the Black Mountains

Milord Sir Smith = Campano

Mimi (Boucicault, D., 1872), v. 269

Mimic Art and Attic Science = Scheming and Seeming

Mina (Linley, G., 1849), IV. 504, 633

Minc'd Pie (Moser, J., 1806), IV. 364

Mind's Magnet = Riches

Mind the Shop (Reece, R. and Righton, E., 1878), v. 538

Mind your Letters (1833), IV. 504

Mind Your Own Business (Lemon, M., 1852), v. 455

Mind your Points (1869), v. 719

— = Line of Life

Mind your Stops (1850), v. 719

Mine (Cross, J. C., 1800), IV. 286

— (Sargent, J., 1785), III. 304

— = Married for Money

Mine and Countermine = Plot and Passion

Mine Friend and the Lake Fay (1852), v. 719

Mine Girl of Kebal (1846), IV. 504

Mine Hostess (Webster, D., 1899), v. 618

Mine Host of the Flagon = Baron's Daughter

Mine of Wealth (Towers, E., 1867), v. 600

Minerali (Grattan, H. P., 1835), IV. 383

— (1835), IV. 504, 633

Miner of Mexico = Ocean Grave

Miner's Dog (1872), v. 719

Miner's Luck (Edwards, F., 1894), v. 355

Miners' Queen (Jarman, F., 1892), v. 434

Miners' Strike = Strike

Minerva and Ulysses (1746), II. 379

Minerva's Triumph = Don Sancho

Minerva's Triumphs = Words made visible

Mines of Ischinski = Iwan

Mines of Poland (1822), IV. 82, 504

Mines of Rubies = Orphan of Hindoostan

Minette's Birthday (André, R., 1889), v. 241

Miniature (1836), IV. 504

Miniature Picture (Craven, E., 1780), III. 20, 41, 170, 249

Minister (Lewis, M. G., 1797), III. 63, 281, 390

Minister and the Favourite (1856), v. 841

Minister and the Mercer (Bunn, A., 1834), IV. 19, 38, 84, 183, 276

Ministering Angel (Doone, N. and Newte, H. C. W., 1893), v. 347

Minister of Finance (1849), IV. 504

Minister of Spain (Wooler, J. P., 1863), v. 632

Minister's Call (Symons, A., 1892), v. 589

Minkalay (Leeds, A. and Reade, G., 1896), v. 453

Minna (Edwards, H. S., 1886), v. 355

Minna von Barnhelm (Holcroft, F., 1805), IV. 326

Minnie (Byron, H. J., 1869), v. 297

Minnie Grey (Davis, S., 1856), v. 787

— (Johnstone, J. B., 1852), v. 438

— (Young, H. and Roberts, G., 1886), v. 636

— (1852), v. 719

Miseries of Civil War = Misery of Civil War

Miseries of Human Life (Dibdin, T. J., 1807), IV. 298

— (Webster, B. N., 1845), IV. 418

Miseries of Love (1732), II. 379

Miser of Bagdad = Crazy Old Slippers

Miser of Clerkenwell = Colonel Jack

Miser of Coventry = Edmund Atherton

Miser of Eltham Green (1867), V. 719

— = Last Man

Miser of Lewes (1823), IV. 633

Miser of Madrid (1831), IV. 504

Miser of Shoreditch (Prest, T. P., 1854), V. 530, 811

Miser of Tewkesbury (1854), V. 719

Miser of the Hill Fort = Inundation

Miser of Walden = Young Courier

Miser Outwitted (1848), IV. 504

— = He must be Married

Miser Reformed (1812), IV. 504

— = Temple of Plutus

Miser's Daughter (Millingen, J. G., 1835), IV. 356

— (Stirling, E., 1842), IV. 407

— (Taylor, T. P., 1835), IV. 411

— (1885), V. 719

— = (1) Avarice; (2) Hilda; (3) Jew's Daughter

Miser Smoked (1823), IV. 504

Misers of Smyrna (1810), IV. 504

Miser's Resolve upon the Lowering of Interest = Fame

Miser's Retreat = Whim

Miser's Treasure (Mortimer, J., 1878), V. 494

Miser's Warning = Christmas Carol

Miser's Will (Craven, T., 1889), V. 329

— (Peake, R. B., 1844), IV. 504, 633

Miser, the Maid and the Mangle = Ingomar the Idiotic

Miser Tricked = Stratagem of Harlequin

Misery of Civil-War (Crowne, J., 1680), I. 79, 399

Misfortunes of an Exile = Charles Edward Stuart the Pretender in Scotland

Misjudged (Gilbert, E., 1884), V. 378

Misled (Wilmot, A. A., 1887), V. 628

Misogynist = Woman Hater

Misplaced Affections (1863), V. 719

Misrepresentor Represented (1755), III. 402

Miss Betty (1898), V. 719

Miss Chester (Young, Sir C. L. and Marryatt, F., 1872), V. 635

Miss Chiquita (Sims, G. R., 1899), V. 570

Miss Cinderella (Walkes, W. R., 1890), V. 611

Miss Decima (Burnand, F. C., 1891), V. 292, 782

Miss Eily O'Connor (Byron, H. J., 1861), V. 296

Miss Eliza Cook (1846), IV. 505

Miss Esmeralda (Leslie, F. and Mills, H., 1887), V. 456

Miss Formosa (1870), V. 719

Miss Forrester (1876), V. 719

Miss Francis of Yale = Leading Lady

Miss Galatea of Oregon (Cleveland, E. A., 1894), V. 314

Miss Gwilt (Collins, W. W., 1875), V. 318

Miss Hobbs (Jerome, J. K., 1899), V. 436

Miss Hoyden's Husband (Daly, A., 1890), V. 333

Miss Impudence (Morton, E. A., 1892), V. 494

Missing (Gibney, S., 1894), V. 378

— (Melford, M., 1890), V. 484

— (Newbound, E., 1881), V. 503

Missing Duchess = Night in Paris

Missing Link (Collier, H., 1886), V. 317

— (Shirley, A., 1894), V. 564

— (1893), V. 719

Missing Mortgage (1883), V. 719

Missing Waterloo (1880), V. 719

Missing Witness (Braddon, M. E., 1880), V. 273

Miss in her Breeches = Country Coquet

Miss in her Teens (Garrick, D., 1747), II. 138, 216, 330, 419, 437

Mission from Rome into Great Britain in the Cause of Popery and the Pretender (?1746), II. 379

Mission of Mercury (Rede, W. L., 1841), IV. 390

— = King's Pledge

Mission to Borneo (1848), IV. 505

Missis Brown of the "Missis" sippi = "Grin" Bushes

Mississipi (1720), II. 379
Missive from the Clouds (1871), V. 719
Miss-judgment of Paris = Siege of Troy
Miss Leer (Dutnall, M. and Shelley,
    A. C., 1864), V. 720, 841
Miss Letty = Belle of the Bath
Miss Lucy in Town (Fielding, H.,
    1742), II. 23–4, 246, 328, 436
Miss Macpherson (1880), V. 720
Miss Maritana (Nugent, G. and Whit-
    bread, J. W., 1890), V. 506
Miss Metamorphoses = Puss! Puss!!
    Puss!!!
Miss Michaelmass (Dibdin, C. I. M.,
    1818), IV. 294
Miss Mite = On the Briny
Miss Multon (?Cazauran, A. R., 1878),
    V. 720, 841
— = Her Atonement
Miss Pop (1827), IV. 505
Miss Poppy (Dibdin, C. I. M., 1826), V.
    286
Miss Prudentia Single's Soirée (1858),
    V. 720
Miss Red Riding Hood (1850), V. 720
Miss Rutland (Pryce, R., 1894), V. 531
Miss Sootie's Masquerade = Folly Ex-
    posed!
Miss-Terry-ous = Vicar of Wideawake-
    field
Miss Tibbett's Back Hair (Robinson,
    N., 1870), V. 547
Miss Tomboy (Buchanan, R., 1890), V.
    285
Miss Wright (1828), IV. 505
Mist (1893), V. 720
Mistake (Vanbrugh, Sir J., 1705), II. 35,
    46, 135, 136, 145, 151, 362, 445; III.
    115, 390
— (1740), II. 379
— (1823), IV. 505
— = Young King
Mistaken (Field, W. F., 1888), V. 366
— (Killick, J. M., 1872), V. 444
— (1880), V. 720
Mistaken Beauty (1684), I. 190, 443; III.
    173
Mistaken Husband (1675), I. 232, 443
Mistaken Idea (1898), V. 720
Mistaken Identity (Bannister, T. B.,
    1883), V. 248
— (Murray, A., 1886), V. 499

Mistaken Story (Wilks, T. E., 1843),
    IV. 421
Mistakes (Dening, Mrs C., 1893), V. 342
— (Harris, J. and Mountfort, W.,
    1690), I. 37, 225, 412
— (Hyde, H., 1758), III. 275
— (1730), II. 379
Mistakes in Madrid = Eccentricities
Mistakes in the Dark = Adventures of a
    Night
Mistakes of a Day (1787), III. 336, 402
Mistakes of a Minute (1787), III. 336,
    402, 404
Mistakes of a Night = She Stoops to
    Conquer
Mistakes of the Heart = Coquette
Mistakes will happen (1898), V. 720
Mistake upon Mistake (1828), IV. 505
— = (1) Perplex'd Couple; (2) Widow's
    Vow
Mist before the Dawn (1868), V. 720
Mister Horatio Sparkins (Stirling, E.,
    1840), IV. 407
Mistletoe Bough (Farnie, H. B., 1870),
    V. 361
— (Marchant, F., 1861), V. 720, 805,
    841
— (Somerset, C. A., 1834), IV. 404
Mistress = Bellamira
Mistress and Maid = Down the Area
Mistress Doggrell in her Altitudes
    (1795), III. 336
Mistress Dorcas (1895), V. 720
Mistress Nonsuch's Nonsense (1790),
    III. 336
Mistress of Arts (1838), IV. 505
Mistress of Hawk's Crag (Towers, E.,
    1865), V. 720, 821, 841
Mistress of the Mill (Moncrieff, W. T.,
    1849), IV. 361
Mistress of the Seas (Douglass, J. T.,
    1899), V. 349
Mistress Peg (Smith, L., 1892), V. 573
Mistress Prynne (1888), V. 720
Misunderstandings (1888), V. 720
Misunderstood (Nordon, J. B., 1899),
    V. 505
Mithridates (Kemble, J. P., 1802), IV.
    335
Mithridates, King of Pontus (Lee, N.,
    1678), I. 67, 329, 419
Mixed (Clarance, L., 1884), V. 311

Moncrieff (Millard, A., 1896), v. 488

Money (Lytton, Lord, 1840), IV. 45, 173–5, 349, 596; V. 120, 121, 126, 194

Money and Misery (Wilkins, J. H., 1855), v. 623

Money and Music = Honest Frauds

Money at a Pinch (Robson, H., 1793), III. 302

Money Bags (Pemberton, T. E. and Shannon, 1885), v. 519

Money Diggers (Milner, H. M., 1829), IV. 505, 633

Money is an Asse (Jordan, T., 1668), I. 415

Money Lender (Ford, T. M., 1888), v. 370

— (Lee, N., Jr., 1861), v. 720, 802

Money Mad (Mackaye, J. S., 1890), v. 471

Money Spider (Eliot, A., 1897), v. 356

Money Spinner (Pinero, Sir A. W., 1880), v. 173, 524

Money the Mistress (Southerne, T., 1726), II. 356

Money works Wonders = Bird in a Cage

Monica (Swarbreck, J. W., 1893), v. 589

Monk = Aurelio and Miranda

Monkeyana = Jack Robinson and his Monkey

Monkey and the Murder = Easter Fair

Monkey Island (1824), IV. 505

Monkey of the Wreck = Treacherous Black

Monkey that has seen the World (Moncrieff, W. T., 1831), IV. 505, 633

Monkey, the Mask and the Murderer = Who Owns the Head?

Monkish Warriors = Victims of Tyranny

Monk of Palluzi = False Penitent

Monks and Smugglers (1820), IV. 505

Monks' Cowl (Moncrieff, W. T., 1818), IV. 505, 633

Monks of St Nicholas = Mystery

Monks of the Great St Bernard = Julian and Agnes

Monk's Room (Lart, J., 1887), v. 449

Monk, the Friend and the Enemy = Daemon of the Drachenfalls

Monk, the Mask and the Murderer (Amherst, J. H.), v. 254

Monmouth Up-to-Date (Mackay, D., 1895), v. 469

Monomania (1838), IV. 505

Monopolizer Outwitted (McLaren, A., 1800), III. 284; IV. 350

Monopoly (1782), III. 336, 402

Monseigneur (Archer, T., 1845), IV. 255

— (Reynoldson, T. H., 1844), IV. 393

— (1845), IV. 505

Monsieur Alphonse (Vaughan, Mrs, 1875), v. 607

Monsieur de Paris = Executioner's Daughter

Monsieur de Pourceaugnac (Ozell, J., 1704), II. 144, 152, 216, 442

— = Squire Trelooby

Monsieur in the Suds = Harlequin Sclavonian

Monsieur Jacques (Barnett, M., 1836), IV. 261

Monsieur Laroche (Bellingham, H., 1878), v. 257

Monsieur La Saxe's Disappointment = Schemes of Harlequin

Monsieur le Duc (Prinsep, V., 1879), v. 531

Monsieur Malbrouk (1827), IV. 505

Monsieur Mallet (Moncrieff, W. T., 1829), IV. 183, 359

Monsieur Raggou = Old Troop

Monsieur Tonson (Moncrieff, W. T., 1821), IV. 359

Mons. Moulan = Fisher Girl

Monster (1790), III. 337

Monster and the Magician (Kerr, J., 1826), IV. 592

Monster Ballroom of 1837 = Elements— Earth, Air, Fire, Water

Monster of Mysore and the Fiend of the Whirlpool = Kerim the Pearl Diver

Monster of the Cave (1798), III. 337

Monster of the Eddystone (Pitt, G. D., 1834), IV. 372

Monster of the Glen (Dibdin, C. I. M., 1826), IV. 296

Monster of the Woods (1772), III. 337

Monstrum Horrendum (1732), II. 379

Montagu (Gemmell, R., 1868), v. 377

Montalbert (1815), IV. 505

Montaldi (1818), IV. 505

Montaleoni (Young, H., 1853), v. 636

Montalto (À Court, W., 1821), IV. 505, 567, 633

— = Guerilla Chief

Montbar (Moore, T., 1804), IV. 361
Mont Blanc (Campbell, A., 1853), V. 301
— (Mayhew, A., 1874), V. 483
— (Wilks, T. E., 1853), V. 623
Montcalm (Young, Sir C. L., 1872), V. 635
Monte Carlo (Carlton, S., 1894), V. 303
— (1887), V. 720
— (1891), V. 720
Monte Cristo (Henry, R., 1886), V. 417, 797
— (1860), V. 720
— (1868), V. 720
— (1888), V. 720
— (1899), V. 720
Monte d'Or (1828), IV. 505
Montem (Rowe, H., 1808), IV. 396
Monte the Prisoner (1856), V. 720
Montezuma (Brooke, H., 1778), III. 240
— (Sladden, D., 1838), IV. 402
— (Stephens, G., 1823), IV. 612
Month after Date = Divided Duty
Month from Home (1857), V. 720
Months and Mummery = April Fools
Montilladios (1897), V. 721
Montoni (Sheil, R. L., 1820), IV. 401, 610
Montrano, the Pirate Lord of Sicily (Atkyns, S., 1845), IV. 257
Montrezar (1840), IV. 633
Montrose (Atkinson, 1829), IV. 569
— (Dibdin, T. J., 1819), IV. 94, 302, 505, 580, 633
— (Murray, W. H., 1823), IV. 94, 365
— (Pocock, I., 1822), IV. 94, 384
— (1820), IV. 94, 505
— (1826), IV. 94, 633
— (1827), IV. 94, 505
— (1847), IV. 94, 505
Mont St Michel (Bernard, W. B., 1852), V. 259
Monument in Arcadia (Keate, G., 1773), III. 278
Mooltan and Googerat (1849), IV. 505
Moonbeams (Russell, E. H., 1891), V. 553
Moonflowers: A Cobweb (1891), V. 721
Moonlight Blossom (Fernald, C. B., 1899), V. 211, 365
Moonlight Jack (Travers, W., 1866), V. 721, 821, 841

Moonlight Knight = Sir Marigold the Dottie
Moonlight Night = Fairy Legends
Moon Maiden (1845), IV. 505
Moon Queen and King Knight (Crowquill, A., 1849), IV. 287
Moon's Age (Addison, H. R., 1835), IV. 505, 633
Moonshine (Booth, J. H., 1892), V. 267
— (Stuart-Wortley, Lady E., 1843), IV. 506, 633
Moonstone (Collins, W. W., 1877), V. 318
Moonstruck (Reece, R., 1873), V. 538
Moorish Banditti (1806), IV. 506
Moor of Sicily = Avenger
Moor of Toledo (1836), IV. 506
Moors and Africans = Fair Slave
Moors in Grenada = Alonzo the Patriot
Moors in Spain = Florinda
Moors of Spain (1841), IV. 82, 506
— = Charlemagne
Moor's Revenge = Abdelazer
Moor the Merrier = Boabdil el Chico
Morah, the Beast Tamer (1848), IV. 506
Moral Brand = Alice Grey
Morality (1882), V. 721
Moral Philosopher (Selby, C., 1843), IV. 399
Moral Quack (Bacon, P., 1757), III. 235
Moral Suasion (Palmer, T. A., 1875), V. 512
Mora's Love (D'Egville, 1809), IV. 506, 633
Morass of the Murdered = Will o' the Wisp
Morays (1884), V. 721
Mordecai (1851), V. 841
Mordecai Lyons (Harrigan, E., 1882), V. 404
Mordecai's Beard (1790), III. 337
Morden Grange (Burnand, F. C., 1869), V. 289
More Blunders = Advertisement for a Husband
More Blunders than One (Rodwell, G. H., 1824), IV. 395
Moreen and Sham Van Voght (1862), V. 721
More Ethiopians (1847), IV. 506
More Flirts than One = Belle Have at Ye All

More Free than Welcome (Suter, W. E.), v., 588

More Frightened than Hurt (Jerrold, D. W., 1821), IV. 331, 590

— (1785), III. 337

— = (1) Execution; (2) Wife's Stratagem

More Good News = Orange Boven

More Jonathans = Tarnation Strange

More Kotzebue (1799), III. 337

More Laugh than Love = Gay Deceivers

More Marriages than One = Count of Anjou

More Merry than Wise (1837), IV. 506

More Precious than Gold (Cheltnam, C. S., 1861), v. 309

More Reform! (1831), IV. 506

More Sacks than One (1817), IV. 506

More Scenes in Town = Mirror

More Secrets than One = Man and Wife

More Sinned against than Sinning (1892), v. 721

More than ever (Matthison, A., 1882), v. 481

More than meets the Eye = Laurette's Bridal

More the Merrier = Wives in Plenty

More Visitors in Town (1838), IV. 506

More Ways than Means (Colman, G., the Younger, 1786) = Ways and Means, III. 337, 379, 403

More Ways than One (Cowley, Mrs H., 1783) = New Ways to Catch Hearts, III. 167, 249

— (1819), IV. 506

— = (1) Contrivances; (2) Simon

More Ways than One for a Wife = Petticoat-Plotter

More Ways than One to Win Her (1745), II. 379

More Wives than One = Thelyphthora

Morgiana (Du Maurier, G., 1892), v. 352

Morgue (1828), IV. 506

Morilda's Wand (1821), IV. 506

Morlais Castle in the Olden Time = Lily of Pontsarn

Mormon (Calthorpe, W. D., 1887), v. 300

Mormons (1881), v. 721

Morna of the Glen (Prest, T. P.), v. 811

Morning at Margate = Fortune Hunter

Morning at Versailles in 1750 = Promotion

Morning Call (Dance, C., 1851), IV. 289; v. 335

Morning Drive (Plant, F. W., 1896), v. 528

Morning, Noon and Night (Dibdin, T. J., 1822), IV. 303

Morning of Life (1852), v. 721

Morning Post and the Morning Herald (Pocock, I., 1811), IV. 383

Morning Ramble (Payne, H. N., 1672), I. 77, 216–17, 347, 423

Morning Star and the Gipsey's Brick = Michael Ceno

Moro (Barrett, W., 1882), v. 250

Morocco Bound (Branscombe, A., 1893), v. 274

Morphia Maniac = White Devil

Mortgage Deeds (Hazlewood, C. H., 1875), v. 415

Moscow (Moncrieff, W. T., 1810), IV 358

— (1819), IV. 506

Moses and Mammon (Dibdin, C. I. M., 1800), IV. 290

Moses and Shadrac (1780), III. 337, 403

Moses and Son (Gordon, J., 1892), v. 385

Moses in the Bulrushes (More, Mrs H., 1782), III. 288

— (1793), III. 337

Moslem's Oath = Alp, the Renegade

Mossoo in London (Grain, R. C., 1888), v. 387

Moss Rose Rent (Law, A., 1883), v. 450

Most Excellent Story = Prisoner of War

Most Unwarrantable Intrusion (Morton, J. M., 1849), IV. 363

Most Votes (Dibdin, C., 1804), IV. 290

Most Votes carry it = Love at a Loss

Moth and Flame (Moore, F. F., 1878), v. 492

Mother (Harvey, F., 1879), v. 408

— (Jerrold, D. W., 1838), IV. 333

— = Domenica

Mother and Child (Morton, J. M., 1879), v. 497

Mother and Child are doing well (Morton, J. M., 1845), IV. 362

— (1855), v. 721

Mother and Daughter = Star of my Home

Mother and Son (Bell, S., 1883), v. 256

Mother and Son (Moncrieff, W. T., 1821), IV. 359

— (1844), IV. 506

— = Elmine

Mother and the Mistress = Victim

Mother Brownrigg, the Painter's Wife of Fetter Lane (1863), V. 721

Mother Bunch (1843), IV. 633

Mother Bunch and the Man with the Hunch (Conquest, G. and Spry, H., 1881), V. 322

Mother Bunch and the Yellow Dwarf (1807), IV. 506

Mother Goose (Aylmer, J., 1868), V. 246

— (Jones, J. W., 1896), V. 441

— (Lane, P., 1864), V. 802

— (1848), IV. 633

— (1883, 1889, 1891, 1892), V. 721

Mother Goose and the Enchanted Beauty (Blanchard, E. L., 1880), V. 265

Mother Goose and the Sleeping Beauty (1887), V. 721

Mother Hubbard (1888), V. 721

Mother in Fashion = Disappointment

Mother-in-law (Dibdin, C. I. M., 1815), IV. 293

— (Miller, J., 1734), II. 135, 144, 203, 344

— (Sims, G. R., 1881), V. 568

Mother Ludlam, the Witch of Epping = Old Bogie

Mother of Three (Graves, C., 1896), V. 389

Mother Redcap (Garston, L., 1873), V. 376

— (1824, 1834), V. 506

— (1841), IV. 633

— (1858), V. 721

Mothers (1805), IV. 506

— (1884), V. 721

Mothers and Daughters (Bell, R., 1843), IV. 264

— (1805), IV. 506

Mother's Bequest (Stirling, E., 1849), IV. 409

Mother's Courage = Eagle and Child

Mother's Crime = Martha

Mother's Curse = (1) Jane Lomax; (2) Jerry Abershaw

Mother's Dream (Jerrold, D. W., 1850), V. 436

Mother's Dream = Shadow

Mother's Dying Child (Hazlewood, C. H., 1864), V. 413

Mother's Dying Words = Orphan's Legacy

Mother Shipton (Thompson, C. T., 1857), V. 597

— (Thomson, T.), I. 435

— (1770), III. 337

Mother Shipton's Prophecy, Seven Women to One Man (1855), V. 721

Mother Shipton's Review of the Audience (1787), III. 337

Mother Shipton's Wish = Jupiter and Io

Mother's Honour = Marriage Certificate

Mother's Love = (1) Haven of Rest; (2) Lota

Mother's Prayer = (1) Marie de Chamouni; (2) Struggle for Gold

Mother's Sacrifice = Henry de Fleurville

Mother's Secret (1849), IV. 506

Mother's Sin (Reynolds, W., 1885), V. 541

— = Torture of Shame

Mother's Sorrows = (1) Little Captive King; (2) Terrible Peak

Mother's Statue = Ruby Ruins

Mother's Tragedy = Videna

Mother's Vengeance = Adrian and Orrila

Mother, the Maid and the Mistletoe = Pretty Druidess

Mother, the Maiden and the Musician = Ill-treated Il Trovatore

Mother Whitecap (1809), IV. 506

Moths (Chute, J., 1882), V. 80, 310

— (Dallas, M., 1883), V. 80, 332

— (Hamilton, H., 1882), V. 80, 401

— (Lyon, W. F., 1883), V. 80, 465

— (Seaton, A. M., 1883), V. 80, 559

— (1882), V. 721

Moths à la Mode (Herbert, F. H., 1883), V. 80, 418

Moths Quitoes (Edgar, D. W., 1882), V. 80, 353

Motto: "I am all there" (Byron, H. J., 1863), V. 296

Motto of Nevers (Rousby, W., 1863), V. 814

Motto on the Duke's Coat (Conquest, G., 1863), V. 721, 785

Moulds of the Mould Manor (1856), v. 721

Mountain Bandit (1824), IV. 506

Mountain Cataract (1844), IV. 506

Mountain Cataran (Barnett, C. Z.), IV. 570

Mountain Chief (1818), IV. 506

Mountain Cottager = Mouse-traps

Mountain Devil (Reeves, G., 1879), v. 540

— (1854), v. 721

Mountain Dhu (Halliday, A., 1866), v. 400

Mountaineers (Colman, G., the Younger, 1793), III. 104, 123, 247; IV. 32

— = Maniac of the Sierra Morena

Mountaineers' Dance (1859), v. 721

Mountain Farm = Blind Sister

Mountain Flower (Travers, W., 1864), v. 721, 821

Mountain Guide (1895), v. 721

Mountain Haunt = Bandit of Sicily

Mountain Heiress (À Beckett, G. A., 1883), v. 234

Mountain Home = Fall of the Avalanche

Mountain Hut (Planché, J. R., 1821), IV. 377

Mountain King (Almar, G.), IV. 253

— (Nance, A. and Winterbottom, J., 1875), v. 501

— = Castle Burners

Mountain Maid (1837), IV. 506

Mountain Monarch (1855), v. 721

Mountain of Miseries (1797), III. 337

Mountain Pass = (1) Alp, the Tartar Khan; (2) Guerilla Chief

Mountain Robber = (1) Camilla the Amazon; (2) Maid of Genoa

Mountain Robbers (1806), IV. 506

— (1863), v. 721

Mountain Smugglers = Manslayer

Mountains of Modena (1826), IV. 506

Mountains of Saxony = Adrian and Orrila

Mountain Sylph (Thackeray, T. J., 1834), IV. 412

Mountain Torrents (1861), v. 721

Mountebank (Motteux, P. A., 1705), II. 346

— (1715), II. 379

— (1805), IV. 506

Mountebank (1851), v. 721

Mountebank of Ravenna = Love Spell

Mountebanks (Gilbert, W. S., 1892), v. 381

Mounted Brigands of the Abruzzi = (1) Carlo Brunari; (2) Horse of the Cavern

Mounted Brigands of Valentia = Manuel of Spain

Mounting Sylph (Rogers, W., 1844), IV. 396

— (1838), IV. 506

— (1839), IV. 507

Mount St Bernard (Moncrieff, W. T., 1839), v. 507, 600, 633

— (1834), IV. 507

Mournful Nuptials (Cooke, T., 1739), II. 123, 316

Mourning Bride (Congreve, W., 1697), I. 69, 73, 143-4, 180, 398

— = School for Greybeards

Mouse Trap (White, J., 1853), v. 620

— (1897), v. 721

— = (1) Fool's Paradise; (2) Mars and Venus

Mouse-traps (Dibdin, T. J., 1819), IV. 302

Mousquetaires au Couvent (Farnie, H. B., 1880), v. 362, 791

Moustache Movement (Brough, R. B., 1854), v. 278

Mouth of the Nile (Dibdin, T. J., 1798) = News from the Nile, III. 256, 383

Mouth of the Pit (Miller, W. F., 1892), v. 489

Move on (Mortimer, J., 1883), v. 494

Moving Statues (1840), IV. 634

Moving Tale (Lemon, M., 1854), v. 455

Mowbray Chase (1859), v. 721

Moyna-a-Roon (Levey, J. C., 1875), v. 458

Moyra (Pitt, G. D., 1845), IV. 374

Moyra the Doomed (1854), v. 721

M.P. (Moore, T., 1811), IV. 361

— (Robertson, T. W., 1870), v. 546

— = Love and Laugh

M.P. for Puddlepool (Summers, K., 1868), v. 587

M.P. for the Rotten Borough (Lemon, M., 1838), IV. 343

M.P.'s Wife (1895), v. 721

Mr Albert Smith's Ascent of Mont Blanc (Smith, A. R., 1854), v. 572

Mr Albert Smith's Ascent of Mont Blanc; Holland and up the Rhine (Smith, A. R., 1854), v. 572

Mr and Mrs Briggs (Rodwell, G. H. and Lee, N., 1851), v. 548

Mr and Mrs Grubb (1840), iv. 507

Mr and Mrs Gulliver (1870), v. 721

Mr and Mrs Muffet (Smith, L., 1892), v. 573

Mr and Mrs Pringle (De Trueba, J. T., 1832), iv. 414

Mr and Mrs Toodles = Farmer's Daughter of the Severnside

Mr and Mrs White (1854), v. 721

Mr Anthony (Boyle, R., 1672), i. 17, 69, 257, 393

Mr B— (Stafford, J. J., 1833), iv. 612

Mr Barnes of New York (Barrington, R., 1888), v. 251

Mr Bayes Practice = Prunella

Mr Bony's Wedding = Empress and No Empress

Mr Briggs (1849), iv. 507

Mr Briggs in his Pleasures of House Keeping (1854), v. 721

Mr Buckstone at Home (Coyne, J. S., 1863), v. 328

Mr Buckstone's Ascent of Mount Parnassus (Planché, J. R., 1853), v. 9, 527

Mr Buckstone's Voyage round the Globe (Planché, J. R., 1854), v. 527

Mr Busy (1832), iv. 507

Mr Chairman (Fitzball, E., 1829), iv. 313

Mr Cynic (Locke, W. J. and Roper, G., 1893), v. 462

Mr Dick's Heir (Crofton, C. and Brooke, H., 1895), v. 330

Mr Donnithorpe's Rent (Seaton, R., 1890), v. 559

Mr Fitz W—? (Newte, H. C. W., 1894), v. 503

Mr Flimsey's Family (1868), v. 721

Mr Gorilla (Addison, H. R., 1861), v. 235

Mr Greenfinch (Bayly, T. H., 1838), iv. 263

Mr Greenlea's Courtship (Mudie, G., 1891), v. 498

Mr Guffin's Elopement (Law, A. and Grossmith, G., 1882), v. 450

Mr H— (Lamb, C., 1806), iv. 123-4, 341

Mr Hughes at Home (1856), v. 721

Mr Jarley at Court (1899), v. 721

Mr Jericho (Greenbank, H., 1893), v. 392

Mr Joffin's Latchkey (Robinson, N., 1875), v. 547

Mr Jolliboy's Conjugal Woes (1878), v. 722

Mr Limberham = Kind Keeper

Mr Martin (Hawtrey, C., 1896), v. 410

Mr Midshipman Easy (Oxenford, J., 1836) = Midshipman Easy, iv. 507, 634

Mr Napie's Reception in Elba (McLaren, A., 1814), iv. 351

Mr Neville's Sheep = Follow the Leader

Mr Nightingale's Diary (Lemon, M., 1851), v. 455

Mr N'Importe (Dibdin, C. I. M., 1825), iv. 296

Mr Paul Pry (1826), iv. 507

Mr Pep (1835), iv. 634

Mr Peppercorn at Home = Gallantee Showman

Mr Pickwick's Little Mistake (1892), v. 722

Mr Potter of Texas (Stephens, W., 1888), v. 581

Mr Richards (Bourchier, A. and Blair, J., 1892), v. 270

Mr Robert Roy, Hielan Helen, his Wife and Dougald the Dodger (Lowe, W., 1880), v. 464

Mrs Annesley (Cooke, J. F., 1891), v. 324

Mrs Beflat's Blunder (Routledge, W., 1869), v. 552

Mrs Brown (Wilton, J. H., 1874), v. 629

Mrs Brown at the Play (Sketchley, A., 1863), v. 570

Mrs Bunbury's Spoons (Coyne, J. S., 1849), iv. 507, 634

Mrs Caudle (Barnett, C. Z., 1845), iv. 507, 634

Mrs Caudle Abroad and at Home (1845), iv. 507

Mrs Caudle's Adventures in France = Mrs Caudle Abroad and at Home

Mrs Caudle's Curtain Lectures (Jerrold, D. J., 1845), IV. 507, 590, 634
— (Stirling, E., 1845), IV. 407
Mrs Chesterfield Thinskin (1853), V. 722
Mrs Colonel Fitzsmythe's Bal Costumé (1850), V. 722
Mrs Confusion's Travail and Hard Labour = Rehearsal
Mr Scroggins = Change of Name
Mrs Daintree's Daughter (1894), V. 722
Mrs Dane's Defence (Jones, H. A., 1900), V. 170, 191, 197
Mrs Dexter (Darnley, J. H., 1891), V. 337
Mrs Eversley—Wednesdays (Bell, M., 1893), V. 256
Mrs G. (Barnett, M., 1831), IV. 261
Mrs Gamp and Mrs Harris (1846), IV. 507
+ Mrs Gamp's Party (12°, n.d., Manchester)
Mrs Gardiner (1888), V. 722
Mrs Gray's Secret (1896), V. 722
Mrs Green's Snug Little Business (Cheltnam, C. S., 1865), V. 119, 309
Mrs H. (Lee, N., 1832), IV. 507, 634
Mrs Hardup's Advertisement = Caroline's Pupils
Mrs Harris (Stirling, E., 1846), IV. 408
Mrs Hilary Regrets (Smith, S. T., 1892), V. 573
Mrs H— will give Lessons in Lovemaking (Atwood, A. and Vaun, R., 1897), V. 245
Mr Simpson and Company = Simpson and Co.
Mr Simpson, M.C. (Cooper, F. F., 1833), IV. 283
Mr Sims (Hood, T., 1829), IV. 327
Mrs Jane Shore (Lee, N., 1845), IV. 507, 634
+ Mrs Jarley's Far-famed Collection of Wax-works (Bartlett, G. B., 8°, 1873)
Mrs Jarman's Profession = Mrs Warren's Profession
Mrs Jarramie's Genie (Desprez, F., 1888), V. 343
Mrs Johnson (O'Neil, J. R., 1852), V. 507
Mrs Jollybutt's Out (Brown, W., 1876), V. 282

Mrs Lessingham (Fleming, G., 1894), V. 369
Mrs Mackenzie No. 2 (Harrison, K., 1896), V. 407
Mr Smith (1831), IV. 507
— (1899), V. 722
Mrs M.P. (Vezin, H., 1891), V. 608
Mrs Mullins (Dibdin, C. I. M., 1815), IV. 293
Mrs Normer (1842), IV. 507
Mrs Othello (Leslie, F. and Shirley, A., 1893), V. 456
Mrs Peaspod (1846), IV. 507
Mrs Ponderbury = Mrs Ponderbury's Past
Mrs Ponderbury's Past (Burnand, F. C., 1895), V. 292
Mrs Rawdon's Rehearsal (1898), V. 722
Mrs Rip Van Winkle (1899), V. 722
Mrs Sarah Gamp's Tea and Turn Out (Webster, B. N., 1846), IV. 418
Mrs Scaite in the Seraglio = Odd Fish
Mr Scroggins (Hancock, W., 1867), V. 402
Mrs Slimmer's Lodgers (Holles, W., 1893), V. 424
Mrs Smiffin's Carte de Visite = Doing the Shah
Mrs Smith (Payne, J. H., 1823), IV. 369
Mrs Speaker (1885), V. 722
Mrs Trictrac (1837), IV. 507
Mrs Veal's Ghost (1823), IV. 507
Mrs W. (Dibdin, T. J., 1826), IV. 304
Mrs Warren's Profession (Shaw, G. B., 1898), V. 195, 203, 562
Mrs Weakly's Difficulty (Poel, W., 1886), V. 529, 811
Mrs White (Raymond, R. J., 1836), IV. 389
Mrs Wiggins (Allingham, J. T., 1803), IV. 252
Mr Wilkins = Wives and Partners
+ Mrs Willis's Will (French)
Mr Sympkyn (Flaxman, A. J. and Younge, W., 1897), V. 369
Mr Taste the Poetical Fop (1732), II. 379
Mr Tibbs (Thomson, J., 1821), IV. 413
Mr Timms (1842), IV. 507
Mr Turbulent (1682), I. 217, 443
Mr versus Mrs (Bourchier, A. and "Mountjoy", 1895), V. 270

Mr Walker's Trunks (Ebsworth, J., 1837), IV. 308

Mr Webster's Company is requested at a photographic Soirée (Yates, E. and Harrington, N. H., 1858), V. 722, 795, 825, 841

Mr Weller's Watch (1840), IV. 97, 507

Much Ado about Nothing (Kemble, J. P., 1797), III. 279, 389; IV. 335

— = Cabinet

Much Ado about Nothing (as usual) = Competition

Much too clever (Oxenford, J. and Hatton, J., 1874), V. 510

Mudborough Election (Brough, W. and Halliday, A., 1865), V. 280

Muddled and Mixed = Sock and Buckskin

Muddler (Hill, H., 1890), V. 421

Muddles (Jessup, 1885), V. 437

Muette de Portici (1845), IV. 507, 634

Muffled Bells of Paris = Dead Duchess

Muff of the Regiment (Ganthony, R., 1898), V. 376

— = Goodbye

Mufti's Tomb (1828), IV. 507

— = Misers of Smyrna

Mugwump (1898), V. 722

Mulatto = Mathilde

Mulatto Murderer (1854), V. 722

Mulatto Nobleman = Serpent on the Hearth

Mulberry Bush (Albery, J., 1882), V. 238

Mulberry-Garden (Sedley, Sir C., 1668), I. 27, 187, 214, 234–5, 344, 427

Muldoon's Picnic (Pleon, H., 1886), V. 183, 528

Mule-driver and his Dogs (1846), IV. 507

Muleteer (Frazer, T. J., 1844), IV. 318

Muleteer and his Monkey = Napoleon's Godson

Muleteer of Toledo (Morton, J. M., 1855), V. 495

— (Robertson, T. W., 1856), V. 546

Muleteer's Vow (Haines, J. T. or Serle, T. J., 1835), IV. 507, 634

Mulic the Slave (1802), IV. 507

Mullibaloo (Green, F. W., 1874), V. 390

Multum in Parvo = Two Thumbs

Mummies and Marriage (Mackinnon, A. M. and Adderley, J. G., 1888), V. 471

Mummy (Bernard, W. B., 1833), IV. 265

— (Brand, O., 1884), V. 273

— (Day, G. D. and Bowkett, S., 1895), V. 339

Mummy and the Study of Living Pictures = Raphael's Dream

Mumps the Masher (Craven, T. and Nelson, R., 1884), V. 329

Mungo Park (Corri, M.?, 1844), IV. 578

— (1819), IV. 507

— (1824), IV. 507

— (1841), IV. 507

Mungo Parke (Bernard, B., 1840), IV. 507, 634

Murat (1843), IV. 507

Murder and Madness (Dibdin, C. I. M., 1825), IV. 295, 507, 580, 634

Murder at Sadlers Wells = Ruby Ring

Murder at the Black Farm = John Stafford

Murder at the Dead Man's Pool = Dark Night's Work

Murder at the Hall = Crock of Gold

Murder at the Mansion = Clock House

Murder at the Old Crook Farm = Silas Bruton

Murder at the Pit's Bank = Miner's Dog

Murder at the Roadside Inn = Jonathan Bradford

Murder at the Turnpike Gate 100 Years Ago = Tollcross

Murder Brought to Light = Iron Chest

Murder Cellar of Fleet Ditch = Thieves' House

Murdered Guest (Dibdin, T. J., 1818), IV. 301

— (1826), IV. 507

— = Fatal Experiment

Murdered Heir = Glenarvon

Murdered Maid (E., S. N., 1820), IV. 507, 634

Murdered Monk (1827), IV. 507

Murderer (Amherst, J. H., 1822), IV. 507, 634

— (1823) = Father and the Son, IV. 507, 634

Murderer of the Pyrenees = (1) Belphegor the Buffoon; (2) Geneviève

Murderers at the Desolate Cottage = Gamblers

Murderer's Doom = Tomb of Sigismond

Murderer's Dream (1818), IV. 507

Music has Charms (McLaren, A., 1824), IV. 352

Music hath Charms (Fisher, D., 1856), V. 367

— (1823), IV. 508

Musician of Venice (1838), IV. 508

Musician's Daughter (1850), V. 722

Musician's Romance (Harvey, F., 1898), V. 409

Music Mad (Hook, T. E., 1807), IV. 327

— (1829), IV. 508

Music Master (Howard, F., 1887), V. 428

— (1892), V. 722

— = Sham Fight

Musico (Jodrell, R. P., 1787), III. 277

Music's Fascination = Travellers

Music's the Language = Operamania

Music the Food of Love = Modern Orpheus

Musketeers (Grundy, S., 1898), V. 397

Musquetaire (1834), IV. 508

Mustapha (Boyle, R., 1665), I. 38, 39, 66, 80, 107–9, 127, 305, 321, 346, 351, 393; II. 70–1

— (Mallet, D., 1739), II. 27, 58, 65, 70–1, 82, 83, 343

— (Wilkinson, T. F., 1829), IV. 617

— (1814), IV. 508

Mustard Plaster (1898), V. 722

Must he die? (1892), V. 722

Mutineer (1744), II. 379

— (1817), IV. 508

Mutineers of 1727 = Casco Bay

Mutineers of the High Seas = John Adams

Mutineer's Widow (Bosworth, J., 1838), IV. 573

Mutines, the Traitor (Downes, J. F., 1898), V. 349

Mutiny at the Nore (Jerrold, D. W., 1830), IV. 332

— = Richard Parker

Mutiny of Spithead and the Nore (1830), IV. 508

Mutiny of the Britannia (1823), IV. 508

Mutiny of the Caroline = Red Rover

Mutiny of the Dolphin = Red Rover

Mutiny of the Isis = Vin Willoughby

Mutius Scaevola (Ireland, S. W. H., 1801), III. 276; IV. 329

Mutual Deception (Atkinson, J., 1785), III. 118, 177, 234

— = Adventurers

Mutual Expense (Fitzball, E., 1836), IV. 315

Mutual Ground (Brockbank, J., 1875), V. 276

Mutual Inconstancy (1795), III. 337

Mutual Mistake (Denny, W. H., 1891) V. 342

Mutual Misunderstanding (Lee, H., 1876), V. 452

Mutual Objections = I'll not have a Wife

Mutual Separation (Compton, E., 1877), V. 319

My Absent Son (1828), IV. 508

My Album (Bayly, T. H., 1838), IV. 14, 263

My American Aunt (1864), V. 722

My Artful Valet = Gloriana

My Astral Body (Hudson, C. and Colthurst, N., 1896), V. 429

My Auld Mare Maggie = Tam o' Shanter

My Aunt (Arnold, S. J., 1815), IV. 508, 634

— (1864), V. 722

My Aunt Grumble (Johnson, E., 1877), V. 437

My Aunt's Bantam = Cockorico

+ My Aunt's Heiress (French)

My Aunt's Hobby = Juniper Jack

My Aunt's Husband (Selby, C., 1858), V. 560

My Aunt's in Town (Grain, R. C., 1889), V. 387

My Aunt's Luggage = Face to Face

My Aunt's Narcotic (Lancaster, E. R.), IV. 593

My Aunt's Secret (Burnand, F. C., 1872), V. 290

My Aunt's Tragedy = Treacle and Mustard

My Aunt, the Dowager = Winterbottoms!

My Awful Dad (Mathews, C. J., 1875), V. 480

My Awful Luck (Doone, N., 1892), V. 347

My Bachelor Days (Morton, J. M., 1883), V. 807

My Beaux (Stack, T. A., 1868), v. 578

My Benefactor (Rose, E., 1883), v. 550

My Best Friend (1827), IV. 508

My Bonny Boy = Our Tuner

My Boy (Lubimoff, A., 1886), v. 464

My Brave Little Wife (Seaton, A. M., 1882), v. 559

My Brother's Sister = Nadine

My Collaborator (Jones, K., 1892), v. 441

My Comrade (Horsman, C., 1885), v. 427

My Cook and Housekeeper (1854), v. 722

My Country Cousin (1827), IV. 508

— = Actress of All Work

My Courier (Leterrier, J., 1886), v. 457

My Cousin (Hewson, J. J., 1885), v. 420

— = (1) False Alarms; (2) False Appearances

My Cousin Peppy (1861), v. 722

My Cousin the Minister (1839), IV. 508

My Dad = Myrtle

My Darling = Light

My Daughter (Bancroft, Lady, 1892), v. 248

— (Chapman, A., 1888), v. 308

My Daughter-in-Law (1899), v. 722

+ My Daughter's Daughter (*French*)

My Daughter's Debut (Craven, H. T.), v. 786

My Daughter's Intended (Suter, W. E.), v. 819

My Daughter, Sir (Planché, J. R., 1832), IV. 379

My Daughter's Letter = Monsieur Mallet

My Daughter the Duchess (Meadow, A., 1884), v. 483

My Dearest Anna Maria (1851), v. 722

My Dear Relations = Brother Tom

My Detective (1876), v. 722

My Dress Boots (Williams, T. J., 1864), v. 625

My Eleventh Day (Bayly, T. H., 1832), IV. 262, 508, 634

— = Cupid

My Enemy (Reece, R., 1880), v. 539

My Father = Twenty per Cent

My Father did so before me (1848), IV. 508

My Father! Methinks I see my Father! = Who's my Father?

My Fellow Clerk (Oxenford, J., 1835), IV. 367, 603

My Fetch (1858), v. 722

My First and Last Courtship (1849), IV. 508

My First Brief (1861), v. 722

My First Case (Courtice, T., 1897), v. 326

My First Client (1890), v. 722

My First Fit of the Gout (Morton, J. M., 1835), IV. 361

My First Patient (Cassel, H. and Ogden, C., 1887), v. 305

Myfisto (Montague, V. and St Clare, F., 1887), v. 491

My Friend (Long, C., 1846), IV. 346

— (Tabrar, J., 1885), v. 589

My Friend from India (1896), v. 722

— = My Friend the Prince

My Friend from Leatherhead (Harrington, N. H. and Yates, E., 1857), v. 404

My Friend from Town (Lunn, J., 1831), IV. 14, 508, 634

My Friend Gomez (Smith, L., 1896), v. 573

My Friend in the Straps (1850), v. 722

My Friend Jarlet (Goldsworthy, A. + in collaboration with Norman, E. B., 1887), v. 384

My Friend's Address (1885), v. 722

My Friend the Captain (Coyne, J. S., 1841), IV. 284

My Friend, the Governor (Planché, J. R., 1834), IV. 380, 605

My Friend the Major (Selby, C., 1854), v. 560

My Friend the Prince (McCarthy, J. H., 1897), v. 467

My Gal at Tea (1889), v. 722

My General (Forrester, S., 1890), v. 371

My Girl = Clergyman's Daughter

My Good Name (Turner, E., 1896), v. 604

My Grandfather (Bayly, T. H., 1834), IV. 508, 634

My Grandfather's Legacy = Wife well won

My Grandfather's Will (Reynolds, F., 1838), IV. 391

My Grandmother (Hoare, P., 1793), III.
197, 269; IV. 140
— (1812), IV. 140, 508
— = All about the Battle of Dorking
My Grandmother's Estate (1840), IV. 508
My Grandmother's Pet = Young Scamp
My Great Aunt (Planché, J. R., 1831),
IV. 379
My Great-great-grandfather = 102
My Guardie (Trevelyan, C., 1896), v.
603
My Heart for Yours = Maids and
Bachelors
My Heart's Darling (Ellis, B., 1876), v.
357
My Heart's Idol (Planché, J. R., 1850),
v. 527
My Heart's in the Highlands (Brough,
W. and Halliday, A., 1863), v. 279
My Home is not my Home (Peake,
R. B., 1840), IV. 371
My Husband's Ghost (Morton, J. M.,
1836), IV. 361
My Husband's Secret (Meadows, T.,
1822), IV. 355
— (Whitty, W. D., 1874), v. 621
— (1858), v. 722
My Husband's Widow = Too late for
the Train
My Husband's Wife (Perry, J., 1885),
v. 520
My Husband's Will (Phillips, Mrs A.,
1853), v. 522
My Idiot (1899), v. 722
My Innocent Boy (Sims, G. R. and
Merrick, L., 1898), v. 570
My Jack (Coffin, E., 1887), v. 316
— (Landeck, B., 1889), v. 447
— (1895), v. 722
My Knuckleduster (Wilson, J. C.,
1863), v. 628, 824 [and see under Anti-
garotte, v. 642]
My Lady Clara (Robertson, T. W.,
1869), v. 546
My Lady Fanciful (Jenner, A., 1899), v.
436
My Lady Help (Macklin, A., 1890), v.
471
My Lady Hilda (Faucit, H. S., 1870), v.
363
My Lady, M.D. (Lynch, G. D., 1895),
v. 465

My Lady of Levenmore (1894), v. 722
My Lady's Lord (Esmond, H. V., 1899),
v. 722, 790
My Lady's Orchard (Beringer, Mrs O.
and Hawtrey, G. P., 1897), v. 259
My Landlady's Daughter (Berton,
P. M., 1893), v. 260
My Landlady's Gown (Oulton, W. C.,
1816), IV. 366
My Landlady's Side Door = In and Out
My Landlord (1894), v. 722
My Last Resource (Newton, J., 1863),
v. 808
My Late Friend (Dance, G., 1835), IV.
508, 634
My Latest Opera (1894), v. 722
My Life (Archer, Miss, 1882), v. 242
My Life by Myself (St Maur, H., 1876),
v. 554
My Little Adopted (Bayly, T. H., 1838),
IV. 263
My Little Brother (1840), IV. 508
My Little Girl (Boucicault, D. G.,
1882), v. 270
My Little Red Riding Hood (Rae, J. and
Sidney, T., 1895), v. 533
My Little William (McCullough, B.,
1876), v. 468
My Lord (Dance, C., 1822), IV. 508,
634
— (1843), IV. 508
My Lord and my Lady (Planché, J. R.,
1861), v. 527
My Lord Cardinal (Alexander, G.,
1894), v. 238
My Lord in Livery (Smith, S. T., 1886),
v. 573
My Lord is not my Lord (+ Dance, C.,
1840), IV. 508, 578
My Love and I (Bellingham, H. and
Best, W., 1886), v. 257
My Lover (1839), IV. 508
My Love the Captain (Thomson, J. E.,
1852), v. 598
My Maggie (Thompson, H., 1884), v.
598
My Maiden Aunts (Sala, F., 1842), IV.
508, 634
My Man and the Barber (Martin, J.),
IV. 597
My Man Tom (Lemon, M., 1842), IV.
344

My Son Get Money = Dissembled Wanton

My Son-in-Law (1850), v. 723

My Son Jack (Soutar, R., 1870), v. 575

My Son's a Daughter (Parselle, J., 1862), v. 515

My Spouse and I (Dibdin, C. I. M., 1815), IV. 293

— (1816), IV. 509

Mysteries and Miseries (1822), IV. 509

Mysteries of Alviano (Milner, H. M., 1829), IV. 509, 634

Mysteries of an American City (Lee, N., 1848), IV. 343

Mysteries of a Private Madhouse = Lady in Black

Mysteries of Audley Court (Brougham, J., 1866), v. 723, 780, 841

Mysteries of Bordercleugh = Life of Ned Cantor

Mysteries of Callow Abbey (1876), v. 723

Mysteries of Carrow (1888), v. 723

Mysteries of Carrow Alley = Will and the Way

Mysteries of Crime = (1) Bohemians of Paris; (2) Rocambole

Mysteries of London (1846), IV. 509

— = Daughter of Midnight

Mysteries of Midnight = Black Band

Mysteries of Old Father Thames (Young, H., 1850), v. 636

Mysteries of Paris (Dillon, C., 1844), IV. 118–19, 305

— (1844), IV. 509

— = Love and Crime

Mysteries of Prince's Tower (Mayne, A., 1879), v. 483

Mysteries of Shoreditch (1860), v. 723

Mysteries of the Black Tower = Fates

Mysteries of the Castle (Andrews, M. P. and Reynolds, F., 1795), III. 29, 31, 100–1, 233

Mysteries of the Cloister (1821), IV. 509

Mysteries of the North (1804), IV. 509

Mysteries of the Temple (1863), v. 723

Mysteries of the Wall (1840), IV. 509

Mysteries of Udulpho (Baylis, J., 1804), IV. 571

Mysteries of Wilton Hall (1858), v. 723

Mysterious Bride (Skeffington, L. St G., 1810), IV. 402

Mysterious Chorus = Discarded Secretary

Mysterious Disappearance (1869), v. 723

Mysterious Family (Rodwell, G. H., 1835), IV. 395

Mysterious Freebooter (1806), IV. 509

Mysterious Hermit (1841), IV. 634

— = Manfred

Mysterious Host = (1) Female Freebooter; (2) Maurice

Mysterious House in Chelsea (Cave, J. A. and Roberts, G., 1876), v. 306

Mysterious Husband (Cumberland, R., 1783), III. 78–9, 90–1, 251

Mysterious Lady (Planché, J. R., 1852), v. 527

Mysterious Letter (1874), v. 723

Mysterious Marriage (Lee, H., 1798), III. 98, 103, 280

— (1821), IV. 509

Mysterious Marriages = Double Perplexity

Mysterious Monitor = Fortress of Paluzzi

Mysterious Mother (Walpole, H., 1768), III. 96, 217, 314

— = Narbonne Castle

Mysterious Mr Buble = Vanishing Husband

Mysterious Murder (Ludlam, G., 1817), IV. 596

— (1824), IV. 634

Mysterious Musician (Eden, G., 1899), v. 353

Mysterious Musician and the Duke of Dis-Guisebury = Bad-Ballad Monger

Mysterious Protector = Retreat of the Mountains

Mysterious Protectress = Youthful Queen, Christine of Sweden

Mysterious Recruit = Clara

Mysterious Stranger (Gordon, F. C., 1812), IV. 319

— (Selby, C., 1844), IV. 399

— (1825), IV. 509

— = (1) Hereditary Honours; (2) Sweet Revenge

Mysterious Tailor (1831), IV. 509

Mysterious Theft (Campbell, A. V., 1815), IV. 278

Mysterious Unknown (1859), v. 723

Mysterious Visit = Earthquake

Mysterious Waiter = Man of Mystery

Mysterious Widow (Fripp, F., 1897), v. 373

Mysterious Wife = Fritz the Outlaw

Mystery (Stephens, W., 1873), v. 581

— (1815), IV. 634

— (1863), v. 723

— = Adele

Mystery and Vengeance = Red Dwarf

Mystery Jairah (Stuart-Wortley, Lady Emmeline, 1840), IV. 613

Mystery, Love and Crime = Blue Dwarf

Mystery of a Gladstone Bag (Francks, F. H., 1889), v. 372

Mystery of a Handsome Cap (André, R., 1888), v. 241

Mystery of a Hansom Cab (Law, A. and Hume, F., 1888), v. 450

— (1888), v. 723

Mystery of Carrow Abbey = Will and the Way

Mystery of Chesney Wold = Jo, the Waif

Mystery of Cloisterham (Stephens, W., 1871) = Mystery of Edwin Drood, v. 581, 723, 817, 841

Mystery of Edwin Drood (Macdermott, G. H., 1872), v. 468

— (Stephens, W., 1871) = Mystery of Cloisterham, v. 581, 723, 817, 841

+ Mystery of Muddlewitz (*French*)

Mystery of Rosedale Hollow = Who did it?

Mystery of the Abbey (Young, H., 1853), v. 636

Mystery of the Ruined Mill = Will o' the Wisp

Mystery of the Seven Sisters (Scudamore, F. A., 1890), v. 559

Mystical Milkman = Camberwell Brothers

Mystical Miss (Klein, C. H., 1899), v. 445

Mystic Branch (1859), v. 723

— = Demon Duke

Mystic Cavern (1803), IV. 509

Mystic Coffer (1812), IV. 509

Mystic Cypress Tree = Demon Bracelets

Mystic Mahatma (Taylor, T. M., 1892), v. 591

Mystic Number VII (1872), v. 723

Mystic Ring (Johnson, E. C., 1893), v. 437

Mystic Tomb (1819), IV. 509

Mystification (Haines, J. T., 1832) = Love and Mystery, IV. 509, 587, 634

— (1821), IV. 509

— (1826), IV. 509

My Sweetheart (Maeder, F. and Gill, W., 1883), v. 472

Mythology run Mad (Moore, T. and Runtz, E., 1893), v. 492

My Turn Next (Williams, T. J., 1866), v. 625

— = Dobson and Company

My Two Nephews (Peake, R. B., 1823) = Duel, IV. 509, 634

My Uncle (Beazley, S., Jr., 1817), IV. 263

— (James, D. S. and Stewart, W. Y., 1883), v. 433

— (Steinberg, A., 1889), v. 580

— (1811), IV. 509

My Uncle Gabriel (Parry, J., 1824), IV. 27, 358, 368

My Uncle's Card (Grattan, H. P., 1840), IV. 320

— (1855), v. 723

My Uncle's House (+ Dibdin, C. I. M., 1815), IV. 509

My Uncle's Parlour (1807), IV. 509

My Uncle's Pet (Archer, T., 1846), IV. 255

— (1845), IV. 509

— (1860), v. 723

My Uncle's Will = Uncle's Will [The play by S. T. Smith, v. 573, has My Uncle's Will on the printed title page, but the running titles read Uncle's Will]

— = Widow

My Uncle Thomas = Dare-Devil

My Uncle Toby (Stafford, J. J., 1828), IV. 405, 612

My Valet and I (Wilks, T. E., 1842), IV. 421

My Vassal's Dog = Cottage of the Lake

My Very Last Proposal (Phipps, A. J., 1874), v. 524

My Villa in Italy (Rae, C. M., 1871), v. 532

My Wife (Cowell, A. E., 1892), v. 327

— (Roberts, G., 1885), v. 544

My Wife and Child (1836), IV. 509

My Wife and First Baby = Club

My Wife and my Umbrella (1857), v. 723

My Wife or my Place (Thackeray, T. J. and Shannon, C., 1831), IV. 412

My Wife Polly = Bamboozling

My Wife's Baby (Hughes, F., 1872), v. 430

— (1898), v. 723

My Wife's Bedroom (1834), IV. 509

My Wife's Bonnet (Morton, J. M., 1864), v. 496

My Wife's Come (Morton, J. M., 1843), IV. 362

My Wife's Cousin (1853), v. 723

My Wife's Daughter (Coyne, J. S., 1850), v. 327

My Wife's Dentist (Wilks, T. E., 1839), IV. 421

My Wife's Diary = Wife's Journal

My Wife's Father's Sister (Pemberton, T. E., 1878), v. 519

My Wife's First Husband (Suter, W. E., 1854), v. 723, 819, 841

My Wife's Future Husband (Mayhew, A. and Edwards, H. S., 1851), v. 482

My Wife shan't act (1850), v. 723

My Wife's Husband (1830), IV. 509

— = Going to my Uncle's

My Wife's Lodgings (1844), IV. 509

My Wife's Lover (1859), v. 723

My Wife's Lovers (1899), v. 723

My Wife's Maid (Williams, T. J., 1864), v. 625

My Wife's Mother (Mathews, C. J., 1833), IV. 354

My Wife's Out (Rodwell, G. H., 1843), IV. 395

My Wife's Party (Grain, R. C., 1892), v. 388

My Wife's Relations (Gordon, W., 1862), v. 385

My Wife's Second Floor (Morton, J. M., 1843), IV. 362

My Wife's Step Husband (Du Souchet, H. A., 1897), v. 352

My Wife! What Wife? (Barrett, E. S., 1815), IV. 261

— (Poole, J., 1829), IV. 386

My Wig and my Wife's Shawl (1855), v. 723

My Young Wife and my Old Umbrella (Webster, B. N., 1837), IV. 417

Nabal (Morell, T., 1764), III. 358, 392

Nabob (Degville, 1809), IV. 509, 634

— (Foote, S., 1772), III. 175, 260

— (1898), v. 723

Nabob for an Hour (Poole, J., 1833), IV. 84, 387

Nabob outwitted (1797), III. 337

Nabob's Fortune (Pettitt, H., 1881), v. 521

Nabob's Pickle (1883), v. 723

Nabob's Return = My Home is not my Home

Nabob, the Farmer and the Miser = Blighted Joys

Nachtigal und der Rabe (1828), IV. 509, 634

Nachtlager von Granada (1849), IV. 510

Nachtteufel (1844), IV. 510

Nadel (Lyon, W. F., 1886), v. 465

Nadeshda (Sturgis, J., 1885), v. 586

Nadeshta, the Slave Girl (1850), v. 723

Nadgy (Murray, A., 1887), v. 500

Nadia (Greville, Lady V., 1892), v. 394

Nadine (Grover, L., 1887), v. 396

— (Rogers, F., 1885), v. 548

Nadir (Wise, J., 1779), III. 316

Nadir Shah (1825), IV. 510

Nadjezda (Barrymore, M., 1886), v. 252

Naiad = Ondine

Naiad Queen (Dalrymple, J. S., 1883), v. 333

— = Reine des Naiades

Naida (1848), IV. 510

Naissance de Flore (1809), IV. 510

Naissance de Venus (Degville, 1826), IV. 579

Nameless (1845), IV. 510

— (1884), v. 723

Namesakes (Lennard, H., 1883), v. 455

— (1835), IV. 510

Name the Winner (Millingen, J. G., 1834), IV. 510, 634

Namouna (1882), v. 723

Nana Sahib (Fenton, F. and Osman, W. R., 1863), v. 723, 841

Nance (Douglass, J. T., 1893), v. 349

Nance Oldfield (Reade, C., 1883), v. 536

Never despair (1875), v. 724

Never Introduce your Dinah to a Pal = Cavalearyer Costercana

Never Judge by Appearances (Drayton, H., 1859), v. 724, 789, 841

— (1857), v. 724

Never Plead's Hopes of being a Lord Chancellor = Fame

Never Reckon your Chickens before they are Hatched (Reeve, W., 1871), v. 540

— (Suter, W. E., 1858), v. 724, 819, 842

Never Satisfied (1886), v. 724

Never say die = Hampshire Hog

Never taste Wine at the Docks (Soutar, R., 1854), v. 575

Never to Know (Fairfax, M., 1899), v. 360

Never too late to learn (Branson, W. S., 1874), v. 274

Never too late to mend (Conquest, G., Jr., 1858), v. 724, 785, 842

— (Hazlewood, C. H., 1859), v. 724, 796, 842

— (Johnstone, J. B., 1858), v. 800

— (1858), v. 724

Never Travel during a Revolution = Lost a Sovereign

New Actress (Drew, E., 1888), v. 350

— (1835), IV. 511

New Adam (Melford, M., 1897), v. 484

New Agent (Lindo, R. H., 1896), v. 460

New Apollo (Grey, C., 1889), v. 394

New Apple of Discord = Not for me!

New Athenian Comedy (Settle, E., 1693), I. 429

New Baby (Bourchier, A., 1896), v. 270

New Babylon (Meritt, P. and Rowe, G. F., 1878), v. 486

New Barmaid (Bowyer, F. and Edwardes-Sprange, W., 1895), v. 272

New Boy (Lumley, R. R., 1893), v. 464

— = Boy

New Brighton Sands (Harrison, W., 1881), v. 407

New Brooms (Byron, H. J., 1881), v. 299

— (Colman, G., 1776), III. 12, 112, 193, 195, 210, 246

— (Dibdin, C. I. M., 1803), IV. 290

New Case for the Lawyers = Will and No Will

Newcastle in an Uproar (?Dodds, R., 1851), v. 842

Newcastle Rider = Ducks and Green Pease

New Cinderella (Simpson J. P., 1879), v. 568

New Comedy (1704), II. 380

New Comedy of Errors = Shakespeare's Festival

New Comic Scene to the Comedy of the Minor (1761), III. 403

New Corsican Brothers (Raleigh, C. and Slaughter, W., 1889), v. 533

New Cosmetic (Pratt, S. J., 1790), III. 299

New Court Legacy = Ladies of the Palace

New Dean (Ellis, H., 1897), v. 357

New Divertisement (1794), III. 337, 403

New Don Juan (1828), IV. 511

New Don Quixote (Buchanan, R. and Jay, H., 1896), v. 285

New Drama (1792), III. 337

New East Lynne (Gurney, E., 1898), v. 398

New Edition of the Corsican Brothers (Mason, W. H., 1870), v. 480

New Edition of the Fairy Tales of Mother Goose, with many Highly Coloured Illustrations (1855), v. 724

New Endimion (1882), v. 724

Newest Woman (Newton, H. C., 1895), v. 503

New Farce (1835), IV. 511 [This has a sub-title, or, A Scene of Confusion]

New Footman (Selby, C., 1842), IV. 398

New Fortune (1853), v. 724

New Found Home = Eugenia Claircille

New Front to an Old Dicky = Rise and Fall of Richard III

Newgate Ned (1834), IV. 511

New Gretna Green (Stuart, C., 1783) = Gretna Green, III. 310, 337, 403

New Groom (Hannan, C., 1899), v. 403

New Hay at the Old Market (Colman, G., the Younger, 1795), III. 23, 156-7, 164, 212, 247

— = Sylvester Daggerwood

New Hand (1885), v. 724

New Haymarket Spring Meeting (Planché, J. R., 1855), v. 527

New Trial of Effie Deans = Heart of Midlothian

New Trick to get a Wife = Litigious Suitor Defeated

New Utopia = Six days Adventure

New Version of Uncle Tom's Cabin (1857), v. 724

New Wags of Windsor (Howard, J. and Cooper, F., 1854), v. 724, 786, 798, 842

New Way of Knowing Things = Telegraph

New Way Old Debts to pay = Sir Giles Overreach

New Way to blow up a King = Guy Fawkes

New Way to Dress an Old Dish = Harlequin turn'd Cook

New Way to get a Husband = Sexes Mismatch'd

New Way to get Married (Dibdin, T. J., 1820), IV. 302

New Way to get rid of a Wife = Bristol Tar

New Way to Keep a Place = I won't go!

New Way to Keep a Wife at Home (Oulton, W. C., 1785), III. 296

— = Letter-Writers

New Way to Obtain Consent = Florenski and Nina

New Way to pay Old Debts (Kemble, J. P., 1810), IV. 335

New Way to Pay the National Debt (1841), IV. 635

New Way to Pay your Rent = Quarter Day

New Way to play an Old Game = False Count

New Ways to Catch Hearts (Cowley, H., 1783) = More Ways than One, III. 338, 380, 403

New Wheat (1795), III. 338

New Wing (Kennedy, H. A., 1890), v. 443

New Wit for a Husband = Modern Prophets

New Woman (Grundy, S., 1894), v. 397

New Wonder (Oulton, W. C., 1784), III. 296

New World (Dawson, F., 1893), v. 339

— (France, E. S., 1880), v. 372

— (Young, H., 1861), v. 825

New World (1801), IV. 511

— = Devil's Mine

New Year (Clarence, R., 1899), v. 311

New Year's Chimes (Shirley, A., 1890), v. 564

New Year's Eve (Lindo, F., 1894), v. 460

— (1861), v. 724

— (1873), v. 724

— = Hogmanay

New Year's Gift (Barrymore, W., 1830), IV. 511, 635

— = Old Customs

New Year's Gifts = Up to Snuff

New York Divorce (Clarke, W., 1895), v. 313

New York Politics (Aikin, J., 1890), v. 236

Next Department (1899), v. 724

Next Door (Wigan, A. S., 1845), IV. 511, 635

— (1897), v. 724

Next Door Neighbours (Inchbald, Mrs E., 1791), III. 118, 144, 275, 388

— (1822), IV. 511

Next of Kin (Falconer, E., 1860), v. 121, 360, 790

— (Overton, R., 1887), v. 509

— = (1) Day of Disasters; (2) Foundling of Fortune

Next Please (1892), v. 725

Next Year's Morning (1899), v. 725

Nibelungen Treasure (1847), IV. 511

Nicandra (Vaun, R., 1898), v. 607

Nice Boy, Jim! (Drinkwater, A. E., 1893), v. 351

Nice Firm (Taylor, T., 1853), v. 592

Nice Girl (Thomas, W. M., 1873), v. 725, 820, 842

Nice Lady (Green, G. S., 1762), III. 265

Nice Mince Pie (1868), v. 725

Nice Quiet Day (Hipkins, T. H. and Murray, G., 1861), v. 422

Nicette (Rose, E., 1879), v. 550

Nice Young Ladies (Stirling, E., 1843), IV. 407

Nicholas Dunks (Lee, N., 1843), IV. 594

Nicholas Flam (Buckstone, J. B., 1833), IV. 274

Nicholas Mendoza (Bromley, F., 1829), IV, 511, 635

Nicholas Nickleby (Halliday, A., 1875), v. 401
— (Stirling, E., 1838), IV. 97, 406
— (1875), v. 725
— (1876), v. 725
— (1885), v. 725
Nicholas Nickleby and Poor Smike (Moncrieff, W. T., 1839), IV. 97, 511, 635
Nicholson's Niece (Bell, Mrs H., 1892), v. 255
Nick Carter = Hue and Cry
Nick of the Woods (Davis, A., 1855), v. 787
— (Medina, L. H. and Haines, J. T., 1839), IV. 323, 365, 587, 598
— (1841), IV. 511
— (1844), IV. 511
Nick of Time (Colville, Sir H., 1896), v. 319
Nicksey (1880), v. 725
Nicodemus in Despair (Craven, E., 1803), IV, 285
Nicolete (Ferris, E. and Stewart, A., 1899), v. 365
Nicomede (Dancer, J., 1671), I. 98, 400
Niewgemaakten Adelman = New-made Nobleman
Nigel (Pocock, I., 1823), IV. 93, 384
Nigger Life in London = Uncle Tom's Crib
Nigger's New Place = Lost Son Found
Nigger's Opera (1861), v. 725
Nigg's Affinity (1896), v. 725
Night (Douglass, J. T., 1863), v. 725, 788, 842
Night-Adventurers = Squire Oldsapp
Night after the Battle (1823), IV. 511
— = (1) Duke's Coat; (2) Wellington
Night after Waterloo = Duke's Coat
Night and Day (1868), v. 725
Night and Morn (Falconer, E., 1864), v. 360
Night and Morning (Boucicault, D., 1871), v. 269
— (Brougham, J., 1855), v. 280
— (Dillon, C., 1844), IV. 581
Night at an Inn = Three Beggars
Night at Dover = Twelve Precisely
Night at Notting Hill (Harrington, N. H. and Yates, E., 1857), v. 404
Night at Sea = Fun on the Bristol

Night at the Bal Masqué (1866), v. 725
Night at the Bastille (Archer, T., 1839), IV. 254 [This appears also as Night in the Bastile, IV. 511]
Night at the Casino = Early Closing
Night at the Widow's (1851), v. 725
Night before the Battle = (1) Advance Guard; (2) Duke
Night before the Wedding (1827), IV. 511
— = Deux nuits
Night Birds (Gordon, G. L. and Mackay, J., 1878), v. 385
— (Travers, W., 1859), v. 821
Night Cometh (Grogan, W. E., 1895), v. 395
Night Dancers = Wilis
Night Errand (1834), IV. 511
Night Express (Holcroft, G., 1890), v. 424
Night Guard (Pitt, C., 1868), v. 526
— = Duke and the Policeman
Night Hag (Barrymore, W., 1820), IV. 511, 635
Night in a Churchyard (1854), v. 725
Night in Fairy Land = Shakespeare's Dream
Nightingale (Melford, M., 1884), v. 484
— (Robertson, T. W., 1870), v. 546
— (1848), IV. 511, 635
Nightingale at Home (1880), v. 725
Nightingale of the Mountain = Rocco Salvioni
Nightingale's Wooing (Rushton, A. and Arlon, F., 1871), v. 553
Night in Granada (1840), IV. 511
Night in La Berlandiere = Gustave Dubarry
Night in Paris (Klein, C. H., 1896), v. 445
— (1889), v. 725
Night in Persia (1851), v. 725
Night in Spain = Matamoros
Night in the Alhambra = Captives
Night in the Bastile = Night at the Bastille
Night in the Bastille = Lady of Belleisle
Night in the Haunted Dell = Wishing Gate
Night in the Tower (1849), IV. 511
Night in Town (Sherburn, H. A., 1891), v. 563
Night in Venice = Gondolier

Night in Wales (Gardner, H., 1885), v. 376 [*See also under* Night on Snowdon]

Nightly Courier of the Air = War Balloon

Night Mail (1893), v. 725

Nightmare (1895), v. 725

Night of Excitement (1846), IV. 511

Night Off (Daly, A., 1885), v. 333

Night of Horrors (1844), IV. 511

Night of Suspense (1843), IV. 511

Night of Terror (Wyndham, Sir C. and Matthison, A., 1877), v. 634

Night of the French Revolution = Robert le Grange

+ Night on Snowdon (Gardner, H., *French*) [Apparently = Night in Wales]

Night on the Big Wheel = Ballyhooley

Night Out = Night in Paris

Night Patrol (Pocock, I., 1835), IV. 385

Night Porter (1861), v. 725

Night Rehearsal (Rede, W. L., 1835), IV. 607

Night's Adventure (Robertson, T. W., 1851), v. 546

— = (1) Black Domino; (2) Cares of Love

Night's Adventures (1819), IV. 511

Night Session (1897), v. 725

Night's Frolic (Thomas, A. and Barry, H., 1891), v. 595

— (1845), IV. 511

— = (1) Couple of Thieves; (2) Devilish Good Joke

Nightshade (Hall, K. E., 1873), v. 399

Night's Intrigue = (1) Evening Adventure; (2) Feign'd Curtizans

Night Surprise (Cromer, W. and Reed, G., 1877), v. 330

— (Law, A.), v. 450

Night's Wonders = Three Cheers for Charity

Night with Burns (1853), v. 725

Night with Punch (Peake, R. B., 1843), IV. 511, 635

Night with Shakespeare = Old House at Home

Night with the Forty Thieves = (1) Ali Baba; (2) Open Sesame

Nihilist (Towers, E. J., 1897), v. 601

Nihilists = Vera

Nihilist's Doom = Scarlet Brotherhood

Nihilists of St Petersburg = Mardo

Nimble Nymph and the Terrible Troglodyte = Xcis and Galatea

Nimble Shilling (Levey, J. C., 1877), v. 458

Nimrod (Jameson, R. W., 1848), IV. 590

Nina (Berkeley, G. M., 1787), III. 236 [By error this is said, III. 377, to have been acted at C.G.]

— (Kennion, Mrs, 1885), v. 443

— (Wolcot, J., 1787), III. 316, 398

— (1787), III. 338

+ — (8°, 1800; or, Love has turned her Head)

— (1837), IV. 511

Nina Sforza (Troughton, R. Z. S., 1841), IV. 414

Nina, the Bride of the Galley Slave (Fitzball, E., 1832), IV. 511, 635

Nincompoop (1898), v. 725

Nine Days' Queen (Buchanan, R., 1880), v. 284

Nine Days' Wonder (Aidé, H., 1875), v. 236

Nine Points of the Law (Jameson, R. F., 1818) = Poor Relations, IV. 331, 521, 590, 637

— (Taylor, T., 1859), v. 593

"1990" (Arthur, B., 1895), v. 244

Nineteenth Century (Morell, H. H. and Mouillot, F., 1894), v. 493

1934 (1834), IV. 511

Nine too many (Buckstone, J. B., 1847), v. 146, 265

Ninetta (Fitzball, E., 1830), IV. 313, 584

Ninette à la cour (1806), IV. 512

Ninety Days (1893), v. 725

'98 (Cooke, F., 1874), v. 323

— = Lord Edward

99 (Boucicault, D., 1891), v. 269

99 victimes = Petites Danaïdes

92 (Macintyre, W. T., 1892), v. 469

Ninon (Wills, W. G., 1880), v. 627, 824

Ninth Hour (1847), IV. 512

Ninth Statue (Dibdin, T. J., 1814), IV. 299

— (1833), IV. 512

— (1849), IV. 512

Niobe (Cross, J. C., 1797), III. 250

Niobe (All Smiles), (Paulton, H. and Paulton, E., 1890), v. 517

Nipkins and the Spectre Steed =
Charmed Charger

Nipped in the Bud (Hewson, J. J.,
1892), v. 420

— (Sullivan, W. C., 1883), v. 587

— = King's Gardener

Nipt in the Bud (1824), IV. 512

Nita's First (Warren, T. G., 1883), v.
615

Nitocris (Collins, C. J., 1855), v. 725,
785

— (Fitzball, E., 1855), v. 368

— (Graves, C., 1887), v. 389

Nitouche (1884), v. 725

Nixie (Burnett, Mrs F. H. and Townsend, S., 1890), v. 292

Nix, the Demon Dwarf (Conquest, G.
and Spry, H., 1872), v. 321

No (Murray, W. H., 1826), IV. 365, 601

— (Pentreath, F. G., 1881), v. 519

— (Reynolds, F., 1828), IV. 391

— (1829), IV. 512

— (1876), v. 725

No Actress (Bartlett, H., 1898), v. 252

Noah's Ark (Paulton, H., 1885), v. 517

Noah's Flood (Ecclestone, E., 1679), I.
101, 410

No Appeal (Craven, W. S., 1897), v. 329

No Assets (1898), v. 725

Noble Art (Norwood, E., 1892), v. 505

Noble Atonement (Cassilis, I. L., 1892),
v. 306

Noble Brother (Summers, W. J., 1889),
v. 587

Noble Coward (Naden, A. T., 1890), v.
501

Noble Deed (1899), v. 725

Noble Englishman (1721), II. 380, 452

Noble Englishman Rewarded = Baronet
Bit

Noble Error = Garcia

Noble Falsehood (Drew, E., 1894), v.
351

Noble Foresters (Smith, A., 1776), III.
111, 308

Noble Foundling (Trotter, T., 1813),
IV. 615

— = Seven Years' Secret

Noble Heart (Lewes, G. H., 1850), v.
458, 804

— (1848), IV. 512

Noble Hero = Heroes

Noble Ingratitude (Lower, Sir W.,
1659), I. 98, 420

Noble Lie (Geisweiler, M., 1799), III.
65, 264, 385

— (Jarman, F., 1890), v. 434

— (1799), III. 338, 403

Noble Love (Clarke, C. A. and Hewson,
J. J., 1890), v. 312

Nobleman (Cooper, Mrs E., 1736), II.
316

Noble Outlaw (1815) = Pilgrim, IV. 512,
635

Noble Peasant (Holcroft, T., 1784), III.
111, 203, 270

Noble Pedlar (Carey, G. S., 1771), III.
242

Noble Pilgrim (1791), III. 403

Noble Revenge = Debating Club

Noble Savage (Corder, F. and Corder,
Mrs F., 1885), v. 325

Noble's Daughter (1897), v. 725

Noble Shepherd = Douglas

Noble Slave (Harwood, T., 1788), III.
267

Noble Soldier (1717), II. 380

Noblesse Oblige (Bright, Mrs A., 1878),
v. 275

— = Our Family Motto

Noble Troubadour (1840), IV. 512

Noble Vagabond (Jones, H. A., 1886),
v. 439

Nobly Won (Bradley, C., 1885), v. 273

+Nobodies at Home; Somebodies
Abroad (Hallett, Mrs, 12°, 1847)

Nobody (Robinson, M., 1794), III. 302

Nobody in London (Blanchard, E. L.,
1873), v. 264

Nobody in Town (1851), v. 725

Nobody's Child (Arnold, H. T., 1868),
v. 243

— (Phillips, W., 1867), v. 523

Nobody's Claim (Lock, E. A., 1886), v.
461

Nobody's Fault (Law, A., 1882), v. 450

Nobody's Fortune (Grattan, H. P.,
1872), v. 389

Nobody's Son (1866), v. 725

Nobs and Snobs = Honour before Titles

No Cards (Gilbert, W. S., 1869), v.
379

— (Oxenford, J., 1872), v. 510

Noce du Village (Aumer, 1823), IV. 569

Noces de Flore = Zéphyr inconstant, puni et fixé

Noces de Gamache = Don Quichotte

No Coronet (Hamilton, H., 1883), v. 401

No Credit (Coffin, E., 1892), v. 316

— (Taylor, Mrs F., 1898), v. 820

No Cross, no Crown (Williams, B. and Sorrell, H., 1896), v. 624

Noctroff's Maid Whipt = Presbyterian Lash

No Cure no Pay (Rowe, H., 1797), III. 207, 303

No Dinner Yet (Rodwell, J. T. G., 1823) = Race for a Dinner, IV. 512, 635

Noe Ainslie (Grogan, W. E. and Norman, N. V., 1897), v. 395

Noemi (1859), v. 842

— = Ernestine

Noemie (Suter, W. E., 1852), v. 587

No Escape (Davies, R. C., 1888), v. 338

No Evidence (Gordon, G. L., 1886), v. 385

No. 50 (Marshall, F., 1876), v. 478

No. 5 (1899), v. 726

No Followers (Oxenford, J., 1837), IV. 367, 603

No Followers Allowed = Cook of Kennington

No Foole like ye Old Foole (1676), I. 346, 443

No Fool like an Old One = Who's to Blame

No Fools Like Wits (1721), II. 380

No. 49 (Lawrence, F., 1860), v. 726, 802, 842

No Harm Done = Tame Tigers

No Irish need apply (1854), v. 725

No Joke like a True Joke (1732), II. 380

Nologoise, King of the Parthenes (1803), IV. 512

No Magick like Love = British Enchanters

No Man's Land (Douglass, J. T., 1890), v. 349

No Matter What (1758) = Politician, III. 338, 340, 403

No Mercy (Melford, M., 1883), v. 484

Nomination Day (1873), v. 725

No Misses (1873), v. 725

No Name (Bernard, W. B., 1863), v. 259

— (Collins, W. W., 1870), v. 318, 785

— (Reeve, W., 1877), v. 540

Nondescript (Hewlings, A., 1813), IV. 325

— (1814), IV. 635

— (1857), v. 725

None but the Brave (Vane, S. and Shirley, A., 1898), v. 607

None but the Brave deserve the Fair (Webster, B. N., 1850), v. 618

None so Blind as those who won't see (Dibdin, C., 1782) = Blind Man, III. 121, 256, 382

Non-Juror (Cibber, C., 1717), II. 14, 132, 163, 189-90, 212, 312, 434; III. 115

Non-marriables = Colonel's Belle

No, no (1846), IV. 512

Non-suited (Rhoades, W. C., 1891), v. 542

Noodledom (Marshall, E., 1877), v. 478

No. 117, Arundel Street, Strand (Addison, R. A., 1860), v. 235

No One's Enemy but His Own (Murphy, A., 1763), III. 7, 119, 181, 290, 392

Noontide Branches (Field, M., 1899), v. 366

Nootka Sound (1790), III. 338

No Pain, no Gain (Cantwell, R. F., 1872), v. 302

No Peace for the Frenchman = He's Here Again

No Play this Night (1797), III. 338

No Plot without Danger (1835), IV. 512

No Prelude (Elliston, R. W., 1803), IV. 309

Nora (Lord, F., 1885), v. 463

— (1894), v. 725

Nora Creina (Stirling, E., 1848), IV. 409

Norah (Henry, R., 1897), v. 417

— (1826), IV. 512

— = Norah's Vows

Norah Creina (1858), v. 725

Norah O'Donnell (Grattan, H. P., 1840), IV. 311

Norah O'Neille (Travers, W., 1876), v. 603

Norah's Vows (Boucicault, D., 1878), v. 269

Nordisa (Corder, F., 1887), v. 325, 786

Nore Light (1834), IV. 512

Norfolk Lass (Murray, C., 1784), III. 392

Norfolk Sharp-shooter = Sure Aim
No Risk, no Gain (1862), V. 725
Norma (Draper, J. F., 1875), V. 350
— (Mildenhall, T., 1842), IV. 598
— (Planché, J. R., 1837), IV. 381
— (Richards, A. B., 1875), V. 542
Norman Conquest = Harold
Normandy Pippins (Byron, H. J., 1874), V. 298
Normandy Sisters (1860), V. 725
Norman Fiend (1820), IV. 512
Norman Invasion (Killick, J. M., 1870), V. 444
Norma Travestie (Oxberry, W. H., 1841), V. 357
No Room to Live = Nell Snooks
No Rose without a Thorn (Melford, M., 1886), V. 484
— = Beast and the Beauty
North and South (Forrest, H., 1877), V. 370
— (Francks, F. H., 1888), V. 372
— = Belgravia
North Briton (Ridgway, J., 1810), IV. 394
Northern Castle (1667), I. 444
Northern Election (1749), II. 380
Northern Feuds = Edgar
Northern Fleet (1801), IV. 512
Northern Heiress (Davys, Mrs M., 1716), II. 163–4, 317, 422
Northern Heroes (1748), II. 380, 386, 448
Northern Imp (1855), V. 725
Northern Inn (Kemble, S., 1791), III. 113, 279
Northern Lass = Northern Inn
Northern Night = Princess Tarakanoff
Northern Star = (1) Jenny Lind; (2) Star of the North
North Pole (Dibdin, C. I. M., 1821), IV. 295
— (Haines, J. T.), IV. 587
— (1818), IV. 512
North Steamer = Death of the Race-Horse
North Tower = Plots!
Northumberland (Meilan, M. A., 1771), III. 85, 287
North West Passage (+ Dibdin, C. I. M., 1820), IV. 512
Norval (Rede, W. L., 1842), IV. 390

Norwegian Wreckers = Floating Beacon
Norwich Festival (1837), IV. 512
Norwich in 1549 = Rebellion
Norwich Lass (Lindoe, 1793), III. 390
Norwood Gipsies (1777), III. 338
Nosegay of Weeds (O'Keeffe, J., 1798), III. 295
No. 17 (Leigh, A.), V. 453
No. 728 = Hurly Burly
No. 70 (1886), V. 726
No. 72 (Patmore, W. J., 1893), V. 515
No. 16 (Mitchell, W. A., 1828), IV. 599
Nos. 1, 2 and 3 (1883), V. 726
No Song, No Supper (Hoare, Prince, 1790), III. 269; IV. 140
— (1812), IV. 140, 512
No Spy = Love Conquers
Not a Bad Judge (Planché, J. R., 1848), IV. 187, 382, 605
Nota Bene (Hookham, 1816), IV. 319
Not a Formosa = Linda of Chamouni
Not a Friend in the World = Blue-eyed Witch
Not All Smoke (McDonald, B. P., 1898), V. 468
Not Alone (Lander, G. and Weldon, Mrs, 1885), V. 448
Not at all Jealous (Robertson, T. W., 1871), V. 546
Not at Home (Aidé, H., 1886), V. 236
— (Dallas, R. C., 1809), III. 253; IV. 11, 130, 288
— = Saracen's Head
Not a Word (Dove, O., 1884), V. 349
— (Kenney, J., 1835), IV. 337
Not Dead (Rousby, A., 1874), V. 552
Not Dead Yet (1863), V. 726
Not Dined Yet = No Dinner Yet
Note at hand = I'll be your Second
Note Forger (Fitzball, E., 1835), IV. 314
Note of Hand (Cumberland, R., 1774), III. 251
— (Keith, H., 1891), V. 442
Notes and Gold (Robbins, A. F., 1885), V. 544
Not false but fickle (Bright, Mrs A., 1878), V. 275
Not for Jo = Miss Maritana
Not for me! (1828), IV. 512
Not Found (Towers, E., 1870), V. 601

Not Guilty (À Beckett, G. A., 1867), v. 233

— (Phillips, W., 1869), v. 523

— (1875), v. 726, 842

— (1884), v. 726

— = Outward Bound

Nothing = Naughtology

Nothing but Nerves (1890), v. 726

Nothing like it at the Zoo (1879), v. 726

Nothing Like Luck (1824), IV. 512

Nothing Superfluous (Dibdin, C. I. M., 1829), IV. 296

— (Thompson, C. P., 1829), IV. 413

Nothing to Do! = Practical Man

Nothing to Nurse (Walcot, C. M., 1858), v. 610

Nothing to wear (Mathews, C. J., 1859), v. 726, 806, 842

Nothing Venture, nothing Win (Coyne, J. S., 1858), v. 328

No. 13 (Townsend, W. T., 1863), v. 726, 842

No Thoroughfare (Dickens, C. and Collins, W. W., 1867), v. 344, 785

— (Grossmith, G., 1869), v. 395

No Thoroughfare beyond Highbury (Hazlewood, H. C., Jr., 1868), v. 415

No. 3, Fig Tree Court, Temple = Our Clerks

Notice to Quit (Conquest, G. and Pettitt, H., 1878), v. 321

Not if I know it (Byron, H. J., 1871), v. 298

Not in Society (Henry, R., 1899), v. 418

Not in Vain (Meritt, P., 1871), v. 485

Not Invited (1820), IV. 512

Not more than I want (1830), IV. 512 [Presumably the same as Satisfied, see IV. 531]

Not on the Strength = Soldier's Wife

Notoriety (Reynolds, F., 1791), III. 132, 301

Notorious Mrs Ebbsmith (Pinero, Sir A. W., 1895), v. 182, 189, 525

Not Proven (Pettitt, H., 1880), v. 521

Notre Dame (Halliday, A., 1871), v. 401

Not Registered (Matthison, A., 1882), v. 481

Not so bad after all (Reeve, W., 1870), v. 540

Not so bad as we seem (Lytton, Baron, 1851), v. 466

Not so mad as he looks (De Frece, M., 1872), v. 341

Not such a Fool as he looks (Byron, H. J., 1868), v. 112–13, 297

— = Lovers on All Sides

Nottingham Castle (Goodyer, F. R., 1873), v. 384

Nottingham Gazette (1873), v. 726

Not to be done (Craven, H. T., 1850), v. 328

No. 20 (Albery, J. and Hatton, J., 1878), v. 238, 796

No 22A Curzon Street (Thomas, B. and Edwards, J., 1898), v. 596

Not Wholly bad (Grogan, W. E., 1893), v. 395

Not wisely but too well (Frith, W., 1898), v. 374

— = Nemesis

No. 2 (Dibdin, C. I. M., 1817), IV. 294

Not yet (Ouseley, M., 1886), v. 508

Noughts and Crosses (1868), v. 726

Noureddin (Edwards, E., 1849), IV. 309

Noureddin and the Fair Persian (1837), IV. 512

Noureddin and the Tartar Robbers (1819), IV. 512

Nourgad (Craven, E., 1803), III. 249

Nourjahad (Arnold, S. J., 1834), IV. 512, 635

Nourmahal Empress of Hindostan (Moser, J., 1808), IV. 364

Novel = She Stoops to Conquer

Novel Effects (1846), IV. 512

— = Story-Telling

Novel Expedient (Webster, B. N., 1852), v. 106, 618

Novel Reader = May and December

Novelty (Motteux, P. A., 1697), I. 144, 252, 263, 421; II. 437

— (Rede, W. L., 1836), IV. 512, 635

Novelty Fair (Taylor, T. and Smith, A. R., 1851), v. 592, 820

Novice (Dimond, W., 1837), IV. 307

Novice of St Mark's = Venoni

Novice of San Martino = Revenge

Nowadays (Barrett, W., 1889), v. 250

— (Craven, W. S., 1882), v. 329

Now in Rehearsal (1852), v. 726

No Wit like a Woman's (1769), III. 117, 338

No Wit like a Woman's = Sir Barnaby
  Whigg
No Work! No Wedding! (1824), IV. 512
Now or Never (Dance, G., 1839), IV.
  512, 635
Now's your Time, Taylors!! (1794), III.
  338
Now Taylors is your Time = Now's
  your Time, Taylors
Noyades (Peake, R. B., 1828), IV. 370
— (1829), IV. 512
Nubby the Q.C. = Fancy Ball
Nubian Captive (1857), V. 726
Nugae Antiquae et Novae = Rowley and
  Chatterton in the Shades
Number Fifty One (Callender, E. R.,
  1880), V. 300
Number Nine = Lady of Ostend
Number Ninety Nine (1882), V. 726
Number Nip (Conquest, G., 1862) =
  Spider and the Fly, V. 320, 753, 785,
  847
— (Cross, J. C., 1803), IV. 286
Number Nip and the Spirit Bride
  (Brooks, C. W. S. and Lemon, M.,
  1853), V. 277
Number One! (Buckstone, J. B., 1831),
  IV. 512, 635
Number 1 A (Talfourd, F.), V. 819
Number One round the Corner
  (Brough, W., 1854), V. 279, 842
Number Six, Duke Street (Becher, M.,
  1871), V. 254
Number Twelve (Français, J., 1886), V.
  371
Number Two (Hiller, H. C., 1890), V.
  421
Number 204 (Burnand, F. C., 1877), V.
  290
Number Two versus Number One
  (1822), IV. 512
Numpo's Courtship (1758), III. 338
Nun (1835), IV. 512
Nunkey (Wilmot, A. A., 1892), V. 628
Nunnery (Pearce, W., 1785), III. 203, 296
Nun of Florence (Sorelli, G., 1840), IV.
  612
Nun of the Bank = Lady in Black
Nun of the Black Convent = Nun
Nuns' Conclave = Punch's Politics
Nuns of Cambray = Fénelon
Nuns of Glossenbury = Maids

Nuns of Minsk (Thompson, R. H.,
  1878), V. 598
— (1877), V. 726
Nuns of St Jago = Terrible Unknown
Nuns turn'd Libertines (1730), II. 380
Nun, the Dun and the Son of a Gun =
  Robert the Devil
Nuovo Figaro (1837), IV. 513
Nuptial Benison = Fairy Favours
Nuptial Masque (1734), II. 380
Nuptial Noose (Brown, W. H., 1884), V.
  282
Nuptials (Christian, T. P., 1791), III.
  243
— (Ramsay, A., 1723), II. 350
— (Shepherd, R., 1761), III. 305
Nurse Charity (1894), V. 726
Nurse Dorothy (1855), V. 726
Nursery Comedies (Bell, Mrs H., 1892),
  V. 255
Nursery Maid Mistress (1812), IV. 513
+ Nursery Pastoral (Paxton, A.,
  French)
+ Nurseryrhymia (Paxton, A., French)
Nursey Chickweed (Williams, T. J.,
  1859), V. 625
Nut-brown Maid = Henry and Emma
Nutting Girls = Witch of the Wood
Nydia, the Blind Girl of Pompeii (Fox,
  G. D., 1892), V. 371
— (1869), V. 726
Nymph of Lurleyburg (Byron, H. J.,
  1859), V. 295
Nymph of Mount Helicon (1819), IV.
  513
Nymph of Nozenaro = Competitors
Nymph of the Danube (Capel, G.,
  1882), V. 302
Nymph of the Fountain (Cross, J. C.,
  1797), III. 250
Nymph of the Grotto (Dimond, W.,
  1829), IV. 307
Nympholept = Amaranthus
Nymphs of the Forest = Marble Bride

Oak and the Bramble = Harry Carley
Oak and the Ivy (Byrne, J., 1808), IV.
  575
Oakdell Mystery (Scudamore, F. A.,
  1884) = Keep to the Right, V. 559, 702
Oakland's Mists = Bought
Oak Leaves and Emeralds (1856), V. 726

Oakmere Hold = Lost for Gold
Oaks (Burgess, Mrs Elizabeth, 1780),
 III. 240
Oakwood Hall (Lane, W., 1871), V. 448
Oath (Meade, J. A., 1887), V. 483
— (1816), IV. 513
Oath and the Hour (1860), V. 726
Oath of Freedom (1831), IV. 513
Oath of the Twelve = Captain Fire-
 brand
Oath of Vengeance = Borderer's Son
Obed Snow's Philanthropy (Newton,
 G., 1887), V. 503
Oberon (Courtney, J., 1858), V. 786
— (Dibdin, C. I. M., 1814), IV. 293
— (Macfarren, G., 1826), IV. 350
— (Planché, J. R., 1826), IV. 378
— (Sotheby, W., 1802), IV. 405
— (1826), IV. 635
— (1841), IV. 513
— (1846), IV. 513
— (1852), V. 726
Oberon and Robin Goodfellow (1832),
 IV. 425, 513
Oberon and the Charmed Horn (1832),
 IV. 513
Oberon and Titania (Dibdin, C. I. M.,
 1829), IV. 296
Oberon's Empire (1858), V. 842
Oberon's Oath (Thompson, B., 1816),
 IV. 412
— (1834), IV. 513
Obi (Fawcett, J., 1800), IV. 311
Obi Sorceress = Tuckitomba
Object of Interest (Stocqueler, J. H.,
 1845), IV. 409
Obliging a Friend (Conquest, G., 1867),
 V. 320
— (Reeve, W., 1872), V. 540
Obliging his Landlady (Hickman, C. B.),
 V. 420
Observations and Flirtation (Wigan, H.,
 1860), V. 622
Obstinate Bretons (1880), V. 726
Obstinate Family (Phelps, S., Jr., 1853),
 V. 522
Obstruction and Effect = Romeo the
 Radical and Juliet the Jingo
Occasional Attempt (1805), IV. 513
Occasional Interlude (1768), III. 338
Occasional Prelude (Colman, G., 1772),
 III. 26, 211, 246

Occasional Prelude (Cumberland, R.,
 1792), III. 252
— (Foote, S., 1767), III. 260
Ocean Birds of Prey = Pirate's Love
Ocean Born (1852), V. 726
Ocean Child = Lookout and the Rescue
Ocean Doomed (Pitt, G. D., 1846), IV.
 374
Ocean Fiend (Dibdin, C. I. M., 1807),
 IV. 292
— (Milner, H. M., 1826), IV. 513, 635
— (1828), IV. 513
Ocean Grave (1833), IV. 513
Ocean Knight (1862), V. 726
Ocean Monarch (Somerset, C. A.),
 V. 846
Ocean of Life (Haines, J. T., 1836), IV.
 322
— = Foundlings
Ocean Queen (1831), IV. 513
— (1858), V. 842
Ocean Queen and the Sleeping Beauty
 of the Deep (Lee, N., 1853), V. 452
Ocean Sylph (1840), IV. 513
Ocean Waif (Temple, G. and Le Blonde,
 H. M., 1893), V. 594
Ocean Wolf (1847), IV. 513
Oceola (Travers, W., 1864), V. 822
— (1859), V. 726
O che bocconi! (1801), IV. 513
Oconesto (Fitzball, E., 1838), IV. 315
Octavia Bragaldi (Barnes, C. M. S.,
 1844), IV. 259, 513, 570, 635
Octavian (1826), IV. 513
Octoroon (Boucicault, D., 1859), V. 86,
 88–9, 268
Octoroon Slave of Louisiana = Cora
Ocular Misfortunes (1837), IV. 513
Oculist (Bacon, P., 1757), III. 235
— (L'Estrange, L., 1894), V. 457
— (1747), II. 380
Odd Affair between Harlequin, his
 Associates and the Vintner of York =
 Trick upon Trick
Odd Fish (Dibdin, C. I. M., 1804), IV.
 291
— (Dibdin, C. I. M., 1813), IV. 293
Odd Fish at Margate (1824), IV. 513
+ Oddities (Burgess, Mrs Elizabeth,
 Canterbury, 17/8/1781)
Oddities of the Olio (1860), V. 726
Odd Lot (Gordon, W., 1864), V. 385

Oh! Susannah! (Ambient, M., Atwood, A. and Vaun, R., 1897), v. 240

Oh! These Widows! (Mortimer, J., 1889), v. 494

Oh! this Love! (Kenney, J., 1810)= Love's Mysteries, IV. 336, 592

Oh! those Babes (Clement, W., 1888), v. 314

Oh! those Girls! (Soutar, R., 1882), v. 575

Oh! What a Night! (Terriss, W., 1898), v. 595

Oh, Woman! (Hardie, F., 1895), v. 403

Oil and Vinegar (Byron, H. J., 1874), v. 298

— (Hook, T. E., 1820), IV. 328

Oil Lamp in a New Light = Aladdin the Third

Oily Collins (1861), v. 726

Oithona (1768), III. 72, 338

Ojitteway Indians = Bounce

O'Jupiter (Hall, F., 1880), v. 399

'Ωκεάνεια (Dibdin, C. I. M., 1804), IV. 42, 291

Okee Pokee Wangee Fum, how do you like your Tartar done? (Travers, W., 1861), v. 726, 821, 842

Old Abbey Ruins = England's Charter

Old Adam (Townsend, W. T., 1853), v. 602

Old Adam's Trust = Grandfather's Clock

Old Admirer (Brookfield, C. H. E., 1899), v. 277

Old and New (1892), v. 726

Old and New Regime = Love's Ordeal

Old and Young (Poole, J., 1822), IV. 386

— (1899), v. 726

Old and Young Stager (Rede, W. L., 1835), IV. 390

Old Bachelor (1830), IV. 513

— = Old Batchelour

Old Bachelor's Birthday (Harvey, F., 1873), v. 408

Old Batchelour (Congreve, W., 1693), I. 193, 199, 241–2, 357, 397; III. 114

Old Bear (Dibdin, C. I. M., 1825), IV. 296

Old Beelzebub and Harlequin (1812), IV. 513

Old Bishop's Gate (1851), v. 726

"Old Blue Lion" in Gray's Inn Lane (Wilks, T. E., 1843), IV. 421

Old Bogie (1844), IV. 513

Old Bogie of the Sea (Addison, J., 1891), v. 236

Old Booty (Mildenhall, T., 1841), IV. 598

— (1860), v. 726

Old Booty of Bishopsgate = Old Booty

Old Boys and the New (Lewis, H. M., 1888), v. 459

Old Bridge of the Isle of Luis = Dead Guest

Old Bureau (Paull, H. M., 1891), v. 516

Old Chapel Ruins = Rose Lendin

Old Chateau (Coyne, J. S., 1854), v. 327

— (1831), IV. 513

Old Cherry Tree (Hazlewood, C. H., 1866), v. 726, 796, 842

Old Christmas Eve = Regicide

Old Chums (Byron, H. J., 1876), v. 298

— (1884), v. 726

+ Old Church Porch; or, John Anderson My Jo (Dillon, C.; C.L. 1841)

Old Church Walls (1852), v. 726

Old City Manners (Lennox, C., 1775), III. 113, 281

Old Clay Pipe (Avondale, J. H., 1878), v. 246

— (Henderson, J., 1883), v. 416

Old Clo' (Mackay, C., 1894), v. 469

Old Clo Man (Mendez, C., 1897), v. 806

Old Clothesman (Holcroft, T., 1799), III. 271

Old Coat (1897), v. 726

Old Coat with a New Lining = Jilted

Old Commodore (1864), v. 726

Old Corporal's Story = Soldier's Legacy

Old Cronies (Smith, S. T., 1880), v. 573

Old Curiosity Shop (Dickens, C., Jr., 1884), v. 344

+ — (Lander, G. (York, 14/5/1877), Dicks)

— (Mackay, J. and Lennard, H., 1881), v. 803

— (Sidney, W., 1871), v. 566

— (Stirling, E., 1840), IV. 97, 407

— (1892), v. 726

— = Nell

Old Customs (Beazley, S., Jr., 1816), IV. 263, 571

Old Daddy Longlegs and Sir Regent Circus (Hazlewood, C. H. and Johnson, D., 1865), v. 727, 796, 800, 842

Old Dame Trot (Allen, O., 1884), v. 239
— (1883), v. 727
Old Dame Trot and her Comical Cat (1864), v. 727
Old Debauchees (Fielding, H., 1732), II. 158, 325
Old England for Ever! (McLaren, A., 1799), III. 284
Old England's Curse = Drop by Drop
Old English Baron (1821), IV. 513
Old English Gentleman (1841), IV. 513
— = Sir Roger de Coverley
Olden Time = (1) Dacre of the South; (2) Henri Quatre
Olden Times (Bain, D., 1841), IV. 258
Oldest Inhabitant (1850), v. 727
Old Fairy of the Woods (1756), III. 403
Old Family Legend = Oliver the Outlaw
Old Farm House on the Common = Kennyngton Crosse
Old Father Thames (Pitt, G. D., 1850), v. 526
Old Father Time (Shute, E. A., 1889), v. 565
— (1847), IV. 513
Old Ferry House (Kingdom, J. M., 1850), v. 444
Old Fidelity = Mysteries of Callow Abbey
Old Figure = No. 2
Old Finsbury (Wilkins, J. H., 1860), v. 823
Old Flame (Blackmore, W. T., 1882), v. 262
Old Flames (Maltby, A., 1884), v. 473
Old Fleet Prison (Cooper, F. F., 1845), IV. 283
Old Folks (Paul, H. M., 1867), v. 516
— (1864), v. 727
Old Folks at Home = March Winds and April Showers
Old Fools (Dibdin, C. I. M., 1800), IV. 290
Old Fools will be medling = Win her and Take her
Old Fool worse than any = He wou'd if he Cou'd
Old Forge (Osborne, C., 1872), v. 508
— (1890), v. 727
Old Fox Caught at Last (1740), II. 367
Old Fox Inn (Hazlewood, C. H., 1875), v. 415

Old Friends (Atkyns, S., 1847), IV. 257
— (Greville, Lady V., 1890), v. 394
— (1890), v. 727
Old Gamul (Newbigging, T., 1892), v. 502
Old Garden (Davies, H., 1895), v. 338
Old Gentleman (Webster, B. N., 1832), IV. 417
Old Gooseberry (Williams, T. J., 1869), v. 626
Old Gossett = Going it
Old Graspall outwitted (1790), III. 338
Old Grimey (Murdoch, J. M., 1872), v. 499
Old Guard (Boucicault, D., 1843), IV. 269
— (Farnie, H. B., 1887), v. 363
Old Harlequin's Fireside (1804), IV. 513
Old Heads and Young Hearts (Boucicault, D., 1844), IV. 270
Old Heads on Young Shoulders (Moncrieff, W. T., 1830), IV. 360 [This is evidently a revised version of Home for the Holidays]
Old Home (Buchanan, R., 1889), v. 285
Old Honesty (Morton, J. M., 1848), IV. 363
Old Horse Pistol = Little Strawbonnet-maker
Old House at Home (Coyne, J. S., 1847) = This House to be Sold, IV. 285, 514
— (1860), v. 727
Old House in the City = Bill-Sticker
Old House in the West = Cead Mille Failthe
Old House of Paris = Partners
Old House on Thames Street (Kingdom, J. M., 1861), v. 444
Old House on the Bridge of Notre Dame (Suter, W. E.), v. 819
Old House on the Thames (1849), IV. 514
Old Hulk = Exiles of France
Old Husbands and Young Wives (Seed, H., 1868), v. 560
Old Interest (1753), III. 338
Old Ireland's Shamrock has not withered yet = Shingawn
Old Isaak Walton (Greenwood, T. L., 1858) = Harlequin and Old Isaac Walton, v. 727, 842

Old Mother Goose and the Golden Eggs (Burnot, W., 1882), v. 293

Old Mother Hubbard (1880), v. 727

Old Mother Hubbard and her Dog (1833), IV. 514

Old Mother Hubbard and her Wonderful Dog, Mother Shipton and her Comical Cat, Jack and Jill, and the Extraordinary Adventures of Master Tommy Tucker and Little Miss Muffet (1871), v. 727

Old Mother Hubbard (Doyle, T. F., 1889), v. 789

Old Nick (Dibdin, T. J., 1822), IV. 304, 581

Old Oak Chest (Scott, J. M., 1816), IV. 397

Old Oak Tree (Raymond, R. J., 1835), IV. 389

— = Criminal

Old Offender (Planché, J. R., 1859), v. 527

Old Old Story (Marchant, F., 1868), v. 475

Old One Caught in a Trick = Harlequin Scapin

Old One in Danger of being Dissected = French Doctor Outwitted

Old Ones and Young Ones (Dibdin, T. J., 1829), IV. 305

Old Pals (Clarance, L., 1884), v. 311

— (Mackersy, W. A.), v. 471

Old Parr (Lemon, M., 1843), IV. 344, 595

Old Parr and the Magic Pills (Pitt, G. D., 1848), IV. 375

Old Partners (1880), v. 727

Old Phil Hardy (Conquest, G., 1863), v. 727, 842

Old Phil's Birthday (Wooler, J. P., 1862), v. 632, 824

+ Old Poz (Edgeworth, Maria; printed in *Juvenile Plays for Home Performance* (French))

Old Promise (Crozier, C., 1898), v. 331

Old Quizzes (Hall, R., 1797), III. 266

Old Ragshop (Marchant, F., 1869), v. 475

Old Regimentals (Bernard, W. B., 1831), IV. 265

Old Robin and his Niece = Deceiver

Old Roscius (McLaren, A., 1805), IV. 351

Old Rugg's Words = Billy Duck

+ Old Sadler's Ghost; or, The Wells in the Days of Queen Bess (Dibdin, C. I. M.; S.W., 1802)

Old Sailors (Byron, H. J., 1874), v. 113, 298

Old St Paul's (1841), IV. 514

— (1859), v. 727

— = Midnight, the Thirteenth Chime

Old Salt (Besemeres, J., 1868), v. 260

Old Sarah (Greenbank, H., 1897), v. 392

Old Sarum (Hough, A. J., 1868), v. 798

Old Scapegoat (Fryers, A., 1884), v. 374

Old School (1846), IV. 514

Old School and the New (1852), v. 727

Old School-fellow = All's Right

Old Score (Gilbert, W. S., 1869), v. 379

Old Servants in New Places = Nosegay of Weeds

Old Shadow (1857), v. 727

Old Sinners (Mortimer, J., 1886), v. 494

Old Soldier (Lemon, M., 1845), IV. 344

— (1810), IV. 514

— = Shepherd of Derwent Vale

Old Soldiers (Byron, H. J., 1873), v. 113, 298

Old Song (Wills, F. and King, A. F., 1894), v. 627

Old Spoons (Smale, Mrs T. E., 1899), v. 571

Old Sport (Rimington, C. and Pryce-Clairemont, J., 1893), v. 543

Old Spanish Guinea = Kate of Dover

Old Steady (Murdoch, J. M., 1881), v. 499

Old Story (Byron, H. J., 1861), v. 296

— (1881), v. 727

Old Strike a Light (1833), IV. 514

Old Swansea Castle (Jones, D. H., 1858), v. 800

Old Swiss Church (1849), IV. 514

Old Times (1878), v. 727

— (1890), v. 727

Old Times and New Times = Wig Reforms

Old Times in Virginia = Yankee Pedlar

Old Toll House (Hazlewood, C. H., 1861), v. 727, 796, 842

— (1845), IV. 514

Old Troop (Lacy, J., 1663), I. 52, 212, 418

Old Trusty (Gordon, W., 1861), v. 385

Old Turtles (1819), IV. 514

On and Off the Stage = Woodleigh

On an Island (Jones, J. W., 1879), v. 153, 440

On an old Harpsichord (1897), v. 728

On Bail (Gilbert, W. S., 1877), v. 380

On Board the Mars (1830), IV. 514

On Business (Desprez, F., 1880), v. 343

Once Again (Broughton, F. W. and Browne, G. W., 1884), v. 281

— (Cuthbert, E., 1879), v. 331

Once a Lover, Always a Lover = She-Gallants

Once a Week (Wilmot, A. A. and Harrison, 1881), v. 628

Once in a Century (À Beckett, G. A. and Bligh, V., 1877), v. 234

Once in a Hundred Years = Night's Frolic

Once too often (Glover H., 1862), v. 728, 793, 842

Once upon a Time (Goodyer, F. R., 1868), v. 384

— (Parker, L. N. and Tree, Sir H. B., 1894), v. 513

— (Russell, E. H. and Furnival, H., 1889), v. 553

Once upon a time there were two kings (Planché, J. R., 1853), v. 527

On 'Change (Lawrence, E., 1885), v. 451

— (1867), v. 728

On Chesil Beach (1894), v. 728

On Condition (Reece, R., 1882), v. 539

Ondine (Fitzball, E., 1843), IV. 83, 316

— (Stirling, E., 1843), IV. 613

— (1843), IV. 514

On Distant Shores (Burnot, W. and Bruce, H. P., 1897), v. 293

On Duty (1845), IV. 514

One and All (Jodrell, R. P., 1787), III. 277

One and Twenty (Dibdin, T. J., 1828), IV. 305

One Bird in the Hand is worth Two in the Bush (1803), IV. 514

One Black Spot (Hazlewood, C. H., 1870), v. 414

One Coat and Two Bodies = Lancers

One Crime (Townsend, W. T., 1839), IV. 414

— = Strange but True

One False Step (Mackay, W. J., 1893), v. 470

One False Step (Travers, W., 1874), v. 603

— (1873), v. 728

— = Guilty Mother

One Fault (Moncrieff, W. T., 1833), IV. 360, 600

— (Selby, C., 1831), IV. 84, 397

— (Warren, E. and Elliott, C., 1885), v. 614

One Fool makes many (1807), IV. 515

One Foot by Land and One Foot by Sea (Male, G., 1811), IV. 515, 635

One for Another = My Landlady's Gown

One for his Nob (Manuel, E., 1874), v. 475

One Good Turn deserves another (Morton, J. M., 1862), v. 496

— = (1) Rival Tars; (2) Rob the Ranter

One Half Hour (Norman, G. T., 1892), v. 505

One-handed Monk = Manfredoni

One Hour (Bayly, T. H., 1836), IV. 263, 571

One Hour from Humphrey's Clock = Old Curiosity Shop

One Hour with Napoleon (Webb, C., 1844) = Hour with Napoleon, IV. 480, 515, 635

£150,000 (Ebsworth, J., 1854), v. 353

102 (Milner, H. M., 1827), IV. 357

— (1834), IV. 515

One Hundred Battle Steeds (1836), IV. 515

One Hundred Cuirassiers (Phillips, R., 1859), v. 728, 810, 842

£100 a Side (Brown, J. R., 1881), v. 282

£100 Note (Peake, R. B., 1827), IV. 370

£100 Reward (1879). v. 728

One Hundred Pounds Reward—A Child Lost (1865), v. 728

One Hundred Years Hence = 1934

One Hundred Years Old (1875), v. 728

One Law for Man (Brookfield, C. H. E., 1899), v. 277

One More (1899), v. 729

One Night at Margate (1828), IV. 515

One O'Clock (Lewis, M. G., 1811), IV. 346

— (1848), IV. 515

One O'Clock=(1) Robber's Wife; (2) Wood Demon

One of Our Girls (Howard, B., 1885), v. 428

One of the Best (Hicks, Sir S. and Edwardes, G., 1895), v. 420

One of the Boys (Summers, W., 1896), v. 587

— =On the Move

One of the Bravest (1895), v. 728

One of the Family (Capel, G. and Benton, F., 1898), v. 302

— =Turtle Doves

One of the Girls (Darnley, J. H. and Dallas, J., 1896), v. 337

One of Them (Chambers, C. H., 1886), v. 205, 307

One of Us (Melford, M., 1884), v. 484

+One of You Must Marry (n.d., *French*)

One Rake in a Thousand (1783), III. 338, 403

One Shade Deeper (1863), v. 728

+One Snowy Night (Ware, J. R., *Dicks*)

One Step from the King's Highway (1885), v. 728

One Summer Afternoon (1894), v. 728

One Summer's Day (Esmond, H. V., 1897), v. 359

One Summer's Night (Broughton, F. W., 1882), v. 281

One Thousand Napoleons (Campbell, A. V., 1862), v. 728, 783, 842

£1000 Reward (Cordyce, and Roberts, G., 1892), v. 325

One Thousand Seven Hundred and Seventy Three=Charlotte

One too many (Burnand, F. C., 1874), v. 290

— (Ryan, D. L., 1836), IV. 396 [where wrongly ascribed to M. D. Ryan]

One too many for him (Williams, T. J., 1868), v. 625

One Touch of Nature (Webster, B. N., 1859), v. 618

One Tree Hill (Craven, H. T., 1865), v. 329

One Tree Square (1865), v. 728

One True Heart (1875), v. 728

One, Two, Three, Four, Five, by Advertisement (?Reeve, J. or ?Reynolds, J. H., 1819), IV. 515, 635

One Witness (Townsend, W. T., 1850), v. 728, 821, 842

One Word (1858), v. 728

On Foreign Service (1898), v. 728

On Guard (Gilbert, W. S., 1871), v. 379

On Guy Fawkes Day (Darnley, J. H. and Bruce, H. P., 1897), v. 337

On Her Majesty's Service (Hatchman, H. W. and May, H. G., 1891), v. 409

On his Oath (Aldin, C. A., 1887), v. 238

On Lease (Dick, C., 1891), v. 344

On Leave (Horner, F., 1897), v. 427

Only a Boy (1899), v. 728

Only a Clod (Simpson, J. P., 1851), v. 567

Only a Clown=Harlequinade

Only a Common Sailor (1896), v. 728

Only a Dream (Brandon, J., 1888), v. 274

— (Forde, A. C., 1885), v. 370

— (1894), v. 728

Only a Farmer's Daughter (Barnes, E. and Levick, F., 1897), v. 249

Only a Governess (Sketchley, A., 1872), v. 571

Only a Half-penny (Oxenford, J., 1855), v. 509, 809

Only a Head (Newbound, E., 1880), v. 503

+Only a Jest (Seymour, M., *French*)

Only a Life=Ethel

Only a Model (Ramsay, C., 1892), v. 728, 812, 842

Only an Actor (1884), v. 728

— =Garrick

Only an Actress (Gratienne, Mlle, 1898), v. 388

Only a Player (Bandmann, D. E., 1873), v. 248

Only a Quaker Maid (Llewellyn, F., 1898), v. 461

Only a Scrap of Paper=Scrap of Paper

Only a Shilling and What became of it (Abel, W. H., 1872), v. 234

Only a Tramp (1880), v. 728

Only a Vagabond (1881), v. 728

Only a Waif (Clement, W., 1888), v. 314

— (1876), v. 728

Only a Woman (Daly, A., 1875), v. 333
— = Clarice
Only a Woman's Hair (Vandenhoff, H., 1873), v. 606
Only for Life (Hazlewood, C. H., 1877), v. 415
— (1874), v. 728
Only Jones (1883), v. 728
Only My Cousin (Newbound, E., 1880), v. 502
Only One (1886), v. 728
Only Six Hours More (1825), IV. 515
Only Three Years Ago (Dickinson, C. H., 1898), v. 344
Only To-night (Russell, E. H., 1888), v. 553
Only Two Common Sailors = Bill and Me
Only Way (Wills, F., 1898), v. 210, 627
On Oath = Wrexford
On Parade (Scarlett, W., 1895), v. 557
On Probation (Matthews, B. and Jessop, G. H., 1889), v. 480
On Ruin's Brink (Newbound, E., 1881), v. 503
On Service (Digges, W., 1878), v. 345
On Shannon's Shore (Cooke, F., 1895), v. 324
On Shore from the Hercules (1880), v. 728
On Strike (À Beckett, A. W., 1873), v. 233
— (Goldschmidt, A., 1894), v. 383
On the Bench (Pemberton, T. E., 1883), v. 519
On the Brain (Pleon, H., 1888), v. 528
On the Brink (Schiff, E., 1875), v. 557
[A play of this name is credited by *French* to J. T. Grein]
On the Briny (1895), v. 728
On the Cards (Thompson, A., 1868), v. 597
On the Clyde (Scott, W. S., 1875), v. 558
On the Continong (Blouet, P., 1897), v. 266
On the Frontier (Johnstone, A. L., 1891), v. 438
On the Indian Ocean (Lee, H., 1878), v. 452
On the Jury (Phillips, W., 1871), v. 523
On the March (Yardley, W., Stephenson, B. C. and Clay, C., 1896), v. 635

On the Move (Tanner, J. T., 1899), v. 591
On the Ranch (Everitt, H., 1896), v. 359
On the Rink (Burnand, F. C., 1876), v. 290
On the Road (Dowsett, E., 1894), v. 350
— = Strollers
On the Sands (Marshall, P. F., 1887), v. 478
On the Sea Shore (1891), v. 729
On the Sly (Morton, J. M., 1864), v. 496
On the Spree (1873), v. 729
On the Spur of the Moment = Spur of the Moment
On the Thames (Grain, R. C., 1883), v. 386
On the Tiles (Stirling, E., 1846), IV. 408
On the Track (Towers, E., 1877), v. 601
— (1878), v. 729
— = Vagabonds
On the Verge (France, E. S. and Dobell, F., 1888), v. 372
— (1885), v. 729
On the Wrong Tack = Anxious Time
On Thorns (Robinson, D., 1880), v. 547
On Toast (Horner, F., 1888), v. 427
On Tour (Field, W. F., 1887), v. 366
— (Mortimer, J., 1886), v. 494
— (1895), v. 729
Ony-na-Pocas (Connor, B., 1879), v. 320
On Zephyr's Wings (Hodgson, A. H. and Hodgson, A. C., 1891), v. 423
Oonagh (Falconer, E., 1866), v. 360
Oonagh of the Broken Heart = Boyne Water
Oonah of the Hills = Deoch and Durass
Oor Geordie = Our Geordie
Opal Ring (Godfrey, G. W., 1885), v. 185, 383
Open Gate (Chambers, C. H., 1887), v. 205, 307
Open House (Buckstone, J. B., 1833), IV. 274
— (Byron, H. J., 1885), v. 299
Opening Night (1814), IV. 515
Opening of London Bridge = August First
Open Sesame (À Beckett, G. A. and Lemon, M., 1844), IV. 250
— (Douglass, J. T., 1876), v. 348
— (Heathcote, A. M., 1892), v. 415

Open Sesame (1855), v. 729
Open to Correction (Brough, R. B., 1870), v. 278
Opera alluding to the Peace (Grimes, 1712), II. 333
Opera Buffers (1838), IV. 515
Opera Cloak (Powles, L. D. and Harris, Sir A., 1883), v. 530
Opera Dancer (1805), IV. 515
Opera Mad (Martell, E., 1877), v. 479
Operamania (1821), IV. 515
Opera of Operas (Haywood, Mrs E. and Hatchett, W., 1733), II. 265, 335, 438
Operator (1740), II. 380
Opiate (Birch, S., 1797) = Fast Asleep, III. 338, 378, 403
— (1824), IV. 515
Opium Eater (Hannan, C., 1894), v. 402
Opposite Neighbours (Paul, H. M., 1854), v. 516
Opposition (Henry, R., 1892), v. 418
— (1790), III. 114, 338
— (1820), IV. 515
Oppression (Thresher, E. H., 1832), IV. 614
Oppression and Reprisal = Cagliostro
Optical Delusion (O'Neil, J. R.), v. 808
O.P. Victorious (1810), IV. 515
Ora and the Red Woodman (1833), IV. 515
Oracle (Cibber, Mrs S-M., 1752), III. 198, 212, 243, 378
— (1741), II. 380
— (1805), IV. 515
— (1826), IV. 515 [This seems to be the same as The Interrupted Sacrifice, IV. 482]
— (1838), IV. 515
— (1865), v. 729, 842
Oracle of Delphi (1799), III. 338
Oracle of Gin = Fall of Bob
Orange Blossoms (Wooler, J. P., 1862), v. 632, 824
Orange Boven (Dibdin, T. J., 1813), IV. 299
— (1813), IV. 515
Orange Girl (Leslie, H. T. and Rowe, N., 1864), v. 457
Oranges and Lemons (1834), IV. 515
Oranges and Lemons, said the Bells of St Clement's (Douglass, J. T., 1867), v. 729, 788, 842

Orange Tree and the Humble Bee (Byron, H. J., 1871), v. 298
Orang Utang of Brazil = Jocko
Ora, the African Slave (1824), IV. 515
Orators (Foote, S., 1762), III. 114, 173, 260, 384
Orbis (Moser, J., 1810), IV. 364
Orchard of the King (Day, E. and Footman, M. H., 1889), v. 339
Ordeal (Wotton, T. S., 1893), v. 632
Ordeal by Touch (Lee, R., 1872), v. 453
Ordeal of the Honeymoon (Burney, E., 1899), v. 293
Order of the Bath (1898), v. 729
Order of the Day = St Patrick's Eve
Order of the Garter = Institution of the Garter
Order of the Night (Mead, T., 1873), v. 483
Orders from Head Quarters = Cornet
Ordsall Hall (Hermann, C., 1883), v. 419
Orestes (Francklin, T., 1769), III. 60, 84, 261
— (Hughes, J., 1717), II. 338
— (Theobald, L., 1731), II. 359
— (Neil, R., 1883), v. 502
— (Sotheby, W., 1802), IV. 405
— (Warren, J. L., 1871), v. 615
Orestes in Argos (Bayley, Mrs P., 1825), IV. 262, 571
Orfa (1860), v. 729
Organ Boy (1860), v. 729
+ Organ Grinder (Edgeworth, Maria: printed in *Juvenile Plays for Home Performance* (*French*))
— (Shirley, A. and Longden, C. H., 1898), v. 565
Organic Affection (Phillips, Mrs A., 1852), v. 522
Organ in the Suds = Justice Triumphant
Organist (Wilton, H. and Moss, A. B., 1887), v. 629
— = Harmony Restored
Organ of Order (1839), IV. 515
Organs of the Brain (Capadose, H., 1838), IV. 87, 279
Oriana (Albery, J., 1873), v. 155, 237
Oriental Magic (1778), III. 338
Orient Express (Burnand, F. C., 1893), v. 292
Original (Morton, J. M., 1837), IV. 362

Original A.B.C. = Arthur's Bakery Co.

Original and Rejected Theatre (1814–15), IV. 635

Original Bloomers (Phillips, A., 1851), v. 522

Origin of a British Tar = Oak and the Ivy

Origin of Doggett's Coat = Waterman of Bankside

Origin of Horn Fair = King John

Origin of Painting (1846), IV. 515

Origin of Shakespeare = Queen Elizabeth

Origin of Swiss Liberty = William Tell

Orioma, the Reclaimed (Inman, J. W., 1858), v. 432

Orlando (Humphreys, S., 1732), II. 396, 439

Orlando and Seraphina (Lathom, F., 1799, 1801), III. 280; IV. 593 [The Larpent MS. is considerably expanded]

Orlando Dando (Hood, B., 1898), v. 425

Orlando the Outcast = Profligate's Career

Ormasdes (Killigrew, Sir W., ?1664), I. 139, 416

Ormond the Unknown (1871), v. 729

Ormshead the Great (Millward, C., 1853), v. 807

Ornano (Hillis, S., 1854), v. 729, 798, 842

Oroonoko (Gentleman, F., 1760), III. 58, 264, 385

— (Hawkesworth, J., 1759), III. 58, 267, 386

— (Southerne, T., 1695), I. 154–5, 337, 433

— (1760), III. 59, 338

Oroonoko, the Royal Slave (1813), IV. 515

Orphan (Ferrar, J., 1765), III. 259

— (Otway, T., 1680), I. 20, 64, 162–3, 272, 338, 351, 352, 357, 422; II. 71

— = Deaf and Dumb

Orphan and the Outcast (Mortimer, J., 1871), v. 494

Orphan Betrayed = Unnatural Brother

Orphan Boy (1825), IV. 515

Orphan Boy of Savoy = Louis XIV

Orphan Cousins = Old Cherry Tree

Orphan Dumb Boy = Spectre Knight

Orphan Girl's Marriage = Gratitude

Orphan Heiress (Jefferson, A., 1895), v. 435

Orphan of Bermondsey = Lighterman of the Bankside

Orphan of China (Francklin, T., 1756), III. 261

— (Murphy, A., 1759), III. 18, 31, 33, 60, 71, 75, 289, 392

— (1755), III. 338, 403

Orphan of Geneva = Thérèse

Orphan of Glencoe (Parselle, J., 1851), v. 515

Orphan of Hindoostan (1831), IV. 515

Orphan of Paris (1831), IV. 515

Orphan of Peru = Vision of the Sun

Orphan of Russia (1831), IV. 515

— = Yelva

Orphan of the Alps (1823), IV. 515

— = Alberto and Lauretta

Orphan of the Frozen Sea (Stirling, E., 1856), v. 584

Orphan of the Mine (Suter, W. E., 1859), v. 729, 819, 842

Orphan of the Pyrenees (1824), IV. 515

Orphan of the Storm = Idle Apprentice

Orphan of the Streets = Ballad Girl

Orphan of Venice (Darcy, J., 1749), II. 317 [This was acted Smock Alley, Dublin, 9/3/1749]

Orphan of War (1842), IV. 515

Orphan Peeress of Greymoor Abbey = Sexton's Bird

Orphan Protected = Deaf and Dumb

Orphans (Dibdin, C. I. M., 1825), IV. 295

— (Shepherd, H., 1800), III. 305; IV. 401

— (Shirley, A., 1898), v. 565

— (1823), IV. 515

— (1862), v. 729

— (1889), v. 729

Orphan's Grave = Bloodhound

Orphan's Legacy (Faucquez, A., 1867), v. 364

— = Industry and Indolence

Orphans of Cyprus = Cherry and Fair Star

Orphans of Fleet Street = Hidden Crime

Orphans of Switzerland = White Pilgrims

Orphans of the Iron Chain = Gitana

Oughts and Crosses (Gordon, G. L., 1884), v. 385

Ought we to visit her? (Gilbert, W. S., 1874), v. 379
— (1877), v. 729

Ouida's Moths = Moths Quitoes

Our Accomplished Domestic (Dale, E., 1878), v. 332

Our Agency (Brumell, R. and Matchem, W. G., 1886), v. 284

Our Amateur Theatricals (Hilliard, H. L., 1894), v. 421

Our American Cousin (Taylor, T., 1858), v. 55, 68, 104–5, 593

Our Angels (Dabbs, G. H. R., 1891), v. 332

Ourang Outang and his Double (Oxberry, W. H., 1833), IV. 602

Our Autumn Manoeuvres (Kenney, C. L., 1871), v. 443

Our Awful Lads (Wyke, E. B., 1878), v. 633

Our Babes in the Wood (Burnand, F. C., 1877), v. 290

Our Babies (Morton, W. E., 1888), v. 497

Our Baby (1878), v. 729

Our Bachelor Friends = Tiffins

Our Bairn (Francks, F. H., 1889), v. 372

Our Beadle (1839), IV. 516

Our Bitterest Foe (Herbert, G. C., 1874), v. 148, 418, 797

Our Boarding School (Rogers, F., 1884), v. 548

Our Bonnie Prince (Chute, J. and Coleman, J., 1887), v. 310

Our Borough Election (Collier, J. W., 1847), IV. 281

Our Bottle (1847), IV. 516

Our Boys (Byron, H. J., 1875), v. 298

Our British Empire (Aldin, C. A., 1898), v. 238

Our Burlesque Baby (De Banzie, E. T., 1895), v. 340

Our Card Basket (Brooks, C. W. S., 1861), v. 277

Our Cinderella (Reece, R., 1883), v. 539

Our Clerks (Taylor, T., 1852), v. 592

Our Club (Burnand, F. C., 1878), v. 291

Our Coastguards (Worden, J., 1892), v. 632

Our Colonial Relative (1886), v. 729

Our Court (Humphrey, E. and Addison, J., 1888), v. 430

Our Cousin German (1839), IV. 516

Our Cousins (Argles, A. and Stayton, F., 1898), v. 243
— (Romer, A., 1869), v. 549

Our Daily Bread (Hazlewood, H. C., Jr., 1885), v. 415

Our Dancing Days (Byrne, J., 1801), IV. 516, 636

Our Daughters = Daughters

Our Dear Boz (1878), v. 729

Our Dear Old Home (Archer, W. J., 1868), v. 242

Our Diva (Rae, C. M., 1886), v. 532, 811

Our Doctors (Roberts, Sir R. and Mackay, J., 1891), v. 545

Our Doll's House = Our Toys

Our Domestics (Hay, F., 1867), v. 411

Our Eldorado (Scudamore, F. A., 1894), v. 559

Our Elsie (1894), v. 729

Our Emmie (Clark, M., 1892), v. 311

Our English Admirals (1854), v. 729

Our Eyes may deceive us = Mew Peerage

Our Family Dentist (1858), v. 729

Our Family Jars (1896), v. 729

Our Family Legend (Stockton, R., 1892), v. 585
— (1862), v. 729

Our Family Motto (Durant, H., 1889), v. 352

Our Farm (Rose, E., 1872), v. 549

Our Father (1897), v. 729

Our Female American Cousin (Galen, C., 1860), v. 729, 793, 843

Our First Visitors = Triple Dilemma

Our Flat (Musgrave, Mrs H., 1889), v. 500

Our Flirt (1897), v. 729

Our Flossie (Field, W. F., 1888), v. 366

Our French Lady's Maid (Morton, J. M., 1858), v. 496

Our Friends (March, M. G., 1872), v. 475
— (Righton, M., 1888), v. 543

Our Friend the Duke (Webb, C., 1848), IV. 516, 636

Our Future Fate (1823), IV. 97, 516

Our Gal (Johnson, G. D., 1856), v. 437

Our Garden (McNamara, A., 1894), v. 471

Our Geordie (Cooper, J. B., 1872), v. 324

Our Girls (Byron, H. J., 1879), v. 299

— (1898), v. 729

Our Goblins (1882), v. 729

Our Golden Wedding (1876), v. 729

Our Great Surprise (Blyth, H., 1890), v. 266

Our Greek Play (1892), v. 729

Our Guardian Angel (Burnette, C., 1895), v. 293

Our Hated Rival (Bayliff, R. L. and Bayliff, C. M. A., 1891), v. 253

Our Helen (Reece, R., 1884), v. 539

Our Hostess (Bartholeyns, A. O'D., 1897), v. 252

Our House (1842), IV. 14, 516

Our Hussars (1862), v. 729

Ourika, the Orphan of Senegal (Ebsworth, J., 1828), IV. 308

Our Irish Lodger (1840), IV. 636

Our Irish Visitors (1894), v. 729

Our Island Home (Gilbert, W. S., 1870), v. 379

Our Joan (Merivale, H. C. and Merivale, Mrs H., 1887), v. 487

Our John (Murray, P., 1899), v. 500

Our Lady of the Willow (1844), IV. 516

— (1854), v. 729

Our Lass (Stephens, W., 1886), v. 581

Our Last Rehearsal (Perry, Mrs, 1893), v. 520

Our Lodger (Blood, J. J., 1885), v. 266

Our Lodgers (Brunner, Mme, 1868), v. 284

Our Lot in Life (Hazlewood, C. H., 1862), v. 412

Our Lottie = For Charity's Sake

Our Lovers (1881), v. 729

Our Luck (Friel, C. D., 1876), v. 373

Our Mary Anne (Buckstone, J. B., 1838), IV. 275

Our M.D. (1881), v. 729

Our Mess (Grain, R. C., 1883), v. 387

Our Mutual Friend = Found Drowned

Our National Defences (?Coyne, J. S. or ?Webster, B. N., 1848), IV. 516, 577, 616

— (1852), v. 729

Our Native Home (Whitlock, C. and Sargent, J., 1892), v. 621

Our Native Land (Cross, J. C., 1803), IV. 286

Our Nelly (Craven, H. T., 1853), v. 328

Our New Governess (Brooks, C. W. S., 1845), IV. 14, 271

Our New Lady's Maid (Coape, H. C., 1852), v. 729, 784, 843

Our New Man = (1) New Groom; (2) Waiter at Cremorne

Our Nurse Dorothy (Harris, A. G., 1855), v. 729, 795, 843

Our Old House at Home (Blake, T. G., 1841), IV. 268

Our Opera (1893), v. 729

Our Own Anthony and Cleopatra (Burnand, F. C., 1873), v. 290

Our Own Correspondent (Strachan, J. S., 1871), v. 585

Our Own Hearth at Home (Wilkins, J. H., 1849), IV. 419

Our Pal (Dabbs, G. H. R., 1889), v. 332

Our Party (Lloyd, A., 1884), v. 461

Our Pet (Edwardes, C. T. M., 1873), v. 354

Our Play (Graham, R. G., 1893), v. 387

Our Pleasant Sins (Barrett, W. and Hannan, C., 1893), v. 251

Our Polly (Towers, E., 1881), v. 601

Our Private Theatricals (1894), v. 730

Our Quiet Chateau (Reece, R., 1867), v. 537

Our Regiment (Hamilton, H., 1883), v. 401

Our Relations (Jarman, F., 1891), v. 434

Our Relatives (Ellis, W., 1880), v. 357

Ours (Robertson, T. W., 1866), v. 546

Our Sailor Lad (Kirke, F. J., 1895), v. 445

Our Seamen = Scuttled Ship

Ourselves (Burnand, F. C., 1880), v. 291

— (Chambers, M., 1811), IV. 279

Our Servant Girl (Lawrence, F. and Vane, C. A., 1896), v. 451

Our Servants' Hall (Grain, R. C., 1887), v. 387

Our Silver Wedding (Willing, J., 1886), v. 626

Our Sisters (1834), IV. 516

Our Social Parlour (Lindon, E., 1892), v. 460

Our Sons and Daughters (Cooke, J. F., 1879), v. 324

Out of his Element (1831), IV. 516

Out of Luck (Stirling, E., 1839), IV. 406

Out of Place (Lemon, M., 1840), IV. 344, 516, 636

— (Reynolds, F., 1805) = Castle of Lausanne, IV. 51, 391, 439, 607

— (1826), IV. 516

— (1870), V. 730

Out of Sight (Stephenson, B. C., 1881), V. 582

Out of Sight, out of 'Erin = Conn

Out of Sight, out of Mind (Summers, K., 1894), V. 587

— (1859), V. 730

Out of Sorts (1884), V. 730

Out of Spirits = Slate Pencillings

Out of the Beaten Track (Milton, M., 1889), V. 490

Out of the Frying Pan (Graves, A. P. and Toft, P., 1872), V. 389

— (Wright, B., 1867), V. 633

Out of the Frying Pan into the Fire = Visit to the Wells

Out of the Hunt (Reece, R. and Thorpe, T., 1881), V. 539

Out of the Past (Grayle, P., 1893), V. 390

— (Nolan, H., 1898), V. 505

Out of the Rain (1847), IV. 516

Out of the Ranks (Reece, R., 1884), V. 539

Out of the Shadow-land (Stuart, M., 1899), V. 586

Out of the World (?Burnett, H. or Smith, L., 1892), V. 292, 782, 817

Out of Town (1896), V. 730

Out on the Loose (Barnett, M. and Barnett, B., 1850), V. 249

Out on the Sly (Selby, C., 1847), IV. 399

Outpost (1838), IV. 516

Outside Passenger (Brewer, G., 1811), IV. 516, 636

Outsider (Dawson, F., 1890), V. 339

Outward Bound (Ganthony, N., 1896), V. 376

— (1875), V. 730, 842, 843

Outwitted (Anderson, G., 1899), V. 240

— (Aylmer, B., 1873), V. 246

— (Praegèr, N., 1890), V. 530

— (Serle, Mrs W., 1889), V. 561

— (Smythies, W. G., 1891), V. 573

— (Vaughan, Mrs, 1871), V. 607

— (1884), V. 730

Outwitted = Woman Outwitted

Outwitted at last (Earle, 1817), IV. 308

— (1864), V. 730

Over Heads and Ears (Reece, R., 1876), V. 538

Overland Journey to Constantinople (Brough, R. B., 1854), V. 278

Overland Mail (1858), V. 730

Overland Route (Taylor, T., 1860), V. 593

Overlooker (1851), V. 730

Over-Proof (Burnand, F. C., 1878), V. 291

Over the Border (1870), V. 730

Over the Bridge = (1) Blue Baron; (2) Modern Collegians

Over the Cliff (Robbins, A. F., 1884), V. 544

Over the Garden Wall (Grundy, S., 1881), V. 396

Over the Garden Wall again (1882), V. 730

Over the Wall = Dinky Doo

Over the Water (Hook, T. E., 1820), IV. 328

Over the Way (Buckingham, L. S., 1856), V. 781

— (Meritt, P., 1878), V. 486

— (Robertson, T. W., 1893), V. 547

Overthrow of Evil Ministers = Majesty Misled

Ovingdean Grange (Cooper, F. F., 1851), V. 324

— (1863), V. 730

Owen Ivan King of Manko (1833), IV. 516

Owen, Prince of Powys (1822) = Henry I, IV. 516

Owl Sisters (Fitzball, E., 1842), IV. 316

Owner of the Works = Man of the World

Oxford Act (1733), II. 380

Oxford Agreement (Hawkins, L., 1897), V. 410

Oxford Roratory = Ragged Uproar

Oxford Scholar = (1) Brazen Nose College; (2) Frolick

Oxonian in Town (Colman, G., 1767), III. 8, 182–3, 246

Oxygen (Reece, R. and Farnie, H. B., 1877), V. 538

Ozmyn and Daraxa (Boaden, J., 1793), III. 118, 238

Paali (1823), IV. 516

Pace that Kills (Hazlewood, C. H., 1870), V. 414

Pacha = Ali Pacha

Pacha's Bridal (Lemon, M., 1836) = Pasha's Bridal, IV. 345, 517, 595

Pacha's Pets (Oxberry, W. H., 1838), IV. 367, 602, 603

Pacha's Revenge = Turkish Lovers

Packet Boat (Birch, S., 1794), III. 238

Packet from England (Tristram, W. O., 1895), V. 604

Pad (Woodbridge, R., 1793), III. 317

Paddy Bull (McLaren, A., 1811), IV. 351

Paddy Carey (1860), V. 843

Paddy Carey's Fortune = Valentine's Day

Paddy Cary, the Boy of Clogheen (Power, T., 1833), IV. 387

Paddy in the Moon = Four Kings

Paddy Miles, the Limerick Boy (Pilgrim, J., 1836), IV. 372

Paddy O'Rafferty (1811), IV. 516

— = Irishman's Fortune

Paddy's Dream = Whiskey and Water

Paddy's Ghost (1863), V. 730

Paddy shooting the Moon (1854), V. 730

Paddy's Portfolio (1854), V. 730

Paddy Whack in Italia (Lover, S., 1841), IV. 347

Padlock (Bickerstaffe, I., 1768), III. 123, 199, 237

Paetus and Arria (Burton, or Nicholson, J., 1809), IV. 277

Pagan King, the Christian Bishop and the Princely Martyrs of Eagle's Hall = Tamworth in A.D. 670

Pageant (O'Keeffe, J.), III. 294

Page from a Novel (1881), V. 730

Page from Balzac = Night Off

Page from History (1850), V. 730

Page from the Life of David Garrick (1895), V. 730

Page from Woman's History = Lady Rosabel

Page of Palermo (1837), IV. 636

Page's Escapade = Which is it?

Page's Revenge = Countess d'Argentine

Page 13 of the Black Book = Hand and Glove

Page 21 (Almar, G., 1838), IV. 253

Page 21 of an Interesting History = Page 21

Pahdre na Mouhl (1830), IV. 516

Paid in Full (Miller, St A., 1887), V. 488

— (1873), V. 730

Painless Dentistry (Becher, M., 1875), V. 254

Painter of Antwerp (1882), V. 730

Painter of Athens (Macnair, A., 1862), V. 471

Painter of Ghent (Jerrold, D. W., 1836), IV. 332

Painter of Rome (Rice, C.), V. 813

Painter of Terracina (1853), V. 730

Painter's Breakfast (Brenan, 1756), III. 239 [This was acted Smock Alley, Dublin, 2/4/1756]

Painter's Study (1841), IV. 516

— = Plots in Madrid

Paint, Poetry and Putty! = Caleb Quotem and his Wife!

Paired Off (Buckle, G., 1885), V. 286

— (Parry, J., 1833), IV. 516

Pair of Boots (1873), V. 730

Pair of Kids (Hewson, J. J., 1888), V. 420

Pair of Knickerbockers (Phillpotts, E., 1899), V. 524

Pair of Lovers (1892), V. 730

Pair of Lunatics (Walkes, W. R., 1889), V. 611

Pair of Pigeons (Stirling, E., 1857), V. 584, 818

Pair of Red Heels (1892), V. 730

Pair of Spectacles (Grundy, S., 1890), V. 206, 397

Pair of Them (Wray, P., 1879), V. 633

Pair o' Wings (Meritt, P. and Girnot, H., 1878), V. 486

Palace of Geneva (1841), IV. 516

Palace of Mirth (1778), III. 339

Palace of Mystery = Zangarotti, the Demon of the Apennines

Palace of Palermo = Heir of Villeroy

Palace of Pearl (Younge, W. and Murray, A., 1886), V. 637

Palace of Plenty = Basket-Maker

Palace of Statues = Morilda's Wand

Palace of the Silver Lake = Witch and the Owl

Palace of the Waters = Two Caliphs

Palace of Truth (Gilbert, W. S., 1870), V. 133-6, 142, 379

Paris (Croly, G., 1830), IV. 285
— (Sketchley, A., 1864), V. 570
Paris and London (Planché, J. R., 1828), IV. 36, 145, 378
Paris and Pleasure (Selby, C., 1859), V. 560, 815
Paris Drag = Delights of the Diligence
Paris Federation (1790), III. 338
Parish Beadle (1831), IV. 517
Parish Boy's Adventures = Oliver Twist
Parish Boy's Progress = (1) "Boz's" Oliver Twist; (2) Oliver Twist
Parish Clerk (Boucicault, D., 1866), V. 268
Parish Revolution (À Beckett, G. A., 1836), IV. 517, 636
Parish Waif (1866), V. 731
Parisian Romance (Cazauran, A. R., 1888), V. 731, 783, 843
Paris in an Uproar (1789), III. 54, 339
Paris in 1750 = Comfortable Lodgings
Paris in 1793 = Delicate Ground
Paris in 1792 (1856), V. 731
Paris in 1720 = Monseigneur
Paris in the Olden Time = Henri Quatre
Paris Robbers = Monseigneur
Paris's Triumph = False Triumph
Parliamentary Express = Railroad of Life
Parlour Maid (1897), V. 731
Parlours (Reece, R., 1880), V. 539
Parma Violets = Baffled
Parnasso in Festa (1734), II. 397
Parole of Honour (Serle, T. J., 1837), IV. 400, 610
Parricide (Allen, R., 1824), IV. 251, 567, 583
— (King, W., 1833), IV. 592
— (Shirley, W., 1739), II. 58, 355
— (Sterling, J., 1736), II. 357
— (1822), IV. 517
— = Battle of Agincourt
Parricide's Curse = (1) Bridge of Notre Dame; (2) Doomed Bridge
Parricide's Return = Doomed House
Parricide, the Lover and the Avenger = Swiss Girl
Parrot (1895), V. 731
Parson (Fizgerald, S. J. A., 1891), V. 369
Parson Jim (Dickinson, C. H., 1889), V. 344

Parson's Nose! (Moncrieff, W. T., 1835), IV. 143, 360, 600
Parson's Play (Battams, J. S., 1889), V. 253
Parson's Wedding (Killigrew, T., 1663), I. 299, 416
Parson Thorn (Challis, R., 1891), V. 307
Parson Wynne's Trust (Heriot, P., 1898), V. 419
Part du demon (1845), IV. 517, 636
Parted (Reeve, W., 1874), V. 540
Parted and Reunited (Hazlewood, C. H., 1872), V. 414
Parted in Crime = Vagabond
Parted on the Bridal Hour (Libby, L. J., 1888), V. 459
Parthenia (1764), III. 339
Parthian Exile (Downing, G., 1773), III. 257
Parthian Hero (Gardiner, M., 1742), II. 329 [This was acted Smock Alley, Dublin, 16/3/1742]
Partial Eclipse (1892), V. 731
Particulars of that Affair at Finchley (Coyne, J. S., 1861), V. 328
Partie de chasse d'Henri Quatre (1816), IV. 517
Parting (Fitzgerald, S. J. A., 1899), V. 369
Parting Lovers = Nancy
Parting of the Ways (Bowyer, F. and Edwardes-Sprange, W., 1890), V. 271
Partisans (Planché, J. R., 1829), IV. 378
Partition War (Pryce, R., 1889), V. 531
Partner for Life (1858), V. 731
Partners (Buchanan, R., 1888), V. 285
— (Hoare, P., 1805), IV. 326
— (1840), IV. 636
Partners for Life (Byron, H. J., 1871), V. 113–14, 298
Partners in Crime = Sons of Toil
Parts and Players (Harlowe, F., 1887), V. 404
Party at Hampton Court = Lie of the Day
Party at Montpellier = World as it Goes
Party Wall = (1) Pyramus and Thisbe; (2) Secret
Parvenu (Godfrey, G. W., 1882), V. 383
Pascal Bruno (À Beckett, G. A., 1837), IV. 250, 567
— (Fitzball, E.), IV. 317

Pascha of Pimlico (Morton, J. M., 1861), v. 496, 807
Pas de Fascination (Coyne, J. S., 1848), IV. 285
— (1855), V. 731
Pas de Pippins = Judgment of Paris
Pasha (Ellis, W. and Greenwood, P., 1899), V. 357
— (Grey, A., 1898), V. 394
Pasha of Paradise Place, Pimlico = Pascha of Pimlico
Pasha's Bridal (Lemon, M., 1836) = Pacha's Bridal, IV. 517, 636
Pa's Odd Trick (Kennedy, J. P., 1897), V. 443
Pa's Pills (Fisher, C. A., 1894), V. 367
Pasquin (Fielding, H., 1736), II. 45–6, 65, 67, 202, 232, 265, 328, 436; III. 116
Pasquin turn'd Drawcansir, Censor of Great Britain = Covent Garden Theatre
Passage in the life of Grace Darling = Humanity
Passage of the Danube = Wallachian
Passage of the Deserts (1838), IV. 517
Passage of the Red Sea = Israelites in Egypt
Passing Cloud (Bernard, W. B., 1850), IV. 266; V. 259
Passing Clouds (1854), V. 843
Passing Fancies (1867), V. 731
Passing Hour (1873), V. 731
Passing the Frontier = Marguerite's Colours
Passing through the Fire (Mead, T., 1873), V. 483
Passion (Roberts, G., 1873), V. 544
— (Stephens, W., 1873), V. 581
Passion and Pride (1853), V. 731
Passion and Principle (Wagner, L., 1883), V. 610
— (1861), V. 731
Passion and Repentance = Love's Frailties
Passionate Mistress = Vice Reclaim'd
Passion Flower = Woman and the Law
Passion Flowers (Robertson, T. W., 1868), V. 546
Passion of Life (Fuller, H., 1899), V. 375
Passion of Sappho (1718), II. 133, 380
Passions (Dibdin, C.), IV. 290

Passions (1899), V. 731
Passion's Battleground = Passing through the Fire
Passions, Love and Jealousy (1823), IV. 517
Passions of the Heart (1876), V. 731
Passion's Paradise = Seven Sins
Passion's Penalty (1884), V. 731
Passion's Peril (Faucquez, A., 1874), v. 364
Passion's Power (Shirley, A., 1886), v. 563
Passion's Slave (Stevens, J. A., 1886), V. 583
— (Stirling, E., 1851), V. 584
Passive Husband = Word for Nature
Pass of Abruzzi = Rat-Trap
Pass of Beresina = Paulina
Pass of Rathconnell = Sylvena! the Rose of Athlone
Passport (Stephenson, B. C. and Yardley, W. 1894), V. 582
Past and Present (Poole, J., 1830), IV. 387
— (1826), IV. 517
Past Four O'Clock (1829), IV. 517
Pasticcio (Arne, T. A., 1773), III. 234
Past Master (Prescott, N., 1899), v. 530
Past Midnight (1855), V. 731
Pastora = Coy Shepherdess
Pastor Fido (Clapperton, W., 1809), IV. 517, 576, 636
— (Fanshawe, Sir R., 1647), I. 138, 410–11
— (Hill, A., 1712), II. 224, 397, 438
— (Settle, E., 1676), I. 101, 118, 428
Pastor's Daughter (Phillips, F. L., 1846), IV. 372
Pastor's Fireside (1831), IV. 517
— = Vicar of Wakefield
Past, Present and Future (Lee, N., 1847), IV. 342
— (1837), IV. 517
— = (1) Scrooge the Miser's Dream; (2) Timely Warning
Past Ten O'Clock and a Rainy Night (Dibdin, T. J., 1815), IV. 299
— (1816), IV. 517
Pat (Roberts, G., Monkhouse, H. and Erwin, H., 1891), V. 545
— (1888), V. 731

Pat a Cake, Pat a Cake, Baker's Man (Douglass, J. T. and Wright, B., 1865), V. 731, 788, 824, 843
— (Lee, N., 1843), IV. 517, 636
Pat and his Potatoes (1838), IV. 517
Patchwork (Paul, H. M., 1859), V. 516
Patent of Gentility (1869), V. 731
Patent Seasons (1820), IV. 517
Paternal Affection (1828), IV. 517
Pater Noster (1898), V. 731
Pa, the Ma and the Padishah = Kissi-Kissi
Path of Life (Dearlove, W. H., 1896), V. 340
Patie and Peggie (Cibber, T., 1730), II. 250, 314, 350
Patie and Roger (1812), IV. 517
Patience (Gilbert, W. S., 1881), V. 144, 380
— (1866), V. 731
Patience the Best Remedy = Wife in the Right
Patient Carried Off = Six Physicians
Patient Griselda (1799), III. 339
Patient Grizill (?1667), I. 446
Patient Penelope (Burnand, F. C. and Williams, M., 1863), V. 288
Patient Wife = Griselda
Pat in Portugal (1837), IV. 517
Patricia in a Quandary (Hamilton, C., 1899), V. 401
Patrician and Parvenu (Poole, J., 1835), IV. 387
Patrician and Pensioners = Seaweed Hall
Patrician's Daughter (Marston, J. W., 1842), IV. 205, 353; V. 103
Patrick Hamilton (Johnston, T. P., 1882), V. 437
Patrick in Prussia (O'Keeffe, J., 1786), III. 293
Patrick's Dream (1835), IV. 517
Patrick's Return (Byrne, O., 1817), IV. 517, 636
Patrick's Vow (Franklin, J., 1873), V. 372
— (1876), V. 731
Patrick the Foreigner (1835), IV. 517
Patriot (Bain, D., 1806), IV. 517, 636
— (Code, H. B., 1811), IV. 577
— (Gildon, C., 1702), II. 22, 71, 76, 333, 437

Patriot (Hamilton, C., 1784), III. 69, 266, 386
— (Harrod, W., 1769), III. 267
— (Simpson, J., 1785), III. 31, 32, 307
— (1736), II. 380
— (1784), III. 339
— (1837), IV. 517
— (1861) V. 731
— = (1) Gustavus Vasa; (2) Martinuzzi
Patriot Father (Shoberl, F., 1830), IV. 87, 401
Patriotism! (+Baillie, 1763), III. 339
Patriot King (Bicknell, A., 1788), III. 52, 59, 87, 238
— (Dobbs, F., 1773), III. 257
— = Alfred the Great
Patriot Martyrs = Laura Dibalzo
Patriot Prince (1809), IV. 517
Patriots (1826), IV. 517
Patriot's Daughter (Stirling, E., 1872), V. 584
Patriots of 1863 = Wrongs of Poland
Patriots of Poland = Oath of Freedom
Patriot Spy (Phillips, F. L., 1859), V. 731, 810, 843
Patron (Foote, S., 1764), III. 156, 173-4, 260
— (Odell, T., 1729), II. 161, 243, 347
— (1793), III. 339
Patronage (1848), IV. 517
— (1849), IV. 517
Patron Saint (Thomas, C., 1888), V. 596
Pat's Thanksgiving (De Frece, M. 1872), V. 341
Pat's Vagaries and the Road-side Inn (1845), IV. 517
Patter versus Clatter (Mathews, C. J., 1838), IV. 354
Pat, the Irish Lancer (1888), V. 731
Patty (1872), V. 731
Paul (1852), V. 731
Paula Lazaro (Lemon, M., 1854), V. 455
Paul and Virginia (Cobb, J., 1800), III. 244-5; IV. 280, 577
— (Davey, R., 1886), V. 338
— (Degville, 1810), IV. 579
— (Neil, R., 1881), V. 502
— (Wood, A., 1870), V. 630
— (1811), IV. 517
— (1818), IV. 517
+ Paul Braintree, the Poacher (Jerrold, D.; Cob. 5/7/1831)

Pay to the Bearer—a Kiss (Gordon, W., 1868), v. 385

Peace (1877), v. 731

Peace and Quiet (Williams, T. J., 1861), v. 625

Peace at any Price (Robertson, T. W., 1856), v. 546

Peaceful War (Scotti, S. and Wagner L., 1887), v. 558

Peace in Europe (1749), II. 397

Peacemaker (1887), v. 731

Peace or War (1878), v. 731

+Peace Triumphant (Smock Alley, Dublin, 15/6/1713)

Peace with Honour = New Year

Peacock and the Crow (Parry, J., 1837), IV. 518, 636

Peacock's Feather (Dibdin, T. J., 1826), IV. 304

Peacock's Holiday (Merivale, H. C., 1874), v. 487

Peal of Belles (1863), v. 731

Pearl among Women (Leslie, H. T., 1870), v. 457

Pearl Darrell (Wilton, K., 1883), v. 629

Pearl of Chamouni (Smith, A. R., 1843), IV. 611

Pearl of Chamouny = Marie

Pearl of Cyprus (1879), v. 731

Pearl of London City = Alice Wingold

Pearl of Paris (Johnstone, J. B., 1871), v. 438

Pearl of Rouen (1852), v. 731

Pearl of Savoy = Marie de Chamouni

Pearl of Spain (1859), v. 731

Pearl of the Drowned = Madeleine

Pearl of the Harem (1842), IV. 518

Pearl of the Ocean (Selby, C., 1847), IV. 399

Pearls of the Rhine = Playing with Water

Pearl, the Peer and the Page = Good Old Queen Bess

Pearly Earl (1895), v. 732

Peasant Boy (Dimond, W., 1811), IV. 47, 306

— (1812), IV. 518

Peasant Bride (1843), IV. 518

Peasant Countess (1843), IV. 518

Peasant Girl of the Pyrenees = Valley of Andoire

Peasant Girl's Dream = Naomi

Peasant Judge (1840), IV. 518

Peasant Marchioness = Blind Father

Peasant of Lucerne (Soane, G., 1815), IV. 403

Peasant Prince = Blindness

+Peasant Queen (Keating, Miss, French)

Peasant Ruffian (1829), IV. 518

Peasant's Dream (1847), IV. 518

Peasant's Frolic (1823), IV. 518

Peasant's Pic-nic = House-warming

Peasant's Revenge = Prisoner of Toulon

Peasant's Wife = Fashionable Fallacy

Peasant Tricked = Stratagems of Harlequin

Pease Porridge Hot (1848), IV. 518

Peccadilloes = Innocent Sins

Pecheur de Portici = Masaniello

Peckham Frolic (Jerningham, E., 1799), III. 187, 277

Peck's Bad Boy (Pleon, H., 1891), v. 183, 528

— = Shop Boy

Pecksniff (Paulton, H., 1876), v. 516

Peculiar Case (Law, A., 1884), v. 450

Peculiar Family (Reed, G., 1865), v. 540

Peculiar Julia = Hunchback back again

Peculiar Position (Planché, J. R., 1837), IV. 380

Peculiar Proposals (Lowry, J. M., 1876), v. 464

Pedantic Apothecary Quizzed (1794), III. 339

Pedagogue Puzzled = Two Pupils

Pedigree (Bowring, C. C. and Court, F. H., 1889), v. 271

Pedlar (Davies, R. C., 1889), v. 338

Pedlar Boy (Harrington, R., 1862), v. 404, 795

Pedlar's Acre (Almar, G., 1831), IV. 252

— (Cross, J. C., 1804), IV. 286

— (Dibdin, T. J., 1816), IV. 300

Pedlar's Dream (1836), IV. 518

Pedlar's Pack (1832), IV. 518

Pedlar's Revenge = Life of a Shingler

Pedlar tricked (1763), III. 339

Pedlar turned Merchant = Caledonia

+Pedrarias (Wilmot, Mrs B.; 8°, 1821 (in Dramas))

Pedrillo (Johnstone, J. B., 1857), v. 438

— (1837), IV. 518

Pedrillo del Campo (1829), IV. 518

Pentheus (Amcotts, V. and Anson, W. R., 1866), v. 240

Pentlands (France, E. S., 1872), v. 372

Pentrobin (1891), v. 732

People made happy = Laoeudaimonos

People's Hero (Poole, W. H., 1889), v. 529

People's Idol (Barrett, W. and Widnell, V., 1890), v. 160-1, 250

People's Lawyer (Jones, J. S., 1856), v. 440, 847

People's William (1884), v. 732

Pepita (Tedde, M., 1886), v. 594

Pepper and Salt (1894), v. 732

Pepper's Diary (Morris, A., 1890), v. 493

Percy (More, Mrs H., 1777), III. 96, 288

— (Towne, L., 1877), v. 602

Perdita, the Royal Milkmaid (Brough, W., 1856), v. 279

Peregrinations of Pickwick (Rede, W. L., 1837), IV. 97, 390, 607

Peregrine Pickle (Reade, C., 1851), v. 536

— (1818), IV. 518

Perequillo (1855), v. 732

Perfect Confidence (1854), v. 732

Perfect Crime (Sapte, Walter, Jr., 1898), v. 556

Perfection (Bayly, T. H., 1830), IV. 262

— (1839), IV. 518

Perfect Love (Reece, R., 1871), v. 537

Perfidious Brother (Mestayer, H., 1716), II. 118, 344

— (Theobald, L., 1716), II. 71, 118, 359

Perfidious Pirate, the Modest Maiden and the Trusty Tar = Lass that loved a Sailor

Perfidious Robinson (Lawrence, W., 1882), v. 451

Perfidy (Falconer, E., 1887), v. 361

Perfidy Punished = (1) Black Knight; (2) Brave Cossack

Performers and Fashionables = Tea and Turn Out

Peri (1843), IV. 518

Periander (Tracy, J., 1731), II. 82, 111, 360

Perichole (Desprez, F., 1870), v. 732, 788, 843

— (Murray, A., 1897), v. 500, 808

Perichon (Stephens, L. E. B., 1882), v. 581

Peril (Scott, C. W. and Stephenson, B. C., 1876), v. 557

Peril of the Sea = Sam Scud

Perilous Cavern (1802), IV. 518

Perilous Pass (Campbell, A. V., 1862), v. 732, 783, 843

Perilous Pass of the Cataract = Gipsy King

Perilous Picnic (Wyke, E. B., 1879), v. 633

Perils by Land and Wave (Travers, W., 1858), v. 732, 821, 843

Perils of a Beauty = One False Step

Perils of a Bride = Wedded and Lost

Perils of a Night = Remorse

Perils of a Sailor = Mutiny of the Britannia

Perils of a Seaman = Mutiny of the Britannia

Perils of a Steam Forge = Orphan and the Outcast

Perils of Certain English Prisoners and their Treasure in Women, Children, Silver and Jewels (1858), v. 732

Perils of Crinoline (Barnett, M., 1857), v. 250

Perils of Life (McGuire, T. C., 1899), v. 469

— = Thugs of Paris

Perils of Paris (Shirley, A., 1897), v. 564

Perils of Penury = Prodigal

Perils of Pippins (Jerrold, D. W., 1836), IV. 333

Perils of the Alps = Night

Perils of the Battle and the Breeze = Yellow Admiral

Perils of the Bush = Ned Kelly

Perils of the Ocean = Fifteen Years of a British Seaman's Life

Perils of the Plague = Old St Paul's

Perils of the Road = Stand and Deliver

Peril, the Pelf and the Pearl = Sylvius

Perinet Leclerc (Almar, G., 1833), IV. 252

Peri of the Mist (Cooper, J. W., 1845), IV. 283

Peri who loved the Prince = Camaralzaman and Badoura

Perizzi (1838), IV. 518

Perjur'd Devotee (Bellamy, D., 1739), II. 143, 261, 297

Perjur'd Husband (Centlivre, Mrs S., 1700), II. 159, 166, 220–1, 303

Perjur'd Lover = Cælia

Perjured Nun (?1680), I. 444

Perjured Prince (1728), II. 380

Per-Juror (Bullock, C., 1717), II. 190, 212, 301

Perkin Warbeck (1836), IV. 518

Perla (Manuel, E., 1875), V. 475

Permit (1831), IV. 518

Perola (1883), V. 732

Perolla and Izadora (Cibber, C., 1705), II. 27, 31, 102–3, 310

Perourou, the Bellows Mender (Moncrieff, W. T., 1842), IV. 175, 361

Perouse (Fawcett, J., 1801), IV. 311

— (1846), IV. 518

Per Parcel's Post (Fox, G. D. and Morton, W. E., 1883), V. 371

Perpetual Motion (1855), V. 843

Perplex'd Couple (Molloy, C., 1715), II. 145, 157, 173, 345, 441

Perplex'd Husband (1748), II. 381

Perplex'd Lovers (Centlivre, Mrs S., 1712), II. 22, 168, 305

Perplexed Husband (Clarke, S., 1811) = Kiss, IV. 518, 636

Perplexed Lovers (1776), III. 339

Perplexities (Hull, T., 1767), III. 114, 274

Persecuted Wife = Needle of Agony

Persecution (1864), V. 732

— (1866), V. 732

— = Don Carlos

Perseus (Suter, W. E., 1864), V. 732, 843

Perseus and Andromeda (Brough, W., 1861), V. 279

— (Theobald, L., 1730), II. 137, 254, 359, 381

— (Weaver, J., 1716), II. 134, 252, 254, 319, 381, 446

— (1765), III. 339

— = (1) Deep Deep Sea; (2) Shipwreck

Perseverance (Oulton, W. C., 1789), III. 296

— (1802), IV. 518

Persian Ambassador and the Beautiful Circassian (1819), IV. 518

Persian Festival (1812), IV. 518

Persian Hero (1741), II. 452

Persian Heroine (Jodrell, R. P., 1786), III. 277

— (Jodrell, R. P., 1819), IV. 333, 590

— (Thornton, B., 1820), IV. 614

Persian Hunters (Noble, T., 1817), IV. 518, 636

Persian Prince = Loyal Brother

Persian Prince and the Moorish Boy (1836), IV. 518

Persian Princess (Theobald, L., 1708), II. 31, 78, 264, 358

Personal Adventures of David Copperfield = Born with a Caul

Personation (Dibdin, T. J., 1828), IV. 305

— (Kemble, M.-T., 1805), IV. 335

Pert (1886), V. 732

Peruvian (Naucaze, A. de, 1891), V. 501

— (1786) = Fair Peruvian, III. 32, 113, 206, 339, 403

Peruvian Boy = Zamor and Zamora

Peruvian Chief = Rolla

Peruvian Clemency = Inca

Peruvian Hero = Rolla

Peruvian Heroes (1825), IV. 519

Peruvian Lovers (1827), IV. 519

Peruvian Nuptials = Telesco and Amgahi

Peruvians (Parker, L. N., 1895), V. 513

Peruvian Virgin = Incas

Peruviens = Zulica

Pestilence of Marseilles (Moncrieff, W. T., 1829), IV. 82, 359

Pest, the Patriot and the Pippin = Tell Re-told

Pet (1855), V. 732

Pet Dove (1870), V. 732

Peter and Paul (Planché, J. R., 1821), IV. 377

— (Webster, B. N., 1842), IV. 418

Peter Bell (Buckstone, J. B., 1836), IV. 519, 636

Peter Bell the Waggoner (Buckstone, J. B., 1829), IV. 273

Peter Fin (Jones, R., 1822), IV. 334, 591

Peter Fin's Trip to Brighton = Peter Fin

Peter Jenkyns (1845), IV. 519

Peterkin (Ladislaw, W., 1893), V. 446

Peter Monk's Dream of the Marble Heart (1851), V. 732

Peter of the Castle = Pahdre na Mouhl

Phæton (Gildon, C., 1698), I. 37, 98, 158, 412

Phæton in the Suds = Tumble-Down Dick

Phanatique Play (1660), I. 444

Phantom (Baillie, J., 1836), IV. 258

— (Boucicault, D., 1862), V. 732, 779, 843

— (Collier-Edwards, H., 1888), V. 317

— = Vampire

Phantom Breakfast (Selby, C., 1846), IV. 399

Phantom Bride (Barnett, C. Z., 1830), IV. 259

Phantom Brides = Phantom Wives

Phantom Captain (Conquest, G., 1864), V. 732, 785, 843

Phantom Corporal (1847), IV. 636

Phantom Dancers (Selby, C., 1846), IV. 399

Phantom Fight (1863), V. 732

Phantom Honour = Break but not bend

Phantom King = Druid's Oak

Phantom Knights of the Charmed Bay = Skeleton Steed

Phantom Love (1867), V. 732

Phantom Lover (1860), V. 732

— = Pauline

Phantom Night Dancers = Giselle

Phantom of the Barque (1852), V. 732

Phantom of the Black Valley = Red Huntsman

Phantom of the Forest = Fountainville Abbey

Phantom of the Nile = Earthquake

Phantom of the Village = Somnambulist

Phantom of the Volcano = Old Booty

Phantoms (Conquest, G. and Shirley, A., 1894), V. 323

— (Jones, T., 1803), IV. 334

Phantom Ship (Haines, J. T., 1839), IV. 323

— (Pitt, G. D., 1839), IV. 604

— = Flying Dutchman

Phantom Voice (1838), IV. 519

Phantom Wives (Buckingham, L. S., 1857), V. 732, 781, 843

Pharaoh (Barrett, W., 1892), V. 251

— (Spink, S., 1848), IV. 612

Pharisee (Watson, T. M. and Lancaster-Wallis, E., 1890), V. 187, 616

Pharisees (Day, J. T., 1884), V. 340

Pharmacopolist = No Cure no Pay

Pharnaces (Hull, T., 1765), III. 274

Pharnaces = Revenge of Athridates

Pharo Table = Faro Table

Pheasant Shooting = Poachers and Petticoats

Phebe (Coffey, C., 1729), II. 243, 314, 375

Phèdre (Momerie, A. W., 1888), V. 490

Phenomenon in a Smock Frock (Brough, W., 1852), V. 278

Philander (Lennox, C., 1758), III. 70, 281, 390

Philander and Rose (Kemble, E., 1785), III. 339, 389, 403

Philanderer (Shaw, G. B., 1898), V. 195, 202, 562

Philandering (Beazley, S., Jr., 1824), IV. 264

Philanthropist (Jones, Capt. J., 1801), IV. 333

Philanthropy (Chandos, A., 1888), V. 307

+ — (Maurice, W. and Rice, W., French)

Philanthropy Rewarded = Nameless

Philaster (Colman, G., 1763), III. 50, 58, 245

Philémon and Baucis (Bennett, J., 1894), V. 778

Philetis and Constantia (Kirkman, F., 1673), I. 418

Philip (Aidé, H., 1874), V. 236

— (1832), IV. 519

Philip II (Holcroft, F., 1805), IV. 326

Philip and his Dog (Dibdin, C. I. M., 1816), IV. 294

— = Rinaldo the Remorseless

Philip of Anjou (1833), IV. 519

Philip of France and Marie de Meranie (Marston, J. W., 1850), V. 478

Philip of Macedon (Lewis, D., 1727), II. 64–5, 91, 341, 440

Philippe (Murray, W. H., 1838), IV. 365

Philippe del Turbillino (1863), V. 732

Philip Quarl (1840), IV. 636

Philip Quarll (Dibdin, C. I. M., 1803), IV. 291

Philip Strong (Neilson, F., 1899), V. 502

Philip the Falconer = Old Father Time

Philip van Artevelde (Taylor, Sir H., 1834), IV. 410

— (Macready, W. C., 1847), IV. 353

Philistines (1793), III. 339

Phillip II (Bliss, H. Q. C., 1849), IV. 573

Phillip IV (Pitt, G. D., 1847), IV. 375

Phillip Quarl (1861), V. 732

Phillis = Nightingale

Phillis at Court (1767), III. 339

Phillis Mayburn (Hazlewood, C. H., 1873), V. 414

Philoclea (Morgan, M., 1754), III. 49, 288

Philoctetes (Sheridan, T., 1725), II. 355, 444

— (Warren, J. L., 1871), V. 615

Philoctetes in Lemnos (Monro, T., 1795), III. 339, 392

Philodamus (Bentley, R., 1767), III. 82, 236

Philomel (Craven, H. T., 1870), V. 329

Philosophe Moderne (Craven, E., 1790), III. 249

Philosopher (?Milner, H. M., 1819), IV. 356, 599

— (1795), III. 339

— = Wheel of Fortune

Philosopher Outwitted = Too Learned by Half

Philosopher Puzzled = Family Party

Philosophers of Berlin (Bernard, W. B., 1841), IV. 266

Philosopher's Opera (Maclaurin, J.), III. 285

— (1757), III. 339

Philosopher's Stone (Taylor, T., 1850), V. 592

Philosophic Whim (Hiffernan, P., 1774), III. 268

Philosophy no Defence against Love = Solon

Philotas (Frowde, P., 1731), II. 29, 34, 70, 75, 92, 329

Philpot and Co. (1827), IV. 519

Phil's Folly (Haywell, F., 1877), V. 412

Phobus' Fix (1870), V. 733

Phoebe (Hoadly, J., 1748), II. 260, 337

Phoebe at Court (Arne, T. A., 1776), III. 200, 234

Phoebe Hersel (Eburne, W. H., 1860), V. 789

Phoebe Hersell (Johnstone, J. B., 1847), IV. 519, 636

Phœnix (Astley, P., Jr., 1802), IV. 257

Phonograph (Wood, A. C. F., 1889), V. 630

Phormio (Rant, H., ?1674), I. 425

Photograph (1861), V. 733

Photographic Fix (Hay, F., 1865), V. 411

Photographic Fog (1898), V. 733

Photographic Fright (Soden, J. E., 1881), V. 817

Photographs (1884), V. 733

Photographs and Ices (Robertson, T. W.), V. 547

Photography (1876), V. 733

Phrenological Philanthropy = Shifts of Genius

Phrenologist (Coyne, J. S., 1835), IV. 284

— (1825), IV. 636

Phrenologists (Wade, T., 1830), IV. 415

Phroso (1898), V. 733

Phunnygraph (Bowyer, F. and Sparling, H., 1894), V. 271

Phyllis (Blatchford, M., 1890), V. 265

— (Burnett, Mrs F. H., 1889), V. 292

— = Double Deception

Phyllis Thorpe (Hazlewood, C. H., 1855), V. 733, 796, 843

Physic (1888), V. 733

Physical Metamorphosis (Streeter, F., 1778), III. 310

Physician (Jones, H. A., 1897), V. 167, 440

— = Dr and Mrs Neill

Physician against his Will (?1667), I. 444

Physician's Daughter = Cruel Kindness

Physician's Wife (Webb, C., 1858), V. 733, 823, 843

— (1845), IV. 519

Physick lies a Bleeding (Brown, T., 1697), I. 394

Pia di Tolomei (Williams, T. J.), V. 824

Piccadilloes (Macfarren, G., 1831), IV. 350

Piccolino (Samuel, S., 1878), V. 815

Piccolomini (Coleridge, S. T., 1800), III. 63, 245; IV. 86, 281

— (Moir, G., 1827), IV. 86, 358

Piccolomini's (1805), IV. 86, 519

Picked up at Sea = Found at Sea

Picking up the Pieces (Sturgis, J., 1882), V. 586

Pickles (Meritt, P., 1879), V. 486

— (Mills, H. and Charles, T. W., 1894), V. 489

Picklock of Paris (1866), V. 733

Pick me up (Capper, M., 1892), v. 303

Pickpocket (Hawtrey, G. P., 1886), v. 410

Pickwick (Albery, J., 1871), v. 237, 238
— (Burnand, F. C., 1889), v. 291
— (Nantz, F. C., 1838), IV. 97, 519, 636

Pickwick Club (Stirling, E., 1837), IV. 97, 406

Pickwickians (Lacy, T. H., IV. 97, 340
— = (1) Perigrinations of Pickwick; (2) Sam Weller

Pickwickians in France = Sam Weller's Tour

Pic Nic (Rodwell, G. H., 1843), IV. 395

Picnic Party = Pic Nic

Picotee's Pledge = Lord Bateman

Picture (Miller, J., 1745), II. 145, 248, 345, 441

Picture Dealer (Reichardt, H. and Goldsworthy, A., 1892), v. 540

Picture of Paris (Bonnor, C., 1790), III. 239

Picture of St Domingo = Wicked Negro

Picturesque (Bayly, T. H., 1831), IV. 519, 571, 636

Picturesque and Beautiful (Bayly, T. H., 1842), IV. 571

Piece cut in the Green Room = Author on the Wheel

+ Pieces of Pleasantry for Private Performance during the Christmas Holidays (Planché, J. R., Dicks (1868))

Piecrust Promises = Gudgeons and Sharks

Piedmontese Alps = Devil's Bridge

Pierette (Fitzball, E., 1858), v. 368, 792

Pierre (Drayton, H., 1853), v. 350

Pierre Bertrand (Lawrance, F., 1837), IV. 519

Pierre Bonnard and his Poor Family (1823), IV. 519

Pierre Brouillard (1865), v. 733

Pierre the Foundling (Boucicault, D., 1854), v. 268

Pierrot (1854), v. 733

Pierrot in a Fix = Statue Blanche

Pierrot of the Minute (1892), v. 733

Pierrot's Dream (Byatt, H., 1893), v. 295

Pierrot's Life (Boissier, F., 1897), v. 266

Pierrot's Sacrifice = Golden Age

Pierrot (the Married Man) and Polichinello (the Gay Single Fellow) (Webster, B. N., 1847), IV. 418

Pietra (Oxenford, J., 1868), v. 510

Pietro il grande (1809), IV. 519

Pietro Wilkini (Eyles, F., 1870), v. 359

Piety in Pattens (Foote, S., 1773), III. 260

Piffardino (1882), v. 733

Piff Paff (Farnie, H. B., 1876), v. 362

Pig and the Pepper-pot (1844), IV. 519

Pigeon Fliers of Spittalfielde = Whytte-Chappelle Byrde Catchers

Pigeons and Crows (Moncrieff, W. T., 1819), IV. 358

Pigeons and Hawks (1856), v. 733

Pigeonwiddy's Perils (1854), v. 733

Pigmalion (1750), III. 339

Pigmy Revels (1772), III. 29, 339, 403

Pike O'Callaghan (Reeve, W., 1866), v. 540

Pilgrim (Kemble, J. P., 1787), III. 113, 278
— (Killigrew, T., 1663), I. 416
— (Vanbrugh, Sir J., 1700), II. 134, 150, 361, 445
— (1815) = Noble Outlaw, IV. 519, 636

Pilgrim from Palestine = Hebrew

Pilgrim of Love (Byron, H. J., 1860), v. 295

Pilgrim Prince = Religious-Rebell

Pilgrims (Harrison, W., 1701), II. 221, 334, 437
— (Jefferson, F., 1884), v. 435

Pilgrim's Progress (Collingham, G. G., 1896), v. 317

Pillars of Society (Archer, W., 1889), v. 242

Pill for Portugals (1831), IV. 519

Pill for the Doctor (1772), III. 339
— (1826), IV. 519

+ Pills of Wisdom (Heighway, W., French)

Pilot (Bernard, W. B., 1826), IV. 19, 97, 265
— (Buckstone, J. B., 1830), IV. 97, 519, 636
— (Fitzball, E., 1825), IV. 97, 313

Pilot's Son (Ebsworth, J., 1840), IV. 309
— (1851), v. 733

Pilule du Diable (1839), IV. 519

Pitman's Daughter (Springate, H. S., 1879), v. 576
Pitman's Secret = Wealth
Pit of Acheron (Bennett, J., 1795), III. 377
Pit's Mouth (Lewis, J., 1895), v. 459
Pity (Shirley, A., 1882), v. 453
Pity is akin to Love (Jerome, J. K., 1888), v. 436
Pity of it (Robertson, I., 1896), v. 545
Pity Poddlechock (Allen, O., 1881), v. 239
Pity the Poor Blind (1858), v. 733
Pity the Sorrows of a Poor Old Man (1866), v. 733
Pizarro (Buckingham, L. S., 1862), v. 286
— (Collins, C. J., 1856), v. 733, 785, 843
— (Geisweiler, C., 1800), III. 264
— (Helme, E., 1800), IV. 324
— (Heron, R., 1799), III. 64, 268, 387
— (Sheridan, R. B., 1799), III. 64, 68, 306, 396
— (Thompson, B., 1800), IV. 412
— (West, M., 1799), III. 64, 315, 398
Pizarro in Peru (Dutton, T., 1799), III. 64, 258, 383
Pizarro, the Great Tyrant (Marchant, F., 1861), v. 733, 805, 843
Pizarro, the Rolla-King Spanish Tyrant = Pizarro, the Great Tyrant
P.L. (Lemon, M., 1836), IV. 343
Place du Palais = Eugenia
Place Hunter (Webster, F., 1840), IV. 520, 637
Place Hunters (1819), IV. 520
Plagiarist Detected (McLaren, A., 1820), IV. 352
Plague (Robertson, I., 1896), v. 545
Plague and the Fire = Woman's Revenge
Plague, Fire and Water = This and the other Hand
Plague o' both your Houses (1856), v. 733
Plague of a Wanton Wife = (1) Amorous Adventure; (2) Harlequin's Contrivance
Plague of Envy = Suspicious Husband Criticized
Plague of Florence (1837), IV. 637
Plague of Marseilles (Raymond, R. J., 1828), IV. 82, 520, 637

Plague of Marseilles (1828), IV. 82, 520
Plague of Plymouth (1845), IV. 520
Plague of Riches = Farmer
Plague of the Family (1854), v. 733
Plagues of Mankind = Pandora's Box
Plaguy Good-natured Friend (1807) = Too Friendly by Half, IV. 520, 637
Plain Cook in the Strand (Stirling, E., 1852), v. 584
Plain Dealer (Bickerstaffe, I., 1765), III. 237, 377
— (Kemble, J. P., 1796), III. 279, 389
— (Wycherley, W., 1676), I. 2, 3, 14, 68, 82, 188, 191, 200, 238-40, 308, 346, 350, 439; III. 389
Plain English (Morton, T., Jr., 1869), v. 497
Plainest Man in France = Ugly Lover
Planchette (1890), v. 733
Plank across the Street (Wilks, T. E., 1848), IV. 617
Planter (Yardley, W., 1891), v. 634
Planter and his Dog (1830), IV. 520
Planters of the Vineyard (1750-1800), III. 340
Planter's Wife (1885), v. 733
Plants and Planets (Dibdin, C. I. M., 1816), IV. 294
Platonic Attachment (Phillpotts, E., 1889), v. 524
Platonic Attachments (Bernard, W. B., 1850), v. 259
Platonic Friendship (Barrie, J. M., 1898), v. 251
Platonick Lady (Centlivre, Mrs S., 1706), II. 166-7, 304
Platonic Wife (Griffith, Mrs E., 1765), III. 121, 266
Play (Robertson, T. W., 1868), v. 125, 128-9, 546
Play-Actress (Dyce-Scott, R., 1896), v. 353
Played and Lost (Wild, W. J., 1887), v. 622
Player Queen (Farren, W., 1892), v. 363
Player's Looking Glass (1751), III. 403
Play Ground and the Battle Field = Wait till I'm a Man
Playhouse hissing Hot = Damnation
Play-House to be Let = Rival Theatres
Play-House to be Lett (D'Avenant, Sir W., 1663), I. 95, 97, 186, 248, 401

Play-House to be Lett = Stage Mutineers

Play-House Wedding = City-Ramble

Playing at Loo Loo (Macdermott, G. H., 1871), v. 468

Playing at Lovers = Mrs Jollybutt's Out

Playing at Marbles = Marble Maiden

Playing First Fiddle (1850), v. 733

Playing the Game (Younge, W. and Flaxman, A. J., 1896), v. 637

Playing their Game = Found in London

Playing with Fire (Brougham, J., 1861), v. 280

Playing with Water (1862), v. 733

Play in Little (Robertson, I., 1892), v. 545

Play in the Pleasure Grounds = Actors al Fresco

Play is Over (Holcroft, T., 1804), IV. 326

Play is the Plot (Breval, J., 1718), II. 213, 266, 299, 300

Playmates (Warburton, H., 1888), v. 613

Play of Genoa = Vandyck

Play's the Thing (Drew, E., 1889), v. 350

Play without a Plot = Cat let out of the Bag

Pleasant Adventures at Brussels = Campaigners

Pleasant and merrye humor off a roge (Cavendish, W., ?1660), I. 396

Pleasant Dreams (Dance, G., 1834), IV. 288, 579

Pleasant Hour (Robbins, A. F., 1878), v. 544

Pleasant Neighbour (Planché, Mrs J. R., 1836), IV. 383

Pleasant Time of it (Buckingham, L. S., 1858), v. 733, 781, 843

Please Copy the Address (Blanchard, E. L., 1859), v. 263

Please to remember the Grotto (Oxenford, J., 1865), v. 510, 809

Pleasure (Meritt, P. and Harris, Sir A., 1887), v. 487

Pleasures of a Country Life = Haymaking

Pleasures of Anarchy (Newnham, F., 1852), v. 503

— (1809), IV. 520

Pleasures of Housekeeping and Horsekeeping = Mr Briggs

Pleasures of London = London Chimes

Pleasures of Memory = Man without a Head

Pleasures of the Town (Fielding, H., 1730), II. 323

— (1757), III. 403

— = Punch's Oratory

Plebeian (Costello, Miss, 1891), v. 325

Plebeian Daughter = Merchant's Honour

Plebeians (Derrick, J., 1886), v. 343

Pledge (Kenney, J., 1831), IV. 337

— (1847), IV. 520

Pledge of Love (1843), IV. 520

Plighted Troth (Darley, C., 1842), IV. 289, 579

Plot (Kelly, J., 1735), II. 237, 256, 340

Plot against Plot (Wilson, T., 1821), IV. 618

Plot and Counterplot (Kemble, C., 1808), IV. 334

Plot, and No Plot (Dennis, J., 1697), I. 32, 59, 337, 402; III. 114, 173

Plot and Passion (Taylor, T. and Lang, J., 1853), v. 98, 592

Plot Discover'd = Venice Preserv'd

Plot for Plot (Young, Sir C. L., 1881), v. 636

Plot of his Story (Beringer, Mrs O., 1899), v. 259

+ Plot of Potzentausend (French)

Plots (Arnold, S. J., 1810) = Bad Neighbours, IV. 255, 429, 569, 620

— (1831), IV. 520

Plots and Plans = Cloris

Plots for Petticoats (Wooler, J. P., 1849), IV. 422

Plots in Madrid (1824), IV. 520

Plots in Spain = Adventurer

Plots of Harlequin (1724), II. 381

Plot Spoil'd = Fatal Mistake

Plotters (1722), II. 448

Plotting Lovers (Shadwell, C., 1720), II. 354, 444

Plotting Managers (?1787), III. 340

Plotting Sisters = Fond Husband

Plotting Wives (Linnecar, R., 1789), III. 282

Ploughman turned Lord = Fortune's Frolic

Plowdens (Rose, E., 1892), v. 550

Pluck: A Story of £50,000 (Pettitt, H. and Harris, Sir A., 1882), v. 521

Plucky Nancy (Thompson, Mrs G. and Sinclair, K., 1889), v. 597

Plucky Parthenia (Reece, R., 1874), v. 538

Plum Pudding and Roast Beef (1853), v. 733

Plum Pudding Pantomime (Mayhew, H., 1847), IV. 520, 637

Plunder Creek (James, C. S., 1851), v. 433

Plunge in the Dark (Roberts, G., 1888), v. 545

— = Brothers

Plunger (Higgins, D. H., 1893), v. 421

— (Sapte, W., Jr. and Spencer, E., 1888), v. 556

— (1899), v. 733

Pluto (Byron, H. J., 1881), v. 299

Pluto and Proserpine (Talfourd, F., 1858) = King Pluto, v. 590, 703, 819, 838

Pluto Furens & Vinctus (Carr, W., 1669), I. 395

Pluto in London = Devil's Walk

Plutus (Theobald, L., 1715), II. 359, 444

Plutus, the God of Riches (Fielding, H. and Young, E., 1742), II. 328

Plymouth in an Uproar (Neville, E., 1779), III. 290

Poacher = Green Gosling

Poacher and his Dog (1835), IV. 520

Poacher and his Son = Little Joey

Poacher Bill (Coates, A., 1872), v. 315

Poachers (Peake, R. B., 1824) = Roebuck, IV. 369, 603

Poachers and Petticoats (Thompson, C. P., 1836) = Farmer and Pheasant, IV. 520, 614, 637

Poacher's Gun = London Carrier

Poacher's Wife (Atkyns, S., 1847), IV. 257

— (Pitt, G. D., 1847), IV. 375

Poala (1889), v. 733

Pocahontas (Barker, J. N., 1820), IV. 259

— (Brougham, J., 1855), v. 280

Pocahontas, the Great White Pearl (Grundy, S., 1884), v. 396

Poccahontas (1857), v. 733

Pocket Book (1837), IV. 520

Poddyhighs (Horncastle, J. H., 1849), IV. 328

+ Podesta (Pemberton, C. R., 8°, 1843 (in *The Life and Literary Remains*))

Poet (Broughton, F. W., 1889), v. 281

Poet and the Puppets (Brookfield, C. H. E., 1892), v. 277

Poetess (1667), I. 344, 444

— (1892), v. 734

Poetical Inventions (1835), IV. 520

Poetical Squire = Sir Hercules Buffoon

Poetic Proposal (Becher, M., 1872), v. 254

Poet in Livery = Intrigues of a Day

Poetry and Poison (1876), v. 734

Poet's Child (Hill, I., 1820), IV. 325

Poet's Dream (Beatty-Kingston, W. B., 1898), v. 444, 778, 801

Poet's Home = Romance and Reality

Poet's Revenge = Wits Led by the Nose

Poet's Slave (1850), v. 734

Poet Stutter = Wit for Money

Point at Herqui (1796), III. 339

Point at Portsmouth = Silver Tankard

Point of Honour (Kemble, C., 1800), IV. 334

— (Roberdeau, J. P., 1792), III. 302

Point of Law (Paxton, and Woodville, 1881), v. 517

Pointsman (Carton, R. C. and Raleigh, C., 1887), v. 305

Poison Doctor of Paris (Ellis, B., 1870), v. 357

Poisoned (Amcotts, V.), v. 240

Poisoned Cup (Ellis, B., 1869), v. 356

— = Chieftain's Banquet

Poisoned Goblet (1831), IV. 520

Poisoned Mask (Suter, W. E., 1864), v. 734, 819

Poisoned Pearl = (1) Half Caste; (2) Taint in the Blood

Poisoned Picalilly = Vokin's Vengeance

Poisoned Ring (1839), IV. 520

Poisoner and his Victim (1845), IV. 520

Poisoner and the Secrets of the Iron Chest = Rupert Dreadnought

Poisoner of Milan (Warren, F. B., 1898), v. 615

Poisoner of Paris = Christine

Poisoner of Venice (1860), v. 734

Poison Flower (Todhunter, J., 1891), v. 600

Poison in Jest (Suter, W. E., 1851), v. 587

Poison Tree (Clarke, S., 1809), IV. 280

— (Scott, J. M., 1811), IV. 520, 637

Poison Tree (1831), IV. 520
Polar Star (1829), IV. 520
Pole-faces and the Put-em-in-the-Cauldron Indians = Ever-so-little Bear
Pole, the Patriot and the Pippin = Tale of Tell
Policeman (Helmore, W. and Phillpotts, E., 1887), V. 416
Police Spy = Spy of the Republic
Polichinel Vampire (1828), IV. 520
Policy (Robertson, T. W., 1871), V. 546
— (Siddons, H., 1814), IV. 401
Polidus (Browne, M.,1723),II.68,84,300
Polish Jew (Emery, S., 1872), V. 358
— (Ware, J. R., 1872), V. 614
Polish Jew polished off = Mathias
Polish Patriot = Siege of Dantzig
Polish Squabble = King and No King
Polish Tyrant (1806), IV. 520
Polite Conversation (Miller, J., 1740), II. 381, 441, 448
Polite Gamester (1753), III. 340
Political Humbug = Sham Fight
Political Pair (Godbold, E. H., 1899), V. 382
Political Woman (1894), V. 734
Politician (1758) = No Matter What, III. 340, 403
— = Polititian
Politician Reformed (1774), III. 340
Politick Whore (1680), I. 443
Politic Queen, I. 388
Politics in Petticoats = Two Queens
Politics on Both Sides (1735), II. 381
Polititian (1677), I. 349, 444
Polititian Cheated (Green, A., 1663), I. 412
Polka (Barnett, C. Z., 1844), IV. 260
— (Vaun, R., 1895), V. 607
Polkamania (Stocqueler, H., 1844), IV. 520, 637
Polka, Polka, Polka (1844), IV. 520
Poll and Partner Joe (Burnand, F. C., 1871), V. 290
Poll Practice (1852), V. 734
Polly (Colman, G., 1777), III. 246
— (Gay, J., 1729), II. 22, 182, 233, 240-1, 332, 437, 447; III. 47
— (Mortimer, J., 1884), V. 494
Polly and Joe Stubbs (1876), V. 734
Polly Honeycombe (Colman, G., 1760), III. 182, 245

Polly in India = Macheath turn'd Pyrate
Polly Middles (1892), V. 734
Polly of Plympton = Constant Maid
Polly of Portsea and Joe the Marine (1831), IV. 520
Polly Plumtree = All a Mistake
Polly's Birthday (Fawcett, C. S., 1884), V. 364
Polly's Venture (Watson, T. M., 1888), V. 616
Poluscenion (1789), III. 340
Polynchinel Vampire (Dibdin, C. I. M., 1823), IV. 295
Polyphonus (Killick, J. M., 1872), V. 444
Polysceine Pasticcio = Egrirophadron
Pomona (Towers, E., 1877), V. 601
Pompadour (Wills, W. G. and Grundy, S., 1888), V. 627
Pompeii (1858), V. 734
Pompey (Philips, K., 1663), I. 98, 106, 347, 423
Pompey the Great (Waller, E., 1663), I. 98, 106, 436
Pong Wong (Mathews, C. J., 1826), IV. 354, 520, 598, 637
Ponsonby Hall (Cartwright, G. L., 1892), V. 305
Ponteach (Rogers, R., 1766), III. 303
Pool of the Four Willows = Who's to win?
Poonowing Kewang (1851), V. 734
Poor and Content (1836), IV. 520
Poor Andrew of the Tyrol = Falling Star
Poor Bess and Little Dick = Outcasts
Poor but honest (1870), V. 734
Poor Carpenter and his Family (1859), V. 734
Poor Cousin Walter (Simpson, J. P., 1850), V. 567
Poor Covent Garden (1792), III. 340
Poor Dick (1890), V. 734
Poor Dog Tray = (1) My Poor Dog Tray; (2) Omadhaun
Poor Em'ly (Ellis, B., 1870), V. 356
Poor Gentleman (Colman, G., the Younger, 1801), IV. 52, 184, 282
— (1812), IV. 520
Poor Gentlewoman (Isdell, S., 1811), IV. 330
Poor Girl (Young, Mrs H., 1863), V. 734, 843

Popish Impostor = King Henry VII

Popocatapetl (Robson, F., 1871), v. 547

Popolino (1841), IV. 521

Poppleton Court Plot = Number Two versus Number One

Poppleton's Predicaments (Rae, C. M., 1870), v. 532

Popping the Question (Buckstone, J. B., 1830), IV. 273, 521

— (1830), IV. 521

Popsey Wopsey (Grundy, S., 1880), v. 396

Popsy (Dabbs, G. H. R., 1888), v. 332

Popular Felons (Jerrold, D. W., 1826), IV. 331

Popularity (Moncrieff, W. T., 1839), IV. 521, 637

Pork Chops (Blanchard, E. L., 1843), IV. 268

Poro, Re dell' Indie (Humphreys, S., 1731), II. 397, 439

Porsenna's Invasion (1748), II. 381

Port Admiral (Bowles, T. G.), v. 271

— (1835), IV. 521 [The probability is that these entries refer to the same play]

Porter of Havre (Oxenford, J., 1875), v. 511, 809

Porter's Knot (Carton, R. C., 1892), v. 305

— (Oxenford, J., 1858), v. 509, 809

Portfolio (Kenney, J., 1816), IV. 336

Portmanteau Predicament (Bingham, F., 1881), v. 261

Port of London (Blake, T. G., 1851), v. 262

Portrait (Colman, G., 1770), III. 121, 195, 207-8, 246, 379

— (Sapte, W., Jr., 1888), v. 556

— (1784), III. 340

— = Love laughs at Locksmiths

Portrait of Cervantes (Greffulhe, 1808), IV. 321, 586

— (Hamilton, W. H., 1810), IV. 324

Portrait of Michael Cervantes = Plot and Counterplot

Portraits (1838), IV. 521

Portraits of Cervantes = Plots

Portsmouth Heiress (1704), II. 170, 381

Poses = Worship of Plutus

Positive and Negative (1899), v. 734

Positive Man (O'Keeffe, J., 1782), III. 292

Possessed = Dominique, the Resolute

Possession (Browne, G. W., 1890) v. 283

— = Nine Points of the Law

Possession Nine Points of the Law = MacCarthy More

Possible Case (1888), v. 734

Possible Exception (1873), v. 734

Postal Card (1871), v. 734

Post Boy (Craven, H. T., 1860), v. 328

Post Captain (Bosworth, J., 1838), IV. 573

— (Townsend, W. T., 1849), IV. 521, 614, 637

Post-chaise Companion (1835), IV. 521

Post-chaise of St Agnes = Wrecker of Cornwall

Posterity (Moore, A. M., 1884), v. 491

Post Haste (Robertson, T. W.), v. 547

Postheen Phewn (Grover, J. H., 1872), v. 395

Post House (1819), IV. 521

Posthumous Man = Lost Life

Postillion (À Beckett, G. A., 1837), IV. 249, 567

— (Hart, J. P., 1837), IV. 521, 637

— (1843), IV. 521, 637

Postillion of Longjumeau (1892), v. 734

Postman (Pemberton, T. E., 1892), v. 519

Postman's Knock (Thornton, L. M., 1856), v. 599

Postmaster's Wife, and the Mayor's Daughter = Diamond Arrow

Post Office Frauds (1870), v. 734

Post of Honour (Mildenhall, T., 1844), IV. 355

Post of Peril (Rede, W. L., 1848), IV. 607

Postscript (Knight, F. H., 1888), v. 445

Potentate (1898), v. 734

Pothooks (1883), v. 734

Potocatapelto (1877), v. 734

Pot of Money (Swift, J., 1881), v. 589

Potpourri (Tanner, J. T., 1899), v. 591

Poul a Dhoil (Hazlewood, C. H., 1865), v. 413

Poule aux Œufs d'or (Hall, F., 1878), v. 399

Pounds, Shillings and Pence (Thompson, Mrs G. and Sinclair, K., 1892), v. 597

Poupée (Sturgess, A., 1897), v. 586, 818

Pouter's Wedding (Morton, J. M., 1865), v. 496

Pouvoir de l'amour = Adolphe et Matilde

Poverty (Blake, T. G., 1844), IV. 268

— (De la Pasture, Mrs H.), v. 341

Poverty and Crime = Two Locksmiths

Poverty and Nobleness of Mind (Geisweiler, M., 1799), III. 65, 138, 264, 385

Poverty and Pride (Reade, C., 1857), v. 536

Poverty and Splendour = Molly Sullivan

Poverty and Temptation (1849), IV. 521

Poverty and Wealth (Wilson, C. H., 1799), III. 69, 316

Poverty, Competence and Riches = Ambition

Poverty Enobled by Virtue = True Patriotism

Poverty of Gold = Incognito

Poverty of Riches (Hendrie, E. and Wood, M., 1899), v. 417

Powder and Ball (Selby, C., 1845), IV. 399

Powder and Shot (Chandler, B., 1896), v. 307

Powder for Peeping = Curiosity Cured

Power and Principle (Barnett, M., 1850), v. 249

— = André the Miner

Power and the Glory (Darrell, C., 1898), v. 337

Powerful Party (1862), v. 734

Power of Conscience (Rutter, R. P., 1891), v. 553

Power of Drink = Del. Trem.

Power of England (Dering, C. E., 1885), v. 343

Power of Gold (Osman, W. R., 1865), v. 734, 808

— (Osman, W. R., 1870), v. 508

— (Sandford, W., 1897), v. 555

Power of Love (Lindley, H., 1888), v. 459

— (1881), v. 734

— = (1) Hercules and Omphale; (2) Satanella

Power of Magic (1783), III. 403

Power of the Heart (Davis, A., 1873), v. 338

Power of the Press (Pitou, A. and Jessop, G. H., 1896), v. 525

Power of Truth (1861), v. 734

Power of Will = Mehalah

P.P. (Parry, T., 1833), IV. 368

P.Q. (1832), IV. 521

Prabod'h Chandro'daya (Taylor), IV. 410

Practical Joker (Hulme, C. L., 1895), v. 430

Practical Jokes (1825), IV. 521

Practical Man (Bernard, W. B., 1849), IV. 266

Practice of a Modern Comic Entertainment = Monstrum Horrendum

Pragmatical Jesuit New-leven'd (Carpenter, R., ?1661), I. 395

Prairie Flower (Ellis, B. and Carlton, A., 1895), v. 357

— (1860), v. 734

Prancing Girl (Rae-Brown, C., 1891), v. 533

Pranks of Puck with the Elfin King (1844), IV. 521

Prawns and Pommery (1884), v. 734

Prayer (Child, H., 1898), v. 309

Prayer in the Storm = Thirst of Gold

Prayer of the Wrecked = Sea of Ice

Precept against Practice = Love's Frailties

Precept without Practice = Gamester Father

Preceptor (Hammond, W., 1739), II. 334

— (Warboys, T., 1777), III. 117, 315

Preciosa, the Spanish Gipsy (?Soane, G. or ?Ball, W., 1825), IV. 521, 637

— (1824), IV. 521

Preciosita (Dorisi, L., 1893), v. 347

Precious Little Crusoe (1894), v. 734

Precious Relics (1796), III. 340

Predestination = Alwyn and Bertholdy

Prediction (1844), IV. 521

— = Second Sight

Predilection (1830), IV. 521

Preference Bond (Maclaren, J. B., 1887), v. 471

Prejudice (Phillips, E., 1848) = Bachelor's Vow, IV. 372, 429, 604

— = Sons of Erin

Prejudice of Fashion (1779), III. 340

Prejudices (Cherensi, B. F., 1796), III. 243

Preludio to the Beggar's Opera (Colman, G., 1781), III. 247

Prentice (1895), v. 735

'Prentice Pillar (Eden, G., 1895), v. 353

Presbyterian Lash (Kirkman, F., 1661), I. 417

Prescription (1833), IV. 521

Presence (Cavendish, M., 1668), I. 396

Presence of Mind (Scudamore, F. A., 1881), v. 558

Presented at Court (Coyne, J. S., 1851), v. 327

Present, Past and Future = White Chateau

President (Fisher, J. M. and Turner, E., 1896), v. 367

President and the Peasant's Daughter (Dibdin, T. J., 1819), IV. 302, 581

Pressed for the Navy = Dead Reckoning

Pressed into the Service = Our Volunteers

Press Gang (Jerrold, D. W., 1830), IV. 332

— (1755), III. 340

— = Nancy

Press Gang at Billingsgate = Nancy

Pres St Gervais (Reece, R., 1874), v. 538

Preston Guild = Jubilee of 1802

Preston in the Olden Time = Cotton Famine

Presumption (Peake, R. B., 1823), IV. 369

Presumptive Evidence (Boucicault, D., 1869), v. 269

— (Buckstone, J. B., 1828), IV. 273

— = Card-Drawing

Presumptuous Love (?Taverner, W., 1716), II. 260, 358, 381

Pretence (Lawrence, S. B., 1891), v. 451

— (1896), v. 735

Pretended Puritan (Horde, T., 1779), III. 273

Pretender (Duncan, G., 1876), v. 352

— (Stafford, J. J., 1828), IV. 405

Pretenders (Dilke, T., 1698), I. 218, 403

— = Kensington-Gardens

Pretender's Flight (Philips, J., 1716), II. 348

Pretty Alice of Portsmouth (Rayner, J., 1852), v. 535

Pretty Bequest (Watson, T. M., 1885), v. 616

Pretty Blue Belle and the Ugly Beast (Hazlewood, C. H., 1860), v. 735, 796, 843

Pretty Couple (Addison, H. R., 1848), IV. 251

Pretty Druidess (Gilbert, W. S., 1869), v. 379

Pretty Esmeralda and Captain Phoebus of Ours (Byron, H. J., 1879), v. 299

Pretty Gipsey and the Bullfighter (1855), v. 735

Pretty Girl of Dundee (1802), IV. 521

Pretty Girl of Stilberg = Regiment of Tartars

Pretty Girls of Stilberg (Webster, B. N., 1842), IV. 616

— (Webster, B., 1855), v. 735, 823, 843

Pretty Horsebreaker (Brough, W. and Halliday, A., 1861), v. 279

Pretty Hunchback = Baden Baden

Pretty Milliners = Trois Fetes de Bois

Pretty Mollie (Rae, J. and Sidney, T., 1892), v. 533

Pretty Perfumeress (Byron, H. J., 1874), v. 298, 782

Pretty Piece of Business (Morton, T., Jr., 1853), v. 497

Pretty Poll (Reece, R., 1876), v. 538

Pretty Poll of Paddington (Coleman, H., 1852), v. 316

Pretty Poll of Portsea, and the Captain with his Whiskers = Mendacious Mariner

Pretty Polly = Our Polly

Pretty Polly, the Farmer's Daughter = Our Polly

Pretty Predicaments (Phipps, A. J., 1876), v. 524

Pretty Princess and the Ugly Beast = Pretty Blue Belle and the Ugly Beast

Pretty Purchase = Love the Leveller

Pretty Request (1885), v. 735

Pretty Sicilian (Blasis, 1847), IV. 521, 637

Pretty White Horn = Bold Robin Hood

Pretty White Mouse (1844), IV. 521

Preux Chevalier (1853), v. 735

Preventive Service (Milner, H. M., 1824), IV. 357

Priceless Jewels = Imperial Guard

Priceless Wife = Devotion

Price of Empire (Hope, A., 1896), v. 425
Price of Existence (Hazlewood, C. H., 1872), v. 414
Price of Freedom = Petrovna
Price of Life = Seventh Hour
Pride (Albery, J., 1874), v. 237
— (Hillyard, J., 1851), v. 422
— (Towers, E., 1872), v. 601
Pride and its Fall (Wilkins, J. H., 1849), IV. 419
Pride and Passion = Honour of the House
Pride and Patience (Pitt, G. D., 1850), v. 526
— (1859), v. 735
— = (1) Twin Brothers; (2) Witches' Weeds
Pride and Poverty = Poacher's Wife
+Pride and Vanity (*French*)
Pride of Birth (Rodwell, G. H., 1843), IV. 395
— = Belphegor the Mountebank
Pride of Fallen Pine (1894), v. 735
Pride of Jerrico (1899), v. 735
Pride of Kildare (1844), IV. 521
Pride of Life (1863), v. 735
Pride of Poverty (Barnett, B. and Johnstone, J. B., 1857), v. 249
Pride of the Alhambra = Zana
+Pride of the Blood; or, The Child of Mystery (Moncrieff, W. T.; Garrick, 15/10/1832)
Pride of the Family (Parry, A., 1878), v. 514
Pride of the Market (Planché, J. R., 1847), IV. 382
Pride, Poverty and Splendour = Seamstress and the Duchess
Pride's Cure = John Woodvil
Pride shall have a Fall (Croly, G., 1824), 174, 285
— (Soane, G., 1832), IV. 30, 404
Priest and the Convict = Out of Evil cometh Good, v. 735
Priest Hunter (O'Grady, H., 1892), v. 506
Priest of Saragossa = De l'Orme
Priest of the Parish = Spanish Dollars
Priest or Painter (Poel, W., 1884), v. 529
Priest's Daughter (Serle, T. J., 1845), IV. 400
Prig of Pimlico = Newgate Ned

Prima Donna (Boucicault, D., 1852), v. 267
— (Farnie, H. B. and Murray, A., 1888), v. 363
Prime Minister (1887), v. 735
Prime Minister a prim-in-a-stir = Eudora
Primitive Wife and Modern Maid = Wives as they Were and Maids as they Are
Primrose Farm (Harvey, F., 1885), v. 408
— (Major, H. A., 1871), v. 472
Primrose Green (1790), III. 340
Primrose Hall (Lacy, M. R., 1863), v. 446
Primrose of Ireland (Pitt, G. D., 1845), IV. 374 [This is the same as Irish Molly: see IV. 483]
Primrose Path (Findon, B. W., 1892), v. 366
Prince (Dibdin, C. I. M., 1812), IV. 292, 521, 580, 637
Prince Amabel (Brough, W., 1862), v. 279
Prince Amabel, Mother Goose (1873), v. 735
Prince and No Prince = German Blunder
Prince and Peasant (1881), v. 735
Prince and the Breeches = Court of Queen Anne
Prince and the Fairy (1857), v. 735
Prince and the Lion King (Suter, W. E., 1863), v. 735, 843
Prince and the Mandarin = Timour Khan
Prince and the Mermaiden = Pearl of the Ocean
Prince and the Ogre (Marchant, F., 1860), v. 735, 805, 844
Prince and the Pauper (Beringer, Mrs O., 1890), v. 259
— (Hatton, J., 1891), v. 409
Prince and the Peasant = Maurice the Woodcutter
Prince and the Peri (O'Neill, J. R., v. 808
Prince and the Piper = King of the Merrows
Prince and the Pirate = Sicilian
Prince and the Player (1823), IV. 521

Prince Blue Cap (1876), v. 735

Prince Brilliantino (1888), v. 735

Prince Camaralzaman (Bellingham, H. and Best, W., 1865), v. 257

Prince Carlo's Party (1887), v. 735

Prince Caruso (1833), IV. 521

Prince Charles Edward Stuart (Crawford, J., 1868), v. 329

Prince Charlie (1830), IV. 637

Prince Cherry and Princess Fair Star (Collins, C. J., 1855), v. 735, 785

Prince Cherrystar (Saunders, T., 1893), v. 556

Prince Chimney-Sweeper, and Chimney-Sweeper Prince = Adventures of the Prince of Seville

Prince Dorus (Taylor, T., 1850), IV. 521, 637; v. 592

+Prince Edward (Mitford, E. L., in Poems, 1869)

Prince et le jardinier (1813), IV. 521

Prince Firoaz, Schah of Persia and the Princess of Bengal = Enchanted Horse

Prince for an Hour (Morton, J. M., 1856), v. 495

Prince Fortune and Prince Fatal (1854), v. 735

Prince in Conceit (Kirkman, F., 1662), I. 417

Prince Karatoff (Dam, H. J. W., 1892), v. 334

Prince Karl (Gunter, A. C., 1888), v. 397

Prince Lardi-Dardi and the Radiant Rosetta = White Cat

Prince Lee Boo (1833), IV. 521

Prince Love (Vandervell, W. F., 1870), v. 606

Prince Lucifer (Austin, A., 1887), v. 245

Princely Peasant and Peasant King = Shepherd King

Princely Shepherd = Royal Revenge

Prince Methuselem (Leigh, H. S., 1883), v. 454, 803

+Prince Nysey Nosey (Keating, Miss, French)

Prince of Agra (Addington, Sir W., 1774), III. 58, 232, 389

Prince of Angola (Ferriar, J., 1788), III. 55, 58, 259, 383

Prince of Arragon = Birth-Day

Prince of Borneo (Herbert, J. W., 1899), v. 418

Prince of Cambria = Welshman

Prince of Cyprus (Broadfoot, J. W., 1846), IV. 271

— (1847), IV. 521

Prince of Darkness (Henry, S. C., 1896), v. 418

Prince of Egypt (Squier, C., 1882), v. 577

Prince of Happy Land (Planché, J. R., 1851), v. 527, 811

Prince of Jerusalem (1899), v. 735

Prince of Madagascar (1884), v. 735

Prince of Mischance (1897), v. 735

Prince of Pearls (1855), v. 735

Prince of Pimlico = Rumfustian Innamorato

Prince of Sauerkrautenberg (Boyce, W., 1895), v. 272

Prince of the Black Mountains = Dinas Bran

Prince of the Lakes = Thierna-na-Oge

Prince of the Orange Islands = Silver Tower

Prince of the Peaceful Islands (Cheatham, F. G., 1863), v. 735, 844

Prince of Tunis (Mackenzie, H., 1773), III. 90, 283

Prince of Wales's Visit (1869), v. 735

Prince Otto (Thalberg, T. B. and Gurney, G., 1888), v. 595

Prince Peacock and the Queen of Spite (1859), v. 735

Prince Pedrillo (Saull, J. A., 1893), v. 556

Prince Peerless (1860), v. 844

Prince Pigmy and Gorillacum (1862), v. 735

Prince Pippo and the Fair Mayde of Islington (Hazlewood, C. H., 1866), v. 735, 796, 844

Prince Pretty-Pet and the Butterfly (Brough, W., 1854), v. 279

Prince's Ball (?1682), I. 447

Prince's Nap and the Snip's Snap = La Ba Kan

Princes of Persia = Zadoc the Sorcerer

Prince Sohobazar (Bowles, E. W., 1885), v. 271

Prince's Park and Scotland Row (Elphinstone, J., 1867), v. 790

Prince's Present = Match-breaking

Princess (Gilbert, W. S., 1870), v. 379

— (Killigrew, T., 1661), I. 416

Princess Amaswazee (Paulton, T., 1895), v. 517

Princess and no Princess = Forest of Hermanstadt

Princess and the Butterfly (Pinero, Sir A. W., 1897), v. 180, 525, 810

Princess and the Swineherd (Hood, B., 1897), v. 425

Princess Badoura (1887), v. 735

Princess Battledore and Harlequin Shuttlecock (De Hayes, W., 1843), IV. 522, 637

Princess Carlo's Plot (Hilton, H., 1887), v. 422

Princess Charming (Arnold, H. T., 1867), v. 243

— (1877), v. 735

Princess Diana (Jones, J. W., 1889), v. 441

Princess Fairlocks (1857), v. 844

Princess Fair Star = Fair Star

Princess George (1885), v. 736

Princess Ida (Gilbert, W. S., 1884), v. 144, 380

Princess in the Tower (Talfourd, F. and Hale, W. P., 1850), v. 590, 819

Princess Liza's Fairy (Wurm, J., 1893), v. 633

Princess of Ashantee = King Coffee

Princess of Cleve (Lee, N., 1681), I. 96, 147, 272, 419

Princess of Georgia (Craven, E., 1799) = Georgian Princess, III. 249, 380

Princess of Orange (James, F., 1896), v. 433

Princess of Parma (Cumberland, R., 1778), III. 78, 251, 381

— (Smith, H., 1699), I. 432

Princess of Parmesan (Millais, W. H., 1898), v. 488

Princess of Persia = Distress'd Innocence

Princess of Poland = Juliana

Princess of Tarento (McDonald, A., 1791), III. 283

Princess of the Burning Eyes (1854), v. 736

Princess of the Pearl Island (Hazlewood, C. H., 1866), v. 736, 796, 844

Princess of Trebizonde (Kenney, C. L., 1870), v. 443, 801

Princess of Zanfara (1789), III. 340

Princess Pansy (1891), v. 736

Princess Pocahontas (1894), v. 736

Princess Primrose and the Four Pretty Princes (Bellingham, H. and Best, W., 1866), v. 257

Princess Radiant (Brough, W. and Brough, R. B., 1851), v. 278

Princess's Idea (Moore, T., 1892), v. 492

Princess Springtime (Byron, H. J., 1864), v. 297, 782

Princess Tarakanoff (Graves, C., 1897), v. 389

Princess, the Peri and the Troubadour = Lalla Rookh

Princess Toto (Gilbert, W. S., 1876), v. 380

Prince's Stratagem = Citizen of Paris

Princess Verita (Cockburn, Mrs T., 1896), v. 315

Princess who lost her Head (1857), v. 736

Princess who was changed into a Deer (1845), IV. 522

Princess with the Raven Locks = Barber and the Bravo

Prince's Trumpeter (Campbell, A. V., 1849), IV. 279

Prince, the Pirate and the Pearl = Bride of Abydos

Prince, the Princess and the Mandarin = Chang Ching Fow, Cream of Tartar

Prince troubadour (1815), IV. 522

— = Joconde

Principal and Interest (1881), v. 736

Principal Boy (D'Lanor, G., 1899), v. 346

Principle and Genius = Edmund Kean

Principle and Practice Combined (1792), III. 340

Printer's Devil (Planché, J. R., 1838), IV. 381

— (1832), IV. 522

Printers' Squabbles (1852), v. 736

Prior Claim (Pye, H. J. and Arnold, S. J., 1805), III. 300; IV. 388

Priscella (1889), v. 736

Prison and Palace (Simpson, J. P., 1853), v. 567, 816

Prison Breaker (1725), II. 244, 381

Prisoner (Hartwell, H., 1799), III. 268
— (Rose, J., 1792), III. 303, 395
— (1805), IV. 522
— (1842), IV. 522
Prisoner at Large (O'Keeffe, J., 1788),
III. 185, 294
Prisoner King = Windsor Castle
Prisoner of Bordeaux = Valerie Duclos
Prisoner of Elville Castle = Marian
Prisoner of France (1849), IV. 522
Prisoner of Ham (1855), v. 736
Prisoner of Lyons (Young, H., 1854), v.
736, 844
Prisoner of Piguerolles (Suter, W. E.),
v. 819
Prisoner of Rochelle (1856), v. 844
Prisoner of Schlussenburg = Lioness of
the North
Prisoner of State = Ulrica
Prisoner of the Bastile = Escape of
Latude
Prisoner of the Seventeenth Century =
Marchioness de Brinvilliers
Prisoner of Toulon (Richards, A. B.,
1868), v. 542
Prisoner of Vincennes = Red Cap
Prisoner of War (Jerrold, D. W., 1842),
IV. 185–6, 333
— (McLaren, A., 1813), IV. 351
Prisoner of Zenda (Rose, E., 1896), v.
11, 210, 550
Prisoners (Killigrew, T., 1641), I. 416
Prisoners at the Bar (Ross, C. H., 1878),
v. 551
— (1881), v. 736
Prisoner's Daughter (1887), v. 736
— = Filial Love
Prisoner's Escape = Castle of Tarento
Prisoners of Lyons (Ebsworth, J., 1823),
IV. 308
Prisoners of the Ball (1860), v. 736
Prisoners' Perils = Island of Silver Store
Prisoners Released = Last Shift
Prisoner's Secret (1847), IV. 637
Private and Confidential (Eldred, J. and
Paulton, H., 1870), v. 356
— = (1) Court Favour; (2) Diplomacy
Private Detective (Leigh, S. and
Pemberton, M., 1886), v. 454
Private Enquiry (Burnand, F. C., 1890),
v. 292
Privateer (Long, C., 1845), IV. 346

Privateer (1812), IV. 522
— = Love and Honour
Privateer and his Friend = Sailor's
Grave
Privateer Invasion (1779), III. 403
Privateer's Venture (Hayman, H.,
1876), v. 411
Private Life (1882), v. 736
Private Makeland (1895), v. 736
Private Secretary (Hawtrey, C., 1883),
v. 182–3, 410
Private Theatre (McLaren, A., 1809),
IV. 351
Private Theatricals (Powell, J., 1787),
III. 21, 186, 299
Private View (Ferrers, E., 1893), v. 365
Private Wire (Desprez, F., 1883), v. 343
— (Felix, A. and Desprez, F., 1883),
v. 364
Prize (Hoare, P., 1793), III. 269
— (1801), IV. 522
Prizefighter's Daughter = Seaside Swells
Prize of Industry (1793), III. 340
Prizes (1891), v. 736
Prizes and Blanks (Booth, O., 1885), v.
267
Prize Wherry (1820), IV. 522
Problem Solved (1843), IV. 522
Procida = Vespers of Palermo
Proclaimed (Manning, W., 1886), v. 474
Procrastination (Payne, J. H., 1829), IV.
369
— (1829), IV. 522
Prodigal (Odell, T., 1744), II. 142, 160,
179, 347
— (Waldron, F. G., 1793), III. 59, 314,
397
— (1794), III. 340
— (1816), IV. 522
— (1827), IV. 522
Prodigal Daughter (Pettitt, H., 1892), v.
521
Prodigal Father (McDonough, G.,
1897), v. 469
Prodigal in London = Azael
Prodigal of Memphis = Azael
Prodigal Parson (Connynghame, F. L.
and Clarke, C. A., 1898), v. 320
Prodigal Reform'd (Jacob, H., 1738),
II. 184, 205, 338
Prodigal Son (Milner, H. M., 1825), IV.
522, 637

Prophet and Loss of Troy = Agamemnon and Cassandra

Prophetess (Dryden, J., 1690), I. 48, 55, 82, 83, 337, 352, 406–7; II. 413

— (Galt, J., 1814), IV. 318, 635

Prophetess of Ordsall Cave = Guido Fawkes

Prophet of Stonehenge = Mad Ruth of Wilton

Prophet of the Caucasus = (1) Questor's Steed; (2) Conqueror's Steed

Prophetess of the Glen = Two Drovers

Prophet of the Moor = Fire Raiser

Prophet of the Rock = Lonely Lighthouse

Prophet's Curse (Markwell, W. R., 1862), V. 477

Prophet's Priest = Maid of Venice

Proposals (Gilmore, J. F., 1887), V. 381

Proscribed (Stanford, G., 1889), V. 578

— = John Wilson

Proscribed Royalist (Seymour, F., 1881), V. 561

Prospect of Peace (Dibdin, T. J., ?1795), III. 382

Prospero (1883), V. 736

Protean Bandit = Reprobate

+Protector at Houghall; or, The Lily and the Rose (Brayshay, J. (Durham, 10/7/1851), 8° (1851; Groombridge))

Protector's Oath = Stanfield Hall

Proteus (Woodward, H., 1755), III. 209, 317

— (1833), IV. 522

Proud Prudence (Atkyns, S., 1849), IV. 257

Proud Shepherd's Tragedy (Downes, J., 1823), IV. 582

Proud Young Porter and the Fair Sophia = Lord Bateman

Proved True (Murdoch, J. M., 1883), V. 499

Provisional Government (Stocqueler, J. H., 1848), IV. 522, 637

Provision for the Convent = Monks and Smugglers

Provocation (1790), III. 340

Provok'd Husband (Cibber, C. and Vanbrugh, Sir J., 1728), II. 10, 15, 40, 134, 135, 137, 138, 152, 158, 183, 189, 190–1, 312, 434

Provok'd Wife (Vanbrugh, Sir J., 1697), I. 244–5, 436

Provoking Predicament = Love Limited

Provost of Bruges (Lovell, G. W., 1836), IV. 347, 596

— (1837), IV. 522

Provost of Paris (1837), IV. 523

Provost's Daughter (Ballantyne, J., 1852), V. 247

Prude (Ryves, E., 1777), III. 304

— (Weeks, J. E., 1791), III. 315

— = Cariboo

Prudes and Pro's (Votieri, A., 1891), V. 609

Prude's Progress (Jerome, J. K. and Phillpotts, E., 1895), V. 436

Prunella (Estcourt, R., 1708), II. 266, 320

Prussian Brothers (Pitt, G. D., 1847), IV. 375

Prussian Camp (1758), III. 340

Prussian Discipline (Abbott, W., 1817) = Youthful Days of Frederick the Great, IV. 249, 523, 567

Prussian Dragoon (1788), III. 340

Prussian Festival (1791), III. 340

Prussian Soldiers = Friendship, Love and Duty

"P.S. Come to Dinner" (Raymond, R. J., 1830), IV. 388

+Prying Little Girl (French)

Psyche (Shadwell, T., 1675), I. 37, 40, 42, 133, 135, 205, 337, 348, 430–1

Psyche Debauch'd (Duffett, T., 1675), I. 37, 135, 249, 407

Psychic Force (1872), V. 736

Public (Maclaurin, J., 1798), III. 285

Public Dinner in aid of a Philanthropic Object (Reece, R., 1868), V. 537

Public House (1787), III. 340

Public Men in Private Life = State Secrets

Public Wooing (Cavendish, M., 1662), I. 396

Pucelle = Maid of Orleans

Puck (Webb, M. G., 1883), V. 617

— (1890), V. 736

Puck in a Pucker = Frolics of the Fairies

Puck's Pantomime (Morton, J. M., 1844), IV. 523

Puddinhead (Mayo, F., 1895), V. 483

Puff of Smoke (Rowe, C. J., 1876), V. 552

Puff! Puff!! Puff!!! = London Characters

Pug (1836), IV. 523

Pugilist Matched = Dreamer Awake

Pull Devil, Pull Baker (1849), IV. 523

Pump (Clowes, W. L., 1886), V. 315

Punch (Byron, H. J., 1881), V. 299

— (Selby, C., 1841), IV. 398

Punch à la Romaine (1852), V. 736

Punch and Fun (Rhys, H., 1862), V. 542

Punch and his Little Dog Toby = Show Folks

Punch and Judy (Collins, C. J., 1859), V. 736, 785, 844

— (Conquest, G. and Spry, H., 1864), V. 736, 844

— (Willard, Mrs E. S., 1893), V. 623

— (1837), IV. 523

— (1853), V. 736

Punch Bowl (Ford, T. M., 1887), V. 370

Punchinello (Dabbs, G. H. R., 1890), V. 332

— (Farnie, H. B., 1864), V. 361

— (?1666), I. 446

— (1843), IV. 523

Punchinello and his Wife Judy (Barlas, J., 1886), V. 249

Punch in Italy (Euston, J. H., 1849), IV. 523, 637

Punch in Naples (1858), V. 736

Punch in Paris (1851), V. 844

Punch's Defeat (1748), II. 381

Punch's Festival (1813), IV. 523

Punch's Oratory (1730), II. 381

Punch's Pantomime (by the writers of *Punch*, 1842), IV. 523, 637

Punch's Politics (1730), II. 381

Punch turn'd Quaker = Town Rake

Punishment in Six Stages (Melville, H., 1849), IV. 355

Punishment of Sacrilege = Blue Man

Puns in Plenty = Will, or the Widow

Pup (1883), V. 736

P.U.P. (Moss, H., 1883), V. 497

Pupil of an Architect (1871), V. 736

Pupil of da Vinci (Lemon, M., 1839), IV. 523, 595, 637

Pupil of Nature = Paulina

Puppet (1897), V. 736

Puppets (McArdle, J. F., 1893), V. 467

Puppet Town (1899), V. 736

Pure as Driven Snow (Hazlewood, C. H., 1869), V. 1, 414

Pure as Snow (Berrie, E., 1873), V. 259

Pure Gold (Marston, J. W., 1863), V. 479

Purely Platonic (De Smart, Mrs A., 1898), V. 343

— = Cocum

Puritan (Murray, D. C. and Shine, J. L., 1894), V. 500

Puritan Girl = In the Days of the Siege

Puritani (À Beckett, G. A., 1843), IV. 523, 637

Puritanical Justice (1698), I. 444

Puritans (Mathews, 1856), V. 806

Puritan's Bride = Queen's Jewels

Puritan's Daughter (Bridgeman, J. V., 1861), V. 275

— (Lavington, W. F., 1875), V. 449

Puritan's Plot (1838), IV. 523

Puritan's Romance (1897), V. 736

Puritan's Sister (1835), IV. 523

Purpose of Life = Patience

Purrah (Moser, J., 1808), IV. 364

Purse (Cross, J. C., 1794), III. 98, 102, 249

+Purse; or, Falstaff (Lewes, L.; Stourbridge, 8/1799)

Purse of Almo (Lunn, J., 1834), IV. 523, 637

Purser (Day, J. T., 1897), V. 340

Pursuit of Vengeance = Vendetta

Puss (1859), V. 736

Puss in a New Pair of Boots (Byron, H. J., 1861), V. 296, 782

Puss in Boots (Blanchard, E. L., 1873), V. 264

— (Blanchard, E. L., 1887), V. 265

— (Bridgeman, J. V., 1859), V. 736, 780, 844

— (Conquest, G. and Spry, H., 1892), V. 322

— (Craven, E., 1799), III. 249

— (Daly, B. and East, J. M., 1898), V. 334

— (Dance, C. and Planché, J. R., 1837), IV. 152, 288, 381, 578, 605

— (Graves, C., 1888), V. 794, 844

— (Hazlewood, C. H., 1859), V. 796

— (Lonsdale, M., 1801), IV. 347

— (Marchant, F., 1873), V. 476

— (Rice, C., 1877), V. 542

Puss in Boots (Russell, F., 1880), v. 553
— (Soutar, R., 1861), v. 737, 817, 844
— (Stainforth, F., 1880), v. 578
— (Tabrar, J., 1884), v. 589
— (Wood, J. H., 1899), v. 824
— (1832), IV. 523
— (1856, 1857, 1858, 1859, 1860, 1862, 1874, 1875), v. 844
— (1875, 1876, 1877, 1878, 1879, 1880, 1881, 1882, 1884), v. 737
— (1888), v. 844
— (1889, 1897, 1898), v. 737
— = Marquis de Carabas
Puss in Boots, the Ogre, the Miller and the King of the Rats (Conquest, G. and Spry, H., 1882), v. 322
Puss in Boots up to Scratch (Byam, M. and Wyke, E. B., 1892), v. 294
Puss in Petticoats (1867), v. 737
Puss! Puss!! Puss!!! (1827), IV. 523
Put Asunder (Wills, F., 1883), v. 627
Putting things right (Zimmerman, H., 1885), v. 637
Put to the Test (Marston, J. W., 1873), v. 479
— = Relations
Put Yourself in his Place (Reade, C., 1870), v. 536
Puzzled and Pleased (1855), v. 737
Puzzles and Penalties = Married or Not?
Pygmalion (1779), III. 120, 340, 404
Pygmalion and Galatea (Gilbert, W. S., 1871), v. 136, 140, 379
Pygmalion and the Statue Fair (Brough, W., 1867), v. 280
Pygmalion Reversed = Galatea
Pyramids (Brooks, C. W. S., 1864), v. 277
— (Dibdin, T. J., ?1796), III. 382
Pyramus and Thisbe (Leveridge, R., 1716), II. 141, 341
— (Mathews, C. J., 1833), IV. 354
— (Oulton, W. C., 1798), III. 296
— (Stephenson, C. H., 1877), v. 583
— (Wigan, H.), v. 622
— (1745), II. 141, 267, 381
— (1804), IV. 523
— (1831), IV. 523
Pyrrhus and Demetrius (MacSwiny, O., 1708), II. 229, 397, 440
Pyrrhus, King of Epirus (Hopkins, C., 1695), I. 152, 413

Q.E.D. (Marshall, F., 1871), v. 478
Q. in the Corner (1810), IV. 523
Q. of Diamonds (Barnett, C. Z., 1846), IV. 260
Q.Q. (Johnson, H. T., 1895), v. 437
Quack (Honig, L., 1887), v. 425
Quack, Quack, Quack (1851), v. 737
Quacks (MacSwiny, O., 1705), II. 22, 129, 144, 208-9, 290, 342, 440
— (1784), III. 340
Quadrille (1819), IV. 145, 523
Quadrilles = Deux âges
Quadroon (1857), v. 737
— (1860), v. 737
Quadroona (Townsend, W. T., 1857), v. 821
— (1857), v. 737
Quadroon and the Secret Tree Cavern = Slave Bride
Quadroon Slave (Webster, B. J., 1841), IV. 523, 637
Quadrupeds (1811), IV. 523
Quadrupeds of Quedlinburgh (Colman, G., the Younger, 1811), IV. 26, 148, 282
Quaker (Dibdin, C., 1777), III. 255
Quakers and Shakers (Doyle, T. F., 1873), v. 350
Quaker's Opera (Walker, T., 1728), II. 244, 363
Quaker's Wedding = Vice Reclaim'd
Quaker's Will = Fox Glove
Quality Binding = Quarter of an Hour before Dinner
Quarantine Ship (1845), IV. 523
Quarrel (Wotton, T. S., 1893), v. 632
Quarrel for what? = Quadrille
+ Quarrel of the Flowers (Hodges, G. S., French)
Quarry Dell (Delafield, J. H., 1868), v. 341
Quarter before Nine (1837), IV. 523
Quarter Day (Sicklemore, R., 1797), III. 307
— (1811), IV. 523
— (1821), IV. 523
— (1855), v. 737
— (1876), v. 737
— = (1) Hermit; (2) She's Eloped
Quarter Deck (1814), IV. 523
Quarter of a Million of Money (Towers, E., 1868), v. 601

Quarter of an Hour before Dinner (Rose, J., 1788), III. 303

Quarters (1887), V. 737

Quarter to Nine (Peake, R. B., 1837), IV. 370

Quartette (1828), IV. 523

Quasimodo (Fitzball, E., 1836), IV. 315

Quasimodo, the Deformed (Spry, H., 1870), V. 576

Quatre Bras (Rice, C., 1853), V. 542

Quatres Fils d'Hemons (1788), III. 341

Quavers and Capers (1817), IV. 523

Queen (Swarbreck, J. W., 1879), V. 589

Queen and Cardinal (Raleigh, W. S., 1881), V. 534

Queen and the Cardinal (1836), IV. 523

Queen and the Knave (1862), V. 737

Queen and the Yeoman (1862), V. 737

Queen Anne's Farthing and the Three Kingdoms of Copper, Silver and Gold (1859), V. 737

Queen Bee (Barrymore, W., 1828), IV. 262

— (1839), IV. 523

— (1869), V. 844

Queen Catharine (Pix, M., 1698), I. 424

Queen Catherine and Cardinal Wolsey (1828), IV. 524

Queen Cock-a-doodle-do, the Dame who lost her Shoe (1866), V. 737

Queen, Crown and Country = Headsman's Axe

Queen Dido (1792), III. 341

Queen Elizabeth (Gregg, T. D., 1872), V. 794

— (1869), V. 737

Queen Elizabeth and the Knight of Sheppey = Sea Horse

Queen Elizabeth's Trumpets = Fame

Queen Elizabeth's Visit to Reading (1862), V. 737

Queen Ellinor (1875), V. 737

Queen! God bless her (1838), IV. 524

Queen Hortensia's Shoe (Krasinski, H., 1857), V. 801

Queen Lady Bird and her Children (1860), V. 737

Queen Lucidora the Fair One with the Golden Locks (Planché, J. R., 1868), V. 528

Queen Mab (Dalby, 1857), V. 332

— (Godfrey, G. W., 1874), V. 382

Queen Mab (Somerset, C. A., 1851), V. 574

— (Vandervell, W. F., 1857), V. 822

— (Woodward, H., 1748), II. 446; III. 209, 317

— (1850), V. 737

— (1851, 1860), V. 844

Queen Mary (Stirling, E., 1840), IV. 80, 524

— (Tennyson, Alfred Lord, 1876), V. 208, 594

— = Tower of London

Queen Mary's Bower (Planché, J. R., 1846), IV. 382

Queen-Mother (Swinburne, A. C., 1860), V. 589

Queen o' Diamonds (Brabner, W. A., 1894), V. 272

Queen of a Day (Haines, J. T., 1841), IV. 323, 587

— (Moncrieff, W. T., 1840), IV. 600

— (1851), V. 738

— = Court of Spain

Queen of an Hour (Douglass, J. T. and Stainforth, F., 1877), V. 348

Queen of Aragon (Paul, H. M., 1854), V. 515, 809

Queen of Argos (Bell, W. B., 1823), IV. 572

Queen of Arts (1884), V. 738

Queen of Beauty = Second Calender

Queen of Bohemia (Blanchard, E. L., 1845), IV. 268

Queen of Brilliants (Thomas, B., 1894), V. 596

Queen of Carthage (Hoare, P., 1792), III. 269

— (1797), III. 341

Queen of Connaught (Jay, H., 1877), V. 738, 799, 844

— (Buchanan, R., 1887), V. 285

Queen of Cyprus (Beazley, S., Jr., 1842), IV. 264

— (Stirling, E., 1842), IV. 613

Queen of Diamonds (Brunton, A., 1882), V. 284

— = Hand of Fate

Queen of England (Clarke, C. A., 1898), V. 312

Queen of Fashion (Cannam, T. and Preston, J. F., 1887), V. 302

Queen of France and England = Eleanor the Amazon

Queen of Golconda (Dibdin, T. J., 1817), IV. 301

Queen of Hearts (Roe, J. E., 1863), v. 814

— (Thomas, C., 1877), v. 596

— (1833), IV. 524

— (1883), v. 738

— (1884), v. 738

— (1894), v. 738

Queen of Hungary = Gertrude and Beatrice

Queen of Hungary Triumphant = Universal Monarch Defeated

Queen of Manoa (Chambers, C. H. and Tristram, W. O., 1892), v. 307

Queen of May (1851), v. 738

Queen of Poland (1847), IV. 524

Queen of Spades (Boucicault, D., 1851), v. 267

— (Worsdale, J., 1744), II. 364

— (1852), v. 738

Queen of the Abruzzi (1846), IV. 524

Queen of the Beggars (Serle, T. J., 1837), IV. 400

Queen of the Butterfly Tower (1828), IV. 524

Queen of the Cannibal Islands = Africaine

Queen of the Clover Field (Lee, N., 1833), IV. 524

Queen of the Frogs (Planché, J. R., 1851), v. 527

Queen of the Hills (Wilkins, J. H.), IV. 420

— = Corsican Maid

Queen of the Market (Coape, H. C. and Webster, B. N., 1852), v. 315

Queen of the May (Legg, F. W., 1896), v. 453

Queen of the Moor (1899), v. 738

Queen of the Night (Tracey, F. T. and Berlin, I., 1897), v. 602

Queen of the Roses (1850), v. 738

Queen of the Silver Lakes = Rodolph and Rosa

Queen of the Thames (Fitzball, E., 1843), IV. 316

Queen of the Vintage and the Courier Prince (1854), v. 738

Queen of Wales = Love's Victim

Queen o' May (1884), v. 738

+ Queen's Ball (À Beckett, G. A., 1838), [Under this title, À Beckett's *Black Domino* was printed in the Duncombe series]

Queen's Bench (Rede, W. L., 1848), IV. 391

Queensberry Fête = Who's your Friend?

Queen's Bounty = Sport

Queen's Bouquet and the Three Cards = Red House

Queen's Champion (Gore, Mrs C. G. F., 1834), IV. 319

Queen's Colours (Conquest, G. and Pettitt, H., 1879), v. 321

Queen's Command ("William Shakespeare", i.e. Walton, 1838), IV. 524, 637

Queen's Counsel (Mortimer, J., 1890), v. 494

Queen's Court = John Duddlestone, the Breeches Maker of Bristol

Queen's Court of Conscience = Royal Twelfth Cake

Queen's Evidence (Conquest, G. and Pettitt, H., 1876), v. 321

Queen's Favourite (Grundy, S., 1883), v. 396

— = Lady of the Louvre

Queen's First Move = Check to the King

Queen's Horse (Planché, J. R. and Honan, M. B., 1838), IV. 381

Queen's Jewel (Collier, W., 1835), IV. 281

Queen's Jewels (Dodson, R., 1876), v. 346

Queen's Lieutenant = Laura

Queen's Love (Hilles, M. W., 1879), v. 421

— = St Bartholomew

Queen's Lover (1834), IV. 524

— = (1) Marie Antoinette; (2) Salvoisy

Queen's Masque (Osborn, H., 1842), IV. 602

Queen's Messenger (Manners, J. H., 1899), v. 474

Queen's Musketeers (1856), v. 844

Queen's Necklace (Ford, D. M., 1899), v. 370

— = Marie Antoinette

Quixote Junior (Buckingham, L. S., 1859), v. 286
Quixotte and Sancho (1800), IV. 524
Quizes (Dibdin, C., 1795), III. 256
Quoniam (1831), IV. 524
Quoz (1789), III. 341
Quywic (1887), v. 738
Qwong-Hi (Mackay, R. F., 1895), v. 470

Rabbi of York (1852), v. 844
Rabbi's Son (Manuel, E., 1879), v. 475
Raby Rattler (Courtney, J., 1847), IV. 284
— (Stirling, E., 1847), IV. 408
— (1847), IV. 524
— (1865), v. 738
Race Ball = Chaos is come again
Racecourse of Life = Sharps and Flats
Race for a Cup (1873), v. 738
Race for a Dinner (Rodwell, J. T. G., 1828, 1844) = No Dinner Yet, IV. 395, 512, 524, 608, 638
Race for a Rarity (1838), IV. 524
Race for a Widow (Williams, T. J., 1860), v. 625, 824
Race for a Wife (Challis, H. W., 1820), IV. 405, 524, 576, 638
— (Cooper, F. F., 1876), v. 324
— (Darnley, J. H., 1897), v. 337
— (1823), IV. 524
— = Win Her and Wear Her
Race for Life = (1) Death Warrant; (2) Varley the Vulture
Race for Life through Flood and Flame = Under Two Flags
Race-horse of the Desert = Godolphin Arabian
Race of Life (Whitbread, J. W., 1887), v. 620
Race to Hampstead (1840), IV. 524
Rachael Ryland = Momentous Question
Rachel (Graves, C., 1890) = Death and Rachel, v. 389, 794
— (Grundy, S., 1883), v. 396
— (1871), v. 738
Rachel's Choice (1889), v. 738
Rachel's Messenger (Watson, T. M., 1891), v. 616
Rachel's Penance (Manuel, E., 1878), v. 475
Rachel the Reaper (Reade, C., 1874), v. 37, 536

Racing Star (Macdermott, G. H., 1886), v. 468
Racket Court (1841), IV. 524
Radical (Genet, E., 1888), v. 377
Radical Candidate (Fryers, A., 1899), v. 374
Radical Cure (Boucicault, D., 1850), v. 267
Rafael the Libertine (Almar, G., 1838), IV. 524, 638
Raffaele Cimaro (Serle, T. J., 1819), IV. 399
Raffaelle the Reprobate (Wilks, T. E., 1841), IV. 421
Raffle for an Elephant (1855), v. 738
Raft (Cross, J. C., 1798), III. 250
Rage (Reynolds, F., 1794), III. 31, 46, 132–3, 301
Rag Fair (Wigan, H., 1872), v. 622
Ragged Fortune = Joe Sterling
Ragged Jack (Stanley, H. J., 1880), v. 579
Ragged Robin (Bowyer, F. and Edwardes-Sprange, W., 1893), v. 271
— (Parker, L. N., 1898), v. 513
Ragged School (Stirling, E., 1852), v. 584
Ragged Uproar (1754), III. 341
Raging Devil = Pluto Furens & Vinctus
Rag-picker of Paris (Lucas, W. J., 1847), IV. 348
— (Stirling, E., 1847), IV. 408
Rags and Bones (Scudamore, F. A., 1883), v. 558
Raid in the Transvaal = King of Diamonds
Rail, River and Road (1868), v. 738
Railroad for Ever (Carr, 1836), IV. 524, 638
Railroad of Life (Johnstone, J. B., 1859), v. 738, 800, 844
— (1878), v. 738
Railroad of Love (Daly, A., 1887), v. 333
— = Clutterbucks
Railroads for Ever = Lucky Hit
Railroad Station (Wilks, T. E., 1840), IV. 421
Railroad to Ruin = Formosa
Railroad Trip (Morton, T., Jr. and Morton, J. M., 1843), IV. 364
+ Railway Adventure (Cheltnam, C. S., French)

Railway Belle (Lemon, M., 1854), v. 455
Railway Bubbles (Coyne, J. S., 1845), iv. 524, 578, 638
Railway King (Stirling, E., 1845), iv. 408
— (1845), iv. 524
— (1851), v. 738
Railway Mania (1845), iv. 524
Railway Train (1840), iv. 524
Raiment and Agonies of that most Amiable Pair, Raimond and Agnes (Marchant, F., 1860), v. 738, 805, 844
Rain Clouds (Walkes, W. R., 1894), v. 612
Rainy Day (Smith, Miss A., 1868), v. 571
Raised from the Ashes (Fuller, F., 1879), v. 374
Raising the Wind (Kenney, J., 1803), iv. 131, 336
— (1811), iv. 524
— = Enchanted Isle
Raitchpoot (1876), v. 738
Rajah of Chutneypore = Nautch Girl
Rajah of Nagpore (1846), iv. 524
— (1862), v. 738
Rajah of Ram Jain Poore = Indian Prince
Rajah's Daughter = Cataract of the Ganges
Rajah's Vengeance = Farmer's Daughter
Rake = Suspicious Husband
Rake and his Pupil (Buckstone, J. B., 1833), iv. 70. 182–3, 274
Rake Demolish'd = Bawdy-House School
Rake Husband = Giovanni in the Country
Rake Reclaimed = Love at a Venture
Rake's Progress (Dibdin, C. I. M., 1826), iv. 296
— (Rede, W. L., 1833), iv. 389
— (Rede, W. L., 1841), iv. 390
— = Peasant Ruffian
Rake's Will (Grattan, H. P., 1889), v. 389
+ Raleigh's Queer Dream (Croft; R. Polytechnic, 1873; 8° [1873])
Ralph de Bigod, Earl of Norwich (Smith, J., 1829), iv. 403
Ralph Gaston (1860), v. 738
Ralph's London (1766), iii. 404
Ramah Droog (Cobb, J., 1798), iii. 205, 244 [The entry of a Dublin edition should be deleted]

Ramblers (1836), iv. 524
Rambles in Bagdad = Caliph and the Cadi
Rambles in Dorsetshire = London Hermit
Rambles of Covent Garden = Harlequin's Frolics
Ramble through London = Touch at the Times
Ramble to Bath (1796) = Jacob's Ramble, iii. 404
Ramble to Oxford = Humours of the Road
Rambling Justice (Leanerd, J., 1678), i. 23, 43, 57, 269, 418–19
Rambling Lady = Sir Anthony Love
Rambling Shepheard = Constant Nymph
Ramiro (Clarke, J. B., 1822), iv. 576
Rampant Alderman (1685), i. 217, 444
Ramsbottoms at Rheims (Peake, R. B., 1825), iv. 524
Ranache King (1891), v. 738
Randall's Thumb (Gilbert, W. S., 1871), v. 136, 379
Ran-Dan Club (Worrell, 1840), iv. 618 [This is the same as The Female Waterman's Society, see iv. 460]
Randolph the Reckless (Stephens, V., 1888), v. 581
Random Shot (1898), v. 738
Random Shots (1830), iv. 524
Randy the (W)Reckless and the Grand Old Man of the Sea = People's William
Ranelagh (Simpson, J. P. and Wray, C., 1854), v. 567
Ranger in Wedlock (Silvester, 1788), iii. 307
Ranger of the Forest = Mysterious Murder
Ranger's Daughter (Fitzball, E., 1843), iv. 316
Rank (1871), v. 738
Rank and Fame (Rae, L. and Stainforth, F., 1875), v. 533
Rank and Riches (Collins, W. W., 1883), v. 318
Ransom (Planché, Mrs J. R., 1836), iv. 383
Ransom of Manilla (Lee, R. G., 1793), iii. 281

Reading for the Bar (Grundy, S., 1876), v. 205, 396

Reading of the Will = Forgery

Ready and Willing (Towers, E., 1867), v. 600, 821

— (1880), v. 739

Ready Money Mortiboy (Maurice, W. and Rice, J., 1874) = My Son Dick, v. 482, 723, 806, 841

Real and Ideal (Wigan, H., 1862), v. 622

Real Case of Hide and Seekyl (Grossmith, G., 1888), v. 395

Realities of Life (Conquest, G., 1862), v. 739, 785, 844

Reality (Rogers, C., 1889), v. 548

Real John Bull (1822), iv. 525

— = Mysteries and Miseries

Real Lady Macbeth (Copping, E., 1889), v. 324

Real Life (Bleakley, E. O., 1872), v. 265

— (Dodson, R., 1882), v. 347

Real Life in London (Amherst, J. H.), iv. 254

Real Little Lord Fauntleroy (Burnett, Mrs F. H., 1888), v. 292, 782

Realm of Joy (Gilbert, W. S., 1873), v. 379

Real Mr Potter of Texas (1890), v. 739

Real Poor of London = Pride of Poverty

Real Prince (Greet, D. V., 1894), v. 393

Real Truth about Ivanhoe (Nugent, E. C., 1889), v. 506

Reapers (Pritt, S., 1897), v. 531

— (Stirling, E., 1856), v. 584, 818

— (1770), iii. 121, 341

Reaping the Harvest = (1) Life's Harvest; (2) True Grit

Reaping the Whirlwind (Lennard, H., 1884), v. 455

Rear Admiral (Emden, W. S., 1839), iv. 310

— (1866), v. 739

Reasonable Animals (1780), iii. 341

Reasonable Fool (1789), iii. 341

— (1811), iv. 525

Reasonable Lover (Kelly, H., 1776) = Man of Reason, iii. 341, 389, 404

Rebecca (Barber, J., 1845), iv. 259

— (Halliday, A., 1871), v. 401

Rebecca and her Daughters (1843), iv. 525

Rebecca of York (1874), v. 739

Rebecca, the Jewish Wanderer (Garthwaite, F., 1864), v. 739, 844

Rebel (1849), iv. 525

Rebel Chief (Grattan, H. P., 1836), iv. 525, 586, 638

Rebel for Love = Waverley

Rebellion (Bromley, G. P., 1815), iv. 271

— (1819), iv. 525 [The date is 1819, not 1809]

Rebellion Defeated (Cutts, J., 1745), ii. 317

Rebellion of Lowland's Creek = Armourer's Forge

Rebellion of Norwich in 1549 (1815), iv. 525

Rebel of 1745 = Life of James Dawson

Rebel Rose (1899), v. 739

Rebels (Fagan, J. B., 1899), v. 359

Rebels and Guerillas = Spain and Portugal

Rebel's Gauntlet = Students

Rebel's Heir = Haunted Hulk

Rebel Spirits (1894), v. 739

Rebel's Wife (Jarman, F., 1898), v. 434

Recalled to Life (Hewson, J. J., 1885), v. 420

Receipt for Beauty = Blind Girl

Receipt for Mirth (Burton, 1811) = Right and Wrong, iv. 277, 525, 636

Receipt Tax (Dent, C., 1783), iii. 254

Receipt to make a Benefit = Hodge Podge

Recent Event (1832), iv. 525

Reception (1799), iii. 341

Reckless Temple (1890), v. 739

Reckoning (Dauncy, S., 1891), v. 337

— (Genet, E., 1891), v. 377

Reckoning Day (1885), v. 739

Reclaimed (Mortimer, J., 1881), v. 494

— = Nance

Recluse (Feist, C., 1823), iv. 525, 638

— (1825), iv. 95, 525, 638

— = Misanthropy and Repentance

Recluse of the Alps = Solitaire

Recluse of the Cavern (1830), iv. 525

Recluse of the Forest (1863), v. 739

Recluse of the Monastery = Caledonian Assassin

Recluta por Fuerza (1832), iv. 525

Recollections which may or may not have happened = Strand-ed Actor

Recommendations (1823), IV. 525

Recommended to Mercy (Jones, J. W., 1882), V. 440

Recompense = Louise

Reconciled (Gwynne, P. and Harrison, C., 1888), V. 398

— = Howard Howard

Reconciliation (Ludger, C., 1799), III. 65, 283, 391

— (Neville, G. F., 1876), V. 502

+ — (Render, W., 8°, 1799)

— (1813), IV. 525

Recrimination (Clarke, C., 1813), IV. 280

Recruit (1788), III. 341

— (1794), III. 341

— (1829), IV. 525

— (1892), V. 739

Recruiting Manager (Oulton, W. C., 1785), III. 296

Recruiting Officer (Farquhar, G., 1706), II. 4, 21, 37, 41, 131, 132, 133, 134, 135, 136, 137, 138, 149, 157, 322

Recruiting Party (Kilmorey, Earl of, 1895), V. 444

Recruiting Serjeant (Bickerstaffe, I., 1770), III. 199, 237

Recruits for the King of Prussia = She Gallant

Recruits for the Queen of Hungary = Prodigal

Rector (Pinero, Sir A. W., 1883), V. 525

Rector's Daughter (Strettell, J. D. C., 1898), V. 585

Rectory (1673), I. 348, 444

Red and Blue (Fanshaw, F., 1892), V. 361

— = Passing Fancies

Red and White (André, R., 1891), V. 241

Red Banner (1831), IV. 525

Red Barn (Mildenhall, T., 1829), IV. 598

— (Comer, G. and Ellis, L., 1892), V. 319

— (1830), IV. 638

Red Bob the Coiner (Towers, E., 1863), V. 821

Red Bridge (Suter, W. E., 1860), V. 739, 819, 844

Red Brigade (1856), V. 739

Red Buoy (1851), V. 739

Red Cap (Archer, T., 1846), IV. 255

Redcliff (1845), IV. 525

Red Coat (Williams, B., 1899), V. 624

Red-Cross Knights (Holman, J. G., 1799), III. 62, 272

— = Harold the Renegade

Red Cross of Burgundy = Perinet Leclerc

Red Crow (Wilks, T. E., 1834), IV. 420

Red Daemon of the Harz Forest (1821), IV. 525

Red Dick (1873), V. 739

Red Dwarf (1871), V. 739

— (1873), V. 739

Redeemed (Coggan, J., 1883), V. 316

Redeeming Spark = Honour

Redemption (1882), V. 739

— (1897), V. 739

Red Eric, the Sea King (1837), IV. 638

Red Farm (Moncrieff, W. T., 1842), IV. 361

Redgauntlet (Murray, W. H., 1825), IV. 94, 365

— (1824), IV. 94, 525

— (1835), IV. 94, 525

Red Hand (Lyon, T., 1865), V. 739, 845

— = (1) Brian, the Probationer; (2) Desmore; (3) Desmoro; (4) Exiled

Red Hand of Fontainebleau (1857), V. 739

Red Hand of Justice (1878), V. 739

Red Hands (À Beckett, G. A., 1869), V. 233

— (Dibdin, C. I. M., 1805), IV. 291

— (Dibdin, C. I. M., 1815), IV. 291

Red House (1849), IV. 525

— (1850), V. 739

Red Huntsman (1858), V. 739

Red Hussar (Stephens, H. P., 1889), V. 580

Red Indian (1822), IV. 525

— (1824), IV. 525

Red John the Daring (1861), V. 739

Red Josephine (Lane, Mrs S., 1880), V. 448

Red Knave (Drinkwater, A. E., 1892), V. 351

Red Lamp (Travers, W., 1862), V. 739, 821, 845

— (Tristram, W. O., 1887), V. 604

Red Lance (Lancaster, E. R., 1841), IV. 593

Redland the Robber (1833), IV. 525

Red Light (Stanley, H. J., 1874), V. 579

Red Maid (1834), IV. 525

Red Man (Phillips, F. L., 1844), IV. 372

Red Man (1847), IV. 525 [The sub-title should be The Sachem's Vow]

Red Man and the Headsman (1857), V. 739

Red Man and the Savage (Dibdin, T. J., 1817), IV. 300

Red Man of Glatz (1849), IV. 525

Red Man's Rifle (Hazlewood, C. H., 1874), V. 415

Redman the Reckless (Lee, N., Jr., 1859), V. 802

Red Mantle (Taylor, T. P., 1841), IV. 525, 638

Red Marine (Cottingham, C. W., 1896), V. 325

Red Mask (Planché, J. R., 1834), IV. 380, 605

Redmond of the Hills (1860), V. 739

Redoutable Don Pierrot (1788), III. 341

Redowald (Hazard, J., 1767), III. 268

Red Rag (McCarthy, J. H., 1888), V. 467

Red Reaver (Dibdin, C. I. M., 1811), IV. 292

Red Reef (Bannister, T. B. and Woods, 1884), V. 248

Red Ribbon (1861), V. 739

Red Rider (Davey, P. and Poley, A. P., 1895), V. 338

Red Riding Hood (Addison, J., 1898), V. 236

— (Barrett, O. and Daly, C., 1886), V. 250

— (Conquest G. and Spry, H., 1894), V. 323

— (Dibdin, C. I. M., 1803), IV. 291

— (Dibdin, C. I. M., 1818), IV. 301

— (French, G. H., 1861), V. 793

— (Keating, M., 1858), V. 739, 800, 845

— (Lanner, K., 1892), V. 448

— (Logan, W. H., 1861), V. 804

— (Rice, C., 1873), V. 542

— (Stephens, V., 1896), V. 581

— (Younge, W., 1879), V. 637

— (1860), V. 845

— (1876, 1880, 1881, 1882, 1883), V. 739

— (1884, 1886, 1887, 1892, 1894, 1895, 1896, 1897, 1898, 1899), V. 740

Red Riding Hood and Baron von Wolf (1858), V. 740

Red Riven (1816), IV. 526

Red Robber (Scott, J. M., 1808), V. 526, 638

Red Robbers = Jersey Girl

Red Robin (1846), IV. 526

Red Rob the Coiner (1863), V. 740

Red Roses (Parker, L. B., 1898), V. 513

Red Rover (Burnand, F. C., 1877), V. 290, 782

— (Fitzball, E., 1829), IV. 97, 313

— (Weaver, R. T., 1829), IV. 97, 616

— (1829), IV. 97, 526

Red Roy (1803), IV. 526

— (1809), IV. 526

Red Rufus (Lee, N., 1851), V. 452

— (1851), V. 740

Red Ruthven (1859), V. 740

Red Savage (1830), IV. 526

Red Signal (Lampard, E. J., 1892), V. 446

Red Snow (Mandeville, H., 1873), V. 474

Reds of the Midi (1896), V. 740

Red Sorcerer (1810), IV. 526

Red Spider (Baring-Gould, S., 1898), V. 249

Red Squadron (Harkins, T. and Macmahon, J., 1894), V. 404

Red Star (1894), V. 740

Red Vial (Collins, W. W., 1858), V. 318

Red, White and Blue (Bush, E. H., 1875), V. 294

Red Witch of Moravia (1820), IV. 526

Reefer's Wrongs = Merry Terry

Reel Smuggled = Ruth Tudor

Referee = Undergraduates

Reflection (1834), IV. 526

— (1877), V. 740

Reform (Moncrieff, W. T., 1831), IV. 360

— (Wrangham, F., 1792), III. 317

Reformation (Arrowsmith, J., 1673), I. 85, 388

— (Pulham, 1815), IV. 388

— (1830), IV. 526

Reform'd Wife (Burnaby, W., 1700), II. 47, 153, 162, 301, 421

Reformed Coquette (1787), III. 341

Reformed in Time (1798), III. 341

Refuge (1837), IV. 526

Refugees (Campbell, J. M., 1888), V. 301

Refusal (Cibber, C., 1721), II. 15, 144, 163, 312, 434; III. 115

— = Rejection

Refusal of Harlequin (Dibdin, C.), IV. 290

Regan-na-Glenna (Addersley, F., 1878), V. 235

Regatta (Bew, C., 1834), IV. 572
— (1847), IV. 638
— = Tom Tug

Regenerates (Post, W. H., 1899), V. 529

Regent (Greatheed, B., 1788), III. 265
— (Planché, J. R., 1834), IV. 380
— (Young, Sir C. L., 1879), V. 636
— (1855), V. 740

Regent of Sparta = Pausanius

Regent's Daughter = True as Steel

Regicide (Dodson, H., 1853), V. 346
— (Smollett, T., 1749), II. 114, 355
— (1842), IV. 638

Regiment (Osborn, S., 1888), V. 508

Regiment of Tartars (1842), IV. 526

Regina, B. A. (Sturgess, A., 1897), V. 586

Regions of Accomplishment (Dibdin, C.), III. 202; IV. 290

Regions of Fancy (1782), III. 341

Registered Lodging House (1851), V. 740

Register Office (Morton, E., 1758) = Universal Register Office, III. 288
— (Reed, J., 1761), III. 19, 300, 394

Regular Fix (Morton, J. M., 1860), V. 496

Regular Scamp (1860), V. 740

Regular Thing (1886), V. 740

Regular Turk (Soutar, R., 1877), V. 575

Regulus (Crowne, J., 1692), I. 56, 124, 151, 400; II. 71
— (Havard, W., 1744), II. 71, 83, 334, 438

Regulus, the Noblest Roman of Them All (Jones, J., 1841), IV. 591

Rehearsal (Clive, C., 1750), III. 194–5, 214, 243, 379
— (Villiers, G., 1671), I. 2, 32, 85, 248, 345, 351, 436; II. 126; III. 215; IV. 147
— (Wilson, R., 1786), III. 316
— (1718), II. 381
— (1882), V. 740

Rehearsal at Goatham (Gay, J., 1754), II. 146, 214, 332; III. 264

Rehearsalization (1899), V. 740

Rehearsal of Kings (1737), II. 381

Rehearsal Rehearsed = Crumlesses

Reigning Favourite (Oxenford, J., 1849), IV. 367

Reign of Blood (Newbound, E., 1880), V. 502

Reign of Hellebore (1760), III. 341

Reign of Terror (Milner, H. M., 1824), IV. 526, 638
— = (1) Burglars; (2) Delicate Ground; (3) Genevieve; (4) Paul the Brazier

Reign of Twelve Hours (1824), IV. 526

Reign of Woman (1892), V. 740

Reimkennar of Zetland = Pirate

Reincarnated Robber = Mystic Mahatma

Reine de Chypre (1845), IV. 526

Reine de Golconde (1812), IV. 526

Reine de la Glace (Smith, F. S., 1897), V. 572

Reine des Naiades (Coles, E., 1870), V. 317

Reinhard and Leonora (1856), V. 740

Reiver of Westburn Flat = Black Dwarf

Rejected Addresses (Cooper, F. F., 1833), IV. 526, 638
— (Stanley, 1812), IV. 406
— (1836), IV. 526

Rejected Addresses Received (1813), IV. 526

Rejection (1811), IV. 526

Relapse (Vanbrugh, Sir G., 1696), I. 18–19, 23, 244, 337, 338, 436; III. 115, 161

Relations (Marston, W., 1869), V. 479

Released (Dickinson, C. H., 1890), V. 344

Released Convict (1857), V. 740

Relief of Lucknow = (1) Indian Revolt; (2) Jessie Brown

Relief of Williamstadt (1793), III. 341

Religious (Cavendish, M., 1662), I. 396

Relvindez and Elzora = Spaniard

Rely on my Discretion (Palmer, T. A., 1870), V. 512

Remarkable Cure (Heriot, P., 1833), V. 419, 797

Remember the Grotto (1854), V. 740

Remembrance (Robinson, M., 1899), V. 547

Remorse (Appleyard, C., 1871), V. 242
— (Coleridge, S. T., 1813), III. 55, 138, 224, 245; IV. 59, 156, 192–3, 281, 577
— (Whiting, G. L., 1873), V. 621

Renaissance (1897), V. 740

Retort Courteous (1834), IV. 526
Retour de Corsair = Bazzard d'Algier
Retour du printemps = Zéphyr
Retreat of the Mountains (Ebsworth, J., 1824), IV. 308
Retribution (Bennett, G. J., 1850), V. 258
— (Dillon, J., 1818), IV. 306
— (Taylor, T., 1856), V. 100, 593
— (1859), V. 740
— = Justifiable Homicide
Retributive Justice (Ashton, J., 1813), IV. 256
— (Burton, E. G., 1863), V. 740, 782
Returned (Pitt, H. M., 1869), V. 526
Returned Captive = Don Rafaelle
Returned from India (1859), V. 741
Returned from Trafalgar (1811), IV. 526
Returned Killed (Planché, J. R., 1826), IV. 378
Returned Outcast (Lee, N., Jr., 1859), V. 802
Return from Navarino = Welcome Home
Return from Siberia = Forced Marriage
Return from Slavery = Native Land
Return from the Baltic (1855), V. 740
Return from Victory = Relief of Williamstadt
Returning the Compliment (Waldan, O. and Palmer, F. G., 1890), V. 610
Return of a Ticket-of-Leave (1863), V. 741
Return of Peace = Speed the Plough
Return of Perouse (1836), IV. 526
Return of the Druses (Browning, R., 1843), IV. 272
Return of the Season = Invitation
Return of the Wanderer = Jessy Vere
Return of Ulysses (Bridges, R. S., 1890), V. 275
— = Patient Penelope
Return Ticket to the International Exhibition (Spencer, G. and James, W., 1862), V. 119, 576
Return to Ithaca = Adventures of Ulysses
Reuben Blight (Panton, J., 1861), V. 741, 809, 845
Reunited (1888), V. 741
Revanche des Cigales (1897), V. 741

Revelations of London (Stevenson, 1868), V. 583
— = Elixir of Life
Revell of Aldford = Countrey Revell
Revels by Moonlight = Millers
Revenge (?Behn, A., 1680), I. 65, 391, 392
— (Chatterton, T., 1770), III. 243
— (Kemble, J. P., 1814), IV. 335
— (Parlby, B. B., 1818), IV. 368
— (Young, E., 1721), II. 59, 70, 71, 113, 264, 364
Revenge and Love = Ellie Brandon
Revengeful Queen (Phillips, W., 1698), I. 170, 266, 423
Revenge of Athridates (1765), III. 341
Revenge of Ceres (Moser, J., 1810), IV. 364
Revenge of Taran (Fitzball, E., IV. 584
Revenge of the Blighted One = Alice Home
Reverse of a Day = Ups and Downs
Reverses (Farnie, H. B., 1867), V. 361
— = Shepherd of Derwent Vale
Review (Colman, G., 1800), IV. 282
— (1837), IV. 526
— = Clump and Cudden
Revolt at Cabul and British Triumphs in India = Afghanistan War
Revolt at Naples = Masaniello
Revolt at Sea (1847), IV. 526
Revolt in the East (1859), V. 741
Revolt of Bruges (Smith, A. R., 1842), IV. 526, 638
Revolt of Flanders (Robinson, E., 1848), IV. 526, 638
Revolt of Genoa = (1) Fiesco; (2) Republican Duke
Revolt of Moscow = Emissary
Revolt of Surinam (1825), IV. 526
Revolt of the Angels (Reade, E., 1830), IV. 607
Revolt of the Chummies (Lighterness, W. B.), IV. 595
— = "Sweep Sweep Sweep!"
Revolt of the Greeks (Walker, C. E., 1824), IV. 526, 638
Revolt of the Harem (1834), IV. 526
Revolt of the Naiades = Lurline
Revolt of the Players = Night Rehearsal

Revolt of the Seraglio on the other Side of the Pole (Moncrieff, W. T., 1834), IV. 526, 638

Revolt of the Water Nymphs = Naiad Queen

Revolt of the Workhouse (À Beckett, G. A., 1834), IV. 249, 567

Revolution (Christian, T. P., 1791), III. 243

— = (1) Gone Away; (2) Timoleon

Revolutionist (1882), V. 741

Revolution of Paris (Pitt, G. D., 1848), IV. 375

Revolution of 1688 = King James the Second

Revolution of Sweden (Trotter, Mrs C., 1706), II. 104, 361

Reward = Mariette

Rewards of Virtue (Fountain, J., 1661), I. 138, 412

Rex and Pontifex (Dodsley, R., 1745), II. 319

Rex Cann, the Whipper-in (Thompson, H., 1884), V. 598

Rhampsinitus (Hamilton, E., 1876), V. 401

Rhine and its Rhino = Lurline

Rhinocerus (1775), III. 404

Rhoda (Parke, W., 1886), V. 512

Rhyme and Reason (Lunn, J., 1828), IV. 348

Ribston's Ride (Chandler, W. A., 1897), V. 307

+ Ricciarda; A Tragedy...from the Italian of Ugo Foscolo, 8°, 1823 (Calcutta) [By James Atkinson]

Rich and Poor (Hazlewood, C. H., 1866), V. 741, 796, 845

— (Lewis, M. G., 1812), IV. 346, 454, 595

— (Price, E., 1873), V. 530

— (1854), V. 741

— (1866), V. 741

Richard I (Dibdin, T. J., 1819), IV. 302

Richard I, King of England (Sewell, G., 1728), II. 354

Richard II (Cumberland, R., 1792), III. 341, 381, 404

— (Gentleman, F., 1754), III. 57, 264, 385

— (Theobald, L., 1719), II. 6, 359

— (Wroughton, R., 1815), IV. 422

Richard III (Coyne, J. S., 1844), IV. 284

— (Kemble, J. P., 1801), IV. 335

— (1815), IV. 527

— (1821), IV. 527

— (1854), V. 741

Richard III Travestie (1823), IV. 527

Richard and Betty (Lane, L., 1848), IV. 527, 638

Richard Armstrong (Poole, W., 1876), V. 529

Richard Cœur de Lion (Burgoyne, J., 1786), III. 44, 98, 102, 241, 378

— (Halliday, A., 1874), V. 401

— (Macnally, L., 1786), III. 44, 102, 285

Richard Cœur de Lion taking in Wolverhampton on his Road to Palestine (1857), V. 845

Richard Darlington (1836), IV. 527

Richard, Duke of York (Kean, E., 1817), IV. 334

— (Merivale, J. H., 1817), IV. 355

Richard in Cyprus (Teres, T., 1769), III. 311

Richard Lovelace (Irving, L. B., 1898) V. 432

Richard Markham (1846), IV. 527

Richard of the Lion Heart (Byron, H. J., 1857), V. 295

Richard Parker (1830), IV. 527

Richard Plantagenet (Haines, J. T., 1836), IV. 322

Richard Savage (Barrie, J. M. and Watson, H. B. M., 1891), V. 211, 251

— (Whitehead, D. C., 1842), IV. 419

— (1897), V. 741

Richard's Play (Rowsell, M. C. and Dilley, J. J., 1891), V. 552

Richard the Lyon (1801), IV. 527

Richard Turpin (1840), IV. 638

Richard Turpin and Tom King = Dick Turpin and Tom King

Richard Turpin, the Highwayman (1819), IV. 527

Richard Whittington and his Cat (Stephens, V., 1897), V. 581

Richard Whittington, Esq. (Payne, E., 1892), V. 518

Richelieu (Lytton, Lord, 1839), IV. 173, 218, 349

— (1888), V. 741

— = French Libertine

Richelieu in Love (Robinson, E., 1844, 1852), IV. 608; V. 547

Richelieu Redressed (Reece, R., 1873), V. 538

Richelieu's Wager = Woman's Secret

Riches (Burges, Sir J. B., 1810), IV. 276

Riches and Poverty (1861), V. 741

Rich in Love but Poor in Pocket (1859), V. 741

Rich Man of Frankfort (Reynoldson, T. H., 1838), IV. 393

Richmond Gardener (1790), III. 341

Richmond Heiress (D'Urfey, T., 1693), I. 273, 276, 409; III. 114

— (Waldron, F. G., 1777), III. 114, 313

Richmond Hill (Grattan, H. P., 1827), IV. 527, 638

Richmond in the Olden Time = Court Masque

Richmond Market = Martha

Richmond Wells (Williams, J., 1722), II. 364

Rick Burners (Rede, W. L., 1833), IV. 607

Riddle Me, Riddle me Ree (1842), IV. 527

— = Harlequin Riddle Me, Riddle me Ree

Ride a Cock Horse (1835), IV. 527

Ride-a-cock-horse to Banbury (1874), V. 741

Ride-a-cock-horse to Banbury Cross (Douglass, J. T., 1870), V. 348

— (1870), V. 571

Ride of Death = Headless Horseman

Rider (1768), III. 341

Ridicule (1795), III. 341

Ridiculous Guardian (1761), III. 341

Ridiculous Lovers = Generous Enemies

Ridotto al' Fresco = Harlot's Progress

Rienzi (Jackson, J. P., 1879), V. 432, 799

— (Mitford, M. R., 1828), IV. 176, 358

Rienzi Reinstated (Allan, A. W., 1874), V. 238

Rienzi, The Last of the Tribunes (Buckstone, J. B., 1836), IV. 275

Rienzi the Patriot = Last of the Romans

Riever of Barry Hill (1842), IV. 638

Riever's Ransom (1846), IV. 638

Rifle and how to use it (Bridgeman, J. V., 1859), V. 275

Rifle Brigade (Selby, C., 1838), IV. 610

Rifle Club (Jerrold, M. W. B., 1852), V. 436

Rifle Manœuvres (1838), IV. 527

Riflemen (1860), V. 741

Riflemen! Riflemen! Riflemen! = Rifle Volunteers

Rifles (1847), IV. 527

Rifle-Shot (Milner, H. M., 1834), IV. 599

Rifle Volunteer = Double Dealing

Rifle Volunteers (Stirling, E., 1859), V. 584

Rift Within the Lute (Dickinson, C. H. and Griffiths, A., 1898), V. 344

Right (Killick, J. M., 1881), V. 444

Right against Might (White, M., 1891), V. 621

— = (1) Alta; (2) Guy Mannering

Right and Might (Waldron, W. R., 1864), V. 610

— (1852), V. 741

Right and Wrong (Burton, 1812) = Receipt for Mirth, IV. 277, 525, 575, 638

— (Harvey, F., 1883), V. 408

— (1858), V. 741

— (1868), V. 741

— = Two Roads of Life

Right at Last (Gibbon, G. C., 1828), IV. 319

— (1887), V. 741

Right Fellow (Marshall, W. F., 1868), V. 478

Rightful Heir (Lytton, Baron, 1868), V. 466

— (Sturgess, A., 1899), V. 586

— (1871), V. 741

Rightful Heiress (Field, H. J., 1895), V. 365

Right-full Heir (Arnold, H. T.), V. 244

Right Man (Comer, G. and Ellis, L., 1887), V. 319

Right Man in the Right Place (1860), V. 741

Right must conquer = Fathoms Deep

Right of Common (Dibdin, T. J., 1811), IV. 299

Right of Possession (1813), IV. 527

Right or Wrong (Bisgood, J. J., 1887), V. 262

— (Jarman, F., 1896), V. 434

Rights and Privileges (McDonald, B. P., 1898), v. 468
Rights and Wrongs of Woman (Morton, J. M., 1856), v. 495
Rights of Hospitality = Wanderer
Rights of Man (Sullivan, W. F., 1791), III. 310, 401
— (1791), III. 401, 404
Rights of Woman (Lunn, J., 1843), IV. 348
— (1792), III. 341, 404
Rights of Women (Schiff, E., 1871), v. 557
Right's Right (Clarke, C. A. and Stewart, J. O., 1886), v. 311
Right will take Place = Restauration
Rigoletti (1861), v. 741
Rigolo (1855), v. 741
Rimonia (1808), IV. 527
Rinaldo (Hill, A., 1711), II. 230, 398, 438
— (Humphreys, S., 1731), II. 439
Rinaldo and Armida (Dennis, J., 1698), I. 402; II. 85
Rinaldo Rinaldini (Cross, J. C., 1801), IV. 36, 286
— (Wilks, T. E., 1836), IV. 420
Rinaldo the Remorseless (1822), IV. 527
Ring (Linley, W., 1800), III. 282, 390; IV. 346, 595
— (Turnbull, Mrs W., 1833), IV. 527, 615, 638
— (1895), v. 741
Ring and its Moral = Champion Belt
Ring and the Keeper (Wooler, J. P., 1862), v. 632, 824
Ring Doves (Mathews, C. J., 1837), IV. 354
Ring Fence (Stannard, Mrs, 1893), v. 579
Ringing the Changes (1862), v. 741
Ring of Iron (Harvey, F., 1884), v. 408
Ring of Polycrates (McCarthy, J. H., 1892), v. 467
— (1890), v. 741
Ring's End (1795), III. 341
Rings on her Fingers (1896), v. 741
Ring, the Statue and the Tournament = Cream White Woman
Riots of '80 = Dolly Varden
Ripe Fruit (Stuart, C., 1781), III. 310
Ripples (Browne, G. W. and Moss, H., 1880), v. 282
Ripplings (Balcour, C., 1883), v. 247

Rip van Winkle (Akerman, W., 1897), v. 236
— (Bernard, W. B., 1832), IV. 265
— (Boucicault, D. and Jefferson, J., 1865), v. 268
— (Burke, 1833), IV. 277
— (Clarke, H. S., 1880), v. 312
— (Farnie, H. B., 1882), v. 363, 791
— (Fitzgerald, S. J. A., 1899), v. 369
— (Kerr, J.), v. 443
— (Manley, J., 1871), v. 805
— (Marchant, F., 1871), v. 476
— (Strachan, W., Jr., 1866), v. 741, 818, 845
— (1866), v. 741
Riquet with the Tuft (Blanchard, E. L., 1862), v. 263
— (Planché, J. R. and Dance, C., 1836), IV. 152, 380
— (1816), IV. 527
Rise and Fall (Dibdin, T. J., 1821), IV. 303
Rise and Fall of Massaniello (D'Urfey, T., 1699), I. 55, 410
Rise and Fall of Richard III (Burnand, F. C., 1868), v. 289, 781
Rise of Dick Halward (Jerome, J. K., 1895), v. 436
Rise of the Moon of Intellect = Prabod'h Chandro' daya
Rise of the Rothschilds (Barnett, C. Z., 1836), IV. 260
Rising Generation (1861), v. 741
Rising of 1745 = Prince Charles Edward Stuart
Rising of the Session = Olden Times
Rising of the Tide (Fitzball, E., 1853), v. 368
Rising Sun (1882), v. 741
Rites of Hecate (Love, J., 1763), III. 209, 282
Rites of Memphis = Prodigal Son
Rival Artisans (1854), v. 741
Rival Artistes (Kingthorne, M., 1873), v. 445
Rival Brothers (1704), II. 71, 115, 116, 117–18, 382
— (1816), IV. 527
— = (1) Election; (2) Iver and Hengo; (3) Rodogune
Rival Candidates (Bate, H., 1775), III. 235

Rival Soldiers (1814), IV. 527
Rival Sorcerers (1790), III. 342
Rival's Rendezvous (1861), v. 742
Rival's Revenge = Patrick's Vow
Rival Statues (Cross, J. C., 1803), IV. 286
Rival Tars (Dibdin, C. I. M., 1802), IV. 290
Rival Theatres (Stayley, G., 1759), III. 309 [This was acted Smock Alley, Dublin, 21/2/1759]
Rival Tinkers (Ward, H. R., 1848), IV. 416
Rival Valets (Ebsworth, J., 1825), IV. 308
— = Painter's Study
Rival Widows (Cooper, Mrs E., 1735), II. 142, 205–6, 316
Riven Clouds (1880), v. 742
River God (1835), IV. 527
River of Life (Shirley, A. and Landeck, B., 1894), v. 564
— = Great Temptation
Riverside Story (Bancroft, Lady, 1890), v. 248
River Sprite (Linley, G., 1865), v. 460
Rizpah Misery (Campbell, Mrs V., 1894), v. 301
Rizzio (Graham, D., 1898), v. 386
Road and the Riders = Scarlet Dick
Road of Life (Blanchard, E. L., 1843), IV. 268
— = Up and Down
Roadside Cottage = Day after the Fair
Roadside Inn (Douglass, J. T.), v. 789
— (Simpson, J. P., 1865), v. 576
Roadside Inn turned inside out = Robert Macaire
Road, the River and the Rail (Spencer, G., 1868), v. 576
Road to Bath = Night's Adventures
Road to Blue Ruin = Miss Formosa
Road to Fame (White, A. and Grunfeld, P., 1885), v. 620
Road to Fortune (Dering, C. E., 1893), v. 343
Road to Happiness (Melville, H., 1848), IV. 355
— = Forget and Forgive
Road to Odiham = 'Tis an ill Wind that blows nobody good

Road to Ridicule (Streatfield, T., 1799), III. 310
Road to Ruin (Holcroft, T., 1792), III. 49, 55, 136, 141, 271
— (1897), v. 742
— = High-mettled Racer
Road to Transportation (Courtney, J., 1862), v. 786
Road to Yaroslaf = Narensky
Roaring Dick & Co. (1896), v. 742
Roasted Emperor = Jenny's Whim
Roasting a Rogue (Palmer, T. A., 1882), v. 512
Robber (Cumberland, R., 1809), IV. 287
Robber Knight = Hans von Stein
Robber of Epping Forest (1831), IV. 527
Robber of Genoa = Great Devil
Robber of the Alps (Nicholson, J., 1820), IV. 366
Robber of the Rhine (Almar, G., 1833), IV. 252
Robbers (Anderson, J. R., 1851), IV. 254; v. 240
— (Render, W., 1799), III. 62, 301
— (Thompson, B., 1800), III. 62, 311, 397; IV. 412
— (Tytler, A. F., 1800), III. 62, 313; IV. 615
— (1724), II. 382
— (1797), III. 62, 342, 404
— (1820), IV. 527
— = Cartouche
Robber's Bride (Pocock, I., 1829), IV. 115–16, 385
— = (1) Abelino; (2) Rauberbraut
Robber's Mother = Band of Death
Robbers of Normandy = Florence Montaubon
Robbers of the Caucasus = Zulema the Circassian Beauty
Robbers of the Mail Post = Courier of Lyons
Robbers of the Pyrenees (Suter, W. E., 1862), v. 588
— = Gallant Moriscoes
Robber's Sister (Fitzball, E., 1841), IV. 316
Robber's Wife (1831), IV. 527
— = Robber's Bride
Robber's Wife of the Apennines = Sparbuto

Robbery at the Tower of London = Colonel Blood

Robbery of the Cape Diamonds = Kimberley Mail

Robbery of the Mail = Courier of Lyons

Robbery under Arms (Dampier, A. and Walch, G., 1894), v. 335

Robbing Robin Hood (1890), v. 742

Robbing Roy (Burnand, F. C., 1879), v. 291

Robbing the Mail = Arrah-ma-Beg

Robers Rob'd = Bouncing Knight

Robert and Bertram (Horton, S. G., 1887), v. 427

Robert and Bertrand (1845), IV. 527

Robert Burns (Lemon, M., 1842), IV. 344

— (1896), v. 742

Robert Emmet (Digges, W., 1881), v. 345

Robert Emmett (Boucicault, D., 1884), v. 269

Robert Emmett, the Irish Patriot of 1803 (1873), v. 742

Robert La Grange (1861), v. 742

Robert le Diable (Fitzball, E. and Buckstone, J. B., 1832), IV. 83, 314

— (1832), IV. 83, 527

Robert le Grange (Webb, C., 1843), IV. 417

Robert Macaire (Byron, H. J., 1870), v. 297

— (Selby, C., 1835), IV. 397, 610

— (Simpson, C. and Simpson, J. P., 1867), v. 816

— (1887), v. 742

Robert Macaire Renovated (Clarance, L., 1884), v. 311

Robert of Normandy = Fiend Father

Robert Rabagas (Fiske, S., 1873), v. 367

Robert Richborne (1871), v. 742

Robert Ryland (Glynn, G., 1849), IV. 319

Robert the Bruce (1819), IV. 92, 527

— (1834), IV. 92, 528

Robert the Devil (Beazley, S., Jr.), IV. 264

— (Gilbert, W. S., 1868), v. 379

— (?Lacy, M. R., 1830), IV. 340, 592

— (Raymond, R. J., 1830), IV. 388

— (1830), IV. 528

— (1888), v. 742

Robespierre (Bernard, W. B., 1840), IV. 266

— (Bliss, H., 1854), v. 265

— (Irving, L. B., 1899), v. 210, 432

— (Patterson, R. H., 1877), v. 809

— (Springate, H. S., 1879), v. 576

Robin and Marion (1819), IV. 528

Robin Bullcalf's Readings (1785), III. 342

Robin Goodfellow (Carton, R. C., 1893), v. 305

— (Loder, E. J., 1848), IV. 346

— (1738), II. 136, 382, 448

Robin Gray (1814), IV. 528

Robin Hood (Barri, H., 1890), v. 251

— (Blanchard, E. L., 1858), v. 742, 779, 845

— (Burnand, F. C., 1862), v. 288

— (Douglass, J. T., 1878), v. 348

— (Fitzball, E., 1860), v. 368

— (Hall, F., 1880), v. 399

— (Jones, R. S., 1848), IV. 591

— (McCardle, J. F., 1880), v. 742, 804, 845

— (Macnally, L., 1784), III. 285

— (Mendez, M., 1750), III. 287

— (Mills, H. and Horton, S. G., 1888), v. 798, 807, 845

— (Oxenford, J., 1860), v. 510

— (1730), II. 448

+ — (D.L., 1750), II. 260

— (1810), IV. 528

— (1857, 1859), v. 845

— (1861), v. 742

— (1876), v. 742

— (1878), v. 845

— (1879, 1881, 1896), v. 742

Robin Hood and his Merry Little Men (Blanchard, E. L., 1877), v. 265

Robin Hood and his Merry Men (Hazlewood, C. H., 1867), v. 413

— (1867), v. 742

Robin Hood and Little John (1730), II. 365

— (1896), v. 742

Robin Hood and Maid Marion (Hood, B., 1899), v. 425

Robin Hood and Richard Cœur de Lion! (Stocqueler, J. H., Brooks, C. W. S. and Kenney, C., 1846), v. 528, 591

Robin Hood and ye Curtall Fryer (Dawtrey, R. A., 1892), v. 339

Robin Hood Esq. (Rogers, T. S., 1894),
v. 549

Robin Hood, Little John and Friar
Tuck (1854), v. 742

Robin Redbreast = Ruddy George

Robin's Art of Money-Catching = Fox
Uncas'd

Robinson Crusoe (Barrett, O., 1895), v.
250

— (Blanchard, E. L., 1845), IV. 268

— (Blanchard, E. L., 1881), v. 265

— (Byam, M. and Melville, A., 1891),
v. 294

— (Byron, H. J., 1860), v. 296, 782

— (Byron, H. J., 1868), v. 297

— (Conquest, G. and Spry, H., 1885),
v. 322

— (Edlin, H., 1897), v. 354

— (England, A. and Noble, C. R.,
1897), v. 358

— (Farnie, H. B., 1876), v. 362

— (Farnie, H. B. and Reece, R., 1886),
v. 363

— (George, G. H., 1872), v. 377

— (Gilbert, W. S., Byron, H. J., Hood,
T., Leigh, H. S. and Sketchley, A.,
1867), v. 379

— (Harris, Sir A. H. G., 1878), v. 405

— (Hewson, J. J., 1898), v. 420

— (Jones, J. W., 1894), v. 441

— (Lee, N., 1836), IV. 594

— (Lemon, M., 1842), IV. 82, 344

— (Lennard, H., 1887), v. 455, 803

— (Lennard, H., 1895), v. 456

— (Lennard, H., 1896), v. 456

— (Locke, F., 1894), v. 743, 804, 845

— (McArdle, J. F., 1876), v. 466

— (Muskerry, W., 1888), v. 501

— (Muskerry, W., 1891), v. 501

— (Nichols, H. and Harris, Sir A. H. G.,
1893), v. 504, 808

— (Nie, J., 1892), v. 504

— (North, W. S., 1895), v. 505

— (Pocock, I., 1817), IV. 82, 113, 384

— (Pratt, F. W., 1890), v. 743, 811, 845

— (Rogers, T. S., 1897), v. 744, 814,
845

— (Rogers, T. S., 1898), v. 549

— (Sheridan, R. B., 1781), III. 396

— (Thorne, G., 1886), v. 598

— (Thorne, G., 1887), v. 598

— (Thorne, G., 1894), v. 599

Robinson Crusoe (Thorne, G., 1895),
v. 821

— (Walton, W., 1891), v. 613

— (1781), III. 342

— (1791), III. 342, 404

— (1857), v. 845

— (1865), v. 744

— (1867, 1876, 1877, 1878), v. 742

— (1878), v. 845

— (1880, 1881, 1882, 1883), v. 743

— (1883), v. 744

— (1884, 1885, 1886, 1888, 1889, 1890,
1891, 1892, 1893, 1894), v. 743

— (1894), v. 845

— (1895, 1896, 1897), v. 743

— (1897), v. 845

— (1897, 1898, 1899), v. 744, 845

Robinson Crusoe and Billie Taylor
(Palmer, G. and Palmer, F. G., 1882),
v. 511

Robinson Crusoe and Gulliver's
Travels = Gulliver on his Travels

Robinson Crusoe and his Man Friday
(Douglass, J. T., 1874), v. 348

Robinson Crusoe, Esq. (1874), v. 744

Robinson Crusoe Junior (McCabe,
C. W. and Barrington, E., 1893), v.
467

Robinson Crusoe Rewigged (1878), v.
744

Robinson Crusoe Rewived (Bertrand,
E. C., 1877), v. 260

Robinson Crusoe up-to-date (1890), v.
744

Robin the Rover (McGuire, T. C.,
1897), v. 469

Rob of the Fen (Lemon, M., 1838), IV.
528, 594, 638

Rob Roy (French, S., 1867), v. 373

— (Milner, H. M., 1818), IV. 92, 528,
638

— (Murray, W. H., 1818), IV. 92, 365

— (Ryder, C., 1825), IV. 396

— (Smith, H. B., 1894), v. 572

— (1818), IV. 92, 528

— (1825), IV. 92, 528

— (1857), v. 744

Rob Roy MacGregor (Pocock, I., 1818),
IV. 92, 384

— (1828), IV. 92, 528

Rob Roy, the Bold Outlaw (Hazlewood,
C. H., 1864), v. 744, 845

Roman Actor (?Betterton, T., 1722), II. 448

— (Kemble, J. P., 1794), III. 279

Roman Awry = Paw Clawdian

Roman Bride's Revenge (Gildon, C., 1696), I. 158, 412

Roman Brother (Heraud, J. A., 1840), IV. 588

Roman Catacombs = Mysteries of Alviano

Romance (Simpson, J. P., 1860), v. 567, 816

Romance and Reality (Brougham, J., 1847), IV. 272

— (Brougham, J., 1860), v. 280

— (Folkard, H., 1870), v. 370

— (1833), IV. 528

— (1860), v. 744

— = Road of Life

Romance and Romancers = In Statu Quo!

Romance in the Life of Sixtus V = Sixtus V

Romance of a Court = Jewels and Dust

Romance of a Day (Planché, J. R., 1831), IV. 379, 605

— = Morning, Noon and Night

Romance of a French Marriage = Vivianne

Romance of an Hour (Kelly, H., 1774), III. 120, 131, 278, 389

— = Wager

Romance of a Patent = Aretoeus

Romance of a Poor Young Man (Hazlewood, C. H., 1862), v. 744, 796, 845

— (Wallack, L., 1860), v. 612

— = Honour before Wealth

Romance of City Life = George Geith

Romance of Love (Steven, A., 1891), v. 583

Romance of Marriage = (1) Marah; (2) Tender Precautions

Romance of Real Life = Geneviève

Romance of Runnymede = Magna Charta

Romance of the Coast (1830), IV. 528

— = Preventive Service

Romance of the Harem (Sketchley, A. 1872), v. 571

Romance of the New Beer Bill = Bona Fide Travellers

Romance of the Nose = Prince Dorus

Romance of the Pyrenees (1830), IV. 528

Romance of the Rhine (1847), IV. 528

Romance of the Rose (Beverley, H. R., 1850), v. 261

— = Prince Dorus

Romance of the Shopwalker (Buchanan, R. and Jay, H., 1896), v. 285

Romance under Difficulties (Burnand, F. C., 1856), v. 287

Roman Empress (Joyner, W., 1670), I. 416

Roman Father (Whitehead, W., 1750), II. 72, 95, 180, 364, 446; III. 60, 315, 398

Roman Generalls (Dover, J., 1667), I. 233, 312, 403

Roman Ladies (1840), IV. 528

— = Vestal-Virgin

Roman Maid (Hurst, R., 1724), II. 26, 31, 74, 84, 338

Roman Matron = Coriolanus

Roman Matron's Jewels = Cornelia

+ Roman Mutiny (Cobbold, Elizabeth. 8°, 1825, Ipswich, in *Poems*)

Roman Nose (1835), IV. 528

— = Good-looking Fellow

Roman Patriot = Mutius Scaevola

Roman Revenge (Hill, A., 1753), II. 110, 438; III. 268

Roman Sacrifice (Shirley, W., 1777), III. 306

Roman Slave = Caius Silius

Romantic Affair (1892), v. 744

Romantic Attachment (Wood, A., 1866), v. 630

Romantic Caroline (Hatton, J., 1874), v. 409

Romantic Idea (Planché, J. R., 1849), IV. 129–30, 383

Romantic Lady (1671), I. 347, 444

Romantic Lover (Allingham, J. T., 1806) = Legacy, IV. 252, 491, 568

Romantic Ruy Blas (1873), v. 744

Romantic Tale (Johnstone, J. B., 1871), v. 438

Romantic Widow (Ranger, 1837), IV. 528, 638

— (1856), v. 845

Roman Victim (Shirley, W.), III. 306

Roman Virgin = Appius and Virginia

Rose and Colin (Dibdin, C., 1778), III. 255, 381

Rose and the Lily (1873), V. 745

Rose and the Ring (Clarke, H. S., 1890), V. 313

— (Heyne, M., 1878), V. 420

— = Ambassador's Lady

Rose and Thistle = Rights of Woman

Rose Ashford (1848), IV. 529

Rose Brilliant (1899), V. 745

Rosebud of Stinging-nettle Farm (Byron, H. J., 1863), V. 296

Rosebuds (Bradley, C., 1885), V. 273

Rose Clinton (Courtney, J., 1848), IV. 284; V. 845

— (1854), V. 745, 845

Rosedale (Arnold, C., 1893), V. 243

— (Wallack, L., 1876), V. 612

Rose d'Amour (1818), IV. 529

Rose Graham (1860), V. 745

Rose Lendin (1842), IV. 529

Rosemary (Parker, L. N. and Carson, S. M., 1896), V. 513

+ Rose Maythorn (Lee, N., Jr., 1867)

Rose Michel (Clarke, C., 1875), V. 311

— (Millward, C., 1886), V. 489

Rosenberg (1828), IV. 529

Rosencrantz and Guildenstern (Gilbert, W. S., 1891), V. 381

Rose of Alvey = Pretender

Rose of Altenheim = Hunter's Bride

Rose of Amiens = Our Wife

Rose of Arragon (Knowles, J. S., 1842), IV. 339

Rose of Auvergne (Farnie, H. B., 1869), V. 790

Rose of Balsora = Noureddin and the Tartar Robbers

Rose of Blarney (Rhys, H., 1862), V. 542

Rose of Castile (Harris, A. G. and Falconer, E., 1857), V. 405

Rose of Castille = Queen and the Knave

Rose of Corbeil (Stirling, E., 1837), IV. 406

Rose of Devon (Jourdain, J., 1889), V. 442

Rose of Ettrick Vale (Lynch, T. J., 1825), IV. 92, 529, 596

Rose of Gurgistan = Persian Hunters

Rose of Ireland and the Fairies of O'Donoghue's Lakes = Brother's Revenge

Rose of Ispahan (1897), V. 745

Rose of Kerry = Ireland

Rose of Killarney (1894), V. 745

— = Aline

Rose of Morven = Beautiful Insane

Rose of Persia (Hood, B., 1899), V. 425

Rose of Rathboy (Fitzgerald, D., 1899), V. 368

Rose of Romford (Martin, J. R., 1885), V. 479

Rose of St Fleur (1867), V. 745

Rose of Salency (1866), V. 745

Rose of Stepney (1838), IV. 529

Rose of the Alhambra (Fitzball, E., 1836), IV. 315

— (Parker, C. S., 1891), V. 513

Rose of the Ferry (1860), V. 745

Rose of the Village (1856), V. 745

Rose of Tuscany = Three Dons

Rose of Windsor (Parke, W., 1889), V. 512

— = Herne's Oak

Rose Queen (1898), V. 745

— = Philandering

Rose Roy (Pitt, G. D., 1835), IV. 372

— (1835), IV. 529

Roses (Valpy, R., 1795), III. 313

Roses and Thorns (Lunn, J., 1825), IV. 348

Rose, Shamrock and Thistle (Lee, N., Jr., 1865), V. 803

— (1845), IV. 529

— = Frolics of the Fairies

Roses of Shadow (Raffalovich, A., 1893), V. 533

Rose's Victory (1871), V. 745

Rose, Thistle and Shamrock (Edgeworth, M., 1817), IV. 209, 309

Rose without a Thorn = Chrystabelle

Rose Wreath (?Palmer, J., 1781), III. 342, 393, 404

Rosicrucian Student = Daemon Owl

Rosière (Monkhouse, H., 1892), V. 491

Rosimunda (Preston, W., 1793), III. 300

Rosina (Brooke, F., 1782), III. 206, 240, 378

Rosine (1836), IV. 529

Roslin Castle (Ebsworth, J.), IV. 309

Rosmer of Rosmersholm (1891), V. 79, 745

Rosmersholm (Archer, C., 1891), V. 79, 187, 242

Rosmersholm (1893), v. 745
Rosamunda (1856), v. 745
Rossignol (1825), IV. 529
Roth (Ross, C. H. and Richards, P.,
  1871), v. 551
Rotherhithe in the Olden Time (1854),
  v. 745
Rotherick O'Connor, King of Con-
  naught (Shadwell, J., 1720), II. 354
Rothomago (Farnie, H. B., 1879), v.
  362
Roué Brother = Adèle
Roué Reformed = Jupiter and Juno
Rouge et Noir (Ebsworth, J., 1838), IV.
  308
— (Leslie, H. T., 1866), v. 745, 803, 845
— (1838), IV. 529
Rougemont = French Libertine
Rougemont the French Robber (John-
  stone, J. B., 1860), v. 800
Rough and Ready (Glendinning, J.,
  1897), v. 382
— (Meritt, P., 1873), v. 485
— (1860), v. 745
Rough and Smooth (1827), IV. 529
Rough Diamond (Buckstone, J. B.,
  1847), IV. 130, 275
— (1836), IV. 529
Rough Hands and Honest Hearts (1873),
  v. 745
Rough Honesty (Pitt, W. H., 1877), v.
  527
Roughly Woo'd and Gently Won
  (1878), v. 745
Rough Road tests the Mettle = Adversity
Rough Road to a Golden Land = Tiger
  of Mexico
Rough Rob, the Gipsy Thief of Hang-
  man's Hollow (Thorne, R. L., 1850),
  v. 599
Round a Tree (Risque, W. H., 1896), v.
  544
Roundhead (Bussy, B. F. and Black-
  more, W. T., 1883), v. 294
Roundheads (Behn, A., 1681), I. 79, 224,
  391
Round of Intrigue (Clarance, J., 1847),
  IV. 280
Round of Wrong (Bernard, W. B.,
  1846), IV. 266
Round Robin (Dibdin, C. I. M., 1811),
  IV. 292

Round the Clock (McArdle, J. F., 1878),
  v. 466
Round the Globe (McArdle, J. F.,
  1875), v. 466
Round the Globe in Eighty Days (1875),
  v. 745
Round the Links (Overbeck, E., 1895),
  v. 509
Round the Ring (Meritt, P., 1891), v.
  487
Round the World (Murray, A., 1886), v.
  499
Round the World in Eighty Days (1875),
  v. 745
Round the World in W'Eighty Days
  (FitzGeorge, Capt., 1877), v. 368
Round Tower (Cross, J. C., 1797), III.
  250, 342, 380, 404 [The date on p. 250
  should be 1797]
— (McCarthy, J. H., 1892), v. 467
Roused Lion (Webster, B. N., 1847), IV.
  418
Rout (Hill, Sir J., 1758), III. 269
Rout Routed (1800), IV. 529
Rover (Behn, A., 1677, 1681), I. 57,
  222–3, 231, 252, 348, 349, 350, 351,
  352, 390, 391; III. 114
— (Boyce, S., 1752), III. 239
— (1757), III. 114, 342
Rover from Many Lands = Bitter
  Reckoning
Rover of the Isles (1833), IV. 529
Rover of the North Sea = False Earl
Rover Reclaim'd = (1) Damon and
  Phillida; (2) Lady's Revenge
Rover Reclaimed = Breakfast of Love
Rovers (Canning, G., 1798), III. 67, 241
Rover's Bride (Almar, G., 1830), IV. 252
Rover's Cruise = Wapping Old Stairs
Rovers of Weimar = Quadrupeds of
  Quedlinburgh
Rover's Secret (Stirling, E., 1845), IV.
  408
— (1860), v. 745
Roving Commission (Besemeres, J.,
  1869), v. 260
Roving Husband Reclaim'd (1706), II.
  182, 382
Roving Meg (Clarke, A. H., 1899), v.
  311
Row in the Buildings (Greenwood, T.,
  1844), IV. 321

Rule a Wife and Have a Wife (Love, J., 1776), III. 283, 391
Rule Britannia (Becher, M., 1870), v. 254
— (Campbell, A. V. 1836), IV. 278, 575
— (Roberts, J., 1794), III. 302
— (1846), IV. 530
— (1868), v. 745
— (1895), v. 745
Rule of Contrary = Sayings and Doings
Rule of Three (Le Clercq, P., 1891), v. 452
— (Talfourd, F., 1858), v. 590
Ruling Passion (Macnally, L., 1778), III. 285 [This was acted on 24/2/1778 at Crow-street, not Capel-street, Dublin]
— (Willing, J., 1882), v. 626
Rumbelow (1888), v. 745
Rum Duke and the Queer Duke (1730), II. 382
Rumfuskin King of Bythnyphorbia (1818), IV. 530
Rumfustian Innamorato (Walker, C. E., 1824), IV. 416, 615
Rummin's Reputation (Rae, C. M., 1879), v. 532
Rummio and Judy (Logan, W. H., 1841), IV. 595
Rum Ones (1822), IV. 530
Rumour (Stannard, Mrs, 1889), v. 579
Rump (Tatham, J., 1660), I. 211, 224, 292, 391, 434
Rumpelstiltskin and the Maid (Burnand, F. C., 1864), v. 288
Rumpus in Ashan-T = King Koffee
Rum'uns from Rome (1881), v. 745
Runaway (Cowley, Mrs H., 1776), III. 248
Runaway Bride (McLaren, A., 1823), IV. 352
Runaway Girl (Hicks, Sir S. and Nichols, H., 1898), v. 421
Runaway Goddess and the Enchanted Daffodil = Diana's Chase
Runaway Horse = Hut of Valais
Runaway Husbands (Jackson, W. H., 1893), v. 432
— (1849), IV. 530
— = Ladies of St Cyr
Runaway Match (Mayne, A., 1872), v. 483

Runaway Match (1854), v. 745
— (1880), v. 745
Runaways (Aria, E., 1898), v. 243
— (Broughton, F. W., 1880), v. 281
— (1894), v. 745
Run down to Brighton (Meadows, A. M., 1893), v. 483
Run for your Life (1820), IV. 530
Run in (Gaskell, Mrs P., 1899), v. 376
Runnamede (Logan, J., 1784), III. 61, 282, 391
Running of the Rat = Brisket Family
Runnymede (Richards, A. B., 1846), IV. 608
Run of Luck (Pettitt, H. and Harris, Sir A., 1886), v. 521
— (1877), v. 745
Run to Earth (Macdonough, G. F., 1874), v. 469
— (Roberts, G., 1887), v. 544
— (Saunders, C., 1873), v. 556
— = (1) Day at Boulogne; (2) Scarlet Sins
Run wild (Coffin, E., 1888), v. 316
Rupert Dreadnought (Beverley, H. R., 1871), v. 261
Rupert of Hentzau (Hope, A., 1898), v. 425
Rural Felicity (Buckstone, J. B., 1834), IV. 274
Ruralising (Carlyle, G., 1872), v. 303
Rural Love (1732), II. 382
— (1764), III. 342
Rural Sports (1740), II. 382
Rural Visitors (1807), IV. 530
Ruse de guerre (Selby, C., 1835), IV. 610
Ruse de Guerre on the Banks of the Tagus = Lisbon
Rushford's Last Ruse (Lawrence, W., 1878), v. 451
Rush Light (1795), III. 404
Russell (1839), IV. 638
Russia (Farnie, H. B. and Reece, R., 1877), v. 362
Russia against Turkey, now on Trial at Cook's Arena of Chivalry before Britannia assisted by immortal Punch (1854), v. 745
Russian (Sheridan, T., 1813), IV. 401
Russian Ambassador (Shield, H., 1871), v. 563

Russian Brothers = Serf
Russian Bride (Hazlewood, C. H., 1874), v. 415
Russian Captive (Haines, J. T., 1831), IV. 530, 639
Russian Daughter (1820), IV. 530
— = Zelma
Russian Festival (Noble, 1817), IV. 530, 639
Russian Impostor (Siddons, H., 1809), IV. 401
Russian Mandate = Ivan Daniloff
Russian Perfidy = Boor's Hut
Russian Sacrifice (Code, H. B., 1813), IV. 281
Russian Slaves = Day in Turkey
Russian Stratagem = Love in Wrinkles
Russian Tyranny (1854), v. 845
— (1884), v. 745
— = Nadeshta, the Slave Girl
Russian Village (Brown, C. A., 1813) = Narensky, IV. 530, 639
Rustic (Halley, W. F., 1896), v. 400
— (Siedle, A. E., 1888), v. 566
Rustic Adonis (1837), IV. 530
Rustic Chivalry (Weatherley, F. E., 1892), v. 617
Rustic Heroine = Loyal Shepherds
Rusticity (1750–1800), III. 342
Rustic Maiden (Gordon, G. L., 1882), v. 385
Rustic Roses (1873), v. 745
Ruth (Bright, A. A. and Jerome, J. K., 1890), v. 275
— (Haines, J. T., 1843), IV. 323
— (Lancaster, E. R.), IV. 593
— (Moore, R., 1868), v. 492
— (1840), IV. 530
— (1883), v. 745
Ruth Lee (Waldron, W. R., 1869), v. 611
Ruth Martin, the Fatal Dreamer (Barnett, C. Z., 1846), IV. 261
Ruth Oakley (Harris, A. G. and Williams, T. J., 1856), v. 405
Ruth of Rosedale (1848), IV. 530
Ruth's Lovers (1898), v. 745
Ruth's Romance (Broughton, F. W., 1876), v. 152, 281
Ruth the Jewess = Ruth
Ruth the Mountain Rose = When the Clock strikes Nine

Ruth Tudor (1837), IV. 530
Ruth Underwood (Mitchell, L. E., 1892), v. 490
Ruthven (Harris, A. G., 1859), v. 405
Ruy Blas (Alexander, W. D. S., 1890), v. 238
— (Crosland, Mrs N., 1887), v. 787
— (Falconer, E., 1860), v. 360
— (Gilbert, W. S., 1866), v. 379
— (Glover, W. H., 1861), v. 793
— (Grist, W., 1886), v. 395, 795
— (Leslie, F. and Clark, H. F., 1889), v. 456
— (O'Rourke, E., ?1861), v. 808
— (1860), v. 745
— (1861), v. 745
Ruy Blas Righted (Reece, R., 1874), v. 538
Rye House Plot (Haines, J. T., 1838), IV. 322
— (1861), v. 745
— (1865), v. 745

Sabbioneta (1896), v. 746
Sabine War = Romulus and Remus
Sabotiers (1806), IV. 530
Sachem's Vow = Red Man
Sacontalá (Jones, W., 1789), III. 70, 277
— (1870), v. 746
Sacrament of Judas (Parker, L. N., 1899), v. 514
Sacred Elephants of the Pagoda = Rajah of Nagpore
Sacred Standard and the Chinese Prince (Milner, H. M., 1828), IV. 530, 639
Sacred Trust (Faucquez, A., 1861), v. 746, 791, 845
Sacrifice (Fane, Sir F., 1686), I. 101, 410
— (Victor, B., 1776), III. 313
— (1857), v. 746
Sacrificed (Lloyd, M. F., 1891), v. 461
Sacrifice of Iphigenia (1750), III. 342
Sadak and Kalasrade (Dibdin, T. J., 1797), III. 342, 382
— (Mitford, M. R., 1835), IV. 358
— (1814), IV. 530
Saddled for the Field = White Surrey
Saddler of Bantry = Black Tom of Tyburn
Sad Memories (Withers, F., 1895), v. 630

Saint Cecily (Medbourne, M., 1666), I. 420

St Clair of the Isles (Polack, E., 1838), IV. 385

St Clara's Eve = Conquest of Taranto

St Clare and the Happy Days of Uncle Tom = Slave Hunt

St Clement's Eve (Taylor, Sir H., 1862), v. 820

St Cupid (Jerrold, D. W., 1853), v. 69, 104, 436

St Cuthbert's Eve (1820), IV. 530

St Cyr = Ninon

St David's Day (Dibdin, T. J., 1800), IV. 297

St Dru, the Accused (1836), IV. 530

St George and the Dragon (À Beckett, G. A. and Lemon, M., 1845), IV. 250

— (Bayliff, R. L., 1891), v. 253

— (Bernard, W. B., 1833), IV. 572

— (Blanchard, E. L. and Greenwood, T. L., 1877), v. 265

— (Cheetham, G. F., 1864), v. 746, 783, 846

— (Dibdin, C. I. M., 1802), IV. 290

— (Dibdin, C. I. M., 1822), IV. 295

— (Ducrow, A., 1833), IV. 307

— (Henry, A., 1884), v. 417

— (Lee, N., 1843), IV. 530, 639

— (Osman, W. R., 1869), v. 508

— (?1688), I. 447

— (1822), IV. 530

— (1855, 1857), v. 746

— (1857), v. 846

— (1883, 1884, 1888, 1896), v. 746

St George for England = Royal Champion

St George's Day (1789), III. 342

— = Knights of the Garter

St Giles's Scrutiny (1785), III. 342

St Gothard's Mount (1824), IV. 530, 639

St Helena (Thompson, E., 1776), III. 311

St Hilda's Cave (1824), IV. 530, 639

St James's and St Giles's (Wilkins, J. H., 1853), v. 623

— = Rubber of Life

St James's Park (1733), II. 382

— = Love in a Wood

St John's Priory (1839), IV. 530

St Kilda in Edinburgh (Heron, R., 1798), III. 268 [The date 1728 for the Larpent MS. is given in error]

St Leger (Fox, G. D., 1877), v. 371

St Leon (Caunter, J. H., 1835), IV. 576

St Marc (Wilkins, J. H., 1853), v. 623

St Margaret's Cave (Carr, G. C., 1804), IV. 279

St Mark's Day = Zenaldi

St Mark's Eve (À Beckett, G. A., 1834), IV. 249

St Mary's Eve (Bernard, W. B., 1838), IV. 266

St Monday (1788), III. 343

Saint or Sinner? (Dampier, A., 1881), v. 335

St Patrick's Day (Sheridan, R. B., 1775), III. 184, 305, 395

— = Shamrock

St Patrick's Eve (Power, T., 1832), IV. 387

— = (1) Kathleen Mavourneen; (2) Lost Bride of Garryowen

St Patrick's Oak = Devil's Punch Bowl

St Robert's Cave = Eugene Aram

St Ronan's Well (Davey, R. and Pollock, W. H., 1893), v. 338

— (Fisher, D., 1876), v. 367

— (McNeill, A. D., 1871), v. 472

— (Planché, J. R., 1824), IV. 95, 377

— (1824), IV. 95, 530

Saints and Sinners (Jones, H. A., 1884), v. 71, 163–5, 172, 439

St Stephen's Green (Phillips, W., 1700), II. 176, 349

St Stephen's Well (1844), IV. 530

St Swithin's Chair = Night Hag

St Tibb's Eve = Powder and Ball

St Valentine (Sharpe, G. F., 1892), v. 562

St Valentine's (Aitken, J. E. M. and Bergne, H. à C., 1897), v. 236

St Valentine's Day (McCabe, C. W., 1891), v. 467

— (Travers, W., 1869), v. 603

St Valentine's Eve (Milner, H. M., 1828), IV. 95, 357

Sakuntala (1899), v. 746

Salamanca Doctor Outplotted = Stolen Heiress

Salamandrine (1847), IV. 530

Salammbo (1885), v. 746

Salammbo, the Lovely Queen of Carthage (1871), v. 746

Salem's Sorrow (1872), v. 746

Sally Cavanagh (Mansfield, J. G., 1871), v. 475

Sally in our Alley (Jerrold, D. W., 1830), IV. 332

— (Lyster, F. and Heriot, P., 1888), v. 466

Sally Smart (1855), v. 746

Salmagundi (Dibdin, C. I. M., 1818), IV. 294

Salomé (Wilde, O. F. O'F. W., 1893), v. 190, 622

Saloon (Dibdin, C.), IV. 290

Saloon and Cellar (Rede, W. L., 1845), IV. 390

Saloons of Paris = Ecarté

Salopian Esquire (Dower, E., 1739), II. 44, 215, 319

Salthello Ovini (1875), v. 746

Saltimbanco (Sicklemore, R., 1797), III. 307

Salt Mine of Cracow = Zorinski

Salt Tears (Speight, T. W., 1873), v. 576

Salvator (Heraud, J. A., 1845), IV. 588

— (1820), IV. 531

Salvatori (Barnett, M., 1853), v. 250

Salvator Rosa (1866), v. 746

Salve (Beringer, Mrs O., 1895), v. 259

Salviniana (Gordon, G. L., 1877), v. 385

+ Salvoisy; or, The Queen's Lover (8°, 1834)

Sambodampalus (Tully, J. H., 1853), v. 604

Sam Carr, the Man in Possession (1872), v. 746

Sam'l of Posen (Jessop, G. H., 1895), v. 437

Samor (Milman, H. H., 1818), IV. 356

Sam Patch (1844), IV. 531

— (1855), v. 746

Sample versus Pattern (Sapte, Walter, Jr., 1887), v. 556

Sampson's Wedding (Rowe, G. F., 1869), v. 552

Sampson the Serjeant = May Queen

Sam's Arrival (Oxenford, J., 1862), v. 510

Sam Scud (1842), IV. 531

Samson (Hamilton, N., 1743), II. 398, 437

Samson Agonistes (Milton, J., 1670), I. 420

Samuel in Search of Himself (Coyne, J. S. and Coape, H. C., 1858), v. 328, 784, 786

Sam Weller (Moncrieff, W. T., 1837), IV. 97, 360

Sam Weller's Tour (Moncrieff, W. T., 1838), IV. 97, 531, 639

Sancho at Court (Ayres, J., 1742), II. 44, 233, 237, 247, 296

Sancho the Great (1799), III. 343

Sancho turn'd Governor = Barataria

Sanctuary (Carpenter, J. E., 1855), v. 303

Sandford and Merton (Burnand, F. C., 1893), v. 292

Sandford and Merton's Christmas Party (Burnand, F. C., 1880), v. 291

Sands of Time (Jenkins, T. J. P., 1894), v. 436

Sang Bleu (Yeldham, Major, 1888), v. 635

San Lin (Blau, H., 1899), v. 265

Sans Culottes and the Grand Culottes (1793), III. 343

Santa Claus (Daly, C., 1898), v. 334

— (Lennard, H., 1894), v. 456, 803

Santon's Cave = Greek Amazon

San Toy (Morton, E. A., 1899), v. 495

Santuzza (1897), v. 746

+ Sapho and Phao (Didelot, music Mazzinghi; H¹ 6/4/1797; 8°, 1797)

Sappho (Braunsen, J., 1820), IV. 270, 574

— (Collingham, G. G., 1899) = Idol of an Hour, v. 317, 746, 785, 846

— (Lee, E. B., 1846), IV. 594

— (Lobb, H., 1886), v. 461

— (Mason, W., 1796), III. 286

— (Serle, T. J., 1843), IV. 400

— (Wills, W. G., 1875), v. 627

— (1866), v. 746

Saracen's Head (1814), IV. 531

Saracen's Head removed from Snow Hill (Beazley, S., 1818) = Bull's Head, IV. 531, 571

Sarah (Jarman, F., 1892), v. 434

— = Warranted Burglar Proof

Sarah Blange (Barnett, M., 1852), v. 250

Sarah Jane in the Harem (Akhurst, W. M., 1875), v. 237

Sarah's Young Man (Suter, W. E., 1856), v. 587

Sarah the Creole = Sarah Blange

Sarah, the Fair Maiden of the Rhine (Bluth, R. J., 1879), v. 266

Sarah the Jewess (1861), v. 746

— = Dream of Fate

Saratoga = Brighton

Sardanapalus (Byron, Lord G. G., 1821), IV. 169–70, 278

— (Granville, H. S., 1868), v. 388

Sardanapalus, the "Fast" King of Assyria (À Beckett, G. A. and Lemon, M., 1853), v. 233

Satan (Grattan, H. and Jones, E., 1899), v. 389

— (1844), IV. 531

— (1897), v. 746

Satanas and the Spirit of Beauty (Coyne, J. S., 1841), IV. 284

Satan Bound (Boulding, J. W., 1881), v. 270

Satanella (Harris, A. G. and Falconer, E., 1858), v. 405

Satan's Daughter (Avondale, W., 1882), v. 246

Satisfaction (Blake, T. G., 1845), IV. 268

— (Bridgman, C., 1880), v. 275

Satisfactory Settlement = Business is Business

Satisfied (1831), IV. 531 [Presumably the same as Not more than I want, see IV. 512]

Saturday Night = Quarter Deck

Saturday Night and Sunday Morning = Touch and Take

Saturday Night at Sea = Armstrong the Shipwright

Saturday Night at Sea = Forecastle Fun

Saturday Night in London (Wilkinson, M., 1899), v. 623

Saturnalia (1873), v. 746

Sauce of Old Nile = Cheek and Plant

Saucy Housemaid = Robust Invalid

Saucy Lass (Haines, J. T., 1843), IV. 587

Saucy May (1884), v. 746

Saucy Nabob (1886), v. 746

Saucy Sally (Burnand, F. C., 1892), v. 292

Saucy Sultana (Stephens, V., 1894), v. 581

Saul (Heavysege, C., 1859), v. 416

Saul (Hill, A., 1760), II. 438; III. 268

— (1738), II. 398

— (1820), IV. 639

Saul and Jonathan (Crane, E., 1761), III. 249

Saul Braintree the Poacher (Ebsworth, J., 1831), IV. 308

Saul of Tarsus (Paley, G. B., 1885), v. 511

Saul the Servant (Almar, G., 1841), IV. 568

Sauny the Scott (Lacy, J., 1667), I. 69, 172, 212, 288, 418

Savage (1727), II. 383

Savage and Civilization (Anderson, J. R. and Wilkins, J. H., 1864), v. 746, 777, 823, 846

— = Huron Chief

Savage and the Maiden (Horncastle, J. H., 1844), IV. 328

Savage as a Bear (Wigan, H., 1860), v. 622

Savage Chieftain (Eyre, E. J., 1814), IV. 310

— (1816), IV. 531

Savage Lovers (Dibdin, C. I. M., 1826), IV. 296, 531, 580, 639

Savages (1792), III. 343

Savages of America = Ponteach

Savannah (Douglass, J. T., 1861), v. 788

— (Mathews, C. J., 1861), v. 746, 806, 846

Saved (Douglass, J. T.), v. 789

— (Granville, H. S., 1868), v. 388

— (Shirley, A., 1833), v. 563

— (1889), v. 746

Saved by a Child = Bab

Saved by an Irishman's Pluck = In the Hands of the Redskins

Saved by a Song (Addison, H. R., 1868), v. 236

Saved by a Word (Newbound, E., 1877), v. 502

Saved by the Sword = Life Boat

Saved from Death = Woman's Peril

Saved from Sin (Selby, H. C., 1884), v. 560

— (1891), v. 746

Saved from the Jaws of Death = Balaclava Joe

Saved from the Scaffold (Carson, L., 1897), v. 304

445

Saved from the Scaffold = Missing

Saved from the Sea (Shirley, A., 1895), v. 564

— = Not Dead

Saved from the Streets (Conquest, G. and Eaton, R. H., 1886), v. 322

Saved from the Wreck (1869), v. 746

Saved from the Yardarm (1890), v. 746

Saved on the Post (Fenton, C., 1893), v. 365

Savonarola (À Beckett, G. A., 1884), v. 234

— (Austin, A., 1881), v. 245

Savourneen Deelish (Blake, T. G., 1839), IV. 268

— = Peep o' Day

Savourneen Delishus = Peep of Day by a new (Lime) light

Savoyard (1815), IV. 531, 636

Savoyard Assassin = Lelia the Betrothed

Savoyard Travellers (1749), II. 383

Sawney Beane (1839), IV. 531

Sawney Bean, the Cannibal (1864), v. 746

Sawney Bean, the Terror of the North (1823), IV. 531

Saw ye Bony coming? (McLaren, A., 1804), IV. 350

Saxon Chief = Ivanhoe

Saxon King = Enchanted Raven

Saxon Maid (1842), IV. 639

Saxon Outlaw = Osric the Lion

Saxon Princes = Offa and Ethelbert

Saxons and Normans in England = Isaac of York

Saxon Slave = (1) Walsha; (2) Warlsha

Sayings and Doings (Morton, J. M., 1839), IV. 362

Sayings and Doings of Sam Weller = Pickwick

Scalded Back (Yardley, W., 1884), v. 634

Scales of Justice (Waldron, W. R., 1894), v. 611

— (1857), v. 746

— = Cotton King

Scalp Hunters (Wilkins, J. H., 1861), v. 823

Scamp = Wild Goose

Scamps of London (Moncrieff, W. T., 1843), IV. 103-4, 118-19, 361

— (1843), IV. 531

Scamps of London (1877), v. 746

— = Ups and Downs of Life

Scamps of Society (Carte, C., 1896), v. 305

Scamp, the Tramp and the Lamp = Aladdin

Scandal (Matthison, A., 1878), v. 481

Scandinavian Sketch (1851), v. 746

Scanderbeg (Dibdin, T. J., 1819), IV. 302

— (Havard, W., 1733), II. 17, 74, 75, 83, 334

— (Whincop, T., 1747), II. 84, 364

Scan. Mag. (Pocock, I., 1833), IV. 385

Scapegoat (Jones, J. W., 1891), v. 161, 441

— (Lawrence, W., 1890), v. 451

— (Poole, J., 1825), IV. 386

Scapegrace (Beazley, S., Jr., 1832), IV. 255, 571

— (Miller, W. F., 1893), v. 489

— (1828), IV. 531

Scapegrace of Paris (1844), IV. 531

— (1855), v. 746

Scapin (1753), III. 343

Scapin in Masquerade (1803), IV. 531

Scaramouch a Philosopher (Ravenscroft, E., 1677), I. 188, 252, 255, 346, 426

Scaramouch in Naxos (Davidson, J., 1889), v. 338

Scaramouch Scapin (1742), II. 383

Scaramuccia (Fitzball, E., 1839), IV. 316

Scarecrow (Thomas, C., 1889), v. 596

— (1848), IV. 531

Scarf of Flight and the Mirror of Light = Dragon's Gift

Scarlet Brotherhood (Darbey, E. and Manning, W., 1893), v. 336

Scarlet Coat (Grogan, W. E., 1899), v. 395

Scarlet Dick (Howe, J. B., 1867), v. 428

Scarlet Dye (Masters, J. C., 1887), v. 480

Scarlet Feather (Greenbank, H., 1897), v. 392, 794

Scarlet Flower (1862), v. 746

Scarlet Letter (Aveling, E. B., 1888), v. 246

— (Coleridge, S. and Forbes, N., 1888), v. 317

— (Rayner, A., 1863), v. 535

Scotch (Dawson, F., 1895), V. 339
Scotched and Kilt = Robbing Roy
Scotch Figaries (1747), II. 383
Scotch Ghost (1796), III. 343
— (1800), IV. 531
— (1801), IV. 531
Scotch Lovers (1800), IV. 531
Scotch Marriage = Man and Wife
Scotch Marriage Laws (Jones, 1823),
    IV. 531, 590, 639
Scotch Mist (Shepherd, E., 1886), V.
    562
— (Wills, H., 1842), IV. 531, 639
Scotch Œconomy (1750–1800), III. 404
Scotch Reformation = Assembly
Scotch Regalia = Oliver Cromwell
Scotch Sisters (1863), V. 747
Scotch Tocsin sounded = Philistines
Scotland and Algiers = Vacant Chair
Scotland's Ancient Days = Weird
    Woman of the Isles
Scotland's Patriot King (1820), IV. 531
Scotland Yard (1895), V. 747
Scotsman in London = Conjuror
Scots wha ha'e wi' Wallace bled
    (Stevens, E., 1895), V. 583
Scottish Chief and the Maid of Ellerslie
    (Anderson, J. R., 1863), V. 240
Scottish Chiefs (Egan, F. B., 1868), V.
    356
Scottish Chiefs (not Miss Porter's)
    (Stirling, E., 1839), IV. 531, 639
Scottish Gentleman who was good all
    round = Crichton
Scottish Gold Mine = Belford Castle
Scottish Outlaw = Jonnie Armstrong
Scottish Outlaws = Gordon Gray
Scottish Volunteers (McLaren, A.,
    1795), III. 284, 391
— = Highland Drover
Scott Scotched = Real Truth about
    Ivanhoe
Scourged Page = Castle Cauldron
Scourge of Denmark = Rodar the Raven
Scourge of the North = Alabama,
    Privateer
Scowrers (Shadwell, T., 1691), I. 209,
    431
Scrap of Paper (Simpson, J. P., 1861),
    V. 567
Scraps (Dibdin, T. J., 1818), IV. 301
Screw Loose (Melford, M., 1893), V. 484

Scribe (Hayman, P., 1891), V. 411
— (Hope, P., 1899), V. 426
— (1899), V. 747
Scribler (1751), III. 343
Scrivener's Daughter = Spendthrift
Scrooge the Miser's Dream (1844), IV.
    97, 531
Scrub's Trip to the Jubilee (Gentleman,
    F., 1769), III. 264
Sculptor (Warren, T. G. and Craft, J.,
    1893), V. 615
— (1821), IV. 531
Sculptor of Frankfort (1849), IV. 532
— (1850), V. 846
Sculptor's Dream: A Romance of Real
    Life = Marble Heart
Sculptor's Workshop (1837), IV. 532
Scuttled Ship (Reade, C., 1874), V. 536,
    812
Sea (Somerset, C. A., 1842), IV. 405
Sea and Land (Lemon, M., 1852), V.
    455
Sea Bathing a Cure for Roguery =
    Voyage to Margate
Sea-Captain (Lytton, Lord, 1839), IV.
    349
Sea Captain of Dundee = Grizzel
    Jamphray
Sea Captains (1674), I. 445
Sea Devil (Moreton, 1822), IV. 601
— (1830), IV. 532
— (1839), IV. 532
Sea Flower (Law, A., 1898), V. 450
Sea Fruit (Moss, H., 1893), V. 498
— (1887), V. 747
Sea-girt Cliff (Douglass, J. T.), V. 789
Seagull Rock (Gunton, R. T., 1895), V.
    397
Sea Gulls (Maltby, A. and Stainforth,
    F., 1869), V. 473
Sea Horse (1839), IV. 532
Sea is England's Glory (Marchant, F.,
    1875), V. 476
Sea-King's Daughter = Frozen Hands
Sea King's Vow (Stirling, E., 1846), IV.
    408
Sealed (1876), V. 747
Sealed Lips (1888), V. 747
Sealed Packet = Prisoner of Ham
Sealed Sentence (Stirling, E., 1844), IV.
    407
— (1857), V. 747

Secret (Beerbohm, C., 1888), v. 255
— (Moncrieff, W. T., 1823), IV. 359, 600
— (Morris, E., 1799), III. 138-9, 288; IV. 112
— = Haydee
Secret Agent (Coyne, J. S., 1855), v. 327
Secret Agreement (Gregory, E., 1886), v. 394
Secret Arch = Highgate Tunnel
Secretary (Knowles, J. S., 1843), IV. 339
— (Webb, C., 1848), IV. 417
Secretary and the Cook (1821), IV. 532
Secret Avengers = Rinaldo Rinaldini
Secret Blabbed = Female Freemason
Secret Castle (1799), III. 343
Secret Crime (Dobson, M. S., 1892), v. 346
Secret Death Union of South America = Ku-Klux-Klan
Secret Discovered = Masonry
Secret Enemy = (1) Banished Brother; (2) Brave Cossack
Secret Expedition (1757), III. 343
Secret Foe (Stevens, J. A., 1887), v. 583
— (Stirling, E., 1845), IV. 407
Secret-Love (Dryden, J., 1667), I. 27, 140, 186, 192, 227-8, 231, 307, 343, 344, 346, 351, 404; II. 142
Secret Marriage (1842), IV. 532
— (1860), v. 747
— (1877), v. 747
— = (1) Philippe; (2) Proof Presumptive
Secret Memoirs (Webb, C.), IV. 616
Secret Mine (Dibdin, T. J. and Fawcett, J., 1812), IV. 299
Secret Mission (1877), v. 747
Secret Mission and the Signet Ring = Raffaelle the Reprobate
Secret Muse (1814), IV. 532
Secret Nuptials = Louisa of Lombardy
Secret of a Life (Williams, A. and Roberts, G., 1886), v. 624
— = Adrienne
Secret of Life = Bridal Phantom
Secret of State (Anstruther, E., 1898), v. 241
Secret of the Five Masks = Night Guard
Secret of the Guilde Court = Musette
Secret of the Holly Bough = Bitter Cold
Secret of the Iron Cabinet = Dead Hand

Secret of the Keep (Raleigh, C., 1898), v. 534
Secret of the Lodge Room = Freemason
Secret of the Sea (Muskerry, W., 1870), v. 500
Secret of Twenty Years = Leonard
Secret Pass (Fitzball, E., 1852), v. 368
Secret Passion (1858), v. 747
Secret Plot (Green, R., 1777), III. 266
Secrets (?D'Avenant, Sir W.), I. 402
Secrets at Court = Hush!
Secret Service (Gillette, W., 1895), v. 381
— (Planché, J. R., 1834), IV. 182, 380
Secret Society (Hannan, C., 1895), v. 402
Secrets of an Old Iron Safe = Foundered Fortune
Secrets of a Palace = Doubtful Son
Secrets of Office = Alcaid
Secrets of the Abbey = Eugenio
Secrets of the Bastille = Man in the Iron Mask
Secrets of the Devil (Osman, W. R. and Fenton, F., 1864), v. 747, 792, 808, 846
Secrets of the Harem (Goldberg, M., 1896), v. 383
Secrets of the Night (1821), IV. 532
Secrets of the Past = Travers' Secret
Secrets of the Police (Melford, M., 1886), v. 484
Secrets of Thornfield Manor = Jane Eyre
Secrets of Thornfield Manor House = Jane Eyre
Secrets of War (1855), v. 747
Secret Sorrow (Dowse, G. D., 1890), v. 350
Secret Springs (1811), IV. 532
Secrets Worth Knowing (Morton, T., 1797), III. 142-3, 289
Secret Tribunal (Boaden, J., 1795), III. 238
— = Vehme Gericht
Secret Twelve (1855), v. 747
Secret Vault and the Voice of Death = Will and the Way
Secret Vaults of Tilney Castle (1806), IV. 639
Secular Masque (Dryden, J., 1700), I. 407

Senekos the Greek (1833), IV. 532
+ Senior Wranglers (Whitmore, E. H., *French*)
Sensational Novel in Three Volumes (Clay, F., 1871), V. 313
+ Sensation Dramas for the Back Drawing Room (Byron, H. J., *Lacy*)
"Sensation" Goat = Esmeralda
Sensation Hunt (1868), V. 747
Sensation Novel (Gilbert, W. S., 1871), V. 379
Sensation Scene = Brumley's Wife
Sensations of the Past Season = 1863
Sense and Sensation (Taylor, T., 1864), V. 593
Sensualist (Buenn, M. and Laidlaw, F. A., 1891), V. 287
Sentence (Webster, A., 1887), V. 617
Sentenced, but not Guilty (1876), V. 747
Sentenced to Death (Conquest, G. and Pettitt, H., 1875), V. 321
— (Stanley, H. J., 1873), V. 579
Sentimental Mother (Baretti, J., 1789), III. 235
Sentimental Waiter = Animal Sympathy
Sentinel (Boucicault, D., 1853), V. 267, 779
— (Morton, J. M., 1837), IV. 362
Sentinel of the Alma (Lover, S., 1854), V. 463
Sentry (Rémo, F. and Watson, T. M., 1890), V. 541
Sentry-Go (1896), V. 747
Sent to the Tower (Morton, J. M., 1850), V. 495
Separate Maintenance (Colman, G., 1779), III. 246
— (Coyne, J. S., 1849), IV. 285
Separation (Baillie, J., 1836), IV. 258
— (Roberts, Sir R., 1886), V. 545
Separation and Reparation (Morton, T., 1830), IV. 364
Sequel (Parker, L. N., 1891), V. 161, 513
Sequel to Nicholas Nickleby = Fortunes of Smike
Sequel to the Bottle = Drunkard's Children
Sequin the Scalp-hunter (1853), V. 747
Seraglio (Dibdin, C., 1776), III. 255
— (Dimond, W., 1827), IV. 307, 581
— (Noble, 1816), V. 522
Seraglio in an Uproar = British Beauty

Seraphina the Fair (Laidlaw, C. W., 1874), V. 446
Seraphine (Boucicault, D., 1869), V. 269
Serbelloni (1833), IV. 532
Serenade (Taylor, S., 1669), I. 435
— (1894), V. 747
Serenaders (Harris, Sir A. H. G. and Parker, W., 1892), V. 406
Serenading (Rede, T. L., 1836), IV. 532
Serenata (Machale, L., 1888), V. 469
Serf (Talbot, R., 1828), IV. 410
— (Taylor, T., 1865), V. 593
Sergeant's Daughter (Massinger, G., 1888), V. 480
Serge Panine (Thorp, J. H., 1891), V. 599
— = Justifiable Homicide
Serious Family (Barnett, M., 1849), IV. 131, 261
Serious Mistake = Lay Figure
Serious Youth (Suter, W. E., 1857), V. 819
Serjeant's Wedding (Wilks, T. E., 1840), IV. 421
Serjeant's Whim (Dibdin, C. I. M., 1804), IV. 291
Serjeant's Wife (Arnold, S. J., 1835), IV. 256
— (Banim, J., 1827), IV. 258
— (1840), IV. 532
Serpent and the Doves = Gipsy Boy
Serpent Lady (1833), IV. 532
Serpent of the Jungle = Attar Gull
Serpent of the Nile (Stirling, E., 1840), IV. 407
Serpent on the Hearth (Mead, T., 1861), V. 747, 806
— (Simpson, J. P., 1869), V. 568
Serpent Play (Hake, T. G., 1883), V. 795
Serpent's Coil = Victims of Power
Sertorius (Bancroft, J., 1679), I. 143, 388
Servant Mistress (1770), III. 123, 343
— = (1) Maid the Mistress; (2) Serva Padrona
Servant of All Work (Bernard, W. B., 1830), IV. 532, 572, 639
Servant or Suitor (1872), V. 747
Servant with Two Masters = Hotel
Serva Padrona (Baker, D. E., 1763), III. 235
— (Storace, S., 1758), III. 123, 310, 396

Serve him right (Barnett, M. and Mathews, C. J., 1850), v. 249

Service in London = Martha Willis, the Servant Maid

Serving the Queen (Leonard, H., 1898), v. 456

Sesostris (Sturmy, J., 1728), II. 90, 358

— (Williams, G. H., 1853), v. 823

— (1899), v. 747

Seth Green (1884), v. 748

Sethona (Dow, A., 1774), III. 257

Seth Slope (1839), IV. 532

Set of Horses (1792), III. 122, 325

Set of Rogues (1899), v. 748

Setting of the Sun (Hannan, C., 1892), v. 402

Setting Sun (Hogg, C., 1809), IV. 326

Settled in Full (Maxwell, H. B., 1898), v. 482

Settled out of Court (Burney, E., 1897), v. 293

Settlers and Natives = Van Dieman's Land

Settlers in America = Omala

Settler's Perils = Red John the Daring

Settler's Struggles = Indian Maid

Settling Day (Scudamore, F. A., 1893), v. 559

— (Taylor, T., 1865), v. 593

+ Settling the Verdict (*French*)

Seven Adventures = Carl Carlsruhe

Seven Ages (Jerrold, D. W., 1823), IV. 331

Seven Ages of Man (Webb, T. H., 1844), IV. 532, 639, 846

— (Webb, T. H., 1859), v. 748, 823

Seven Ages of Woman (Blanchard, E. L., 1855), v. 779

— = Maids and Matrons

Seven Brazen Towers of Tepelini = Aslan the Lion

Seven Capes (1808), IV. 532

Seven Castles of the Passions (Stirling, E., 1844), IV. 532, 612, 639

Seven Champions of Christendom (Dibdin, T. J., 1821), IV. 303

— (Osman, W. R., 1870), v. 508

— (Planché, J. R., 1849), IV. 383

— (Stocqueler, J. H., 1845), IV. 532, 639

— (1829), IV. 532

— (1853), v. 748

— = St George and the Dragon

Seven Champions of Christendom and the Storm Demon (1844), IV. 532

Seven Charmed Spuds (Quayle, C., 1872), v. 532

Seven Clerks (Wilks, T. E., 1834), IV. 420

Seven Clerks of Marseilles = Denouncer

Seven Dials (James, C. S., 1849), IV. 330

Seven Fairies of the Grotto = Doctor Faustus and the Black Demon

Seven Gifted Servants = Fortunio

Seven in One (1822), IV. 533

Seven Islands = Seven Capes

Seven Maids of Munich (Rodwell, G. H., 1846), IV. 395

Seven Mannikins and the Magic Mirror = Snowdrop

Seven Merry Maids of Marylebone = Light and Shade

Seven or Seventeen [IV. 533 should be Seventy or Seventeen]

Seven Poor Travellers (Duval, C., 1869), v. 353

— (Johnstone, J. B., 1855), v. 748, 800, 846

— (1855), v. 748

Seven Saints of Thule = Sense and Sensation

Seven Sins (Meritt, P. and Conquest, G., 1874), v. 486

Seven Sisters (Almar, G., 1835), IV. 253

Seven Steps to Ruin (1859), v. 748

— = Man

Seven's the Main = Winning a Husband

Seven Swan Princes and the Fair Melusine = Wittikind and his Brothers

Seventeen and Seventy (1837), IV. 533

Seventeen Hundred and Eighty One (1781), III. 343

Seventeen Hundred and Ninety (Hunt, H., 1894), v. 430

Seventeen Hundred Fifty Seven = Male Coquette

Seventeen Hundred Years Ago = Last Days of Pompeii

1792 = Robur Ragabas

Seven Temptations (Howitt, M., 1834), IV. 589

Seventh Bullet = Freischutz

Seventh Hour (Hughes, B. and Faucquez, A., 1861), v. 748, 792, 846

Seventh Night = Daft Meg of the Cliff

Shadow-tree Shaft (Robertson, T. W., 1867), v. 546

Shadrack (1805), IV. 533

Shadragh the Hunchback (Williamson, H. W., 1878), v. 626

Shadragh the Shingawn (1862), v. 748

Shadroch the Shingawn and Ailleen the Rose of Kilkenny = Rathboys

Shaft No. 2 (1897), v. 748

Shah (Hall, K. E., 1873), v. 399

Shah's Festival = Night in Persia

Shake Hands (Buckingham, L. S., 1864), v. 748, 846

Shakers and Quakers = Rival Artistes

Shakespeare (Greville, E. E., 1891), v. 394

Shakespeare and Burbage (Moncrieff, W. T., 1838), IV. 91, 533, 639

Shakespeare and the Fairies = Midsummer Night

Shakespeare Converted into Bacon (Cox, S. A., 1899), v. 786

Shakespeare, his Life and Times (1847), IV. 533

Shakespeare-ience Teaches = What's it on?

Shakespeare in the Shades (Cumberland, R., ?1744), III. 251

Shakespeare Jubilee = Man and Wife

Shakespeare's Choice Spirits (1768), III. 343

Shakespeare's Dream (Maynard, M., 1861), v. 806

— (1831), IV. 91, 533

Shakespeare's Early Days (Somerset, C. A., 1829), IV. 91, 404

Shakespeare's Festival (Moncrieff, W. T., 1830), IV. 91, 360

Shakespeare's House (Coyne, J. S., 1864), v. 786

Shakespeare's Jubilee (Carey, G. S., 1769), III. 242

Shakespeare Versus Harlequin (Dibdin, C. I. M. or Dibdin, T. J., 1820), IV. 91, 294, 580

Shakespearian Reverie (Brough, W., 1864), v. 279

Shakespear's Garland = Jubilee

Shakey Page, more Funkey than Flunkey = Don Giovanni Jr.

Shakspeare's Dream (Brougham, J., 1858), v. 280

Shakspere and Company (Bradshaw, C. B., 1845), IV. 573

Shall he forgive her? (Harvey, F., 1894), v. 408

Shall I Kill Myself? (Dibdin, T. J., 1826), IV. 305

Shall we remember? (Turnbull, W. and Ellis, R. C., 1893), v. 604

Shamacda (1814), IV. 533

Sham Beggar (1756), III. 343

Sham Captain (1848), IV. 533

— = Boarding School

Sham Conjurer (1741), II. 383

Sham Doctor (1740), II. 383

— = Anatomist

Sham Duke (1896), v. 748

Shame (Chapin, A. and Oliphant, E. H. C., 1892), v. 308

— (Noble, C., 1883), v. 504

Shameful Behaviour (Troughton, A. C., 1859), v. 604

Sham Fight (1756), III. 343

— (1836), IV. 533

Sham Funeral = Two English Gentlemen

Sham Ghost (1790), III. 343

Sham Lawyer (Drake, J., 1697), I. 63, 337, 403

Sham Marquis = Younger Brother

Sham Pilgrims (1734), II. 140, 383

Sham Prince (Shadwell, C., 1719), II. 354 [This was acted Smock Alley, Dublin about June 1719]

— (1836), IV. 533

Shamrock (O'Keeffe, J., 1777), III. 292

Shamrock and the Rose (Reynolds, W., 1891), v. 541

Shamrock of Chelsea = Fine Old British Veterans

Shamrock of Ireland (Howe, J. B., 1867), v. 428

Sham Solicitor (Tabrar, J., 1883), v. 589

Shamus-na-Glanna (Aylmer, B., 1876), v. 246

Shamus-na-Lena (Towers, E., 1876), v. 601

Shamus O'Brien (Jessop, G. H., 1896), v. 437

— (Maeder, F. and Vernon, C., 1897), v. 472

Shepherd's Lottery (Mendez, M., 1751), III. 287

Shepherd's Mount (1735), II. 383

Shepherd's Opera (Maxwell, J., 1739), II. 343

Shepherd's Star (Johnstone, J. B., 1879), V. 438

Shepherd's Wedding (Steele, A., 1789), III. 309
— = Arcadia

Shepherd's Welcome to the Spring = Flora's Holiday

Shepherd's Well (Powell, T., 1844), IV. 387

Sheriff of the County (Peake, R. B., 1845), IV. 371

Sherlock Homes (Gillette, W., 1899), V. 381
— (Rogers, C., 1894), V. 548

Sherlock Holmes—Private Detective (1894), V. 748

Sherwood Forest (Planché, J. R., 1821), IV. 376
— = Robin Hood

Sherwood Forest, that's where the Foresters lodge = Robin Hood

She's a Man = Nelly's Sister

She's Eloped (O'Keeffe, J., 1798), III. 295, 393

She's mad for a Husband (Dibdin, C.), IV. 290
— (1778), III. 343

She's mine for a Thousand (Lucas, W. J., 1845), IV. 533, 639

She's not to be managed (Dibdin, C. I. M., 1825), IV. 295, 533, 580, 639

She's not Him and He's not Her (Erskine, A., 1764), III. 258

She's not to Blame (1842), IV. 533

She Stoops to Conquer (Fitzball, E., 1864), V. 368, 792
— (Goldsmith, O., 1773), III. 159–60, 167, 265, 386

She's very like her Mother = Night and Morning

She Took the Will for the Deed = She Wants a Guardian

She Ventures, and He Wins (1695), I. 445

She Wants a Guardian (Coyne, J. S., 1837), IV. 533

She Wou'd and She Wou'd Not (Cibber, C., 1702), I. 269; II. 36, 132, 134, 135, 136, 137, 169, 308, 433

She wou'd if she cou'd (Etherege, Sir G., 1668), I. 14, 15, 43, 63, 204, 235–6, 347, 348, 350, 410

She Would and He Wouldn't (Morton, J. M., 1862), V. 496

She Would Be a Duchess = Irishman in Spain

She would be a Soldier (1790), III. 343

Shield of David (1899), V. 748

Shifting Scenes of a Workman's Life = Honest Labour

Shifting Scenes of a Workman's Life = Mercy's Choice

Shifts of Genius (Roxby, S., 1843), IV. 533, 639

Shilling Day at the Great Exhibition (Brough, W. and Halliday, A., 1862), V. 279

Shilling Hop = School for Tigers

Shilly Shally (Reade, C., 1872), V. 536

Shindy in a Shanty (O'Grady, H., 1876), V. 506

Shingawn (Stirling, E., 1872), V. 584
— (1862), V. 748
— (1869), V. 748

Ship Ahoy (Roberts, G., 1874), V. 544

Ship and the Plough = Mast and the Ploughshare

Ship Boy (1847), IV. 533
— (1854), V. 748

Shipbuilder's Daughter = Helen Fortescue

Ship Launch (1804), IV. 533
— (1851), V. 748

Ship Launching (1749), II. 383

Shipmates (Bridgeman, J. V., 1873), V. 275

Ship of Glass (Mildenhall, T., 1847), IV. 356

Ship on Fire (Barnett, C. Z., 1845), IV. 260
— (1861), V. 748, 817, 846
— = (1) Loss of the Monarch; (2) Ocean Monarch

Shipped by the Light of the Moon (Sims, G. R., 1896), V. 570

Shipwreck (Arnold, S. J., 1796), III. 234
— (Hyland, W., 1746), II. 338

Sicilian Hussars (1840), IV. 534

Sicilian Idyll (Todhunter, J., 1890), V. 600

Sicilian Lover (Robinson, M., 1796), III. 302

Sicilian Mother (1829), IV. 534

Sicilian Outlaw (1824), IV. 639

Sicilian Peasants (1762), III. 343

Sicilian Queen, *see* Orphan of the Pyrenees

Sicilian Romance (Siddons, H., 1794) = Castle of Otranto, III. 72, 99, 102, 307

Sicilian Usurper = King Richard the Second

Sicilian Vespers (Kenney, J., 1840), IV. 180, 338

Sick Lady's Cure = Double Gallant

Sid (Meritt, P., 1871), V. 485, 806

Sidecraft (1883), V. 749

Sidi Hamet Muley Ben Ismael and Peggy Larkins = Beauty and the Bey

Sidney and his Dog = Red Savage

Sidonia di Molina (1844), IV. 534

Sidonie (Lyster, F. and Heriot, P., 1887), V. 466

Siege (Baillie, J., 1812), IV. 258

Siege and Surrender of Mons (1691), I. 445

Siège de Cythère (Degville, 1827), IV. 579

Siege of Abydos (1844), IV. 534

Siege of Acre (Milner, H. M., 1824), IV. 534

— = Sir Sidney Smith

Siege of Alençon = King and the Duke

Siege of Aleppo (Hawkins, W., 1758), III. 267

Siege of Antwerp (Kennedy, W., 1833), IV. 336

Siege of Ancona (Landor, W. S., 1846), IV. 199, 341

Siege of Aquileia (Home, J., 1760), III. 93, 272

Siege of Babylon (Pordage, S., 1677), I. 40, 83, 119, 424

Siege of Bangalore = Tippoo Sahib

Siege of Barcelona (1706), II. 383

Siege of Beauvais = Jane of the Hatchet

Siege of Belgrade (Cobb, J., 1791), III. 206, 244, 379

— (1828), IV. 534

— (1836), IV. 534

Siege of Berwick (Jerningham, E., 1793), III. 84, 277

— (McLaren, A., 1818), IV. 352

— (Millar, J., 1824), IV. 599

Siege of Bethulia (1721), II. 383

Siege of Bradford (Nicholson, J., 1821), IV. 366

Siege of Calais (Denis, C., 1765), III. 254, 381

— (1823), IV. 534

Siege of Carthage (Fitzgerald, P., 1819), IV. 317

— = Scipio's Triumph

Siege of Carthagena (1741), II. 384

Siege of Constantina = French Spy

Siege of Constantinople (Payne, H. N., 1674), I. 54, 130, 348, 423

Siege of Corinth (Planché, J. R., 1836), IV. 380, 605

Siege of Curzola (O'Keeffe, J., 1785), III. 293

Siege of Cuzco (Sotheby, W., 1800), III. 308; IV. 405

Siege of Damascus (Hughes, J., 1720), II. 58, 59, 107–8, 275, 338

Siege of Dantsic = Stanislaus

Siege of Dantzig (1837), IV. 534

Siege of Derry (1692), I. 445

Siege of Dresden = Katitzka

Siege of Dumbarton Castle = Sir William Wallace, of Ellerslie

Siege of Dunkerque = Buccaneer's Wife

Siege of Estakhar = Zembuca and the Net-maker of Persia

Siege of Flushing (1809), IV. 534

Siege of Gibraltar (Pilon, F., 1780), III. 19, 207, 298

— (1835), IV. 534

— = Ὠκεάνεια

Siege of Granada = (1) Ethiop; (2) Leila, the Maid of the Alhambra

Siege of Hennebonne = Jane of Flanders

Siege of Hyderabad = Conquest of Scinde

Siege of Isca (Kemp, J., 1810), IV. 336

Siege of Ismail Preston, W. 1794), III. 300

Siege of Jerusalem (Bowes, M. E., 1774), III. 239

— (Gregory, G.), III. 266

Six Months Ago (Dale, F., 1867), v. 106, 332

Sixpenny Telegram (Bell, Mrs H.), v. 256

Sixpenny Wire (Rae-Brown, C., 1887), v. 533

Six Persons (Zangwill, I., 1893), v. 637

Six Physicians (1818), IV. 535

Six Simpletons (Amherst, J. H., 1825), IV. 254

Six Spaniards (1787), III. 344

Six Steps of Punishment (1849), IV. 535

Sixteen and Sixty (1815), IV. 535, 636

Sixteen and Sixty-three = Modern Misses

Sixteen—not out (Blair, J., 1892), v. 262

1679 (Webb, C., 1872), v. 617

Sixteen String Jack (Rede, W. L., 1823), 389, 607

— (Rede, W. L., 1841), IV. 18, 390

— (Wilks, T. E., 1842), IV. 421

Sixteen Years Ago (Wolff, J., 1871), v. 630

Sixteen Years Since = (1) Eleventh Hour; (2) Leontine; (2) Horrors of War

Sixth Commandment (Buchanan, R., 1890), v. 285

6000 a Year = German Silver

Sixth Victim = Necromancer

Six to Four on the Colonel (Dance, G., 1832), IV. 579

Six to One against you = Transformation

Sixtus V (Boucicault, D. and Bridgeman, J. V., 1851), v. 267

— (Phillips, F. L., 1860), v. 810

Sixty-Six (1876), v. 751

Sixty-third Letter (Oulton, W. C., 1802), IV. 366

Sixty Years Ago (1852), v. 751

Sixty Years Since = Waverley

Six Voyages of Sinbad the Eastern Mariner (1820), IV. 535

Six Years After (Cheltnam, C. S., 1866), v. 309

Six Years More = Hearts at Fault

Skeleton (Stephens, Y. and Graves, C., 1887), v. 581

Skeleton Crew (Hazlewood, C. H., 1867) = Wilfred Ned, v. 768, 850

Skeleton Hand (Barnett, C. Z., 1833), IV. 259, 570

Skeleton in the Cupboard (1885), v. 751

— = Zenobia

Skeleton Lover (1830), IV. 535

— = Love and Anatomy

Skeleton of the Wave (1852), v. 751

Skeleton Robber (1861), v. 751

Skeleton Steed (Ramsay, T. J., 1843), IV. 388

Skeleton Witness (Rede, W. L., 1835), IV. 390

Sketches from Life (Frome, S. B., 1809), IV. 318

— (Sicklemore, R., 1802), IV. 401

Sketches in 1840 = Devil in London

Sketches in India (1846), IV. 535

— (1854), v. 751

Sketches of Character = Proteus

Sketches of Northern Mythology (Sawyers, F., 1789), III. 304

Sketch from the Louvre (Major, H. A., 1860), v. 805, 846

— (1867), v. 751, 805

Sketch of a Fine Lady's Return from a Rout (Clive, C., 1763), III. 243

Sketch of the Times = Detection

Skilful Practitioner (1861), v. 751

— (1868), v. 751

Skimmer of the Sea (1830), IV. 535

— = Water Witch

Skip Jack Joe (Evans, F., 1874), v. 790

Skipper of the Two Sisters (1884), v, 751

Skipper's Secret (1878), v. 751

Skirt Dancer (Ridgwell, G., Mansell, E. and Mackay, R. F., 1898), v. 543

Skirts of the Camp = Hartford-Bridge

Skittles Limited (Thompson, R. H., 1895), v. 598

Skyward Guide (Bradshaw, Mrs A. and Melford, M., 1895), v. 273

Slander (Wyke, E. B., 1878), v. 633

— (1882), v. 751

Slanderer (Wallace, J., 1823), IV. 416

Slasher & Crasher (Morton, J. M., 1848), IV. 363

Slate Pencillings (Hay, F., 1876), v. 411

Slave (Morton, T., 1816) = Freedom and Slavery, IV. 364, 464, 601, 626

— = Gambia

Slave Bride (Young, H., 1861), v. 825

Slave Brother = First Love
Slave by Choice = Chains of the Heart
Slave Daughter = Louisiana
Slave Girl = Deborah
Slave Hunt (Young, H., 1853), v. 636
Slave Hunter and the Half Caste (1866), v. 751
Slave King (1833), IV. 535
Slave Life (Taylor, T. and Lemon, M., 1852), v. 592
Slave Lost (1867), v. 751
Slave Merchant (1818), IV. 535
Slave of Drink (Reynolds, W., 1890), v. 541
Slave of Wealth (1844), IV. 535
Slave Pirate = Kaloc
Slave Queen = Valsha
Slavery and Freedom = Woman of Colour
Slavery of Drink = Fairy Madge
Slaves (McLaren, A., 1807), IV. 351
Slave Sale (1838), IV. 535
Slaves in Barbary (Dibdin, T. J., 1816), IV. 300
Slaves of Centa = Chains of the Heart
Slaves of Crime (Hazlewood, C. H., 1864), v. 751, 796, 846
Slaves of Drink = Drunkard
Slaves of Duty = Pirates of Penzance
Slaves of London (1851), v. 751
Slaves of Mammon = Common Sense
Slaves of Passion = (1) Avenger; (2) Cross of Olga
Slaves of the Ring (Grundy, S., 1894), v. 397
Slaves of the South = Cora
Slave's Ransom (Osborne, C., 1874), v. 508
Slave's Revenge = (1) Foulahs; (2) Planter and his Dog; (3) Revolt of Surinam
Slaves' Revolt (1827), IV. 535
— = Walsha
Slave Trade (1814), IV. 535
Slave's Triangle = Ida May
Slave's Tribute = Kamtchatka
Slave Trade Cruelty = African
Slaviana (Hay, F., 1875), v. 411
Sledge Bells (1877), v. 751
— = Polish Jew
Sledge Driver (Planché, Mrs J. R., 1834), IV. 383

Sledge-Driver and his Dogs = Land Storm
Sledgehammer (Barrett, W., 1897), v. 251
Sleeper = Doldrum
Sleeper Awake = Abou Hassan
Sleeper Awakened (Harris, Sir A. H. G. and Henry, R., 1892), v. 406
— (Oxenford, J., 1850), v. 509
— = Abon
Sleeper wide awake = Abou Hassan
Sleeping Beauty (À Beckett, G. A. and Ross, C. H., 1870), v. 233
— (Chambers, T. and Hyde, W. S., 1863), v. 783
— (Daly, C., 1891), v. 334
— (George, G. H., 1874), v. 377
— (Harris, Sir A. H. G. and Osman, W. R., 1877), v. 405
— (Skeffington, L. S., 1805), IV. 402, 611
— (Soutar, R., 1862), v. 751, 817, 862
— (1812), v. 535
— (1841), v. 536
— (1855), v. 846
— (1871, 1876, 1879, 1880, 1886, 1897, 1898, 1899), v. 751
— = Camillus and Columna
Sleeping Beauty and the Mystic Yellow Dwarf (Walton, W., 1895), v. 613
Sleeping Beauty; Her Seven Fairy Godmothers and a Wicked Fairy (Daly, C. and Chatterton, B., 1885), v. 334
Sleeping Beauty in the Wood (Buckstone, J. B., 1857), v. 287
— (James, C. S., 1849), IV. 330
— (Planché, J. R., 1840), IV. 381
— (1858, 1859), v. 846
— (1861, 1878), v. 751
— = Enchanted Castle
Sleeping Beauty with the Golden Hair (Conquest, G. and Spry, H., 1890), v. 322
Sleeping Dogs (Melford, M., 1897), v. 484
Sleeping Draught (Penley, S., 1818), IV. 130, 371
— = Popolino
Sleeping Hare (Dilley, J. J., 1868), v. 345

Sleeping Partner (Morton, M., 1897), v. 497

Sleeping Queen (Farnie, H. B., 1864), v. 752, 790

Sleepless Woman (1833), IV. 536

Sleepwalker (Abbott, C. H., 1893), v. 233

— (Craven, E., 1778), III. 20, 120, 177, 249, 380

— (Ellis, W., 1898), v. 357

— (Oulton, W. C., 1812), IV. 366

— = Matrimony

Sleigh Bells (Rowe, G. F., 1872), v. 552

Slender Thread (Stuart-Smith, E., 1896), v. 586

Slice of Luck (Morton, J. M., 1867), v. 496

Slighted Maid (Stapylton, Sir R., 1663), I. 35, 38, 95, 139, 264, 433

+ Slighted Treasures (Suter, W., French)

Slight Headache (Barrow, P. J., 1898), v. 252

Slightly Suspicious (Byron, J., 1891), v. 299

Slightly Touched (1868), v. 752

Slight Mistake (Eames, C. C., 1840), IV. 308

— (Fraser, J. A., 1873), v. 372

— (Stirling, E., 1869), v. 584

— (Wise, J., 1897), v. 629

— = Baby

Slight Mistakes (Herman, H., 1876), v. 419

— (Morton, J. M., 1843), IV. 362

Slip (Bullock, C., 1715), II. 140, 211, 300

Slippers = Hide and Seek

Slippers and Soothing Syrup = Man and Woman

Slocum's Perplexities (1898), v. 752

Slow and Sure (Abel, W. H., 1876), v. 235

Slow Man (Lemon, M., 1854), v. 455

Slowstop's Engagements (Cheltnam, C. S., 1862), v. 309

Slumbering Beauty (1883), v. 752

Slumber my Darling (Gee, L., 1868), v. 752, 793, 847

Slumbernambula (1844), IV. 536

Slumber of Wonders = Giant's Causeway

Slums of London (Aldin, C. A., 1892), v. 238

Slur of Slander (1889), v. 752

Sly and Shy (Manby, F. H., 1870), v. 474

— (Phillips, A. R., 1883), v. 522

Sly Dogs (Daly, C., 1887), v. 334

Smack for a Smack (Simpson, J. P., 1860), v. 567

Small and Early (Grain, R. C., 1882), v. 387

Small Profits do Great Things (Dibdin, T. J., 1819), IV. 302

Small Talk (Topham, E., 1786), III. 312

Smiles and Kisses (1885), v. 752

Smiles and Tears (Kemble, M.-T., 1815) = Law Suit, IV. 336, 491, 591, 630

— (1884), v. 752

— = (1) Right and Wrong; (2) Vicar's Daughter

Smith (Davidson, J., 1888), v. 338

— (1871), v. 752

Smith of Sheerness = Nore Light

Smith's Mixture (Crauford, J. R., 1879), v. 328

Smiths of Norwood (1863), v. 752

Smock Alley Secrets (Lefanu, P., 1780), III. 281

Smoke (Webster, B., the Younger, 1870), v. 618

Smoked Miser (Jerrold, D. W., 1823), IV. 331

Smouldering Fires (Avondale, W., 1883), v. 246

Smuggler and the Jew = Black Phantom

Smuggler Boy (Peake, R. B., 1833), IV. 370

Smuggler Count (Peake, R. B., 1833), IV. 603

Smuggler of the Abbey = St Anne's Night

Smuggler of the Blue Crag Rock = Mark the Mulatto

Smugglers (Birch, S., 1796), III. 98, 101-2, 238

— (Odell, T., 1729), II. 215, 347

Smugglers and the Preventive Service = Romance of the Coast

Smuggler's Boy = Woodriffe

Smuggler's Cave = Up All Night

Smuggler's Daughter (Bird, J., 1835), IV. 118, 267

— (1898), v. 752

Soldier's Widow (Fitzball, E., 1833), IV. 314 [This was printed in the Cumberland series as The Deserted Mill]

— (M°Laren, A., 1800), III. 284; IV. 350

Soldier, the Monk and the Assassin = Secret Marriage

Sold to Advantage (Wooler, J. P., 1853), V. 632

Sold Up (Goldberg, M., 1890), V. 383

Sole Survivor (Conquest, G. and Pettitt, H., 1876), V. 321

Sol Gandy (Bellingham, H. and Best, W., 1887), V. 257

Solicitor (Darnley, J. H., 1890), V. 337

Solid Silver (1880), V. 752

Solitaire (Planché, J. R., 1821), IV. 377, 604

Solitary of Lambeth (1849), IV. 536

Solitary of Mount Savage (1822), IV. 82, 536

Solitary of the Desert Mountains = Solitaire

Solitary of the Heath (1830), IV. 536

Solomon (Morell, T., 1749), II. 399

Solomon's Twins (Peile, F. K., 1897), V. 518

Solon (Bladen, M., 1705), II. 298

Solon Shingle (Owens, J. E., 1865), V. 752, 809, 847

Solway Mariner = Paul Jones

Solyman (1807), IV. 536

Some Bells that ring the Old Year out and a New One in (Hazlewood, C. H., 1862), V. 752, 796, 847

Somebody Else (Planché, J. R., 1844), IV. 382, 605

Somebody's in the House with Dinah (1847), IV. 536

Somebody's Sweetheart = Sunny Florida

Some Day (Phillips, Mrs N. and Tresahar, J., 1889), V. 523

Some Passages in the Diary of a Physician (1847), IV. 640

Some Passages in the Life of Love = Cupid in London

Something Forgotten (1874), V. 752

Something like a Nugget (1869), V. 752

Something like History = Charles II

Something New (Dibdin, T. J., 1792), III. 382; IV. 297, 580

Something of All Sorts (1871), V. 752

Something Singular = Is She his Wife?

Something to Do (Hoare, P., 1808), IV. 326

— (Morton, J. M., French)

Something to live for = Reuben Blight

Somewhat (Barnard, E., 1757), III. 235

Somnambula (Beazley, S., Jr., 1833), IV. 84, 264

— (Greenwood, T., 1841), IV. 321

— (Rede, W. L., 1844), IV. 391

— (1835), IV. 536

— (1854), V. 752

Somnambulist (Moncrieff, W. T., 1828), IV. 84, 359

— = Somnambula

Somnambulistic Knickerbockers = Rip Van Winkle

Somnambulists = Village Phantom

Somnambulo and Lively Little Alessio (Byron, H. J., 1878), V. 299

Sonambula (1859), V. 752

Son and Stranger (Chorley, H. F., 1851), V. 310

— (1896), V. 752

Songe d'Ossian (1824), IV. 536

Song of Fortunis (1876), V. 847

Song of Solomon (Bland, J., 1750), III. 238

Song of the River (Loader, M. and Ellis, F. R., 1898), V. 461

Songs of the Birds (Fitzball, E.), IV. 313

Sonia (Overbeck, E., 1895), V. 509

Son-in-Law (O'Keeffe, J., 1779), III. 42, 292, 393

Son of a Sailor = False Light

Son of a Sinner (Forshaw, F., 1896), V. 371

Son of Clanronald = Infant Heir

Son of Erin (Burges, G., 1823), IV. 575

Son of Neptune (1791), III. 344

Son of Night (1856), V. 752

— (1857), V. 752

— (1872), V. 752

Son of the Desert (Charlton, W. H., 1858), V. 783

— (Rede, W. L., 1843), IV. 390

Son of the Navy (1848), IV. 536

Son of the Night = Del Ombra

Son of the Sea (1866), V. 753

Son of the Sun (À Beckett, G. A., 1834), IV. 249

Son of the Wilderness, IV. 536

— = Oceola

Sons (Jones, Capt. J., 1809), IV. 333

Sons and Systems (Dance, C., 1838), IV. 288

— (1859), V. 753

Sons of Altona = Watch Tower

Sons of Anacreon (1785), III. 344

Sons of Britannia (Shirrefs, A., 1796), III. 307

— (1794), III. 344

Sons of Columbia (1862), V. 753

Sons of Erin (Lefanu, A., 1812), IV. 343

— (Patmore, W. J., 1893), V. 515

Sons of France (Kean, L., 1873), V. 442

Sons of Freedom (Faucquez, A., 1868), V. 364

— (1866), V. 753

Sons of Mars (1849), IV. 536

Sons of Neptune (Smithyes, W. G., 1858), V. 817

Sons of the Empire (Mackay, J. W., 1899), V. 469

Sons of the Forge (Hazlewood, C. H., 1870), V. 414

Sons of the Ocean (1843), IV. 536

Sons of the Sea (Wilkinson, M., 1895), V. 623

— = Sons of the Ocean

Son of the Soil (Merivale, H. C., 1872), V. 487

Sons of Toil (Gilbert, H. P., 1899), V. 378

— (Levey, J. C., 1873), V. 458

— = (1) Miner's Luck; (2) Under the Earth

Son's Revenge (Haines, J. T., 1836), IV. 536, 640

— = Osbert

Sophia (Buchanan, R., 1886), V. 285

Sophia's Supper (Addison, H. R., 1849), IV. 251

Sophonisba (Lee, N., 1675), I. 15, 37, 67, 96, 122-3, 125, 128, 129, 345, 346, 419

— (Thomson, J., 1730), II. 92-3, 360

Sophy (Denham, Sir J., 1642), I. 402

Sophy, Lucy, and Lucy, Sophy = My Own Rival

Sophy of Brabant (1802), IV. 536

Sop in the Pan (Oliphant, R., 1790), III. 115, 295

Sorcerer (Gilbert, W. S., 1877), V. 142-3, 380

— (Rich, J., 1724), II. 253, 256, 443

— (1831), IV. 537

Sorcerer of Candahar = Queen of the Roses

Sorcerer of Tewkesbury = Lansdowne Castle

Sorcerer's Three Golden Hairs (1830), IV. 537

Sorceress (Fitzball, E., 1831), IV. 313

— (1766), III. 344

— (1814), IV. 537, 636

Sorceress of Derncleuch = Dick Hatteraick, the Dutch Smuggler

Sorceress of Love (Parker, L. N., 1894), V. 513

Sorceress of Strozzi (1806), IV. 537

Sorrow and Crime = Charlotte Hanwell

Sorrowful Satan (Chapin, A., 1897), V. 308

Sorrow of a Secret (Buckland, W., 1892), V. 286

Sorrows and Death of Cleopatra (1805), IV. 537

Sorrows of a Sister = Pawnbroker

Sorrows of Margaret Forster = Satan

Sorrows of Satan (Dacre, H. S., 1897), V. 332

— (Woodgate, H. and Berton, P. M., 1897), V. 631

— (1897), V. 753

— = (1) Lucifer, Son of the Morning; (2) Prince of Darkness

Sorrows of Susan = Daft Dora

Sorrows of Werter (1825), IV. 537

Sorrows of Werther (Lunn, J., 1818), IV. 348

So runs the World away (Phillipson, G., 1889), V. 524

Sosarme, Re di Media (Humphreys, S., 1732), II. 399, 439

Sot (Arne, T. A., 1772), III. 47, 199-200, 234

So the World goes (1860), V. 753

Souldiers Fortune (Otway, T., 1680), I. 68, 79, 187, 191, 258, 262, 268, 308, 349, 422

Soul of Honour (Farnie, H. B.), V. 363

— = Might of Right

Soul's Tragedy (Browning, R., 1846), IV. 272

Souls Warfare (Tuke, R., 1672), I. 435

Source of the Nile = Mungo Park

Sour Grapes (Byron, H. J., 1873), V. 298

— (Gray, J., 1894), V. 390

Souterrain of Heidelburg = Poor Idiot

South Briton (1773), III. 344

Southdown, A.D. Society's Dress Rehearsal of East Lynne (Hoffman, M. H., 1896), V. 423

Southern Climes (Beyruth, P., 1876), V. 261

Southern Cross (Peel, G., 1873), V. 518

Southerner just arrived (Wigan, H., 1862), V. 622

South-Sea (Chetwood, W., 1720), II. 214, 262, 306

South-sea Director (Rich, J., 1720), II. 253, 443

South Sea Mutineers = Neuha's Cave

Southwark Fair (Coffey, C., 1729), II. 315

Southwark Ferry = John Overy, the Miser

Sovereign Remedy (Woodrooffe, S., 1847), IV. 422

So very obliging (Buckingham, L. S., 1857), V. 753, 781, 847

Sowers (1897), V. 753

Sowing and Reaping (Vernon, C., 1890), V. 608

— = Living Lie

Sowing the Whirlwind and Reaping the Storm = Slaves of Crime

Sowing the Wind (Grundy, S., 1893), V. 206, 397

Spadra the Satirist (1869), V. 753

Spae Wife (Boucicault, D., 1886), V. 269

Spain and Portugal (Dibdin, T. J., 1827), IV. 305

— (1827), IV. 537

Spain in Devonshire (1829), IV. 537

Spalpeen (Braham, H., 1875), V. 273

Spaniard (Gray, S., 1839), IV. 321

— (1819), IV. 537

Spaniard and Siorlamh (Fitzgerald, P., 1810), IV. 317

Spaniard Out-witted = (1) Intriguing Footman; (2) Tricks of Harlequin

Spaniards (1814), IV. 537, 636

Spaniards dismayed (1780), III. 116, 344

Spaniards in Denmark (Gazul, C., 1825), IV. 318

Spaniards in Peru (Plumptre, A., 1799), III. 64, 298, 393

Spaniard's Secret = Army of the North

Spaniard's Vow = Son's Revenge

Spanish Adventure = Gibraltar

Spanish Armada (1834), IV. 537

— = (1) 1588; (2) Rose of Devon; (3) Tilbury Fort

Spanish Bandit = Gonzalo

Spanish Banditti = Olivia

Spanish Barber (Colman, G., 1777), III. 119, 246, 379

Spanish Bond (À Beckett, G. A. and Reed, G., 1875), V. 234

Spanish Bonds (1823), IV. 537

Spanish Bridal (Johnstone, A. S., 1883), V. 438

Spanish Bride = Home, Out and Home

Spanish Brothers (1830), IV. 537

Spanish Bull-fight (1834), IV. 537

Spanish Coquettes (1788), III. 344

Spanish Curate (Planché, J. R., 1840), IV. 381

— (1749), II. 384

— (1783), III. 113, 344

Spanish Dancers (Selby, C., 1854), V. 560

Spanish Daughter = Theodora

Spanish Dollars (Cherry, A., 1805), IV. 279

Spanish Duel = Curiosity

Spanish Father (Mackenzie, T. H., 1808), IV. 350

Spanish Friar = Spanish Fryar

Spanish Fryar (Dryden, J., 1680), I. 10, 17, 68, 78, 79, 230–1, 308, 349, 352, 356, 406; III. 114

Spanish Gala (Dibdin, C. I. M., 1813), IV. 293, 537, 580, 640

Spanish Gallantries (Blasis, 1847), IV. 537, 640

Spanish Gallants (Byrne, O. and Noble, 1824), IV. 537, 640

Spanish Gipsy (Eliot, G., 1868), V. 356

— = Preciosa

Spanish Gipsy and the Assassin = Viceroy

Spanish Girl (Pitt, G. D., 1857), V. 526

Spanish Heroine (McLaren, A., 1808), IV. 351

Spectre on the White Horse = Conlath of the Isles

Spectre Pilot (1829), IV. 537

Spectre's Compact = Red Marine

Spectresheim (Reece, R., 1875), V. 538

Spectres of the Past (Whitbread, J. W., 1893), V. 620

+ Speculation (Farrell, J.; Pav. 10/11/1828)

— (Freeman, 1830), IV. 537, 640

— (Reynolds, F., 1795), III. 132, 301

— (Sapte, W., Jr., 1886), V. 555

Speechless Wife (1794) = Colin and Susan, III. 344, 404

Speech of the Dumb Restored = Torrent of the Valley

Speed the Plough (Dibdin, C. I. M., 1802), IV. 290

— (Morton, T., 1800), III. 142-4, 289; IV. 184, 363

Speedy Settlement (1896), V. 753

Speidhair = Shamus-na-Lena

Speidhoir = Shamas-na-Glanna

Spell (1756), III. 404

Spell-bound (Faucit, H. S., 1871), V. 363

— (Mackay, R. F., 1892), V. 470

Spell-bound Garden (Parker, L. N. and Carson, S. M., 1896), V. 513

Spelling Bee (Reece, R., 1876), V. 538

Spell of the Cloud King = Bronze Horse

Spells of Love = Truth

Spendthrift (Albery, J., 1875), V. 155, 237

— (Blake, T. G., 1844), IV. 537, 640

— (Draper, M., 1731), II. 178-9, 319

— (Foote, S., 1762), III. 384

— (Jerrold, D. W., 1839, 1850), IV. 333; V. 436

— (Kenrick, W., 1778), III. 113, 279

— = Legacy

Spendthrift Husband = Frank Wildeye

Spendthrift's Folly and Fortune (1751), III. 404

Sphinx (Boult, W., 1872), V. 270

— (Brough, W. and Brough, R. B., 1849), IV. 271

— (Clarke, C., 1874), V. 311

Spider and the Fly (Addison, J., 1890), V. 236

— (Conquest, G. and Spry, H., 1862) = Number Nip, V. 320, 753, 785, 847

Spider and the Fly (1862), V. 753

Spider King = Tarantula

Spiders and Flies (Galer, E. J. N., 1868), V. 375

Spider's Web (Henry, B., 1876), V. 417

— (1881), V. 753

— = In the Spider's Web

Spider, the Fly and the Butterfly = Village Nightingale

Spightful Sister (Bailey, A., 1667), I. 388

Spindlepops (1854), V. 753

Spin for Life (Carriden, W., 1897), V. 304

Spinster (Gwynne, P. and Harrison, C., 1887), V. 398

— (1883), V. 753

Spinsters Beware! (1873), V. 753

Spirit Bride (1850), V. 753

Spirit Captain (Holt, C., 1864), V. 798

Spirit Child's Prayer (Travers, W., 1865) = Neglected Home, V. 724, 753, 821, 841, 847

Spirit Haunted (Townsend, W. T., 1845), IV. 414

Spirit Medium (1862), V. 753

Spirit of Air (1838), IV. 537

Spirit of Avarice = Devil of Marseilles

Spirit of Avenel = White Lady

Spirit of Beauty (1841), IV. 537

Spirit of Conscience = Old Shadow

Spirit of Contradiction (Rich, J., 1760), III. 301, 394

Spirit of Death (Suter, W. E., 1861) = Angel of Midnight, V. 588, 753, 819, 847

Spirit of Evil = Legend of the Headless Man

Spirit of Gold (1848), IV. 537

Spirit of Good and Evil = Doom of Morana

Spirit of Liberty (Hazlewood, C. H., 1859), V. 753, 796, 847

Spirit of Mercy (1863), V. 753

Spirit of Peace = Angel's Whisper

Spirit of Punch = Arcadian Brothers

Spirit of Revenge (Suter, W. E., 1860), V. 753, 819, 847

Spirit of the Air = Étoile

Spirit of the Bell (Kenney, J., 1835), IV. 338

Spirit of the Black Mantle = Wenlock of Wenlock

Spirit of the Boreen = Banshee
Spirit of the Chimes = Bell Ringer
Spirit of the Elbe = Blackenberg
Spirit of the Fountain (Courtney, J., 1843), IV. 537, 640
Spirit of the Grotto (1796), III. 344
Spirit of the Haunted Room (1855), V. 753
Spirit of the Hill (1828), IV. 537
Spirit of the Lake = All Hallows' Eve
Spirit of the Loom (1848), IV. 538
— = Mary of Manchester
Spirit of the Mist (Keppell, 1831), IV. 538, 640
Spirit of the Moon (Farley, C., 1824), IV. 538, 640
— (1830), IV. 538
Spirit of the Reclining Stone = Ombra
Spirit of the Rhine (Barnett, M., 1835), IV. 261
Spirit of the Star = Zoroaster
Spirit of the Valley (Markwell, H., 1853), V. 476
Spirit of the Vault = Palace of Geneva
Spirit of the Waters (Milner, H. M., 1829), IV. 357
— = Undine
Spirit of Water = Demon of the Drachenfels
Spirit Rappers (Pitt, G. D., 1853), V. 526
Spirit Rapping and Table Moving (1853), V. 753
Spirit Rappings and Table Moving (1853), V. 753
Spirits and Water (Reynoldson, T. H., 1845), IV. 393
Spirits in Bond = Bottle Imp
Spirits of Donan the Goblin Page = Water Queen
Spirits of Good and Evil (1857), V. 753
Spirits of the Departed (1863) = Wishing Glen, V. 753, 769, 847, 850
Spirits of the Night (Markwell, W. R., 1853), V. 477
Spirit's Song (Haines, J. T., 1843), IV. 323
Spirit Trapper (1853), V. 753
Spiritualist (Durez, H., 1891), V. 352
Spiritual Minor (1762), III. 344
Spiritual Mountebank Detected = Female Enthusiast

Spirit Warning (Brougham, J., 1863), V. 780
Spirit World (1888), V. 753
Spitalfields Weaver (Bayly, T. H., 1838), IV. 263
Spite and Malice (McLaren, A., 1811), IV. 351
Spitfire (Morton, J. M., 1837), IV. 362
Spitz-Spitze (Conquest, G. and Spry, H., 1875), V. 321
Spleen (Colman, G., 1776), III. 12, 117, 183, 246, 379
Splendid Investment (Bernard, W. B., 1857), V. 259
Splendid Mrs Wichels (1898), V. 753
Spoglioni (1832), IV. 538
Spoil'd Child (Bickerstaffe, I., 1790), III. 238
Spoiled Child (1836), IV. 538
Spoiled Children (Dibdin, T. J., 1819), IV. 302
Spoilt Spree (1892), V. 753
Sponge in the Country = No Dinner Yet
Sponge out of Town = No Dinner Yet
Spoons (Lowe, W., 1881), V. 464
Sport (Nicholson, G. A., 1876), V. 504
— (Turner, M. and Edwardes-Sprange, W., 1895), V. 605
— (1883), V. 753
Sport after Rain = Angler
Sporting Boots of the Inn = Lad of the Village
Sporting Intelligence Extraordinary (1861), V. 753
Sporting in the Dark (1855), V. 753
Sporting Life (Raleigh, C. and Hicks, Sir S., 1897), V. 534
— = St Leger
Sporting Youth from the Counting House to the Hulks = Grand National
Sport of Fate (1895), V. 753
Sport of Kings = Favourite
Sports and Pastimes of London 200 Years Ago = City Games
Sportsman (Lestocq, W., 1892), V. 457
Sportsman and the Shepherd (1816), IV. 538
— = Dinner of Madelon [Evidently a revised title of the above]
Sportsman Pearl = Derry Driscoll
Sport upon Sport = Mad Lovers

Spotted Lion (Sapte, W., Jr., 1888), v. 556

Spottie, the Terror of Wearside (Langlois, H. A., 1877), v. 448

Spouse Trap (East, J. M., 1899) = Kitchen Girl, v. 353, 754, 789, 847

Spouter (Dell, H., 1756), III. 253

— (Murphy, A., 1756), III. 180, 289

Spread Eagle (Dibdin, T. J., 1826), IV. 304

Sprees Alongshore = Mat Mizen and Tom Tiller

Sprightly Romance of Marsac (Seawell, E., 1898), v. 559

Sprig of Shillelah (Mildenhall, T., 1836), IV. 355

Sprigs of Laurel (O'Keeffe, J., 1793), III. 200, 294

Spring (Harris, J., 1762) = Daphne and Amyrillis, III. 213, 266

Spring and Autumn (Kenney, J., 1827), IV. 337

Spring and Fall of Life (1866), v. 754

Spring Gardens (Planché, J. R., 1846), IV. 382

Spring-Guns and Man-Traps (1832), IV. 538

Spring-heeled Jack (Stewart, D., 1863), v. 754, 818, 847

— (Travers, W., 1868), v. 603

Spring Leaves (Grein, J. T. and Jarvis, C. W., 1891), v. 394

Spring Legend (Colnaghi, C. P., 1891), v. 318

Spring Lock (Peake, R. B., 1829), IV. 370

Spring of Life and the Spring of Death = Rival Fountains

Spring or Autumn (1833), IV. 538

Spring's Delights (Grain, R. C., 1884), v. 387

Spring Valley (1787), III. 344

Sprite of the Snowdrift (1844), IV. 538

Sprung from the Streets = Waif

Spur of the Moment (Byron, H. J., 1872), v. 298

Spy (Paull, H. M., 1896), v. 516

— (Raleigh, C., 1888), v. 533

— (Turner, G., 1889), v. 605

Spy and Counter Spy = Finesse

Spy in the Crimea = Shelah from Cork

Spy of Naples = Spanish Girl

Spy of Paris (1858), v. 754

Spy of the Neutral Ground (1825), IV. 538

Spy of the Republic (Stirling, E., 1861), v. 584, 818

Spy of Venice (Duncan, J., 1845), IV. 308

Squabbles (Rogers, T. S., 1881), v. 549

Squall in the Downs = William that married Susan

Square-Toes Outwitted = She Gallant

Squaring the Circle (Drake, F., 1876), v. 350

Squeaker (1894), v. 754

— (1895), v. 754

Squeeze for St Paul's = British Loyalty

Squeeze to the Coronation (Thomson, J., 1821), IV. 538

Squib for the Fifth of November (Mayhew, A. and Edwards, H. S., 1851), v. 482

Squire (Pinero, Sir A. W., 1881), v. 173, 174, 176, 525, 810

Squire and Someone Elsa = Elsa's Hand

Squire Badger = Sot

Squire Basinghall (1735), II. 384

Squire Brainless (1710), II. 384

Squire Burlesqued (1765), III. 344

Squire Crossmate's Vow (Macintyre, W. T., 1892), v. 469

Squireen, the Informer and the Illicit Distiller = Green Grow the Rushes, Oh!

Squire Humphrey (Blackmore, W. T., 1887), v. 262

Squire of Alsatia (Shadwell, T., 1688), I. 69, 84, 198, 200, 208, 308, 431; III. 168

Squire of Burleigh (Seddon, F. H., 1892), v. 559

Squire of Dames (Carlton, R. C., 1895), v. 305

Squire of Ringwood Chace (Wooler, J. P., 1865), v. 632

Squire of Undercliff (James, S. T., 1895), v. 434

Squire Oldsapp (D'Urfey, T., 1678), I. 33, 39, 273–4, 408

Squire's Daughter (Bloomer, J. E., 1879), v. 266

Squire's Last Shilling = English Gentleman

Squire's Maria (Adams, H., 1882), v. 235

Squire's Return (Cumberland, R., 1772), III. 381

Squire's Wife (Jarman, F., 1889), V. 434

Squire's Will (Russell, E. H., 1897), V. 553

Squire Trelooby (Vanbrugh, Sir J., 1704), II. x, 144, 147, 152, 362, 443, 445

Staff of Diamonds (Hazlewood, C. H., 1861), V. 412

Stage (Digges, W., 1877), V. 345

Stage and State (Simpson, J. P., 1868), V. 568

Stage Arrivals = Favourites in Town

Stage-Beaux toss'd in a Blanket (Brown, T., 1704), II. 262, 300

Stage Coach (De Lara, F., 1887), V. 341
— (Farquhar, G., 1704), II. 131, 132, 133, 134, 137, 145, 148–9, 321, 435–6
— (1787), III. 344

Stage Coach Opera (?Chetwood, W. R., 1730), II. 384, 448

Stage Dora (Burnand, F. C., 1883), V. 291

Stage Land (Douglas, G. R., 1875), V. 347

Stage Letter (1806), IV. 538

Stage Mutineers (1733), II. 384

Stage Overturned = Jew and the Robbers

Stage Pretenders (1720), II. 384

Stage Struck (Dimond, W., 1835), IV. 307
— (1837), IV. 538

Stage-Struck Apothecary (1827), IV. 538

Stage-Struck Butler = He Would Be a Player

Stage-Struck Lady (1819), IV. 538

Stage-Struck Yankee (Markwell, W. R., 1845), IV. 538, 640

Stain upon the Hand = Wait and Hope

Stallion (Kirkman, F., 1662), I. 417

Stand and Deliver (Archer, W. J., 1885), V. 242

Standard of England (Young, H., 1863), V. 754, 847

Stanfield Hall (Dodson, R., 1851), V. 346

Stanislaus (Milner, H. M., 1823), IV. 538, 640

Stanislaus of Poland (1835), IV. 538

Star and a Stroller = Stella and Leather-lungs

Star and the Flame = Moths

Starling of the Old Saloup = Tom Moor of Fleet Street

Star of Andalusia (1854), V. 754

Star of Destiny (1898), V. 754
— = Renowned Mandarin, Whang Fong Long Tong Chang Song Ho

Star of India (Sims, G. R. and Shirley, A., 1896), V. 569

Star of my Home (1846), IV. 538

Star of Seville (Kemble, F. A., 1837), IV. 335

Star of the North (Pratt, F. W., 1889), V. 530
— (Robertson, T. W., 1855), V. 123, 546

Star of the Rhine (Barrez, M., 1852), V. 251
— (1853), V. 847

Star of the Street (1860), V. 754

Star of the Woodlands (Lee, N., Jr., 1861), V. 452

Stars (Rede, W. L., 1835), IV. 538, 640

Stars and Garters (Reece, R. and Farnie, H. B., 1878), V. 538

Star-Spangled Banner (Patmore, W. J., 1892), V. 515

Starting Price (Clarke, C. A., 1894), V. 312

Star Turn (Leuberts, H., 1893), V. 458

Starved to Death (1872), V. 754

State Courier (Weston, J. P., 1871), V. 619

State Farce (1757), III. 344

State Jewels = Blood Royal

State Juggler (1733), II. 384

State Menders = Wat Tyler

State of Innocence (Dryden, J., 1677), I. 23, 99, 237, 405–6
— (1712), II. 384, 448

State of Physic (1742), II. 384

State Prisoner (Gowing, W. A., 1851), V. 386
— (Raymond, R. J., 1819), IV. 388
— (Stirling, E., 1847), IV. 408

State Prisoner of Austria = Fortress of Ganzbrough

State Prisoner of the Iron Den = Fidelio

State Secret (Cassel, H. and Duckworth, H. C., 1889), V. 305
— = Peg Woffington

State Secrets (Snodgrass, A., 1821), IV. 538, 640

State Secrets (Wilks, T. E., 1836), IV. 420

Statesman (Dent, J., 1782), III. 254

Statesman Foil'd (Dossie, R., 1768) = Trial of Skill, III. 257, 383

Statesman's Opera = Patron

State Tower = Unknown Guest

State Trial (Irving, L. B., 1896), v. 432

Station House (Dance, G., 1833), IV. 288, 579

— (1854), v. 754

Station Master's Daughter = Last Express

Statue (Dibdin, C.), IV. 290

— = Evadne

Statue Blanche (1856), v. 847

Statue Bride (Amcotts, V., 1868), v. 240

— = Elves

Statue Feast (Craven, E., 1782), III. 117, 249, 366, 380

Statue in the Wood = Red Robber

Statue Lover (Jerrold, D. W., 1828), IV. 331

— (1854), v. 754

Statue of Clay (1892), v. 754

Statue Shop = Helen of Troy up-to-date

Statue Steed (1832), IV. 538

Statute (1777), III. 344

Statute Fair = Lady Henrietta

Statute of Albemarle (Whishaw, Mrs B., 1892), v. 620

Statutory Duel = Grand Duke

Stay at Home (Lewes, G. H., 1856), v. 459

Steamboating on the Mississippi = Down the River

Steed of the Silver Star and the Last Struggle of the Moors = Conquest of Granada

Steel Castle (1845), IV. 538

Steel Hand and his Nine Thieves (1857), v. 754

Steel Pavilion (Peake, R. B., 1836), IV. 370

Steeple Chase (Morton, J. M., 1865), v. 496

Steeple Jack (Pemberton, T. E., 1888), v. 519

Stella (Findon, B. W., 1889), v. 366

— (Shoberl, F., 1804), IV. 86, 401

— (Thompson, B., 1800), IV. 86, 412

— (1798), III. 344, 404

Stella (1852), v. 754

Stella and Leatherlungs (Colman, G., 1823), IV. 282

Stella de Rittersdorf (Barnett, C. Z., 1844), IV. 260

Stella Gordon (1893), v. 754

Stella, the Female Pirate (1859), v. 754

Step Brothers = Actor

Step by Step (1862), v. 754

— = Sybilla

Stephania (Field, M., 1892), v. 366

Stephen (Denny, J., 1851), v. 788

Stephen Arncliffe = Honour among Thieves

Stephen Digges (Oxenford, J., 1864), v. 510

Stepmother (Gillies, R. P., 1814), IV. 538, 585

— (Howard, F., 1800), III. 273; IV. 329

— (Jones, J., 1829), IV. 333

— (Lacy, M. R., 1828), IV. 84, 340

— (Sketchley, A., 1880), v. 571

— (Stapylton, Sir R., 1663), I. 38, 139-40, 264, 433

— (1882), v. 754

— = Forced from Home

Stepmothers (1877), v. 754

Stepmother's Vengeance = Belinda the Blind

Stepping Stones (Fox, G. D., 1887), v. 371

Step-Sister (Sapte, Walter, Jr., 1887), v. 556

Stern Resolve (Masterton, C., 1837), IV. 353

Steward (Beazley, S., Jr., 1819), IV. 263, 571

— (Spicer, H., 1844), IV. 405

Stick, the Pole and the Tartar = Mazourka

Still Alarm (Arthur, J. and Wheeler, A. C., 1888), v. 244

Still Waters run deep (Taylor, T., 1855), v. 100–101, 592

+ Stirring the Pudding (Planché, J. R.: Dicks (1868, in Pieces of Pleasantry))

Stirring Times (Celli, F. H. and Daly, B., 1897), v. 307

Stock Exchange (Dance, C., 1858), v. 335

Stock-Jobbers (Chetwood, W., 1720), II. 214, 306

Stock-Jobbers = Volunteers

Stock-Jobber turn'd Gentleman = Exchange Alley

Stolen (Hancock, W. 1863), v. 402

— (1868), v. 754

Stolen Away (Dodson, R., 1875), v. 346

Stolen Birthright (Spencer, S., 1896), v. 576

Stolen Bonds (1897), v. 754

Stolen Diamonds (Glen, I., 1876) = Woman's Error, v. 382, 754, 793, 847

Stolen Fortune (Clarke, F., 1877), v. 312

Stolen from Home (1891), v. 754

Stolen Heiress (Centlivre, Mrs S., 1702), II. 166, 303, 433; III. 115

— = Under the Stars

Stolen Jewess (Hazlewood, C. H., 1872), v. 414

Stolen Kiss (1856), v. 754

Stolen Kisses (Meritt, P., 1876), v. 486

Stolen Lamb = Innocence and Love

Stolen Marriage = Iron Arm

Stolen Sheep (1832), IV. 538

— (1849), IV. 538

Stolen Will (Mildenhall, T., 1846), IV. 355

Stone-broke (Sievier, R. S., 1892), v. 566

— (1895), v. 754

Stone Eater (Stuart, C., 1788), III. 310

Stone Jug (1873), v. 754

Stone Man (1854), v. 754

Stone-Masons' Strike (1848), IV. 538

Stoney Batter (1825), IV. 538

Stoney Broke (1897), v. 754

Stop for Dinner (1894), v. 754

Stop her who can = Female Adventurer

Stop him who can (1840), IV. 538

— = Dramatist

Stopped at Rochester = Grand Tour

Stop Thief! (Dibdin, T. J., 1820), IV. 302

— (Melford, M., 1889), v. 484

Stores (Rose, E. and Harris, Sir A., 1881), v. 550

Storm (Burges, Sir J. B., 1817), IV. 277

— (Holford, G., 1799), III. 271

— (Robertson, I., 1896), v. 545

— (1834), IV. 538

Storm and Sunshine (1889), v. 754

Storm at Sea = Pilot

Storm Beaten (Buchanan, R., 1883), v. 284

Stormcoast (Vanneck, F., 1888), v. 607

Storm Deed (Seaman, W., 1877), v. 559

Storm Fiend = Fantisticuff

Storm Fiend of the Apennines (1847), IV. 538

Storm in a Teacup (Bernard, W. B., 1854), v. 259

— (Corder, Mrs F., 1882), v. 325

— (1875), v. 754

Storming and Capture of Delhi (1857), v. 754

Storming of Fort Omoa (Sheridan, R. B., 1780), III. 396

Storming of Mezanderan = Zohrab the Hostage

Storming of Quito (1840), IV. 538

Storming of St Sebastian = Guerillas

Storming of Seringapatam (1829), IV. 538

Storming of Seringapatan = Tippoo Sahib

Storm King's Dream (1860), v. 847

Storm-Light of Anzasca = Lelia's Lamp

Storm of Life (1886), v. 754

Storm of Mussel Craig = Antiquary and the Bluegown Beggar

Storm on the Thames = Jonathan Wild

Storm Sails Set = Boatswain's Whistle

Storms by Sea and Land = Postillion

Storm Signal (1866), v. 754

Storm, the Fire and the Ball = House on the Bridge

Storm Visitor (Travers, W., 1856), v. 754, 821, 847

Story of a Big Diamond = Courage

Story of a Coffin Shop = Insurance Money

Story of a Feather (Webb, C., 1845), IV. 417

Story of a Flag = Napoleon

Story of Agnes Primrose = Wrack of the Heart

Story of a Great Diamond = Dark Continent

Story of a Heart = (1) Lucille; (2) Nina

Story of a Lyre = Arion

Story of a Night (Mead, T., 1859), v. 754, 806, 847

Story of a Pastoral Life = Luck

Stratagem = (1) Juan Fernandez; (2) Stratagemma

Stratagem for Stratagem = Hamlet and Zelina

Stratagemma (1759), III. 404

Stratagem of Harlequin (1732), II. 384

Stratagem on Stratagem = Witchcraft of Love

Stratagems (1816), IV. 539

Stratagems of Harlequin (1730), II. 384

Stratford Jubilee (Garrick, D., 1769), III. 264

Stratford Wake = Man like himself

Strathlogan (Overton, C. and Moss, H., 1892), v. 509

Strathmore (Marston, J. W., 1849), IV. 93, 353

Strawberries and Cream (De Banzie and Grant, J., 1890), v. 340

Strawberry Girl = Fashion and Famine

Strawberry Pickers (1796), III. 344

Straw Hat (1873), v. 755

Strayed Away (Travers, W., 1870), v. 603

Strayed from the Fold (Murdoch, J. M., 1878), v. 499

Streak o' Sunshine (Don, L., 1888), v. 347

Streaks of Gold (Randford, M., 1878), v. 534

Streanshall Abbey (Gibson, F., 1799), III. 264; IV. 319

Street Arab = Outcast Joe

Street Ballad Singer = Stolen

Street Juggler = Grimaldi

Streets (Gordon, G. L., 1884), v. 385

Street-singer, the Sailor, and the Noble = Little Ned

Streets of London (Boucicault, D., 1857), v. 85, 92-3, 268

— = Poor of Liverpool

Streets of New York = Streets of London

Streets to the Hulks (Conquest, G., 1869), v. 320

Stricken Oak (1863), v. 755

Stricken Down (Dillon, C., 1870), v. 345

Strike (Herbert, L., 1873), v. 418

— (Stanley, H. J., 1875), v. 579

— (1885), v. 755

Strike = Long Strike

Strike at Arlingford (Moore, G., 1893), v. 161, 187, 492

Strike at the Mill and the Mutineers = Lashed to the Helm

Strike of the Cantons = William Tell

Striking Beauty (1836), IV. 539

Striking Feature = Man in the Moon

Striking Similarity (Hay, F., 1870), v. 411

Striking the Hour (Pitt, W. H., 1867), v. 527

Striking Widow (1858), v. 755

String of Pearls (Clarke, C. A. and Silva, H. R., 1892), v. 312

— (Pitt, G. D., 1847), IV. 374

— (Young, Mrs H., 1862), v. 755, 825, 847

— (1861), v. 755

— = Sweeney Todd, the Barber of Fleet Street

Stripling (Baillie, J., 1836), IV. 162, 258

Stroke of Luck (Bagot, A. E. and Murray, J. K., 1899), v. 247

Stroke of the Pen = Fool's Fidelity

Strolers (Breval, J., 1723), II. 49, 134, 213, 299, 432

Strolers Pacquet open'd (1742), II. 4, 172, 211, 216, 384, 385

Stroller (Dick, C., 1887), v. 344

— (Logan, Mrs O., 1878), v. 462

Strollers (Glenny, G. W., 1888), v. 382

Strolling and Stratagem = Counter Attractions

Strolling Country Actors = Country Actors

Strolling Gentleman = Wild Oats

Strolling Players (1823), IV. 539

Strong as Death (Ford, D. M., 1899), v. 370

Strongbow (French, W. P., 1892), v. 373

Stronger than Hate = Zola

Stronger than Love (1894), v. 755

Strong Man of the West = Trapper of the Hills

Strozzi (1824), IV. 539

Struck in the Dark (Moore, R., 1875), v. 492

Struck Oil (1876), v. 755

Struck Oil at Last = Seth Green

Struggle for a Crown (1846), IV. 539

Struggle for Gold and the Orphan of
the Frozen Sea (Stirling, E., 1854), v.
584, 755, 818, 847

Struggle for Liberty = (1) Sea King's
Vow; (2) Spy of Paris; (3) War in
Turkey

Struggle for Life (Buchanan, R. and
Horner, F., 1890), v. 285

— (Drayton, E., 1884), v. 350

Struggle of Seventy Years = Phoebe
Hersell

Struggles at Starting = Professionals
Puzzled

Struggles of a Poor Engineer = Dora's
Love

Struggles of the Poor (Hazlewood,
C. H., 1857), v. 755, 796, 847

Struggling for Wealth (Gosnay, W. A.,
1880), v. 386

Student (1823), IV. 539

Student of Blackfriars (1836), IV. 539

Student of Bonn = Blind Wife

Student of Gottingen = Death Fetch

Student of Jena (Cooper, W., 1842), IV.
539, 640

Students (Courtney, J., 1861), v. 755,
786, 847

— (Smith, G., 1837), IV. 539

— (Stewart, J., 1777), III. 309

— (1762), III. 344

— (1779), III. 344

Student's Dream (Blake, T. G., 1845),
IV. 268

— = Pandemonium

Student's Frolic (Molloy, J. L., 1864),
v. 807

Student's Grave (Seaman, W., 1853), v.
559

Students of Bonn (Rodwell, G. H.,
1842), IV. 395

Students of Jena (Planché, J. R., 1833),
IV. 379

Students of Salamanca (Jameson, R. F.,
1813), IV. 330

Students Whim = Don Sancho

Study of Two Women (Wilton, Mrs,
1898), v. 629

Stuffed Dog (Knox, J. A. and Atwell,
E., 1889), v. 446

Sturdy Beggars (1733), II. 385

Sub-Editor (Payne, E. and Harrison,
C., 1896), v. 518

Subject's Joy for the King's Restoration
(Sadler, A., 1660), I. 427

Sublime and Beautiful (Morton, T.,
1828), IV. 364

Substance and the Shadow (Mullen,
F. and Atkinson, T., 1894), v. 499

Substitute (Bell, M., 1893), v. 256

— (Payn, J., 1876), v. 518

Subterfuge (1857), v. 755

Suburban Spectre (1898), v. 755

Suburb-Justice = Town-Shifts

Success (Hyde, H. F., 1879), v. 431,
846

— (Knight, F. H., 1892), v. 445

— (Planché, J. R., 1825), IV. 12, 78,
135-6, 149, 378; v. 133

— = Stowaway

Successful Mission (1894), v. 755

Successful Pyrate (Johnson, C., 1712),
II. 45, 142, 221-2, 339

Successful Straingers (Mountfort, W.,
1689), I. 225, 421

Such a Good Man (Besant, W. and
Rice, J., 1879), v. 260

Such a Guy Mannering (Strachan, W.,
Jr., 1868), v. 585

Such is Life (Rignold, H. H., 1893), v.
543

— (Young, H., 1864), v. 755, 847

— (1885), v. 755

Such is Love (Mond, A. M., 1894), v.
491

Such is the Law (Taylor, T. and
Merritt, P., 1878), v. 594

Such Stuff as Dreams are made of
(Fitzgerald, E., 1899), v. 368

Such Things Are (Inchbald, Mrs E.,
1787), III. 55, 145-7, 148, 150,
275

Such Things Have Been (Ryder, W.,
1789), III. 304

Such Things Were (Hoare, P., 1787),
III. 269

— = Highland Robbers

+ Sudden Arrival (Hay, F., French)

Sudden Arrivals (Cobb, J., 1809) = Man
of Business, IV. 281, 500, 577,
632

Sudden Attack (1863), v. 755

Sudden Shower (1895), v. 755

+ Sudden Squall (Lancaster-Wallis, E.,
French)

Sudden Thoughts (Wilks, T. E., 1837), IV. 420, 617
— (1843), IV. 539
Sue (Harte, B. and Pemberton, T. E., 1896), V. 407
Sugar and Cream (Hurst, J. P., 1883), V. 431
Sugar and Spice (McArdle, J. F., 1882), V. 466
Sugar and Spice and all that's nice (Thorne, R. L., 1850), V. 599
Suggestion (Collins, M. and Brown, W. H., 1891), V. 318
Suggs in Danger (Atkinson, T., 1882), V. 245
Suicide (Colman, G., 1778), III. 112, 246
Suicide's Tree (Marchant, F., 1863), V. 755, 847
Suil Dhuv the Coiner (Dibdin, T. J., 1828), IV. 305
Suitable Match (1879), V. 755
Suited at Last (Bedford, E., 1895), V. 255
Suit for the Season = Lawyer
Suit of Tweeds (Hay, F., 1867), V. 411
Suitor at Sea (1870), V. 755
Suitors in Abergavenny = Welsh Dairy
Sulamite (1884), V. 755
Sulieman (1814), IV. 539, 635
Suliote (1829), IV. 539
Sullen Lovers (Shadwell, T., 1668), I. 7, 26, 68, 85, 90, 187, 193, 198, 202–3, 347, 429–30
Sultan (Bickerstaffe, I., 1775), III. 27, 238
— (Gentleman, F., ?1754), III. 264
— (1729), II. 385
— (1759), III. 344
Sultana (Gardiner, W., 1806), IV. 318
— (Goff, R., 1848), IV. 539, 640
Sultan and the Slave (1830), IV. 539
Sultan and the Soldier = Nadir Shah
Sultan and the Tsar (1854), V. 755
Sultaness (Johnson, C., 1717), II. 53, 72, 81, 89, 117, 339, 439
Sultan of Curdistan = Enchanted Courser
Sultan of Mocha (Lestocq, W., 1874), V. 457
— (1876), V. 847
Sultan's Dream (1850), V. 755
Sultan's Favourite = Bruno

Sultan, the Gardener and the Odalisque (Krasinski, H., 1857), V. 801
Sumachaun (Connor, B., 1878), V. 320
Summer Amusement (Andrews, M. P. and Miles, W. A., 1779), III. 204, 233, 377
Summer and Winter (Ebsworth, J., 1840), IV. 308
— = Summer and Winter of Life
Summer and Winter of Life (Marchant, F., 1864), V. 805
Summer Cloud (1880), V. 755
— (1899), V. 755
Summer Clouds (Doone, N., 1891), V. 347
— (Lancaster-Wallis, E., 1899), V. 447
Summer Festival (1873), V. 755
Summer Fête (1837), IV. 539
Summer Flies (Dibdin, T. J., 1823), IV. 304
Summer Flowers (1854), V. 755
Summer House (1815), IV. 539
Summerland's Mistake (1873), V. 755
Summer Moths (Heinemann, W., 1898), V. 416
Summer's Dream (Meller, R., 1891), V. 485
Summer's Morn of 1660 = White Wreath
Summer's Tale (Cumberland, R., 1765), III. 251
Summer Storm (Parry, T., 1854), V. 515
Summer Storms (Jennings, H. J., 1876), V. 436
Summoned to Court (Dilley, J. J. and Clifton, L., 1880), V. 345
Sun and the Wind (1860), V. 755
Sunbeams and Shadows = First Love and False Hearts
Sunbury Scandal (Horner, F., 1896), V. 427
Sundown till Dawn (Mortimer, J., 1875), V. 494
Sunken Treasure = Beneath the Waters
Sunlight and Shadow (Carton, R. C., 1890), V. 305
Sunlight through the Mist = Rescue on the Raft
Sunny Florida (Marris, H., 1896), V. 477

Sunny Side (Rae, C. M., 1885), v. 532

Sunny South (Darrell, G., 1884), v. 337

Sunny Vale Farm (Bridgeman, J. V., 1864), v. 275, 780

Sun Picture = Quadroon

Sunset (Jerome, J. K., 1888), v. 186, 436

Sunshine (Broughton, F. W., 1880), v. 281

Sunshine after Rain = (1) Cry To-day and Laugh To-morrow; (2) Mad Guardian

Sunshine and Shade (Rede, W. L., 1843) = Faith and Falsehood, IV. 539, 607, 640

Sunshine and Shadow (Thomson, A., 1867), v. 598, 820

— = Sunlight and Shadow

Sunshine in Season = Happy Hours

Sunshine through the Clouds (Lewes, G. H., 1854), v. 458

Sunshine through the Mist = My Wife

Super (Heathcote, A. M., 1894), v. 415

Superannuated Gallant (Reed, J., 1745), II. 351; III. 300

Superfluous Lady (Bell, Mrs H., 1891), v. 255

Super-Natural = Hurlothrumbo

Supernatural Warning = Death Fetch

Supper (Binyon, R. L., 1877), v. 261

Supper Dances (Young, Sir W. L., 1891), v. 637

Supper for Three = Tourists

Supper for Two (Gifford, J. W., 1883), v. 184, 378

Supper Gratis (Reeve, W., 1871), v. 540

Supper Party (1861), v. 755

Supper's Over (Barnett, M., 1830), IV. 261

Supper the Night before the Coronation (1831), IV. 539

Supper, the Sleeper and the Merry Swiss Boy = La! Somnambula

Supreme Moment (Clifford, Mrs W. K., 1899). v. 755, 784, 847

Sure Aim (1807), IV. 539

Sure Bait for a Good Husband = Female Angler

Sure to Win (Goldsmith, W. H., 1896), v. 383

— (1876), v. 755

Surgeon of Paris (Jones, J., 1849), IV. 334

Surooj Seeing (1820), IV. 539

Surprisal (Howard, Sir R., 1662), I. 55, 214, 414

Surprise (Calvert, W., 1897), v. 300

— (Kirkman, F., 1662), I. 418

— (1899), v. 755

Surprises (Burnette, C., 1890), v. 293

Surrender of Calais (Colman, G., the Younger, 1791), III. 247

— (1801), IV. 539

Surrender of Conde (1793), III. 344

Surrender of Trinidad (1797), III. 344

Surrender of Valenciennes (1793), III. 344

Surrey Toll-Gate = Stoney Batter

Surrounded = War—the Fugitives

Susan Hapley (Denvil, Mrs, 1841), IV. 579

Susan Hopley (Pitt, G. D., 1841), IV. 373

Susanna (Tollet, E., 1755), III. 312

Susan's Lovers (1878), v. 755

Susan Smith (Harris, A. G., 1860), v. 405

Susian Captive = Panthea

Suspicion (1843), IV. 539

— (1875), v. 755

Suspicious Brother (1789) = Try Again, III. 344, 405

Suspicious Husband (Hoadly, B., 1747), II. 137, 206, 207–8, 337, 439

Suspicious Husband Criticized (Macklin, C., 1747), II. 207, 342

Suzanne (Leigh, H. S., 1884), v. 454, 803

— (Lucas, W. J., 1838), IV. 539, 640

Suzette (1832), IV. 539

Swallows' Nest (Young, Mrs H., 1863) = Ben Child, v. 648, 755, 827, 847

Swallows of Paris = Game of Life

Swamp Hall (Jerrold, D. W., 1833), IV. 332

Swan and Edgar (Edwards, H. S. and Kenney, C., 1859), v. 755, 789, 801, 847

Swansea Castle in 1327 = Regicide

Swarry Dansong (Barrington, R., 1890), v. 251

Swedish Ferryman (Poole, J., 1843), IV. 539, 640

Swedish Nightingale = Jenny Lind at Last

Swedish Patriotism (Abbot, W., 1819), IV. 249, 567

Swedish Patriots = Swedish Patriotism

Sweeney Todd = String of Pearls

Sweeney Todd, the Barber of Fleet Street (Hazleton, F., 1865), v. 412

Sweep for a King (Bruce, H. P., 1888), v. 283

Sweepstakes (Lake, E., 1891), v. 446

Sweep Sweep Sweep! (Faucit, J. S., 1834), IV. 311

Sweet Belle of the Period = Timour the Tartar

Sweet Bells Jangled (Hastings, G., 1879), v. 409

Sweet Brier (Shelley, H., 1898), v. 562

Sweet Cinderella (Thorne, G., 1888), v. 598

— (1889), v. 755

Sweet Cupid's Net (Cross, J., 1892), v. 330

Sweet Deception (Doone, N., 1896), v. 347

Sweetheart, Good-bye (Fairbairn, Mrs R., 1881), v. 359

Sweethearting (1827), IV. 539

Sweethearts (Gilbert, W. S., 1874), v. 138, 380

Sweethearts and Wives (Kenney, J., 1823), IV. 337

Sweet Innisfail (Reynolds, W., 1886), v. 541

Sweet Lavender (Pinero, Sir A. W., 1888), v. 178–9, 525

Sweet Nancy (Buchanan, R., 1890), v. 285

Sweet Olden Days (Dalroy, H., 1894), v. 333

Sweet Poll of Horsleydown (1841), IV. 640

Sweet Revenge (Fox, J. and McArdle, J. F., 1876), v. 371

— (1835), IV. 539

Sweet Roses = Try before you Buy

Sweet Seventeen (De Lara, F., 1894), v. 341

— (1898), v. 755

Sweet Simplicity (Field, W. F., 1891), v. 366

Sweet Sorrow (1899), v. 755

Sweet Will (Jones, H. A., 1887), v. 165, 440

Swellfoot the Tyrant = Œdipus Tyrannus

Swell Miss Fitzwell (1897), v. 755

Swindler (Campbell, A., 1873), v. 301

— (1785), III. 344

Swindlers (Baddeley, R., 1774), III. 344, 377, 405

— (McLaren, A., 1812), IV. 351

Swing (Barnett, C. Z., 1831), IV. 259

Swing Bridge (1823), IV. 539

Swiss (1805), IV. 539

Swiss Banditti = Maniac

Swiss Boys (1828), IV. 539

Swiss Church (1859), v. 755

Swiss Cottage = Why don't she marry?

Swiss Express (Gilbert, A. H. and Read, C., 1891), v. 378

Swiss Family (1828), IV. 539

Swiss Father (1836), IV. 539

Swiss Girl (Wilkins, J. H., 1849), IV. 420

— (1897), v. 755

Swiss Huntress (Oxberry, W. H., 1840), IV. 366

Swiss Milkman = Nathalie

Swiss Patriots = Forest of Rotzberg

Swiss Revels (1806), IV. 539

Swiss Swains (Webster, B. N., 1837), IV. 417

Swiss Villagers (1823), IV. 539

Switzerland (Porter, A. M., 1819), IV. 387

Switzer's Curse (1859), v. 847

Swop (1789), III. 344

Sword of Damocles (Darwin, P., 1889), v. 337

Sword of Peace (Starke, M., 1788), III. 308, 405 [The plays entered under M. Starke and UA are identical]

Sword of Whitefriars = Watchdog of the Castle

Swords into Anchors (Blanch, J., 1725), II. 261, 299

Swordsman's Daughter (Thomas, B. and Scott, C. W., 1895), v. 596

Sworn at Highgate (Daniel, G., 1832), IV. 289

Sworn to Secrecy (1873), v. 755

Sybil (Cumberland, R., 1818), IV. 287

— (Haxell, E. N., 1889), v. 410

Sybil Clare (1840), IV. 640

Sybilla (Simpson, J. P., 1864), v. 567

Sybil of the Camp = Norah O'Donnell

Sybil's Warning (Fitzball, E.), IV. 584

Sybil the Hunchback (Ford, F., 1873), V. 370

Sybyle (1873), V. 755

Sydney Carton (Pemberton, T. E., 1893), V. 519

Sylla (Banim, J., 1826), IV. 258

— (Brandreth, H., 1824), IV. 574

— (Derrick, S., 1753), III. 254, 381

Sylph (Leftly, C.), IV. 343

— (1771), III. 344, 347, 405

Sylphide (Brough, W., 1860), V. 279

Sylph of the Glen (1871), V. 755

Sylph of the Sunflower (1831), IV. 539

Sylphs (1774), III. 345

Sylvana (Somerset, C. A., 1828), IV. 404

Sylvan Statue (Arnold, H. T., 1872), V. 244

Sylvena! the Rose of Athlone (1832), IV. 539

Sylvester Daggerwood (Colman, G., the Younger, 1808), IV. 282

— (1810), IV. 540

— (1837), IV. 540

Sylvia (Blatchford, M., 1891), V. 265

— (Darley, G., 1827), IV. 289

— (Parry, M., 1895), V. 514

— (1866), V. 756

Sylvia's Exchange (1899), V. 756

Sylvia's Romance (Young, Sir W. L., 1899), V. 637

Sylvius (1866), V. 756

Sympathy (Dubourg, A. W., 1872), V. 351

Symptoms (1849), IV. 540

Syndicate (Votieri, A., 1897), V. 609

Syren (Bunn, A., 1844), IV. 83, 276

— (Soane, G., 1844), IV. 404

— (Webb, C., 1844), IV. 83, 417

— (1846), IV. 83, 540

Syren of Paris (Suter, W. E., 1861), V. 588

Syrens (Thompson, E., 1776), III. 311

Systematic or Imaginary Philosopher (1800), III. 345; IV. 540

System of Lavater (1797), III. 345

Tabitha's Courtship (Bright, E. and Bright, F., 1890), V. 276

Table Moving = Media

Tables Turned (Lancaster, E. R.), IV. 593

Tables Turned = Tit for Tat

Table Talk (1827), IV. 540

Taboo (Carnes, M., 1894), V. 303

Tact (Barnett, M., 1831), IV. 261

— (Bellamy, G. S. and Romer, F., 1885), V. 256

Tactic out of Place (1835), IV. 540

Taffy's Triumph (McArdle, J. F., 1874), V. 466

— (1876), V. 756

Taffy was a Welchman (Parley, P., 1854), V. 756, 809, 847

+ Taffy was a Welshman; or, The Child, the Chouse and the Cheese (Byron, H. J.: *Dicks* (in *Sensation Dramas*))

Tag in Tribulation (Dibbin, T. J., 1799), III. 257

— (Dibdin, T. J., 1814), IV. 299, 580

Tailor makes a Man (Heathcote, A. M., 1892), V. 415

Tailor makes the Man (Soden, J. E., 1876), V. 573

Tailor of Tamworth = State Secrets

Tailors (1767) = Wet Weather, III. 345, 405

— = Devil among the Tailors

Tailor's Strike (1859), V. 756

Taint in the Blood (1856), V. 756

Take back the Heart (1886), V. 756

Take care of Dowb (Morton, J. M., 1857), V. 496

Take care of your Pockets (Collins, C. J., 1858), V. 317

Take Care of your Wife! (1847), IV. 640

Taken by Force (Rodgers, W., 1897), V. 547

Taken by Storm (Collier, H., 1889), V. 317

— (Maltby, A., 1884), V. 184, 473

Taken by Surprise (Courtney, J., 1844), IV. 283

— (1831), IV. 540

Taken for Granted (Cann, R. W., 1898), V. 302

Taken from Life (Pettitt, H., 1881), V. 521

Taken from Memory (Lane, Mrs S., 1873), V. 448

Taken from the Greek = Helen

Taken in and Done for (Selby, C., 1849), IV. 399

Taken Up and Taken In = Disagreeable
Surprise
Take that Girl Away (Buckingham,
L. S., 1855), v. 286
Take Warning! (1805), IV. 540
Take your Choice (1839), IV. 540
Taking by Storm (Lewes, G. H., 1852),
v. 458, 804
Taking it easy (1882), v. 756
Taking of the Bastille (1844), IV. 540
Taking of the Pledge (1844), IV. 540
Taking Possession (1845), IV. 540
Takings and Mistakings = Married and
Single
Taking the Bull by the Horns (Newte,
H. C. W., 1889), v. 503
Taking the Census (Blanchard, E. L.,
1851), v. 262
Taking the Veil (Hazlewood, C. H.,
1870), v. 414
Taking the Waters (1886), v. 756
Talbot's Trust (Tharp, T. A., 1875), v.
595
Tale in a Tub (Reiss, F. R., 1893), v.
541
Tale of a Coat (Brough, W. and
Franck, 1858), v. 756, 780, 793, 847
Tale of a Comet (Horne, F. L., 1873), v.
426
Tale of a Copper (1871), v. 756
Tale of Africa = Gorilla Hunt in the
Forest of Gabon
Tale of a Palace = Ladies at Court
Tale of a Reaper's Fireside = Our Own
Hearth at Home
Tale of a Tar = Gale Breezeley
Tale of a Telegram (1888), v. 756
Tale of a Telephone (Clarke, H. S.,
1879), v. 312
Tale of a Tub (Gore, Mrs C. G. F.,
1837), IV. 319
— (Vaun, R., Atwood, A. and Booth,
W., 1896), v. 607
— = Marforio
Tale of a Tubb (Girnot, H. and Meritt,
P., 1876), v. 382
Tale of a Wig = Professor Wiggles
Tale of Blood = (1) Idiot Witness; (2)
Solitary of the Heath
Tale of Dartmoor (1891), v. 756
Tale of Eighteen Hundred and Five =
Days we live in

Tale of India = Fugitives
Tale of Malkin Tower = Witch-Wife
Tale of Manchester Life = Mary Barton
Tale of Mantua = Wife
Tale of Mystery (Holcroft, T., 1802),
IV. 81, 326
— (1812), IV. 540
— = Cœlina
Tale of New Zealand = Emigrant
Family
Tale of Old China (Burnand, F. C. and
Molloy, J. L., 1875), v. 290
Tale of Other Days = Second Sight
Tale of Other Times (Dibdin, T. J.,
1822) = Minstrel Maid, IV. 303, 581
Tale of Pisa = Italian Boys
Tale of Seville = Loretta
Tale of Sorrows = Mary Graham
Tale of Tell (Clarance, L., 1883), v. 310
Tale of Terror (Siddons, H., 1803), IV.
401
Tale of the Abruzzi = Francesca Doria
Tale of the Castle (1793) = Who is she
like? III. 345, 406
Tale of the Commune = No. 50
Tale of the Eleventh Century = Old
Man of the Mountain
Tale of the French Police = Dutch
Anna
Tale of the Goodwin Sands = Sole
Survivor
Tale of the Highlands = Second Sight
Tale of the Irish Rebellion = Raymond
the Rebel
Tale of the Kitchen (1862), v. 756
Tale of the Neutral Ground = Emi-
grant's Daughter
Tale of the O'Hara Family (1827), IV.
540
Tale of the Old and New Year = Right
and Wrong
Tale of the Past = Mark Drummond
Tale of the Sea = Pilot
Tale of the Seaside = Broadsea Cliffs
Tale of the Spanish War (Lee, N.,
1854), v. 452
Tale of the Thames (Conquest, G. and
Shirley, A., 1895), v. 323
— = Pilot
Tale of the Thames Valley = Dark
Secret
Tale of the Times = Counterfeit

Tale of Tipperary = Sally Cavanagh

Tale of Trials and Temptations = Flower Makers and Heart Breakers

Tale of Troy (1886), v. 756

Tale of Two Cities (Cooper, F. F., 1860: +*Dicks*), v. 786

— (Rivers, H., 1861), v. 814

— (Taylor, T., 1860), v. 593

— (1860), v. 847

Tales in Verse = My Night-Gown and Slippers

Tales of the Holly Tree Inn (1856), v. 756

Talisman (Dibdin, T. J., 1796), III. 345, 382, 405

— (McArdle, J. F., 1875), v. 466

— (Macfarren, G., 1828), IV. 350

— (Swanwick, C., 1864), v. 819

— (1784), III. 345

— (1806), IV. 540

— (1825), IV. 540

— = Lion of England

Talisman of Oromanes = Abudah

Talisman of Orosmanes = Abudah

Talking Bird (Dibdin, C. I. M., 1805), IV. 291

— (Dibdin, C. I. M., 1819), IV. 294

Talking Fish (Coyne, J. S., 1859), v. 328, 786

Talk of the Devil! (Beazley, S., 1831), IV. 540, 640

Talk of the Town (Drinkwater, A. E., 1896), v. 351

Tallow-chandler Bewitched (Rhodes, A., 1868), v. 542

Tally-Ho! (Watson, T. M., 1887), v. 616

Tallyho, the Modern Mephistopheles (Pitt, G. D., 1845), IV. 374

Talons and Claws (1886), v. 756

Tamar, Prince of Nubia (Clancy, M., 1740), II. 314 [This was acted Aungier-street, Dublin, 19/2/1740]

Tame Cat (Parker, L. N., 1898), v. 513

Tame Cats (Yates, E., 1868), v. 635

Tamerlane (Rowe, N., 1701), II. 19, 57, 58, 59, 98–99, 100, 101, 351, 417, 443; III. 59

Tamerlane the Beneficent (1692), I. 445

Tamerlane the Great (Saunders, C., 1681), I. 54, 156, 427

— (1733), II. 385

Tamer Tam'd (1757), III. 112, 345

Tamer Tam'd (1795), III. 345

— = Wedding Night

Tame Tigers (Dance, C., 1835), IV. 288

— (1838), IV. 540

Taming a Tartar (Selby, C., 1845), IV. 540, 640

+ Taming a Tiger (*French*) [A revised version of Twenty Minutes with a Tiger]

Taming of Bucephalus (1827), IV. 540

Taming of the Shrew (Kemble, J. P., 1815), IV. 335

— (Troutbeck, J., 1878), v. 822

— (1828), IV. 540

— = Sauny the Scott

Taming the Truant (Wigan, H., 1863), v. 622, 823

Tamlin (Campbell, Lady A., 1899), v. 301

Tam o' Shanter (Addison, H. R., 1834), IV. 99, 251

— (Ebsworth, J., 1820), IV. 99, 308

— (Elliott, W., 1857), v. 790

— (Lowe, W., 1873), v. 464

— (1828), IV. 99, 540

— (1858, 1868, 1876), v. 756

Tamworth in A.D. 670 (1894), v. 756

Tancred (Kingdom, J. M., 1852), v. 444

Tancred and Sigismunda (Thomson, J., 1745), II. 59, 65, 93–4, 360, 445; III. 78

Tancredi (1843), IV. 540

Tangle (Knight, G., 1894), v. 445

Tangled Path (Hume, H., 1863), v. 430

Tangled Skein (Allen, O. and Fleck, D., 1872), v. 239

Tangled Web (Chester, V., 1884), v. 309

— (1891), v. 756

Tanner of York = Lucky Discovery

Tannhäuser (1882), v. 756

Tantalus (Matthison, A. and Wyndham, Sir C., 1878), v. 481

Tantalus at Law (Holcroft, T., 1789), III. 271

Tantara-Rara, Rogues All (O'Keeffe, J., 1788), III. 293

Taradiddles (Stones-Davidson, T. W., 1896) = White Lies, v. 585, 767, 818, 849

Tar and the Ticket = Blank

Tarantula (Coralli, 1846), IV. 578

— (Dent, J.), III. 254

Tarantula (Scott, M. A., 1897), V. 558
— (Talfourd, F. and Smith, A., 1850),
v. 590
— (1831), IV. 540
Tarare (James, C., 1787), III. 119, 276,
388
Tar Ashore and Afloat = Life on the
Ocean Wave
Tarempon and Serinda (1810), IV. 540
Tares (Beringer, Mrs O., 1888), v. 259
Tar for All Weathers = Blue Anchor
Tarnation Strange (Moncrieff, W. T.,
1838), IV. 131, 361
Tar of Trinidad and the Spirit of the
Ocean = Red Buoy
Tarquin and Lucretia = Judgment of
Brutus
Tarquin's Overthrow = Tuscan Treaty
Tarrare, the Tartar Chief (Arnold,
S. J., 1825), IV. 540, 640
Tars at Anchor = Jolly Crew
Tars at Torbay (1799), III. 345
Tars in Port (1801), IV. 540
Tars of England (1852), V. 756
Tars of Old England = Reprisal
Tars on Shore (1818), IV. 540
Tars regaling = Rendezvous
Tar's Revenge = Jeffery the Seaman
Tartar Hordes = Adalna
Tartars Tartar'd = Baghran-Ho
Tartærs Tarter'd = One Foot by Land
and One Foot by Sea
Tartar's Vengeance = Black Tower
Tartar Witch and the Pedlar Boy (1832),
IV. 540
Tartar Woman (1829), IV. 540
Tar that was "pitched" into = Sinbad
the Sailor
Tartuffe (Medbourne, M., 1670), I. 188,
258-9, 420
— (Oxenford, J., 1851), v. 509
Tarugo's Wiles (St Serfe, Sir T., 1667),
I. 192, 220, 250, 271, 346, 427
Tasso (Neil, R., 1879), v. 502
Taste (Foote, S., 1752, 1761) = Virtuoso,
III. 172, 259, 260, 383
Taste a la Mode = (1) Fall of Phæton;
(2) Tittle Tattle
Taste and Feeling (1790), III. 345
Taste in the Upper Story = High Life
Taste of the Age = Fool's Opera
Tasting Order (1854), V. 756

Tatlers (Hoadley, B., 1797), III. 269
Tatterley (Shirley, A. and Gallon, T.,
1898), V. 565
Taunton Vale (Parker, L. N., 1890), v.
513
Tavern Bilkers (Weaver, J., 1702), II.
252, 385, 425, 446
— = Cheats
Tawno's Bride (Bowles, E. W. and
Phillips, G. R., 1892), v. 271
Taxes (Bacon, P., 1757), III. 235
Taylor made a Man = Humours of
Greenock Fair
Taylor of Brussels (Neil, R., 1874), v. 501
— = Duke for a Day
Taylors, to Arms! = Volunteers
Tea (Noel, M., 1887), v. 505 [The entry
IV. 366 is in error, and should be
deleted]
Tea and Turn Out (1823), IV. 541
Teacher Taught (Stirling, E., 1850), v.
584
Teaching made Easy (1823), IV. 541
Teague (1821), IV. 541
Teague's Ramble to London (1770), III.
345
Teaman's Car = Brown Fanny
Tea-Room (1811), IV. 541
Tears (Scott, C. W. and Stephenson,
B. C., 1874), v. 557
Tears and Smiles (Eyre, E. J., 1809) =
Vintagers, IV. 541, 640
Tears and Triumphs of Parnassus
(Lloyd, R., 1760), III. 282
Tears, idle Tears (Scott, C. W., 1872),
V. 557
Tears of Britain (Eyre, E. J.), IV. 310
Tears of Virtue = Such Things Were
Teasing made Easy (Jameson, R. F.,
1817), IV. 331
Tea's the Twaddle = Twisting and
Twining
Tea-totallers versus Wittelers (1840),
IV. 541
Tecalco (Spicer, M. H., 1889), v. 576
Teddy O'Connor (1876), v. 756
Teddy Roe (Stirling, E., 1841), IV. 407
Teddy's Wives (Hume, F., 1896), v. 430
Teddy the Rollicker = Foster Sisters of
Wicklow
Teddy the Tiler (Rodwell, G. H., 1830),
IV. 395

Tempter (Jones, H. A., 1893), v. 165–6, 169, 172, 440

— (Lee, N., Jr., 1859), v. 756, 802, 847

Tempter and the Betrayer = Belinda Seagrave

Tempter and the Disowned (1860), v. 756

Tempter and the Tempted = Annie Tyrell

Tempting Bait (Austin, W. J., 1875), v. 246

Tenant for Life (Phelps, W., 1858), v. 756, 810, 847

Tenant of the Tomb (1830), IV. 541

— = (1) Hour of Retribution; (2) Raymond de Percy; (3) Vampire Bride

Tenants (James, H., 1894), v. 433

Tenants in Common (1885), v. 756

Ten Daughters and No Husband (1871), v. 756

Tender Chord (Maltby, A., 1899), v. 473

— (Mortimer, J., 1873), v. 494

— (Somerset, C. A., 1853), v. 574

Tender Husband (Steele, Sir R., 1705), II. 129, 130, 131, 132, 134, 135, 136, 144, 157, 183, 192, 231, 356, 444

Tender Precautions (Serle, T. J., 1851), v. 561

Tender Sisters (Gilbert, 1805), IV. 319

Ten Minutes for Refreshments (Mansfield, R., 1882), v. 475

Ten Nights in a Bar-room (Pratt, W., 1867), v. 530

Tennis (Eastwood, L. B., 1893), v. 353

Ten of 'em (Matthison, A., 1874), v. 481, 806

+Ten Pounds (Emson, F. E., 8°, 1873)

Tenterhooks (Paull, H. M., 1889), v. 516

10.30 Down Express (Stanley, H., 1899), v. 579

10th of October = Threepence a Pot

£10,000 a Year (Peake, R. B., 1844), IV. 371

— (Somerset, C. A., 1841), IV. 612

Ten Thousand Pounds for a Pregnancy = Wanton Countess

Ten Thousand Top-sail Sheet Blocks (Bosworth, J., 1838), IV. 573

Ten Thousand Years (1841), IV. 541

Ten to One = Nettlewig Hall

+Ten Tortured Tutors (Heighway, W., French)

Ten Years' Blunder (1824), IV. 541

— = Botheration

+Ten Years Hence (Seymour, M., French)

Ten Years of a Woman's Life (1834), IV. 541

Teraminta (Carey, H., 1732), II. 30, 31, 235–6, 302

Teresa (Bancroft, G. P., 1897), v. 248

Teresa Tomkins (Moncrieff, W. T., 1821), IV. 359

Termagant (Parker, L. N. and Carson, S. M., 1899), v. 514

Termagant Mistress = Prussian Dragoon

Termagant tam'd = Gingerbread Nut

Termagant Wife (1793), III. 345

Term Day (Houston, T., 1803), IV. 329

Terpsichore (McCarthy, J. H., 1894), v. 467

— (1855), v. 756

Terpsichore's Return (Degville, 1805), IV. 579

Terrible Fright (Law, A., 1884), v. 450

Terrible Hymen (À Beckett, G. A., 1866), v. 233

Terrible Peak (Dibdin, C. I. M., 1817), IV. 294

Terrible Revenge = Cruel Father

Terrible Secret (Coyne, J. S., 1861), v. 328

— (Waldron, W. R., 1889), v. 611

Terrible Tinker (Williams, T. J., 1869), v. 626

Terrible Trilby (Pleon, H., 1895), v. 528

Terrible Twins = Oliver Grumble

Terrible Unknown (1836), IV. 541

Terrific Brothers = Zambo and Cadjoc

Terrific Horn = Mountain Robbers

Terrific Register (1824), IV. 541

Territor of St Faust = Desrues the Deceiver

Terror of France = Gabrielle the Girondist

Terror of London (James, W. and Whyte, H., 1879), v. 434

— = Spring-heeled Jack

Terror of Normandy = Robert the Devil

Terror of Paris (Hill-Mitchelson, E. and Longden, C. H., 1894), v. 422

Terrors of a Gay City (Lyttleton, G., 1897), v. 466

Terrors of Conscience (1816), IV. 541

Terry (Vane, S., 1891), v. 606

Tess of the D'Urbervilles (Stoddard, L., 1897), v. 585

— (1899), v. 756

Test (Aveling, E. B. and Marston, P. B. 1885), v. 246

Tested, Tried and True (1872), v. 756

Test of Affection = What Would She Not?

Test of Good Fellowship = Liberty-Hall

Test of Guilt (Strutt, J., 1808), IV. 409

— = Alfred and Matilda

Test of Love (Robinson, 1787), III. 302, 394

Test of Truth (Suter, W. E., 1860), v. 588 [*see also* It's a Long Lane]

Test of Union and Loyalty (Sullivan, W. F., 1797), III. 310

Test of Virtue = Dorval

Testy Lord (Kirkman, F., 1662), I. 418

Texan (Power, T., 1894), v. 530

Texan's Revenge (1896), v. 756

Thad (Meritt, P., 1872), v. 485

Thalaba the Destroyer (Fitzball, E., 1823), IV. 99, 541, 584, 640

— (Fitzball, E., 1836), IV. 25, 99, 315

Thalia (1878), v. 756

Thalia's Sketch Book (1836), IV. 541

Thalia's Tears (Cherry, A., 1806), IV. 280

Thamas Kouli Kan, the Persian Hero (1741), II. 385

Thames (Dodson, R., 1879), v. 347

Thames Tunnel (1827), IV. 541

Thane and the Throne = Wierd Sisters

Thanks to Jack (Hardy, E., 1891), v. 403

That Awful Boy (Miller, W. F., 1891), v. 489

That Awful Legacy (Warlow, P., 1898), v. 614

That Awful Yankee = Lynch Law

That Beastly Child (Melford, M., 1899), v. 484

That Beautiful Biceps (Clarke, H. S., 1876), v. 312

That Beautiful Wretch (1881), v. 756

That Blessed Baby (Moore, F., 1856), v. 492

That Boy Pete (1881), v. 757

That Charming Mrs Spencer (Votieri, A., 1897), v. 609

That Couple from Cuba (Johnson, H. T., 1898), v. 437

That Dancing Dog (1855), v. 757

That Doctor Cupid (Buchanan, R., 1889), v. 285

That Dreadful Boy (À Beckett, G. A., 1882), v. 234, 777

That Dreadful Doctor (Young, Sir C. L., 1881), v. 636

That Fatal Hour (Curry, C. F., 1895), v. 331

That Fatal Menu (Grain, R. C., 1894), v. 388

That Girl (Hamilton, H. and Beringer, Mrs O., 1890), v. 402

That Horrid Biggins (Allen, F., 1860), v. 757, 777, 848

That House in High Street (Stuart, M., 1856), v. 757, 818, 848

That Idiot Carlo (Hayman, P., 1891), v. 411

That Lass o' Lowrie's = (1) Jean; (2) Liz

That Mysterious Novel (1897), v. 757

That Naughty Can-Can (Sorrell, W. J., 1873), v. 574

That Odious Captain Cutter (Simpson, J. P., 1851), v. 567

That Rascal Jack (Greenwood, T., 1843), IV. 321, 541, 640

— (1861), v. 757, 848

That Rascal Pat (Grover, J. H.), v. 396

That Rascal Rudolph (Summers, K., 1897), v. 587

That Ring (Rolfe, V. C., 1893), v. 549

That's How He Told the Tale = Captain J. D. Pitman

That's Poz = Not more than I want

That's the Manager (1815), IV. 541

That's why she loved him (Granville, H. S., 1876), v. 388

That Telegram (Sapte, Walter, Jr., 1888), v. 556

That Terrible Girl (Stephens, J., 1895), v. 581

That Terrible Turk and his Loving Legacy (Sidney, F. W., 1898), v. 565

That Woman in Pink (Harraden, H., 1891), v. 404

Theatre (1720), II. 385
Theatres (1733), II. 385
Theatrical Candidates (Garrick, D., 1775), III. 155, 211, 264
Theatrical Duchess (1896), v. 757
— = Chorus Girl
Theatrical Manager (1751), III. 345
Theatrical Museum (1776), III. 405
Theatrical Scenes for Children (Angus, J. K., 1880), v. 241
Theatric Count (1809), IV. 541
Theban Brothers = Antigone
Theban Sister = Antigone
Theban Twins = Ino
Theckla (Bliss, H., 1866), v. 265
Theft for a Life (Bannister, T. B., 1877), v. 248
"The Greatest of These—" (Grundy, S., 1895), v. 397
Thelyphthora (Knight, T., 1783), III. 279
— (Pilon, F., 1781), III. 298
Themis (Stephens, H. P., 1880), v. 580
Themistocles (Hoole, J., 1800), III. 388
Themistocles and Aristides = Lovers of their Country
Themistocles, the Lover of his Country (Madden, S., 1729), II. 58, 343
Then and Now! (Grain, R. C., 1891), v. 388
Then Flowers grew fairer (Vane, S., 1892), v. 606
Theo (1894), v. 757
Theodora (Buchanan, R., 1889), v. 285
— (Burrell, Lady S. R., 1800), III. 241; IV. 277
— (Morell, T., 1750), III. 362, 392
— (1814), IV. 635
Theodora, Actress and Empress (Phillips, W., 1866), v. 523
Theodore (Colls, J. H.), III. 245
Theodore of Ritzberg (1857), v. 757
Theodore the Brigand (Buckstone, J. B., 1828), IV. 273
Theodorick King of Denmark (1752), III. 345
Theodosius (Lee, N., 1680), I. 96, 146–7, 419; III. 59
Theory and Practice (Benham, A., 1893), v. 257
There and Back (Arliss, G., 1895), v. 243

There and Back Again = Belford and Minton
There are Secrets in all Families (1862), v. 757
Thereby hangs a Tale = Apollo turn'd Stroller
There he goes (Upton, 1805), IV. 415
There never was such Times = What are you at? What are you after?
Theresa (Thomas, W. L., 1843), IV. 614
Theresa's Vow = Maid of Croissey
Theresa Vorschner (Pitt, G. D., 1845), IV. 374
Thérèse (Jeffers, C., 1850), v. 435
— (Kerr, J.), IV. 110–11, 338
— (1821), IV. 541
Thérèse Raquin (Mattos, A. T. de, 1891), v. 481
Therese, the Orphan of Geneva (Payne, J. H., 1821), IV. 368, 603
There she goes (Sapte, W., Jr., 1896), v. 556
There's Many a Slip 'twixt the Cup and the Lip (Hall, R. W., 1877), v. 400
There's nothing like a Friend at Court when a Man is in Search of Relations (Prest, T. P., 1854), v. 757, 811, 848
There's Spirit in Punch = Odd Volume
Thermopylae (Roberdeau, J. P., 1805), IV. 394
— (1814), IV. 635
Theseus and Ariadne (Planché, J. R., 1848), IV. 383
— (1836), IV. 541
Thespian from Tanderagee = Arrived at Crow-Street
Thespian Panorama (1795), III. 345
Thespis (Gilbert, W. S., 1871), v. 379
Thespis in Distress = Hobson's Choice
Thetis and Peleus (Hale, W. P. and Talfourd, F., 1851), v. 398
Theusia (1892), v. 757
They all love Jack (Clarke, C. A., 1898), v. 312
They are all come Home = State Farce
They're all alike (1898), v. 757
They're both to blame (1859), v. 757
— = Wealthy Widow
They Took the Will for the Deed = She Wants a Guardian

They've bit the old one (Cross, J. C., 1798), III. 345, 380, 405

They were Friends (1889), v. 757

They were married (Crauford, J. R. and Hawley, F., 1892), v. 328

They would if they could (1803), IV. 542

Thief Maker (Towers, E., 1878), v. 601

Thief's Shoe = Ankle Jack

Thief-taker of Paris = Vidcoq

Thief, the Artist, the Doctor and the Banker = Realities of Life

Thierna-na-Oge (Planché, J. R., 1829), IV. 378

Thieves' House (Atkyns, S., 1844), IV. 19, 257

Thieves of Dijon = Beggar and the Soldier

Thieves of Paris (Stirling, E., 1853), v. 584

— = Bohemians

Thieves! Thieves! (1857), v. 757

Thimble Rig (Buckstone, J. B., 1844), IV. 275

Thimble's Flight from his Shopboard (1789), III. 345

Things that happen every Hour = How Time flies

Third Class and First Class (Seaman, W., 1859), v. 757, 815, 848

Third Day = Hussars of Hesse

Third Time (Dickinson, C. H., 1896), v. 344

Third Time the Best = Perseverance

Thirst of Gold (Webster, B. N., 1853), v. 618

1395 (1855), v. 848

Thirteenth Chime (1859), v. 757

1313 (Desprez, F., 1879), v. 343

Thirteen to the Dozen (Kenney, J., 1826), IV. 337

Thirteen Years' Labour Lost (Bennett, J. M., 1821), IV. 265 [The correct title is as here, not Thirteen Years of Labour Lost]

— (1855), v. 757

Thirty Nine Thieves (1863), v. 757

— (1877), v. 757

— = Ali Baba

30 Strand = P.L.

Thirty Thousand (Dibdin, C. I. M., 1808), IV. 292

— (Dibdin, T. J., 1804), IV. 52, 298

Thirty Thousand Pounds (Harleigh, L. W., 1875), v. 404

Thirty Three Next Birthday (Morton, J. M., 1858), v. 496

Thirty Years (1827), IV. 542

Thirty Years of a Gambler's Life (1827), IV. 542

— (1831), IV. 542

— = Hut of the Red Mountains

Thirty Years of a Rattler's Life = Elbow Shakers

Thirty Years of a Woman's Life = Isabelle

This and the other Hand (1863), v. 757

Thisbe and Pyramus (1889), v. 757

This Horse will be sold to pay the Expenses, if not claimed within Fourteen Days (1854), v. 757

This House to be Sold (Coyne, J. S., 1847) = Old House at Home, IV. 285

This House to let (Oxenford, E., 1884) = In Ladbroke Square, v. 509, 696, 809, 836

— (Towers, E., 1869), v. 601

This is the House that Jack built (Akhurst, W. M., 1871), v. 236

This Little Back Parlour (Mowbray, T., 1857), v. 498

This Plot of Ground to let, a Capital Site for a Theatre (1874), v. 757

This Side of the Water = Champion's Belt

This Side Up (Rae, L., 1874), v. 757, 811, 848

Thistle and the Rampant Lion (1872), v. 757

Thistle and the Rose = Caledonia

This Woman and That (Le Clercq, P., 1890), v. 452

This World of Ours (Hicks, Sir S., 1891), v. 420

Thomas à Becket (Darley, G., 1840), IV. 289

— (Jerrold, D. W., 1829), IV. 180, 332

Thomas and Sally (Bickerstaffe, I., 1760), III. 197-8, 237

Thomas and Susan (1787), III. 345

Thomaso (Killigrew, T., 1663), I. 416

Thomas the Rhymer (Thomas, E. L., 1894), v. 596

Thompkins in North-Street (Rennell, C. R. 1865), v. 813

Thompson and Co. (1831), IV. 542

Thompson's Visit (Douglass, J. T., 1872), V. 348

Thomyris, Queen of Scythia (Motteux, P. A., 1707), II. 58, 228–9, 399

Thorgrim (Bennett, J., 1890), V. 258

Thorneycroft Cousins (Thorneycroft, Lieut-Col., 1888), V. 599

Thorney, Laben and Dobin (Carey, G. S., 1770), III. 242

Thorough Base (Pemberton, T. E., 1884), V. 519

Thorough-bred (Lumley, R. R., 1895), V. 465

Those Dear Blacks! (Brough, W., 1852), V. 278

Those Horrid Garotters (1873), V. 757

Those Landladies (Cassilis, I. L.), V. 306

Those Mysterious Shots (Deane, C., 1894), V. 340

Those...put asunder (Trevelyan, C., 1897), V. 603

Those Terrible Twins (1899), V. 757

Those Volunteers (Ellis, B., 1875), V. 357

Tho' Strange 'Tis True (1732), II. 385

Though out of Sight, ne'er out of Mind = Constant Couple

£1000 Reward = (1) Condemned; (2) Legacy

Thou shalt not kill (Scudamore, F. A., 1899), V. 559

— = Two Christmas Eves

Thread of Silk (Matthison, A., 1881), V. 481

Threatening Eye (Knight, E. F. and Jourdain, J., 1885), V. 445

Threat for Threat = Shadow of Wrong

Three Adventures = Day well Spent

Three Ambassadors = Czar of Muscovy

Three and One (1839), IV. 542

Three and the Ace (Dibdin, C. I. M., 1810), IV. 292

Three and the Deuce (Hoare, P., 1795), III. 270

— (Lawler, D., 1810), IV. 542, 641

— (1862), V. 757

Three Bachelors (1862), V. 848

Three Banished Men of Milan = Gaspardo the Gondolier

Three Beauties of Dresden (1831), IV. 542

Three Beggars (Dunn, S., 1883), V. 352

Three Black Seals (Stirling, E., 1864), V. 584

Three Blind Eyes (Amherst, J. H.), IV. 254

Three Blind Mice (Ellis, B., 1883), V. 357

— (French, H. P., 1896), V. 373

Three Brothers = Black King

Three Brothers of Bagdad = Golden Lily

Three Brothers of Brevannes (Mead, T., 1863), V. 757, 806, 848

Three Brothers of Mystery (Suter, W. E., 1861), V. 757, 819, 848

Three Brothers of Normandy (1859), V. 757

Three Brothers of Paris (Rayner, A., 1858), V. 812

Three Brothers of the Old Chateau (Rayner, E., 1860), V. 757, 812, 848

Three Caskets (1827), IV. 542

— = Courtship

Three Charcoal Burners = (1) Fire Goblin; (2) Red Daemon of the Harz Forest

Three Cheers for Charity (1853), V. 757

Three Clerks (Oxberry, W. H.), IV. 602

Three Cloaks = Sparks in the Dark

Three Conjurers (1767), III. 345

Three Conscripts = Weaver of Lyons

Three Conspirators (Thompson, A., 1874), V. 597

Three Criminals = Two Men

Three Cripples and the Queen of Billingsgate (Amherst, J. H., 1822), IV. 253, 542, 568, 641

Three Crumpies (Dibdin, T. J., 1825), IV. 304

Three Crumps (1818), IV. 542

Three Cuckoos (Morton, J. M., 1850), V. 107, 495

Three Days at a Well-known Hotel = Incog.

Three Days at Hatchett's = (1) Exeter Mail; (2) Incog.

Three Days at Long's = Arrivals

Three Days' Trial = Magic Car

Three Deep (Lunn, J., 1826), IV. 348

Three Degrees of Crime = Progress of a Rake

Three Doctors (Gammon, R. T., 1896), V. 375

Three Doctors (Peacock, T. L.), IV. 369
Three Dons (1828), IV. 542
Three Dukes of Dunstable = Fool's Preferment
Three Dummies (1859), V. 757
Three Entertainments (Thurmond, J., 1727), II. 360
Three Fairy Gifts (Adams, F. D., 1896), V. 235
Three Fast Men (1860), V. 757
Three Fathers and One Son (1827), IV. 542
Three-Fingered Jack (1860), V. 757
— = (1) Karfa the Slave; (2) Obi
Three Fishermen (1822), IV. 542
Three Fives (1812), IV. 542
Three Flats (1880), V. 757
Three Fra Diavolos (Stocqueler, J. H., 1844), IV. 542
Three Furies (Roberts, G., 1865), V. 544
Three Generations (1830), IV. 542
— = Rogues All!
Three Glass Distaffs = Discreet Princess
Three Golden Apples = Atalanta
Three Golden Lamps (1825), IV. 542
Three Graces (À Beckett, G. A., 1843), IV. 250
— (Collins, H. B., 1898), V. 318
— (1859), V. 848
— (1891), V. 757
— = Hobbs, Dodds and Stubbs
Three Great Worthies (Anderson, J. R., 1866), V. 241
Three Hats (Dove, O. and Maltby, A. 1883), V. 349
— (Woodrow, H. C., 1896), V. 631
Three Hours after Marriage (Gay, J., 1717), II. 13, 25, 29, 41–2, 144, 213–14, 331, 423
Three Hunchbacks (De Frece, M., 1872), V. 341
— (Fitzball, E., 1826), IV. 313, 584
Three Hundred a Year (1863), V. 758
Three Jacks (1883), V. 759
Three Johns (1819), IV. 542
Three Keys (Hiller, H. C., 1888), V. 421
Three Legs, King of Man (1853), V. 848
Three Lives (Hazlewood, C. H., 1860), V. 758, 796, 848
— = (1) Fair Lilias; (2) Ralph Gaston
Three Magic Wands (Amherst, J. H.), IV. 254

Three Merry Boyes (Kirkman, F., 1662), I. 417
Three Miles from Paris (Dibdin, C. I. M., 1818), IV. 294
Three Millions of Money (Lyster, F. and Mackay, J., 1876), V. 466
Three Moorish Princesses = Alhambra
Three Musket Dears, and a Little One In (Paulton, J. and Paulton, H., 1871), V. 517
Three Musketeers (Brown, W. H., 1898), V. 210, 282
— (Carl, F., 1899), V. 303
— (Daly, B. and East, J. M., 1898), V. 210, 334
— (Goldberg, M., 1892), V. 383
— (Hamilton, H., 1898), V. 210, 402
— (Rice, C., 1850), V. 210, 542, 813
— (Saintsbury, H. A., 1898), V. 210, 554
— (Whitney, H., 1899), V. 621
Three Musqueteers (1899), V. 758
Three Mutineers (1828), IV. 542
Three Naughty Boys = Brown, Jones and Robinson
Three O'Clock = Camelford
Three of a Kind (1894), V. 758
Three of Them (Dibdin, T. J., 1821), IV. 303
Three Old Women Weatherwise = Old Women Weatherwise
Three Paddies (Dibdin, T. J., 1817), IV. 300
Three Pairs of Lovers (1852), V. 758
Threepence a Pot (1830), IV. 542
Threepenny Bit (Morton, J. M. and Young, A. W., 1870), V. 496
Threepenny Bits (Zangwill, I., 1895), V. 637
Three Per Cents (Reynolds, F., 1803), IV. 391
Three Perils (Marchant, F., 1870), V. 476
Three Perils of Man (Blanchard, E. L., 1852), V. 262
Three Phases of a Life = Marlborough
Three Princes (Kingdom, J. M., 1850), V. 444
Three Red Men (Archer, T., 1848), IV. 255
— (1848), IV. 542
Three Secrets (Lemon, M., 1840), IV. 344

Three Secrets (1849), IV. 345, 595
Three Shots from a Carbine (Suter, W. E., 1865), v. 758, 819
Three Singles (1862), v. 758
Three Smugglers of Kent (Barnett, C. Z., 1843), IV. 260
Three Spectres (1831), IV. 542
Three Spectres of the Castle of St Valori = Man and the Marquis
Three Strangers (Lee, H., 1825), IV. 342
Three Suitors (1805), IV. 542
Three Sultanas (1826), IV. 542
Three Talismans (Dibdin, T. J., 1818), IV. 301
Three Temptations = (1) Better Self; (2) Demon of Darkness
Three Tenants (À Beckett, G. A. and Reed, G., 1874), v. 234
Three Thieves and the Dreamer = Seven Clerks
Three Thieves of Lambetti (1854), v. 758
Three Times Three (Dibdin, T. J., 1816), IV. 300
Three to One (1831), IV. 542
— (1850), v. 848
— (1853), v. 758
— (1893), v. 758
— = (1) I'm Puzzled; (2) What would the Man be at?
Three Transformed Princes = Enchanted Wood
Three Travellers of the Tyrol = Accusing Spirit
Three Trials = (1) Bianca; (2) Woman's Worth
Three Turkish Razor Grinders (1854), v. 758
Three Vampires (1823), IV. 542
Three Warnings (Rayner, A., 1872), v. 535
— (Warner, A., 1873), v. 614
Three Wayfarers (Hardy, T., 1893), v. 404
Three Ways of Living = Lesson of Life
Three Weavers (Pitt, G. D., 1851), v. 526
Three Weeks After Marriage (Murphy, A., 1776), III. 15, 181–2, 290
— (1812), IV. 542
Three Weeks at a Well-known Hotel = Incog.

Three Wishes (McLaren, A., 1823), IV. 352
— (1819), IV. 542
— = (1) Court of Oberon; (2) Don't you wish you may get it?
Three Wives of Madrid (Peake, R. B., 1844), IV. 33, 371
Three Women (1866), v. 758
Three Yards of Broadcloth (1826), IV. 542
Three Years in a Man Trap (Morton, C. H., 1879), v. 494
— (Stephens, W., 1874), v. 581
Three Years' System (Maynard, W., 1887), v. 483
Thrice Married (Paul, H. M., 1854), v. 515
— = Escaped
Thrillby (Muskerry, W., 1896), v. 501
Throne and the Tomb = Ambition
Throne, the Tomb and the Cottage = Rudolpho the Hungarian
Through a Glass, darkly (Seymour, E. M., 1896), v. 561
Through Fire and Snow (Goldberg, M., 1886), v. 383
Through Fire and Water (Gordon, W., 1865), v. 385
Through Life = Deceived
Through my Heart First (Campbell, J. M., 1884), v. 301
Through Shot and Shell (1896), v. 758
Through the Fire (Hastings, G., 1879), v. 409
— (Lestocq, W. and Stephens, Y. 1888), v. 457
Through the Furnace (Howell-Poole, W., 1885), v. 429
Through the Looking Glass (Stephens, H. P., 1882), v. 580
Through the World (Wray, C., 1874), v. 633
Thrown on the World = Cruel Destiny
Thrown Together (Greet, D. V.), v. 393
Throw of the Dice (Kennedy, H. A., 1890), v. 443
Throw Physic to the Dogs (Lee, H. 1798), III. 280, 390
Throwster's Opera (1731), II. 385
Thugs of Paris (Ellis, B., 1887), v. 357
Thumbscrew (Byron, H. J., 1874), v. 298

Thumping Legacy (Morton, J. M., 1843), IV. 362

Thunderbolt (Belac, D. and Hamilton, W., 1894), V. 255
— (1835), IV. 542

Thus runs the World away = Policy

Thyestes (Crowne, J., 1681), I. 24, 56, 124, 150, 399
— (Wright, J., 1674), I. 438

Thyra (Pertence, E., 1896), V. 520

Thyrsis (Oldmixon, J., 1697), I. 263, 421

Thyrza Fleming (Leighton, D., 1895), V. 454

Tibby and Tabby (1829), IV. 542

Tiberius in Capreae (Cumberland, R., 1813), IV. 287

Tib, Pat, Joe, the Three Butcher Boys all of a Row (1858), V. 758

Tic doloureuse (Craven, H. T., 1847), IV. 285

Ticket-of (French)-Leave Man = Cartouche and Co. Ltd.

Ticket of Leave (Phillips, W., 1862), v. 523
— (1859), V. 758

Ticket-of-Leave Man (Taylor, T., 1863), V. 101-2, 150, 163, 593
— = Repentant

Ticket-of-Leave Man's Wife = Six Years After

Ticket-of-leave's Career = Detective

Ticket Porter (1825), IV. 542

Tickets (1882), V. 758

Tickle and Scrubbs (Penley, W. S., 1893), V. 519

Ticklish Times (Morton, J. M., 1858), v. 496

Tidal Hour (Watney, R., 1890), V. 615

Tiddlediwink (De Freece, M., 1874), V. 341

Tide and Time (Leslie, H. T., 1867), v. 457

Tide of Time (Bernard, W. B., 1858), V. 259

Tiffins (1858), V. 758

Tiger (Burnand, F. C., 1890), V. 291

Tiger at Large (1837), IV. 543

Tiger Crew = Pirate Minister

Tiger Horde (1814), IV. 543

Tiger Hunt = Zuluca and the Rival Warriors

Tiger Hunters of the Prairies = Pirates of the Savannah

Tiger Lilies = Husband and Wife

Tiger Lily (Wallace, M., 1892), V. 612

Tiger of Mexico (Johnstone, J. B., 1881), V. 438

Tiger of the North (1833), IV. 543

Tiger of the Sea = Rattlin the Reefer

Tiger's Claw (1899), V. 758

Tiger's Grip (Goldberg, M. and Comer, G., 1898), V. 383

Tiger Slayer of the Savannah (1861), v. 758

Tigers of Paris (Frampton, 1841), IV. 585

Tigers of the Sea = Death's Head Dick, the Skeleton Pirate

Tiger Tom (1873), V. 758

Tiger Tribe = Demon of the Ganges

Tight Rein (1879), V. 758

Tigress (Morris, R., 1889), V. 493

Tilbury Fort (Atkyns, S., 1844), IV. 257
— (Stirling, E., 1829), IV. 406
— (1851), V. 758

Till Death do us part (Comer, G., 1885), V. 319

Till the Half Hour (Heathcote, A. M., 1891), V. 415

Till we meet again (Saker, M. E., 1898), V. 554

Timanthes (Hoole, J., 1770), III. 70, 83, 272, 387

Time and the Hour (Simpson, J. P. and Merivale, H. C., 1868), V. 568, 787, 816

Time and Tide = Tide and Time

Time, Hunger and the Law (Irving, L. B., 1894), V. 432

Time is Money (Bell, Mrs H. and Cecil, A., 1890), V. 255

Timely Discovery = Generous Conqueror

Timely Moment (Andrews, E., 1888), V. 241

Timely Warning (1856), V. 758

Time o' Day = Mr Weller's Watch

Timepiece (1836), IV. 543

Times (Besemeres, J., 1853), V. 260
— (Griffith, Mrs E., 1779), III. 266, 386
— (Pinero, Sir A. W., 1891), V. 177-8, 525
— (1797), III. 345

Times (1831), IV. 543

Time's a Tell-Tale (Siddons, H., 1807) = Mark the End On't, IV. 142, 401, 500, 611, 632

Times of Oliver Cromwell = Esdale Hall

Time's Revenge (Edwardes-Sprange, W., 1890), V. 354

— (Henry, S. C., 1898), V. 418

— (1875), V. 758

Time's Story = Heir of Ashmore

Time's Triumph (Byron, H. J., 1872), V. 298

— (1889), V. 758

Times we live in = Gin and Water

Time Tells Tales = Devil's Gap

Time the Avenger (Craven, T., 1892), V. 329

— (1877), V. 758

Time tries all (Courtney, J., 1848), IV. 284

Time Turned Occulist = Albion Restored

Time will tell (Gardner, H., 1882), V. 376

— = Father's Sin

Time Works Wonders (Jerrold, D. W., 1845), IV. 185–6, 333

Timoleon (Jameson, R. W., 1852), V. 799

— (Martyn, B., 1730), II. 31, 63, 68, 81, 233, 343

— (Southby, 1697), I. 171, 432

Timon in Love (Kelly, J., 1733), II. 145, 249, 340, 440

Timon of Athens (Cumberland, R., 1771), III. 57, 78, 251

— (Hull, T., 1786), III. 57, 86, 274

— (Lambe, G., 1816), IV. 341

— (Love, J., 1768), III. 57, 283

— (Shadwell, T., 1678), I. 85, 173, 337, 431

Timothy to the Rescue (Byron, H. J., 1864), V. 296

Timour Khan (1826), IV. 543

Timour the Cream of all the Tartars (À Beckett, G. A., 1845), IV. 250, 567

Timour the Tartar (Chamberlaine, E., 1869), V. 307

— (Lewis, M. G., 1811), IV. 346

— (Oxenford, J. and Brooks, C. W. S., 1860), V. 510

— (1829), IV. 543

Timson's Little Holiday (+ Nicholls, H., 1884: *French*), V. 758

Tin Box (Fenn, G. M., 1892), V. 365

Tinder Box (1823), IV. 543

Tinker (1791), III. 345

Tinker and his Son = Mountain Hut

Tinker's Holiday (1886), V. 758

Tinker's Son = Mountain Hut

Tinsel Queen (Morton, W. E., 1883), V. 497

Tinted Venus (Bessle, E., 1889), V. 260

Tipperary Legacy (Coyne, J. S., 1847), V. 275

Tippitywitchet (1845), IV. 543

Tipplers (1730), II. 452

Tippoo Sahib (Milner, H. M., 1823), IV. 599

— (1791), III. 345

— (1792), III. 345

Tipster (Fitzhamon, L., 1898), V. 369

— = Round the Links

Tipsy Gipsy and the Pipsy Wipsy = Merry Zingara

'Tis All a Farce (Allingham, J. T., 1800), III. 232; IV. 251

'Tis all a Mistake = See if you like it

'Tis an Ill Wind that Blows nobody Good (Markwell, W. R.), V. 477

— (1788), III. 345

'Tis a strange World (Holcroft, T., 1795) = Deserted Daughter, III. 345, 387, 405

'Tis a Wise Child knowns his own Father (Waldron, F. G., 1795), III. 314

'Tis a Wise Child that knows its own Father = Match-making

'Tis better than it was (Digby, G., 1662–5), I. 192, 403

'Tis She (Wilks, T. E., 1838), IV. 420

'Tis so reported = Law for Ladies

'Tis Well if it Take = Amorous Old-woman

'Tis Well if it Takes (Taverner, W., 1719), II. 133, 358

'Tis Well it's no Worse (Bickerstaffe, I., 1770), III. 123, 178, 237

— = Haunted Chamber

'Tis well they are married (1804), IV. 543

Tita in Tibet (Desprez, F., 1879), V. 343

Tit Bit for a nice Palate = Top of the Tree

Tomb, the Throne and the Scaffold = Catherine Howard

Tom Cobb (Gilbert, W. S., 1875), v. 140, 380

Tom Cringle (Fitzball, E., 1834), IV. 314

Tom, Dick and Harry (Pacheco, Mrs R., 1873), v. 511

To meet Mr Stripling (1895), v. 758

Tom Essence (Rawlins, 1676), I. 23, 215–16, 426

Tom, Jerry and Logic (1822), IV. 543

Tom, Jerry and Logic in 1845 = Our Future Fate

Tom, Jerry and Logick Hop at Brighton (1834), IV. 543

Tom Jones (Dibdin, T. J., 1818), IV. 301

— (Jones, F., 1826), IV. 591

— (Reed, J., 1768), III. 119, 300

— (1843), IV. 543

— (1848), IV. 543

Tomkins the Troubadour (1868), v. 758

Tom Moor of Fleet Street (1841), IV. 543

Tommy (Willard, Mrs E. S., 1891), v. 623

Tommy and Harry (Merion, C., 1872), v. 485

Tommy and Jerry t'other Side the Water = Vive la Bagatelle

Tommy at College (Grain, R. C., 1890), v. 387

Tommy Atkins (Shirley, A. and Landeck, B., 1895), v. 564

— (1895), v. 758

Tommy Dodd (Shillingford, O., 1897), v. 563

Tommy's Tutors (Wyke, E. B., 1881), v. 633

Tom Noddy's Secret (Bayly, T. H., 1838), IV. 263

Tom of Bedlam = Mad Tom of Bedlam

Tom of Chelsea Ferry = Lucky Waterman

Tom Pinch (Dilley, J. J. and Clifton, L., 1880), v. 345

Tom Sheppard (1866), v. 758

Tom Smart (Craven, H. T., 1847), IV. 543 [The date is given wrongly at IV. 543 as 1827: printed in Duncombe's series as Tom Smart, The Adventurer! Apparently it was given on a benefit night at the Str. 1/5/1848]

Tom's Mother-in-Law (Jones, C. F., 1894), v. 439

Tom's Revenge (Bandmann, D. E., 1874), v. 248

Tom's Wife (Parker, N., 1896), v. 514

— (1862), v. 758

Tom Thrasher (Harris, A. G., 1868), v. 405

Tom Thumb (Faucit, H. S., 1862), v. 791

— (Fielding, H., 1730), II. 138, 263–5, 324

— (O'Hara, K., 1780), III. 291

Tom Thumb the Great (Blanchard, E. L., 1871), v. 264

— = Opera of Operas

Tom Tiddler (Hall, F., 1878), v. 399

Tom Tiddler's Ground (James, C. S., 1846), IV. 330

Tom Titler's Ground (Pitt, G. D., 1844), IV. 373

Tom Tom the Piper's Son (Akhurst, W. M., 1875), v. 237

— (Suter, W. E., 1860), v. 758, 819, 848

— (1876, 1878, 1885, 1887), v. 758

Tom Trim (Courtney, J., 1843), IV. 543, 641

Tom Truant (Stewart, D., 1874), v. 583

Tom Tug (1816), IV. 543

Ton (Wallace, Lady E., 1788), III. 314

Ton and Antiquity (?Streatfield, T., 1795), III. 405

Tong-li-Too (1899), v. 758

Tongue of Slander (Warren, T. G. and Douglass, J. T., 1887), v. 615

Tongue-tied Tragedian = Lindamira

Tonight at 8 (McCloskey, J. and Toplis, G. A., 1887), v. 468

Ton of Gold (1866), v. 759

Tony Lumpkin in Town (O'Keeffe, J., 1774), III. 292 [This was first acted at Smock Alley, Dublin, 13/4/1774]

Tony Lumpkin's Ramble to London (1792), III. 346, 405

Too agreeable by Half = Fascinating Individual

Too Agreeable to be True (Reeve, W., 1870), v. 540

To Oblige Benson (Taylor, T., 1854), v. 105, 592

Too Busy by Half (1832), IV. 543

— = Sudden Arrivals

Too Careful by Half (Ebsworth, J., 1838), IV. 543

Too Civil by Half (Dent, J., 1782), III. 254

Too Clever (1876), V. 759

Too Clever by Half (1868), V. 759

— = Much too clever

Too Curious by Half (Planché, J. R., 1823) = Marplot in Spain, IV. 377, 500, 605, 632

Toodles (?Raymond, R. J., 1832), IV. 543

— (1862), V. 759

Too Fatiguing (1885), V. 759

Too Friendly by Half (1807) = Plaguy Good-natured Friend, IV. 543, 641

Too Handsome for Anything = Cousin Adonis

Too Happy by Half (Field, J., 1895), V. 365

— (Simpson, J. P.), V. 816

Too Kind (Fenibond, P., 1876), V. 364

Too Late (Quayle, C., 1876), V. 532

— (Thompson, G. F., 1881), V. 597

— (1868), V. 759

— = Shall we remember?

Too Late for Dinner (Jones, R., 1820), IV. 334, 591

— (1835), IV. 543

— (1844), IV. 543

Too late for the Train (Morton, J. M., 1852), V. 495

Too late to save (Palmer, T. A., 1861), V. 511

Too Learned by Half (Sharpe, J., 1793), III. 305

Toole at Sea (Reece, R., 1875), V. 538

Toole up-to-date = Ibsen's Ghost

Toolooloo and Woolooloo (1858), V. 759

Too Lovely Black-Eyed Susan (Lennard, H., 1888), V. 455

Too Loving by Half (Robson, H., 1784), III. 302

Too Many by One (Burnand, F. C. and Cowan, F., 1865), V. 288

Too many Cooks (Kenney, J., 1805), IV. 336

— (Reed, G., 1863), V. 759, 813, 848

Too many Cooks spoil the Broth (1846), IV. 543

Too much for Friendship = Joke's a Joke

Too much for Good Nature (Falconer, E., 1858), V. 360

Too much Johnson (Gillette, W., 1898), V. 759, 793, 848

Too much married (Melford, M., 1886), V. 484

Too much of a good thing (Harris, A. G., 1855), V. 404

Too much the Way of the World (Herbert, J., 1817), IV. 325

Too too far from the Madding Crowd = Squire's Maria

Too True (Craven, H. T., 1876), V. 329

Tootsie (Townley, A. H., 1888), V. 602

Tootsie's Lovers (Le Quex, W. T., 1886), V. 456

To Parents and Guardians (Taylor, T., 1846), IV. 411; V. 592, 820

To Paris and back for Five Pounds (Morton, J. M., 1853), V. 495

Top Boots (1834), IV. 543

To Persons about to Marry (1844), IV. 543

Top of the Ladder = Man of the People

Top of the Tree (1739), II. 385

Topsail Sheet Blocks (Townsend, W. T., 1838), IV. 414

Topsy Turvy (1885), V. 759

Topsey Turveydom (Gilbert, W. S., 1874), V. 380

Topsy Turvey Hotel (Sturgess, A., 1898), V. 586

Topsyturvydom (Byford, R., 1895), V. 295

Toretta [By error this appears at IV. 543 for Loretta, see IV. 276]

Tornado (Carter, L. J., 1899), V. 305

Torneo (1838), IV. 544, 641

Torquato (Swanwick, C., 1850), V. 819.

Torrendal (Cumberland, R., 1813), IV. 287

Torrent of La Charbonnière = Forest Savage

Torrent of the Valley (1816), IV. 544

— (1821), IV. 544

Torrid Zone (Clarke, S., 1809), IV. 280

Tortesa the Usurer (Wilks, T. E., 1839), IV. 421

Torture of Shame (Gannon, J., 1896), V. 376

Tosca (Grove, F. C. and Hamilton, H., 1889), V. 395

Toss up (Addison, J., 1876), V. 236

— (1897), V. 759

Tradesman's Son (Shepherd, R., 1862), v. 563

Trafalgar (Campbell, A. V., 1845), IV. 279

— (1807), IV. 544

— (1849), IV. 544

Trafalgar Medal (Buckstone, J. B., 1863), v. 781

Tragedy (Fawcett, C. S., 1887), v. 364

Tragedy à la Mode = (1) First Act of Taste; (2) Lindamira

Tragedy Expell'd = Art of Management

Tragedy for Warm Weather = Devil among the Tailors

Tragedy in Trousers = Irvingmania

Tragedy in True Taste = Distress upon Distress

Tragedy of Amidea = Traytor

Tragedy of Love = Cyrus the Great

Tragedy of Ovid (Cockain, Sir A., 1662), I. 397

Tragedy of Tragedies = Tom Thumb

Tragedy of Vortigern Rehearsed = Precious Relics

Tragedy Queen (Oxenford, J., 1855), v. 759, 848

— (Robson, W., 1847), IV. 395

Tragedy rehearsed = Critic

Tragical Actors (1660), I. 445

Tragic Mary (Field, M., 1890), v. 366

Tragopodagra (Francklin, T., 1780), III. 261

Traill the Anarchist (1896), v. 759

Trail of Sin (Leslie, H. T., 1863), v. 457

Trail of the Serpent (Lander, G., 1879), v. 448

— (Walker, W., 1881), v. 611

— (Watson, F. M., 1896), v. 616

Trained to Crime (Towers, E., 1878), v. 601

Training a Husband (Dening, Mrs C., 1892), v. 342

Traitor = (1) Maurice the Woodcutter; (2) Traytor

Traitor Doubts (1887), v. 759

Traitor's Doom = Destiny

Traitor's Gate (Lucas, W. J., 1834), IV. 347

Traitors of Ferrara = Florinda Salviati, the White Devil

Traitor's Touch = Wedding Eve

Traitor, the Jew and the Gypsey = Casper Duverade

Traitor to Himself (Johns, W., 1678), I. 101, 415

Traits of Ancient Superstition = Test of Guilt

Tra-la-la Tosca (Burnand, F. C., 1890), v. 291

Tramp (Harrison, C., 1889), v. 407

Tramp and the Treasure of the Seven Seas = Pauper of Lambeth

Tramps (Stephens, W. and McCullough, B., 1896), v. 581

Tramp's Adventure (Phillips, F. L., 1860) = Dying Gift, v. 522, 671, 810, 831

Trances of Nourjahad = Illusion

Transferred Ghost (Lynn, N., 1894), v. 465

Transferring a Licence (1852), v. 759

Transformation (Allingham, J. T., 1810), IV. 252, 568

— (1787), III. 346

— (1816), IV. 544

— (1822), IV. 544

Transformations (1821), IV. 544

Transformations in Olympus = Low Life below Stairs

Transformed (1854), v. 759

Transformed Lover (1850), v. 848

Transgressor (Gattie, A. W., 1894), v. 377

Transit of Venus (Tanner, J. T., 1898), v. 591

Transmogrification = Crockery's Misfortunes

Transported for Life (Murdoch, J. M., 1880), v. 499

Trap of Gold (Higgie, T. H., 1864), v. 421

Trapolin's Vagaries = Devil of a Duke

Trapped (1885), v. 759

— (1898), v. 759

Trapped at Last (Neville, G. F., 1882), v. 502

Trapper (Roberts, G., 1888), v. 545

Trapper of the Hills (1845), IV. 544

Trappers of the Mountains = Year and a Day

Trapper Trapped = Caught in his own Trap

Trapping a Tartar (Stirling, E., 1864),
v. 584
Trappolin's Vagaries = Enchantment
Traveller (1809), IV. 544
Traveller and his Host = Spread Eagle
Travellers (Cherry, A., 1806), IV. 280
— (Harrison, N. B., 1788), III. 266
— (1819), IV. 544
— (1897), v. 759
— = Adventurers
Traveller's Adventure = Hebrew Family
Travellers Benighted (1811), IV. 544
Travellers from Threadneedle-street =
Caribee
Travellers in Switzerland (Bate, H.,
1794), III. 47, 206, 236
Traveller's Portmanteau = Rob Roy
Travellers' Rest (1887), v. 759
Traveller's Room (Fitzball, E., 1847),
IV. 317
Traveller's Tale = Murder and Madness
Travelling Carriage (Planché, J. R.,
1835), IV. 380
Travelling Incog. (Milner, H. M.,
1824), IV. 544, 641
Travelling in Ireland = Transformations
Travels of a Sailor = Progress of a Law-
suit
Travers' Secret (Thorrington, J. E.,
1899), v. 599
Traviata (Buckingham, L. S., 1857), v.
286
— (Jefferys, C., 1858), v. 800
— (Reynoldson, T. H., 1857), v. 759, 848
Traviata, the Lost One (Hazlewood,
C. H., 1857), v. 759, 796, 848
Traytor (Bullock, C., 1718), II. 301
— (Rivers, A., 1692), I. 427
Treacherous Baron (1812), IV. 544
Treacherous Black (1829), IV. 544
Treacherous Brothers (Powell, G.,
1689), I. 27, 39, 130, 156–7, 425
Treacherous Esquimaux = Frozen Re-
gions
Treacherous Friend = Marcelia
Treacherous Guide = Mungo Park
Treacherous Husband (Davey, S.,
1737), II. 317
Treacherous Moor = Alonzo of Castile
Treacherous Son-in-Law (Pierson, T.,
1785), III. 297
Treacherous Uncle (1826), IV. 544

Treacle and Mustard (1820), IV. 545
Treadmill (1822), IV. 545, 641
Treasure (Carton, R. C. and Raleigh,
C., 1888), v. 305
Treasurers (Cooke, J., 1843), IV. 282
Treasure Seeker (1847), IV. 641
Treasure Seekers = Votaries of the Ruby
Cross
Treasure Seekers' Dream = Long Finn
Treasures of the Weeping Rock = Frank
the Fool
Treasure Trove (Law, A., 1883), v. 450
— = Cries of London
Treaty of Limerick = Rapparee
Treaty of Peace (Gordon, G. L., 1878),
v. 385
— (1860), v. 759
Treble Discovery = Physical Metamor-
phosis
Treble Lover (1813), IV. 545
Tree of Fate = Rookwood
Tree of Health = Zuma
Tree of Knowledge (Carton, R. C.,
1897), v. 305
Trelawney = King's Password
Trelawny of the "Wells" (Pinero, Sir
A. W., 1898), v. 1, 179–80, 189, 525, 810
Tremendous 1824 = Terrific Register
Tremendous Mystery (Burnand, F. C.
and Hall, K., 1878), v. 291
Trenck the Pandour (1823), IV. 545
Trepan (Maxwell, J., 1739), II. 343
Trespassers Beware (Thomas, C., 1888),
v. 596
Trevanion (Bernard, B., ?1849), IV. 545,
641
Tria juncta in uno (1822), IV. 545
Trial by Battle (Barrymore, W., 1818),
IV. 261
Trial by Jury (Gilbert, W. S., 1875), v.
141–2, 147, 380
— (Hook, T. E., 1811), IV. 132, 328
Trial for Infanticide = Jessie Farleigh
Trial for Life = Infanticide
Triall of the Three Politick Ghosts =
Hell's Higher Court of Justice
Trial of Abraham (Farrer, 1790), III.
259
Trial of Effie Deans (Boucicault, D.,
1860), v. 268
Trial of Friendship (1825), IV. 545
Trial of Hum-bug = Court of Nassau

Trial of Love (Lovell, G. W., 1852), IV.
347; V. 463
— (Soane, G., 1827), IV. 545, 641
Trial of Poverty = Love Gift
Trial of Skill (Dossie, R., 1768) =
Statesman Foil'd, III. 346, 383, 405
— (Wilcox, W. T. W., 1837), IV. 419
— (1835), IV. 545
Trials and Triumphs of Temperance
(Pitt, G. D., 1851), V. 526
Trials and Troubles of Claude and
Pauline = Extraordinary Version of
the Lady of Lyons
Trials of a Fond Papa = Virginius
Trials of a Merry-Andrew = Belphegor
Trials of Life = Wealth and Poverty
Trials of Love = Angel's Visit
Trials of Poverty (1843), IV. 545
Trials of the Heart (1799), III. 346
— = (1) Avalanche; (2) Woman's Life
Trials of the Poor (1887), V. 759
Trials of Tomkins (Williams, T. J.,
1863), V. 625
Trials of Youth = Resolution
Tribulation (Poole, J., 1825), IV. 184,
386
Tribunal of Blood = Black Banner
Tribunal of Death = Maid of Grenada
Tribute of a Hundred Virgins (Mon-
crieff, W. T., 1840), IV. 600
Trick and Trap (1859), V. 759
Tricked (Dalrymple, L., 1884), V. 333
Trick for Trick (Dibdin, T. J., 1817),
IV. 300
— (D'Urfey, T., 1678), I. 273, 408
— (Fabian, R., 1735), II. 321
— (Forrest, A., 1889), V. 370
— (Gathercole, Mrs, 1877), V. 376
— (Stanley, H. J., 1874), V. 579
— (1812), IV. 545, 641
— (1827), IV. 545
— = Comical Resentment
Tricking a 'Tec (Drew, E., 1891), V. 350
Tricking's Fair in Love (1814), IV. 545
Tricks (Field, W. F., 1889), V. 366
— (Wyke, E. B., 1878), V. 633
Tricks and Blunders (Dobbs, J., 1823),
IV. 545
— (1822), IV. 545
— (1825), IV. 545
Tricks and Honours (Gray, L., 1897), v.
390

Tricks and Trials (1850), V. 759
Tricksey Monarch and the Wicksey
Warrior = Louis XI
Tricks of Harlequin (Downing, G.,
1739), II. 319
Tricks of London (McLaren, A., 1812)
= Ways of London, IV. 351
Tricks of the Turf (1867), V. 759
Tricks of Timothy = Castle of Lausanne
Tricks upon Travellers (Brassington,
R., Jr., 1816), IV. 270
— (Burges, Sir J. B., 1810), IV. 276
Trick to Cheat the Devil = Imposture
Defeated
Trick upon Trick (Yarrow, J., 1742), II.
364, 385, 386
— (1739), II. 364, 385, 447-8
— = (1) Hymen's Triumph; (2) Sor-
ceress; (3) Squire Brainless
Tricky Esmeralda (Bailey, W. E. and
Ward, E., 1897), V. 247
Tried and True = Patriot's Daughter
Tried for Life (1896), V. 759
Tried in the Fire = Mary Warner
Triermain (Ellerton, J. L., 1831), IV.
92, 309
Trifles light as Air (1850), V. 759
Trifling Mistake = Prince and the
Player
Trilby (Potter, P. M., 1895), V. 530
— (1896), V. 759
Trilby the Model (1896), V. 759
Trinummi Imitated (Barnes, J., ?1684),
I. 389
Trip across the Herring Pond = Paris
and London
Trip by Railway = Look to your Lug-
gage
Trip from the North = Lowland Lassie
in London
Triple Alliance (Oxenford, J., 1862), V.
510
— (1897), V. 759
— = Poor Tommy
Triple Bill (Adams-Acton, Mrs, 1894),
V. 235
Triple Dilemma (1863), V. 759
Triple Discovery (1800), IV. 545
Triple Marriage (Foote, S., 1762), III.
384
Triple Revenge = Spouter
Triple Wedding = Pill for the Doctor

Trip to Bath (Sheridan, F.), III. 395
— = Snuff Box
Trip to Bengal (Smith, C., 1802), IV. 402
Trip to Blackheath = Past Four O'Clock
Trip to Blackpool (1899), V. 759
Trip to Brighthelmstone = Invasion
Trip to Brighton (Seymour, T., 1899), V. 561
— (Soden, J. E., 1874), V. 573
— = Lewes Maid
Trip to Calais (Foote, S., 1776), III. 19, 175, 260
Trip to California = Voyage to California
Trip to Cambridge = Grateful Fair
Trip to Chicago (1893), V. 759
Trip to Chinatown (Hoyt, C. H., 1891), V. 429
Trip to Dover = Ways and Means
Trip to Elysium (1791), III. 346
— = Quizes
Trip to Exmouth = High Notions
Trip to Gretna (D'Almeida, W. B., 1891), V. 333
Trip to Hampton (1847), IV. 545
Trip to Heidelberg = On Tour
Trip to India (Bennett, 1875), V. 258
Trip to Ireland (1777), III. 346 [The date of production should be 8/2/1777]
Trip to Jamaica = Sailor's Opera
Trip to Kissingen (Taylor, T., 1844), IV. 411; V. 592 [A. A. Knox collaborated in writing this play]
Trip to Klondyke (1897) = Kiss Me Quick, V. 703, 759, 838, 848
Trip to London = Man of Parts
Trip to Margate = Ar-rivals
Trip to Marseilles (Waldron, F. G., 1806), IV. 615
Trip to Midget-town (Breitenbach, R., 1899), V. 274
Trip to Newmarket = Note of Hand
Trip to New York = Kentuckian
Trip to Paddington = Grand Junction Canal
Trip to Paris (1892), V. 760
— = Aderman's Gown
Trip to Plymouth Dock (Robinson, 1793), III. 302
Trip to Portsmouth (Stevens, G. A., 1773), III. 309

Trip to Portsmouth = Britain's Glory
Trip to Richmond (1861), V. 760
Trip to Scarborough (Sheridan, R. B., 1777), III. 115, 160, 161, 305
— (Soden, J. E., 1874), V. 573
— (1813), IV. 545
Trip to Scotland (Whitehead, W., 1770), III. 154-5, 187, 315
Trip to Tenby = High Notions
Trip to the Ball (Milner, H. M., 1823), IV. 545, 641
Trip to the Coronation = Courting by Mistake
Trip to the Danube (Dibdin, C. I. M., 1804), IV. 291
Trip to the Garden of Love at Vauxhall = Alexis's Paradise
Trip to the Isle of Man (Bailey, S. F., 1898), V. 247
Trip to the Jubilee = Constant Couple
Trip to the Nile = Abyssinia
+ Trip to the Nore (Dibdin, C. I. M.: R.A., 1798)
— (Franklin, A., 1797), III. 261
Trip to Tunbridge (1831), IV. 545
Trip to Wales (Parry, J., 1826), IV. 368
Tristan (Hilton, B. H., 1882), V. 422
Tristan and Isolde (Corder, F. and Corder, H., 1882), V. 786
— (Forman, A., 1891), V. 792
— (Jameson, F., 1886), V. 799
— (1898), V. 760, 848
Tristernagh (Ouseley, M., 1883), V. 508
Tristram Shandy (Macnally, L., 1783), III. 285
Triumphant Widow (Cavendish, W. and Shadwell, T., 1674), I. 86, 215, 348, 396; II. 238
Triumph of Arms (Foulton, W., 1872), V. 371
Triumph of Bacchus = Ariadne
Triumph of Beauty = (1) Judgment of Paris; (2) New Cosmetic
Triumph of Constancy = Nologoise, King of the Parthenes
Triumph of Cupid (1787), III. 346
Triumph of Fidelity (Harpley, T., 1790), III. 266, 405
— (1790), III. 346, 405
— (1832), IV. 545
— = Recluse of the Cavern
Triumph of Friendship (1752), III. 346

Troubadour (1831), IV. 545
— = Laura et Linza
Troubadours (Planché, J. R., 1819), IV. 376
Trouble at the Court of King Bulbous (1896), v. 760
Troubled Hearts (1866), v. 760
Troubled Waters (Brock, F., 1899), v. 276
— (Hume, H., 1864), v. 760, 799, 848
— (1878), v. 760
— (1893), v. 760
Troubles (Findon, B. W., 1888), v. 366
Troubles of a Tourist (Grain, R. C., 1884), v. 387
Troublesome Lodger (Mayhew, H. and Baylis, H., 1839), IV. 545, 641
Troublesome Twins = Corsican "Bothers"
Trovatore (Byron, H. J., 1880), v., 299
— (Suter, W. E. and Travers, W., 1855), v. 587
Troy Again (Bowles, E. W., 1888), v. 271
Truant Chief (?Oxberry, W. H., 1837), IV. 367, 602, 603
— = Provost of Paris
Trudge and Wowski (Knight, T., 1790), III. 279
True as Steel (Hazlewood, C. H., 1869), v. 414
— (Reeve, W., 1871), v. 540
— (Romaine, E., 1871), v. 549
True as Truth (Drinkwater, A. E., 1891), v. 351
True at Last (Reynoldson, T. H., 1866) = Gitano Boy, v. 683, 813, 833
True Blue (Outram, L. S. and Gordon, S., 1896), v. 509
— (1787), III. 346
— = Nancy
True Blue for Ever = Spaniards dismayed
True-born Irishman (Macklin, C., 1762), III. 284, 391
True-born Scotsman (Macklin, C., 1764), III. 284 [This seems to have been acted first at Smock Alley, Dublin, 10/7/1764]
True British Tar (Hull, T., 1786), III. 274
True Briton (Cranke, 1782), III. 249

True Colours (Hartley, C., 1889), v. 408
— (Hurst, J. P., 1888), v. 431
True Friends (Dibdin, T. J., 1800), IV. 297
True Grit (Pettitt, H. and Flaxman, A. J., 1894), v. 521
— (Stafford, A., 1887), v. 578
True Heart (Byatt, H. and Magnay, W., 1889), v. 295
True Hearts (Bell, F., 1874), v. 255
True Irish Girl = Kathleen
True Lesson of Life = Temperance Pledge
True Life in the Brickfields = Bright Beam at Last
True Love (Goodrich, A., 1885), v. 384
True Lovers' Knots (Pettitt, H., 1874), v. 520
True Nobility (Ford, T. M., 1892), v. 370
True Patriot = Vortimer
True Patriotism (1799), III. 346
True Revenge = Abbot of San Martino
True Ring of the Genuine Metal = Gold and Guilt
True Satisfaction (1815), IV. 545
True Story told in Two Cities (Galer, E. J. N., 1884), v. 375
True Tale of the Twelfth Century = Who's the Murderer?
True Test of Gold = Voyage to California
True till Death (Dix, F., 1896), v. 345
— (Marston, H., 1876), v. 478
— = Lord Darcy
True to his Colours (Bean, F., 1892), v. 254
True to his Trust = Terry
True to the Core (Slous, A. R., 1866), v. 571
— = Will Tell
True to the Corps = Vivandière
True to the Last (Whitbread, J. W., 1888), v. 620
— = Tramp's Adventure
True Touch of the Times = Harlequin's Whim
True Virgin Prophetess = Virgin Prophetess
True Way to be Happy = Darby and Joan

True Widow (Shadwell, T., 1678), I. 12, 23, 193, 207, 431

True Woman (Dodson, R., 1878), V. 346

— (Wild, W. J., 1897), V. 622

— (1883), V. 760

True Woman's Heart = Twixt Gold and Love

True Women (Braekstad, H. L., 1890), V. 780

Trulla's Triumph = Hudibras

Trump Card (Broughton, F. W. and Jones, J. W., 1882), V. 281

— (1878), V. 760

Trumpet Call (Sims, G. R. and Buchanan, R., 1891), V. 569

Trumpeter's Daughter (Coyne, J. S., 1843), IV. 284, 578

— (Webster, B., the Younger, 1863), V. 618

Trumpeter's Wedding (Morton, J. M., 1849), IV. 363

Trumps in the Dumps (1823), IV. 545

Trust (Breck, C., 1808), IV. 270

— (Newte, H. C. W., 1891), V. 503

— (1871), V. 760

— (1877), V. 760

Trust and Trial (Calmour, A. C., 1880), V. 300

Trust Each Other = Joe and Nolly Stubbs

Trustee (Allingham, J. T., 1809) = Independence, IV. 545, 641

— (Lovel, G. W., 1841), IV. 347

— (1854), V. 760

— = Noah's Ark

Trust to Luck (Clarke, C. A., 1891), V. 312

Truth (Howard, B., 1879), V. 428

— (Mathews, C. J., 1834), IV. 354

— (Pitt, W. H., 1871), V. 527

— (1821), IV. 545

Truth against the World (Spencer, G., 1870), V. 576

Truth and Fiction (Williams, T. J. and Harris, A. G., 1861), V. 625, 824

— = Romance and Reality

Truth and Filial Love (1797), III. 346

Truth and Treachery = Angiolina del' Albano

Truth and Treason = Foresters

Truth Found too Late = Troilus and Cressida

Truthful James (Mortimer, J. and Klein, C. H., 1894), V. 494

Truth is a lie = 'Twas I

Truth may be blamed but cannot be shamed = Family Treason

Truth Will Out = All-Hallows' Eve

Try Again (1821), IV. 545

— (1790) = Suspicious Brother, III. 346, 405

— = Jack Mingo, the London Street-Boy

Tryal (Baillie, J., 1798), III. 224, 235

Tryal of Conjugal Love (Jacob, H., 1738), II. 205, 338

Tryall of Samuel Foote, Esq. for a Libel on Peter Paragraph (Foote, S., 1763), III. 260

Tryal of Abraham (1790), III. 346

Tryal of the Time-Killers (Bacon, P., 1757), III. 235

Tryal's All (Herbert, 1802), IV. 325

Try before you Buy (1806), IV. 545

Try Before You Trust (?1660–1700), I. 445

Trying a Magistrate (Toole, J. L., 1877), V. 600

Trying it on (Brough, W., 1853), V. 278

Trying Scenes of Life (Gardner, C., 1876), V. 376

Tryphon (Boyle, R., 1668), I. 38, 39, 55, 99, 107–8, 393

T.T.S. (1829), IV. 545

T.T.T.—Tom Trimmer's Trials = My Husband's Wife

Tuckitomba (Pocock, I., 1828), IV. 385

Tufelhausen (Johnstone, J. B., 1856), V. 438

Tully's Rambles (1794), III. 405

Tumble-Down Dick (Fielding, H., 1736), II. 34, 67, 255–6, 263, 328

Tumble Down Naps = Man in the Moon

Tummus and Meary (1773), III. 346

Tunbridge-Walks (Baker, T., 1703), II. 60, 129, 135, 143, 175, 216, 231, 296, 432

Tunbridge-Wells (Rawlins, 1678), I. 216, 234, 426

Tuppins and Co. (Watson, T. M., 1889), V. 616

Turandot, Princess of China (Gurney, A. T., 1836), IV. 322; V. 397

Turf (Lemon, H., 1884), V. 454

Turf (Lemon, M., 1842), IV. 344

Turgesius (Banim, J.), IV. 258

+Turk (Dibdin, C. I. M.: R.A., 1798)

Turk and No Turk (Colman, G., the Younger, 1785), III. 247

Turkey and a Bear=Peace

Turkington's Talisman (Banks, B., 1893), V. 248

Turkish Bath (Burnand, F. C. and Williams, M., 1861), V. 288

— (1897), V. 760

Turkish Delight=Turkish Bath

Turkish Life in London=Pascha of Pimlico

Turkish Lovers (Armstrong, W. H., 1853), V. 243

— (Lacy, M. R., 1827), IV. 340, 592

Turkish Misers=Mufti's Tomb

Turkish War (1853), V. 760

Turko the Terrible (Brough, W., 1868), V. 280

Turlututu (Marchant, F., 1876), V. 476

Turn again, Whittington (1895), V. 760

Turn among the Knights of Chivalry (Somerset, C. A., 1839), IV. 404

Turn and Turn (Dibdin, T. J., 1827), =Clown and the Captain, IV. 545

Turned Head (À Beckett, G. A., 1834), IV. 249

Turned out to starve (Webb, T. H., 1870), V. 617

Turned Up=Too much married

Turn Hands and Change Partners (1825)=Change Partners, IV. 440, 545

Turn Him Out (Kenney, J., 1812)= Tyrant and Parrasite, IV. 144, 336, 547, 592, 641

— (Williams, T. J., 1863), V. 625

Turning the Tables (Poole, J., 1830), IV. 387, 606

— (1836), IV. 545

Turn of Fortune=Happy Marriage

Turn of the Lane (1899), V. 760

Turn of the Tide (Burnand, F. C., 1869), V. 289

Turnpike Gate (Knight, T., 1799), III. 280

Turn Round (1870), V. 760

Turns and Returns (Jameson, R. F., 1814)=Love and Gout, IV. 546

Turns of Fortune=Philosopher

+Turnus (Aungier-street, Dublin, 21/5/1739]

Turpin à la mode (Huntley, G. P. and Gray, G., 1897), V. 431

Turpin's Ride to York (1855)=Rook-wood, V. 744, 760

Turpin's Ride to York and the Death of Black Bess (1835), IV. 546

Turquoise Ring (Godfrey, G. W. and Benson, L., 1880), V. 382

Turret Clock (Earle, 1818), IV. 546, 641

Turret Demon (Barrett, C. F., 1810), IV. 546, 641

Turtle Doves (1880), V. 760

Tuscan Orphan=Clemenza

Tuscan Treaty (Bond, W., 1733), II. 299

Tutor (Townley, J., 1765), III. 312

— (1759), III. 346

Tutor for the Beaus (Hewitt, J., 1737), II. 335, 419, 438

Tutor's Assistant=Court Guide

Twa Ghaists (1835), IV. 546

'Twas all for Love (Granville, H. S., 1877), V. 388

'Twas I (Payne, J. H., 1825), IV. 369

'Twas in Trafalgar's Bay (Henderson, J., 1889), V. 416

'Twas Time to Counterfeit=London Stars

Tweedie's Rights (Albery, J., 1871), V. 69, 237

Tweedleton's Tail Coat (Williams, T. J., 1866), V. 625

Twelfth Night (Kemble, J. P., 1811), IV. 335

— (Reynolds, F., 1820), IV. 392

Twelfth of August (1805), IV. 546

— =Hope of Britain [This is evidently an earlier version of the above, see IV. 479]

Twelve Angels (Towers, E., 1869), V. 601

+Twelve at Night; or, The Alarm Bell (Royalty, 10/1820)

Twelve Hours in India=Calcutta

Twelve Hours in New York=Flight to America

Twelve Labours of Hercules (Brough, R. B., 1851), V. 278

Twelve Months (À Beckett, G. A., 1834), IV. 546, 641

Twins, Paul and Philip (Pitt, G. D., 1836), IV. 373

Twin Tars = Wizard Schooner

Twin Venturers (1710), II. 386

Twisting and Twining (1785), III. 346, 405

'Twixt Axe and Crown (Taylor, T., 1870), V. 98-9, 594

'Twixt Crime and Prison (Parry, P. F., 1897), V. 514

'Twixt Cup and Lip (De la Plume, C. A., 1873), V. 341

— (Sapte, W., Jr., 1889), V. 556

'Twixt Gold and Love (1883), V. 760

'Twixt Kith and Kin (Blood, J. J., 1887), V. 266

'Twixt Love and Art (Cooper, H. B., 1882), V. 324

'Twixt Love and Duty (Curtin, J. M., 1894), V. 331

— (Harvey, Sir J. M., 1885), V. 409

— (Worden, J. and Johnston, R., 1889), V. 632

'Twixt Love and War (Miles, R., 1892), V. 488

'Twixt Night and Morn (Seymour, E. M., 1896), V. 561

'Twixt the Cup and the Lip (Poole, J., 1826), IV. 386

Twm John Catty, the Welsh Rob Roy (Milner, H. M., 1823), IV. 546, 641

Two Adolphuses = Carry's Breach of Promise

Two Apprentices (Oulton, W. C., 1798), III. 296

Two at a Time = Odd Whims

Two Bears (1822), IV. 546

Two Bears in Smyrna (1831), IV. 546

Two Blighted Loves = Constancy

Two Blinds (Clements, A., 1874), V. 314

Two Bloomers (Courtney, J., 1851), V. 326

Two Boat Makers (1788), III. 346

Two Bodkins (1837), IV. 546

Two Bonnycastles (Morton, J. M., 1851), V. 495

+ Two Brothers (*French*)

Two Brothers of Catania = Sorcerer

Two Brothers of Pisa (1822), IV. 546

Two Bumpkins = Margery Daw

Two Caliphs (Dibdin, C. I. M., 1814), IV. 293

Two can play at that Game (Gordon, W., 1857), V. 760, 794, 848

— (Pinero, Sir A. W., 1878), V. 524

+ Two Catherines (Pemberton, C. R.; 8°, 1843 (in *The Life and Literary Remains*))

Two Centuries Ago = Forest Princess

Two Christmas Eves (Drinkwater, A. E., 1888), V. 351

— (1859), V. 760

Two Clerks (1846), IV. 546

Two College Friends (1857), V. 760

Two Common Sailors (Overton, R., 1883), V. 509

Two Confessions (Fenn, F., 1899), V. 364

Two Connoisseurs (Hayley, W., 1784), III. 226, 267, 386

Two Coquettes (Albery, J., 1870), V. 237

Two Crispins (1826), IV. 546

Two Curious by Half = Middle Dish

Two Daughters (1881), V. 760

Two Days at the Hall = Country Squire

Two Days of the Revolution = Robespierre

Two Doctor Hobbs's (1815), IV. 546

Two Dogs of Ravensdale (1838), IV. 546

Two Drovers (Goff, H., 1841), IV. 95, 319, 585

— (Murray, W. H., 1828), IV. 95, 365

— (1828), IV. 95, 546

— = Predilection

Two D's (1899), V. 760

Two Dumas Skiteers (Day, G. D., 1899), V. 340

Two English Gentlemen (Stewart, J., 1774), III. 309

Two Eyes between Two (Jerrold, D. W., 1828), IV. 331

Two Faces under a Hood (Dibdin, T. J., 1807) = How happy could I be with either, IV. 52, 298, 480, 580, 628

Two Families = Pocket Book

Two Farmers (Dibdin, T. J., 1800), IV. 297

— (1823), IV. 546

Two Fathers (1836), IV. 546

Two Figaros (Planché, J. R., 1836), IV. 380

Two Fishermen of Lynn (Lancaster, E. R.), IV. 593

Two make a Pair (Raymond, R. J., 1827), IV. 388

Two Marriages (Barlow, G., 1878), V. 249

Two Masters Better than One = English Plum-Pudding

Two Mean Husbands (1894), V. 761

Two Men (Bourne, W., 1896), V. 270

Two Men and a Maid (Purchase, F. H. and Webster, J., 1893), V. 531

Two Men and a Woman (1899), V. 761

Two Men in One Coat = Uniform

Two Merry Milk-maids (1661), I. 445

Two Misers (O'Hara, K., 1775), III. 120, 207, 291

Two More Slaves = Two Gallows Slaves

Two Mothers (Mayer, 1877), V. 482

— = Heiress of Daventry

Two Mothers to One Child = Devil at the Elbow

Two Mr Browns (1825), IV. 547

"Two" Much Alike (Rogers, A. R. and Grossmith, G., 1870), V. 548

Two Murderers (Selby, C., 1835), IV. 398

— = Auberge des Adrets

Two Murders but Nobody Hurt (1822), IV. 547

Two Nannys (Dent, J., 1788), III. 346, 381, 405

Two Neighbours and their Wives (1837), IV. 547

Two Nights (1829), IV. 547

Two Nights in Madrid = Deuce is in Her!

Twonkey and Son (1842), IV. 547

Two Noble Kinsmen = Love and Valour

Two o'Clock in the Morning (1841), IV. 547

Two of a Trade (1896), V. 761

Two Old Blokes (1871), V. 761

Two Old Boys (Capel, G. and Benton, F., 1880), V. 302

Two Old Maids of Florence (1808), IV. 547

Two Old Pals (1895), V. 761

Two or One (Wishaw, Mrs B., 1891), V. 629

Two Orphan Girls (1899), V. 761

Two Orphans (Oxenford, J., 1874), V. 510

— (1883), V. 761

— = Blind Girl's Fortune

Two Orphans of Paris (1892), V. 761

— (1897), V. 761

Two Owls in One Ivy Bush (1848), IV. 547

Two Pages of Frederick the Great (Poole, J., 1821), IV. 386

Two Paths of Life (Callender, E. R., 1875), V. 300

Two Pence (Peake, R. B., 1821), IV. 547, 641

Two Penitents (1894), V. 761

Twopenny Pride and Pennytence = Lady of Lyons

Two Peters = Burgomaster of Sardaam

Two Photographs (Clements, A., 1884), V. 314

Two Places at Once = Queen of Golconda

Two Poets (Germain, J. E., 1886), V. 378

Two Polts (Courtney, J., 1850), V. 326

Two Precious Scoundrels (Buckingham, L. S., 1856), V. 761, 781, 848

Two Pretty Women (1855), V. 761

Two Prima Donnas (Ebsworth, J.), IV. 309

Two Prisoners (Kenney, J., 1804) = Matrimony, IV. 547, 641

— = (1) Adolf and Clara; (2) Adolphus and Clara; (3) False Friend

Two Pros (Bowyer, F., 1886), V. 271

Two Puddifoots (Morton, J. M., 1867), V. 496

Two Pupils (1831), IV. 547

Two Q.C.'s (Fox, F., 1881), V. 371

Two Queens (Buckstone, J. B., 1835), IV. 275

Two Queens of Brentford (D'Urfey, T., 1721), II. 267, 320

Two Rainbows (1846), IV. 547

Two Recruits (Wyatt, F., 1890), V. 633

Two Reefers = Life Raft

Two Revolutions (1854), V. 761

Two Rings (Range, I., 1885), V. 534

Two Rivals and the Small Boar = Venus and Adonis

Two Roads of Life (1871), V. 761

— = (1) Gitano Boy; (2) Idle Apprentice; (3) Jolly Dogs of London

Uncle Tom's Cabin (Dampier, A. and Sheridan, J. F., 1887), v. 335
— (Fitzball, E.(3 versions, 1852)), v. 368
— (Hermann, C., 1853), v. 419
— (Rowe, G. F., 1878), v. 552
— (Young, H., 1852), v. 636
— (1852), v. 761, 762
— (1853), v. 761
— (1882), v. 761
— = Slave Life
Uncle Tom's Crib (Brough, W., 1852), v. 278
Uncle too many (Thomson, J., 1828), IV. 413
Uncle True (1872), v. 762
Uncle Yank's Mishaps (Wilmot, C. and Mannon, C. H., 1892), v. 628
Uncle Zac = Mad Revenge
Uncle Zachary (Oxenford, J., 1860), v. 510, 809
Unconscious Counterfeit (Greffulhe, 1809), IV. 547, 641
Un-dead = Dracula
Undecided Voter (1871), v. 762
Under a Ban (Duckworth, W., 1870), v. 351
Under a Cliff (1897), v. 762
Under a Cloud (Hazlewood, C. H., 1859), v. 762, 796, 848
— (Johnstone, J. B., 1859), v. 762, 800, 848
— (1863), v. 762
Under a Crimson Crown = Catharine Howard
Under a Mask (1881), v. 762
— = Mask of Guilt
Under Arrest = Captain Sabertache
Under a Veil (Roberts, Sir R., 1876), v. 545
Under Compulsion (Vane, S., 1895), v. 606
Under Cover (Bridgman, C., 1886), v. 275
— (1865), v. 762
Under False Colours (De Pass, E. A., 1870), v. 342
— (Steele, Mrs, 1869), v. 580
— (Taylor, F. C., 1870), v. 591
Under Fire (Marston, J. W., 1885), v. 184-5, 479
— (1888), v. 762
Undergraduate (Freund, J. C., 1872), v. 373

Undergraduates (Tristram, W. O., 1886), v. 604
Underground Journey (Bell, Mrs H. and Brookfield, C. H. E., 1893), v. 256
Under his Thumb = Randall's Thumb
Under Proof (Rose, E., 1879), v. 550
Under Remand = Handcuffs
Understudy (Bessle, E., 1892), v. 260
— (Dabbs, G. G. R., 1887), v. 332
Under Suspicion (1894), v. 762
— = New Boy
Under the Ban (1895), v. 762
Under the British Flag (Curtin, J. M., 1896), v. 331
Under the Clock (Brookfield, C. H. E. and Hicks, S., 1893), v. 277
Under the Czar (Jarman, F., 1894), v. 434
Under the Earth (Nation, W. H. C., 1867), v. 762, 808, 848
Under the Flag (1879), v. 762
Under the Gaslight (Daly, A., 1867), v. 333
— (1869), v. 762
Under the Lamps (Mead, T., 1862), v. 762, 806, 848
Under the Line (Green, J., 1881), v. 392
Under the Mask of Truth = Mask of Guilt
Under the Mistletoe (Molyneux, St J. and Jephson, R. M., 1881), v. 490
Under the Oak (1830), IV. 547
Under the Old Church Porch = Hallowmas Eve
Under the Old Name (Pritt, S., 1896), v. 531
Under the Red Flag = Wicked Paris
Under the Red Robe (Rose, E., 1896), v. 550
— (1896), v. 762
— (1897), v. 762
Under the Rose (Roberts, G., 1862), v. 544, 814
— = Great Gentleman in the Little Parlour
Under the Screw (Mead, T., 1873), v. 483
Under the Shadow (1884), v. 762
Under the Shadow of Old St Paul's (Marchant, F., 1872), v. 476
Under the Snow (1877), v. 762

Union of the Clans = Highland Fair

Union of the Seven Kingdoms = King Egbert, King of Kent and Monarch of England

Union of the Three Sister Arts (1723), II. 386

Union Wheel (Fox, J., 1870), V. 371

United (Harley, J. N. and Creamer, A., 1886), V. 404

— (Selwyn, A., 1890), V. 561

United Britons (Byrne, J., 1805), IV. 548, 641

United Kingdoms (Howard, H., 1664), I. 414

United Pair (Carr, J. W. C., 1886), V. 304

United Service (Townsend, W. T., 1845), IV. 414

— (1841), IV. 548

— (1855) = Lion of England and the Eagle of France, V. 707, 762

United Service of England and France (Stirling, E., 1854), V. 762, 818, 849

United Services (O'Neil, J. F., 1852), V. 507

United we stand (Dickson, J. H., 1892), V. 344

Universal Bandits = Caitiff of Corsica

Universal Gallant (Fielding, H., 1735), II. 328, 436

Universal Monarch Defeated (1742), II. 452

Universal Passion (Miller, J., 1737), II. 65, 141, 144, 203, 233, 344, 423

Universal Register Office (Reed, J., 1761) = Register Office, III. 347, 394, 405

Unjust Judge = Roman Virgin

Unjust Steward = Term Day

Unknown (Dimond, W., 1831), IV. 581

— (1819), IV. 548

— (1859), V. 762

— = (1) Mill of Aldervon; (2) Two Galley Slaves

Unknown and the Bayedere (1855), V. 762

Unknown, a River Mystery (Stevens, J. A., 1882), V. 583

Unknown Female = Eugenia

Unknown Friend = Gambler's Dupe

Unknown Guest (Arnold, S. J., 1815), IV. 256, 569

Unknown Knight = Hebrew Patriarch

Unknown of the Mountain = Solitaire

Unknown Quantity (Votieri, A., 1897), V. 609

Unlawful Present (Hazlewood, C. H., 1872), V. 414

Unlimited Cash (Burnand, F. C., 1879), V. 291

Unlimited Confidence (Troughton, A. C., 1864), V. 604

Unlucky Coincidence (Crozier, C., 1897), V. 331

Unlucky Friday (Craven, H. T., 1858), V. 328

Unlucky Leap Year (1858), V. 762

Unlucky Lovers (1717), II. 386

Unlucky Mortal (1863), V. 762

Unmasked (Merton, C., 1875), V. 488

— (Waldie, C., 1899), V. 610

— (1886), V. 762

— (1888), V. 762

— = Hope Deferred

Unnatural Brother (Filmer, E., 1697), I. 142, 263, 411

— (1712), II. 386

Unnatural Brothers = Sins of the Fathers

Unnatural Combat (1834), IV. 548

— = Fatal Passion

Unnatural Mother (1697), I. 28, 171, 445

Unnatural Parents (1727), II. 386

Unnatural Tragedie (Cavendish, M., 1662), I. 396

Unpaid Debt (Dickinson, C. H., 1893), V. 344

Unprotected Female (Coyne, J. S., 1850), V. 327

Unready Gentleman = Procrastination

Unreal Riches (Raleigh, C., 1890), V. 533

Unrequited Love = Mountain Flower

Unreserved Young Lady (1788), III. 347

Unrivalled Blondin = Caught in a Line

Unsanctified Garment (Gray, and Martin, 1895), V. 390

Unseen Helmsman (Alma-Tadema, L., 1897), V. 240

Unstable as Water (1899), V. 762

Until the Day Break (Beresford, I., 1898), V. 258

— (1891), V. 762

+ Unwarrantable Intrusion (Morton, J. M., French)

Valley of Wolves (1830), IV. 548

Valmonde the Merchant of Calais (1860), v. 763

Valmondi (Rodwell, J. T. G., 1824), IV. 548, 642

Valsha (Coyne, J. S., 1837), IV. 284

Valshi (1824), IV. 548

+ Value of Truth (*French*)

Valvoni (1823), IV. 548

Vampire (Boucicault, D., 1852), v. 86, 267

— (Moncrieff, W. T., 1820), IV. 359

— (Reece, R., 1872), v. 537

— (Stephens, G., 1821), IV. 612

Vampire and the Bride of the Isles = Spirit of the Moon

Vampire and the Water Kelpie = Hallowe'en

Vampire Bride (1834), IV. 642

— = Tenant of the Tomb

Vampyr (Planché, J. R., 1829), IV. 378

Vampyre (Planché, J. R., 1820), IV. 376, 605

Van der Decken (Edgar, W., 1885), v. 354

— (Taylor, T. P., 1846), IV. 411

Vanderdicken (Wills, W. G. and Fitzgerald, P., 1878), v. 627

Van Dieman's Land (Moncrieff, W. T., 1830), IV. 360

Van Donderman (1829), IV. 548

Vandyck (Richards, A. B., 1850), IV. 394; v. 542

Vandyke Brown (Troughton, A. C., 1859), v. 604

Vanelia (?Miller, J., 1732), II. 377, 386, 448

Vanella (1736), II. 386

Vanguard (1799), III. 347

Vanishing Husband (Ryley, M. L., 1897), v. 554

Vanity (McCarthy, J. H., 1886), v. 467

— (Micklethwaite, T. D. F., 1882), v. 488

— (1861), v. 763

— = What will the World say?

Vanity Cured (Ranger, 1853), v. 534

Vanity Fair (Godfrey, G. W., 1895), v. 383

— (Reynolds, W., 1888), v. 541

Vanity of Vanities (McCarthy, J. H., 1890), v. 467

Vanquish'd Love (Bellamy, D., 1723), II. 297

Vanrick of Voorn (1835), IV. 548

— = Executioner

Van the Virginian (1879), v. 763

Variations (Young, M., 1899), v. 636

Varietie (Cavendish, W., 1649), I. 396

Variety (Griffith, R., 1782), III. 44, 142, 266

— (1850), v. 763

Varley the Vulture (1845), IV. 548

— (1860), v. 763

Varney the Vampyre (Young, H., 1846), IV. 423

Varsity Belle (Jarman, F., 1898), v. 434

Varsity Boat Race (Stephenson, C. H. and Robson, F., 1870), v. 582

Varsity Girl = Varsity Belle

Vaulted Cavern = Orsino

Vaults of Mount St Bernard = Three Weavers

Vauxhall Gardens = Mr Simpson, M.C.

V.C. (Vane, S., 1891), v. 606

Vedah (1886), v. 763

Veemah Kareeda (Young, H., 1857) = Keereda and Nana Sahib, v. 702, 763, 825, 838, 849

Vegetarians (1851), v. 763

Vehme Gericht (1830), IV. 548

Veiled Lady = Diadeste

Veiled Picture (Lyon, W. F., 1883), v. 465

Veiled Portrait (1838), IV. 548

Veiled Prophet (Squire, B., 1893), v. 578

Veiled Prophet of Korassan (Walford, H. L., 1870), v. 611

— (1820), IV. 548

— = Mokana

Velvet and Rags (Meritt, P. and Conquest, G., 1874), v. 485

Venceslao (Humphreys, S., 1731), II. 400, 439

Vendetta (Calvert, W., 1888), v. 300

— (Cheetham, F. G., 1858), v. 763, 849

— (Stephens, W., 1868), v. 581

— (1854), v. 763

— (1863), v. 763

— (1878), v. 763

— (1896), v. 763

Venditore d'Aceto (1812), IV. 548

Venetian (Reynoldson, T. H., 1840), IV. 393

Very Good Wife (Powell, G., 1693), I.
261, 425
Very Grand Dutch—s (Bernard, C.,
1869), v. 763, 778, 849
Very Last Days of Pompeii (Reece, R.,
1872), v. 537
Very Latest Edition of the Gathering of
the Clans (Hunt, G. W., 1873), v. 430
Very Latest Edition of the Lady of
Lyons (Byron, H. J., 1859), v. 295
Very Little Faust and More Mephisto-
pheles (Burnand, F. C., 1869), v. 289
Very Little Hamlet (Yardley, W., 1884),
v. 634
Very Low Spirits (Bourne, W., 1876), v.
270
Very much above Pa = Under Proof
Very Picture = Speaking Likeness
Very Pleasant Living (Suter, W. E.),
v. 588
Very Queer Lover (1884), v. 763
Very Serious Affair (Harris, A. G.,
1857), v. 405
Very Suspicious (Simpson, J. P., 1852),
v. 567
— = Decorum
Very, very much engaged (Haworth, J.
and Buchanan, R. C., 1895), v. 410
Very Wilful Maid of Venice = Count
Tremolio
Vesper Bell = Lodovic the Corsican
Vespers of Palermo (Hemans, Mrs F. D.,
1823), IV. 324
Vesta (Farnie, H. B., 1871), v. 361
Vestal Virgin (Brooke, H., 1778), III. 240
— (Howard, Sir R., 1665), I. 40, 99, 126,
127, 137, 414–15
Vesta's Temple (1872), v. 763
Vetah (Santley, K., 1886), v. 555
Veteran (1804), IV. 549
— (1827), IV. 549
— = Veteran Soldier
Veteran and his Dog = Conscript
Veteran and his Progeny (1865), v. 763
— = 102
Veteran and his Son (1860), v. 763
— = Ben Block
Veteran Ashore (1851), v. 763
+ Veteran of 102 (Milner, H. M.,
French)
Veteran of the Old Guard (1847), IV.
642

Veterans (Dibdin, T. J., 1821), IV. 303
— (1888), v. 763
— = Veteran Soldier
Veteran Serjeant (1839), IV. 549
Veteran Soldier (Knight, E. P., 1822),
IV. 338 [This was printed 8°, 1822 as
The Veteran]
Veteran Tar (Arnold, S. J., 1801), IV.
255
Veva (O'Neil, C., 1883), v. 507
Vicar (Hannan, C., 1893), v. 402
— (Hatton, J. and Albery, J., 1885), v.
409
Vicarage (Scott, C. W., 1877), v. 557
Vicar of Bray (Grundy, S., 1882), v. 396
Vicar of Wakefield (Coyne, J. S., 1850),
v. 763, 786, 849
— (Dibdin, T. J., 1817), IV. 301, 549,
642
— (Douglass, J. T., 1870), v. 348
— (Farren, W., 1888), v. 363
— (Taylor, T., 1850), v. 592
— (1850), v. 764
Vicar of Wideawakefield (Stephens,
H. P. and Yardley, W., 1885), v. 580
Vicar Primrose = Vicar of Wakefield
Vicar's Daughter (Corney, M., 1896),
v. 325
— (Drew, E., 1889), v. 350
— = Betrayed
Vicar's Dilemma (Vicarson, A., 1898),
v. 608
Vicar's Fireside = Strayed from the Fold
Vice and its Consequences = Red
Brigade
Vice in Liverpool = Prince's Park and
Scotland Row
Vice Reclaim'd (Wilkinson, R., 1703),
II. 171, 233, 364
Viceroy (Dibdin, C. I. M., 1817), IV.
294, 549, 580, 642
— (Hayley, W., 1811), IV. 324
Vices of the Age Displayed (1711), II.
386
Vice Versa (Rose, E., 1883), v. 550
Vice versus Virtue (Barker, J., 1891), v.
249
Vicissitudes (Sicklemore, R., 1817), IV.
611
Vicissitudes of a Servant Girl = Susan
Hopley
Vicissitudes of Life = George Vernet

Vicissitudes of Sir Roger Tichbourne (1872), v. 764

Victim (Dibdin, T. J., 1820), IV. 549, 642

— (Johnson, C., 1714), II. 39, 63, 72, 89, 264, 339, 439

— (1819), IV. 549

— (1833), IV. 549

— = (1) Achilles; (2) Iphigenia

Victim of Ambition = Napoleon

Victim of Circumstances = Charlotte Hayden

Victim of Circumstantial Evidence = Rose Clinton

Victim of Constancy = Albert and Adelaide

Victim of Delusion (1865), v. 764

Victim of Drink = Road to Ruin

Victim of Falsehood (Pitt, G. D., 1847), IV. 375

Victim of Malice (Dibdin, C. I. M., 1826), IV. 296

Victim of Perjury = Martin Hayward

Victim of St Vincent (Serle, T. J., 1831), IV. 399, 610

Victim of Seduction = (1) Adeline; (2) Father and Daughter

Victim of the Star Chamber = Masked Man

Victim of the Vault = Casper the Doomed

Victim of the Violet = Prussian Brothers

Victim of the Yorkshire School = Nicholas Nickleby and Poor Smike

Victim of Unmerited Persecution = Jane Paul

Victims (Taylor, T., 1857), v. 105, 593

Victims of Fraud (Coyne, J. S., 1857) = Fraud and its Victims, v. 327

Victims of Gaming = Hertfordshire Tragedy

Victims of Love and Honour (Brooke, H., 1762), III. 240

Victims of Power (Hill-Mitchelson, E. and Longden, C. H., 1895), v. 422

Victims of Tyranny (1802), IV. 549

Victim's Tomb = Father's Guilt

Victoire (Smythe, A., 1893), v. 573

— (1837), IV. 549

Victor and Hortense (1843), IV. 549

Victor Dene (Moncrieff, W. T., 1832), IV. 549, 642

Victor Durand (Carleton, H. G., 1884), v. 303

Victor Hugh (1840), IV. 642

Victoria Cross (Whitbread, J. W., 1886), v. 620

Victorian (Anderson, J. T. R., 1883), v. 241

Victoria Stakes (Skuse, E., 1896), v. 571

Victories of Edward the Black Prince (1839), IV. 549

Victories of Joan of Arc (1839), IV. 549

Victorine (Barnett, C. Z., 1831), IV. 259

— (Buckstone, J. B., 1831), IV. 182–3, 274

— (Falconer, E., 1859), v. 360

— (Milner, H. M., 1832), IV. 357, 599

Victorious British Tar = Caravan

Victorious Love (Walker, W., 1698), I. 157, 436

Victorious Tars (1791), III. 347

Victor Vanquished (Dance, C., 1845, 1856), IV. 289; v. 335

Victory (Porter, J. H., 1890), v. 529

Victory and Death of Lord Viscount Nelson (Cumberland, R., 1805), IV. 287

Victory of the Heart (1861), v. 764

Victory of the Sunbeam = Legend of Spring

Vida (Cassilis, I. L. and Lander, C., 1891), v. 306

Videna (Heraud, J. A., 1854), v. 418, 797

Vidocq (Marchant, F., 1860), v. 764, 805, 849

Vidocq, the French Police Spy (Buckstone, J. B., 1829), IV. 273

— (Jerrold, D. W., 1829), IV. 331

Vie (Farnie, H. B., 1883), v. 363

Vienna Besieged (?1688), I. 447

Vie Parisienne in London (Burnand, F. C., 1872), v. 290, 781

Views in the Country and Views in Town = Gambler's Life in London

Vigilant Detectives (Hawkins, W. T., 1883), v. 410

Village (Cherry, A., 1805), IV. 279

Village Belles (Wilkins, J. H., 1845), IV. 419

Village Bells (1892), v. 764

Village Blacksmith (Leslie, H. T., 1868), v. 457

— (Marchant, F., 1868), v. 475

Village Blacksmith (1857), v. 764
Village Cobbler = Port Admiral
Village Conjurer (1767), III. 120, 347, 405
Village Coquette (Simon, 1792), III. 307
— (1884), v. 764
— = Love Charm
Village Coquettes (Dickens, C., 1836), IV. 146, 305
Village Doctor (Cross, J. C., 1796), III. 250
— (Montignani, F. A., 1810), IV. 600
— = Alcantara
Village Festival (1855), v. 764
— = Chip of the Old Block
Village Fete (Cumberland, R., 1797), III. 252
— (1802), IV. 549
— (1810), IV. 549, 642
Village Forge (Conquest, G. and Craven, T., 1890), v. 322
Village Frolics = (1) Goody Two Shoes; (2) Serjeant's Whim
Village Ghost (Dibdin, T. J., ?1794), III. 382
Village Gossip = Scan. Mag.
Village Heiress (Dibdin, C. I. M., 1814), IV. 293
Village Hotel = Sharp Set
Village Inn and the Count Out = Allario and Adelina
Village Lawyer (Macready, W., 1787), III. 285, 391
Village Life in France (1837), IV. 549
Village Madcap (Mervyn, E., 1898), v. 488
Village Maid (1792), III. 347
Village Nightingale (Craven, H. T., 1851), v. 328
Village of Youth (Hatton, B., 1899), v. 409
Village Opera (Johnson, C., 1729), II. 134, 242, 339; III. 116
Village Outcast (Taylor, T. P., 1846), IV. 411
— (1844), IV. 549
+ Village Pearl (Wilson, J. C.)
Village Phantom (1833), IV. 549
— (1839), IV. 549
— = White Spectre
Village Politicians = (1) Electioneering; (2) Wealth and Want

Village Post-Office (Dabbs, G. H. R. 1889), v. 332
Village Practitioner (1824), IV. 549
Village Pride = Jeannette and Jeannot
Village Priest (Grundy, S., 1890), v. 397
Village Rejoicing Day = Prize of Industry
Village Rivals = Pierette
Village Romps (1765), III. 347
Villagers (Earle, W.), III. 258
— (Worgan, T. D., 1808), IV. 422
— (1756), III. 347
— = Augustus and Gulielmus
Villagers of San Quintino = Scaramuccia
Village Smithy (1894), v. 764
Village Somnambulist = Spirit of the Hill
Village Story (Raymond, R. J., 1838), IV. 389
— (Serle, T. J., 1859), v. 561
Village Tale (Reade, C., 1852), v. 535
— (Younge, A. 1850), v. 637
— = Rachel the Reaper
Village Theatre = Scraps
Village, the Voyage and the Bush = Emigration
Village Torment (1870), v. 849
Village Vauxhall = How to take up a Bill
Village Venus (Stephens, V. and Birch, A., 1895), v. 581
+ Village Virtue; or, The Libertine Lord, and the Damsel of Daisy Farm (Byron, H. J.: *Dicks* (in *Sensation Dramas*))
Village Virtues (Lewis, M. G., 1796), III. 281
Village Washerwoman = Bubbles in the Sudds
Village Wedding (Love, J., 1767), III. 283
Villain (Porter, T., 1662), I. 38, 62, 69, 136, 346, 351, 425
Villain and Victim (Walkes, W. R., 1894), v. 612
Villainous Squire and the Village Rose (Byron, H. J., 1882), v. 299
Villainous Squire and the Virtuous Villager = Rosebud of Stinging-nettle Farm
Villain Reclaimed = Chance of War
Villain Unmask'd = Lost Child

Villario (1814), IV. 635

Villekyns and his Dinah (Eyles, F., 1873), V. 359

Villi (1897), V. 764

Villiam the Vicious (Hall, H., 1895), V. 399

Villikins and his Dinah (Burnand, F. C., 1854), V. 287

— (1854), V. 764

Villon: Poet and Cut-throat (Courte, S. X., 1894), V. 325

Vimonda (McDonald, A., 1787), III. 283, 391

Vincent Veriphleet (Vynne, C., 1869), V. 609

+ Vincenzo, Prince of Mantua; or, The Death of Chrichton. A Tragic Drama (Godmond, Christopher, 8°, 1840 (privately printed)), IV. 585

Vinda de Padilla (1832), IV. 549

Vindictive Man (Holcroft, T., 1806), IV. 326

Vine-dresser's Daughter (1846), IV. 549

Vineyard Revels (Gardner, 1791), III. 385

— (1777), III. 347

Vintage (1767), III. 347

Vintagers (Eyre, E. J., 1809) = Tears and Smiles, IV. 310, 541, 640

Vintager's Frolic = Innkeeper's Disaster

Vintner in the Suds (1740), II. 386

Vintner Outwitted = (1) Love and Revenge; (2) Trick upon Trick

Vintner Trick'd (Ward, H., 1746), II. 363

— = Revenge

Vin Willoughby (Fitzball, E., 1851), V. 367

Viola (Price, M., 1870), V. 531

Violante (1864), V. 764

Violated Bed Avenged = Italian Husband

Violence of Love = Rival Sisters

Violenza (Roscoe, W. C., 1851), V. 814

Violet (Maddox, F. M., 1845), IV. 353 [+Lacy]

— = Life of an Actress

Violet's Perils (1862), V. 764, 797

Violet's Playthings (Thomson, A., 1867), V. 598

Violette (1868), V. 764

Violette la Grande (Suter, W. E., 1853) = Life of an Actress, V. 587, 764, 819, 849

Violin Maker of Cremona (Neville, H., 1877), V. 502

Violin Players (Berlyn, A., 1890), V. 259

Viper on the Hearth (Campbell, J. M., 1888), V. 301

Virgin her own Rival = Modern Wife

Virginia (Bidlake, J., 1800), III. 238

— (Brooke, F., 1754), III. 83, 240

— (Cole, E. F., 1889), V. 316

— (Crisp, H., 1754), III. 81-2, 249

— (Jones, Major, 1883), V. 438

— (Oxenford, J., 1849), IV. 549, 603, 642

— (Plowden, Mrs F., 1800), IV. 383

— = Paul and Virginia

Virginia and Paul (Stephens, H. P., 1883), V. 580

Virginia Mummy (Rice, T. D., 1837), IV. 549, 642

Virginian (Campbell, B., 1873), V. 301

Virginian Courtship (1897), V. 764

Virginian Mummy (1854), V. 764

— (1872), V. 764

Virginibus Puerisque (1894), V. 764

Virginius (Bidlake, J., 1820), IV. 267

— (Buckingham, L. S., 1859), V. 286

— (Knowles, J. S., 1820), IV. 53, 171-2, 176, 339

Virgin Martyr = (1) Injured Love; (2) Injured Virtue

Virgin of the Sun (Plumptre, A., 1799), III. 64, 298, 394

— (Reynolds, F., 1812), IV. 87, 392, 607

— (1815), IV. 87, 549

Virgin Prophetess (Settle, E., 1701), I. 42; II. 233-4, 353, 443-4

Virgin Queen (Barford, R., 1728), II. 39, 58, 75, 91, 297

— (Waldron, F. G., 1797), III. 314

Virgin Sacrifice = Jephtha's Rash Vow

Virgin's Sacrifice = Jephtha's Rash Vow

Virgin Unmask'd (1786), III. 347

— = Old Man Taught Wisdom

Virgin Victim (1750-1800), III. 347

Virgin Widow (Taylor, Sir H., 1850), V. 820

Viricatus, the Lusitanian Hero (1826), IV. 548

Wait a Little Longer = Hard Times

Wait and Hope (Byron, H. J., 1871), v. 297

— (Nanton, L., 1869), v. 501

— = Checkmated

Waiter (Henry, R., 1887), v. 417

— (Pleon, H., 1891), v. 528

Waiter at Cremorne (Suter, W. E., 1855), v. 107, 587

Waiter at the Eagle = Waiter at Cremorne

Wait for an Answer (Lemon, H., 1869), v. 454

Wait for a Year and a Day (1876), v. 764

Wait for the End (1877), v. 764

Waiting (1887), v. 764

— (1899), v. 764

Waiting Consent (Fairbairn, Mrs R., 1881), v. 359

Waiting for an Omnibus in Lowther Arcade on a Rainy Day (Morton, J. M., 1854), v. 495

Waiting for an Omnibus on a Rainy Day = Lowther Arcade

Waiting for Dead Men's Shoes (1875), v. 764

Waiting for Death (Robertson, L. and Comerford, M., 1877), v. 545

Waiting for the Coach (Clement, F. A., 1891), v. 314

Waiting for the Dawn (Moore, R., 1870), v. 492

Waiting for the Train (Fitzgerald, S. J. A., 1899), v. 369

— (Wilmot, A. A., 1891), v. 628

Waiting for the Underground (Du Terreaux, L. H., 1866), v. 765, 789, 849

Waiting for the Verdict (Hazlewood, C. H., 1859), v. 97, 412

Waiting Game (1891), v. 765

Waits (Taylor, T. P., 1849), IV. 411

Wait till I'm a Man (Hazlewood, C. H., 1868), v. 413

Wake not the Dead (Almar, G., 1824), IV. 550, 642

+ Walberg; or, Temptation (Smith, Sophia Mary: printed in *The Eastern Princess and Other Poems*)

Walcot Castle (Goldsmith, M., 1804) = Angelina, IV. 550, 642

Waldeck (Slous, A. R., 1852), v. 816

+ Waldemar, surnamed Seir (Chapman, J. F., 12° 1841 [Translated from a play by B. S. Ingemann]

Walker, London (Barrie, J. M., 1892), v. 187, 211, 251

Walker's Trunks (1837), IV. 550

Walk for a Wager! (Peake, R. B., 1819), IV. 369

Walking Statue (Hill, A., 1710), II. 133, 336

— = Devil in the Wine-Cellar

Wallace (Buchanan, R., 1856), v. 284

— (Grahame, J., 1799), III. 347; IV. 586

— (Waddie, C., 1898), v. 610

— (Walker, C. E., 1820), IV. 416

— (1833), IV. 550

— = (1) Caledon's Tears; (2) Patriot

Wallace and Bruce (Robe, 1869), v. 544

Wallace the Brave (McLaren, A., 1819), IV. 352

Wallace, the Hero of Scotland (Barrymore, W., 1817), IV. 262, 570

Wallachian (1854), v. 765

Wallenstein (1799, 1800), IV. 87, 550

— = Piccolomini

Wallenstein's Camp (Gower, Lord F. L., 1830), IV. 320

Wall of China (Matthison, A., 1876), v. 481

Walls have Ears (Grain, R. C., 1894), v, 388

Walloons (Cumberland, R., 1782), III. 126, 251

Walooka and Noomahee (1825), IV. 550

Walpole (Lytton, Baron, 1869), v. 466, 804

Walpurghi's Eve (1830), IV. 550

Walpurgis Night (Atkyns, S., 1844), IV. 257

— (1859), v. 849

Walsha (Haines, J. T., 1841) = Warlsha, IV. 551, 587 [The title appears both as Warlsha and Walsha: the correct date is 26/4/41]

— (1837), IV. 550, 587

Walter (Warmington, G., 1846), IV. 616

Walter Brand (Fitzball, E., 1833), IV. 314

Walter Lorimer (1845), IV. 550

Walter, the Mechanic (1854), v. 765

Walter Tyrrel (Fitzball, E., 1837), IV. 315

Waltham Blacks (1832), IV. 550

Waltheof (Robson, W. J., 1851), V. 547

Waltz (Arnold, S. J., 1813), IV. 550, 642

— (1895), V. 765

Waltz by Arditi (Oxenford, J., 1874), V. 510

Wanderer (Kemble, C., 1808), IV. 87, 334

— (Travers, W., 1869), V. 603

— (1894), V. 765

— (1899), V. 765

— = Thomaso

Wanderer and Traveller (Hunter, J., 1733), II. 338

Wanderer from Venus (Buchanan, R. and Jay, H., 1896), V. 285

Wanderer of Malabar (1830), IV. 550

Wanderers (1885), V. 765

— = Swiss Boys

Wanderer's Fortune (1863), V. 765

Wandering Bard = Sketches from Life

Wandering Boys (Kerr, J., 1814), IV. 81, 338, 592

— (Pocock, I., 1814), IV. 550, 642

Wandering Deities (1740), II. 366

Wandering Heir (Reade, C., 1873), V. 536

— = Desperate Adventures of the Baby

Wandering Janet (1873), V. 765

Wandering Jew (Atkyns, S., 1844), IV. 257

— (Franklin, A., 1797), III. 187, 261

— (Lewis, L. D., 1873), V. 459

— (Paulton, T. G., 1873), V. 517

— (Whiting, G. L., 1873), V. 621

— (1835), IV. 551

— = Sea Devil

Wandering Knight (1810), IV. 551

Wandering Ladies = Mulberry-Garden

Wandering Magician = Fairy Land

Wandering Minstrel (Mayhew, H., 1834), IV. 355, 598

— (1827), IV. 551

— = Campano

Wanderings of Little Nell = Quilp

Wandering Tribe (Rede, W. L., 1837), IV. 551, 642

Wand of Wedlock (Lancaster-Wallis, E. and Macpherson, H., 1896), V. 447

Want and Vice = London Labour and London Poor

Want, Crime and Retribution = Factory Strike

Wanted (Williamson, H. W., 1884), V. 626

— (1881), V. 765

Wanted a Bravo (Webb, C., 1846), IV. 551, 642

Wanted, a Brigand (À Beckett, G. A., 1837), IV. 249, 567

Wanted, a Companion (Levey, J. C., 1873), V. 458

Wanted, a Curate (1894), V. 765

Wanted a Governess! (Peake, R. B., 1817), IV. 369

Wanted a Hermit (Taylor, T., 1847), IV. 551, 614, 642

Wanted, a Husband (Holt, N., 1850), V. 424

Wanted, an Actor (1830), IV. 551

Wanted, an Enemy (Grattan, H. P., 1886), V. 389

Wanted, an Errand Boy (1857), V. 765

Wanted, an Heir (Watson, T. M., 1888), V. 616

Wanted, an Heiress (McCabe, C. W., 1897), V. 467

Wanted, a Partner (Buckstone, J. B., 1828), IV. 273, 571, 575

Wanted, a She Wolf (Lewes, G. H., 1854), V. 458

Wanted, a Situation (Talfourd, F., 1853), V. 590

Wanted, a Title (1849), IV. 551

Wanted, a Typewriter (Harris-Burland, J. R. and Weatherley, A., 1896), V. 407

Wanted, a Wife (Darnley, J. H., 1889), V. 337

— (Moncrieff, W. T., 1819), IV. 358

— (Spencer, E., 1871), V. 576

— (Stirling, E., 1843), IV. 407

— (1897), V. 765

Wanted, a Wife and Child (Soden, J. E., 1871), V. 573

— (1860), V. 765

Wanted, a Young Lady (Suter, W. E.), V. 588

Wanted by the Police (Brooke, C., 1898), V. 276

Wanted £5 = Absence of Mind

Wanted, Husbands for Six (Kenney, C. L., 1867), v. 443

Wanted Immediately (1895), v. 765

Wanted 1000 Spirited Young Milliners (Coyne, J. S., 1852), v. 327

Wanted to Marry (Sawyer, W., 1849), IV. 397

Wanton Countess (1733), II. 386

Wanton Jesuit (1731), II. 387

Wanton Trick'd (1743), II. 387

Wanton Wife = Amorous Widow

Wants and Superfluities = Azim

Wapping Landlady (1748), II. 387

— = (1) All Alive at Liverpool; (2) Sailor's Wedding

Wapping Old Stairs (Blake, T. G., 1834), IV. 268

— (Faucit, J. S., 1837), IV. 311

— (Holl, H., 1834), IV. 326

— (Robertson, S., 1894), v. 545

War (Daly, C., 1871), v. 334

— (Robertson, T. W., 1871), v. 129–31, 546

War and Peace (Barrymore, W., 1814), IV. 261

— (1855), v. 765

War Balloon (Lovegrove, W., 1871), v. 463

War Cloud (Barrs, H., 1895), v. 252

War Correspondent (Corbett, Mrs G. and Boyne, W., 1898), v. 324

Ward and Brother = Outwitted at Last

Warden (1855), v. 765

Warden of Galway (Groves, E., 1831), IV. 321, 586

— = Lynch Law

Wardock Kennilson (Fitzball, E., 1824), IV. 312, 584

Ward of France (1897), v. 765

Ward of the Castle (Burke, Miss, 1793) III. 241, 378

Wards and Wardens (1830), IV. 551

Wards in Chancery = Irish Dragoon

War in Abyssinia (1868), v. 765

War in India = (1) Burmese War; (2) Sikh's Invasion

War in Syria (1840), IV. 551

War in Turkey (1854), v. 765

War in Zululand (1879), v. 765

Warlock (Smythe, A., 1892), v. 573

Warlock of the Glen (Walker, C. E., 1820), IV. 416, 615

Warlock of the Glen (1827), IV. 551

Warlocks of the Border = Chevy Chase

War, Love and Duty = Africans

War, Love and Peace (Lee, N., 1848), IV. 343

Warlsha (Harris, J. T., 1841) = Walsha, IV. 587 [The title appears both as Warlsha and Walsha: the correct date is 26/4/41]

Warming Pan = My Lord

Warm Member (Seaton, P., 1898), v. 559

— = Ballyhooley

Warm Members (1891), v. 765

Warm Reception = Bobby No. 1

Warning Bell of Ronguerall = Memoirs of the D—l

Warning Dream (Pitt, G. D., 1851), v. 526

Warning Spirit = Lady Anne's Well

Warning to Bachelors (Mortimer, J., 1871), v. 494

Warning to Mesmerists = Baby

Warning to Parents (Roberts, G., 1877), v. 544

Warning to Wives (1849), IV. 551

Warning Vision = Twin Brothers

Warning Voice (Lee, N., Jr., 1864), v. 765, 849

— = Bletchington House

War of Paris in 1649 = Partisans

War of Wealth (Dazey, C. T. and Vane, S., 1898), v. 340

War of Wits = Midnight Hour

Warranted (1875), v. 765

Warranted Burglar Proof (Stephenson, B. C., 1888), v. 582

Warranted Sound and Quiet in Harness (Douglass, J. T., 1871), v. 348

Warrior and his Child (1843), IV. 642

Warrior and the Crescent = Enchanted Palfrey

Warrior Bold (1879), v. 765

Warrior Boy (Burton, E. G., 1851), v. 294

Warrior Kings (1835), IV. 551

Warrior of the Sun = Storming of Quito

Warrior Peasant (1847), IV. 642

Warrior's Career = Emperor's Decree

Warrior's Faith (1834), IV. 551

Warrior Slaves (1841), IV. 551

Warrior's Steed = Corasco

Warrior Women = Last of the Race
Wars in China = Chinese War
Wars in Spain (Corn, G. E., 1844), IV. 283
— (1837), IV. 551
Wars in Wedlock = Spanish Bonds
Wars of the Jews (Blake, T. G., 1848), IV. 551, 642
Wars of the Punjab (1846), IV. 551
Wars of the Roses = King Maker
Wars of Wellington (Amherst, J. H., 1834), IV. 551, 642
War—the Fugitives (Abel, W. H., 1871), v. 234
War Time (1867), v. 765
War to the Knife (Byron, H. J., 1865), v. 297
War Trail (Townsend, W. T., 1857), v. 765, 821, 849
War versus Art (Wilson, M., 1898), v. 628
War versus Law = Quits
War Whoop = Americans
Warwickshire Jubilee = Shakespear's Garland
Warwick the Kingmaker (Lancaster, E. R.), IV. 593
Warwick the King Maker and the Battle of Barnet = Last of the Barons
+ War with the Danes; or, Wild Eric of the Hills (Pav. 15/2/1864) [A revised version of The Sea King's Vow, by E. Stirling]
War with the Waves (Stirling, E., 1864), v. 584
War Wolf = Zapolyta
War Woolf of Tlascala (1828), IV. 551
Wary Widdow (Higden, R., 1693), I. 13, 16, 18, 27, 218, 413
Washed Ashore (1894), v. 765
Washerwoman of St Remy (1846), IV. 551
Was he the Man? (1870), v. 765
Washington Watts (Schonberg, J., 1879), v. 557
Was it a Dream? (Staples, E. B., 1896), v. 579
Was I to blame? (Rodwell, G. H., 1830), IV. 395
Wasted Life (Osmond, L. and Herbert, F. H., 1894), v. 508
Wasted Lives (France, E. S.), v. 792

Wasted Lives (1875), v. 765
— = Nell Snooks
Wastrel (Byatt, H. and Moss, H., 1894), v. 295
Watch and Wait (Higgie, T. H. and Shepherd, R., 1871),
Watch and Ward (Wigan, A. S., 1844), IV. 419, 617
Watch Cry (Simpson, J. P., 1865), v. 110, 567
Watchdog (1854), v. 765
— = Carlo
Watchdog of the Castle (1844), IV. 551
Watchdog of the Walsinghams (Simpson, J. P., 1869), v. 568
Watchers on the Longships (1885), v. 765
Watchful Mother Duped = Kate of Brockmoor
Watch-house (Galt, J., 1814), IV. 318, 635
Watching and Waiting (Hodgson, A. H. and Hodgson, A. C., 1891), v. 423
Watching and Winning = Brought to Light
Watching the Body (1848), IV. 551
Watchmaker of Clerkenwell (Wilks, T. E., 1843), IV. 421
Watchman (1829), IV. 551
Watchman of New York (1856), v. 765
Watchman's Secret = Found Dying
Watch Tower (1859), v. 849
Watch-word (Bell, R., 1816) = Assassin, IV. 112, 264, 428, 572
Watchwords of Old London = Young Apprentice
Water and Fire = Drenched and Dried
Water Babes (Bowles, E. W., 1887), v. 271
Water Carnival (1890), v. 765
Water Carrier (1875), v. 765
— = Escapes
Water-carrier and the Beauty (1831), IV. 551
Watercress Girl (Travers, W., 1865), v. 765, 821, 849
Water Cure (Felix, A., 1883), v. 364
Water Kelpie (1844), IV. 551
Water King = Flying Fish
Waterloo (Akhurst, W. M., 1876), v. 237
Waterloo Bridge (Dibdin, T. J., 1817), IV. 300

Waterloo Cup (1897), v. 765
— =Won by a Head
Waterloo in 1835 = Gertrude's Cherries
Waterman (Dibdin, C., 1774), III. 202, 254
— (1844), IV. 551
Waterman of Bankside (1879), v. 765
Water Monster and Fire Spectre = Invisible Ring
Water Pageant = Wild Man
Waterpail Rebellion = Jack and Jill Up-to-date
Water Party (Dance, C., 1832), IV. 288
Water Queen (1835), IV. 551
Waters (1863), v. 765
Waters of Oblivion = Sadak and Kalasrade
Water Spectre = Bratach
Water Spirit and the Magic Axe = Eve of St John
Water Sprite and the Fire Fiend = Ondine
Water's Water (Young, 1801), IV. 422
Water Witch (Bernard, W. B., 1830), IV. 97, 551, 642
— = Skimmer of the Sea
Water Witches (Coyne, J. S., 1842), IV. 284
Wattie and Meg (Lowe, W., 1873), v. 464
Wat Tyler (Lee, N., Jr., 1867), v. 453
— (Southey, R., 1817), IV. 192, 405
— (1733), II. 387
— (1844), IV. 551
Wat Tyler and Jack Straw (1730), II. 387
— (1831), IV. 551
— = Life and Death of King Richard II
Wat Tyler, M.P. (Sala, G. A., 1869), v. 555, 815
Wave (1847), IV. 551
Waverley (Calcraft, J. W., 1824), IV. 94, 278
— (Fitzball, E., 1824), IV. 94, 312, 584
— (1822), IV. 94, 551
— (1824), IV. 94, 551
— (1827), IV. 94, 552
— (1831), IV. 94, 642
— (1871), v. 765
Wave of War (Chesterley, F. and Piffard, H., 1887), v. 309
Wax and Wonders (Lemon, M., 1842), IV. 344

Waxwork Man (Clarke, C. A., 1871), v. 311
Waxwork Wooing (1884), v. 765
Wayfarers (Swears, H., 1898), v. 589
Way of the Wicked (Grover, J. H., 1871), v. 395
— = I.O.U.
Way of the Wind (Mackay, W., 1876), v. 470
Way of the World (Congreve, W., 1700), I. 74, 190, 193, 236, 242–3, 341, 398; II. 125, 147
— (Kemble, J. P., 1800), IV. 335
— (McNair, A., 1860), v. 805
— (Payne, W. B., 1883), v. 518
— (Planché, J. R., 1842), IV. 382
— (1846), IV. 552
— (1857), v. 765
— (1892), v. 766
— = Bound for Life
Ways and Means (Colman, G., the Younger, 1788) = More Ways than Means, III. 247, 379
— (1785), III. 347
— = (1) On Guy Fawkes Day; (2) Wife, the Bone of Contention
Wayside Cottage (Poel, W., 1881), v. 529, 811
+ Wayside Wiolets; or, The Gipsy Girl and the Guilty Conscience (Byron, H. J.: Dicks (in Sensation Dramas))
Ways of London (McLaren, A., 1812) = Tricks of London, IV. 597
Way Things Turn (Reade, C.), v. 812
Way to be Happy = Haunted Village
Way to Get Married (Morton, T., 1796), III. 142, 289
Way to get Un-Married (Cross, J. C., 1796), III. 250
Way to Keep Him (Murphy, A., 1760), III. 12, 120, 162–3, 289, 392
Way to Win and Tame a Shrew = Mad Wooing
Way to Win Her (1814), IV. 552, 635
Way to Win Him = Inconstant
Weaker Sex (Pinero, Sir A. W., 1888), v. 177, 525
Weaker Vessel = Twentieth-Century Girl
Weak Points (Buckstone, J. B., 1838), IV. 275

What's bred in the Bone = Who's to Father Her?

What shall I do for a Ticket? = Bal Masqué

What shall I sing? (Blunt, R., 1892), v. 266

What's in a Name? (Green, K., 1895), v. 392

— (Moncrieff, W. T., 1835), IV. 552, 642

— (1829), IV. 552

— (1880), v. 766

What's in the Wind? = (1) Up the Flue; (2) Who did it?

What's it on? (Routledge, W., 1870), v. 552

What's the Clock? = Mysterious Murder

What's the Matter? (Oulton, W. C., 1789), III. 296

What's the News? = Old Quizzes

What's the Odds? (Jones, J. W., 1882), v. 440

What's the Result? = All in One

What's to be Seen? = Bill of Fare

What's your Game? (Bruton, H., 1858), v. 284

What! The Devil Again! (Murray, W. H., 1833), IV. 552, 642

What to Eat, Drink and Avoid (1848), IV. 552

What was found in a Celebrated Case = Over-Proof

What We Have Been and What We May Be (Siddons, H., 1796), III. 307

What We Must All Come To (Murphy, A., 1763), III. 7, 181, 290, 392

— = Three Weeks after Marriage

What will become of him? (Marchant, F., 1872), v. 476

What Will be the End of It? = Emmeline of Hungary

What will he do next? (1825), IV. 552

What will he do with it? (Lightfoot, 1871), v. 459

— (Phillips, F. L., 1859), v. 766, 810, 849

What will my Aunt say? (1850) = Forbidden Fruit, v. 679, 766, 832, 849

What will my Lady say? = Knight of the Boots

What will my Wife say? = Assignation

What will the Neighbours say? (Douglass, J. T., 1873), v. 348

What will the World say? (Bancroft, G. P., 1899), v. 248

— (Gillum, W., 1787), III. 265

— (Lemon, M., 1841), IV. 344

— = Captain Tarradiddle

What will they say at Brompton? (Coyne, J. S., 1857), v. 328

What Women will do (Jerome, J. K., 1890), v. 436

What won't a Woman do? = Venus in Arms

What Would She Not? (Ross, W., 1790), III. 303

What would the Man be at? (1801), IV. 552

What you please (1750–1800), III. 405

— (1788), III. 347

— = Crisis

Wheedling (Lunn, J., 1832), IV. 552, 642

Wheel of Death = Black Vulture

Wheel of Fortune (Collier, H., 1883), v. 317

— (Cumberland, R., 1795), III. 128–9, 252, 381

— (Howell-Poole, W., 1890), v. 429

— = Fool's Expectation

Wheel of Life (1856), v. 766

Wheel of Time (Bannister, T. B., 1892), v. 248

Wheels within Wheels (Carton, R. C., 1899), v. 305

— (Dibdin, T. J., 1820), IV. 302

— (1873), v. 766

When a Man's in Love (Hope, A. and Rose, E., 1898), v. 425

— = Man in Love

When George was King = Master of Hope

When George III was King (Rimington, C., 1893), v. 543

When George IV was King (Moore, F. W., 1896), v. 492

When Greek meets Greek = Roll of the Drum

When it takes Place (1820), IV. 552

When London Sleeps (Darrell, C., 1896), v. 337

When one Door shuts another opens (Thomas, C., 1885), v. 596

When Poverty comes in at the Door = Love and Poverty

When Rogues fall out (1898), v. 766

When the Bell Tolls (1819), IV. 552
When the Cat's Away (Matthews, A. K., 1896), v. 480
When the Clock Strikes (1820), IV. 552
— = Golden Farmer
When the Clock strikes Nine (Hazlewood, C. H., 1869), v. 413
When the Lamps are lighted (Sims, G. R. and Merrick, L., 1897), v. 570
When the Wheels run down (Rogers, M. M., 1899), v. 548
When Widows wooed (Chevalier, A., 1899), v. 309
Where are you going to, my Pretty Maid? = Naomi's Sin
Where did the Money come from? = Two Gregories
Where have you been? (1888), v. 766
Where is Eliza? (1847), IV. 552
Where is She? = Who Wants a Guinea
Where is she gone? (Baron-Wilson, Mrs C., 1832), IV. 570
Where is the Note? = Miss Pop
Where's Brown? (Legg, J., 1859), v. 766, 803, 835, 849
— (1859), v. 766
Where's Crevelli? (Howard, J. and Cooper, F. F., 1854), v. 766, 786, 798, 849
Where's Eliza? (James, C. S., 1847), IV. 330, 552, 590, 642
Where shall I dine? (Rodwell, G. H., 1819), IV. 395
Where's Mr Smith (Conquest, G., 1858), v. 766, 785, 849
Where's Prodgers? (Hester, E., 1896), v. 420
Where's the Cat? (Albery, J., 1880), v. 238
Where's the Child? = Philip and his Dog
Where's the Wig? = Sportsman and the Shepherd
Where's your Wife? (Bridgeman, J. V., 1863), v. 275
Where there's a Will = My Great Aunt
Where there's a Will there's a Way (Morton, J. M., 1849), IV. 363
— = Black Squire
Where to find a Friend (Leigh, R., 1811), IV. 343, 553, 594
Which? (Bagot, A. G., 1886), v. 247
Which can be the Man? (1821), IV. 553

Which is He? = (1) Snake in the Grass; (2) William Thompson
Which is it? (Robertson, T. W., 1881), v. 546
— (Tully, J. H., 1862), v. 604, 822
Which is Mine? = Old Soldier
Which is my Cousin? (Raymond, R. J., 1825), IV. 388
— = Love and Mystery
Which is my Husband? (1861), v. 766
— = Giralda
Which is my Love? (1846), IV. 553
Which is my Son? = (1) Middle Temple; (2) Tricks and Blunders
Which is the Bride? = Tale of Other Times
Which is the Dandy? = Ultra Exquisite
Which is the Girl? = Irish Tar
Which is the King? (Watts, W., 1848), IV. 417
Which is the Lady? = Sleepwalker
Which is the Man (Cowley, Mrs H., 1782), III. 141, 166–7, 248
Which is the Manager? = Odds and Ends
Which is the Miller? = Peter Smink
Which is the Real Dog (1799), III. 347
Which is the Right One? = Round of Intrigue
Which is the Thief? (Barber, J., 1843), IV. 259
— = Maid and the Magpye
Which is the Uncle? (Watts, W., 1841), IV. 417, 616
Which is the Woman? (1833), IV. 553
Which is Thomas? = Black and White
Which is which? (Smith, S. T., 1871), v. 573
— (1810), IV. 553
— (1878), v. 766
— = (1) Fire of London; (2) King and the Duke; (3) Twins
Which Mr Smith? (Reach, A. B., 1846), IV. 389
Which of the Two? (Morton, J. M., 1859), v. 496
Which shall I marry? = Whom shall I marry?
While there's Life there's Hope = False Accusation
Which wins? (Piggott, J. W., 1889), v. 524
Whiffin and Co. (1893), v. 766

Whitefeet (1832), IV. 553
White Fox (1779), III. 406
Whitefriars (Townsend, W. T., 1844), IV. 414, 615
— (1838), IV. 643
White Goat = Fifteenth Carbineers
White-Hands (Spicer, H., 1856), v. 817
White Hat (1873), v. 767
White Hawk Lady (Bew, C., 1831) = Brighton Cliff, IV. 572, 436, 621
White Heather (Raleigh, C. and Hamilton, H., 1897), v. 534
White Hood (Planché, J. R., 1850), v. 527
White Hoods (1838), IV. 553
White Horse = Mrs H.
White Horse of Nick of the Woods = Jibbenainosay
White Horse of the Peppers (Lover, S., 1838), IV. 347
White Hypocrite (Mackenzie, H.), III. 284
White Indian (Towers, E., 1860), v. 767, 821, 849
White Joke (1730), II. 387
White Knight (Ogilvie, G. S., 1898), v. 506
White Lady (Beazley, S., 1826), IV. 84, 93, 553, 642
— (1892), v. 767
— (1893), v. 767
White Lie (Grundy, S., 1889), v. 397
— (Mortimer, J., 1888), v. 494
White Lies (Lunn, J., 1826), IV. 348
— (Stones-Davidson, T. W., 1896) = Taradiddles, v. 585, 767, 818, 849
— (1886), v. 767
White Lily (1891), v. 767
White Lion (1833), IV. 553
White Magic (Chorley, H. F., 1852), v. 310, 783
White Maid (Payne, J. H., 1827), IV. 84, 93, 369
White Maid of Avenel = Monastery
White Maiden of California (Fitzball, E., 1849), IV. 317
White Maiden of Tiernaboul = Cluricanne's Tower
White Mask = May Dudley
White Milliner (Jerrold, D. W., 1841), IV. 333
White Nun (1831), IV. 553

White Nun of Wakefield (Pitt, G. D., 1849), IV. 376
White of the Prairie = War Trail
White Palfrey (Suter, W. E., 1858) = Roland and his Steed, v. 744, 767, 819, 845, 849
White Passport (1869), v. 767
White Phantom (Pitt, C., 1867), v. 525
White Pilgrim (Merivale, H. C., 1874), v. 487
White Pilgrims (1820), IV. 553
White Plume (Dibdin, T. J., 1806), IV. 52, 298
White Queen (Boulding, J. W., 1883), v. 270
— (1889), v. 767
White Rabbit of Edinburgh = Royal Scots Fusiliers
White Rose (Sims, G. R. and Buchanan, R., 1892), v. 569
— = Housekeeper
White Rose and the Red Rose (1835), IV. 553
+ White Rose of the Plantation; or, Lubly Rosa, Sambo don't come (Byron, H. J.: Dicks (in Sensation Dramas))
White Roses (Gilbert, E., 1891), v. 378
Whiter than Snow (Lee, K., 1885), v. 452
White Scarf (1864), v. 767
— = Louise
White Serjeants (Selby, C., 1850) = Buttermilk Volunteers, v. 560, 654
White Silk Dress (Dam, H. J. W., 1896), v. 334
White Slave (Campbell, B., 1882), v. 301
— (Pitt, G. D., 1845), IV. 374
— (Stirling, E., 1849), IV. 409
White Slave of Guadeloupe = Ship Boy
White Spectre (Amherst, J. H., 1828), IV. 254
White Spirit (Burton, E. G., 1850), v. 294
White Squall (Haines, J. T.?, 1839), IV. 553, 643
White Star (1891), v. 767
White Stocking (Ferris, E. and Stewart, A., 1896), v. 365
White Stockings (Hannon, G. W., 1888), v. 403

Who Owns the Head? (1821), IV. 554
Who Pays the Bill? = Blind Man's Buff
Who Pays the Piper? (1803) = Bad Customers, IV. 554, 643
— (1810), IV. 554
— = Blind Man's Buff
Who Pays the Reckoning? (Arnold, S. J., 1795), III. 234, 377
Who pays the Rent? (1797), III. 347
— = Quarter Day
Who Rules? = Sultan and the Slave
Who's Afraid? (Carr, Sir J., 1805), IV. 279
— (Jodrell, R. P., 1787), III. 277
— = Hop
Who's Afraid? Ha! Ha! Ha! = Who's Afraid
Who's at Home? (1825), IV. 554
Who's a Traveller? (Howard, J. and Cooper, F. F., 1854), V. 767, 786, 798, 849
Who's Drowned? = Hoax
Whose Baby? (1885), V. 767
Whose Wife? (Horridge, F., 1898), v. 427
— = Spiritualist
Who's for India? = Drapery Question
Who Shot the Dog? = Frightful Hair
Who's Married? (Adams-Acton, Mrs, 1893), V. 235
Who's my Father? (Morton, T., 1818), IV. 364
Who's my Husband? (Morton, J. M., 1847), IV. 363
— (1861), V. 767
Who's my Papa? (1845), IV. 554
Who speaks first? (Dance, C., 1849), IV. 289
Who's the Composer? (Morton, J. M., 1845), IV. 362
Who's the Dupe? (Cowley, Mrs H., 1779), III. 115, 186, 248
Who's the Heir? (March, M. G., 1869), V. 475
— = Prince Pedrillo
Who's the Murderer? (Dibdin, T. J., 1816), IV. 300
— = (1) Angeline; (2) Martin Faber
Who's the Richest? = Thirty Thousand
Who's the Rogue? (1801), IV. 554, 643
Who's the Victim? (Hazlewood, C. H., 1856), V. 797

Who's the Winner? = Game and Game
Who's to be Master? (1886), V. 767
Who's to Blame? (Meadows, T., 1805), IV. 355
— (1880), V. 767
Who stole the Pocketbook? (Morton, J. M., 1852), V. 495
Who stole the Tarts? (Silvester, F., 1894), V. 566
Who's to Father Her! (Planché, J. R., 1820), IV. 376
Who's to have her? (Dibdin, T. J., 1813), IV. 299
— (Sharpe, J., 1791) = Laura, III. 348, 395, 406
Who's to have him? (1831), IV. 554
— = Woman's Wit
Who's to inherit? = Poor Relations
+ Who Stole the Clock? (Lucas, W. J., French)
Who stole the Ducks? = Proscribed Royalist
Who Stole the Partridge? = Man and the Monkey
Who's to Teach? = Polka, Polka, Polka
Who's to win? (Branson, W. S., 1877), v. 274
— (1878), V. 767
Who's to Win her? = Woman's Whims
Who's to win him? (Williams, T. J., 1868), V. 118–19, 625
Who's who? (Poole, J., 1815), IV. 386
— (1853), V. 767
Who's Wife is She? (O'Neil, J. R., 1852), V. 507
Who's your Friend? (Planché, J. R., 1843), IV. 382
Who's your Hatter? (1855), V. 767
Who wants a Guinea? (Colman, G. the Younger, 1805), IV. 52, 282, 577
Who wants a Wife (Bishop, Sir H. R., 1816), IV. 267
Who will get her out? = Veteran
Who will he have? = Rifles
Who Wins? (Allingham, J. T., 1808) = Widow's Choice, IV. 252, 568
— (1866), V. 767
— = Loyal Lovers
Who would be married? (Addison, H. R., 1833), IV. 251
Who would have thought it? = Too Careful by Half

Wild Dog of the Cape (1846), IV. 555
Wild Doings in the South = Leopard
Wild Duck (1894), V. 768
Wild Ducks (Stirling, E., 1850), V. 584
Wild Eric of the Hills = War with the Danes
Wildfang (1805), IV. 555
Wildfire (Farnie, H. B. and Reece, R., 1877), V. 362
Wildfire Dick (Pitt, G. D., 1847), IV. 374
Wild Flower of Hazlebrook = Mark Jarrett's Dairy
Wild Flower of Mexico (1860), V. 768
— = Jura
Wild Flower of the Prairie (Fuller, F. and Richardson, H., 1877), V. 374
Wild Flowers (Rose, E., 1880), V. 550
Wild Gallant (Dryden, J., 1663), I. 192, 227, 248, 249, 403-4
Wild Gipsy Girl (1857), V. 768
Wild Girl (Dibdin, C. I. M., 1811), IV. 292
— (1804), IV. 555
— (1819), IV. 555
Wild Goose (Boucicault, D. and Wallack, J. L., 1867), V. 269
Wild Goose Chase (Jameson, H., 1820), IV. 330
Wild Hag of the Mountain (1831), IV. 643
Wild Herde of the Wolf's Lair = Jessie Holes
Wild Herdsman of the Hills = Drover Boy
Wild Horse, Mazeppa (1841), IV. 555
Wild Horse of Tartary = Mazeppa
Wild Horse of the Ukraine = Mazeppa
Wild Huntsman of Bohemia = Freischutz
Wild Indian Girl (1815), IV. 555
Wild Irish Girl (Pilgrim, J., 1850), V. 524
— (1842), IV. 555
— = Too Clever by Half
Wild Irishman (1820), IV. 555
Wild Islanders (Byrne, J., 1805), IV. 555, 643
Wild Love (Dietz, L., 1881), V. 344
Wild Man (Dibdin, C. I. M., 1809), IV. 292
Wild Man, Fair Maniac and Dumb Brother and Sister (Dibdin, C. I. M., 1823), IV. 295

Wild Man of Andalusia (Pitt, G. D., 1846), IV. 374
Wild Man of Orleans = Valentine and Orson
Wild Man of the Mountain (1846), IV. 555
Wild Oats (O'Keeffe, J., 1791), III. 294
Wild Primrose (1891), V. 768
Wild Rabbit = Deputy
Wild Steed of the Prairies = Lightning's Flash
Wild Tribe of a Mountain Torrent = Zerago
Wild Tribes of London (Hazlewood, C. H., 1856), V. 768, 796
Wild Violet (Bruce, J., 1894), V. 283
Wild Violets (Maxwell, W. B., 1891), V. 482
Wild West (Stafford, A., 1887), V. 578
+ Wild Wolf of Tartary; or, The Empty Khan and the Khurdish Conspirators (Byron, H. J.: Dicks (in Sensation Dramas))
Wild Woman (1859), V. 768
Wild Woman of Languedoc (1829), IV. 555
Wild Woman of the Fens = King Stephen
Wild Woman of Zetland = Pirate
Wild Zebra Hunt (1832), IV. 555
Wiles (1898), V. 768
Wilfred Ned (Hazlewood, C. H., 1866) = Skeleton Crew, V. 768, 850
Wilfred of Ivanhoe (1881), V. 768
Wilfred's Choice (Cullum, H. H., 1894), V. 331
Wilful Beauty (Burton, A. E., 1885), V. 294
Wilful Murder (Higgie, T. H., 1844), IV. 325
— (Preston, J. F., 1888), V. 530
Wilful Ward (Wooler, J. P., 1864), V. 632
Wilis (Soane, G., 1846), IV. 404
— = Giselle
Wili's Bride = Phantom Dancers
Wilkes (Foote, S., 1769), III. 384
Wilkins the Weaver (1834), IV. 555
Will (Reynolds, F., 1797) = Will and the Deed, III. 31, 133, 301, 394
Will and a Way = Man Proposes

Will, or the Widow (Hook, T. E., 1810), IV. 328

Will o' the Wisp (Addison, J., 1897), v. 236

— (Johnstone, J. B., 1859), v. 768, 800, 850

— (Seaman, W., 1859), v. 768, 815, 850

— (1869), v. 768

— (1879), v. 768

— (1890), v. 768

— = (1) Fanchette; (2) Fanchonette the Cricket; (3) Zelma

Willow Copse (Boucicault, D., 1849), IV. 270

Willow Grove (1824), IV. 555

— (1850), v. 768

Willow Marsh (Faucquez, A., 1862) = Forced Marriage, v. 768, 792, 832, 850

Willow Pattern Plate (Bowkett, S. and Day, G. D., 1897), v. 271

— (Hale, W. P. and Talfourd, F., 1851), v. 398

Willow Pool (1870), v. 769

Will Pontypridd (1875), v. 769

Will Reckless (1836), IV. 555

Will Tell (1895), v. 769

Will Watch (Amherst, J. H., ?1825), IV. 568

Will Watch, the Bold Smuggler = Blood demands its Victim

Will with a Vengeance (Hay, F., 1876), v. 411

Willy Reilly and his Own Dear Colleen Bawn (Brady, F., 1861), v. 273

Wilmore Castle (Houlton, R., 1800), III. 273; IV. 329

Wiltshire Tom (Kirkman, F., 1673), I. 418

Win and Wear (Berwick, E. L. A., 1859), v. 779

Wind and Wave (Moore, R., 1868), v. 492

Windmill (Morton, T., Jr., 1842), IV. 364, 601

Windmill Hill = Merry Pranks

Windmill Turrett = Bonifacio and Bridgetina

Window Curtain (1849), IV. 555

Windsor Castle (Burnand, F. C. and Williams, M., 1865), v. 288

— (Marchant, F., 1873), v. 476

Windsor Castle (Pearce, W., 1795), III. 297

— (1838), IV. 555

Windsor Installation = Knights of St George

Wind Up = Ghosts of Tom and Jerry

Wine and Passion = Amour

Wine does Wonders (1820), IV. 555

— = Ramah Droog

Wine Dresser's Daughter = Village Life in France

Wine Drinkers of Paris = Isabel Bertrand

Wine House (Taylor, T. P., 1839), IV. 411

Wine, Women and Gambling = Three Perils

Wings of the Storm (Barlow, R. J. and North, W., 1891), v. 249

Wings of Wealth (Clarke, A. H., 1894), v. 311

Win her and Take her (Smythe, J., 1691), I. 260, 432

Win Her and Wear Her (1832), IV. 555

— = Race for a Wife

Winifred's Vow (Douglass, J. T., 1892), v. 349

Winkelried (McAlister, J., 1837), IV. 349

Winkhopper's Plot (Rolfe, V. C., 1897), v. 549

Winki the Witch and the Ladies of Samarcand = Enchanted Girdles

Winkle's Waxworks (1883), v. 769

Winner (1894), v. 769

Winning a Husband (Macfarren, G., 1819), v. 339

Winning a Widow (1856), v. 769

Winning a Wife (1888), v. 769

Winning Card (Wood, A., 1867), v. 630

Winning Defeat (Campbell, D. and Quaire, M., 1891), v. 301

Winning Hand (Conquest, G. and Miller, St A., 1895), v. 323

Winning Hazard (Wooler, J. P., 1865), v. 119, 632

Winning Post (1885), v. 769

Winning Suit (Filmore, L., 1863), v. 366,

Winning the Winner = Jockey

Winona, the Sioux Queen (1880), v. 769

Winterbottoms (Moncrieff, W. T., 1837), IV. 131-2, 360

— (1859), v. 769

Winter in London (1854), v. 769

Woman's Worth (Whitehead, D. C., 1846), IV. 419
Woman's Worth and Woman's Ways = Four Sisters
Woman's Wrongs (Courtney, J., 1859), v. 786
— (Heathcote, A. M., 1887), v. 415
— = Felon's Son
Woman Tamer (Doone, N., 1896), v. 347
Woman that was a Cat (Suter, W. E., 1859), v. 587
Woman turn'd Bully (1675), I. 216, 446
Woman wears the Breeches = Semiramis, Queen of Babylon
Woman who wooed (Ashlyn, Q., 1897), v. 245
+ Duologue. A Woman will be a Woman (Ware, J. R.: *Dicks*)
Woman will have her Will (1713), II. 387
Woman wronged by Woman = Madeline Martel
Women and Men (Dubourg, A. W., 1871), v. 351
Women and Wine (Landeck, B. and Shirley, A., 1897), v. 447
— (1834), IV. 556
Women of Shunem = Elisha
Womens Conquest (Howard, E., 1670), I. 61, 138, 414
Women Three (1866), v. 770
Won at Last (Reeve, W., 1869), v. 118, 540
Won by a Head (Clarke, C. A., 1887), v. 311
— (Taylor, T., 1869), v. 593
— (1897), v. 770
Won by a Neck (Horsman, C., 1879), v. 427
— (1880), v. 770
Won by a Trick (Wilson, S., 1885), v. 770, 824, 850
Won by Honours (Brunton, A., 1882), v. 284
Won by Wit (Attenborough, F. G., 1895), v. 245
Wonder = Honest Yorkshire-Man
Wonder: A Woman Keeps a Secret (Centlivre, Mrs S., 1714), II. 20, 142, 168, 305, 433; III. 205
Wonderful Adventures of Daddy Daddles = Great Metropolis

Wonderful Cousin (1874), v. 770
+ Wonderful Cure (*French*)
Wonderful Duck (Kenney, C. L., 1873), v. 443, 801
Wonderful Lamp (1830), IV. 556
Wonderful Lamp in a New Light (À Beckett, G. A., 1844), IV. 250
Wonderful Lamp of Aladdin (1827), IV. 556
Wonderful Travels of Gulliver (Byron, H. J., 1867), v. 782
Wonderful Visit (Wells, H. S., 1896), v. 619
Wonderful Wall and the Wise Elephants of the East = Chinese Insurrection
Wonderful Water Cure (Webster, B. N., 1846), IV. 418, 616
Wonderful Woman (Dance, C., 1849), IV. 289
Wonders in St Helena = Napoleon's Glory
Wonders in the Sun (D'Urfey, T., 1706), II. 233, 320
Wonders of Derbyshire (1779), III. 27, 29, 348, 367
Wonders of Wales = Penmaenmawr
Wonder-Worker (Cumberland, S., 1894), v. 331
Wonga of the Branded Hand (Atkyns, S., 1844), IV. 257
Won, not Wooed (Lodge, A., 1874), v. 462, 804
Woodbarrow Farm (Jerome, J. K., 1888), v. 436
Wood Carver of Bruges = Midnight
Woodcock's Little Game (Morton, J. M., 1864), v. 496
Wood Daemon (Lewis, M. G., 1807) = Demon of the Woods, IV. 345, 346, 450
Wood Demon (Conquest, G. and Spry, H., 1873), v. 321
— (Kenney, C. and Smith, A. R., 1847), IV. 556, 643
— (Marchant, F., 1867), v. 475
— (1813), IV. 556
Wood Devil (Fitzball, E., 1836), IV. 315
Wooden Spoon (Burgess, G., 1892), v. 287
Wooden Spoon Maker (Halliday, A. and Brough, W., 1863), v. 400

Wooden Walls (Cherry, A., 1806)= Peter the Great, IV. 556, 643
Woodin's Carpet-bag and Sketchbook (1854), v. 770
Woodleigh (1883), v. 770
Woodman (Bate, H., 1791), III. 236
Woodman and his Ass (1835), IV. 643
Woodman and his Dog = Bruin the Brave
Woodman Prince (1817), IV. 556
Woodman's Daughter = Zittau, the Cruel
Woodman's Dream = Lesson of Life
Woodman's Horse (1854), v. 770
Woodman's Hut (Arnold, S. J., 1814), IV. 256
Woodman's Spell (Stirling, E., 1850), v. 584
Woodriffe (Dibdin, C. I. M., 1822), IV. 295
Woodstock (?Pocock, I. or Dibdin, C. I. M., 1826), IV. 33, 94, 296, 385
— (1826), IV. 94, 556
Woodstock Bower = (1) Fair Rosamond; (2) Fall of Fair Rosamond
Wood Wolf of the Black Mountains (Moncrieff, W. T., 1842), IV. 361
Wooer, the Waitress and the Willain = Belle of the Barley Mow
Wooing = Florentine Wedding
Wooing and Waiting (Levy, E. L., 1895), v. 458
Wooing a Widow (Bernard, W. B., 1832), IV. 265
— (1833), IV. 556
— (1836), IV. 556
Wooing in Jest and Loving in Earnest (Troughton, A. C., 1858), v. 604
Wooing One's Wife (Morton, J. M., 1861), v. 496
— (1870), v. 770
Wooings and Weddings = Look before you Leap
Wool (Linden, H., 1878), v. 459
Woolcomber's Progress (1879), v. 770
Wool-gathering (Brayley, 1826), IV. 270
— (Longride, A., 1888), v. 463
Worcester Fight (Dalton, M., 1890), v. 333
Worcester Sauce (1872), v. 770
Word for Nature (Cumberland, R., 1798), III. 252

Word for the Ladies (Kenney, J., 1818), IV. 337
Word of Honour (Meritt, P., 1874), v. 486
— (Skeffington, L. S., 1802), IV. 402
— (1814), IV. 635
— = Seigneur's Daughter
Words made visible (Shaw, S., 1679), I. 432
Word to the Wise (Kelly, H., 1770), III. 7, 18, 130–1, 132, 155, 278, 389
— = Historical Register
Worga (Haines, J. T., 1824), IV. 556, 643
Work and Wages (Bourne, W., 1890), v. 161, 270
Workbox (Craven, T., 1890), v. 329
Work for the Bailiffs = Broken Stock-Jobbers
Work for the Upholders = Bickerstaff's Burying
Work Girl (Conquest, G. and Shirley, A., 1895), v. 323
Work Girl of Cardiff = Welsh Orphan
Workgirls of London (Hazlewood, C. H., 1864), v. 770, 796, 850
Workhouse Life = Casual Ward
Workhouse, the Palace and the Grave (Seaman, W., 1858), v. 770, 815, 850
Working in the Dark = Waifs
Working Man (Hardy, H., 1890), v. 403
— (1852), v. 770
Working Man's Story = Ready and Willing
Working the Oracle (1862), v. 770
Workman (Harvey, F., 1880), v. 408
— (Towers, E., 1880), v. 601
Workman's Dream = Rich and Poor
Workman's Wife (1875), v. 770
Workmen of Paris (1864), v. 770
Work of Mercy (Racer, F., 1892), v. 532
World (Meritt, P., Pettitt, H. and Harris, Sir A., 1880), v. 486
— (Kenney, J., 1808), IV. 184, 336
World against her (Harvey, F., 1887), v. 408
World and Stage (Simpson, J. P., 1859), v. 567
World as it Goes (Colls, J. H., 1792), III. 245
— (Cowley, Mrs H., 1781) = Second Thoughts are Best, III. 248, 380
— = (1) Fashion; (2) Touchstone

World as it Runs (Moncrieff, W. T., 1832), IV. 600

World as it Wags (Moore, S., 1792), III. 288

World at Auction (Field, M., 1898), v. 366

World between them = Pilgrims

World bewitched = Venus's Girdle

World Discovered = Columbus

World for Novelty = Old Roscius

World in a Village (O'Keeffe, J., 1793), III. 294

World in London = World of Fashion

World in the Moon (Settle, E., 1697), I. 42, 48–9, 81, 135, 161–2, 429; III. 192

— = (1) Celestia; (2) Orbis

Worldliness (Moore, G., 1874), v. 492

World of Dreams (Coyne, J. S., 1841), IV. 284

World of Fashion (Barnett, C. Z., 1846), IV. 261

— (Oxenford, J., 1862), v. 510, 809

World of Silence (Mortimer, L. and Wilson, P., 1898), v. 494

World of Trouble in a Locket (Paulton, H. and Paulton, E., 1894), v. 517

World of Wonders (1847), IV. 556

World's Epitome = Village

World's Games (Courtney, J., 1851), v. 326

World's Idol = Plutus

World's Verdict (Jefferson, A., 1890), v. 435

World's Waif = Little Ragamuffin

World's War (1854), v. 770

World turn'd Upside Down (1777), III. 406

World turned Upside Down (1873), v. 770

World Underground (À Beckett, G. A., 1847), IV. 251

World Unmask'd = Fortune Tellers

World upside down = Female Government

World We Live In (Hunt, G. W., ?1879), v. 799

World well lost = All for Love

Worm of Lambton (Barnett, C. Z., 1835), IV. 259

Worried to Death (1885), v. 770

Worryburry's Whims (Ross, C. H. and Murray, D., 1865), v. 551

Worse and Worse (Digby, G., 1664), I. 192, 346, 403

Worse Plague than the Dragon = Margery

Worse than Ever (Farmer, E., 1849), IV. 311

Worship of Bacchus (Meritt, P. and Pettitt, H., 1879), v. 486

Worship of Plutus (Clevedon, A., 1888), v. 314

Worst not always true = Elvira

Worst Woman in London (Melville, W., 1899), v. 485

Worth a Struggle (Waldron, W. R., 1871), v. 611

Wortigerne (1800), IV. 556

Wounded Horse (1861), v. 850

Wounded Ladies = Monster

Wounded Lion = Androcles, the Slave

Wounded Sailor = Adventures of Tom Trip

Wrack of the Heart (Pitt, G. D., 1841), IV. 373

Wraith of the Lake (Haines, J. T., 1829), IV. 322

Wrangling Deities (1741), II. 387

Wrangling Lawyers = Whackham and Windham

Wrangling Lovers (Lyon, W., 1745), II. 342

— (Ravenscroft, E., 1676), I. 192, 254, 426

Wrath (Stephenson, C. H., 1882), v. 583

Wrath's Whirlwind (1853), v. 770

Wreck (Campbell, A. V., 1831), IV. 556, 643

— (Masterton, C., 1824), IV. 353

Wreckage (Hein, G.), v. 416

Wreck and Rescue (Mead, T., 1863), v. 770, 850

— = Jack Stedfast

Wreck and the Reef (Fitzball, E., 1847), IV. 317

Wreck and the Rescue = Philippe del Turbillino

Wreck Ashore (Buckstone, J. B., 1830), IV. 273

Wreck at New Brighton (1882), v. 770

Wreck at Sea (Stirling, E., 1838), IV. 406

Wrecked (Edwardes-Sprange, W., 1884), v. 354

Ye Merrie Days of Olde Englande =
 Good Queen Bess
Ye Merrie England (Webb, G., 1877),
 v. 617
— = Merrie England
Ye Miller and hys Man (Thorne, G.,
 1893), v. 599
Ye Mysseltoe Boughe (1861), v. 771
Yeoman of Kent = Tunbridge-Walks
Yeoman's Daughter (Serle, T. J., 1833),
 IV. 399
— (1833), IV. 557
— (1834), IV. 557
Yeoman's Service (Pemberton, T. E.,
 1885), v. 519
Yeomen of the Guard (Gilbert, W. S.,
 1888), v. 145, 380
Ye Queene, ye Earle and ye Maydenne
 = Kenilworth
"Yes!" (Somerset, C. A., 1829), IV. 145,
 404
Ye Siege of Liverpool (Millward, C.,
 1852), v. 807
Ye Signe of ye Golden Ship (1881), v.
 771
Yes or No (Beauchamp, E., 1877), v.
 254
— (Pocock, I., 1808), IV. 144, 383
— (Poel, W., 1892), v. 771, 811
Yew Tree Ruins (Haines, J. T., 1841),
 IV. 323
Ye Wyn-Wyn-Wyn (McArdle, J. F.,
 1875), v. 466
Y'lang, Y'lang (Cohen, G. M., 1893), v.
 316
Yogi's Daughter (Hopkins, J. B., 1854),
 v. 426
Yolande (1877), v. 771
Yorick's Love (Howells, W. D., 1878),
 v. 429
Yorick, the King's Jester (Somerset,
 C. A., 1836), v. 394
York and Lancaster (Hood, T., 1829),
 IV. 327
York Roses (Markwell, W. R.), v.
 477
Yorkshire Attorney = (1) Sheep Stealer;
 (2) Three Yards of Broadcloth
Yorkshire Bonfire = Make a Noise Tom
Yorkshire Brothers (1852), v. 771
Yorkshire Ghost (Craven, E., 1794), III.
 249

Yorkshire Grey (1833), IV. 557
Yorkshire Highwayman and the Twin
 Brothers = Nat Graves
Yorkshire Hoyden (1797), III. 406
Yorkshire Lady = (1) Female Rake;
 (2) Woman of Taste
Yorkshire Lass (Jones, J. W., 1891), v.
 441
— = Luck
Yorkshire Lover = Change upon Change
Yorkshire-Man   Bit = Industrious
 Lovers
Yorkshire Miller = Ellen and Alberto
Yorkshire School (Pitt, G. D., 1847),
 IV. 374
York, you are not wanted = Lubin Log's
 Journey to London
You can't marry your Grandmother
 (Bayly, T. H., 1838), IV. 14, 263
You know what (Beazley, S., Jr., 1842),
 IV. 14, 264
You know who (Morton, J. M., 1864), v.
 496
You may like it, or let it alone (1791),
 III. 348
You May Say That = Fortune Hunters
You must be buried (Planché, J. R.,
 1827), IV. 378
You must be married (Selby, C., 1846),
 IV. 399
You mustn't laugh (Lubimoff, A.,
 1892), v. 464
You Never Can Tell (Shaw, G. B.,
 1899), v. 195, 562
You Never Know (Dale, G., 1899), v.
 332
Young Actress (Boucicault, D., 1853),
 v. 268
— (1860), v. 771
Young America (1897), v. 771
Young and Handsome (Planché, J. R.,
 1856), v. 527
Young Apprentice (Hazlewood, C. H.,
 1868), v. 413
Young at Sixty (1829), IV. 557
Young Burglar (1891), v. 771
Young Chasseur = Romance of the
 Pyrenees
Young Colonel = Military Promotion
Young Coquette (1705), II. 387, 448
Young Country Widow (Gray, S.,
 1839), IV. 321